Betty Crocker
Cookbook

Everything you need to know to cook from scratch

Houghton Mifflin Harcourt

Boston · New York

GENERAL MILLS

Owned Media and Publishing Director:
Amy Halford

Owned Media and Publishing Manager:
Audra Carson

Senior Editors: Grace Wells and Cathy Swanson

Food Editor: Lori Fox

Recipe Development and Testing:
Betty Crocker Kitchens

Photography: General Mills Photography Studios and Image Library

Photographers: Val Bourassa, Mike Jensen, Chuck Nields, Kayla Pieper, Maja Sahlberg

Photo Assistants: Dusty Hoskovec, Olga Ivanova, Morgan Marks, Kayla Pieper, Brie Rinkel, Kevin Santavy, Kacey Wyrick

Food Stylists: Junita Bognanni, Sue Brosious, Carol Grones, Sharon Harding, Nancy Johnson, Stacey LeNeave, Karen Linden, Cindy Lund, Alynna Malson, Betsy Nelson, Amy Peterson, Beth Rosendahl, Cindy Syme

Food Styling Assistants: Susan Barrientos Hevey, Sara Bartus, Jerry David Dudycha, Patty Gabbert, Phyllis Kral, Alynna Malson, Kari Setterholm

HOUGHTON MIFFLIN HARCOURT

Editorial Director: Cindy Kitchel

Executive Editor: Anne Ficklen

Senior Editor: Adam Kowit

Editorial Assistant: Melissa Fisch

Editorial Associate: Molly Aronica

Managing Editor: Marina Padakis Lowry

Associate Production Editor: Helen Seachrist

Cover Design: Tai Blanche

Interior Design and Layout: Tai Blanche

Director of Production Technologies:
David Futato

Senior Production Coordinator: Kimberly Kiefer

The Betty Crocker Kitchens seal guarantees success in your kitchen. Every recipe has been tested in America's Most Trusted Kitchens™ to meet our high standards of reliability, easy preparation and great taste.

Find more great ideas at
BettyCrocker.com

CONTENTS

Dear Friends,

Whether you are just learning to cook or know your way around the kitchen, you'll find *Betty Crocker Cookbook* to be an indispensable resource you'll consistently reach for. It's like having a trusted cook nearby whenever you have a cooking question!

Betty Crocker still provides the expertise you need to make cooking approachable and rewarding—everything you'd expect from America's most-trusted test kitchens. This is the 12th edition of the popular cookbook that's been helping cooks for more than 75 years—but it isn't your grandmother's version. Loaded with over 1500 recipes, this edition has hand-selected, frequently requested traditional favorites plus brand new, taste-tempting recipes utilizing fresh ingredients and the wide variety of flavors available today.

In addition, you'll love the breadth and depth of cooking information, provided by means of the many features woven throughout. Our "Quick Technique" photos and descriptions will show you how to easily master cooking skills. Each "Make Ahead" feature highlights one recipe and several simple ways to use it. "Betty's Staples" shows how to use ingredients typically found in your pantry, in easy ways that are sure to please.

Whether you cook with others or for others, food brings people together; conversations are richer, laughter erupts and guests linger. Each time in the kitchen can be a fun, rewarding and satisfying experience! Let us help you make delicious meals and memories with your family and friends.

Sincerely,

Betty Crocker

Getting Started

GETTING STARTED

Whether you are just learning to cook or to want to make cooking more inspirational, a little organization can be just what you need.

A PLACE IN YOUR KITCHEN CALLED HOME

- Store items where you use them—pans by the stove, spices near where you mix, tableware near where you serve.

- Keep items you use frequently in easy-to-grab spaces and store things you rarely use in a different spot.

- Use cabinet organizers so everything can be located quickly.

- Install roll-out shelves if you don't already have them—they make it easier to see and grab items.

- Keep your counters clutter-free so they are open for cooking.

KEEPING YOUR KITCHEN SANITY

Are you tired of looking for an item you know you have but can't locate it? Keeping things in order lets you cook more easily and effortlessly:

- **Use Prime Real Estate Well:** Reserve the front and center parts of any space for the ingredients you reach for most often. Group items by how often your family uses items. Use the space around (higher and lower shelves) for those items you use occasionally.

- **Label Liberally:** Leave no question as to what things are and where they are stored. Mark foods with name and date.

- **Tame Clutter:** Use containers to keep foods together easily and neatly, such as sauce and seasoning packets or bags of pasta.

- **Use Trays:** Place raw meats on trays or in containers with sides to catch any meat juice drips in the refrigerator. Store these items separately from produce to prevent bacterial contamination.

- **First In, First Out:** Avoid food waste and missed expiration dates by placing newer, unopened packages behind older ones. What you buy first should be used first.

Smart and Creative Storage

Here are some of our favorite unexpected household storage ideas:

- Store snacks or bulk spices in leftover food containers or baby food jars.

- Use canning jars to store for rice, grains, pasta and other dry goods.

- Use plastic shoe boxes to store sauce and seasoning packets, as well as herbs and spices.

- Use magazine holders with holes to store potatoes and onions.

- Use an over-the-door clear plastic shoe organizer to store individual snacks.

SMART SHOPPING STRATEGIES

Set aside time for weekly meal planning to avoid last-minute dashes to the store or take-out splurges. Also, be strategic about grocery shopping, to save money and cut down on food waste. Shopping will be more efficient, helping you stick to your list and budget. It will also be easier, so you'll have the energy and time to enjoy cooking and eating at home.

Meal Planning

- **Start Fresh:** Before you shop, do a quick cleanup and inventory of your fridge, freezer and pantry so you know what you have, as well as what you need to use soon.

- **Keep a Running List:** Keep a dry-erase board inside your pantry or cupboard door. As you finish an item, add it to the board. Each time you go shopping, start a shopping list from this list.

- **Create a Chart:** Map out a chart of the week's needed meals, snacks and brown-bag lunches. Consider your schedule and the time you can spend to make each meal.

- **Strategize Your List:** Plan meals that help you make use of foods you already have—especially those items you noted need to be used soon.

- **A Meal and Recipe at a Time:** As you consider each item on your chart, add any needed ingredients to your shopping list.

Shop Smart

- If possible, shop alone so that you aren't distracted.

- Bring your own bags—many stores offer a reusable bag discount.

- Clip coupons ahead of time and read store ads, both print and online.

- Know your budget and stick to it.

- Always shop with a list.

Supermarket Skills

- Shop and cook seasonally to get the freshest food at the best prices.

- Shop the perimeter of the store for the most healthful items (dairy, produce, meats).

- Check out the discount shelves for bargains.

- Buy in bulk for those items you use often.

- Check the **unit price per ounce** to compare package sizes or brands for the best price. Many stores offer this information on the shelf labels, right below the item. If not, you can determine the unit price with this equation: **price/number of units (such as ounces) = cost per unit**. Use the calculator feature on your phone to do the math for you.

INGREDIENTS

Baking Ingredients

Baking Powder: A leavening mixture made from baking soda and a moisture absorber. When mixed with liquid, carbon dioxide gas bubbles are released, causing baked goods to rise. Not interchangeable with baking soda.

Baking Soda: A leavening ingredient that must be mixed with an acid ingredient, such as lemon juice or buttermilk, in order for it to cause baked goods to rise.

Butter: Available salted or unsalted and must contain at least 80 percent butterfat. Recipes in this book were tested with salted butter unless unsalted butter is noted. Butter (not margarine) was tested for recipes in this book for the best taste, texture, appearance and performance. See Cake Basics, page 553; Cookie and Bar Basics, page 519; Quick Bread Basics, page 481.

Chocolate: Cocoa beans are made into a thick paste called chocolate liquor, and then processed to make the various forms of chocolate:

- **Baking Cocoa:** Made from dried chocolate liquor with cocoa butter removed; unsweetened.

- **Bittersweet, Sweet (German), Milk and Semisweet Chocolate:** Available in bars and chips (German chocolate in bars only) for baking and eating.

Photo (at right): 1 Brown Sugar **2** Granulated Sugar **3** Egg **4** Yeast **5** White Baking Chips **6** Coconut **7** Sweet Baking (German) Chocolate **8** Baking Cocoa **9** Chocolate Chips **10** Butter **11** Whole Wheat Flour **12** All-Purpose Flour **13** Salt **14** Ground Cinnamon **15** Baking Powder

- **Dark Chocolate:** Contains a higher percentage of cocoa solids (more than 60 percent) and little or no added sugar. A rich, intense flavor; available as baking chocolate, chocolate bars and candies.

- **Unsweetened Chocolate:** Bitter in flavor, so use just for baking; available in bars.

- **White Chocolate:** Contains no chocolate liquor and so it is not truly chocolate. Labeled as white baking chips or vanilla baking bar.

Coconut: Made from the fruit of the coconut palm tree; available sweetened or unsweetened. **Shredded Coconut** is moist and therefore best for baking. **Dried (desiccated) Flaked Coconut** is used mostly for decorating.

Corn Syrup: A sweetener made from corn sugar processed with acid or enzymes. **Dark Corn Syrup** has a caramel-like flavor and dark color; it can be used interchangeably with **Light Corn Syrup**, although flavor and color of the finished dish may be affected.

Cornstarch: A thickener derived from corn; good for making clear (rather than opaque) sauces.

Cream of Tartar: An acid ingredient that adds stability and volume when beating eggs.

Eggs: Adds richness, moisture and structure to baked goods.

Flour: A primary baking ingredient; comes in many varieties. Below are the varieties of wheat flour. (See Quick Bread Basics, page 481, Yeast Bread Basics, page 496, and Cookie and Bar Basics, page 519.) In addition, many other non-wheat flour choices are either gluten-free or low in gluten. Follow recipes specifically designed for these products, as they are not directly interchangeable with wheat flour.

- **All-Purpose:** The most common flour; available bleached and unbleached.

- **Bread Flour:** Higher in protein so it gives more structure to bread.

- **Cake Flour:** Made from soft wheat; makes tender, fine-textured cakes.

- **Quick-Mixing Flour:** Processed to blend easily; used for sauces and gravies.

- **Self-Rising Flour:** Flour combined with baking powder and salt. Not interchangeable with other flours.

- **Whole Wheat Flour:** Made from the whole grain; gives foods a nutty flavor and heartier texture. **White Whole Wheat Flour** is whole-grain flour made with white wheat.

Molasses: Made from the sugar-refining process; available in light and dark varieties, which are interchangeable unless specified otherwise.

Salt: Adds flavor, controls the growth of yeast in breads.

Shortening: Sold in sticks and cans, this solid all-vegetable product is available in regular and butter-flavored varieties. Used to grease pans, make pie pastry and sometimes as all or part of the fat in cookies.

Spices: Adds flavor to baked goods. See Spices/Seasonings, page 474.

Sugar: Made from sugar beets or sugarcane.

- **Brown Sugar:** Made from granulated sugar plus molasses. Light or dark brown in color; use interchangeably unless one is specified in a recipe.

- **Coarse, Decorating or Pearl Sugar:** Large grained; use for decorating.

- **Colored Sugar:** Use for decorating.

- **Granulated Sugar:** Available in boxes or bags, cubes or packets. **Superfine Sugar** dissolves quickly and is great for beverages, meringues and frostings.

- **Powdered Sugar:** Granulated sugar that has been processed to a fine powder and contains a very small amount of cornstarch to keep it from clumping.

- **Raw or Turbinado Sugar:** This golden brown–colored sugar is coarser than granulated sugar. Use to sprinkle on cookies and pies before baking.

Yeast: A leavening ingredient used to make breads rise. There are several varieties available:

- **Bread Machine Yeast:** Finely granulated yeast for bread machine recipes.

- **Fast-Acting Dry Yeast:** Dehydrated yeast that allows bread to rise in less time than regular yeast.

- **Regular Active Dry Yeast:** Dehydrated yeast that can be used in most bread recipes.

Dairy/Refrigerated Ingredients

Butter: See Butter, page 5.

Cheese: See Cheese Types, page 27.

Cream: Smooth, rich dairy product made from milk; churned to make butter and buttermilk; pasteurized and processed into several forms:

- **Half-and-Half:** Contains 10 to 20 percent butterfat and does not whip. To save on fat and calories, look for fat-free half-and-half: although not recommended for baking, it is great for soups and beverages.

- **Sour Cream:** Regular sour cream has 18 to 20 percent butterfat. Low-fat and fat-free varieties are available and can often be substituted for regular.

- **Whipping Cream:** Available in light and heavy varieties. Contains 36 to 40 percent butterfat and doubles in volume when whipped. **Ultra-Pasteurized Cream** has a longer shelf life than regular cream.

Eggs: See Egg Basics, page 90.

Milk: Pasteurized dairy milk is available in many types. Today there are also many nondairy options to choose from. See There Is More to Milk, page 66. Read labels to compare protein, calcium and calories. Common forms of milk:

- **Buttermilk:** Fat-free or low-fat product adds a tangy taste to baked goods. See Betty's Staples: Buttermilk, page 70.

- **Dulce de Leche:** Sweetened milk that's slowly heated to caramelize the sugar, changing the flavor and thickness to be more like caramel sauce. Common in Mexican, Central and South American cooking; meaning "sweet milk" or "milk candy."

- **Evaporated Milk:** Milk with at least half of the water removed. Available in cans, typically in the baking aisle; whole, low-fat and skim varieties.

- **Fat-Free (Skim) Milk:** Contains little or no fat.

- **Low-Fat Milk:** Available as 1% milk (99% of milk fat removed) and 2% milk (98% of milk fat removed). Recipes in this book were tested with 2% milk.

- **Sweetened Condensed Milk:** A highly sweetened milk product used mostly for baking.

Dairy Ingredients

- **Whole Milk:** Contains at least 3.5% milk fat.

Yogurt: Product made from milk heated and combined with healthful bacteria. A variety of yogurts are available with a range of fat content, sugar and possibly added fruit for flavor. Look for yogurt with "live and active cultures" to be sure you are getting the most from your yogurt.

Thick, creamy Greek yogurt is regular yogurt with the whey strained off, resulting in yogurt with generally higher protein content and less sugar than regular yogurt. See Betty's Staples: Yogurt, page 49; to make your own, see page 444.

Pantry Ingredients

Bouillon/Broth/Stock: Bouillon is available in cubes or granules. **Broth** and **Stock** are available in cans and larger-quantity boxes. **Soup Base** is a highly concentrated stock available near the broth in supermarkets.

Coffee: Available as whole beans or ground and instant. See Beverage Basics, page 65.

Cooking Oil: The healthiest oils are those that are high in monounsaturated and polyunsaturated fats, such as **Vegetable Oil** and **Olive Oil**. When cooking, not all oils are equal. Choose the right oil, depending on what you will use it for.

- **For High-Heat Cooking:** For frying and stir-frying, choose Corn, Soybean, Peanut or Sesame Oil.

Pantry Ingredients

- **For Moderate-Heat Cooking:** For sautéing, choose Olive, Canola or Grapeseed Oil.

- **Other Oils:** Some oils don't perform well with heat, such as Flaxseed or Walnut. They can be used when no heat is required, such as in making dressings or dips.

Gelatin: Colorless, tasteless thickening agent used to thicken foods when dissolved in liquid and refrigerated. Also available in sweetened fruit flavors.

Herbs and Spices: See Herbs, page 472, and Spices/Seasonings, page 474.

Honey: A sweetener produced by bees. Store it at room temperature.

Legumes: See Bean Basics, page 252, and Betty's Staples: Canned Beans, page 163.

Maple Syrup: Made from maple tree sap. Maple-flavored syrup and pancake syrup are made from corn syrup and other sweeteners with some maple syrup or maple flavor added.

Pasta: See Pasta Basics, page 167.

Rice: See Grains and Rice Basics, page 199.

Sun-Dried Tomatoes: Available dehydrated and in jars packed in oil; use the type specified in the recipe.

Tea: Available in a variety of loose tea, tea bags and instant products; both regular and decaffeinated. See Beverage Basics, page 65.

Tortillas: Corn and flour tortillas are often used for sandwich wraps and in recipes.

Condiments, Sauces and Seasonings

Capers: Unopened buds of a Mediterranean plant with a sharp, tangy flavor; packed in vinegar brine. Use in appetizers and cooking.

Ketchup: Thick, spicy sauce made from tomatoes, vinegar and seasonings. Use it as sauce or in cooking. To make your own, see page 446. Sriracha is the hot, spicy Thai "ketchup"; see Asian Flavors, page 464. To make your own, see page 463.

Mayonnaise/Salad Dressing: Creamy sauce used in cooking and for salads and sandwiches. Salad dressing is usually sweeter than mayonnaise. To make your own, see page 460.

Mustard: A range of flavors available from yellow to darker, more highly flavored varieties; adds a sharp flavor to dishes.

Pesto: Italian sauce traditionally made from basil, Parmesan cheese, olive oil and pine nuts. Make your own, page 456, or look for it in the refrigerated area and in jars near the spaghetti sauce.

Photo (above): 1 Red Pepper Sauce **2** Worcestershire Sauce **3** Balsamic Vinegar **4** Red Wine Vinegar **5** Mayonnaise **6 and 7** Mustards **8** Salsa **9** Roasted Bell Peppers **10** Pesto **11** Capers

Red Pepper Sauce: Spicy sauce made from hot peppers.

Roasted Bell Peppers: Both red and yellow bell peppers are available packed in jars for salads, sandwiches, snacking and cooking.

Salsa: Sauce made from tomatoes and a variety of other ingredients. Make your own, page 458, or look for varieties ranging from mild to spicy.

Soy Sauce: Asian sauce made from fermented soybeans.

Vinegar: Many varieties with different flavors that can balance other ingredients in salad dressings and other recipes. Varieties include: apple cider, wine (both red and white), balsamic (both dark and white), rice and rice wine.

Worcestershire Sauce: Highly flavored sauce containing garlic, soy sauce, onions, molasses and vinegar; for stew and meat dishes.

Nuts and Seeds

Nuts and seeds are great sources of protein, and also contain vitamins, minerals and other components that may contribute to good health. Perfect for eating out of hand or adding to recipes for flavor and crunch. They naturally contain oil, so they may spoil easily; store at room temperature 1 month or see Refrigerator and Freezer Food Storage Chart, page 33.

Almonds: Available whole in shell or shelled, blanched, sliced or slivered. Also ground into almond flour and meal or made into almond milk.

Cashews: Rich, buttery flavor. Also made into cashew milk.

Hazelnuts (Filberts): Available whole or chopped. Use in a variety of desserts, salads and main dishes.

Macadamia Nuts: Available shelled, either roasted or raw; rich, buttery, sweet flavor.

Pecans: Available shelled (halves or chopped) or unshelled. Unshelled should be blemish- and crack-free and shouldn't rattle when shaken.

Pine Nuts: From the pinecones of several varieties of pine trees. Commonly used in pesto.

Pistachios: Available raw, roasted, salted or unsalted. Available shelled or unshelled (partially open) in tan, red (dyed) or white.

Pumpkin Seeds (Pepitas): Available with or without hulls, raw, roasted or salted. Delicious, delicate flavor; common in Mexican cooking.

Walnuts: English (most common) or black varieties. Unshelled walnuts should have shells free from cracks or holes; shelled walnuts should be crisp and meaty (not shriveled).

THE RIGHT TOOL FOR THE JOB

Just imagine trying to cut a lawn with a pair of scissors—it wouldn't be easy, quick or enjoyable, right? Similarly, having the right tools in the kitchen can help make cooking easier, quicker and more a lot more fun! Don't worry—you won't necessarily need everything listed below. Start by stocking your kitchen with items you'll use often or that can slash prep time. As you expand your cooking abilities, you can continue to add to your kitchen tool collection.

Cooking Tools and Handy Gadgets

Baster: Use to baste meat and poultry when roasting to keep it moist. The bulb draws up liquid into the stem. Squeeze the bulb again over the meat to release the liquid.

Bowls (Large, Medium and Small): Use for combining ingredients.

Brushes: A wide variety of sizes and materials are available. Keep brushes used for pastry separate from those used to baste meat.

Can Opener: Available in handheld and electric versions.

Cheese Servers: Sets of **Cheese Knives** are available; use a **Spreader** for soft cheese, a **Curved Blade Knife** for hard cheese, a **Cheese Plane** or **Wide Blade Knife** for semi-hard cheese and a **Thin Blade Knife** for semi-soft cheeses.

Citrus Reamer and Juicer: Both remove juice easily from citrus fruits; juicers also keep seeds from getting into the juice.

Colanders and Strainers: Use colanders for draining pasta and vegetables. Use strainers to drain liquid from canned goods.

Cooling Racks: Use to cool baked goods so that air can get underneath hot pans or foods.

Cutting Boards: See note at right.

Fat Separator: Made with a special spout so that as fat rises to the top, juices can be poured off, leaving the fat behind.

Graters: Many styles with a variety of hole sizes for grating/shredding. A handheld **Plane Grater** is sharp with many very small holes.

Jar Opener: Aids in opening jars and bottles.

Kitchen Towels: Dish and hand towels should be absorbent; tea towels are made for drying stemware and cutlery without scratching or leaving lint.

Meat Mallet: Breaks down tough meat fibers for more tender meat, among other tasks.

Oven Mitt/Pot Holder: Use to remove hot pans from oven or stovetop. **Barbecue Mitts** cover more of the forearm for grilling.

Pastry Blender: Handy for making pastry, but you can substitute a potato masher or fork.

Potato Masher: Handheld tool for mashing potatoes, cooked vegetables and apples (for applesauce); also used for making pie pastry.

Rolling Pin: Use for rolling cookies, pastry and bread dough. Look for one with sturdy, easy-to-hold handles.

Ruler: Use to measure dough and in other recipes requiring food to be shaped to a certain size; also use for determining correct pan sizes.

Salad Spinner: Quickly removes the water from lettuce and leafy herbs after washing.

Scrubbing Brush: Aids in pan/dish washing to remove stuck-on food while keeping hands dry.

Silicone Mat: Use to line cookie sheets when baking cookies or pastries, as an alternate to waxed paper or as a floured surface for rolling out pie pastry.

Rubber Spatulas or Scrapers: A must-have for folding, stirring and scraping food from bowls, jars or saucepans. Look for those that are heat resistant.

Spatula or Pancake Turner: Use to turn foods such as burgers or pancakes, remove cookies from baking sheets or serve desserts. Offset Metal Spatulas frost baked goods while keeping fingers from marking the frosted surface.

Spoons: Use to stir thick batters and dough. Use wooden spoons for nonstick cookware and for hot items on the stove, such as soups and

Photo (at left): 1 Colanders and Strainers **2** Pancake Turner **3** Graters **4** Spoons **5** Timer **6** Kitchen Towel **7** Salad Spinner **8** Cooling Racks **9** Zester **10** Offset Metal Spatula **11** Basting Brushes **12** Whisks **13** Rolling Pin **14** Pastry Blender **15** Jar Opener **16** Ruler **17** Citrus Reamer **18** Scrubbing Brush **19** Silicone Mat **20** Rubber Spatulas **21** Bowls **22** Meat Mallet **23** Potato Masher **24** Silicone Pot Holder

Cutting Board Smarts

- Have at least two boards—one for raw meats and poultry and one for vegetables and fruit.
- Hard plastic or glass cutting boards are the best choices for raw meat, poultry and seafood as they are less porous than other types.
- Avoid cutting cooked foods with the same knife and board used to cut raw foods.

sauces. Slotted Spoons allow liquid to drain away from food.

Timer: Alerts you when food is finished cooking or baking and for timed directions in recipes.

Tongs: Use to handle raw cuts of meat without touching, for turning foods when cooking and serving or for tossing and serving green salads. (Do not let tongs that have touched raw meat contact other foods until thoroughly washed.)

Vegetable Peeler: Used to peel any vegetable or fruit, and to make vegetable ribbons and chocolate curls.

Whisk: Cuts the time to beat eggs, sauces and dressings, and to smooth lumpy batters.

Zester: Removes the peel from citrus fruit, leaving the bitter pith below it.

Knives and Related Tools

An integral part of cooking, a good set of knives is a worthwhile investment. Because you'll use them daily, invest in the best quality that you can afford. Wash them by hand; keep them sharp and they will last many years. Choose knives that feel good in your hand. Look for stainless steel blades with sturdy, durable handles. If you can't afford an entire set of knives, these three knives would get you by: a chef's knife, a paring knife and a serrated knife. As you can afford more, check out the variety of choices and select those that fit your needs.

Carving Knife: The long, thin blade of this knife makes it the perfect choice for carving meat and poultry or slicing cooked meats.

Chef's Knife: Use for chopping, slicing and dicing foods. Choose an 8- or 10-inch blade for your first chef's knife; later, add shorter-blade versions for other specific tasks.

Kitchen Scissors: Great for snipping herbs, cutting up chicken, cutting fat from chicken pieces and other tasks.

Paring Knife: The short, small blade of this knife is great for peeling vegetables and fruits, removing the seeds of fruit or cutting small food items such as grapes.

Santoku Knife: Similar in size to a chef's knife but with a different-shaped blade for a slightly different cutting action. Typically has a thinner, sharper blade, which gives more precise control when slicing dense food such as carrots.

Serrated (Bread) Knife: Use a longer-blade serrated knife to cut bread or angel food cake without tearing or compressing it.

Sharpening Steel: A quick way to occasionally sharpen knives by gently scraping blade back and forth several times across it; rinse and wipe blade before using.

Steak Knife: Use to cut meat into bite-size pieces while dining.

Utility Knife: Smaller than a chef's knife, larger than a paring knife; use for many kitchen tasks when these other knives aren't the right size.

Photo (at right): 1 Sharpening Steel **2** Chef's Knife **3** Carving or Utility Knife **4** Kitchen Scissors **5** Serrated Knives **6** Paring Knives **7** Steak Knives

Cutting Techniques

Chop: Gather food into close cluster. Hold down top of knife with fingers from one hand while holding knife handle in other hand. Manipulate knife (holding tip of knife on board) up and down over food, until evenly chopped.

Slice: Hold food with fingers of one hand tucking fingers under. Slice with knife held in the other hand.

Julienne: Slice long, thin, uniform strips of food, using slicing method.

Dice or Cube: Hold food with fingers of one hand, tucking fingers under. With knife in other hand, cut into strips; rotate, then cut into small squares.

Cookware

A variety of cookware is essential. Often, you are able to purchase sets of cookware with an assortment of pieces to provide for basic cooking needs.

The best heat conductors are copper and aluminum, so buying pans made of these materials ensures better cooking results. Avoid purchasing uncoated aluminum pans, as the aluminum can react with acidic foods, causing off flavors in the food as well as discoloring the pans. Also avoid pans made entirely of stainless steel, as they can get hot spots when heated, causing food to cook unevenly.

Dutch Oven: A large pot with a tight-fitting lid used mostly for moist, slow-cooking methods such as braising and stewing or a large batch of chili or soup, if you don't have a stockpot. Sides are shorter than a stockpot.

Griddle: Large, heavy, flat pan with very short sides; great for pancakes, bacon, sandwiches and fried potatoes. Regular pans are used on the stovetop; electric versions are also available.

Grill Pan: Heavy pan with shallow sides and ridged cooking surface that allows fat to drain away from food as it cooks and leaves grill marks on the food. Regular grill pans are used on the stovetop; electric versions are also available.

Saucepan: Comes in a range of sizes from 1- to 4-quart and should have tight-fitting lid. Having a variety of sizes will ensure you have you have the right size for cooking or reheating food. Using the wrong size can be a reason a recipe isn't successful.

Sauté Pan: Similar to skillets, sauté pans generally have sides that are a little higher. The sides can be straight or slightly sloped. In addition to a long handle, these pans typically have a loop handle on the side opposite the long handle so the pan can be lifted easily. Use to brown and cook meats or almost any other kind of food on the stovetop.

Skillet: Usually available in 8-, 10- and 12-inch sizes. Skillets generally have low, gently sloping sides that allow steam to escape. Use to pan-fry or cook almost any kind of food on the stovetop.

Stockpot: Large pan with tall sides; perfect for making stocks and soups or cooking pasta.

Wok: A rounded, flat-bottomed pan with high, sloping sides; popular for Asian cooking, for stir-frying, steaming and deep frying. Electric woks are also available.

Bakeware

Bakeware is available in many materials, including aluminum, glass, ceramic and terra-cotta (clay). For the recipes in this book, *pan* refers to a shiny metal pan and *baking dish* refers to a heat-resistant glass or ceramic dish.

Baking Dish: Made of heat-resistant glass or ceramic, usually round, square or rectangular. Use for desserts, egg bakes, casseroles and main dishes.

Baking Pans: Metal baking pans are available in a variety of sizes—round, square, rectangular and loaf shapes. Use for cakes, breads and desserts. See below for specific types of cake pans.

Cake Pans:

* **Angel Food Cake Pan (Tube Pan):** Round metal 10-inch pan with a hollow tube in the middle. The bottom is usually removable, making it easy to remove the cake from the pan. Use for angel food, chiffon and sponge cakes.

* **Fluted Tube Cake Pan:** Round, fluted pan; typically metal pan with center tube. Use for cakes and coffee cakes.

* **Jelly Roll Pan:** The 15x10-inch pan has 1-inch sides and is technically used for baking thin, rectangular cakes (called jelly rolls when filled and rolled up) or bars. Some refer to this pan as a *sheet pan, baking sheet* or *cookie sheet*. While these pans can be used for baking cookies, the sides can cause cookies near the edges to brown more quickly and the edges of the pan can make removing cookies without damaging them more difficult.

Casserole: Glass or ceramic cookware for baking and serving food; may come with a matching cover.

Photo (at right): 1 Baking Dish **2** Baking Pans **3** Roasting Pan and Rack **4** Muffin Pan **5** Fluted Tube Cake Pan **6** Baking Dish **7** Cookie Sheet **8** Broiler Pan and Rack **9** Pie Plate and Pie Pan **10** Tart Pan **11** Jelly Roll Pan

Cookie Sheet: Flat, rectangular aluminum sheets of various sizes with very short sides on one or more edges. The open sides allow for good air circulation while baking cookies, biscuits, scones, shortcakes or bread.

Custard Cup or Ramekin: Custard Cups are small, deep, glass or ceramic heatproof individual dishes (6- and 8-ounce) with flat bottoms. Ramekins are similar but come in a variety of shapes and sizes—and can be short or tall and deep, like custard cups—and are made of a variety of materials. Use for baking individual custards or other desserts.

Muffin Pan: Pan with 6 or 12 individual cups for baking muffins or cupcakes. Cups can range in size from miniature to jumbo.

Pie and Tart Pans:

- **Pie Plate or Pan:** A pie plate is glass with a flared side, designed for baking pies with flaky (not soggy) crusts. A pie pan is the metal version.

- **Tart Pan:** Available in a variety of shapes and sizes, typically metal with a removable bottom.

Pizza Pan: Round metal pan with no sides or low sides (deep-dish) for baking pizza. Some are perforated to help crisp the crust. A **Pizza Stone** is typically flat and should be preheated in the oven; the unbaked pizza is slid onto the hot stone to help crisp pizza crust while it bakes.

Popover Pan: Pan with 6 or 12 individual extra-deep cups especially designed for baking popovers.

Soufflé Dish: Round, open dish with high sides, especially designed for making soufflés.

Springform Pan: Round, deep pan with a removable side; available in various sizes. Use for cheesecakes and desserts that can't be turned upside down to remove from pan.

Other Ovenware

Broiler Pan and Rack: Rack has slits to allow fat to drip away from food as it cooks, falling into the pan below. For easier cleanup, line pan and rack separately with foil; cut through foil over broiler rack slits with knife.

Microwavable Cooking Dishes: Specifically made and designated to be microwavable.

Use only dishes labeled "microwave-safe" in the microwave.

Roasting Pan: Large, rectangular pan with short sides so that the oven heat can reach as much of the food as possible. Typically comes with a roasting rack to elevate the food and allow the fat to drain away from the food as it cooks. Use to roast whole chicken, turkey, pork and tender cuts of meat with little or no liquid.

Measuring Utensils

Using the correct measuring equipment can make a difference in how a recipe turns out:

- **Glass Measuring Cups:** Use to measure liquids. To measure accurately, pour liquid to desired mark on cup; set on counter and read at eye level.

- **Plastic and Metal Measuring Cups:** Use to measure dry ingredients. Spoon dry ingredient into cup; level off with metal spatula or flat side of a knife.

- **Measuring Spoons:** Use to measure small amounts of liquid, such as extracts or food color, and dry ingredients, such as salt, baking soda and baking powder. For dry ingredients, fill and level off. For liquid ingredients, fill to rim.

Measuring Correctly

Spoon in dry ingredients, then level off top using a flat-edged utensil such as a knife or metal spatula.

Spoon brown sugar into measuring cup; firmly pack with back of spoon.

Check amount of liquid by looking at it at eye level while cup sits steady on counter.

Dip measuring spoon into food; level off (if dry) or fill to rim (if liquid).

Thermometers

Look for a variety of thermometers in domestic retail stores and kitchen specialty stores.

Candy Thermometer: Use to check temperature of candy while it cooks and to check liquid temperature for bread making and deep frying.

Digital Oven Probe Thermometer: Temperature readout goes on your counter or oven door and has a long cord with a probe that allows the thermometer to measure temperature of food without opening the oven door. You can set the temperature you wish to cook your food to and an alarm will sound when the food has reached temperature.

Instant-Read Thermometer: Gives an accurate reading of food's temperature in seconds. These thermometers are not heat-safe: Don't leave in oven or on grill while cooking.

Photo (below): **1** Oven Thermometers **2** Regular and Digital Candy/Deep Fry Thermometers **3** Ovenproof Meat Thermometers **4** Digital Thermometer **5** Refrigerator/Freezer Thermometer **6** Digital Oven Probe Thermometer **7** Instant-Read Thermometer

Oven Thermometer: Ovens can run hot or cool over time—the wrong temperature can affect the success of a recipe. Use to ensure oven is at the proper temperature; nudge the heat up or down as needed to get the temperature to where it needs to be.

Ovenproof Meat Thermometer: Heat-safe so they can be left in the food while in the oven.

Is My Thermometer Accurate?

Thermometers can lose accuracy over time. To check whether your food thermometer is reading accurately, heat 2 cups water in 1-quart saucepan to boiling. Immerse the stem of the thermometer 2 inches into the boiling water; it should read 212°F after 30 seconds. If the thermometer is off a few degrees, calibrate it according to the manufacturer's directions or allow for this adjustment when measuring the temperature of food. Check thermometers once or twice a year for accuracy.

Thermometers

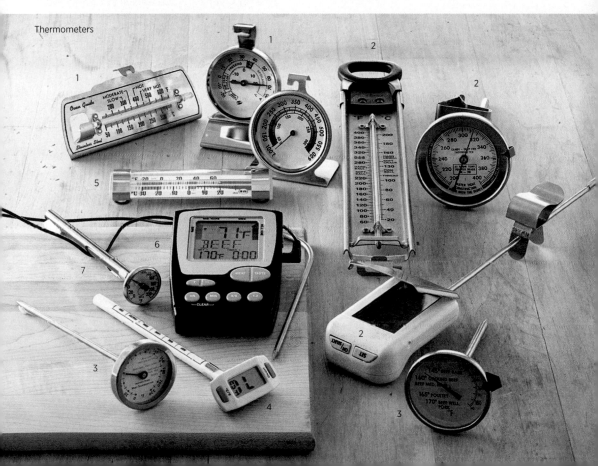

Small Electric Appliances

Some appliances are necessary if you want to make a recipe—making waffles is impossible if you don't have a waffle iron, for example. Many times small appliances aren't essential, but they certainly can make your time in the kitchen easier, quicker and a lot more enjoyable. As you think about equipment for your kitchen, consider purchasing these items as you need them.

Blender: Use to blend, liquefy and puree. An **Immersion Blender** is a handheld appliance used to puree soups and sauces right in the pan.

Bread Machine: Mixes, kneads, rises and bakes bread or can be used to make dough to shape for other foods such as rolls and pizza crust to be baked in your oven.

Coffee Grinder: Quickly grinds whole beans for making coffee.

Coffee Maker: Makes coffee automatically; available in models ranging from making coffee a cup at a time to a full pot, or the option of both.

Food Processor: Handles a host of cooking tasks quickly: chopping, slicing, mixing, shredding, pureeing and kneading.

Photo (below): 1 Electric Hand Mixer **2** Food Processor **3** Stand Mixer **4** Waffle Maker **5** Mini Chopper **6** Blender

Hand Mixer: Use to whip and mix liquid foods or thin batters quickly. Not good for heavy batters or dough.

Mini Chopper: Much smaller than a food processor. Use to chop small amounts of food or grind whole dried spices quickly.

Pressure Cooker: Meals cook in much less time than if prepared on the stovetop or in the oven. Moisture from the food builds up pressure inside the cooker, causing the temperature to rise above what it could if cooked conventionally, so it can cook faster.

Slow Cooker: An easy way to make meals with little preparation, as the food cooks for long periods with little attention or electricity, and without heating up your kitchen. Great for less tender cuts of meat.

Stand Mixer: Preferred by professional chefs over hand mixers for ease of use (hands-free) and power (heavy-duty and quicker).Handles thicker, stiffer mixtures, such as bread dough.

Toaster or Toaster Oven: For toasting bread, bagels and frozen waffles, use a **Toaster.** A **Toaster Oven** can toast as well as heat up, broil or toast foods (such as garlic bread and frozen snacks) more quickly and with less energy than if done in the regular oven.

Waffle Maker: Bakes waffles and is available in a variety of shapes and sizes.

Quick Techniques

We've gathered the best ways to tackle the most-used cooking skills you'll need to know when cooking. Refer back to this feature any time you come across a technique that's unfamiliar. It's an easy way to build your cooking prowess. Many techniques have more in-depth instructions elsewhere in this book. See Index for specific techniques.

Basting

Brushing foods with liquid adds flavor to the food while also keeping it moist during cooking.

Blanching

Immerse food into boiling water to loosen skins, partially cook or brighten color.

Immediately immerse food into ice water to stop the cooking process.

Boiling and Simmering

Boil liquid or cook food in liquid at a temperature that causes bubbles to rise continuously and break on surface.

Simmer food in liquid at a temperature just below boiling point. Bubbles rise slowly and break just below surface.

Broiling

Broil food directly under heated broiler element at a specified distance to keep from burning.

Coring Fruit

Pierce fruit at stem end with corer; twist into fruit and pull out to remove core.

With paring knife, cut fruit into quarters; cut out core with knife.

Crushing

Place food to be crushed into resealable plastic bag; seal. Roll over bag with rolling pin until food is in small, even pieces.

Deep-Frying

Heat oil to desired temperature.

Drop food carefully into oil; do not crowd.

Drain fried food on paper towel–lined plate.

Drizzling

With spoon, drop glaze in a thin stream while moving over food.

Cut tiny (⅛-inch) corner from bag of glaze. Squeeze glaze over food in thin stream.

Hulling

Gently press huller into fruit. Squeeze while twisting and pulling hull away from fruit.

Making Soft and Stiff Peaks

Soft Peaks: Beat just until peaks form but curl over.

Stiff Peaks: Continue beating until peaks stand upright.

Straining

Place food in sieve; with back of spoon, press liquid through.

Peeling Fruit

Cut into top of fruit just below the skin. Turn the fruit, carefully peeling off skin in strip(s).

Using Kitchen Scissors

Snipping: Place small items such as herbs into small cup. Snip with scissors into uniform size.

Cutting: Use scissors to cut small pieces of food into even smaller, similar-shaped pieces.

COOKING TERMS

Al Dente: Used to describe pasta or other food cooked just enough—neither soft nor underdone.

Bake: To cook food in the oven with dry heat. Bake uncovered for a dry, crisp top or covered to keep food moist.

Baste: To add liquid or fat over surface of food during cooking to keep food moist. Use a spoon, pastry brush or bulb baster to baste.

Batter: Mixture of flour, eggs, liquid and other ingredients that is thin enough to be spooned or poured.

Beat: To combine ingredients vigorously with a spoon, fork, whisk or electric mixer. When electric mixer is specified, mixer speed is included. See Learn to Beat, Whip and Fold, page 572.

Blanch: To place food in boiling water briefly and then into ice water to stop the cooking process as a way to preserve color and texture, or to remove skin. See Learn to Blanch, page 130.

Blend: To combine ingredients using a spoon, whisk or rubber spatula, or using a blender or food processor.

Boil: To heat liquid or cook food at a temperature that causes bubbles to rise continuously and break the surface.

Braise: Less tender cuts of meat are seared and then cooked in a large amount of liquid to make them tender. See Learn to Braise, page 330.

Bread or Coat: To cover food with a coating by dipping or brushing with a liquid (like beaten egg or milk), then dipping or rolling in bread or cracker crumbs or cornmeal before frying or baking.

Broil: To cook food from a measured distance directly under the heat source in the oven. See Learn to Broil, page 358.

Brown: To cook quickly, usually over high heat, causing surface of food to turn brown and adding color and flavor to the finished dish.

Caramelize: To melt sugar slowly over low heat until golden brown and syrupy. Sugar can be caramelized on top of food with a kitchen torch or by placing it under the broiler.

Chill: To place food in the refrigerator until thoroughly cold.

Chop: To cut food into coarse or fine pieces of irregular shapes, using a knife, food processor or chopper.

Core: To remove the center of a fruit (apple, pear, pineapple).

Crisp-Tender: Describes doneness of cooked vegetables when they are between completely soft and hard and crunchy.

Crush: To smash into small pieces using the side of a knife blade (garlic), a meat mallet, mortar and pestle (dried herbs and seeds) or rolling pin.

Cube: To cut food with a knife into uniform squares, ½ inch or larger.

Cut In: To work butter or shortening into dry ingredients. Use a pastry blender, potato masher or fork, lifting up and down with a rocking motion, until particles are of desired size.

Cut Up: To cut food into small pieces of irregular sizes, using a knife or kitchen scissors. Or to cut a large food, like whole chicken, into smaller pieces.

Dash: Refers to less than ⅛ teaspoon of an ingredient.

Deep-Fry: Cooking in hot fat that's deep enough to cover and float the food being fried. See also Fry and Panfry, and Learn to Deep-Fry, page 50.

Deglaze: After food has been fried, a small amount of liquid is added to a hot pan to loosen the brown bits, which are full of flavor. See Learn to Deglaze, page 466.

Dice: To cut food with a knife into uniform ¼-inch squares.

Dip: To moisten or coat food by submerging into liquid mixture to cover completely.

Dissolve: To stir a dry ingredient, like gelatin, into a liquid, like boiling water, until dry ingredient disappears.

Dot: To drop small pieces of an ingredient, like butter, randomly over another food.

Dough: A stiff but pliable mixture of flour, liquid and other ingredients that can be dropped from a spoon, rolled or kneaded.

Using Silicone Mats

Silicone mats prevent food from sticking to pans (and no greasing is necessary). Placed in a baking pan on a lower racks in oven, they catch juices bubbling out of pies or casseroles to prevent burning on the bottom of the oven. They're also great for rolling dough, since the dough will release from the mat easily.

Drain: To pour off liquid by putting food into a colander or strainer. To drain fat from meat, place strainer over a disposable container.

Drizzle: To pour a thin stream over food from a spoon, a bag, a squeeze bottle with a tip or a liquid measuring cup.

Dust: To sprinkle lightly with flour, granulated sugar, powdered sugar or baking cocoa.

Flake: Using a fork to break off pieces or layers of food.

Flute: Using fingers to squeeze pastry, making a decorative edge.

Fold: To combine ingredients without losing volume. See Learn to Beat, Whip and Fold, page 572.

Fry: To cook in hot fat over medium to high heat. See also Deep-Fry and Panfry.

Garnish: A decorative, edible accessory added when serving a dish to enhance its visual appeal with color, flavor or texture. Garnishes may be placed under, around or on top of finished dishes.

Glaze: To spread, drizzle or brush an ingredient on hot or cold food, adding a thin, glossy coating.

Grate: To rub a hard-textured food across the holes of a grater to make tiny particles.

Grease: To coat the bottom and sides of a pan with shortening, using a pastry brush or paper towel, to prevent food from sticking. Cooking spray can often be used. Don't use butter unless specified in a recipe, as it may make foods stick.

Grease and Flour: After greasing pan, sprinkle with a small amount of flour and shake pan to distribute evenly on bottom and sides.

Turn pan upside down over sink; tap bottom to remove excess flour. See Flouring Pan, page 557.

Grill: See Grilling Basics, page 405.

Hull: To remove stems and leaves from strawberries with a paring knife or huller.

Husk: To remove leaves and silk from fresh ears of corn.

Juice: To extract the juice from fruit and vegetables. See Learn to Juice, page 74.

Julienne: To cut into long, thin slices. Stack slices; cut into match-like sticks.

Knead: See Learn to Knead, page 498.

Marinate: To soak food in a flavorful liquid (called a marinade), which infuses flavor into and/or tenderizes food. Meat, fish or vegetables can be marinated. See Marinade Success, page 477.

Melt: To turn a solid into a liquid or semiliquid by heating.

Microwave: To cook, reheat or thaw food in a microwave oven. See Microwave Cooking, page 28.

Mince: To cut food with a knife into very fine pieces that are smaller than chopped but bigger than crushed.

Mix: To combine ingredients to distribute evenly.

Panfry: To crisp or brown meat or other food in an uncovered skillet, using less fat than with deep frying (if fat is necessary). See also Deep-Fry and Fry.

Peel: To cut off an outer covering with a paring knife, vegetable peeler or citrus zester, or to remove peel with your fingers. Also refers to the outside colored layer of citrus fruit that contains aromatic oils and flavor.

Poach: To cook in simmering liquid just below the boiling point.

Process: To use a blender, food processor or mini chopper to liquefy, blend, chop, grind or knead food.

Puree: See Learn to Puree, page 158.

Reduce: To boil liquid uncovered in order to reduce volume as a way to thicken it and/or intensify the flavor.

Roast: To cook meat or vegetables in the oven in a shallow, uncovered pan to achieve a brown exterior and moist interior. A dry-heat cooking method, using little to no liquid, it is great for more tender cuts of meat, poultry, potatoes and vegetables. See Learn to Roast, page 240.

Roll: To use a rolling pin to flatten dough into a thin, even layer. Also means to shape food into balls or to turn over in all directions to coat food.

Roll Up: To roll a flat food that's spread with filling or with filling placed at one end. Begin at one end and turning food over and over, until food is log-shaped.

Sauté: To cook food over medium-high heat in a small amount of fat, frequently tossing or turning.

Score: To cut shallow lines, about ¼ inch deep, through surface of food such as meat or bread to decorate, tenderize or let fat drain away as food cooks or bakes.

Sear: See Learn to Sear, page 302.

Season: To add flavor with salt, pepper, herbs, spices or seasoning mixes.

Shred: To cut food into thin strips with a knife or with a food processor fitted with a shredding disk. Or to pull apart very tender cooked meat using two forks.

Simmer: See Learn to Simmer, page 208.

Skim: To remove fat or foam from soup, broth, stock or jam, using a spoon, ladle or skimmer (a flat utensil with small holes).

Slice: To cut into flat pieces of about the same size.

Smoke: See Smoking Basics, page 424.

Snip: To cut into very small pieces with kitchen scissors.

Soft Peaks: Refers to egg whites or whipping cream beaten until peaks curl over when beaters are lifted from bowl. See Learn to Beat, Whip and Fold, page 572.

Steam: To cook food by placing it in a steamer basket or steamer pan insert over a small amount of boiling or simmering water in a covered pan.

Stew: To cook slowly in a covered pot, pan or casserole in a small amount of liquid to tenderize less tender cuts of meat and/or to blend flavors.

Stiff Peaks: Refers to egg whites or whipping cream beaten until peaks stand up straight when beaters are lifted from the bowl. See also Soft Peaks. See Learn to Beat, Whip and Fold, page 572.

Stir: To combine ingredients with a circular or figure-eight motion until thoroughly blended.

Stir-Fry: Method of cooking small, similar-size pieces of food in a small amount of hot oil in a wok or skillet over high heat while stirring constantly.

Strain: To pour a mixture or liquid through a fine-mesh strainer or cheesecloth to remove unwanted larger particles.

Tear: To break into pieces with your fingers.

Toast: To brown lightly in a toaster, oven, broiler or skillet. See below.

Toss: To gently combine ingredients by lifting and dropping using hands or utensils.

Whip: To add air by beating ingredients; whipping increases the volume until ingredients are light and fluffy. See Learn to Beat, Whip and Fold, page 572.

Toasting Coconut

To toast coconut, heat the oven to 350°F. Spread the coconut in an ungreased shallow pan. Bake uncovered 5 to 7 minutes, stirring occasionally, until golden brown. Or, sprinkle in an ungreased skillet. Cook over medium-low heat 6 to 14 minutes, stirring frequently until coconut begins to brown, then stirring constantly until golden brown.

Toasting Nuts and Sesame Seed

To toast nuts, heat the oven to 350°F. Spread the nuts in an ungreased shallow pan. Bake uncovered 6 to 10 minutes, stirring occasionally, until light brown. Or, sprinkle in an ungreased skillet. Cook over medium heat 5 to 7 minutes, stirring frequently until nuts begin to brown, then stirring constantly until light brown.

To toast sesame seed, sprinkle in an ungreased skillet. Cook over medium-low heat 5 to 7 minutes, stirring frequently until seed begins to brown, then stirring constantly until golden brown.

COOKING AT HIGHER ALTITUDES

For elevations of 3,500 feet or higher, there are unique cooking challenges. Air pressure is lower, so water has a lower boiling point and liquids evaporate faster. That means recipes for conventional and microwave cooking may need to be adjusted.

Unfortunately, no set of rules applies to all recipes; sometimes the only way to make improvements is through trial and error. Here are some guidelines to help you with high-altitude cooking challenges:

- **Boiling foods** such as pasta, rice and vegetables will take longer.

- **Microwave cooking** may require more liquid and foods may need to be microwaved longer; the type and amount of food, the water content of the food and the elevation may affect how much.

- **Meat and poultry cooking** when braising (see page 330) or boiling takes longer— possibly 50 to 100 percent longer. Cooking large meat cuts such as roasts and turkeys in the oven also take longer.

- **Grilling foods** will take longer.

- **Baked goods** made with baking powder or baking soda (but not yeast) can be improved with one or more of these changes:

  - Increase oven temperature by 25°F

  - Increase liquid

  - Decrease baking powder or baking soda

  - Decrease sugar and/or use larger pan

- **High-fat baked** goods such as pound cakes will turn out better if you decrease the fat. Quick breads and cookies usually don't require as many adjustments.

- **Yeast bread dough** may need less flour, as flour dries out more quickly at high altitudes. Use the minimum amount called for or decrease the amount by ¼ to ½ cup. Dough rises faster at high altitudes and can easily overrise: let dough rise just until doubled in size.

Specific High Altitude Cooking Adjustments

Slow Cooking: Meats may take twice as long as specified to get tender. To shorten meat cooking times, use High heat setting. Cut vegetable into smaller pieces than the recipe specifies so that they cook more quickly.

Deep-Fried Foods: May brown too quickly on the outside before the centers are cooked. Reduce oil temperature by 3°F for every 1,000 feet of elevation and increase fry time, if necessary.

Cooked Sugar Mixtures: Any cooked sugar mixtures, such as **boiled candy** or **cooked frostings**, will concentrate faster because water evaporates quicker. Watch the recipe closely during cooking so that it doesn't scorch. You can try reducing the recipe temperature by 2°F for every 1,000 feet of elevation or use the cold water test for candy (see Testing Candy Temperatures, page 545).

More Cooking Help

If you're new to high-altitude cooking, go to the **U.S. Department of Agriculture website** for more information: http://www.fsis.usda.gov/wps/portal /fsis/topics/food-safety-education/get-answers/ food-safety-fact-sheets/safe-food-handling/high -altitude-cooking-and-food-safety/ct_index.

Or visit the **Colorado State University website**: http://www.extension.colostate.edu/SEA/High%20 Altitude%20Cooking.pdf

EASY ENTERTAINING STRATEGIES

Great food and good friends are the perfect ingredients for a memorable event. Relationships are formed and deepened and conversations flow when people can relax and be themselves. But the secret to pulling off a successful gathering starts with a relaxed host or hostess. Use these strategies to entertain with minimal fuss so you can enjoy the party, too.

- Sometimes there isn't time to make everything. Select a few "wow" recipes to prepare that will make a delicious statement, then fill in the rest with go-to prepared foods.

- Consider local delis, specialty bakeries, gourmet shops, ethnic grocers and organic food stores as your behind-the-scenes food providers. Scope them out ahead of time, making sure any unusual items you are interested in will be available when you need them (not just on certain days or for certain occasions).

- Consider asking guests to bring a food item to the party. It's a great way to slash the cost of entertaining if you are on a budget. People will be happy to bring something because you are doing the hosting. If ask them to bring something specifically, it will be easy to round out the menu.

CREATING A CHEESE TRAY

From simple and inexpensive to impressive showstoppers, cheese trays offer limitless variety and are a perfectly-easy choice for an appetizer or dessert.

- Start with at least 3 types of cheese on a tray. For larger groups or buffets, add more varieties and/or larger quantities (plan on at least 2 ounces per person).

- Aim for a variety of flavors and textures (see Cheese Types, page 27). Many specialty grocery stores offer countless types and can provide samples for you to try as well as pairing suggestions.

- Cheese is easier to cut when cold but tastes better at room temperature. Remove from the refrigerator and unwrap 30 to 60 minutes before eating.

- Provide appropriate servers or butter knives appropriate for each type of cheese (see Cheese Servers, page 11).

- Offer crackers or bread to go with the cheese. Consider also adding other foods for more color, interest and flavors, such as dried or fresh fruit, nuts, olives, preserves, mustard, chutney, honey, fig spread or quince paste.

Cheese tray arrangement with a variety of items

CHEESE TYPES

Very Hard (Grating)

Asiago: Mild when young; nutty and semisharp when aged. Melts best when grated. Use with pasta, potatoes, rice salads, vegetables.

Cotija: Firm, dry, crumbly. Salty, sharp flavor. **Cotija Añejo** (aged) is firmer and harder than regular cotija. Both will soften but do not change shape when heated. Crumble over salads or Mexican dishes such as tacos or refried beans.

Parmesan: Sharp, savory, salty. Flavor intensifies with age. Melts best when grated. Use in salads, cooked dishes or casseroles, or sprinkle on pizza.

Romano: Sharp, robust; similar to but richer than Parmesan. **Pecorino Romano** is made from sheep's milk. Melts best when grated. Use in pasta, soups, salads, egg dishes and stuffings, or sprinkle on pizza.

Hard

Cheddar: Rich, nutty flavor ranging from mild to full-bodied (sharp Cheddar also has a bite). **Smoked Cheddar** contains smoked hardwood flavor. Other ingredients may be added.

Gouda: Mellow, rich caramel flavor. **Smoked Gouda** contains smoked hardwood flavor. Melts best when shredded. Use in sandwiches, soups, salads and snacks.

Gruyère: Mellow, buttery, nutty. Melts well. Use in fondues, baked dishes and onion soup.

Jarlsberg: Similar to Swiss. Slightly sweet, nutty. Use in baked dishes, sandwiches and snacks.

Manchego: Creamy, mildly nutty. Melts well. Use as any meal course or in sandwiches, salads, baked dishes and snacks.

Semisoft

Blue: Rich, robust, salty with a lingering tang. Melts best when crumbled. Use in vegetable, green, fruit and pasta salads, spreads, dressings, dips and with grilled meats.

Feta: Very sharp, salty flavor. Melts best in sauces. Use in salads, Greek or egg dishes and hot or cold pasta dishes.

Fontina: Delicate, nutty, with a hint of honey flavor. Melts well. Use in sandwiches, baked dishes and snacks.

Gorgonzola: Italian blue cheese; spicy flavor becomes more pronounced as it ages. Melts best when crumbled. Use in salads, pasta, soufflés, spreads, dressings and dips.

Paneer: Indian cheese, similar to queso blanco. Mild, fresh, mozzarella-like flavor. Unaged, nonmelting, it's customarily diced and used in a variety of dishes including vegetables and salads.

Queso Blanco: Fresh (unripened), with a crumbly, curdy texture. Commonly fried. Softens but holds its shape when heated. Use in soups, salads, stuffings and snacks.

Queso Fresco: Spongy, fresh (unripened), with a grainy texture and slightly acidic flavor. Softens but holds its shape when heated. Crumble over enchiladas or refried beans.

Roquefort: French blue cheese made from sheep's milk. Similar in flavor to blue cheese with a melt-in-your-mouth texture. See Blue cheese for uses.

Soft

Brie: Rich, buttery. Softens and flows when heated. Use as an appetizer and in sandwiches or snacks.

Chèvre (Goat): Creamy, fresh, mildly tangy. Made with goat's milk. Softens but holds its shape when heated. Use in appetizers, salads, baked dishes and sauces.

Fresh Mozzarella: Creamy, soft texture with a delicate, milky flavor. Use in salads, sandwiches, as an appetizer or as a pizza topping.

Mascarpone: Very soft, sweet, mild with a buttery texture. Melts best in sauces. Use in fillings, toppings, dips, spreads and sauces.

Ricotta: Mild, slightly sweet. Use in fillings, stuffings, spreads and cheesecakes.

HEALTH AND NUTRITION

What is healthy eating? It means eating foods that are good for you and also enjoying them. Trendy diets come and go, as does frequently changing nutrition research, leaving a haze of questions. Bottom line: Common sense and balance are the pillars of good health, and good food choices can have a positive effect on our health.

Small but Mighty Changes

Start with small changes that build positive habits over time. Try these easy ways based on *www.choosemyplate.gov* to up your healthy eating game:

- **Don't Skip Meals:** When meals are missed, it's harder to maintain blood glucose levels, making it easy to overeat at the next meal or overindulge in anything just to take away the hunger. Stick to your food plan, but if you don't have time for a meal, have satisfying snacks on hand.

- **Plan Meals and Snacks:** Planning what you eat might seem a little over the top at first, but in time, you'll become aware of what foods keep you satisfied and when your hunger tends to hit, so you can be armed with healthy foods that keep you on track. Plan to grocery shop when you aren't hungry, with a list of the healthy foods you need, so you won't be tempted to purchase foods that aren't part of your plan.

- **Make Half Your Plate Fruits and Vegetables:** Focus on whole fruits (rather than juice). Satisfy your sweet tooth with fresh, frozen, canned or dried fruits instead of cookies or candies; they also make a healthy dessert choice. Vary your veggies to include greens as well as other colorful choices like red and orange. Add veggies to salads, side dishes and main dishes as a way to increase your consumption.

- **Reduce Sugar, Saturated Fat and Sodium:** The USDA Dietary Guidelines recommend consuming: less than 10 percent of calories per day from added sugar, less than 10 percent of calories per day from saturated fats and less than 2,300 milligrams (mg) per day of sodium. Guidelines are based on gender and age; to find out more information visit **http://health.gov/dietary/guidelines/**

- One way to help keep your sodium, saturated fat and added sugars in check is to prepare your veggies without sauces or glazes.

- **Make Half Your Grains Whole Grains:** Choose whole-grain foods, such as oats, whole wheat flour and popcorn, over refined grains for at least half of the grains you eat each day. Read Nutrition Facts labels and ingredient lists on packages to be sure foods are whole grain.

- **Move to Low-Fat and Fat-Free Dairy:** Choose low-fat or fat-free milk and yogurt and low-fat varieties of cheese more often than full-fat varieties.

- **Vary Your Protein Routine:** Mix up your protein choices to include seafood, beans, nuts, seeds, soy, eggs, lean meats and poultry. Eat fish and seafood twice a week. Add beans or peas, unsalted nuts or seeds and soy to main dishes and snacks to add protein.

MICROWAVE COOKING

Convenient to use and great for many tasks, the microwave oven is an indispensable, time-saving appliance for any kitchen. It's perfect to use for reheating but it can be used to cook many food items with little time or fuss. Look here to get great microwave tips and a chart for cooking a variety of foods.

Microwaving Tips

- Increase the cooking time stated in the chart on the next two pages if you increase the amount of food.

- Check food at the minimum time to avoid overcooking. Microwave longer if necessary.

- Stir food from the outer edge to the center so food cooks evenly.

- If food cannot be stirred (or the microwave doesn't have a turntable), rotate dish one-quarter to one-half turn during cooking.

- Foods that contain high amounts of sugar, fat or moisture may cook more quickly.

- Small pieces of food cook faster than larger pieces.

- For even cooking, arrange food in a circle with thickest parts to the outside of the dish.

- Use standing time to help finish cooking and distribute heat through food.

- For microwaving vegetables, see Fresh Vegetable Cooking Chart, page 234.

Microwave Testing for this Book

Recipes in this book that are cooked or heated in a microwave oven were tested in consumer ovens with 700 to 800 watts of power. Find the wattage of your microwave inside the door or unit, on the back near the UL tag or in your Use and Care Manual. Adjust your cooking times if the wattage of your oven is more or less than ours.

MICROWAVE COOKING AND HEATING CHART

Here are at-a-glance times for cooking, warming and softening many favorite foods. Be sure to use microwavable dishes and microwave-safe paper towels or plastic wrap. Follow any directions that follow microwave times for stirring or standing.

FOOD, UTENSIL AND TIPS	POWER LEVEL	AMOUNT	TIME
Bacon (cook) Place on plate or bacon rack lined with paper towels. Place paper towels between layers; cover with paper towel. Microwave until crisp.	High	1 slice 2 slices 4 slices 6 slices 8 slices	30 seconds to 1½ minutes 1 to 2 minutes 2 to 3 minutes 3 to 5 minutes 4 to 6 minutes
Brown Sugar (soften) Place in glass bowl; cover with damp paper towel, then plastic wrap.	High	1 to 3 cups	1 minute Let stand 2 minutes, until softened. Repeat heating once or twice.
Butter (melt) Remove wrapper. Place in glass bowl; cover with paper towel.	High	1 to 8 tablespoons ½ to 1 cup	10 to 50 seconds 60 to 75 seconds
Butter (soften) Remove wrapper. Place in glass bowl, uncovered.	Low (30%)	1 to 8 tablespoons ½ to 1 cup	10 to 40 seconds 30 seconds to 1 minute
Caramels (melt) Remove wrappers. Place in a 4-cup glass measuring cup, uncovered.	High	1 bag (11 ounces) plus 2 to 4 tablespoons milk	2 to 3 minutes, stirring once or twice.
Baking Chocolate (melt) Remove wrappers. Place in glass dish, covered.	Medium (50%)	1 to 3 ounces	1½ to 2½ minutes, until can be stirred smooth.
Chocolate Chips (melt) Place in glass bowl, uncovered.	Medium (50%)	½ to 1 cup	2 to 3 minutes, until can be stirred smooth.
Coconut (toast) Place in pie plate, uncovered.	High	¼ to ½ cup 1 cup	1½ to 2 minutes 2 to 3 minutes Stir every 30 seconds.
Cream Cheese (soften) Remove wrapper or tub. Place in glass bowl, uncovered.	Medium (50%)	8-oz package 8-oz tub	1 to 1½ minutes 45 seconds to 1 minute

Continued on next page.

Continued from previous page.

MICROWAVE COOKING AND HEATING CHART

FOOD, UTENSIL AND TIPS	POWER LEVEL	AMOUNT	TIME
Fruit, Dried (soften) Place in 2-cup glass measuring cup; add ½ teaspoon water for each ½ cup fruit. Cover with plastic wrap, turning back a corner or ¼-inch edge to vent steam.	High	¼ to ½ cup ½ to 1 cup	30 to 45 seconds 45 seconds to 1 minute Let stand 2 minutes.
Fruit, Frozen (thaw) Place in glass bowl.	Medium (50%)	16-oz bag	3 to 5 minutes Thaw until most of the ice is gone, stirring or rearranging twice.
Fruit, Refrigerated (warm) Place on turntable or floor of microwave.	High	1 medium 2 medium	15 seconds 20 to 30 seconds Let stand 2 minutes.
Honey (dissolve crystals) Leave in jar with lid removed, uncovered.	High	½ to 1 cup	45 seconds to 1½ minutes, stirring every 20 to 30 seconds or until crystals dissolve.
Ice Cream (soften) Leave in original container; remove any foil or plastic covering and loosen the lid (whether cardboard or plastic).	Low (10%)	½ gallon	2 to 3 minutes Let stand 2 to 3 minutes.
Muffins or Rolls, Small to Medium (heat) Place on plate, napkin or napkin-lined non-metal basket, uncovered.	High	1 2 3 4	5 to 10 seconds 10 to 15 seconds 12 to 20 seconds 20 to 30 seconds
Muffins, Large to Jumbo (heat) Place on plate or napkin, uncovered.	High	1 2 3 4	10 to 20 seconds 20 to 30 seconds 30 to 40 seconds 40 to 50 seconds Let stand 1 minute.
Nuts, Chopped (toasted) Place in glass measuring cup, uncovered; add ¼ teaspoon vegetable oil for each ¼ cup nuts.	High	¼ to ½ cup ½ to 1 cup	2½ to 3½ minutes 3 to 4 minutes Stir every 30 seconds, until light brown.
Snack, Popcorn, Pretzels, Corn or Potato Chips (crisp) Place in paper towel–lined non-metal basket, uncovered.	High	2 cups 4 cups	20 to 40 seconds 40 seconds to 1 minute
Syrup (heat) Place in glass measuring cup or pitcher, uncovered.	High	½ cup 1 cup	30 to 45 seconds 45 seconds to 1 minute Stir every 30 seconds.
Water (boil) Place in glass measuring cup, uncovered.	High	1 cup	2 to 3 minutes

FOOD SAFETY

America's food supply is one of the safest in the world. Farmers, ranchers, food processors, supermarkets and restaurants must follow strict rules and regulations while getting food to you. Once food leaves the grocery store, care must be taken to keep it safe.

Why worry about food safety? Because most illnesses reported from "bad food" are caused by bacterial contamination. Nearly all cases can be linked to improper food handling and could have been prevented.

Microorganisms are always with us: They are on us and on animals, in the air and water and on raw food. Some bacteria are useful, like those used to make cheese or ferment beer. But other bacteria cause foods to spoil or cause food poisoning.

Bacteria that can cause food to spoil can grow at refrigerator temperatures (below 40°F). They usually make the food look or smell bad, raising a red flag that it should be thrown out. Food poisoning bacteria grow at temperatures between 40°F and 140°F—those temperatures between hot-from-the-oven and chilled. These are pathogens that you can't see, smell or taste, which if eaten may lead to illness, disease or even death.

To prevent this type of bacteria from becoming harmful, they must be stopped from multiplying. If contaminated food is eaten, people most often get sick within 4 to 48 hours. It's not always easy to determine if the problem is the flu or food poisoning. Call a doctor or go to a hospital immediately if symptoms are severe.

Basic Food Safety Rules

Wash Your Hands

Proper hand washing could eliminate nearly half of all causes of food-borne illness. Always wash hands:

- Before handling food and utensils and serving and eating food.
- After handling food—especially raw meat, poultry, fish, shellfish and eggs.
- Between jobs like cutting up raw chicken and making a salad.

- After using the bathroom, blowing your nose, changing diapers, touching pets, or handling garbage, dirty dishes, hair, dirty laundry and phones.
- If you have any kind of skin cut or infection on your hands; and wear protective plastic or rubber gloves.

Keep It Clean

- Wash all utensils and surfaces with hot, soapy water after contact with raw meat, poultry, fish or seafood. Use paper towels when working with these foods.
- Bleach and commercial kitchen-cleaning agents are the most effective at killing bacteria. Hot water and soap or hot water alone may not kill all strains of bacteria that are present.
- Keep dishcloths and sponges clean and dry because when wet, these materials harbor bacteria and may promote their growth. Wash them often in hot water in the washing machine and, for added safety, sanitize them three times a week by soaking them in a mixture of ¾ cup bleach to 1 gallon water.
- Clean refrigerator surfaces inside and out. Sort through perishable foods each week, tossing out anything past its prime.
- Keep pets out the kitchen and away from food.

Don't Cross-Contaminate

Cross-contamination happens when cooked or ready-to-eat foods pick up bacteria from other foods, hands, cutting boards and utensils. Raw meat, poultry, shellfish, fish and eggs require special handling to keep them from contaminating other foods:

- Keep them separate from cooked or ready-to-eat foods in your grocery cart.
- Prevent leaks by repacking leaky packages and thawing foods in the refrigerator on a tray with sides to catch any juices.
- It's best to have at least two cutting boards—one for raw meats and so forth and one for vegetables and fruit. Don't cut raw meat on wooden boards, as the raw juices can get into the wood, where bacteria can grow.

- Don't put cooked food on an unwashed plate that was used for raw meats.

- Wash sinks and sink mats with hot, soapy water if they've come in contact with raw meat.

Keep Hot Food Hot

- Hot foods can't be left at room temperature for more than 2 hours, including preparation time. Keeping foods hot means keeping them at 140°F or higher.

- Don't partially cook perishable foods and then set them aside or refrigerate to finish them later. It's okay to cook them with one appliance if they are immediately completed with another—grilling recipes will frequently use this technique.

- Keep cooked food hot, or refrigerate until ready to serve. This includes take-out foods, too.

- Reheat leftovers, stirring often, until steaming hot (165°F), using a cover to get the food hot in the center and retain moisture. Heat soups, sauces and gravies to a rolling boil, then boil 1 minute, stirring frequently, before serving.

Keep Cold Food Cold

- Cold foods can't be left at room temperature for more than 2 hours, including preparation time. Keeping foods cold means keeping them at 40°F or lower.

- When shopping, put perishable foods (eggs, milk, seafood, fish, meat and poultry or items that contain them) in your cart last. Make sure they are cold to the touch when you select them. Put packages that can leak into plastic bags to prevent dripping on other foods in your cart.

- Perishable foods should be taken home and refrigerated immediately. If the trip is longer than 30 minutes or it is a hot day, bring freezer shopping bags or a cooler with freezer packs for these items to prevent them from reaching unsafe temperatures.

- Purchase frozen foods that are free from ice crystals, because ice crystals may mean the food had been partially thawed and refrozen.

- Foods will chill faster if stored in smaller, shallow containers and there is space between them in the refrigerator or freezer.

- Never thaw foods at room temperature—thaw only in the refrigerator or microwave following manufacturer's directions. If food is thawed in the microwave, cook it immediately.

Safe Buffets

- Serve food in family-size dishes rather than larger, catering-size ones. Put out new dishes of food as they become empty.

- Keep foods hot (at least 140°F) by using slow cookers, chafing dishes, fondue pots or a warming tray. Use warming units heated by electricity or canned cooking fuel—not candles, as they don't get hot enough to keep foods safe.

- Chill both salads made with seafood, poultry, meat or dairy products and the dish before serving; they will stay cold longer.

- Hot or cold foods shouldn't stand at room temperature for more than 2 hours. Toss it if you don't know how long it's been out.

- At restaurants or potlucks, salad bars and buffets should look clean. Make sure cold foods are cold and hot foods are steaming before putting them on your plate.

Safe Picnics and Packed Lunches

- Pack lunches in insulated lunch bags or in a small cooler with a freezer pack, frozen juice box or frozen small plastic bottle of water to keep food cold. Keep out of the sun. Perishable foods packed in an uninsulated bag should be refrigerated.

- Wash thermal containers and rinse well with boiling water after each use. Be sure hot foods are boiling when poured into these containers.

- Wash fruits and vegetables before packing.

- Chill picnic food before packing it in freezer shopping bags or an ice-filled cooler. Because beverage coolers will be opened more frequently, use one cooler for beverages and one for perishable food.

- Tightly wrap raw meat, poultry, fish and seafood or pack them in a separate cooler to keep them from dripping on other foods. Bring along hand sanitizer for washing hands after handling raw poultry, meat, fish or seafood.

STORING FOOD IN THE REFRIGERATOR AND FREEZER

REFRIGERATOR AND FREEZER FOOD STORAGE CHART

FOODS	REFRIGERATOR (35°F TO 40°F)	FREEZER (0°F OR BELOW)
Baked Products		
Breads, coffee cakes, muffins, quick and yeast breads Cool completely; wrap tightly after frostings have set at room temperature. Freeze muffins uncovered before packaging together.	5 to 7 days Refrigerate bread during hot, humid weather or if it contains perishable ingredients like meat or cheese.	2 to 3 months Freeze tightly wrapped in freezer plastic bags. Thaw by loosening wrap; let stand 2 to 3 hours.
Cakes (unfrosted or frosted) Cool completely; wrap tightly. Do not freeze cakes with fruit filling. Thaw by loosening wrap; thaw unfrosted cakes at room temperature. For frosted cakes, place in refrigerator overnight.	3 to 5 days Refrigerate cakes that contain dairy products in the filling (like custard filling) or frosting.	3 to 4 months (unfrosted) 2 to 3 months (frosted) Cakes filled and frosted with plain sweetened whipped cream can be frozen. Freeze unwrapped on a plate. When frozen, wrap and freeze.
Cheesecakes (baked)	3 to 5 days	4 to 5 months Thaw wrapped in refrigerator 4 to 6 hours.
Cookies (baked) Place delicate or frosted cookies between layers of waxed paper. Do not freeze meringue, custard-filled or cream-filled cookies.	Only if stated in recipe	Up to 12 months (unfrosted) Up to 3 months (frosted) Thaw most cookies, covered, in container at room temperature 1 to 2 hours. Crisp cookies: Remove from container to thaw.
Pies (unbaked or baked fruit pies, baked pecan and baked pumpkin pies) Thaw frozen baked fruit and pecan pies unwrapped at room temperature or unwrap and thaw at room temperature 1 hour, then heat in 375°F oven 35 to 40 minutes or until warm. Thaw frozen baked pecan pie unwrapped 3 to 4 hours in refrigerator.	3 to 5 days (baked pumpkin pie) 2-3 days (baked fruit pie) 1-2 days (unbaked fruit pie) 3-5 days (pecan pie)	Up to 4 months (unbaked and baked fruit pies, baked pecan pie) 1 month (baked pumpkin pie) To thaw unbaked fruit pies, unwrap and cut slits in top crust. Bake at 425°F for 15 minutes. Reduce oven to 375°F; bake 30 to 45 minutes longer or until juices begin to bubble through slits.
Dairy Products		
Cottage cheese and creamy ricotta	Up to 10 days	Not recommended
Hard cheese If hard cheese is moldy, trim ½ inch from the affected area and rewrap tightly.	3 to 4 weeks	6 to 8 weeks Thaw wrapped cheeses in refrigerator. Texture will be crumbly; use in baked goods.
Buttermilk, cream and milk	Up to 5 days 1 day (sweetened whipped cream).	Not recommended Unsweetened and sweetened whipped cream can be frozen by dropping small mounds onto waxed paper; freeze and store in airtight container 1 to 2 weeks. To thaw, let stand at room temperature about 15 minutes.
Sour cream and yogurt	Up to 1 week	Not recommended
Eggs		
Fresh eggs in shell **Cooked eggs in shell**	2 weeks 1 week	Not recommended Not recommended

Continued on next page.

Continued from previous page.

REFRIGERATOR AND FREEZER FOOD STORAGE CHART

FOODS	REFRIGERATOR (35°F TO 40°F)	FREEZER (0°F OR BELOW)
Fats and Oils		
Butter	No longer than 2 weeks	No longer than 2 months
Margarine and spreads	No longer than 1 month	No longer than 2 months
Mayonnaise and salad dressing	No longer than 6 months	Not recommended
Meats		
If wrapped in white butcher paper, rewrap tightly in plastic wrap, foil or plastic freezer bags.		
Chops (uncooked)	3 to 5 days	4 to 6 months
Ground (uncooked)	1 to 2 days	3 to 4 months
Roasts and steaks (uncooked)	3 to 5 days	6 to 12 months
Cooked	3 to 4 days	2 to 3 months
Cold cuts	3 to 5 days (opened)	Not recommended
	2 weeks (unopened)	Not recommended
Bacon, cured	5 to 7 days	No longer than 1 month
Hot dogs	1 week (opened)	1 to 2 months
	2 weeks (unopened)	1 to 2 months
Ham, whole or half (cooked)	5 to 7 days	1 to 2 months
Ham slices (cooked)	3 to 4 days	1 to 2 months
Nuts		
Store nuts in airtight container		
	6 months	1 year
Poultry		
Whole, including game birds, ducks and geese (uncooked)	1 to 2 days	No longer than 12 months
Cut up (cooked)	5 to 7 days	No longer than 9 months
Cooked	3 to 4 days	1 to 2 months
Seafood		
Fish (uncooked)	1 to 2 days	3 to 6 months
Fish (breaded, cooked)	Store in freezer	2 to 3 months
Shellfish (uncooked)	Up to 1 to 2 days	3 to 4 months
Shellfish (cooked)	3 to 4 days	1 to 2 months

Appetizers

CALORIE SMART = See Helpful Nutrition and Cooking Information, page 643   FAST = Ready in 30 minutes or less
EASY = Prep in 10 minutes or less **plus** five ingredients or less   LIGHTER = 25% fewer calories or grams of fat
MAKE AHEAD = Make-ahead directions   SLOW COOKER = Slow cooker directions

APPETIZER BASICS

Whether you call them appetizers or hors d'oeuvres, variety is the name of the game when these tasty morsels are part of the occasion. And it doesn't need to be a special occasion to enjoy their amazing versatility.

The word "appetizers" simply refers to any food served before a meal to entice the appetite. Often we think of appetizers as being small plates served at the table and hors d'oeuvres as small finger foods that are served separately from the meal—a subtle difference. But the terms are used interchangeably and include all snack-type foods, whether they are served as a meal itself, or simply to awaken taste buds.

The array of appetizers ranges from dips and spreads to elegant choices such as tapas and fancy canapés. But whether you are serving one or two or expecting a crowd, planning is key.

CHOOSING APPETIZERS

- Depending on the occasion, you might want to make a meal of appetizers or just snack on one or two tasty morsels before the meal.

- Select a menu with an eye toward different foods, flavors and textures. For larger groups, choose both hot and cold appetizers for variety and ease of serving. Be mindful of oven space when planning hot choices.

- Allow for 2 or 3 pieces of each appetizer per person. Many recipes can be doubled or tripled easily.

- Map out how many guests will attend, what you want to serve and when and where you will serve food before deciding what to make.

- Make recipes or parts of recipes ahead as much as possible.

SERVING WITH STYLE

- Choose a place for the food that guests can access easily. For a larger gathering, set up several areas with different appetizers so guests can help themselves at their leisure.

- Consider your theme and who will attend, then decorate and set the table or buffet area ahead of time. Think about serving—will the event require equipment such as a fondue pot, slow cooker or hot plate?

- Make cutlery bundles wrapped in paper or cloth napkins for foods that require utensils. Add small trays for guests to gather appetizers—often beverages will fit on these trays, too.

- Unless it is a sit-down occasion, choose appetizers that are easy to pick up.

- Serve foods in interesting containers—pretty plates/bowls, hollowed out loaves of bread, fun baskets.

Tomato-Basil Crostini (page 59)

CHARCUTERIE

If you have never assembled a charcuterie board, a wonderful experience awaits you. This crowd-pleasing appetizer is simply a tasty combination of cured meats and other delicious foods to round out the display. Like a cheese platter, a charcuterie board is low maintenance and can serve a crowd easily.

Make your display stand out by including a few other foods tucked in around the meats, adding visual interest, flavors and textures to the board. You'll find good ideas both in this chapter and the Do It Yourself chapter. Most can be made ahead and then simply spooned into serving dishes.

Start by adding bread to the board. Choose toasted French bread, breadsticks, small cocktail breads or even hearty crackers. Add a spicy food, such as spiced nuts or spicy pickles. Offer a sweet sauce, like Sweet Tomato Jam, page 435, or chutney. Sour, crunchy foods like Pickled Red Onions (right) or other pickled vegetables add delightful contrast to the rich meats. Or check out gourmet food shops for unique finds when you're short on time. Cheeses can be added, too, for variety. (See page 27 for cheese types.)

Cutting boards of many shapes and sizes are available, a large flat tray, marble or other smooth surfaces make visually interesting and practical choices for serving charcuterie.

For the meats, check out a good deli, ethnic market or butcher shop. Be sure to ask for samples so that you can try any meats that are unfamiliar. Here are some popular choices, but there are many more options available.

Bacon: Smoked pork belly

Bresaola: Cured beef tenderloin that is air-dried and salted

Capicola (Capocollo): Dry-cured rolled pork shoulder

Cesina: Spanish version of bresaola

Chorizo: Cured hard sausage with a spicy garlicky flavor

Finocchiona: Cured Italian salami flavored with fennel seed

Lomo de Cerdo: Cured pork tenderloin

Mortadella: Large Italian hard sausage made with pork

Pancetta: Italian bacon made from cured pork belly

Pâté or Terrine: Cooked ground meat and fat minced into a spreadable paste—mixture in a terrine will be more coarsely chopped

Pepperoni: Variety of salami, usually made with pork and beef

Prosciutto: Dry-cured ham

Rillettes: Rustic pâté made from meat that has been poached in its own fat, then shredded and combined with some of the fat.

Salami: Cured sausage made from fermented and air-dried beef or pork

Serrano Ham: Spanish dry-cured ham similar to prosciutto

Smoked Country Ham: Salty cured ham

Sopressata: Cured hard spicy sausage

Speck and Lardo: German and Italian types of salted and seasoned lard

Pickled Red Onions CALORIE SMART

PREP 20 min **TOTAL** 8 hr 20 min • 16 servings

3 medium red onions, thinly sliced
2 tablespoons vegetable oil
2 cloves garlic, finely chopped
1 cup cider vinegar or ⅓ cup fresh lime juice
4 black peppercorns
1 teaspoon salt
⅛ teaspoon dried oregano leaves
⅛ teaspoon dried thyme leaves
⅛ teaspoon dried marjoram leaves
3 dried bay leaves

1 In large bowl, place onions. Cover with boiling water; let stand about 10 minutes. Drain well.

2 In 12-inch skillet, heat oil over medium-high heat. Add onions and garlic; cook 5 to 8 minutes, stirring frequently, until onions are crisp-tender. Transfer onions to medium bowl. Stir in remaining ingredients until blended.

3 Cover tightly; refrigerate at least 8 hours. Remove bay leaves before serving. Store in refrigerator up to 3 days.

1 Serving: Calories 25 (Calories from Fat 15); Total Fat 2g (Saturated Fat 0g, Trans Fat 0g); Cholesterol 0mg; Sodium 150mg; Total Carbohydrate 2g (Dietary Fiber 0g, Sugars 2g); Protein 0g **Exchanges:** ½ Vegetable **Carbohydrate Choices:** 0

Smoked Country Ham

Capocollo

Mortadella

Prosciutto

Finocchiona

Cana de Cabra

Prosciutto

Chorizo

Smoked Country Ham

Bacon

Pâté

Mahón

Pepperoni

Pancetta

Asiago with Rosemary

Manchego

Roasted Garlic

Southwestern Spiced Party Nuts

Roasted Garlic CALORIE SMART • EASY

Roasting garlic turns it into a sweet and delicious spread. Garlic bulbs (heads of garlic) are made up of as many as 15 sections, called cloves.

PREP 10 min **TOTAL** 1 hr • 2 to 8 tablespoons

- 1 to 4 bulbs garlic
- 2 teaspoons olive or vegetable oil for each bulb garlic
  Salt and pepper to taste
  Sliced French bread, if desired

1 Heat oven to 350°F. Carefully peel paperlike skin from around each bulb of garlic, leaving just enough to hold cloves together. Cut ¼- to ½-inch slice from top of each bulb to expose cloves. Place each bulb, cut side up, on 12-inch square of foil.

2 Drizzle 2 teaspoons oil over each bulb. Sprinkle with salt and pepper. Wrap securely in foil. Place in pie plate or shallow baking pan.

3 Bake 45 to 50 minutes or until garlic is tender when pierced with toothpick or fork. Let stand until cool enough to handle. To serve, gently squeeze soft garlic out of cloves. Spread garlic on bread.

1 Tablespoon: Calories 70; Total Fat 4.5g (Saturated Fat 0.5g, Trans Fat 0g); Cholesterol 0mg; Sodium 300mg; Total Carbohydrate 6g (Dietary Fiber 0g, Sugars 0g); Protein 1g **Exchanges:** 1 Vegetable, 1 Fat **Carbohydrate Choices:** ½

Southwestern Spiced Party Nuts FAST

PREP 10 min **TOTAL** 20 min • 2¼ cups nuts

- 1 can (9.5 to 11.5 oz) salted mixed nuts
- 1 tablespoon butter, melted
- 2 teaspoons chili powder
- ½ teaspoon garlic powder
- ½ teaspoon onion powder
- ¼ teaspoon ground cinnamon
- ¼ teaspoon ground red pepper (cayenne)
- 2 tablespoons sugar

1 Heat oven to 300°F. In medium bowl, mix nuts and butter until nuts are coated. In small bowl, mix remaining ingredients except sugar; sprinkle over nuts. Stir until nuts are completely coated. In ungreased 15x10x1-inch pan, spread nuts in single layer.

2 Bake uncovered about 10 minutes or until nuts are toasted. Return to medium bowl. While nuts are still hot, sprinkle with sugar and toss to coat. Serve warm, or cool completely, about 1 hour. Store in airtight container at room temperature up to 3 weeks.

¼ Cup: Calories 250; Total Fat 21g (Saturated Fat 3.5g, Trans Fat 0g); Cholesterol 0mg; Sodium 240mg; Total Carbohydrate 11g (Dietary Fiber 3g, Sugars 4g); Protein 6g **Exchanges:** 1 Starch, ½ High-Fat Meat, 3 Fat **Carbohydrate Choices:** 1

Southwestern Spiced Cashews Substitute salted whole cashews for the mixed nuts.

Guacamole

Cinnamon-Sugared Nuts

PREP 10 min **TOTAL** 40 min • 2 cups nuts

- 1 tablespoon slightly beaten egg white
- 2 cups pecan halves, unblanched whole almonds or walnut halves
- ¼ cup sugar
- 2 teaspoons ground cinnamon
- ¼ teaspoon ground nutmeg
- ¼ teaspoon ground cloves

1 Heat oven to 300°F. In medium bowl, stir egg white and nuts until nuts are coated and sticky.

2 In small bowl, stir remaining ingredients until well mixed; sprinkle over nuts. Stir until nuts are coated. In ungreased 15x10x1-inch pan, spread nuts in single layer.

3 Bake uncovered about 30 minutes or until toasted (nut coating becomes crunchy during baking and cooling). Serve warm, or cool completely, about 1 hour. Store in airtight container at room temperature up to 3 weeks.

¼ **Cup:** Calories 210; Total Fat 18g (Saturated Fat 1.5g, Trans Fat 0g); Cholesterol 0mg; Sodium 0mg; Total Carbohydrate 10g (Dietary Fiber 3g, Sugars 7g); Protein 3g **Exchanges:** ½ Other Carbohydrate, ½ High-Fat Meat, 3 Fat **Carbohydrate Choices:** ½

Cinnamon-Cardamom Mixed Nuts Substitute lightly salted mixed nuts for the pecans and ground cardamom for the nutmeg. Omit cloves.

Guacamole CALORIE SMART • FAST

Ripe avocados yield to gentle pressure. To ripen, let stand at room temperature in a closed paper bag until ripe.

PREP 15 min **TOTAL** 15 min • 2 cups dip

- 1 small jalapeño chile*
- 2 large ripe avocados
- 2 tablespoons fresh lime or lemon juice
- 2 tablespoons finely chopped fresh cilantro
- ¼ to ½ teaspoon salt
  Dash pepper
- 1 small clove garlic, finely chopped
- 1 small tomato, seeded, chopped (½ cup)
- 2 tablespoons finely chopped red onion
  Tortilla chips, if desired

1 Remove stems, seeds and ribs from chile; chop chile. Cut avocados lengthwise in half; remove pit and peel. In medium glass or plastic bowl, mash avocados with fork. Gently stir in chile and remaining ingredients except tortilla chips until mixed.

2 Serve with tortilla chips. Press and smooth plastic wrap directly on surface of leftover guacamole to help prevent discoloration.

*Or substitute 1 tablespoon canned chopped green chiles for the jalapeño chile.

1 Tablespoon: Calories 15; Total Fat 1g (Saturated Fat 0g, Trans Fat 0g); Cholesterol 0mg; Sodium 15mg; Total Carbohydrate 0g (Dietary Fiber 0g, Sugars 0g); Protein 0g **Exchanges:** Free **Carbohydrate Choices:** 0

Cotija Guacamole Stir in ½ cup crumbled Cotija cheese with remaining ingredients in Step 1.

Chipotle Guacamole Omit the jalapeño and add 1 chopped chipotle chile in adobo sauce instead.

Cutting an Avocado

Cut avocado lengthwise through skin around pit.

With hands, slowly twist both sides to separate.

Slide flatware tablespoon under pit to remove.

Make cuts through flesh; remove with spoon.

Hummus CALORIE SMART • FAST

Tahini, a thick paste made from ground sesame seed, gives this dip its distinctive flavor. Look for it in the condiment, ethnic foods or pickle aisle.

PREP 5 min **TOTAL** 5 min • 2 cups dip

- 1 can (15 to 16 oz) chickpeas, drained, ¼ cup liquid reserved
- ½ cup tahini*
- ¼ cup olive oil
- 2 cloves garlic, finely chopped
- 3 tablespoons lemon juice
- 1 teaspoon salt
- ⅛ teaspoon pepper
   Chopped fresh parsley
   Pita bread wedges, crackers or fresh vegetables, if desired

1 In blender or food processor, place beans, reserved bean liquid, tahini, oil, garlic, lemon juice, salt and pepper. Cover and blend on high speed, stopping occasionally to scrape side, until smooth.

2 Spoon into serving dish. Garnish with parsley. Serve with pita bread wedges.

* Or substitute ½ cup sesame seed for the tahini, but the hummus will not be smooth.

2 Tablespoons: Calories 60; Total Fat 3g (Saturated Fat 0g, Trans Fat 0g); Cholesterol 0mg; Sodium 85mg; Total Carbohydrate 6g (Dietary Fiber 1g, Sugars 0g); Protein 2g **Exchanges:** 1 Vegetable, ½ Fat **Carbohydrate Choices:** ½

Cumin Hummus Add ¼ teaspoon ground cumin with the salt and pepper. Omit parsley. Sprinkle with cumin seed, if desired.

Roasted Garlic Hummus Stir 1 to 2 table-spoons Roasted Garlic (page 40) into blended mixture.

Sun-Dried Tomato Hummus Stir ⅓ cup chopped drained sun-dried tomatoes (packed in oil) into blended mixture.

Baba Ghanoush CALORIE SMART

This heathly vegan dip comes together easily and is a flavorful way to enjoy eggplant—even for those who don't like eggplant!

PREP 10 min **TOTAL** 1 hr 35 min • 1½ cups dip

- 1 large eggplant (about 1½ lb)*
- 1 tablespoon olive oil

- 2 tablespoons sesame tahini paste
- 1 tablespoon fresh lemon juice
- 1 clove garlic, minced
- ¾ teaspoon salt
- ½ teaspoon ground cumin
- ⅛ teaspoon pepper
   Pomegranate seeds and chopped fresh parsley, if desired
   Toasted baguette slices or pita wedges, if desired

1 Heat oven to 450°F. Line 15x10x1-inch pan with foil. Pierce eggplant in several places with tip of sharp knife; place on pan. Roast uncovered 45 to 55 minutes, turning once, until skin is blackened and inside begins to soften. Let stand until cool enough to handle, about 30 minutes.

2 Cut eggplant lengthwise in half. Scoop out flesh and place on several layers of paper towel to absorb excess moisture. In food processor, place eggplant, oil, tahini, lemon juice, garlic, salt, cumin and pepper. Cover and process until smooth.

3 Spoon into serving bowl. Sprinkle with pomegranate seeds and parsley. Serve with toasted baguette slices.

*Choose dark purple, smooth, glossy, taut-skinned eggplant that is free from blemishes and rust spots. Caps and stems should be intact and free of mold.

2 Tablespoons: Calories 45; Total Fat 2.5g (Saturated Fat 0g, Trans Fat 0g); Cholesterol 0mg; Sodium 150mg; Total Carbohydrate 4g (Dietary Fiber 2g, Sugars 2g); Protein 1g **Exchanges:** 1 Vegetable, ½ Fat **Carbohydrate Choices:** 0

Charring Eggplant

Roast eggplant until skin is blackened and insides begin to soften.

Scoop out flesh and place on several layers of paper towel to absorb excess moisture.

Tzatziki Dip (page 44),
Baba Ghanoush, Hummus

Tzatziki Dip CALORIE SMART • EASY

A classic Greek yogurt dip, tzatziki typically includes cucumber and mint.

PREP 10 min **TOTAL** 2 hr 10 min • 2 cups dip

- 1½ cups plain Greek yogurt (to make your own, see page 444)
- ⅔ cup finely chopped peeled, seeded English (hothouse) cucumber
- 3 tablespoons finely chopped fresh mint leaves
- 1½ teaspoons fresh lemon juice
- 1 teaspoon olive oil
- ½ teaspoon salt
  Additional fresh mint leaves, if desired
  Pita fold breads or pita (pocket) breads, cut into wedges, if desired
  Fresh vegetables, if desired

1 In medium bowl, gently mix yogurt, cucumber, chopped mint, lemon juice, oil and salt until blended. Cover and refrigerate 2 hours to blend flavors.

2 Garnish with mint leaves. Serve with pita wedges and vegetables.

2 Tablespoons: Calories 20; Total Fat 1g (Saturated Fat 0g, Trans Fat 0g); Cholesterol 0mg; Sodium 85mg; Total Carbohydrate 1g (Dietary Fiber 0g, Sugars 1g); Protein 2g **Exchanges:** Free **Carbohydrate Choices:** 0

Greek Layered Dip

CALORIE SMART • FAST

PREP 20 min **TOTAL** 20 min • 12 servings

- 2 whole wheat pita (pocket) breads (6 inch)
  Cooking spray
- 1 container (8 oz) plain hummus (to make your own, see page 42)
- 1 container (6 oz) plain Greek yogurt (to make your own, see page 444)
- 1 tablespoon chopped fresh parsley
- 1 teaspoon lemon juice
- ⅛ teaspoon pepper
- 1 medium plum (Roma) tomato, seeded, chopped
- ⅓ cup pitted kalamata or ripe olives, quartered
- ⅓ cup finely chopped seeded cucumber
- 1 cup crumbled feta cheese (4 oz)
- 4 medium green onions, chopped (¼ cup)
- 1 tablespoon olive oil
- ½ medium cucumber, sliced
- 1 medium green or red bell pepper, cut into strips

1 Heat oven to 350°F. Split each pita bread horizontally to make 2 rounds. Cut each round into 6 wedges. Place bread, rough surface up, on ungreased cookie sheet. Spray with cooking spray. Bake 8 to 10 minutes or until golden brown and crisp; cool.

2 Meanwhile, spread hummus on shallow serving platter or in pie plate. In small bowl, mix yogurt, parsley, lemon juice and pepper; spread evenly over hummus. Top with tomato, olives, chopped cucumber, cheese and onions. Drizzle with oil. Serve with pita chips, sliced cucumber and bell pepper strips.

1 Serving (¼ Cup Dip, 2 Chips and 4 Veggies): Calories 100; Total Fat 4.5g (Saturated Fat 1g, Trans Fat 0g); Cholesterol 5mg; Sodium 270mg; Total Carbohydrate 12g (Dietary Fiber 2g, Sugars 3g); Protein 4g **Exchanges:** ½ Starch, ½ Skim Milk, ½ Fat **Carbohydrate Choices:** 1

LIGHTER Directions To reduce the fat and calories in this recipe, use fat-free plain Greek yogurt. Reduce feta cheese to ½ cup and olive oil to 1 teaspoon.

Greek Layered Dip

Steamed Edamame in the Shell with Dipping Sauces

CALORIE SMART • FAST

PREP 15 min **TOTAL** 15 min • 10 servings

GINGER-SOY DIPPING SAUCE

⅔ cup reduced-sodium or regular soy sauce

2 tablespoons honey

2 teaspoons finely chopped gingerroot

½ teaspoon crushed red pepper flakes

2 green onions with green tops, thinly sliced

CREAMY WASABI DIPPING SAUCE

½ cup mayonnaise

⅓ cup sour cream

2 teaspoons wasabi powder*

¼ teaspoon salt

Toasted sesame seed and black sesame seed, if desired

EDAMAME

1 bag (12 oz) frozen edamame soybeans (in the pod)**

1 In small bowl, mix soy sauce, honey, gingerroot and pepper flakes until well blended; stir in onions. In another small bowl, mix mayonnaise, sour cream, wasabi powder and salt until smooth; sprinkle with sesame seed. Set sauces aside.

2 In 4-quart saucepan, place steamer basket. Add 1 cup water; heat to boiling. Add edamame to basket; cover and cook 3 to 6 minutes or until crisp-tender. Remove from basket to serving bowl; let stand until cool enough to handle. Serve warm or room temperature with dipping sauces.

*Wasabi, also called Japanese horseradish, has a sharp, pungent, fiery flavor. It comes in both powder and paste form and is available in the Asian-foods aisle of large supermarkets. If you can't find it, regular prepared horseradish makes a great substitute.

**Fresh edamame (green soybeans), found in the produce section, can be substituted for frozen edamame. Increase steaming time to 20 minutes.

1 Serving (10 Edamame and 1 Tablespoon of Each Sauce):
Calories 150; Total Fat 11g (Saturated Fat 2.5g, Trans Fat 0g); Cholesterol 10mg; Sodium 710mg; Total Carbohydrate 8g (Dietary Fiber 1g, Sugars 5g); Protein 3g **Exchanges:** ½ Other Carbohydrate, ½ Vegetable, 2 Fat **Carbohydrate Choices:** ½

Olive Tapenade **CALORIE SMART • FAST**

Tapenade is a French condiment often served with vegetables, fish and meat. The flavor is tangy, rich and strong. Fresh rosemary is delicious in this version, but you could use parsley instead.

PREP 10 min **TOTAL** 10 min • 1¾ cups dip

1½ cups pitted kalamata or ripe olives

¼ cup chopped walnuts

3 tablespoons olive oil

3 tablespoons capers, drained

1½ teaspoons fresh rosemary leaves

1 teaspoon Italian seasoning

2 cloves garlic, peeled

Chopped red bell pepper, if desired

Assorted crackers, if desired

1 In food processor or blender, place all ingredients except bell pepper and crackers. Cover; process, using quick on-and-off motions, until slightly coarse.

2 Spoon into serving dish. Sprinkle with bell pepper. Serve with crackers.

2 Tablespoons: Calories 60; Total Fat 6g (Saturated Fat 1g, Trans Fat 0g); Cholesterol 0mg; Sodium 190mg; Total Carbohydrate 2g (Dietary Fiber 0g, Sugars 0g); Protein 0g **Exchanges:** 1 Fat **Carbohydrate Choices:** 0

Steamed Edamame in Shell with Dipping Sauces

Heirloom Recipe and New Twist

This classic cheese ball has been a favorite in the Betty Crocker Kitchens for many years. It is ideal for any occasion and is even easy to tote if you are asked to bring along an appetizer. Often it is the first item on a buffet to be gone. The new twist provides ideas for a variety of mini cheese balls that can be customized for a theme party. Enjoy!

HEIRLOOM

Cheese Ball CALORIE SMART

PREP 15 min **TOTAL** 10 hr 45 min • 16 servings

- 2 packages (8 oz each) cream cheese
- 1 cup shredded sharp Cheddar cheese (4 oz)
- ¾ cup crumbled blue, Gorgonzola or feta cheese (3 oz)
- 1 small onion, finely chopped (¼ cup)
- 1 tablespoon Worcestershire sauce
- ½ cup chopped fresh parsley
  Assorted crackers, if desired

1 Place cheeses in medium bowl; let stand at room temperature about 30 minutes or until softened. Add onion and Worcestershire sauce. Beat with electric mixer on low speed until mixed. Beat on medium speed 1 to 2 minutes, scraping bowl frequently, until fluffy. Cover and refrigerate at least 8 hours or until firm enough to shape into ball.

2 Shape cheese mixture into 1 large ball. Roll in parsley; place on serving plate. Cover and refrigerate about 2 hours or until firm. Serve with crackers.

1 Serving (2 Tablespoons): Calories 160; Total Fat 14g (Saturated Fat 9g, Trans Fat 0g); Cholesterol 45mg; Sodium 240mg; Total Carbohydrate 2g (Dietary Fiber 0g, Sugars 0g); Protein 6g **Exchanges:** 1 High-Fat Meat, 1 Fat **Carbohydrate Choices:** 0

LIGHTER Directions For 3 grams of fat and 65 calories per serving, use fat-free cream cheese and reduced-fat Cheddar cheese.

Pepper Jack Cheese Ball Substitute ¾ cup shredded pepper Jack cheese for the blue cheese. Omit Worcestershire sauce. Substitute cilantro for the parsley.

Pecan-Coated Cheese Ball Omit the parsley and roll the cheese ball in ¼ cup finely chopped pecans.

Bell Pepper Cheese Ball Omit the onion and stir in ¼ cup finely chopped red bell pepper instead.

Dill Havarti Cheese Ball Substitute dill Havarti cheese for the blue cheese and roll the cheese ball in chopped fresh dill weed instead of parsley.

Cheese Ball

Mini French Cheese Balls

CALORIE SMART

PREP 1 hr **TOTAL** 2 hr • 75 cheese balls

BASIC CHEESE BALL

2 packages (8 oz each) cream cheese, softened
1 package (10 to 11 oz) chèvre (goat)
    cheese, softened
1 teaspoon fresh lemon juice
½ teaspoon Worcestershire sauce
¼ teaspoon kosher (coarse) salt
¼ teaspoon freshly ground black pepper

FLAVOR STIR-INS

3 cups crumbled Roquefort cheese (12 oz)
2 tablespoons honey
3 tablespoons finely chopped shallot
¼ cup chopped fresh parsley

COATING

¾ cup chopped fresh parsley
¼ cup finely chopped Marcona almonds

SERVE-WITH, IF DESIRED

Toasted baguette slices

1 Line large cookie sheet with waxed paper or cooking parchment paper. In large bowl, beat all basic cheese ball ingredients with electric mixer on medium speed until combined. Stir in Roquefort cheese, honey, shallot and ¼ cup parsley.

2 With moistened hands, shape mixture into 1-inch balls. (If mixture is too soft to shape, refrigerate 30 minutes.) Place cheese balls on cookie sheet. Refrigerate until firm, about 1 hour.

3 In small bowl, stir together ¾ cup parsley and the almonds. Roll cheese balls in coating before serving. Serve with baguette slices.

1 Cheese Ball: Calories 60; Total Fat 5g (Saturated Fat 3g, Trans Fat 0g); Cholesterol 15mg; Sodium 130mg; Total Carbohydrate 1g (Dietary Fiber 0g, Sugars 0g); Protein 2g **Exchanges:** ½ Medium-Fat Meat, ½ Fat **Carbohydrate Choices:** 0

MAKE-AHEAD Directions Make cheese balls as directed through Step 2. Cover and refrigerate up to 3 days or freeze up to 1 month. If frozen, allow cheese balls to thaw in the refrigerator before rolling in coating and serving.

Mini Indian Cheese Balls Omit flavor stir-ins, coating and serve-with. Beat cheese ball ingredients as directed in Step 1. Stir in 3 cups finely shredded paneer cheese (12 ounces), 1 tablespoon each grated lime peel and curry powder and ¼ cup chopped fresh cilantro. Continue as directed in Step 2. In small bowl, stir together ¾ cup chopped fresh cilantro and ¾ cup finely chopped roasted salted cashews. Before serving, roll cheese balls in cashew mixture. Serve with naan bread if desired.

Mini Korean Cheese Balls Omit flavor stir-ins, coating and serve-with. Beat cheese ball ingredients as directed in Step 1. Stir in 3 cups shredded mozzarella cheese (12 ounces), 1½ teaspoons chili paste, ¾ cup finely chopped mild kimchi, 6 tablespoons finely chopped green onions (6 medium) and 1 tablespoon grated lime peel. Continue as directed in Step 2. Before serving, roll cheese balls in 2¼ cups black sesame seed. Serve with rice crackers if desired.

Mini Mexican Cheese Balls Omit flavor stir-ins, coating and serve-with. Beat cheese ball ingredients as directed in Step 1. Stir in 3 cups crumbled queso fresco cheese, 1½ teaspoons ancho chile powder, 2 tablespoons chopped chipotle chiles in adobo sauce (from 7-ounce can) and 6 tablespoons chopped green onions (6 medium). Continue as directed in Step 2. Before serving, roll cheese balls in 1½ cups finely chopped pepitas (pumpkin seeds). Serve with tortilla chips if desired.

Mini Korean Cheese Balls

Hot Artichoke Dip   CALORIE SMART •
EASY

PREP 10 min **TOTAL** 35 min • About 1½ cups

- ½ cup mayonnaise or salad dressing
- ½ cup grated Parmesan cheese
- 4 medium green onions, chopped (¼ cup)
- 1 can (14 oz) artichoke hearts, drained, coarsely chopped
  Crackers or cocktail rye bread, if desired

1 Heat oven to 350°F. In small bowl, stir mayonnaise and cheese until well mixed. Stir in onions and artichoke hearts. Spoon into ungreased 1-quart casserole.

2 Cover and bake 20 to 25 minutes or until hot. Serve warm with crackers.

1 Tablespoon: Calories 50; Total Fat 4.5g (Saturated Fat 1g, Trans Fat 0g); Cholesterol 0mg; Sodium 115mg; Total Carbohydrate 2g (Dietary Fiber 0g, Sugars 0g); Protein 2g **Exchanges:** 1 Fat **Carbohydrate Choices:** 0

Hot Artichoke-Spinach Dip Increase mayonnaise and Parmesan cheese to 1 cup each. Stir in 1 box (9 ounces) frozen chopped spinach, thawed (squeeze to drain; spread on paper towels and pat dry).

Roasted Vegetable Dip with Baked Pita Crisps   CALORIE SMART

PREP 20 min **TOTAL** 1 hr • 6 servings

BAKED PITA CRISPS
- 2 pita (pocket) breads (6 inch)
- 1 tablespoon olive oil or melted butter
- 1¼ teaspoons dried basil leaves
- 3 tablespoons grated Parmesan cheese

ROASTED VEGETABLE DIP
- 1 medium zucchini, sliced (2 cups)
- 1 medium yellow summer squash, sliced (1½ cups)
- 1 medium red bell pepper, sliced
- 1 medium red onion, thinly sliced
- 2 cloves garlic, peeled
  Cooking spray
- ½ teaspoon salt
- ¼ teaspoon ground red pepper (cayenne)

1 Heat oven to 375°F. Split each pita bread horizontally to make 2 rounds. Cut each round into 6 wedges. Lightly brush oil over smooth surface of bread; sprinkle with basil and cheese.

Place bread, cheese side up, on ungreased cookie sheet. Bake 6 to 8 minutes or until golden brown and crisp; cool.

2 Increase oven temperature to 400°F. In 15x10x1-inch pan, spread zucchini, yellow squash, bell pepper, onion and garlic in single layer. Spray vegetables with cooking spray. Sprinkle with salt and red pepper.

3 Roast about 30 minutes, turning vegetables once, until tender and light brown.

4 Place roasted vegetables in blender or food processor. Cover and blend on high speed about 1 minute, stopping occasionally to scrape side, until smooth. Spoon dip into serving bowl. Serve warm with pita crisps, or refrigerate at least 2 hours or until chilled.

1 Serving (1/4 Cup Dip and 4 Chips): Calories 25; Total Fat 0g (Saturated Fat 0g, Trans Fat 0g); Cholesterol 0mg; Sodium 170mg; Total Carbohydrate 5g (Dietary Fiber 1g, Sugars 2g); Protein 1g **Exchanges:** 1 Vegetable **Carbohydrate Choices:** 1/2

Fig-Hazelnut Tapenade
CALORIE SMART • FAST

PREP 15 min **TOTAL** 15 min • 16 servings

- 1 cup dried Mission figs
- ⅓ cup water
- ½ cup pitted kalamata olives, chopped
- ½ cup roasted red bell peppers (from a jar), drained, chopped
- 2 tablespoons olive oil
- ¼ cup chopped hazelnuts (filberts)
- 1 tablespoon chopped fresh thyme leaves
- 1 container (8 oz) mascarpone cheese or 1 package (8 oz) cream cheese, softened
  Crisp wheat crackers

1 In small saucepan, heat figs and water to boiling over medium-high heat. Reduce heat; simmer 5 minutes, stirring occasionally, until liquid is absorbed and figs are soft. Cool; chop.

2 In medium bowl, stir together figs, olives, roasted peppers, oil and nuts until well combined. Sprinkle with thyme. To serve, spread cheese on crackers; spoon fig mixture over cheese.

1 Serving: Calories 190; Total Fat 11g (Saturated Fat 3g, Trans Fat 0g); Cholesterol 10mg; Sodium 210mg; Total Carbohydrate 20g (Dietary Fiber 2g, Sugars 7g); Protein 2g **Exchanges:** 1 Starch, ½ Other Carbohydrate, 2 Fat **Carbohydrate Choices:** 1

Betty's Staples
Yogurt

A favorite food for many, yogurt is wonderful all by itself as part of a breakfast or lunch, or just simply as a snack. But this versatile food is also useful to have on hand for impromptu quick recipes. These ideas suggest a type or flavor and sometimes an amount, but you can certainly vary the recipe to suit your taste or what you might have on hand.

1. Apple-Yogurt Snacks: Place plain Greek yogurt in small bowl; top with apple slices and a drizzle of caramel sauce.

2. Blue Cheese Yogurt Dressing: In small bowl, mix ¼ cup each plain Greek yogurt, mayonnaise and crumbled blue cheese until blended. Add 1 to 2 tablespoons milk to thin if desired. Serve on tossed green salads or use as dip for vegetables.

3. Frozen Yogurt Pops: Place any flavor yogurt in small (5-ounce) paper cups. Insert wooden craft stick into center of yogurt; freeze until firm. To serve, remove paper cup.

4. Granola-Blueberry Parfaits: Layer Greek yogurt with granola cereal and fresh blueberries in parfait glasses or small bowls.

5. Orange-Pineapple Smoothies: To make 2 smoothies, place 1 cup orange juice, 1 cup orange or vanilla yogurt, 1 small banana and ½ cup fresh or canned pineapple chunks in blender; blend until smooth.

6. Peanut Butter–Yogurt Dip: In medium serving bowl, mix 1 cup vanilla yogurt with 2 tablespoons creamy or crunchy peanut butter. Sprinkle with chopped peanuts and serve with sliced pears, celery pieces and baby-cut carrots for dipping.

7. Personal Taco Dip: Layer equal amounts of plain Greek yogurt, guacamole, chunky salsa, shredded lettuce and just a sprinkle of shredded Cheddar cheese in individual custard cups or small glasses. Serve with tortilla chips.

8. Spicy Vegetable Dip: In medium serving bowl, mix 1 cup plain Greek or regular yogurt, 2 tablespoons chili sauce and 1 tablespoon prepared horseradish until well blended. Serve with cut-up fresh vegetables.

Granola-Blueberry Parfaits, Spicy Vegetable Dip, Apple-Yogurt Snacks

Learn to DEEP-FRY

Cooking food in enough hot oil to cover it is called deep-frying. You want to be sure that your food is very dry before frying, as water can cause the oil to splatter. Start with fresh oil—a neutral-flavored oil such as canola, peanut, safflower or sunflower works best so you only taste the flavor of the food and not the oil. These oils also have a high smoke point, which means that the oil can be kept at a fairly high temperature without smoking. A deep-fry thermometer is a must for monitoring the temperature of the cooking oil. Follow recipe directions carefully to bring the oil to the proper temperature for the recipe.

Use a deep fryer or a large pot with a heavy bottom for frying. The vessel should be tall enough to have at least 2 inches between the top of the oil and the top of the pan, as the oil will rise and bubble as the food cooks. Follow these basic steps to crispy-cooked food:

- Heat oil to desired temperature and maintain it using deep-fry thermometer.

- Be sure food to be fried is dry; pat with paper towels if necessary.

- Carefully place food into hot oil using metal slotted spoon or tongs; do not crowd.

- Remove food from oil with slotted spoon to drain on paper towel–lined plate.

When done at the correct temperature, deep-frying produces a deliciously crispy exterior without the food being greasy.

Shrimp Egg Rolls

Shredded cooked chicken or pork can be substituted for the shrimp. Thaw frozen egg roll skins at room temperature.

PREP 1 hr 15 min **TOTAL** 1 hr 15 min • 8 egg rolls

- 1 teaspoon cornstarch
- ¼ teaspoon five-spice powder
- 4 teaspoons soy sauce
- 1 tablespoon vegetable oil
- 4 cups coleslaw mix (from 1-lb bag)
- 1 cup fresh bean sprouts
- 2 tablespoons sliced green onions
- ½ teaspoon grated gingerroot
- ½ cup finely chopped cooked shrimp
  Vegetable oil for frying
- 8 egg roll skins (from 1-lb package)
- 1 egg, beaten
  Sweet-and-sour sauce

1 In small bowl, mix cornstarch, five-spice powder and soy sauce until blended.

2 In large skillet or wok, heat 1 tablespoon oil over medium-high heat until hot. Add coleslaw mix, bean sprouts, onions and gingerroot; cook 3 to 4 minutes, stirring constantly, until tender. Add shrimp and cornstarch mixture; cook 1 to 2 minutes, stirring constantly, until mixture is thoroughly coated. Remove from skillet; cool to room temperature. In deep fryer or 4-quart Dutch oven, heat 3 to 4 inches oil to 350°F.

3 Meanwhile, place 1 egg roll skin on work surface with 1 corner facing you. (Cover remaining skins with damp paper towel to prevent drying out.) Place ¼ cup coleslaw mixture slightly below center of egg roll skin. Fold corner of egg roll skin closest to filling over filling, tucking point under. Fold in and overlap right and left corners. Brush remaining corner with egg; gently roll egg roll toward remaining corner and press to seal. (Cover filled egg roll with damp paper towel to prevent drying out.) Repeat with remaining egg roll skins and coleslaw mixture.

4 Fry egg rolls, a few at a time, in hot oil 4 to 6 minutes, turning once, until golden brown. Drain on paper towels. Serve with sweet-and-sour sauce.

1 Egg Roll: Calories 220; Total Fat 11g (Saturated Fat 2g, Trans Fat 0g); Cholesterol 60mg; Sodium 220mg; Total Carbohydrate 22g (Dietary Fiber 2g, Sugars 2g); Protein 8g **Exchanges:** 1½ Starch, ½ Very Lean Meat, 2 Fat **Carbohydrate Choices:** 1½

Shrimp Egg Rolls

Forming Egg Rolls

Fold corner of egg roll skin over filling, tucking in corner.

Fold in and overlap left and right corners.

Brush remaining corner with egg; gently roll egg roll toward remaining corner and press to seal.

Make-Ahead
MEATBALLS

CALORIE SMART

Homemade meatballs are a versatile snack that can be served in a variety of ways. They are ideal for appetizers or added to soups, but can be served as a main dish too.

PREP 20 min **TOTAL** 40 min • 60 meatballs

      1 lb lean (at least 80%) ground beef
    ½ lb ground pork
      1 medium onion, finely chopped (½ cup)
    ¼ cup unseasoned dry bread crumbs
    ½ teaspoon ground mustard
    ½ teaspoon seasoned salt
    ⅛ teaspoon pepper
      1 egg

1 Heat oven to 375°F. Spray 15x10x1-inch pan with cooking spray. In large bowl, mix all ingredients. Shape into 1-inch meatballs. Place in pan.

2 Bake 15 to 20 minutes or until no longer pink in center and meat thermometer inserted in center of meatball reads 160°F. Cool completely. Cover tightly and refrigerate 3 to 4 days or freeze 2 to 3 months. Reheat in desired sauce.

1 Meatball: Calories 25; Total Fat 1.5g (Saturated Fat 0.5g, Trans Fat 0g); Cholesterol 10mg; Sodium 20mg; Total Carbohydrate 0g (Dietary Fiber 0g, Sugars 0g); Protein 2g **Exchanges:** ½ Fat **Carbohydrate Choices:** 0

Ways to Use Meatballs

Make up a batch or two of these easy meatballs and store in the refrigerator for up to 3 days or in the freezer for up to 3 months. The meatballs are easy to heat and can be served as they are with a little ketchup or chili sauce, or try the ideas below.

1. Cheeseburger Hoagies: Fill individual small hoagie buns with 3 or 4 warm meatballs, 2 to 3 tablespoons barbecue sauce or ketchup and 3 or 4 dill pickle slices. Sprinkle with 2 to 3 tablespoons shredded Cheddar cheese. Microwave each sandwich on plate for 30 to 60 seconds or until cheese is melted.

2. Meatball Pizza: Top a purchased pizza crust (or make your own, page 192) with 1 cup each canned diced tomatoes with basil, garlic and oregano, halved meatballs and shredded mozzarella cheese. Bake as directed on pizza package.

3. Pesto Pasta and Meatballs: For 4 servings, toss 6 ounces hot cooked linguine with ½ cup refrigerated pesto; toss with about 20 warm meatballs.

4. Salsa Tacos: Fill individual taco shells with 1 or 2 meatballs, ¼ cup shredded lettuce, 2 tablespoons chunky-style salsa and 2 tablespoons shredded Monterey Jack cheese.

5. Sweet Chili Kabobs: Thread meatballs on skewers with strips of any color bell pepper and whole fresh mushrooms. Brush with sweet chili sauce. Place kabobs on a cookie sheet. Bake 15 to 20 minutes at 350°F or until hot and vegetables are crisp-tender.

6. Teriyaki Sliders: Fill individual slider buns with 1 or 2 warm meatballs, 1 tablespoon teriyaki baste and glaze, 1 slice drained canned pineapple and 1 to 2 tablespoons sliced roasted red bell pepper.

Making Meatballs

Shape mixture into 1-inch balls, place in pan.

Bake until no longer pink in center and thermometer reads 160°F.

Easy Square Meatballs

Here is a quick way to make meatballs without making balls. Make the meat mixture. In a 13x9-inch pan, shape the meat mixture into a rectangle, 10x6 inches. With a knife dipped in water, cut the mixture into 60 squares (6 squares x 10 squares) but do not separate. Bake 20 to 25 minutes or until no longer pink. Cool slightly and separate meatballs by cutting apart.

Bas

CALOR

PREP

1
2
¼

¼
1

⅓

1 He
with s
chees
Stir in

2 Cu
strips
towel
1 leve
1 strip
end i
Place
strips
lightl

3 Ba
golde

*Finely
cheese.

**Chopp
substitu

**1 Appet
Cholest
(Dietary
**Carboh

MAKE
unba
bakin

Cut phy
wise int
Place 1
mixture

Make-Ahead Meatballs, Sweet Chili Kabobs

Deviled Eggs CALORIE SMART • FAST

PREP 15 min **TOTAL** 30 min • 12 appetizers

- 6 **eggs**
- 3 **tablespoons mayonnaise, salad dressing or half-and-half**
- 1 **teaspoon prepared yellow, Dijon or spicy brown mustard***
- ⅛ **teaspoon pepper**

1 In 2-quart saucepan, place eggs in single layer. Cover with cold water at least 1 inch above eggs. Cover saucepan; heat to boiling.

2 Immediately remove from heat; let stand covered 15 minutes for large eggs (12 minutes for medium eggs and 18 minutes for extra-large eggs).

3 Drain. Immediately place eggs in cold water with ice cubes or run cold water over eggs until completely cooled.

4 To peel, gently tap egg on countertop until entire shell is finely crackled. Roll gently between hands to loosen shell. Starting at large end, peel egg under cold running water to help remove shell.

5 Cut lengthwise in half. Slip out yolks into small bowl; mash with fork. To prevent eggs from tipping on serving plate, cut a thin slice from bottom of each egg white half before filling. Or, to stand eggs upright, cut crosswise slice about two-thirds from top of narrow end of egg to remove yolk; cut thin slice from bottom of wide end of egg white to rest on serving platter.

6 Stir mayonnaise, mustard and pepper into yolks. Fill whites with egg yolk mixture, heaping lightly. Cover and refrigerate up to 24 hours.

*Any flavored prepared mustard can be used, or ½ teaspoon ground mustard can be substituted for yellow mustard.

1 Appetizer: Calories 60; Total Fat 5g (Saturated Fat 1g, Trans Fat 0g); Cholesterol 110mg; Sodium 75mg; Total Carbohydrate 0g (Dietary Fiber 0g, Sugars 0g); Protein 3g **Exchanges:** ½ Medium-Fat Meat, ½ Fat **Carbohydrate Choices:** 0

LIGHTER **Directions** For 1 gram of fat and 25 calories per serving, mash only 6 yolk halves in Step 5 (reserve remaining yolks for another use or discard). Use fat-free mayonnaise. Stir in ⅓ cup finely chopped zucchini.

Bacon-Cheddar Deviled Eggs Mix 2 slices crisply cooked crumbled bacon and 2 tablespoons finely shredded Cheddar cheese into yolk mixture. Garnish with additional crumbled bacon or chopped fresh chives or parsley.

Blue Cheese Deviled Eggs Omit mustard. Mix ¼ cup crumbled blue cheese into yolk mixture. Garnish with coarse ground black pepper and small celery leaves.

Chipotle Deviled Eggs Omit mustard. Mix 1½ to 2 teaspoons finely chopped chipotle chiles in adobo sauce (from 7-ounce can), drained, and 1 thinly sliced green onion into yolk mixture. Garnish with whole or chopped fresh cilantro leaves.

Reuben Deviled Eggs Omit mustard. Substitute Thousand Island dressing for the mayonnaise. Stir in 2 tablespoons each finely chopped thinly sliced deli corned beef and finely chopped sauerkraut (squeezed in paper towel to drain). Garnish with shredded Swiss cheese and caraway seed.

Making Deviled Eggs

Cut a thin slice from bottom of egg half so that egg sits on a platter.

Spoon prepared filling into egg halves.

Deviled Eggs

Brie in Puff Pastry with Cranberry Sauce

uncovered 15 to 20 minutes, stirring frequently, until mixture thickens and cranberries are tender. Stir in orange peel; remove from heat and set aside.

2 In 8-inch skillet, melt butter over medium heat. Cook almonds in butter, stirring frequently, until golden brown; remove from heat and set aside.

3 Heat oven to 400°F. Spray cookie sheet with cooking spray. On lightly floured surface, roll pastry into 16x9-inch rectangle; cut out 2 circles, 1 (8½-inch) round and 1 (7-inch) round.

4 Remove paper from cheese; leave rind on. Place cheese round on center of 8½-inch pastry round. Spoon cranberry sauce and almonds over cheese. Bring pastry up and press around side of cheese. Brush top edge of pastry with egg. Place 7-inch pastry round on top, pressing around edge to seal. Brush top and side of pastry with egg. Cut decorations from remaining pastry and arrange on top; brush with egg. Place on cookie sheet.

5 Bake 20 to 25 minutes or until golden brown. Cool on cookie sheet on cooling rack 30 minutes before serving. Serve with crackers.

*Or substitute 1 cup purchased whole berry cranberry sauce for the cranberry sauce.

1 Serving: Calories 270; Total Fat 19g (Saturated Fat 9g, Trans Fat 1g); Cholesterol 75mg; Sodium 270mg; Total Carbohydrate 17g (Dietary Fiber 0g, Sugars 8g); Protein 9g **Exchanges:** 1 Starch, 1 High-Fat Meat, 2 Fat **Carbohydrate Choices:** 1

Brie in Puff Pastry with Double-Orange Cranberry Sauce Add 1 tablespoon orange-flavored liqueur or chai-flavored liqueur to the cranberry mixture before cooking.

Brie in Puff Pastry with Cranberry Sauce

PREP 30 min **TOTAL** 1 hr 25 min • 12 servings

CRANBERRY SAUCE*
- 1 cup fresh cranberries
- 6 tablespoons packed brown sugar
- 1 tablespoon orange juice
- ½ teaspoon grated orange peel

BRIE IN PASTRY
- 1 tablespoon butter
- ⅓ cup sliced almonds
- 1 frozen (thawed) puff pastry sheet (from a 17.3-oz package)
- 1 round (14 to 15 oz) Brie cheese
- 1 egg, beaten
- Assorted crackers or sliced fresh fruit, if desired

1 In 1-quart saucepan, stir cranberries, brown sugar and orange juice until well mixed. Heat to boiling, stirring frequently; reduce heat. Simmer

Wrapping Brie in Puff Pastry

Center cheese on puff pastry. Spoon sauce and almonds over cheese, and wrap pastry around sides of cheese.

Place 7-inch round on top, pressing around edge to seal.

Brush top and sides of pastry with egg.

Cut garnish from pastry scraps; place on top, and press lightly to secure.

Black Bean Sliders

Black Bean Sliders CALORIE SMART

PREP 45 min **TOTAL** 2 hr 45 min •
20 sandwiches

BUNS
5 frozen stone-ground 100% whole wheat Texas rolls (from 3-lb bag)
2 tablespoons butter, melted

CORN SALSA
1 can (7 oz) whole kernel corn with red and green peppers, drained
⅔ cup chunky-style medium salsa

BEAN PATTIES
5 teaspoons olive oil
¼ cup finely chopped red or yellow onion
1 can (15 oz) black beans, drained, rinsed*
1 egg, beaten
½ cup unseasoned dry bread crumbs
2 cloves garlic, finely chopped
1 teaspoon ground cumin
½ teaspoon salt
¼ teaspoon freshly ground pepper
20 small pieces Bibb or leaf lettuce
5 slices (¾ oz each) Cheddar cheese, cut into quarters

1 Thaw rolls at room temperature until soft but still cold, about 10 minutes. Spray cookie sheet with cooking spray. Cut each roll into quarters; shape dough pieces into balls. Place on cookie sheet. Brush tops of dough balls with butter. Cover with plastic wrap sprayed with cooking spray. Let rise in warm place 2 hours to 2 hours 30 minutes or until doubled in size.

2 Heat oven to 350°F. Remove plastic wrap. Bake buns 12 to 15 minutes or until golden brown. Remove from pan to cooling rack.

3 Meanwhile, in medium bowl, mix corn salsa ingredients. Cover and refrigerate until serving time.

4 In 10-inch nonstick skillet, heat 1 teaspoon of the oil over medium heat. Add onion; cook 3 to 4 minutes, stirring frequently, until softened. Remove from heat; cool slightly.

5 In medium bowl, mash beans with potato masher, leaving a few beans whole. Stir in egg, bread crumbs, garlic, cumin, salt and pepper. Add cooled onion; mix until thoroughly combined. Shape mixture into 20 (1-inch) balls, using slightly less than 1 tablespoon per ball.

6 In same skillet, heat 2 teaspoons oil over medium heat. Place half of the bean balls in skillet; with back of spatula, flatten balls into patties, about 1½ inches in diameter. Cook 4 to 6 minutes, turning once, until browned. Remove from skillet; cover to keep warm. Repeat with remaining 2 teaspoons oil and bean balls.

7 Split buns in half. On bottom half of each bun, place lettuce piece, bean patty, cheese quarter and 1 heaping tablespoon corn salsa. Cover with top halves of buns.

*Cannellini beans or chickpeas (garbanzo beans) can be substituted for the black beans.

1 Sandwich: Calories 130; Total Fat 5g (Saturated Fat 2g, Trans Fat 0g); Cholesterol 20mg; Sodium 270mg; Total Carbohydrate 17g (Dietary Fiber 3g, Sugars 2g); Protein 5g **Exchanges:** 1 Starch, ½ Vegetable, 1 Fat **Carbohydrate Choices:** 1

Making Black Bean Sliders

Slightly flatten bean balls to about 1½ inches in diameter.

Top each slider with prepared corn salsa.

CHAPTER 3

Beverages

CALORIE SMART = See Helpful Nutrition and Cooking Information, page 643   FAST = Ready in 30 minutes or less
EASY = Prep in 10 minutes or less **plus** five ingredients or less   LIGHTER = 25% fewer calories or grams of fat
MAKE AHEAD = Make-ahead directions   SLOW COOKER = Slow cooker directions

< Martini Cocktails, page 80

BEVERAGE BASICS

Having coffee in the morning, tea in the afternoon or even milk with a meal are all traditional choices for beverages. Why not shake things up a bit? Break out of your routine with flavored coffee, tangy chai tea or almond milk. Or you might even want to try a creamy smoothie or tall glass of lemonade for a refreshing change of pace.

COFFEE ANYTIME

Coffee is grown in more than 50 countries around the world in tropical climates at high altitudes and in rich soil. *Arabica* is the most common variety, as well as the highest quality, and is a descendent of the original coffee beans grown in Ethiopia hundreds of years ago. *Robusta* is another coffee variety that is becoming more common, particularly in blends and instant coffees. This coffee has a higher caffeine level than Arabica.

There are many methods for brewing coffee and a large selection of coffeemakers to choose from. You might choose an automatic drip coffeemaker, a French press, cone and filter, percolator or even a cappuccino machine. However you make coffee, here some tips:

- Purchase coffee in small amounts that can be used within one to two weeks.

- French or dark roast yields a dark, rich cup of coffee, ideal for espresso. Lighter roasts will be better for a mild morning cup of coffee.

- Store unopened packages of coffee in the freezer for up to 1 month.

- If you grind whole beans, do it as close to brew time as possible.

- Be conscious of the grind you are using in relation to how you are making coffee. If coffee is bitter, it may be ground too finely. If it is flat tasting, the grind may be too coarse. Check with professionals where you purchase beans for the correct grind. Here are some general guidelines:

  - **Automatic drip:** medium grind
  - **Espresso maker:** fine grind
  - **Percolator:** coarse grind
  - **French press:** coarse grind

- Use good water for best flavor—filtered or bottled water are good choices.

- For regular-strength coffee, use 1 level tablespoon coffee for 6 ounces water. If you like stronger coffee, use 2 tablespoons coffee for 6 ounces water.

TEA FOR RELAXATION

This simple beverage is the most-commonly consumed drink in the world because it is delicious, healthful, easy to make and just plain relaxing. The thousands of different varieties of tea vary by where they are grown, the time of year they are picked and how they are processed. Black and green teas contain a good amount of antioxidants. Some common varieties of tea include:

- **Black tea:** This tea contains the most caffeine of all tea, 50 to 65 percent of the amount in coffee. It is processed by crushing and fermenting the leaves. Common black teas include Darjeeling and English Breakfast.

- **Green tea:** Pale green with a light, fresh flavor, green tea is favored in Asia. The leaves are steamed and dried but not fermented. Varieties include Gunpowder and Tencha.

- **White tea:** Pale in color with a light, sweet flavor, white tea is the purest and least processed of all teas, and contains very little caffeine. Familiar varieties include Silver Needle and White Peony.

- **Oolong tea:** Partially fermented and a cross between black and green teas, it is also known as Chinese restaurant tea. Oolong is full bodied with a sweet aroma. Imperial oolong is prized for honey flavor and Formosa oolong tastes a bit like peaches.

- **Herbal teas:** Because these teas do not contain any leaves from the Camellia sinensis plant, they are referred to as tisanes. These blends consist of herbs, flowers and fruits.

For brewing tea, some equipment you might want on hand includes:

- Tea kettle for boiling water.

- Teapot for brewing.

- Infuser for holding tea leaves in a teapot.

- Strainer for pouring if there is no infuser.

To brew tea:

- Start with cold water in a tea kettle. For black or oolong tea, bring water to a boil. For green or white tea, water should reach between 170°F and 190°F.

- Warm a teapot by filling with hot water and letting it stand for a few minutes; drain.

- Place desired tea in teapot, using about 1 teaspoon loose tea or 1 teabag for each 6 ounces of water. Pour boiling or hot water over tea; steep 3 to 5 minutes.

- Pour tea into cups; use a strainer to catch loose tea leaves.

THERE IS MORE TO MILK

Milk has come a long way, with many varieties to choose from. Look for organic, lactose-free (for those who cannot drink regular milk) and milk with added calcium or omega-3 fatty acids. Goat's milk is easy to digest, has less lactose than cow's milk and is less allergenic.

There are many tasty nondairy choices, which are delicious and healthful:

- **Soymilk:** Made from soybeans and available unsweetened, sweetened and flavored. Often organic, it has a nutrition profile and protein content similar to dairy milk

- **Almond and cashew milks:** Although these have less protein than dairy milk, they contain about ⅓ fewer calories than 2% milk. They are made with ground almonds or cashews, water and often a sweetener.

- **Rice milk:** Made from boiled rice, brown rice syrup and brown rice starch, this alternative is low in protein compared to dairy milk. Look for rice milk that is calcium fortified.

- **Coconut milk:** This alternative is the closest to dairy milk in texture but is high in fat content. It is a good choice for those with multiple food allergies and does not contain soy or gluten. It has fewer calories, less protein and less calcium than dairy milk.

- **Hemp milk:** Sometimes available, this alternative is another choice for those with multiple allergies. It is made from hemp seeds, water and sweeteners and is often free of soy, nuts and gluten.

Iced Coffee CALORIE SMART • EASY

The coffee concentrate base in this recipe uses ground coffee and water. In addition to making iced coffee, you can use it for ice cubes so that cold coffee-flavored drinks are not diluted by regular ice cubes.

PREP 5 min **TOTAL** 12 hr 35 min • 4 cups

COFFEE CONCENTRATE
1 package (12 oz) medium or coarsely ground medium to dark roasted coffee beans*

8 cups cold water

ICED COFFEE
Ice cubes

½ cup Coffee Concentrate

½ cup cold whole milk

1 In large bowl, stir coffee grounds and water until coffee grounds are completely moistened. Cover and let stand at room temperature 12 to 15 hours. The longer it stands, the stronger the flavor will be.

2 Line fine-mesh strainer with paper coffee filter or several layers of cheesecloth; place over 2-quart pitcher. Pour coffee mixture through strainer, in batches, allowing all the liquid to drain through without pressing on the grounds (this may take up to 30 minutes; replace cheesecloth or coffee filter as needed). Pressing on the grounds can cause cloudy coffee. Discard grounds.

3 Cover pitcher and store coffee concentrate in refrigerator up to 2 weeks. Stir concentrate before each use. To make iced coffee, fill a glass with ice. Mix ½ cup coffee concentrate with ½ cup milk, or if desired, water.

*Medium or coarsely ground coffee is recommended because the concentrate will be clearer. Using finely ground coffee will result in a cloudy concentrate.

½ **Cup:** Calories 80; Total Fat 4g (Saturated Fat 2.5g, Trans Fat 0g); Cholesterol 10mg; Sodium 70mg; Total Carbohydrate 8g (Dietary Fiber 0g, Sugars 6g); Protein 4g **Exchanges:** ½ Milk **Carbohydrate Choices:** ½

Sweetened Iced Coffee In coffee mug or glass, mix ¾ cup coffee concentrate with ¼ cup water and 1 to 2 tablespoons Simple Syrup (page 81). Stir well and add ice cubes.

Hazelnut Iced Coffee In coffee mug or glass, mix ¾ cup Coffee Concentrate with ¼ to ⅓ cup hazelnut-flavored liquid nondairy creamer. Add ice cubes. If you don't prefer hazelnut, use your favorite flavor of liquid coffee creamer.

Vietnamese Iced Coffee In coffee mug or glass, mix ¾ cup Coffee Concentrate with 2 to 3 tablespoons sweetened condensed milk. Add ice cubes.

Straining Iced Coffee

Line fine-mesh strainer with several layers of cheesecloth. Pour coffee through cheesecloth to catch all coffee bean particles.

Iced Coffee

Fresh Strawberry Milk FAST • EASY

Because fresh strawberries are used to make this beverage, the flavor is light, fresh and sweet.

PREP 5 min **TOTAL** 5 min • 4 servings

- 4 cups milk
- 4 cups sliced fresh strawberries
- 1 cup powdered sugar
  Additional sliced strawberries, if desired

In blender, place milk, 4 cups strawberries and the powdered sugar. Cover and blend on low speed 30 seconds or until smooth. Pour through fine-mesh strainer, if desired. Pour into 4 glasses. Garnish rim of each glass with strawberry slice.

1 Serving: Calories 300; Total Fat 5g (Saturated Fat 3g, Trans Fat 0g); Cholesterol 20mg; Sodium 115mg; Total Carbohydrate 54g (Dietary Fiber 3g, Sugars 50g); Protein 9g **Exchanges:** 1 Fruit, 2 Other Carbohydrate, 1 Low-Fat Milk **Carbohydrate Choices:** 3½

Chocolate Milk In small microwavable bowl, mix ½ cup milk and ¼ cup unsweetened baking cocoa. Microwave on High 10 to 15 seconds or until warm. Pour into blender; add 3½ cups milk, ⅓ cup powdered sugar and ½ teaspoon vanilla. Cover and blend on low speed about 30 seconds or until well blended. Pour into 4 glasses.

New York Egg Cream In each of 4 (10-ounce) glasses, place 2 tablespoons chocolate-flavored syrup. Add ½ cup cold whole milk or half-and-half to each glass. While beating vigorously, slowly add ½ cup cold club soda to each glass.

Root Beer Milk In blender, place 2 cups cold root beer and 2 cups cold milk. Cover and blend on low speed about 30 seconds or until well blended. Pour into 4 glasses.

Betty's Staples
Buttermilk

In years past, buttermilk was the portion of milk remaining after it was churned to make butter. Today buttermilk is milk "cultured" with lactic acid bacteria. Cultured buttermilk is low in fat and calories but still has the traditional tangy flavor and creamy texture. Store it in the refrigerator and shake the carton before using, as it can separate. Many people drink buttermilk just as it is, but it is also wonderful in a variety of recipes. Here are some ways to use it (and don't miss the Buttermilk Ranch Dressing, page 138).

1. Chopped Salad with Tangy Dressing: In medium bowl, with wire whisk, beat ¼ cup buttermilk and ¼ cup lime juice until blended. Beat in ⅓ cup buttermilk until mixture is smooth. Add 1 cup cooked shelled edamame, 1 cup chopped romaine, ½ cup chopped red bell pepper and ½ cup cooked corn. Toss to mix. Add salt and pepper to taste.

2. Strawberry Pops: Place 2 cups fresh strawberries in blender and blend until smooth. Add 1 cup buttermilk and ¼ cup sugar and blend until smooth. Pour into small paper cups and freeze until slightly firm, about 1 hour. Place wooden craft stick into center of each pop and freeze until firm.

3. Tangy Coleslaw: In medium bowl, mix ¼ cup buttermilk, ¼ cup mayonnaise and 1 tablespoon sugar until blended. Stir in 2 cups coleslaw mix or shredded cabbage and carrot mixture. Season to taste with salt and pepper.

4. Orange Smoothies: In blender, place 1 cup buttermilk, ½ cup orange juice and 1 cup orange sherbet. Blend until smooth; pour into glasses.

New York Egg Cream, Fresh Strawberry Milk

Strawberry Pops

Apple-Mint Iced Green Tea

CALORIE SMART • FAST • EASY

PREP 5 min **TOTAL** 30 min • 6 servings

 6 tea bags green tea with mint
 4 cups boiling water
 2 cups apple juice
 Mint sprigs, if desired

1 In large heatproof bowl or pitcher, place tea bags. Pour boiling water over tea bags. Cover and let steep 10 minutes. Remove tea bags. Cool tea 15 minutes.

2 Stir apple juice into tea. Pour over ice. Garnish with mint.

1 Serving: Calories 40; Total Fat 0g (Saturated Fat 0g, Trans Fat 0g); Cholesterol 0mg; Sodium 10mg; Total Carbohydrate 10g (Dietary Fiber 0g, Sugars 8g); Protein 0g **Exchanges:** ½ Other Carbohydrate **Carbohydrate Choices:** ½

Easy Iced Tea

For iced tea, brew a pot of tea, using double the amount of tea bags. Remove the tea bags and pour into a pitcher. Cool the tea before refrigerating so it does not get cloudy. Refrigerate until very cold. To sweeten iced tea, add Simple Syrup (page 81), or use honey, agave nectar or sugar.

Raspberry-Ginger Tea

CALORIE SMART • FAST • EASY

PREP 5 min **TOTAL** 15 min • 6 servings

 3 cups brewed tea
 3 cups cranberry-raspberry or raspberry juice
 3 slices (¼ inch thick) gingerroot
 Fresh raspberries, if desired
 Mint sprigs, if desired

1 In 3-quart saucepan, heat tea, juice and gingerroot to boiling over medium-high heat; reduce heat to low.

2 Simmer uncovered 10 minutes, stirring occasionally. Remove gingerroot. Serve warm. Garnish with raspberries and mint.

1 Serving: Calories 80; Total Fat 0g (Saturated Fat 0g, Trans Fat 0g); Cholesterol 0mg; Sodium 5mg; Total Carbohydrate 21g (Dietary Fiber 0g, Sugars 17g); Protein 0g **Exchanges:** 1½ Other Carbohydrate **Carbohydrate Choices:** 1½

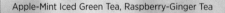

Apple-Mint Iced Green Tea, Raspberry-Ginger Tea

Make-Ahead LEMONADE CONCENTRATE

CALORIE SMART • FAST • EASY

PREP 10 min **TOTAL** 10 min • 5 cups

- 2 cups sugar
- 2 cups water
- 2 cups lemon juice (about 8 medium lemons, at room temperature)
- 2 teaspoons grated lemon peel, if desired

1 In 2-quart saucepan, stir together sugar and water. Heat over medium heat, stirring frequently, until sugar is dissolved. Remove from heat; stir in lemon juice and lemon peel. Store covered in refrigerator up to 1 month or in freezer up to 3 months.

¼ **Cup:** Calories 90; Total Fat 0g (Saturated Fat 0g, Trans Fat 0g); Cholesterol 0mg; Sodium 0mg; Total Carbohydrate 22g (Dietary Fiber 0g, Sugars 21g); Protein 0g **Exchanges:** 1½ Other Carbohydrate **Carbohydrate Choices:** 1½

Lemonade from Concentrate In a pitcher, mix together 1 cup concentrate and 3 cups cold water.

Limeade Concentrate Substitute lime juice for the lemon juice and lime peel for the lemon peel. Continue as directed. Make limeade as directed for lemonade in step 2.

Ways to Use Lemonade Concentrate

It is so easy to make delicious lemonade when you have this concentrate on hand in the refrigerator. But that's not all you can make with the mixture. Try some of these tasty ideas, including a slush, a sangria and a delicious tea. It is such a versatile concentrate that you might decide that one batch is not enough! Be sure to experiment with your own ideas, too.

1. Citrus Splash: Mix 1 cup lemonade concentrate and 2 cups orange juice and pour over ice. Garnish with lemon and orange wedges.

2. Sparkling Lemonade: In pitcher filled with 2 cups ice cubes, mix 1 cup concentrate with 3 cups club soda until well blended.

3. Raspberry Lemonade: In pitcher, mix ½ cup concentrate, 2 cups raspberry juice and 3 cups cold water until blended.

4. Lemonade Sweet Tea: In kettle or saucepan, heat 4 cups water to boiling. In large heatproof container, pour hot water over 6 tea bags of black tea. Stir in 3 cups cold water and 1 cup concentrate. Refrigerate until chilled.

5. Strawberry-Lemonade Slush: Microwave 1 (10-ounce) package frozen strawberries 1 to 2 minutes on High or until partially thawed in syrup. In blender, blend strawberries and syrup with ¾ cup concentrate until smooth. Stir in ½ cup vodka and 1 cup water. Freeze until firm (will not totally freeze because of vodka). To serve, spoon slush mixture into pitcher and add 3 to 4 cups ginger ale, club soda or lemon-lime carbonated beverage.

6. Lemon Sangria: In pitcher, mix 1 cup concentrate, ½ cup orange juice and 1 bottle (750 ml) dry red wine. Stir until mixed.

7. Lemonade Smoothies: In blender, place 1 cup vanilla yogurt, 1 cup orange juice, 1 medium cut-up banana and ¼ cup concentrate. Blend until smooth.

8. Lemonade Ice Cubes: Pour concentrate into ice cube trays and freeze until firm. Place ice cubes in lemonade or tea when serving.

Grating Lemon Zest

Handheld plane grater: Use to grate tiny pieces of citrus peel or whole nutmeg.

Using a sharp paring knife or zester, pull across peel pressing lightly to remove peel, but not the bitter white pith below.

Juicing Lemons

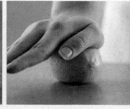

Before squeezing, roll lemon back and forth on counter with palm of hand, using firm pressure, to help burst the cells holding the juice.

Cut lemon in half crosswise. Using citrus reamer, press into center of cut side of lemon and twist to squeeze out juice. Strain juice through mesh strainer.

Lemonade Sweet Tea

Learn to JUICE

Juicing is an easy way to incorporate more fresh produce into your diet. And a diet that is rich in produce can make you feel fabulous, with an added plus that it is fun to blend your own flavors together.

Types of Juicers

There are two main types of juicers:

- **Slow juicer:** Also known as an upright juicer, this type uses a single auger to crush and squeeze produce and extract juice. This juicer takes just a few minutes longer than the other type. Juice from a slow juicer will be fairly thick and a pretty color, with a small amount of foam.

- **Centrifugal juicer:** Sometimes called a high-speed juicer, this juicer separates juice from pulp with high-speed spinning, removing more pulp and making more foam. This appliance is great for making juice in larger quantities.

Prepping Produce

Choose vibrant, fresh produce—juice will only be as good as the produce that it is made from. Here are some tips for produce preparation.

- Wash produce before cutting.

- Cut produce into pieces that will fit in the feed tube. Most fruits and veggies can be juiced with the peel, stems and leaves left on, if they are scrubbed and have not been chemically treated. Peels can add color and boost nutrients.

- Roll leaves such as lettuce and kale into tight balls before adding.

- Remove pits from foods and rind from melon, pineapple and citrus.

- Wrap herbs around other produce before adding so that they are evenly incorporated.

- Have all produce ready before you start juicing so that it is easy to add produce to the juicer.

- Alternate adding different produce pieces to the juicer. For produce stuck in the juicer, add a little juice that has already been made to help unstick the juicer.

Refreshing Green Juice CALORIE
SMART • FAST • EASY

PREP 10 min **TOTAL** 10 min • 2 servings

- 8 large leaves fresh green kale (6 oz), ½ inch cut off stem ends
- 1 medium Bartlett pear (9 oz)
- ¼ bunch fresh cilantro (1 oz)
- ½ medium lemon, peeled

1 Turn juicer on. Alternate adding ingredients, a little at a time, to juicer, until fruit and vegetables are processed into juice.

2 Stir juice well; pour into 2 glasses. Serve immediately. Discard pulp.

1 Serving: Calories 140; Total Fat 1g (Saturated Fat 0g, Trans Fat 0g); Cholesterol 0mg; Sodium 45mg; Total Carbohydrate 29g (Dietary Fiber 6g, Sugars 13g); Protein 3g **Exchanges:** 1½ Fruit, 1½ Vegetable **Carbohydrate Choices:** 2

Raspberry-Lime Juice FAST • EASY

Apples that work well in this juice include Regent, Gala and Fuji. Leave the skin on so it adds to the red color of the juice.

PREP 10 min **TOTAL** 10 min • 2 servings

- 2 unpeeled sweet red apples (about ½ lb each)
- 1 package (6 oz) fresh raspberries (1⅓ cups)
- ½ medium lime, peeled

1 Turn juicer on. Alternate adding ingredients, a little at a time, to juicer, until fruit is processed into juice.

2 Stir juice well; pour into 2 glasses. Serve immediately. Discard pulp.

1 Serving: Calories 170; Total Fat 1g (Saturated Fat 0g, Trans Fat 0g); Cholesterol 0mg; Sodium 0mg; Total Carbohydrate 40g (Dietary Fiber 10g, Sugars 25g); Protein 1g **Exchanges:** 2½ Fruit **Carbohydrate Choices:** 2½

Tips for Success
- If you are new to juicing, start with fruit-based combinations and slowly work into using more vegetables.
- For the best flavor, add fruit to vegetable mixtures. Apples and pears can play a great supporting role in vegetable juices.
- Think about the colors of the produce, as eye appeal makes a difference.

Refreshing Green Juice

CAUTION
UNPLUG BEFORE CLEANING AND BEFORE
ASSEMBLING OR REMOVING PARTS
SHARP BLADE—ALWAYS USE FOOD PUSHER

FRONT

Strawberry Smoothies

CALORIE SMART • FAST • EASY

PREP 5 min **TOTAL** 5 min • 4 servings

>   2   cups fresh strawberries
>   1   cup milk
>   2   containers (6 oz each) strawberry yogurt
>   (1⅓ cups)

Reserve 4 strawberries for garnish. Cut out the hull, or "cap," from remaining strawberries. In blender, place strawberries, milk and yogurt. Cover and blend on high speed about 30 seconds or until smooth. Pour into 4 glasses. Garnish each with reserved strawberry.

1 Serving: Calories 140; Total Fat 2.5g (Saturated Fat 1g, Trans Fat 0g); Cholesterol 10mg; Sodium 80mg; Total Carbohydrate 24g (Dietary Fiber 2g, Sugars 21g); Protein 6g **Exchanges:** 1 Fruit, 1 Skim Milk **Carbohydrate Choices:** 1½

Blueberry Smoothies Substitute 2 cups fresh or frozen blueberries for the strawberries and blueberry yogurt for the strawberry yogurt. Sweeten to taste with honey or agave nectar.

Peach Smoothies Substitute frozen sliced peaches for the strawberries and peach yogurt for the strawberry yogurt.

Raspberry Smoothies Substitute fresh or frozen raspberries for the strawberries and raspberry yogurt for the strawberry yogurt. Sweeten to taste with honey or agave nectar.

Strawberry-Banana Smoothies Substitute 1 medium banana, cut into chunks, for 1 cup of the strawberries.

Easy-Being-Green Smoothies

FAST • EASY

PREP 10 min **TOTAL** 10 min • 2 servings

>   1   box (9 oz) frozen chopped spinach
>   1   container (6 oz) Key lime pie low-fat yogurt
>   2   medium kiwifruit, peeled, quartered
>   ½   cup ice cubes
>   ⅓   cup apple juice
>   Kiwi slices, if desired

1 Microwave spinach as directed on box. Rinse with cold water until cooled. Drain, squeezing out as much liquid as possible.

2 In blender, place ⅓ cup of the cooked spinach and remaining ingredients. (Cover and refrigerate remaining spinach for another use.) Cover and blend on high speed about 30 seconds or until smooth. Pour into 2 glasses. Garnish with kiwi slices. Serve immediately.

1 Serving: Calories 160; Total Fat 1.5g (Saturated Fat 0.5g, Trans Fat 0g); Cholesterol 5mg; Sodium 60mg; Total Carbohydrate 32g (Dietary Fiber 3g, Sugars 24g); Protein 4g **Exchanges:** 1½ Fruit, ½ Skim Milk, 1 Vegetable **Carbohydrate Choices:** 2

Smoothie Success

For the coolest smoothies, start with refrigerated juice and fruit. Be sure to cool cooked vegetables before adding to smoothies. If you like frosty smoothies, chill the glasses in the freezer about 15 minutes ahead of time.

Peach, Strawberry, and Blueberry Smoothies

Easy-Being-Green Smoothies

DRINKS BASICS

Whether you are a cocktail lover, wine drinker or beer aficionado, having a good selection of bar ingredients at hand for gatherings is the secret to being a great host. Start with a sampling of liquors, wines and beers plus a variety of mixers and nonalcoholic beverages and build from there. Also, having the right bar equipment makes it a cinch to whip up drinks quickly and with confidence.

TOOLS FOR THE BAR

- Blender
- Bottle opener
- Cocktail shaker
- Corkscrew
- Ice bucket and tongs
- Pitcher
- Mini measure or shot glass
- Muddler
- Stir sticks and toothpicks
- Coasters and cocktail napkins

GLASSWARE

- Highball tumblers (10 to 14 ounces): used for gin and tonics, Tom Collins, coolers, spritzers, iced tea and soft drinks
- Old-fashioned, lowball or rocks glasses (6 to 10 ounces): used for Scotch or other on-the-rocks drinks and old-fashioned cocktails
- Martini/cocktail glasses: used for martinis, Manhattans, some iced and frozen drinks
- Wine glasses (stemmed or not stemmed): used for white or red wine
- Margarita glasses: used for margaritas, daiquiris and some frozen or slushy drinks
- Champagne flutes
- Beer mugs
- Shot glasses

COCKTAIL MIXOLOGY

Mixology is all about making good drinks, understanding what goes into drinks and using quality ingredients. Most cocktails follow formulas that are fairly classic, and the difference in flavor will be due to the brand of liquor, the mixer or even the garnish used.

Spirits to Stock

- Bourbon and/or whiskey
- Brandy or cognac
- Gin
- Liqueurs as desired
- Scotch
- Tequila
- Vermouth
- Vodka

Mixers to Stock

- Club soda
- Cola
- Ginger ale
- Lemon-lime soda
- Drink mixes (Bloody Mary, margarita, daiquiri)
- Lime and lemon juices
- Bitters

Garnishes to Stock

Most cocktail recipes will suggest a certain garnish, but you can mix it up a bit, too—use decorative toothpicks for spearing cherries, olives and fruit. Small containers are a fun way to showcase garnishes.

- Stuffed cocktail olives
- Maraschino cherries
- Cocktail onions
- Fresh fruit (lemons, limes, oranges, berries)
- Whole hazelnuts
- Coarse salt
- Granulated, coarse and powdered sugar
- Black pepper
- Celery sticks
- Fresh mint or basil

Shaken Cocktails

The best shaken cocktails are always served refreshingly cold, with a very thin layer of ice floating on the surface. Knowing a few tips will make cocktails an easy task and just might make you legendary.

- Chill glasses in the freezer.
- Use correct amounts of the chosen cocktail ingredients.
- Have garnishes ready to add quickly.
- Use a cocktail shaker with a strainer insert so that the drink mixture moves around the ice cubes, chilling it well.
- Strain the drink immediately after mixing so that ice chills the drink but doesn't dilute it.
- Serve shaken drinks immediately.

ABOUT BEER

Although the major ingredients of beer are simple (grain, hops and yeast), the explosion of different flavors of craft beer has made this simple beverage an art, with local breweries sprouting up virtually everywhere. It is truly remarkable that the United States now has more beer styles and brands than any other place in the world!

Here are the basic categories of beer with some varieties (or flavors) you might like to sample:

Ales

Often higher in alcohol than lagers, ales tend to be sweet, tasty beers. Varieties include:

- **India Pale Ale (IPA):** general category of pale ales with hoppy flavor
- **Brown Ale:** generally mellow but flavorful, with a caramel taste
- **Saison/Farmhouse Ale:** refreshing fruity ale with mild to moderate tartness
- **Belgian Pale Ale:** copper colored with a malty, somewhat spicy flavor
- **Berliner Weisse:** wheat based and very pale. but refreshingly sour flavor
- **Lambic:** wheat based, with a complex sour flavor
- **Oatmeal Stout:** dark ale that is full bodied and malty, with a slight oatmeal flavor

Lagers

Most of the mass-produced beers are lagers, but a large variety of styles are available, including:

- **American Pale Lagers:** light color with delicate sweetness; serve very cold
- **Bock Beer:** dark, somewhat strong, with an intense malty flavor
- **Doppelbock:** dark, with a malty, rich flavor and high alcohol content

- **Pilsner:** very aromatic, with a crisp, refreshingly bitter flavor

Specialty

These beers do not fit in the other categories. They are often quite memorable and will have distinct flavors from fruits, herbs and spices to make them unusual but interesting and delicious.

- **Fruit Beers:** usually light- to medium-bodied lagers or ales that have fruit extract or real fruit added, resulting in sweet-flavored beers

- **Smoked Beers:** flavor and aroma are derived from added smoky flavoring

- **Herb and Spice Beers:** beer flavor resembles the ingredients that are added

WINE PRIMER

Three things determine the flavor of wine: the type of grapes, where the grapes were grown and how the grapes are processed for the wine. Whether you are serving wine with a meal or with appetizers, the choice of wine is mostly personal; there are no fixed rules. Wine stores can be very helpful and provide guidance. Experimenting with different wines will be helpful, too, as in the end, it is about what you like and what tastes good!

"Varietal" refers to a particular variety of grape. Some wines are made from a single varietal, and others are blends; here are some general flavor guidelines:

White Grape Varietals

- **Chardonnay:** rich and creamy, with a buttery, full flavor that often has vanilla overtones

- **Chenin Blanc:** light and fruity, this wine often has a spicy peach flavor

- **Pinot Gris or Pinot Grigio:** refreshing wine with a little spice and fruit overtones

- **Riesling:** crisp and fresh with a delightful fruity flavor and notes of peach, apple or apricot

- **Sauvignon Blanc or Fumé Blanc:** often slightly acidic with citrus and herb overtones

Red Grape Varietals

- **Cabernet Sauvignon:** bold with a velvety texture and rich flavor often reminiscent of chocolate, coffee, blackberries and plums

- **Malbec:** dark red, with rich flavor

- **Merlot:** fruity flavor with a medium body and overtones of blackberry and plum

- **Pinot Noir:** light-bodied wine that is often spicy with the flavors of cherries, blackberries and currants

- **Syrah (Shiraz):** dark red, bold and spicy, with overtones of dark fruit like blackberries and plums

- **Zinfandel:** spicy red with earthy overtones of berries and peppers

Other Wines

- **Sparkling wines** include Champagne, Prosecco, and Cava.

- **Fortified wines** have added liquor and include Madeira, Marsala, port, and sherry.

- **Aromatic wines** such as vermouth are flavored with herbs and spices.

Storing and Serving Wine

- Store wine in a cool, dry location away from light. Lay bottles on their sides, not upright, so corks do not dry out and shrink, which can allow air to enter and spoil the wine.

- Serve white and sparkling wines between 45°F and 55°F. Reds should be a bit warmer at 55°F to 60°F for the best flavor.

- Wineglasses are designed to maximize aromas and flavors of wine. A set of all-purpose glasses for both red and white wines is a good place to start.

- If you have wine left over, place the cork back into the bottle or seal with a wine plug. Refrigerate and use within 3 days.

Manhattan Cocktails

CALORIE SMART • FAST • EASY

PREP 5 min **TOTAL** 5 min • 2 servings

> 2 maraschino cherries
> ¼ cup small ice cubes or shaved ice
> ⅓ cup bourbon or whiskey
> ⅓ cup sweet vermouth
> 2 dashes aromatic bitters

1 Chill 2 (3-oz) stemmed glasses in freezer.

2 Place cherry in each chilled glass. Place ice in martini shaker or pitcher. Add bourbon, vermouth and bitters; shake or stir to blend and chill. Pour into glasses, straining out ice.

1 Serving: Calories 130; Total Fat 0g (Saturated Fat 0g, Trans Fat 0g); Cholesterol 0mg; Sodium 0mg; Total Carbohydrate 4g (Dietary Fiber 0g, Sugars 3g); Protein 0g **Carbohydrate Choices:** ½

Martini Cocktails **CALORIE SMART • FAST • EASY**

PREP 5 min **TOTAL** 5 min • 2 servings

> 2 pimiento-stuffed green olives or lemon twists
> ¼ cup small ice cubes or shaved ice
> ⅓ cup gin
> ⅓ cup dry vermouth
> 2 dashes aromatic bitters

1 Chill 2 (3-oz) stemmed glasses in freezer.

2 Place olive in each chilled glass. Place ice in martini shaker or pitcher. Add gin, vermouth and bitters; shake or stir to blend and chill. Pour into glasses, straining out ice.

1 Serving: Calories 150; Total Fat 0.5g (Saturated Fat 0g, Trans Fat 0g); Cholesterol 0mg; Sodium 65mg; Total Carbohydrate 5g (Dietary Fiber 0g, Sugars 0g); Protein 0g **Carbohydrate Choices:** ½

Sweet Martini Cocktails Substitute sweet vermouth for the dry vermouth.

Chocolate Martini Cocktails Omit all ingredients except ice. Swirl about 1 tablespoon chocolate syrup on inside of each chilled glass. To serve, add ⅓ cup chocolate-flavored liqueur, ⅓ cup Irish cream liqueur, ⅓ cup vanilla-flavored vodka and ⅓ cup crème de cacao to ice in martini shaker; shake or stir and pour over swirled chocolate in each glass.

Mango Martini Cocktails Omit all ingredients except ice. Puree 5 slices mango and 5 tablespoons syrup from one jar (24 ounces) refrigerated mango slices in extra-light syrup to make about ½ cup puree. Add ½ cup mango puree, ½ cup peach-flavored vodka, ¼ cup orange-flavored liqueur and 2 tablespoons fresh lime juice to ice in martini shaker; shake or stir and pour as directed. Garnish each cocktail with a slice of mango and slice of lime, if desired.

Pomegranate Martini Cocktails Omit all ingredients except ice. Wet rim of each glass by rubbing with lime wedge; dip into colored sugar. Add 1 cup pomegranate juice, 3 tablespoons citrus-flavored vodka, 2 tablespoons orange-flavored liqueur and 1 tablespoon lime juice to ice in martini shaker; shake or stir and pour as directed.

Green Tea Martini Cocktails Omit all ingredients except ice. Add ½ cup citrus-flavored vodka, ½ cup chilled brewed green tea and ⅓ cup sweet tea–flavored vodka or regular vodka to ice in martini shaker; shake or stir and pour as directed.

Shaking Cocktails

Place ice in shaker. Add liquor; cover and shake vigorously to blend and chill.

Remove shaker cover; place strainer over top of shaker. Pour liquor into glass, straining out ice.

Manhattan Cocktails

Mojitos

PREP 15 min **TOTAL** 40 min • 4 servings

MINT SYRUP

½ cup sugar
¾ cup water
1 cup packed fresh mint leaves,
coarsely chopped

MOJITOS

1 cup rum
¼ cup fresh lime juice (2 medium limes)
1½ cups chilled club soda
Ice cubes or crushed ice
12 thin lime slices (from 2 limes), cut in half
4 mint sprigs

1 In 1-quart saucepan, mix syrup ingredients. Heat to boiling over high heat, stirring occasionally. Reduce heat to low; simmer 5 minutes or until sugar is dissolved. Remove from heat; let stand at room temperature about 20 minutes.

2 Strain mixture into pitcher; do not push on leaves or syrup will turn a dark green color.

3 Stir in rum, lime juice and club soda. Fill 4 lowball glasses with ice. Place lime slices in glasses, pushing down alongside of glass, allowing ice cubes to hold them in place. Pour mint mixture over ice. Garnish with mint sprigs.

1 Serving: Calories 250; Total Fat 0 (Saturated Fat 0, Trans Fat 0); Cholesterol 0; Sodium 25; Total Carbohydrate 30 (Dietary Fiber 1, Sugars 26); Protein 0 **Carbohydrate Choices:** 2

MAKE-AHEAD **Directions** Make a big batch of the Mint Syrup and store it in your refrigerator for up to 1 week. If you make it beforehand, the mojitos will take only a few minutes to make. For more mint flavor, place 1 tablespoon chopped mint leaves in glasses before adding the ice.

Making a Citrus Twist

With vegetable peeler or small knife, cut strip of orange or lemon peel; twist as desired.

Simple Syrup

Use this syrup to sweeten drinks instead of granulated sugar—it works especially well in cold drinks. Use 1 teaspoon per drink or more to taste.

To make simple syrup: In 2-quart saucepan, stir together 2 cups sugar and 2 cups water. Heat over medium heat, stirring frequently, until sugar is dissolved. Store covered in refrigerator up to 1 month. Makes 3 cups.

Dill Simple Syrup: Make as directed— except add 1½ cups lightly packed fresh dill weed. After removing from heat, let stand 30 minutes. Strain through fine-mesh strainer; discard dill.

- **Dill Martini:** Mix up a Martini (page 80) and shake it up with 1 teaspoon syrup. For more dill flavor, try adding a little more of the syrup.

- **Dill Tea:** Make hot black or green tea and stir 1 teaspoon syrup into each serving.

Ginger Simple Syrup: Make as directed —except add ½ pound fresh gingerroot, peeled, cut into ¼-inch slices. After removing from heat, let stand 30 minutes. Strain through fine-mesh strainer; discard gingerroot, or reserve for another use.

- **Ginger Tea:** Make Easy Iced Tea (page 71) and stir in 1 to 2 teaspoons syrup.

- **Ginger Lemonade:** Make Lemonade (page 72) and stir in enough syrup (1 to 2 teaspoons) for desired flavor.

Triple-Berry Simple Syrup: Make as directed—except add 3 cups frozen (thawed) mixed berries. After removing from heat, let stand 30 minutes. Strain through fine-mesh strainer; discard berries or reserve for another use.

- **Berry Tea:** Make Easy Iced Tea (page 71) and stir in 1 to 2 teaspoons syrup.

- **Berry Sangria:** Stir 2 to 3 teaspoons syrup into a pitcher of Sangria (page 83).

Margaritas FAST

PREP 15 min **TOTAL** 15 min • 8 servings

> Margarita salt or kosher (coarse) salt
> 2 cups cracked ice
> 2½ cups sweet-and-sour drink mix or nonalcoholic margarita drink mix
> 1⅓ cups tequila
> 1⅓ cups fresh lime juice (about 9 limes)*
> ¾ cup orange-flavored liqueur (such as Cointreau or triple sec)

Rub rims of 8 stemmed glasses with water; dip rims of glasses into salt. Place ice in pitcher. Add drink mix, tequila, lime juice and liqueur; shake or stir until blended and chilled. Pour into glasses, straining out ice.

*Or substitute ¾ cup frozen (thawed) limeade concentrate for the lime juice.

1 Serving: Calories 180; Total Fat 0g (Saturated Fat 0g, Trans Fat 0g); Cholesterol 0mg; Sodium 0mg; Total Carbohydrate 11g (Dietary Fiber 0g, Sugars 8g); Protein 0g **Carbohydrate Choices:** 3

Frozen Strawberry Margaritas In blender, place 6 ounces (half of 12-ounce can) frozen (thawed) limeade concentrate and 1 box (10 ounces) frozen strawberries. Cover and blend on high speed until smooth. Add 3 cups water and ¾ cup tequila; blend until smooth. Pour into freezer container. Freeze until slushy, at least 24 hours. To serve, stir and spoon ⅔ cup mixture into each glass and fill with ⅓ cup lemon-lime carbonated beverage.

Classic Bloody Mary

CALORIE SMART • FAST

Bloody Marys are very easy to make at home. As with any cocktail, it helps to start with chilled ingredients. Store your vodka in the freezer; it won't freeze but will be icy cold!

PREP 10 min **TOTAL** 10 min • 4 servings

> 1 cup vodka
> ¾ cup chilled tomato juice
> ¼ cup lemon juice
> ¼ teaspoon celery salt
> ¼ teaspoon pepper
> ¼ teaspoon Worcestershire sauce
> Hot pepper sauce, if desired
> Ice cubes
>
> **GARNISHES, IF DESIRED**
> Celery stalk
> Pickle spear
> Cucumber spear
> Beef jerky stick
> Lime or lemon wedge

1 In half-gallon pitcher, mix vodka, tomato juice, lemon juice, celery salt, pepper and Worcestershire sauce until well blended. Add pepper sauce to taste.

2 Fill 4 glasses with ice; add tomato juice mixture. Garnish as desired.

1 Serving: Calories 140; Total Fat 0g (Saturated Fat 0g, Trans Fat 0g); Cholesterol 0mg; Sodium 220mg; Total Carbohydrate 3g (Dietary Fiber 0g, Sugars 2g); Protein 0g **Carbohydrate Choices:** 0

Margarita

Coating the Edge of a Glass

Wet rim of glass with citrus wedge or dip into lemon or lime juice or water on small plate; shake off excess.

Dip wet rim into sugar, coarse (kosher) salt, decorator sugar or chocolate candy sprinkles on small plate.

Mango Mimosas

CALORIE SMART • FAST • EASY

PREP 5 min **TOTAL** 5 min • 12 servings

- 2 **cups chilled orange juice**
- 2 **cups chilled mango nectar***
- 1 **bottle (750 ml) regular or nonalcoholic dry champagne or sparkling white wine, chilled**

In 1½-quart pitcher, mix orange juice and mango nectar. Pour champagne into glasses until half full. Fill glasses with juice mixture.

*Apricot or peach nectar can be substituted for the mango nectar.

1 Serving: Calories 100; Total Fat 0g (Saturated Fat 0g, Trans Fat 0g); Cholesterol 0mg; Sodium 10mg; Total Carbohydrate 11g (Dietary Fiber 0g, Sugars 9g); Protein 0g **Carbohydrate Choices:** 1

Pineapple Mimosas Substitute pineapple juice for the mango nectar. Garnish with a pineapple wedge.

Pomegranate-Mango Mimosas Substitute pomegranate juice for the orange juice. Place a few fresh pomegranate seeds in each glass for a fun garnish.

Sangria **CALORIE SMART • FAST**

Sangria is also lovely made with white or rosé (blush) wine. Try adding fresh peach or plum slices instead of the lemon and orange.

PREP 10 min **TOTAL** 10 min • 8 servings

- ⅔ **cup lemon juice**
- ⅓ **cup orange juice**
- ¼ **cup sugar**
- 1 **lemon, cut into thin slices**
- 1 **orange, cut into thin slices**
- 1 **bottle (750 ml) dry red wine or nonalcoholic red wine**
  Ice cubes, if desired

In half-gallon glass pitcher, mix juices and sugar until sugar is dissolved. Add lemon and orange slices. Stir in wine. Add ice, if desired.

1 Serving: Calories 100; Total Fat 0g (Saturated Fat 0g, Trans Fat 0g); Cholesterol 0mg; Sodium 10mg; Total Carbohydrate 10g (Dietary Fiber 0g, Sugars 8g); Protein 0g **Carbohydrate Choices**: ½

White Sangria Substitute dry white wine, such as Chardonnay or Sauvignon Blanc, for the dry red wine.

Classic Bloody Mary

Heirloom Recipe and New Twist

This classic eggnog recipe is easy to make ahead of time so is ideal for gatherings. It is a favorite among many on our staff. The new twist is made with bacon and bourbon—our taste panel raved about this fun combination. Serve it at your next holiday gathering.

HEIRLOOM

Eggnog

For food safety, our eggnog is made with a cooked egg custard instead of raw eggs.

PREP 35 min **TOTAL** 2 hr 35 min • 10 servings

SOFT CUSTARD

- 3 eggs, slightly beaten
- ⅓ cup granulated sugar
-    Dash salt
- 2½ cups milk
- 1 teaspoon vanilla

EGGNOG

- 1 cup whipping cream
- 2 tablespoons powdered sugar
- ½ teaspoon vanilla
- ½ cup light rum, brandy or whiskey*
- 1 to 2 drops yellow food color, if desired
-    Ground nutmeg

1 In heavy 2-quart saucepan, stir eggs, granulated sugar and salt until well mixed. Gradually stir in milk. Cook over medium heat 10 to 15 minutes, stirring constantly, until mixture just coats a metal spoon; remove from heat. Stir in 1 teaspoon vanilla. Place saucepan in cold water until custard is cool. (If custard curdles, beat vigorously with hand beater until smooth.) Cover and refrigerate at least 2 hours but no longer than 24 hours.

2 Just before serving, in chilled medium bowl, beat whipping cream, powdered sugar and ½ teaspoon vanilla with electric mixer on high speed until stiff. Gently stir 1 cup of the whipped cream, the rum and the food color into custard.

3 Pour custard mixture into small punch bowl. Drop remaining whipped cream in mounds onto custard mixture. Sprinkle with nutmeg. Serve immediately. Store covered in refrigerator up to 2 days.

*Or substitute 2 tablespoons rum extract and ⅓ cup milk for the rum.

1 Serving: Calories 160; Total Fat 10g (Saturated Fat 6g, Trans Fat 0g); Cholesterol 95mg; Sodium 70mg; Total Carbohydrate 12g (Dietary Fiber 0g, Sugars 12g); Protein 4g **Carbohydrate Choices:** 1

NEW TWIST

Bourbon-Maple Eggnog

PREP 35 min **TOTAL** 2 hr 35 min • 10 servings

CUSTARD

- 3 eggs, slightly beaten
- ½ cup real maple syrup
-    Dash salt
- 2½ cups milk
- 1 teaspoon vanilla

EGGNOG

- 1 cup whipping cream
- 2 tablespoons powdered sugar
- 2 tablespoons real maple syrup
- ½ teaspoon vanilla
- ½ cup bourbon
-    Crisply cooked bacon, finely chopped, if desired

1 In 2-quart saucepan, stir eggs, ½ cup syrup and the salt until well mixed. Gradually stir in milk. Cook over medium heat 10 to 15 minutes, stirring constantly, until mixture just coats a metal spoon; remove from heat. Stir in 1 teaspoon vanilla. Place saucepan in cold water until custard is cool. (If custard curdles, beat vigorously with hand beater until smooth.) Cover and refrigerate at least 2 hours but no longer than 24 hours.

2 Just before serving, in chilled medium bowl, beat whipping cream, powdered sugar, 2 tablespoons syrup and ½ teaspoon vanilla with electric mixer on high speed until stiff. Gently stir 1 cup of the whipped cream and the bourbon into custard.

3 Pour custard mixture into small punch bowl. Drop remaining whipped cream in mounds onto custard mixture. Sprinkle each serving with bacon. Serve immediately. Store covered in refrigerator up to 2 days.

1 Serving: Calories 220; Total Fat 12g (Saturated Fat 7g, Trans Fat 0g); Cholesterol 95mg; Sodium 90mg; Total Carbohydrate 19g (Dietary Fiber 0g, Sugars 17g); Protein 4g **Carbohydrate Choices:** 1

Eggnog

Bourbon-Maple Eggnog

Beergaritas FAST • EASY

This takeoff on the classic margarita is a fun alternative to plain beer. For an authentic touch, salt the rims of the glasses. Pour ½ cup margarita salt or coarse salt onto a small flat plate. Rub a lime wedge around the edge of each glass and then dip into salt.

PREP 10 min **TOTAL** 10 min • 8 servings

- 1 can (12 oz) frozen (thawed) limeade concentrate
- 1 cup tequila
- ¼ cup orange-flavored liqueur
- 2 bottles (12 oz each) light-colored beer
  Crushed ice
- 8 lime slices

1 In pitcher, mix limeade concentrate, tequila and liqueur until well blended. Pour beer into pitcher; stir.

2 Fill 8 lowball or margarita glasses with crushed ice. Pour beer mixture over ice. Garnish each with lime slice.

1 Serving: Calories 210; Total Fat 0g (Saturated Fat 0g, Trans Fat 0g); Cholesterol 0mg; Sodium 0mg; Total Carbohydrate 31g (Dietary Fiber 0g, Sugars 20g); Protein 0g **Carbohydrate Choices:** 2

Mulled Wine CALORIE SMART

PREP 5 min **TOTAL** 1 hr 5 min • 12 servings

- 2 bottles (750 ml each) dry red wine
- ½ cup brandy
- 1 cup honey
- 2 oranges, thinly sliced
- 4 cinnamon sticks
- 8 whole cloves
- ½ teaspoon whole allspice
  Cinnamon sticks, if desired
  Orange slices, if desired

1 In 3-quart stainless steel or nonstick saucepan (not aluminum), mix all ingredients. Heat to simmering over low heat. Simmer uncovered 1 hour, being careful not to boil.

2 Pour mixture through strainer into heatproof pitcher or punch bowl; serve warm. Garnish with additional cinnamon sticks and orange slices.

1 Serving: Calories 113; Total Fat 0g (Saturated Fat 0g, Trans Fat 0g); Cholesterol 0mg; Sodium 5mg; Total Carbohydrate 26g (Dietary Fiber 0g, Sugars 0g); Protein 0g **Carbohydrate Choices:** 1½

Beergaritas

CHAPTER 4

Breakfast & Brunch

Potato, Bacon and Egg Scramble CALORIE SMART • FAST

Precooking the potatoes in boiling water helps them cook faster, turning this scramble into a 20-minute meal.

PREP 10 min **TOTAL** 20 min • 5 servings

- 1 lb small red potatoes (6 or 7), cubed
- 6 eggs
- ⅓ cup milk
- ¼ teaspoon salt
- ⅛ teaspoon pepper
- 2 tablespoons butter
- 4 medium green onions, sliced (¼ cup)
- 5 slices bacon, crisply cooked, crumbled

1 In 2-quart saucepan, heat 1 inch water to boiling. Add potatoes. Heat to boiling; reduce heat to medium-low. Cover and cook 6 to 8 minutes or until potatoes are tender; drain.

2 In medium bowl, beat eggs, milk, salt and pepper with fork or whisk until well mixed; set aside.

3 In 10-inch skillet, melt butter over medium-high heat. Cook potatoes in butter 3 to 5 minutes, turning occasionally, until light brown. Stir in onions. Cook 1 minute, stirring constantly.

4 Pour egg mixture into skillet with potatoes and onions. As mixture begins to set at bottom and side, gently lift cooked portions with spatula so that thin, uncooked portion can flow to bottom. Avoid constant stirring. Cook 3 to 4 minutes or until eggs are thickened throughout but still moist. Sprinkle with bacon.

1 Serving: Calories 290; Total Fat 15g (Saturated Fat 6g, Trans Fat 0g); Cholesterol 275mg; Sodium 370mg; Total Carbohydrate 25g (Dietary Fiber 3g, Sugars 3g); Protein 13g **Exchanges:** 1 Starch, 1 Vegetable, 1 High-Fat Meat, 1 Fat **Carbohydrate Choices:** 1½

Chorizo, Potato and Egg Scramble Omit

bacon. In 8-inch skillet, crumble ¼ pound bulk chorizo sausage; add ½ cup chopped green bell pepper. Cook and stir until sausage is no longer pink; drain. Stir into eggs at end of cook time. Garnish each serving with 1 to 2 tablespoons salsa.

Huevos Rancheros

Huevos rancheros is Spanish for "rancher's eggs." When buying tortillas, check for freshness by making sure they are soft and pliable when you bend the package, and check that the edges are not dry or cracked.

PREP 45 min **TOTAL** 45 min • 6 servings

- ½ lb bulk chorizo or pork sausage
  Vegetable oil
- 6 soft corn tortillas (6 to 7 inch)
- 1¼ cups salsa (for homemade salsa, see page 458)
- 6 Fried Eggs (page 90)
- 1½ cups shredded Cheddar cheese (6 oz)

1 In 8-inch skillet, cook sausage over medium heat 8 to 10 minutes, stirring occasionally, until no longer pink; drain. Remove to bowl; cover to keep warm.

2 In same skillet, heat ⅛ inch oil over medium heat just until hot. Cook 1 tortilla at a time in oil about 1 minute, turning once, until crisp; drain on paper towels.

3 In 1-quart saucepan, heat salsa, stirring occasionally, until hot.

4 Spread 1 tablespoon salsa over each tortilla to soften. Place 1 fried egg on each tortilla. Top with sausage, cheese and remaining salsa.

1 Serving: Calories 460; Total Fat 33g (Saturated Fat 14g, Trans Fat 1g); Cholesterol 275mg; Sodium 1100mg; Total Carbohydrate 16g (Dietary Fiber 2g, Sugars 3g); Protein 25g **Exchanges:** 1 Starch, 3 High-Fat Meat, 2 Fat **Carbohydrate Choices:** 1

Potato, Bacon and Egg Scramble

Skillet Eggs with Summer Squash Hash CALORIE SMART

PREP 35 min **TOTAL** 1 hr 15 min • 4 servings

- 2 medium yellow summer squash (1 lb), shredded
- 2 medium zucchini (1 lb), shredded
- 1 teaspoon salt
- 1 tablespoon olive oil
- ¼ cup chopped red onion
- 1 small tomato, chopped (½ cup)
- ½ cup diced cooked 95% fat-free ham
- 1 tablespoon chopped fresh dill weed
- 1 teaspoon grated lemon peel
- 4 eggs
- ⅛ teaspoon pepper

1 In large colander, place yellow squash and zucchini. Sprinkle with salt; stir. Let stand in sink 30 minutes to drain.

2 Gently rinse squash to remove excess salt; squeeze to remove as much liquid as possible. Set aside.

3 In 12-inch nonstick skillet, heat oil over medium-high heat. Add onion; cook 2 minutes, stirring frequently. Stir in squash mixture. Cook 8 minutes, stirring occasionally, until vegetables are crisp-tender. Add tomato, ham, dill and lemon peel. Cook and stir 1 minute longer. Reduce heat to medium.

4 Spread squash mixture evenly in skillet. Make 4 (2½-inch-wide) indentations in mixture with back of spoon. Break eggs, 1 at a time, into custard cup or small glass bowl; carefully slide into indentations. Sprinkle eggs with pepper. Cover and cook 8 to 10 minutes or until whites and yolks are firm, not runny.

Ham 'n Egg Breakfast Sandwich

Make biscuits as directed on page 400 using 3-inch cutter (yield will be 6 biscuits). Split biscuits in half while still warm. Spread with mayonnaise and mustard if desired. For each sandwich, place ½ slice American cheese, 1 Fried Egg (page 90) or Poached Egg (page 91) and 1 thin slice deli ham on bottom half of biscuit. Top each with tops of biscuits. Serve immediately.

Or, cool sandwiches and wrap individually with plastic wrap and refrigerate up to 1 week. To reheat, unwrap sandwich and rewrap with a paper towel. Microwave on High 50 seconds. Let stand 1 minute in microwave before eating.

1 Serving: Calories 260; Total Fat 13g (Saturated Fat 3.5g, Trans Fat 0g); Cholesterol 225mg; Sodium 1550mg; Total Carbohydrate 10g (Dietary Fiber 2g, Sugars 7g); Protein 24g **Exchanges:** 2 Vegetable, 2 Very Lean Meat, 1 Medium-Fat Meat, 1½ Fat **Carbohydrate Choices:** ½

Eggs Benedict FAST

As one story goes, Delmonico's restaurant in New York City was the birthplace of this classic brunch dish. In the late 1800s, when regular patrons Mr. and Mrs. LeGrand Benedict complained of nothing new on the lunch menu, the chef created this now-famous dish and named it after them.

PREP 30 min **TOTAL** 30 min • 6 servings

- Hollandaise Sauce (page 461)
- 3 English muffins, split, toasted
- 7 teaspoons butter, softened
- 6 thin slices Canadian bacon or cooked ham
- 6 Poached Eggs (page 91)
- Paprika, if desired

1 Keep hollandaise sauce warm.

2 Spread each toasted muffin half with 1 teaspoon butter; keep warm.

3 In 10-inch skillet, melt remaining 1 teaspoon butter over medium heat. Cook bacon in butter until light brown on both sides.

4 Place 1 slice bacon on each muffin half; top with 1 poached egg. Spoon warm hollandaise sauce over eggs. Sprinkle with paprika.

1 Serving: Calories 410; Total Fat 33g (Saturated Fat 14g, Trans Fat 1.5g); Cholesterol 400mg; Sodium 670mg; Total Carbohydrate 14g (Dietary Fiber 0g, Sugars 5g); Protein 15g **Exchanges:** 1 Starch, 1½ High-Fat Meat, 4 Fat **Carbohydrate Choices:** 1

Skillet Eggs with Summer Squash Hash

Spinach and Cheddar Quiche

CALORIE SMART

PREP 25 min **TOTAL** 1 hr 10 min • 6 servings

CRUST
- ½ cup all-purpose flour
- ½ cup whole wheat flour
- ¼ teaspoon salt
- ¼ cup butter
- 3 to 4 tablespoons cold water

FILLING
- ½ cup shredded reduced-fat sharp Cheddar cheese (2 oz)
- 1 tablespoon all-purpose flour
- 4 eggs, slightly beaten
- 1½ cups milk
- ½ teaspoon salt
- 1 cup firmly packed fresh spinach leaves, coarsely chopped
- 1 small red bell pepper, chopped (½ cup)

1 Heat oven to 375°F. In medium bowl, mix ½ cup all-purpose flour, the whole wheat flour and ¼ teaspoon salt. Cut in butter, using pastry blender or fork, until mixture looks like small crumbs. Sprinkle with water, 1 tablespoon at a time, tossing with fork just until flour is moistened. Shape into a ball; flatten slightly.

2 On floured surface, roll dough into 12-inch round. Fold dough into fourths; place in 9-inch glass pie plate. Unfold and ease into pie plate, pressing firmly against bottom and side; crimp edge. Trim overhanging edge of pastry 1 inch from rim of pie plate. Fold and roll pastry under, even with plate; flute.

3 In large bowl, mix cheese and 1 tablespoon all-purpose flour. Stir in eggs, milk and ½ teaspoon salt until well blended. Stir in spinach and bell pepper. Pour into pie crust.

4 Bake 15 minutes. Cover edge of crust with pie crust shield or strip of foil to prevent excessive browning. Bake 15 to 20 minutes longer or until knife inserted in center comes out clean. Let stand 10 minutes before cutting.

1 Serving: Calories 250; Total Fat 13g (Saturated Fat 7g, Trans Fat 0.5g); Cholesterol 170mg; Sodium 510mg; Total Carbohydrate 21g (Dietary Fiber 2g, Sugars 4g); Protein 11g **Exchanges:** 1 Starch, ½ Other Carbohydrate, 1 Medium-Fat Meat, 1½ Fat **Carbohydrate Choices:** 1½

Spinach and Cheddar Quiche

Ham and Cheddar Strata

CALORIE SMART

PREP 15 min **TOTAL** 1 hr 35 min • 8 servings

- 12 slices bread
- 2 cups cut-up cooked smoked ham (about 10 oz)
- 2 cups shredded Cheddar cheese (8 oz)
- 8 medium green onions, sliced (½ cup)
- 6 eggs
- 2 cups milk
- 1 teaspoon ground mustard
- ¼ teaspoon red pepper sauce
      Paprika, if desired

1 Heat oven to 300°F. Spray 13x9-inch (3-quart) glass baking dish with cooking spray.

2 Trim crusts from bread. Arrange 6 of the slices in baking dish. Layer ham, cheese and onions on bread in dish. Cut remaining 6 bread slices diagonally in half; arrange on onions.

3 In medium bowl, beat eggs, milk, mustard and pepper sauce with fork or whisk; pour evenly over bread. Sprinkle with paprika.

4 Bake uncovered 1 hour to 1 hour 10 minutes or until center is set and bread is golden brown. Let stand 10 minutes before cutting.

1 Serving: Calories 350; Total Fat 19g (Saturated Fat 9g, Trans Fat 0g); Cholesterol 215mg; Sodium 920mg; Total Carbohydrate 20g (Dietary Fiber 0g, Sugars 5g); Protein 24g **Exchanges:** 1 Starch, 3 Medium-Fat Meat, 1 Fat **Carbohydrate Choices:** 1

Breakfast Burritos

To make 2 burritos, scramble 4 eggs as directed on page 90. On each of 2 (10-inch) flour tortillas, spread ¼ cup refried beans and 2 tablespoons salsa. Top each with ¼ cup shredded Cheddar cheese. Microwave each on microwavable plate 30 to 45 seconds or until cheese is melted. Top each with scrambled eggs and roll up.

`MAKE-AHEAD` **Directions** Prepare recipe as directed through Step 3; cover and refrigerate up to 24 hours. Increase bake time by 5 to 10 minutes if necessary.

Chiles Rellenos Bake CALORIE SMART

PREP 10 min **TOTAL** 55 min • 8 servings

- 8 eggs
- 1 container (8 oz) sour cream
- ¼ teaspoon salt
- 2 drops red pepper sauce
- 2 cups shredded Monterey Jack cheese (8 oz)
- 2 cups shredded Cheddar cheese (8 oz)
- 2 cans (4.5 oz each) chopped green chiles, undrained
- 2 cups salsa (for homemade salsa, see page 458)
- 2 tablespoons chopped fresh cilantro
- ½ cup black beans (from 15-oz can), drained, rinsed
- ½ cup frozen (thawed) or canned (drained) whole kernel corn, cooked as directed on package; drained and cooled

1 Heat oven to 350°F. Spray 13x9-inch (3-quart) glass baking dish with cooking spray.

2 In large bowl, beat eggs, sour cream, salt and pepper sauce with whisk. Stir in cheeses and chiles. Pour into baking dish.

3 Bake uncovered 40 to 45 minutes or until golden brown and set in center.

4 In small bowl, mix 1 cup of the salsa and the cilantro. In another small bowl, mix remaining 1 cup salsa, the beans and corn. Serve casserole with salsa mixtures.

1 Serving: Calories 400; Total Fat 29g (Saturated Fat 17g, Trans Fat 0.5g); Cholesterol 285mg; Sodium 870mg; Total Carbohydrate 12g (Dietary Fiber 2g, Sugars 5g); Protein 23g **Exchanges:** 1 Starch, 3 High Fat Meat, ½ Fat **Carbohydrate Choices:** 1

Roasted Poblanos Rellenos Bake Set oven control to broil. Place 2 fresh poblano chiles (4½x3-inch) on cookie sheet. Broil with tops 2 inches from heat about 10 minutes, turning frequently with tongs, until all sides are blackened and blistered. Place chiles in paper bag; seal bag. Let chiles steam 15 minutes. Wearing food-safe plastic gloves, peel blackened skin from chiles. Cut open chiles and remove stems, seeds and membranes; chop. Substitute for the canned chiles.

Bacon, Kale and Egg Cups

CALORIE SMART

PREP 30 min **TOTAL** 1 hr • 12 servings

- 3 large kale leaves
- 6 slices packaged precooked bacon (from 2.1-oz package)
- ¼ cup finely chopped red bell pepper
- 1 green onion, chopped (1 tablespoon)
- 3 tablespoons grated Parmesan cheese
- 12 eggs
- ¼ teaspoon salt
- ⅛ teaspoon pepper
  Additional grated Parmesan cheese, if desired

Filling Egg Cups

Line muffin cups with several leaves of softened kale. Place bacon in cup over kale.

1 Heat oven to 350°F. Grease 12 regular-size muffin cups with shortening.

2 Cut kale into 2- to 3-inch pieces. In 2-quart saucepan, heat ½ inch water to boiling. Add kale pieces; cover and cook about 5 minutes or until bright green and just tender.

3 Line bottom and side of each muffin cup with several small leaves of steamed kale (leaves should stick up around edge of cup). Cut each bacon slice crosswise in half; place half slice in bottom of each cup or around edge over kale.

4 In small bowl, stir together bell pepper and onion; reserve 1 tablespoon. Stir cheese into remaining bell pepper and onion. Place about 1 teaspoon vegetable-cheese mixture into each muffin cup. Press mixture down slightly with back of spoon. Break eggs 1 at a time into small custard cup; slide into muffin cup over cheese mixture. Top with reserved bell pepper and onion. Sprinkle with salt, pepper and additional cheese.

5 Bake 25 to 30 minutes or until egg yolks are set. Serve immediately.

1 Serving: Calories 110; Total Fat 7g (Saturated Fat 2.5g, Trans Fat 0g); Cholesterol 190mg; Sodium 230mg; Total Carbohydrate 1g (Dietary Fiber 0g, Sugars 0g); Protein 8g **Exchanges:** 1 Medium-Fat Meat, ½ Fat **Carbohydrate Choices:** 0

MIDDLE EASTERN

Take a trip to the other side of the world without even leaving your kitchen! Explore the variety of flavors and diversity of Middle Eastern cuisine.

Dates The fruit of the date palm. Very sweet; contain a long, narrow seed. Available dried, or fresh in late summer through mid-fall.

Figs Fresh figs can be found May to December, depending on the variety, which can range in color and flavor. Dried figs are available year round.

Flatbread There are many varieties that vary slightly in ingredients and technique. Flatbread is used at nearly every meal to scoop up meat, vegetables and rice and to sop up sauces and dips. **Pita** rounds can be split horizontally to form a pocket that is used to stuff ingredients for sandwiches. **Naan** is traditionally baked in a tandoor oven to achieve its characteristic smoky flavor. **Sabaayed** is a grilled Somali flatbread that has a crispy outside and flaky interior.

Harissa A spicy-hot sauce, both green and red; use as accompaniment for couscous and to flavor soups, stews and other dishes. Available canned or jarred. To make your own, see page 445.

Pomegranates Inside the leathery skin of this fruit are hundreds of juicy, tart seeds packed in sections separated by membranes. Typically available August through December; also look for fresh pomegranate seeds, which eliminates peeling and separating the fruit.

Pomegranate Molasses Pomegranate juice reduced to thick, tart-sweet syrup, used as a marinade for grilled meats or in everything from dips to stews.

Preserved Lemons A staple in Moroccan cooking, these lemons have been preserved in salty lemon juice brine—possibly with cinnamon, cloves or other spices —giving them a silky texture and unique flavor.

Sumac Ground dried berries found in Middle Eastern markets, this brick- to dark-purple spice adds fruity, astringent flavor to meat, fish and vegetables.

Tahini A Middle Eastern staple, this thick paste is made from ground sesame seed. Available in many grocery stores near the international ingredients.

Za'atar Both a native spice of the Middle East with the flavors reminiscent of marjoram, oregano and thyme and also the name of a popular dry spice blend containing toasted sesame seed, marjoram and sumac. Mix with olive oil and salt and drizzle over warm bread or use to season meat and vegetables.

Classic Shakshuka

Classic Shakshuka CALORIE SMART

Here is our version of a Middle Eastern favorite.

PREP 25 min **TOTAL** 50 min • 6 servings

- 2 tablespoons olive oil
- 1 large onion, chopped (1 cup)
- 1 medium red bell pepper, chopped
- 3 cloves garlic, finely chopped
- 2 teaspoons ground cumin
- 1 teaspoon paprika
- 1 can (28 oz) crushed tomatoes, undrained
- 1 teaspoon sugar
- 1¼ teaspoons salt
- ¼ teaspoon pepper
- ¼ teaspoon crushed red pepper flakes
- 6 pasteurized eggs (see page 177)
- ¾ cup crumbled feta cheese (3 oz)
  Chopped fresh cilantro or chives, if desired
  Crusty bread, if desired

1 Heat oven to 350°F. In 12-inch ovenproof skillet, heat oil over medium heat. Cook onion, bell pepper and garlic in oil about 8 minutes, stirring occasionally, until tender. Add cumin and paprika; cook 1 minute, stirring once. Stir in tomatoes, sugar, salt, pepper and pepper flakes.

2 Heat to simmer; remove from heat. With back of spoon, make 6 (3-inch) indentations in tomato mixture. Break eggs, 1 at a time, into custard cup; carefully slide egg into each indentation. Place skillet in oven.

3 Bake uncovered 20 to 25 minutes or until whites are firm but yolks are still slightly runny. Bake longer if desired for firm yolks. Sprinkle with cheese and cilantro. Serve with bread.

1 Serving: Calories 220; Total Fat 14g (Saturated Fat 5g, Trans Fat 0g); Cholesterol 205mg; Sodium 960mg; Total Carbohydrate 13g (Dietary Fiber 2g, Sugars 9g); Protein 10g **Exchanges:** 2 Vegetable, 1 Medium-Fat Meat, 2 Fat **Carbohydrate Choices:** 1

Pomegranate

Pomegranate
Molasses

Preserved
Lemons

Sabaayed

Olive
Oil

Dates

Honey

Sumac

Almonds

Fresh Dates

Figs

Dried
Pineapples

Olives

Dried
Apricots

Dried
Mangos

Ground Turmeric

White
Sesame
Seeds

Za'atar

Ground
Ginger

Gingerroot

Feta

Egyptian
Roomi Cheese

Fresh
Turmeric

Tahini

Cinnamon

Saffron

Red Harissa

Green Harissa

Whole
Allspice

Ground
Allspice

Whole
Coriander

Ground
Coriander

Cumin
Seed

Ground
Cumin

Caraway
Seed

Ground
Caraway

Betty's Staples
Cooked Pork Sausage

To cook bulk pork sausage, crumble the sausage and cook in a skillet over medium heat 10 to 15 minutes or until well browned and thoroughly cooked, stirring frequently. Drain in a colander or on a paper towel and store tightly covered in the refrigerator for up to 3 days or freeze for up to 2 months.

1. **Breakfast Roll-Up:** For each roll-up, heat ¼ cup cooked sausage in the microwave for about 20 seconds. Spoon onto center of flour tortilla. Top with 1 sliced hard-cooked egg and ½ cup each shredded lettuce and chopped tomato. Drizzle with taco sauce and roll up.

2. **Sausage Waffles:** Make Waffles, page 104. For each waffle, pour batter onto waffle maker as directed; sprinkle with ¼ cup cooked sausage. Bake waffle as directed.

3. **Sausage 'n Eggs:** Make Scrambled Eggs mixture as directed on page 90. Stir in ½ to ¾ cup cooked sausage. Cook egg and sausage mixture as directed in recipe.

4. **Easy Sausage-Broccoli Pizza:** Sprinkle purchased Italian pizza crust with 1 cup cooked sausage, 1 cup chopped cooked broccoli and 1½ cups shredded Italian cheese blend. Bake as directed on pizza crust package.

5. **Tex-Mex Egg Bake:** Spread 5 cups frozen diced hash brown potatoes in greased 13x9-inch (3-quart) glass baking dish. Top with 1 cup cooked sausage, 1 can (4.5 oz) chopped green chiles and 1½ cups shredded Colby–Monterey Jack cheese. In medium bowl, beat 6 eggs with 1½ cups milk; pour over mixture. Sprinkle with 1½ cups additional cheese. Bake at 350°F for 50 to 60 minutes or until knife inserted in center comes out clean. Serve with salsa.

Oven-Baked Bacon

CALORIE SMART • EASY

PREP 5 min **TOTAL** 40 min • 12 slices

    12   slices bacon

1 Heat oven to 350°F. Line 15x10x1-inch pan with foil. Place metal cooling rack on foil, making sure rack fits within interior of pan so drippings don't fall to bottom of oven. Arrange bacon in single layer on rack.

2 Bake 20 minutes. Turn bacon over. Bake 10 to 15 minutes longer or until crisp and golden brown. Remove from rack to paper towels. Serve warm.

1 Slice: Calories 60; Total Fat 3g (Saturated Fat 1g, Trans Fat 0g); Cholesterol 10mg; Sodium 135mg; Total Carbohydrate 5g (Dietary Fiber 0g, Sugars 5g); Protein 2g **Exchanges:** ½ Other Carbohydrate, ½ Fat **Carbohydrate Choices:** ½

Balsamic and Brown Sugar Bacon In small bowl, mix ¼ cup packed brown sugar and 2 tablespoons balsamic vinegar. Make bacon as directed—except after turning bacon over, brush slices with balsamic mixture.

Honey-Mustard Bacon Brush both sides of bacon with ⅓ cup honey mustard. Arrange bacon in single layer on rack. Bake as directed.

Peppered Brown Sugar Bacon In large resealable food-storage plastic bag, mix ½ cup packed brown sugar, 1 teaspoon coarse ground black pepper and ¼ teaspoon ground red pepper (cayenne). Separate bacon slices and place in bag; seal and shake to coat. Arrange bacon in single layer on rack. Bake as directed.

Praline Bacon In small bowl, mix ¼ cup packed brown sugar and ¼ cup finely chopped pecans. Make bacon as directed—except after turning bacon over, sprinkle evenly with pecan mixture.

Oven-Baked Bacon, Peppered Brown Sugar Bacon, Praline Bacon

Pancakes CALORIE SMART • FAST

This classic pancake recipe has appeared in every Betty Crocker cookbook since 1950.

PREP 25 min **TOTAL** 25 min • 9 pancakes

- 1 egg
- 1 cup all-purpose or whole wheat flour
- 1 tablespoon sugar
- 3 teaspoons baking powder
- ¼ teaspoon salt
- ¾ cup milk
- 2 tablespoons vegetable oil or melted butter

1 In medium bowl, beat egg with whisk until fluffy. Stir in remaining ingredients just until flour is moistened (batter will be slightly lumpy); do not overmix or pancakes will be tough. For thinner pancakes, stir in 1 to 2 tablespoons additional milk.

2 Heat griddle or skillet over medium-high heat (375°F). (To test griddle, sprinkle with a few drops of water. If bubbles jump around, heat is just right.) Brush with vegetable oil if necessary (or spray with cooking spray before heating).

3 For each pancake, pour slightly less than ¼ cup batter onto hot griddle. Cook 2 to 3 minutes or until bubbly on top and dry around edges. Turn; cook other side until golden brown.

1 Pancake: Calories 110; Total Fat 5g (Saturated Fat 1.5g, Trans Fat 0g); Cholesterol 25mg; Sodium 250mg; Total Carbohydrate 13g (Dietary Fiber 0g, Sugars 3g); Protein 3g **Exchanges:** 1 Starch, ½ Fat **Carbohydrate Choices:** 1

Berry Pancakes Stir ½ cup fresh or frozen (thawed and well drained) sliced strawberries, blackberries, blueberries or raspberries into batter. Top pancakes with vanilla yogurt and additional berries.

Buttermilk Pancakes Substitute 1 cup buttermilk for the ¾ cup milk. Reduce baking powder to 1 teaspoon. Add ½ teaspoon baking soda.

Orange-Cranberry Pancakes Substitute orange juice for the milk. Stir in ¼ cup dried cranberries and ¼ cup chopped dried apples after mixing ingredients in Step 1.

Cornbread Pancakes

CALORIE SMART • FAST

Make the syrup first, then the pancakes, so both are warm and ready at the same time.

PREP 30 min **TOTAL** 30 min • 8 servings

- 1¼ cups all-purpose flour
- ¾ cup cornmeal
- ¼ cup sugar
- 2 teaspoons baking powder
- ½ teaspoon salt
- 1⅓ cups milk
- ¼ cup vegetable oil
- 1 egg, beaten
  Butter-Pecan Syrup (page 102)

Turning Pancakes

Pancakes are ready to turn when they are puffed and bubbles form on top.

1 Heat griddle or skillet over medium-high heat (375°F). Brush with vegetable oil if necessary (or spray with cooking spray before heating).

2 In large bowl, mix flour, cornmeal, sugar, baking powder and salt. Stir in milk, oil and egg just until blended.

3 For each pancake, pour about ¼ cup batter onto hot griddle. Cook 2 to 3 minutes or until bubbly on top and dry around edges. Turn; cook other side until golden brown. Top each serving (2 pancakes) with 2 tablespoons syrup.

1 Serving: Calories 380; Total Fat 15g (Saturated Fat 3.5g, Trans Fat 0g); Cholesterol 35mg; Sodium 350mg; Total Carbohydrate 57g (Dietary Fiber 2g, Sugars 20g); Protein 6g **Exchanges:** 1 Starch, 3 Other Carbohydrate, 3 Fat **Carbohydrate Choices:** 4

Cornbread Pancakes

Puffy Oven Pancake

CALORIE SMART • EASY

More like a popover than a pancake, this oven pancake puffs up high around the edges when it's done. Serve it quickly, before it sinks.

PREP 10 min **TOTAL** 40 min • 4 servings

2 tablespoons butter

2 eggs

½ cup all-purpose flour

¼ teaspoon salt

½ cup milk

Lemon juice and powdered sugar or cut-up fruit, if desired

1 Heat oven to 400°F. In 9-inch glass pie plate or cast-iron skillet, melt butter in oven; brush butter over bottom and side of pie plate.

2 In medium bowl, beat eggs slightly with whisk. Stir in flour, salt and milk just until flour is moistened (do not overbeat or pancake may not puff). Pour into pie plate.

3 Bake 25 to 30 minutes or until puffy and deep golden brown. Serve immediately sprinkled with lemon juice and powdered sugar or topped with fruit.

1 Serving: Calories 160; Total Fat 9g (Saturated Fat 5g, Trans Fat 0g); Cholesterol 125mg; Sodium 230mg; Total Carbohydrate 14g (Dietary Fiber 0g, Sugars 2g); Protein 5g **Exchanges:** 1 Starch, 2 Fat **Carbohydrate Choices:** 1

Apple Oven Pancake Make pancake as directed—except sprinkle 2 tablespoons packed brown sugar and ¼ teaspoon ground cinnamon evenly over melted butter in pie plate.

Cast-Iron Skillets

It's worth digging out your heavy cast-iron skillet from the recesses of your cupboard or picking one up at a garage sale (if you are lucky enough to find one). What makes cast iron so special? It holds the heat like no other pan. So it's a perfect choice for the Puffy Oven Pancake because the heat of the pan helps to make the pancake puff up and gives it a delicious crispy exterior.

A cast-iron skillet is also great for meats that need to get a nice sear (see page 302) before being braised, delivering a great deep brown color without getting burnt bits in the bottom of the pan. Also oven compatible, it makes delicious roasted veggies with perfectly golden-brown crispy exteriors. And it's the secret of many for gorgeous fried chicken, as the heat of the pan helps keep the oil very hot, producing crispy chicken while the deep side cuts down on oil splatters.

Arrange 1 cup thinly sliced peeled baking apple (1 medium) over sugar. Pour batter over apple. Bake 30 to 35 minutes. Immediately loosen edge of pancake and turn upside down onto heatproof serving plate.

Double Oven Pancake In 13x9-inch pan, melt ⅓ cup butter. Use 4 eggs, 1 cup all-purpose flour, ¼ teaspoon salt and 1 cup milk. Bake 30 to 35 minutes.

Buckwheat Pancakes

CALORIE SMART • FAST

Store buckwheat tightly covered for up to 1 month in the pantry or in the freezer for up to 2 months.

PREP 30 min **TOTAL** 30 min • 5 servings

1 egg

½ cup buckwheat flour

½ cup whole wheat flour

1 cup milk

1 tablespoon sugar

2 tablespoons vegetable oil

1 tablespoon baking powder

½ teaspoon salt

Whole bran or wheat germ, if desired

Butter-Pecan Syrup (below)

1 Heat griddle or skillet over medium-high heat (375°F). Grease with vegetable oil if necessary (or spray with cooking spray before heating).

2 In medium bowl, beat egg with whisk until fluffy. Beat in remaining pancake ingredients except bran just until smooth.

3 For each pancake, pour about 3 tablespoons batter onto hot griddle. Cook pancakes until puffed and dry around edges. Sprinkle each pancake with 1 teaspoon bran. Turn; cook other side until golden brown.

4 Top each serving (2 pancakes) with about 2 tablespoons syrup.

1 Serving: Calories 340; Total Fat 13g (Saturated Fat 3g, Trans Fat 0g); Cholesterol 50mg; Sodium 620mg; Total Carbohydrate 48g (Dietary Fiber 3g, Sugars 17g); Protein 6g **Exchanges:** 2 Starch, 1 Other Carbohydrate, 2½ Fat **Carbohydrate Choices:** 3

Butter-Pecan Syrup

In 1-quart saucepan, melt 2 tablespoons butter over medium heat. Add ⅓ cup pecans; cook 2 to 3 minutes, stirring frequently, until browned. Stir in ¾ cup real maple syrup; heat until hot. Serve over pancakes.

Apple Oven Pancake

Crepes CALORIE SMART

PREP 35 min **TOTAL** 35 min • 12 crepes

- 1½ cups all-purpose flour
- 1 tablespoon granulated sugar
- ½ teaspoon baking powder
- ½ teaspoon salt
- 2 cups milk
- 2 tablespoons butter, melted
- ½ teaspoon vanilla
- 2 eggs
  Applesauce, sweetened berries, jelly or jam, if desired
  Powdered sugar, if desired

1 In medium bowl, mix flour, granulated sugar, baking powder and salt. Add milk, 2 tablespoons butter, the vanilla and eggs; beat with whisk just until smooth.

2 Lightly butter 6- to 8-inch skillet or crepe pan. Heat over medium heat until bubbly. For each crepe, pour slightly less than ¼ cup batter into hot skillet. Immediately tilt and rotate skillet so thin layer of batter covers bottom. Cook until light brown. Run wide spatula around edge to loosen; turn and cook other side until light brown. Repeat with remaining batter, buttering skillet as needed.

3 Stack crepes, placing waxed paper between each; keep covered. Spread applesauce, sweetened berries, jelly or jam thinly over each warm crepe; roll up. (Fill crepes so when rolled the more attractive side is on the outside.) Sprinkle with powdered sugar.

1 Crepe: Calories 140; Total Fat 8g (Saturated Fat 3.5g, Trans Fat 0g); Cholesterol 55mg; Sodium 190mg; Total Carbohydrate 15g (Dietary Fiber 0g, Sugars 3g); Protein 4g **Exchanges:** 1 Starch, 1½ Fat **Carbohydrate Choices:** 1

MAKE-AHEAD Directions Make crepes as directed and cool completely; do not fill. Stack crepes with plastic wrap between each; wrap tightly and freeze up to 2 months.

Waffles CALORIE SMART

PREP 35 min **TOTAL** 35 min • 6 (7-inch) round waffles

- 2 eggs
- 2 cups all-purpose or whole wheat flour
- 1 tablespoon sugar
- 4 teaspoons baking powder
- ¼ teaspoon salt
- 1¾ cups milk
- ½ cup vegetable oil or melted butter
  Syrup or fresh berries, if desired

1 Heat waffle maker. (Waffle makers without a nonstick coating may need to be brushed with vegetable oil or sprayed with cooking spray before batter for each waffle is added.)

2 In large bowl, beat eggs with whisk until fluffy. Beat in flour, sugar, baking powder, salt, milk and oil just until smooth.

3 Pour slightly less than ¾ cup batter onto center of hot waffle maker. (Check manufacturer's directions for recommended amount of batter.) Close lid of waffle maker.

4 Bake about 5 minutes or until steaming stops. Carefully remove waffle. Serve immediately with syrup. Repeat with remaining batter.

1 Waffle: Calories 380; Total Fat 22g (Saturated Fat 4g, Trans Fat 0g); Cholesterol 75mg; Sodium 480mg; Total Carbohydrate 38g (Dietary Fiber 1g, Sugars 6g); Protein 9g **Exchanges:** 2½ Starch, 4 Fat **Carbohydrate Choices:** 2½

Crepes

Waffles

Apricot Stuffed French Toast

Whole Wheat Waffles with Honey–Peanut Butter Drizzle

CALORIE SMART

PREP 35 min **TOTAL** 35 min • 8 servings

WAFFLES

- 2 eggs
- 1 cup whole wheat flour
- 1 cup all-purpose flour
- 2 cups buttermilk
- 1 tablespoon sugar
- 3 tablespoons vegetable oil
- 2 teaspoons baking powder
- ¼ teaspoon salt

DRIZZLE AND TOPPING

- ½ cup honey
- ¼ cup creamy peanut butter
- ½ cup low-fat granola

1 Heat waffle maker. (Waffle makers without a nonstick coating may need to be brushed with vegetable oil or sprayed with cooking spray before batter for each waffle is added.)

2 In medium bowl, beat eggs with whisk until foamy. Beat in remaining waffle ingredients just until smooth.

3 Pour about 1 cup of batter onto the center of hot waffle maker. (Check manufacturer's directions for recommended amount of batter.) Close lid of waffle maker.

4 Bake about 5 minutes or until steaming stops. Carefully remove waffle. Repeat with remaining batter.

5 Meanwhile, in small microwavable bowl, mix honey and peanut butter. Microwave uncovered on High 40 to 60 seconds or until warm; stir until smooth.

6 Top each serving (2 waffle squares) with 4½ teaspoons honey mixture and 1 tablespoon granola.

1 Serving: Calories 350; Total Fat 12g (Saturated Fat 2g, Trans Fat 0g); Cholesterol 55mg; Sodium 330mg; Total Carbohydrate 52g (Dietary Fiber 3g, Sugars 25g); Protein 10g **Exchanges:** 1½ Starch, 2 Other Carbohydrate, ½ High-Fat Meat, 1½ Fat **Carbohydrate Choices:** 3½

Apricot Stuffed French Toast

CALORIE SMART

PREP 20 min **TOTAL** 1 hr 15 min • 6 servings

- 1 loaf (½-lb size) or ½ loaf (1-lb size) day-old French bread
- 3 oz (from 8-oz package) cream cheese, softened
- 3 tablespoons apricot preserves
- ¼ teaspoon grated lemon peel
- 3 eggs
- ¾ cup half-and-half or milk
- 2 tablespoons granulated sugar
- 1 teaspoon vanilla
- ⅛ teaspoon salt
- ⅛ teaspoon ground nutmeg, if desired
- 2 tablespoons butter, softened
  Powdered sugar, if desired

1 Spray 13x9-inch pan with cooking spray. Cut bread crosswise into 12 (1-inch) slices. Cut a horizontal slit in the side of each bread slice, cutting to but not through the other side.

2 In medium bowl, beat cream cheese, preserves and lemon peel with electric mixer on medium speed about 1 minute or until well mixed. Spread 2 teaspoons cream cheese mixture into slit in each bread slice. Place stuffed bread slices in pan.

3 In medium bowl, beat eggs, half-and-half, granulated sugar, vanilla, salt and nutmeg with fork or whisk until mixed. Pour egg mixture over bread slices in pan; turn slices carefully to coat. Cover and refrigerate at least 30 minutes but no longer than 24 hours.

4 Heat oven to 425°F. Uncover French toast. Bake 20 to 25 minutes or until golden brown. Top with butter and sprinkle with powdered sugar.

1 Serving (2 Slices): Calories 310; Total Fat 16g (Saturated Fat 8g, Trans Fat 1g); Cholesterol 145mg; Sodium 380mg; Total Carbohydrate 32g (Dietary Fiber 1g, Sugars 11g); Protein 9g **Exchanges:** 1 Starch, 1 Other Carbohydrate, 1 High-Fat Meat, 1½ Fat **Carbohydrate Choices:** 2

Heirloom Recipe and New Twist

French toast has been a breakfast favorite for generations, and this recipe has been in our collection for many years. Although there are subtle differences in recipes, this classic fried bread dish is typically crispy on the outside and tender on the inside—and is made and cooked right before serving. The secrets to success are beating the eggs well and having the griddle at the correct temperature. The new twist is ideal for make-ahead occasions. It has wonderful flavor and looks impressive.

HEIRLOOM

French Toast CALORIE SMART • FAST

PREP 25 min **TOTAL** 25 min • 8 slices

- 3   eggs
- ¾   cup milk
- 1   tablespoon sugar
- ¼   teaspoon vanilla
- ⅛   teaspoon salt
- 8   slices firm-textured sandwich bread, Texas toast or 1-inch-thick French bread

1 In medium bowl, beat eggs, milk, sugar, vanilla and salt with whisk until well mixed. Pour into shallow bowl.

2 Heat griddle or skillet over medium-high heat (375°F). (To test griddle, sprinkle with a few drops of water. If bubbles jump around, heat is just right.) Grease griddle with vegetable oil if necessary (or spray with cooking spray before heating).

3 Dip bread into egg mixture. Place on hot griddle. Cook about 4 minutes on each side or until golden brown.

1 Slice: Calories 230; Total Fat 3.5g (Saturated Fat 1g, Trans Fat 0g); Cholesterol 80mg; Sodium 490mg; Total Carbohydrate 39g (Dietary Fiber 1g, Sugars 8g); Protein 10g **Exchanges:** 2 Starch, ½ Other Carbohydrate, ½ Medium-Fat Meat **Carbohydrate Choices:** 2½

LIGHTER Directions For 95 calories and 2 grams of fat per serving, use 1 whole egg and 2 egg whites for the 3 eggs, use ⅔ cup fat-free (skim) milk and increase vanilla to ½ teaspoon.

Oven French Toast Heat oven to 450°F. Generously butter 15x10x1-inch pan. Heat pan in oven 1 minute; remove from oven. Arrange dipped bread in hot pan. Drizzle any remaining egg mixture over bread. Bake 5 to 8 minutes or until bottoms are golden brown; turn bread. Bake 2 to 4 minutes longer or until golden brown.

French Toast Sticks Use 8 slices firm-textured whole-grain sandwich bread. Cut each piece into 3 strips. Dip bread strips into batter. Cook on griddle about 4 minutes on each side or until golden brown. Serve with Spicy Cider Syrup, page 107, or real maple syrup for dipping.

French Toast Sticks

Upside-Down Banana-Walnut French Toast

Upside-Down Banana-Walnut French Toast

PREP 15 min **TOTAL** 2 hr 10 min • 10 servings

- 1½ cups packed brown sugar
- ½ cup butter, melted
- ¼ cup light corn syrup
- ½ cup chopped walnuts
- 3 medium bananas, sliced
- 1 loaf (about 1 lb) sliced unfrosted firm cinnamon bread
- 6 eggs
- 1½ cups milk
- 1 teaspoon vanilla
  Powdered sugar, if desired

1 Spray 13x9-inch (3-quart) glass baking dish with cooking spray. In large bowl, mix brown sugar, butter, corn syrup and walnuts. Gently stir in bananas. Spoon mixture into baking dish.

2 Reserve ends of bread loaf for another use; they do not soak up egg mixture very well. Arrange 2 layers of bread on banana mixture, tearing bread to fit if needed.

3 In medium bowl, beat eggs, milk and vanilla with whisk until well blended. Pour over bread. Cover tightly and refrigerate at least 1 hour but no longer than 24 hours.

4 Heat oven to 325°F. Uncover baking dish; bake 45 to 55 minutes or until knife inserted in center comes out clean. Serve portions upside down, spooning sauce from bottom of dish over each serving. Sprinkle with powdered sugar.

1 Serving: Calories 490; Total Fat 19g (Saturated Fat 7g, Trans Fat 1g); Cholesterol 155mg; Sodium 380mg; Total Carbohydrate 72g (Dietary Fiber 2g, Sugars 42g); Protein 10g **Exchanges:** 3 Starch, 2 Other Carbohydrate, 3½ Fat **Carbohydrate Choices:** 5

Spicy Cider Syrup

In 2-quart saucepan, mix 1 cup sugar, 3 tablespoons all-purpose flour, ¼ teaspoon each ground cinnamon and nutmeg, 2 cups apple cider, and 2 tablespoons lemon juice. Cook and stir over medium heat until mixture thickens and boils. Boil and stir 1 minute; remove from heat. Stir in 4 tablespoons butter, cut into several pieces, until melted.

Triple-Berry Oatmeal-Flax Muesli CALORIE SMART

PREP 10 min **TOTAL** 45 min • 6 servings

- 2¾ cups old-fashioned oats or rolled barley
- ½ cup sliced almonds
- 2 containers (6 oz each) banana crème or French vanilla fat-free yogurt
- 1½ cups fat-free (skim) milk
- ¼ cup ground flaxseed or flaxseed meal
- ½ cup fresh blueberries
- ½ cup fresh raspberries
- ½ cup sliced fresh strawberries

1 Heat oven to 350°F. In ungreased 15x10x1-inch pan, spread oats and almonds.

2 Bake 18 to 20 minutes, stirring occasionally, until light golden brown. Cool 15 minutes.

3 In large bowl, mix yogurt and milk until well blended. Stir in flaxseed and toasted oats and almonds. Top each serving with berries.

1 Serving: Calories 290; Total Fat 8g (Saturated Fat 1g, Trans Fat 0g); Cholesterol 0mg; Sodium 55mg; Total Carbohydrate 42g (Dietary Fiber 7g, Sugars 11g); Protein 11g **Exchanges:** 2½ Starch, ½ Skim Milk, 1 Fat **Carbohydrate Choices:** 3

Is Muesli Really Granola?

Think of muesli as granola's fresher cousin. While both foods contain oats (traditionally), fruit, seeds and nuts, they are not the same food. Muesli combines toasted grains with other fresh ingredients. Granola is baked. Muesli is usually less sweet—not adding any extra sugar or oil. Granola adds sweeteners and oil to make it more clumpy—perfect for eating out of your hand, anytime. Muesli is a loose mixture—meant for eating with milk, yogurt or water, either hot or cold.

Triple-Berry Oatmeal-Flax Muesli

Make-Ahead GRANOLA

PREP 10 min **TOTAL** 1 hr • 8 servings

- 3 cups old-fashioned or quick-cooking oats
- 1 cup whole almonds
- 1 teaspoon ground cinnamon
- ⅓ cup real maple syrup or honey
- ½ cup dried cherries
- ½ cup dried blueberries

1 Heat oven to 300°F. In ungreased 15x10x1-inch pan, spread oats and almonds. Sprinkle evenly with cinnamon; drizzle with syrup. Toss to coat; spread mixture evenly in pan.

2 Bake 15 minutes. Remove from oven. Stir well to mix so granola toasts evenly. Spread mixture evenly in pan. Bake 15 minutes longer or until mixture is dry and lightly toasted. Cool completely.

3 Place granola in container with tight-fitting lid or resealable food-storage plastic bag. Add dried fruit; stir to distribute. Cover tightly and store at room temperature up to 1 month.

1 Serving (½ Cup): Calories 330; Total Fat 11g (Saturated Fat 1g, Trans Fat 0g); Cholesterol 0mg; Sodium 0mg; Total Carbohydrate 50g (Dietary Fiber 7g, Sugars 22g); Protein 8g **Exchanges:** 2 Starch, 1½ Other Carbohydrate, 2 Fat **Carbohydrate Choices:** 3

Ways to Use Granola

1. Granola Cereal: Pour soymilk or almond milk over granola and top with sliced fresh strawberries.

2. Granola Pancakes: Make Pancake batter, page 101, as directed. Stir in ¾ cup granola before spooning pancakes onto griddle.

3. Granola Cookies: Make Oatmeal-Raisin Cookies, page 522. Substitute 1 cup granola for the raisins, nuts and chocolate. Bake as directed.

4. Ice Cream and Granola: For each serving, spoon ice cream or frozen yogurt (any flavor) into bowl. Sprinkle with 2 to 4 tablespoons granola.

5. Yogurt Parfaits: In parfait glasses or dessert dishes, layer vanilla yogurt with granola and sliced bananas.

6. Granola Bars: In medium bowl, mix 1 cup all-purpose or whole wheat flour, 1 teaspoon baking powder, 1 cup packed brown sugar, ⅓ cup vegetable oil and 2 eggs until well blended. Stir in 2 cups granola. Spread mixture in lightly greased 9-inch square pan. Bake at 350°F for 30 minutes or until set. Cool and cut into squares.

7. Granola Fruit Salad: In medium bowl, mix 1 cup sliced strawberries, 1 cup raspberries, 1 sliced banana, 1 or 2 sectioned oranges and 1 cup granola. Toss with ¼ cup honey-mustard salad dressing.

Granola Bars, Granola

Baked Apple Oatmeal

Baked Apple Oatmeal

CALORIE SMART

Steel-cut oats, also known as Scottish or Irish oats, are kernels of the oat sliced lengthwise.

PREP 10 min **TOTAL** 1 hr • 8 servings

- 2⅔ cups old-fashioned or steel-cut oats
- ½ cup raisins, sweetened dried cranberries or dried cherries
- ⅓ cup packed brown sugar
- 1 teaspoon ground cinnamon
- ¼ teaspoon salt
- 4 cups milk
- 2 medium apples or pears, chopped (2 cups)
- ½ cup chopped walnuts, toasted (page 23) if desired

  Additional milk, if desired

1 Heat oven to 350°F. In ungreased 2-quart casserole, mix oats, raisins, brown sugar, cinnamon, salt, 4 cups milk and the apples.

2 Bake uncovered 40 to 50 minutes or until most of the milk is absorbed (a small amount of milk will remain in the center); do not overbake (oats will look chewy). Sprinkle walnuts over top. Serve with additional milk.

1 Serving: Calories 300; Total Fat 9g (Saturated Fat 2.5g, Trans Fat 0g); Cholesterol 10mg; Sodium 130mg; Total Carbohydrate 45g (Dietary Fiber 5g, Sugars 24g); Protein 10g **Exchanges:** 1½ Starch, 1 Other Carbohydrate, ½ Low-Fat Milk, 1 Fat **Carbohydrate Choices:** 3

Steel-Cut Oatmeal

For about 4 servings of oatmeal, stir 1 cup steel-cut oats into 4 cups boiling water or milk. Reduce heat to low and cook uncovered for 20 to 30 minutes or until thickened and oats are tender, stirring occasionally. For firmer oats, use a little less water.

Breakfast Quinoa CALORIE SMART •

FAST • EASY

Quinoa makes a quick and hearty base for this new spin on hot cereal. Experiment with your favorite dried or fresh fruits and nuts. Use more liquid for a creamier cereal, or serve additional milk or cream on the side.

PREP 5 min **TOTAL** 20 min • 4 servings

- 1 cup uncooked quinoa
- 2 cups water, milk or soymilk
- ¼ teaspoon ground cinnamon
- 1 cup fresh or frozen (thawed) blueberries
- ¼ cup pecans or walnuts, toasted (page 23) if desired

  Real maple syrup, if desired

1 Rinse quinoa thoroughly by placing in fine-mesh strainer and holding under cold running water until water runs clear; drain well.

2 In 1-quart saucepan, heat water and quinoa to boiling. Reduce heat to low; cover and simmer 15 minutes or until liquid is absorbed (mixture will still be moist).

3 Stir in cinnamon. Spoon quinoa into bowls. Top with blueberries and pecans. Sweeten to taste with a drizzle of syrup.

1 Serving (½ Cup): Calories 230; Total Fat 7g (Saturated Fat 0.5g, Trans Fat 0g); Cholesterol 0mg; Sodium 5mg; Total Carbohydrate 34g (Dietary Fiber 4g, Sugars 7g); Protein 7g **Exchanges:** 2½ Starch, 1 Fat **Carbohydrate Choices:** 2

What Is Quinoa?

Tiny and bead shaped, quinoa cooks quickly and expands to four times its volume. The flavor is delicate and similar to couscous. Look for this grain at most supermarkets and health food stores.

Breakfast Quinoa

CALORIE SMART = See Helpful Nutrition and Cooking Information, page 643   FAST = Ready in 30 minutes or less
EASY = Prep in 10 minutes or less **plus** five ingredients or less   LIGHTER = 25% fewer calories or grams of fat
MAKE AHEAD = Make-ahead directions   SLOW COOKER = Slow cooker directions

< Heirloom Tomato Caprese Salad, page 122

SALAD BASICS

We love our salads! From mixed greens and fresh fruit to tender pasta and crisp vegetables, salad ingredients span a delicious range of flavors and textures. In this collection of recipes, there are many side salads that will complement other recipes on your menu, as well as salads that can stand alone as a main course.

Looking for ways to break out of your salad rut? Explore some of the newer greens that are available. From mild greens like mesclun, leaf or Bibb lettuce to bolder varieties like kale or radicchio, the many choices let you vary the taste, texture and appearance of salads easily!

ABOUT GREENS

Within the two categories of lettuce (delicate and assertive-flavored), there are four lettuce types: crisphead (iceberg), butterhead (Bibb or Boston), loose leaf (oak leaf) and long leaf (romaine).

Selecting and Handling Greens

- Choose the freshest greens possible—there should be no bruising, discoloration or wilting.

- Keep greens chilled—store unwashed in the refrigerator, wrapped in a paper towel and placed in a plastic bag or tightly covered container for up to 5 days.

- Wash greens well just before using—rinse well in cold water, removing any dirt.

- Dry greens well—use a salad spinner or pat dry with paper towels.

- Trim greens—remove stems and roots as necessary and discard. Serve small leaves whole and cut up larger pieces.

Mild Greens

Butterhead Lettuce (Bibb, Boston): Small rounded heads of soft, tender, buttery leaves; delicate, mild flavor.

Crisphead Lettuce (Iceberg): Solid, compact heads with leaves ranging in color from medium green outer leaves to pale green inner ones; very crisp, mild flavor.

Long Leaf Lettuce (Romaine, Cos): Narrow, elongated, dark green, crisp leaves with tips sometimes tinged with red. The broad white center rib is especially crunchy.

Loose Leaf Lettuce (Green, Red, Oak): Tender, crisp leaves in loose heads. Mildly flavored but stronger than iceberg lettuce.

Mâche (Lamb's Lettuce, Corn Salad): Spoon-shaped medium to dark green leaves with velvety texture; mild, subtly sweet and nutty.

Mesclun (Field or Wild Greens): A mixture of young, tender, small greens often including arugula, chervil, chickweed, dandelion, frisée, mizuna and oak leaf lettuce.

Mixed Salad Greens (Prepackaged): These prewashed greens come in many varieties, some with dressing, croutons or cheese.

Drying Fresh Greens

Salad Spinner: Place washed leaves in basket of spinner; cover spinner and spin until lettuce is dry.

Towel Dry: Place washed leaves on clean kitchen towel or in several layers of paper towels and pat dry.

Bold Greens and Cabbage

Arugula (Rocket): Small, slender, dark green leaves similar to radish leaves; slightly bitter, peppery mustard flavor. Pick smaller leaves for milder flavor.

Belgian Endive (French): Narrow, cupped, cream-colored leaves tinged with green or red; slightly bitter flavor.

Cabbage: Comes in several distinctly flavored varieties. Green and red cabbage are most common; look for compact heads of waxy, tightly wrapped leaves. Savoy cabbage has crinkled leaves and Chinese (or napa) cabbage has long, crisp leaves.

Curly Endive: Frilly, narrow, slightly prickly leaves; slightly bitter taste.

Escarole: Broad, wavy, medium-green leaves; slightly bitter flavor but milder than Belgian or curly endive.

Frisée: Slender, curly leaves ranging in color from yellow-white to yellow-green; slightly bitter flavor.

Greens (Beet, Chard, Collard, Dandelion, Mustard): All have a strong, sharp flavor. Young greens are milder and more tender for tossed salads; older greens are more bitter and should be cooked for best flavor.

Kale: Firm, dark green leaves with frilly edges tinged with shades of blue and purple; mild cabbage taste. Pick young, small leaves for best flavor.

Radicchio: Looks like a small, loose-leaf cabbage with smooth, tender leaves; slightly bitter flavor. The two most common radicchios in the United States are a ruby red variety with broad white veins and one with leaves speckled in shades of pink, red and green.

Sorrel (Sour Grass): Resembles spinach, but with smaller leaves; sharp, lemony flavor.

Spinach: Smooth, tapered, dark green leaves, sometimes with crumpled edges; slightly bitter flavor. Baby spinach leaves are smaller and milder in flavor than regular spinach leaves.

Watercress: Small, crisp, dark green, coin-size leaves; strong, peppery flavor.

Collard Greens

Dandelion Greens

Mustard Greens

Beet Greens

Chard

Mesclun

Escarole

Butterhead
Lettuce
(Boston)

Mâche

Spinach

Frisée

Romaine
Lettuce

Arugula

Watercress

Radicchio

Curly Endive

Iceberg Lettuce

Loose Leaf Lettuce
(Red and Green)

Belgian
Endive

Caesar Salad

2 In salad bowl, mix anchovies, oil, lemon juice, egg yolk, Worcestershire sauce, salt, mustard and pepper with whisk.

3 Add lettuce; toss until coated. Sprinkle with croutons and cheese; toss. Serve immediately.

*2 teaspoons anchovy paste can be substituted for the anchovies. If you prefer, anchovies can be omitted.

**Use only pasteurized eggs in this recipe to prevent the risk of food poisoning that can result from eating (raw or undercooked) eggs.

1 Serving (1¾ Cups): Calories 190; Total Fat 16g (Saturated Fat 3g, Trans Fat 0g); Cholesterol 10mg; Sodium 500mg; Total Carbohydrate 7g (Dietary Fiber 2g, Sugars 2g); Protein 6g **Exchanges:** 1½ Vegetable, ½ High-Fat Meat, 2½ Fat **Carbohydrate Choices:** ½

Caesar Salad CALORIE SMART • FAST

This classic salad is the perfect go-to recipe to accompany most any meal. It's not hard to whip up, but knowing how to make a great dressing and crisp croutons turns a ho-hum Caesar into a specialty salad that folks will ask you to make again and again.

PREP 15 min **TOTAL** 15 min • 6 servings

- 1 clove garlic, cut in half
- 8 anchovy fillets, cut up*
- ⅓ cup olive oil
- 3 tablespoons fresh lemon juice
- 1 pasteurized egg yolk**
- 1 teaspoon Worcestershire sauce
- ¼ teaspoon salt
- ¼ teaspoon ground mustard
-    Freshly ground pepper to taste
- 1 large or 2 small bunches romaine lettuce, torn into bite-size pieces (10 cups)
- 1 cup Garlic Croutons (page 117)
- ⅓ cup freshly grated Parmesan cheese

1 Rub large salad bowl with cut clove of garlic for extra flavor, if desired. Chop garlic and place in bowl.

Chicken Caesar Salad Broil 6 boneless skinless chicken breasts (page 351); slice diagonally and arrange on salads. Serve chicken warm or chilled.

Grilled Caesar Salad Heat gas or charcoal grill. Make dressing as directed in small bowl. Omit halved garlic clove; do not tear lettuce. Carefully cut head of romaine lengthwise in half through stem. Brush each cut side with 1 tablespoon of dressing. Place on grill cut side down; cook 2 to 4 minutes over medium-high heat or until lightly browned. Brush with dressing; turn and cook 2 to 4 minutes or until lightly browned. Place romaine on serving platter. Drizzle with desired amount of remaining dressing; sprinkle with croutons and cheese.

Kale Caesar Salad Substitute baby kale leaves for romaine lettuce.

Shrimp Caesar Salad Broil or grill 1 pound deveined peeled large shrimp (page 370); arrange on salads. Serve shrimp warm or chilled.

Making Caesar Salad

Rub bowl with cut side of garlic.

Mix ingredients with whisk.

Toss lettuce until coated with dressing.

Croutons CALORIE SMART • EASY

Homemade croutons taste so much better than purchased ones and are super easy to make. We've suggested cutting the bread into ½-inch cubes, but by all means, if you love big croutons, cut them larger (they will take longer to get golden and crisp).

PREP 10 min **TOTAL** 55 min • 16 servings

- 10 slices (½ inch thick) firm white or whole-grain bread
- ½ cup butter, melted*

1 Heat oven to 300°F. Cut bread slices into ½-inch cubes. In ungreased 15x10x1-inch pan, spread bread cubes in single layer. Drizzle butter evenly over bread cubes; toss until coated.

2 Bake 30 to 35 minutes, stirring occasionally, until golden brown, dry and crisp. Cool completely. Store tightly covered at room temperature up to 2 days.

*Olive oil can be substituted for the melted butter. After drizzling bread cubes with oil, sprinkle evenly with 1/2 teaspoon coarse (kosher or sea) salt; toss until coated.

1 Serving: Calories 90; Total Fat 6g (Saturated Fat 4g, Trans Fat 0g); Cholesterol 15mg; Sodium 150mg; Total Carbohydrate 8g (Dietary Fiber 0g, Sugars 0g); Protein 1g **Exchanges:** ½ Starch, 1 Fat **Carbohydrate Choices:** ½

Garlic Croutons Add 3 cloves garlic, very finely chopped, or ¼ teaspoon garlic powder to butter before drizzling over bread cubes.

Herbed Croutons Drizzle bread cubes with olive oil instead of butter. Sprinkle with 2 teaspoons Italian seasoning and ½ teaspoon salt; toss until coated.

Pumpernickel or Rye Croutons Substitute pumpernickel or rye bread. Bake as directed or until pumpernickel cubes are dry and crisp or rye cubes are light golden brown, dry and crisp.

Making Tortilla Straws

Cut tortilla in half; cut each half crosswise into ¼-inch strips.

Place on cookie sheet; bake until crisp and golden brown.

Greek Salad CALORIE SMART • FAST

PREP 20 min **TOTAL** 20 min • 8 servings

SALAD

- 5 cups fresh baby spinach leaves
- 1 head Boston lettuce, torn into bite-size pieces (4 cups)
- 1 cup crumbled feta cheese (4 oz)
- 24 pitted kalamata or Greek olives*
- 4 medium green onions, sliced (¼ cup)**
- 3 medium tomatoes, cut into wedges
- 1 medium cucumber, sliced

LEMON DRESSING

- ¼ cup olive oil
- 2 tablespoons fresh lemon juice
- 1½ teaspoons Dijon mustard
- ½ teaspoon sugar
- ¼ teaspoon salt
- ⅛ teaspoon pepper

In large bowl, mix salad ingredients. In tightly covered container, shake dressing ingredients. Pour dressing over salad; toss until coated. Serve immediately.

*Extra-large pitted ripe olives can be substituted for the kalamata or Greek olives.

**Chopped red onion can be substituted for the green onions.

1 Serving (1¾ Cups): Calories 140; Total Fat 11g (Saturated Fat 3.5g, Trans Fat 0g); Cholesterol 15mg; Sodium 680mg; Total Carbohydrate 6g (Dietary Fiber 2g, Sugars 2g); Protein 4g **Exchanges:** 1 Vegetable, 2½ Fat **Carbohydrate Choices:** ½

Other Crispy Toppers

Ideas for other toppings that add crunch and flavor to salads can be as simple as chopped cashews or peanuts, thin or thick chow mein noodles, french-fried crispy onions or shoestring potatoes, or opt for shredded carrots, radishes or cucumber. Here are a couple of other ideas to try:

Tortilla Straws: Brush flour tortillas with vegetable oil and sprinkle each with ¼ teaspoon each chili powder and salt. Cut into ¼-inch-wide strips. Place on cookie sheet and bake at 350°F for 10 to 12 minutes or until crisp.

Bacon Crumbles: Chop bacon and cook in skillet over medium heat until crisp. Drain on paper towels.

Edamame: Cook frozen shelled edamame until crisp-tender as directed on package. Chill in cold water and drain.

Sweet Peppery Pecans: Cook ¼ cup pecan halves and 1 tablespoon brown sugar in skillet over low heat until sugar begins to melt; sprinkle with coarsely ground pepper. Cook and stir until sugar is melted. Remove pecans to plate to cool before using.

Cherry-Walnut Kale Salad

Mandarin Salad with Sugared Almonds

Cherry-Walnut Kale Salad

CALORIE SMART • FAST

Massaging kale means to rub the leaves with a bit of oil, lemon juice and salt. This makes the fibrous green more tender and palatable. Wear plastic gloves to do this if you wish; or instead, toss the leaves with oil, lemon juice and salt and refrigerate overnight. If you like, substitute baby kale for part of the kale and add with the vinaigrette.

PREP 20 min **TOTAL** 20 min • 4 servings

- 1 bunch (8 oz) fresh kale, ribs removed, leaves thinly sliced (6 cups)
- 3 tablespoons lemon juice
- 1 tablespoon olive oil
- ½ teaspoon salt
- 1 tablespoon white balsamic or white wine vinegar
- 1 tablespoon honey
- ½ teaspoon pepper
- 2 tablespoons dried tart cherries
- 2 tablespoons chopped walnuts, toasted (page 23), if desired
- 2 tablespoons crumbled blue cheese

1 In large bowl, mix kale, lemon juice, 1 teaspoon of the oil and the salt. Massage kale with your hands 3 to 5 minutes or until it starts to wilt; set aside.

2 In small bowl, beat vinegar, honey and pepper with whisk. Slowly pour in remaining 2 teaspoons oil while continuing to beat. Pour vinaigrette over kale mixture; toss to coat.

3 Top individual servings with cherries, walnuts and cheese.

1 Serving: Calories 120; Total Fat 5g (Saturated Fat 1.5g, Trans Fat 0g); Cholesterol 0mg; Sodium 380mg; Total Carbohydrate 16g (Dietary Fiber 1g, Sugars 9g); Protein 3g **Exchanges:** ½ Starch, 1 Vegetable, 1 Fat **Carbohydrate Choices:** 1

Mandarin Salad with Sugared Almonds **CALORIE SMART • FAST**

PREP 30 min **TOTAL** 30 min • 6 servings

SUGARED ALMONDS

- ¼ cup sliced almonds
- 4 teaspoons sugar

SWEET-SOUR DRESSING

- ¼ cup vegetable oil
- 2 tablespoons sugar
- 2 tablespoons white or cider vinegar
- 1 tablespoon chopped fresh parsley
- ½ teaspoon salt
  Dash pepper
  Dash red pepper sauce

SALAD

- 3 cups bite-size pieces mixed salad greens or iceberg lettuce
- 3 cups bite-size pieces romaine lettuce
- 2 medium stalks celery, chopped (1 cup)
- 2 medium green onions, thinly sliced (2 tablespoons)
- 1 can (11 oz) mandarin orange segments, drained

Making Sugared Almonds

Cook almonds and sugar over low heat about 10 minutes, stirring constantly.

Cook until sugar is melted and almonds are coated; cool and break apart.

1 In 1-quart saucepan, cook almonds and 4 teaspoons sugar over low heat about 10 minutes, stirring constantly, until sugar is melted and almonds are coated. Cool; break apart.

2 Meanwhile, in tightly covered container, shake dressing ingredients. Refrigerate until serving time.

3 In large bowl, mix salad ingredients. Shake dressing; pour over salad and toss until coated. Sprinkle with sugared almonds. Serve immediately.

1 Serving (1⅓ Cups): Calories 170; Total Fat 12g (Saturated Fat 1.5g, Trans Fat 0g); Cholesterol 0mg; Sodium 220mg; Total Carbohydrate 15g (Dietary Fiber 2g, Sugars 12g); Protein 2g **Exchanges:** ½ Fruit, 2 Vegetable, 2 Fat **Carbohydrate Choices:** 1

Crunchy Chicken-Mandarin Salad Top each serving with a grilled boneless skinless chicken breast, sliced (warm or cold) and sprinkle with 2 tablespoons chow mein noodles.

Roasted Beet Salad

PREP 15 min **TOTAL** 1 hr 25 min • 4 servings

- 1½ lb small beets (1½ to 2 inches in diameter)
- 1 tablespoon olive or vegetable oil
- 4 cups bite-size pieces mixed salad greens
- 1 medium orange, peeled, sliced
- ½ cup walnut halves, toasted (page 23), coarsely chopped
- ¼ cup crumbled chèvre (goat) cheese (1 oz)
- ½ cup Fresh Herb Vinaigrette (page 136)

1 Heat oven to 425°F. Remove greens from beets, leaving about ½ inch of stem. Wash beets well; leave whole with root ends attached. Place beets in ungreased 13x9-inch pan; drizzle with oil. Bake uncovered about 40 minutes or until tender.

2 Remove skins from beets under running water. Let beets cool until easy to handle, about 30 minutes. Cut off root ends and cut beets into slices (cut slices in half if large).

3 On 4 salad plates, arrange salad greens. Top with beets, orange slices, toasted walnuts and cheese. Serve with dressing.

1 Serving: Calories 410; Total Fat 33g (Saturated Fat 5g, Trans Fat 0g); Cholesterol 5mg; Sodium 440mg; Total Carbohydrate 19g (Dietary Fiber 6g, Sugars 11g); Protein 7g **Exchanges:** ½ Other Carbohydrate, 3 Vegetable, 6½ Fat **Carbohydrate Choices:** 1

Betty's Staples
Seeds and Nuts

A touch of something crunchy in a salad can be a wonderful surprise. This can come from crisp vegetables or croutons (page 117), but nuts or seeds are a fun way to add both crunch and some protein. Walnuts, pecans, almonds, cashews, pistachios, sunflower seeds and pumpkin seeds (pepitas)—any of these little treasures can be added plain, toasted (see page 23) or for a special treat, candied, which works well with pecan or walnut halves, whole or slivered almonds and whole cashews.

Candied Nuts: In medium bowl, mix 1 cup nuts, 2 tablespoons corn syrup, 1 tablespoon sugar and ¼ teaspoon salt (unless the nuts are salted). If you want a spicy mixture, include ⅛ teaspoon ground red (cayenne) pepper too. Spread the nuts on a shallow baking pan lined with parchment paper and bake at 350°F for 10 to 15 minutes or until nuts are golden brown and sugar mixture is bubbly, stirring once or twice during baking. Cool completely and store tightly covered.

Sunny Sunflower Salad: Toss kale leaves with torn butter lettuce leaves, small cauliflower florets, sliced roasted red bell pepper pieces (page 247), sliced yellow summer squash, toasted sunflower seeds and Honey-Mustard Dressing (page 137).

Asparagus-Almond Salad: Blanch asparagus spears (see page 130). Arrange spears on individual salad plates. Drizzle with Fresh Herb Vinaigrette (page 136) and sprinkle with chopped toasted sliced almonds.

Beets and Baby Greens Salad: In medium bowl, toss mixed baby greens with chopped cooked beets and crumbled goat cheese. Drizzle with vinaigrette and sprinkle with toasted walnuts. Toss lightly to mix.

Mango-Avocado Salad: On individual salad plates, arrange sliced mango with sliced avocado and fresh raspberries. Sprinkle with toasted slivered almonds and drizzle with Raspberry Vinaigrette (page 137).

Chicken Chopped Salad: In medium bowl, mix chopped romaine, chopped cooked chicken, crumbled bacon, chopped fresh tomato, chopped cauliflower and chopped pistachios. Drizzle with Italian Dressing (page 137) and toss to mix.

Beets and Baby Greens Salad

Ratatouille Salad CALORIE SMART

PREP 30 min **TOTAL** 4 hr 40 min • 8 servings

- 1 cup water
- ¾ teaspoon salt
- 1 small eggplant (1 lb), cut into ½-inch cubes
- ⅓ cup olive or vegetable oil
- 2 tablespoons lemon juice
- 2 teaspoons chopped fresh or ½ teaspoon dried basil leaves
- ½ teaspoon ground mustard
- ⅛ teaspoon pepper
- 2 medium tomatoes, chopped (1½ cups)
- 1 medium zucchini, thinly sliced (2 cups)
- 1 small onion, sliced, separated into rings
- 1 small green bell pepper, chopped (½ cup)
- ⅓ cup chopped fresh parsley

1 In 3-quart saucepan, heat water and ¼ teaspoon of the salt to boiling. Add eggplant. Return to boiling; reduce heat. Simmer uncovered 5 to 8 minutes or until tender; drain.

2 In large glass or plastic bowl, mix the oil, lemon juice, basil, mustard, pepper and remaining ½ teaspoon salt. Add eggplant and remaining ingredients; toss. Cover and refrigerate about 4 hours or until chilled.

1 Serving: Calories 120; Total Fat 9g (Saturated Fat 1.5g, Trans Fat 0g); Cholesterol 0mg; Sodium 230mg; Total Carbohydrate 7g (Dietary Fiber 2g, Sugars 4g); Protein 1g **Exchanges:** 1½ Vegetable, 2 Fat **Carbohydrate Choices:** ½

Panzanella CALORIE SMART

Panzanella, or bread salad, is an Italian classic.

PREP 20 min **TOTAL** 1 hr 20 min • 6 servings

- 4 cups cubed (1 inch) day-old Italian or other firm-textured bread
- 2 medium tomatoes, cut into bite-size pieces (2 cups)
- 2 cloves garlic, finely chopped
- 1 medium green bell pepper, chopped (1 cup)
- ⅓ cup chopped fresh basil leaves
- 2 tablespoons chopped fresh parsley
- ⅓ cup olive oil
- 2 tablespoons red wine vinegar
- ½ teaspoon salt
- ⅛ teaspoon pepper

1 In large glass or plastic bowl, mix bread, tomatoes, garlic, bell pepper, basil and parsley.

Panzanella

2 In tightly covered container, shake remaining ingredients. Pour over bread mixture; toss gently until bread is evenly coated.

3 Cover and refrigerate at least 1 hour, but no longer than 8 hours, until bread is softened and flavors are blended. Toss before serving.

1 Serving: Calories 190; Total Fat 13g (Saturated Fat 2g, Trans Fat 0g); Cholesterol 0mg; Sodium 340mg; Total Carbohydrate 15g (Dietary Fiber 2g, Sugars 1g); Protein 3g **Exchanges:** 1 Starch, 2 Fat **Carbohydrate Choices:** 1

Heirloom Tomato Caprese Salad CALORIE SMART • FAST • EASY

Choose heirloom tomatoes in a variety of colors for a stunning presentation. If you want to splurge with ingredients, buy balsamic vinegar aged over 20 years. It has a syrupy consistency and a heavenly sweet and tangy flavor.

PREP 10 min **TOTAL** 10 min • 8 servings

- 2 containers (8 oz each) bocconcini (small fresh mozzarella cheese balls), drained
- 4 medium to large heirloom or other tomatoes, cut into wedges or slices
- 2 tablespoons balsamic vinegar
- 1 tablespoon olive oil
  Coarse sea salt, flaked salt or colored salt, if desired
  Freshly ground pepper, if desired
- 6 large fresh basil leaves, thinly sliced*

On serving platter, arrange cheese and tomatoes. Drizzle with vinegar and oil; sprinkle with salt and pepper. Sprinkle with basil. Serve immediately.

*Basil leaves cut into thin strips is called "chiffonade." To cut, stack the leaves on top of each other, then roll up. Slice across the roll to form long shreds.

1 Serving: Calories 170; Total Fat 12g (Saturated Fat 0g, Trans Fat 0g); Cholesterol 40mg; Sodium 170mg; Total Carbohydrate 5g (Dietary Fiber 0g, Sugars 2g); Protein 10g **Exchanges:** ½ Vegetable, 1 Lean Meat, 2 Fat **Carbohydrate Choices:** ½

Heirloom Tomato Caprese Salad

Heirloom Recipe and New Twist

Ideal for picnics and gatherings, this Seven-Layer Salad is a classic! The new twist is also layered and shows how versatile this salad style can be.

HEIRLOOM

Seven-Layer Salad

PREP 25 min **TOTAL** 2 hr 25 min • 6 servings

- 6 cups bite-size pieces mixed salad greens
- 2 medium stalks celery, thinly sliced (1 cup)
- 1 cup thinly sliced radishes
- 8 medium green onions, sliced (½ cup)
- 12 slices bacon, crisply cooked, crumbled (¾ cup)
- 1 cup frozen sweet peas, cooked, drained
- 1½ cups mayonnaise or salad dressing (for homemade mayonnaise, see page 460)
- ½ cup grated Parmesan or shredded Cheddar cheese (2 oz)

1 In large glass bowl, layer salad greens, celery, radishes, onions, bacon and peas. Spread mayonnaise over peas, covering top completely all the way to edge of bowl. Sprinkle with cheese.

2 Cover and refrigerate at least 2 hours, but no longer than 12 hours, to blend flavors. Toss before serving, if desired.

1 Serving (1¼ Cups): Calories 580; Total Fat 54g (Saturated Fat 11g, Trans Fat 0g); Cholesterol 55mg; Sodium 790mg; Total Carbohydrate 11g (Dietary Fiber 3g, Sugars 5g); Protein 12g **Exchanges:** ½ Starch, 1 Vegetable, 1 High-Fat Meat, 9 Fat **Carbohydrate Choices:** 1

LIGHTER Directions For 12 grams of fat and 200 calories per serving, substitute ½ cup reduced-fat mayonnaise and 1 cup plain fat-free yogurt for the 1½ cups mayonnaise. Reduce bacon to 6 slices and cheese to ¼ cup.

NEW TWIST

Fennel-Asparagus Seven-Layer Salad

PREP 25 min **TOTAL** 2 hr 25 min • 6 servings

- 6 cups mesclun (field or wild) greens
- 1 cup thinly sliced fennel bulb
- ½ cup thinly sliced radishes
- ½ cup shredded carrot
- ½ cup thinly sliced sweet onion
- 6 slices bacon, crisply cooked, crumbled
- 1 cup (½-inch pieces) fresh asparagus
- 1½ cups reduced-fat mayonnaise or salad dressing
- ½ cup grated Parmesan cheese
- ¼ cup shredded aged Gouda or Swiss cheese (2 oz)

1 In large glass bowl, layer mesclun, fennel, radishes, carrot, onion, bacon and asparagus.

2 In medium bowl, mix mayonnaise and Parmesan cheese. Spread mayonnaise mixture over asparagus, covering top completely and sealing to edge of bowl. Sprinkle with Gouda cheese.

3 Cover and refrigerate at least 2 hours, but no longer than 12 hours, to blend flavors. Toss before serving, if desired.

1 Serving (About 1¼ Cups): Calories 330; Total Fat 27g (Saturated Fat 7g, Trans Fat 0g); Cholesterol 40mg; Sodium 810mg; Total Carbohydrate 11g (Dietary Fiber 2g, Sugars 5g); Protein 9g **Exchanges:** 1½ Vegetable, 1 Very Lean Meat, 5½ Fat **Carbohydrate Choices:** 1

Seven-Layer Salad

Fennel-Asparagus Seven-Layer Salad

Cobb Salad

Santa Fe Salad with Tortilla Straws

Cobb Salad

The original Hollywood Brown Derby restaurant, where owner Robert H. Cobb created the Cobb salad, is gone, but this hearty dish remains popular.

PREP 25 min **TOTAL** 1 hr 25 min • 4 servings

LEMON VINAIGRETTE DRESSING

½ cup vegetable oil

¼ cup fresh lemon juice

1 tablespoon red wine vinegar

1 clove garlic, finely chopped

2 teaspoons sugar

½ teaspoon salt

½ teaspoon ground mustard

½ teaspoon Worcestershire sauce

¼ teaspoon pepper

SALAD

1 medium head iceberg lettuce (about 1 lb), shredded (6 cups)

2 cups cut-up cooked chicken

3 Hard-Cooked Eggs (page 91), chopped

2 medium tomatoes, chopped (1½ cups)

1 medium avocado, pitted, peeled and chopped

¼ cup crumbled blue cheese (1 oz)

4 slices bacon, crisply cooked, crumbled (¼ cup)

1 In tightly covered container, shake all dressing ingredients. Refrigerate at least 1 hour to blend flavors.

2 Divide lettuce among 4 salad plates or shallow bowls. Arrange remaining salad ingredients in rows on lettuce. Serve with dressing.

1 Serving: Calories 610; Total Fat 49g (Saturated Fat 10g, Trans Fat 0g); Cholesterol 230mg; Sodium 650mg; Total Carbohydrate 12g (Dietary Fiber 4g, Sugars 6g); Protein 30g **Exchanges:** 2 Vegetable, 4 High-Fat Meat, 3 Fat **Carbohydrate Choices:** 1

Santa Fe Salad with Tortilla Straws

PREP 25 min **TOTAL** 40 min • 6 servings

TORTILLA STRAWS

1 flour tortilla (7- or 8-inch)

Cooking spray

¼ teaspoon coarse (kosher or sea) salt

¼ teaspoon chili powder

CREAMY AVOCADO DRESSING

½ cup ranch dressing

1 medium ripe avocado, pitted, peeled and cut into chunks

SALAD

2 cups bite-size pieces iceberg lettuce

2 cups bite-size pieces romaine lettuce

1 large tomato, chopped (1 cup)

1 cup diced peeled jicama

¾ cup shredded Cheddar cheese (3 oz)

¼ cup sliced pitted ripe olives

1 Heat oven to 350°F. Spray one side of tortilla with cooking spray; sprinkle with salt and chili powder. Cut tortilla in half, then cut each half crosswise into ¼-inch strips. Place on ungreased cookie sheet. Bake 10 to 12 minutes or until crisp and golden brown.

2 In blender, place ranch dressing and avocado. Cover and blend on medium speed until smooth and creamy. Transfer to small bowl.

3 Place lettuces on shallow serving platter or in large bowl. Top with tomato, jicama, cheese, olives and tortilla straws. Serve with dressing.

1 Serving (1 Cup): Calories 240; Total Fat 20g (Saturated Fat 5g, Trans Fat 0g); Cholesterol 20mg; Sodium 450mg; Total Carbohydrate 11g (Dietary Fiber 3g, Sugars 1g); Protein 5g **Exchanges:** ½ Starch, 1 Vegetable, 4 Fat **Carbohydrate Choices:** 1

MAKE-AHEAD Directions Make Tortilla Straws up to 2 days ahead of time. Cool completely, then store in a resealable food-storage plastic bag. Dressing can be made up to 2 hours ahead of time; cover and refrigerate.

Asparagus-Strawberry Salad

Cranberry-Orange Mold

Asparagus-Strawberry Salad CALORIE SMART · FAST

PREP 15 min **TOTAL** 15 min • 4 servings

- 1 lb fresh asparagus spears, trimmed, cut into 1-inch pieces (2 cups)
- ¼ cup fresh lemon juice
- 2 tablespoons vegetable oil
- 2 tablespoons honey
- 2 cups sliced fresh strawberries

1 In 2-quart saucepan, heat 1 inch water to boiling. Add asparagus. Return to boiling; boil uncovered 2 to 4 minutes or until crisp-tender. Remove asparagus from boiling water; immediately plunge into ice water until cold to stop cooking. Drain.

2 In tightly covered container, shake lemon juice, oil and honey.

3 On salad plates or in bowls, arrange asparagus and strawberries; drizzle with dressing.

1 Serving: Calories 150; Total Fat 7g (Saturated Fat 1g, Trans Fat 0g); Cholesterol 0mg; Sodium 0mg; Total Carbohydrate 19g (Dietary Fiber 3g, Sugars 14g); Protein 2g **Exchanges:** 1 Other Carbohydrate, 1 Vegetable, 1½ Fat **Carbohydrate Choices:** 1

Asparagus-Orange Salad Substitute orange juice for the lemon juice and 2 cups sliced peeled fresh oranges for the strawberries.

Asparagus-Cashew Salad Substitute ¼ cup sliced green onions and 1½ cups small cauliflower florets for the strawberries. Arrange vegetables on salad plates; drizzle with dressing. Sprinkle with ½ cup cashew pieces.

Cranberry-Orange Mold CALORIE SMART · EASY

PREP 10 min **TOTAL** 4 hr 10 min • 8 servings

- 1 can (11 oz) mandarin orange segments, drained, juice reserved
- 1 box (4-serving size) orange-flavored gelatin
- 1 can (14 oz) whole berry cranberry sauce
  Salad greens, if desired

1 Spray 4-cup mold with cooking spray. Add enough water to reserved mandarin orange juice to measure 1¼ cups. In 1-quart saucepan, heat juice mixture to boiling.

2 In medium bowl, pour boiling mixture on gelatin; stir until gelatin is dissolved. Stir in cranberry sauce until sauce is melted. Stir in orange segments. Pour into mold.

3 Refrigerate about 4 hours or until firm. Unmold; serve on salad greens.

1 Serving: Calories 150; Total Fat 0g (Saturated Fat 0g, Trans Fat 0g); Cholesterol 0mg; Sodium 65mg; Total Carbohydrate 35g (Dietary Fiber 1g, Sugars 33g); Protein 1g **Exchanges:** 2½ Fruit **Carbohydrate Choices:** 2

Unmolding Gelatin Salads

Dip mold into warm (not hot) water for several seconds. Dip tip of knife in warm water; carefully run knife around top edge of mold to loosen.

Place chilled serving plate on top of mold. Holding both mold and plate firmly, turn upside down onto plate and gently shake to release gelatin. Carefully lift mold from gelatin.

Cinnamon-Maple Glazed Salmon Salad

Roasted Potato Salad

Cinnamon-Maple Glazed Salmon Salad

PREP 20 min **TOTAL** 35 min • 4 servings

DRESSING
⅓ cup real maple or maple-flavored syrup
⅓ cup vegetable oil
2 tablespoons plus 1 teaspoon balsamic vinegar
½ teaspoon ground cinnamon

SALAD
1 salmon fillet (1¼ lb), cut into 4 serving pieces
6 cups mixed spring greens
⅔ cup crumbled feta cheese
⅓ cup dried cherries
⅓ cup coarsely chopped pecans, toasted (page 23)

1 Heat oven to 400°F. Line 15x10x1-inch pan with foil. In small bowl, beat dressing ingredients with whisk until blended. Place 3 tablespoons dressing in small bowl; reserve for brushing on salmon. Set remaining dressing aside for salad. Place salmon pieces, skin side down, in pan.

2 Bake 10 to 14 minutes, brushing with reserved 3 tablespoons dressing twice during last 5 minutes of baking, until salmon flakes easily with fork. Discard any remaining dressing used for salmon.

3 In large bowl, toss greens with reserved dressing for salad. Divide greens among 4 individual plates; sprinkle evenly with cheese, cherries and toasted pecans. With metal spatula, lift pieces of salmon from skin; place 1 salmon piece on each salad. Discard skin and foil.

1 Serving: Calories 630; Total Fat 39g (Saturated Fat 7g, Trans Fat 0g); Cholesterol 100mg; Sodium 400mg; Total Carbohydrate 35g (Dietary Fiber 3g, Sugars 29g); Protein 34g **Exchanges:** 2 Starch, 1 Vegetable, 3½ Lean Meat, 5½ Fat **Carbohydrate Choices:** 2

Roasted Potato Salad

PREP 15 min **TOTAL** 50 min • 6 servings

POTATOES
6 medium unpeeled Yukon Gold potatoes, each cut into 8 wedges*
2 tablespoons olive oil
½ teaspoon salt
Fresh rosemary leaves for garnish, if desired

HERB VINAIGRETTE DRESSING
¼ cup olive oil
1 tablespoon white balsamic or cider vinegar
2 teaspoons Dijon mustard
2 tablespoons finely chopped shallots
1 tablespoon chopped fresh chives
1 teaspoon fresh thyme leaves
1 teaspoon chopped fresh rosemary leaves
½ teaspoon sugar
¼ teaspoon salt
1 clove garlic, finely chopped

1 Heat oven to 400°F. Place potatoes in center of 15x10x1-inch pan. Drizzle with 2 tablespoons oil; sprinkle with ½ teaspoon salt. Toss to coat. Spread in single layer in pan.

2 Roast uncovered 30 to 35 minutes or until potatoes are light brown and tender, turning occasionally.

3 In small bowl, mix dressing ingredients with whisk. Transfer potatoes to serving bowl; drizzle with dressing. Toss gently to coat. Garnish with rosemary leaves. Serve immediately or let stand 30 minutes at room temperature.

*Red potatoes can be substituted for the Yukon Gold potatoes.

1 Serving: Calories 300; Total Fat 14g (Saturated Fat 2g, Trans Fat 0g); Cholesterol 0mg; Sodium 350mg; Total Carbohydrate 38g (Dietary Fiber 4g, Sugars 3g); Protein 4g **Exchanges:** 2 Starch, ½ Other Carbohydrate, 2½ Fat **Carbohydrate Choices:** 2½

Creamy Potato Salad

This classic potato salad is always a favorite for picnics and potlucks. Make it your own by adding a variety of flavors, such as bacon, capers, herbs or fresh vegetables.

PREP 20 min **TOTAL** 5 hr • 10 servings

6	medium unpeeled round red or Yukon Gold potatoes (2 lb)
1½	cups mayonnaise or salad dressing (for homemade Mayonnaise, see page 460)
1	tablespoon white or cider vinegar
1	tablespoon yellow mustard
1	teaspoon salt
¼	teaspoon pepper
2	medium stalks celery, chopped (1 cup)
1	medium onion, chopped (½ cup)
4	Hard-Cooked Eggs (page 91), chopped
	Paprika, if desired

1 In 3-quart saucepan, place potatoes and just enough water to cover potatoes. Cover and heat to boiling; reduce heat to low.

2 Cook 30 to 35 minutes or until tender; drain. Let stand until cool enough to handle. Peel potatoes; cut into cubes.

3 In large glass or plastic bowl, mix mayonnaise, vinegar, mustard, salt and pepper. Add potatoes, celery and onion; toss. Stir in eggs. Sprinkle with paprika. Cover and refrigerate at least 4 hours to chill and blend flavors.

1 Serving (¾ Cup): Calories 350; Total Fat 28g (Saturated Fat 4.5g, Trans Fat 0g); Cholesterol 105mg; Sodium 480mg; Total Carbohydrate 19g (Dietary Fiber 2g, Sugars 2g); Protein 5g **Exchanges:** 1½ Starch, 5½ Fat **Carbohydrate Choices:** 1

LIGHTER Directions For 13 grams of fat and 210 calories per serving, use reduced-fat mayonnaise and 2 eggs.

Hot German Potato Salad CALORIE SMART

The tangy sweet-sour dressing, which soaks into the velvety cooked potatoes, and the smoky bacon are what give this salad its characteristic flavor.

PREP 30 min **TOTAL** 1 hr 5 min • 6 servings

4	medium unpeeled red or white potatoes (1½ lb)
3	slices bacon, cut into 1-inch pieces
1	medium onion, chopped (½ cup)
1	tablespoon all-purpose flour
1	tablespoon sugar
½	teaspoon salt
¼	teaspoon celery seed
	Dash pepper
½	cup water
¼	cup white or cider vinegar

1 In 3-quart saucepan, place potatoes and just enough water to cover potatoes. Cover and heat to boiling; reduce heat to low. Cook 30 to 35 minutes or until tender; drain. Let stand until cool enough to handle. Cut potatoes into ¼-inch slices.

2 In 10-inch skillet, cook bacon over medium heat 8 to 10 minutes, stirring occasionally, until crisp. Remove bacon with slotted spoon; drain on paper towels.

3 Cook onion in bacon drippings over medium heat, stirring occasionally, until tender. Stir in flour, sugar, salt, celery seed and pepper. Reduce heat to low. Cook and stir until mixture is bubbly; remove from heat.

4 Stir in water and vinegar. Heat to boiling, stirring constantly. Boil and stir 1 minute; remove from heat. Stir in potatoes and bacon. Heat over medium heat, stirring gently to coat potato slices, until hot and bubbly. Serve warm.

1 Serving (⅔ Cup): Calories 120; Total Fat 2g (Saturated Fat 0.5g, Trans Fat 0g); Cholesterol 0mg; Sodium 270mg; Total Carbohydrate 22g (Dietary Fiber 3g, Sugars 5g); Protein 3g **Exchanges:** 1 Starch, 1 Vegetable, ½ Fat **Carbohydrate Choices:** 1½

SLOW-COOKER Directions Cut uncooked potatoes into ¼-inch slices. Cook and drain bacon; refrigerate. Increase flour to 2 tablespoons. Decrease water to ⅓ cup. Spray 3½- to 6-quart slow cooker with cooking spray. In slow cooker, mix all ingredients except bacon. Cover; cook on Low heat setting 8 to 10 hours or until potatoes are tender. Stir in bacon.

Creamy Potato Salad

Hot German Potato Salad

Sweet-and-Sour Coleslaw

Creamy Coleslaw CALORIE SMART

This is a delicious coleslaw to make for any occasion. For variety, you could add ¼ to ½ cup chopped red bell pepper. To serve, garnish with a lemon twist and a little fresh parsley.

PREP 15 min **TOTAL** 1 hr 15 min • 8 servings

- ½ cup mayonnaise or salad dressing (for homemade Mayonnaise, see page 460)
- ¼ cup sour cream
- 1 tablespoon sugar
- 2 teaspoons fresh lemon juice
- 2 teaspoons Dijon mustard
- ½ teaspoon celery seed, if desired
- ¼ teaspoon salt
- ¼ teaspoon pepper
- ½ medium head green cabbage, thinly sliced or chopped (4 cups)
- 1 medium carrot, shredded (½ cup)
- 1 small onion, finely chopped (⅓ cup)

1 In large glass or plastic bowl, mix all ingredients except cabbage, carrot and onion. Add cabbage, carrot and onion; toss until evenly coated.

2 Cover and refrigerate at least 1 hour to blend flavors. Stir before serving.

1 Serving (⅔ Cup): Calories 140; Total Fat 13g (Saturated Fat 2.5g, Trans Fat 0g); Cholesterol 15mg; Sodium 200mg; Total Carbohydrate 6g (Dietary Fiber 1g, Sugars 4g); Protein 1g **Exchanges:** ½ Other Carbohydrate, ½ Vegetable, 2½ Fat **Carbohydrate Choices:** ½

LIGHTER Directions For 6 grams of fat and 85 calories per serving, use reduced-fat mayonnaise and sour cream.

Tropical Creamy Coleslaw Add 1 can (8 ounces) pineapple tidbits or chunks, drained, with the cabbage, carrot and onion. Just before serving, sprinkle with ½ cup chopped macadamia nuts.

Sweet-and-Sour Coleslaw CALORIE SMART

PREP 15 min **TOTAL** 3 hr 15 min • 8 servings

- ½ medium head green cabbage, thinly sliced or chopped (4 cups)
- 1 large carrot, finely shredded (1 cup)
- 1 medium green bell pepper, chopped (1 cup)
- 4 medium green onions, thinly sliced (¼ cup)
- ½ cup sugar
- ½ cup white wine vinegar, white vinegar or cider vinegar
- ¼ cup vegetable oil
- 1 teaspoon ground mustard
- ½ teaspoon celery seed
- ½ teaspoon salt

1 In large glass or plastic bowl, toss cabbage, carrot, bell pepper and onions.

2 In tightly covered container, shake remaining ingredients. Pour over vegetables; toss until evenly coated.

3 Cover and refrigerate at least 3 hours, stirring several times, to blend flavors and chill. Stir before serving; serve with slotted spoon.

1 Serving: Calories 140; Total Fat 7g (Saturated Fat 1g, Trans Fat 0g); Cholesterol 0mg; Sodium 170mg; Total Carbohydrate 17g (Dietary Fiber 1g, Sugars 15g); Protein 1g **Exchanges:** 1 Other Carbohydrate, 1 Vegetable, 1½ Fat **Carbohydrate Choices:** 1

QUICKER Sweet-and-Sour Coleslaw Substitute 6½ cups coleslaw mix (from 1-pound bag) for the cabbage and carrot; omit bell pepper.

Thinly Slicing Cabbage

To thinly slice cabbage, place a flat side of ¼ head of cabbage on cutting board. Cut into thin slices with a large sharp knife. Cut slices several times to make smaller pieces.

Learn to BLANCH

The simple definition of blanching is to place food in boiling water for a brief time to slightly cook it. Blanch foods (typically vegetables and fruits) when you want to preserve their color, crisp texture and nutritional value or as a way to remove skin. Once you realize how simple it is to blanch, it will be easy to see the many ways you can use this technique.

Blanching is most often done in boiling water on the stove top. Although steaming can also be used to blanch a few vegetables, this method does take longer and is not as effective. Microwave blanching is not recommended.

Prepare the vegetables or fruits just before blanching to prevent discoloration. If you are blanching to remove skins (peaches, nectarines, tomatoes), leave whole and wash just before blanching to remove any visible dirt. Some vegetables can be blanched whole (string or wax beans) and some should be cut (carrots). Cut vegetables into uniform sizes.

1. Fill a large pot with water and bring it to a boil. A vegetable blancher will have a basket for holding the vegetables and immersing in the water. Use 1 gallon of water per pound of vegetables (about 2 cups). Salt can be added (1 teaspoon) to help maintain color and flavor but is not necessary.

2. Place the vegetables or fruit in a wire basket or the blancher basket and immerse into the boiling water. (If you don't have a basket, plunge the food into the boiling water and remove with a slotted spoon or small colander.) Bring the water back to a boil. Boil uncovered 2 to 4 minutes for most vegetables or until color brightens. (Exact time will depend on vegetables and size. Watch carefully, as over-blanching can cause loss of flavor and color.) Skin on tomatoes and peaches may start to wrinkle slightly or crack.

3. Remove items from the boiling water and immediately plunge into ice water to cool quickly and stop the cooking process.

4. Drain well when cooled. Use in recipes or refrigerate or freeze as desired. For tomatoes and peaches, use fingers and a small knife to pull skins from fruit.

Asian Salad with Wonton Crisps FAST

This very pretty and fresh-tasting arranged salad would pair great with any grilled meat, chicken, fish or seafood.

PREP 30 min **TOTAL** 30 min • 4 servings

WONTON CRISPS

4 wonton skins (about 3¼-inch square), cut into ¼-inch strips

PEANUTTY SOY DRESSING

¼ cup vegetable oil

2 tablespoons lemon juice

4 teaspoons sugar

4 teaspoons soy sauce

2 teaspoons Dijon mustard

¼ cup chopped dry-roasted peanuts

SALAD

1 cup small fresh broccoli florets

1 cup fresh snow pea pods (4 oz), strings removed

4 cups bite-size pieces mixed salad greens

½ cup shredded red cabbage

½ cup shredded radishes, patted dry

1 Heat oven to 350°F. On ungreased cookie sheet, arrange wonton strips in single layer. Bake 5 to 6 minutes or until lightly browned.

2 Meanwhile, in tightly covered container, shake all dressing ingredients; set aside.

3 In 2-quart saucepan, heat 2 cups water to boiling. Add broccoli and pea pods; boil uncovered 1 to 2 minutes or just until bright green. Remove vegetables from boiling water; immediately place in ice water until cold. Drain well.

4 Divide salad greens among 4 plates. Top evenly with broccoli, pea pods, cabbage and radishes. Drizzle with dressing; top with wonton strips.

1 **Serving:** Calories 270; Total Fat 19g (Saturated Fat 3g, Trans Fat 0g); Cholesterol 0mg; Sodium 500mg; Total Carbohydrate 18g (Dietary Fiber 4g, Sugars 7g); Protein 6g **Exchanges:** ½ Other Carbohydrate, 1½ Vegetable, ½ High-Fat Meat, 3 Fat **Carbohydrate Choices:** 1

Green and Yellow Bean Salad

CALORIE SMART

Three-bean salad gets a vibrant take in this makeover of the classic—with two colors of fresh beans, cannellini beans, grape tomatoes and fresh basil. Garnish with shaved Parmesan cheese, if desired.

PREP 20 min **TOTAL** 1 hr 20 min • 10 servings

SALAD

- 8 oz fresh green beans, trimmed
- 8 oz fresh yellow wax beans, trimmed
- 1 cup grape tomatoes, cut in half
- 1 can (15 oz) cannellini beans, drained, rinsed
- ¼ cup lightly packed fresh basil leaves, torn

SHERRY VINAIGRETTE DRESSING

- ¼ cup olive oil
- 2 tablespoons sherry vinegar
- ½ teaspoon salt
- ¼ teaspoon coarse ground black pepper

1 In 2-quart saucepan, place green and wax beans in 1 inch water. Heat to boiling; reduce heat. Simmer uncovered 8 to 10 minutes or until beans are crisp-tender. Rinse with cold water; drain.

2 In medium bowl, stir together cooked beans, tomatoes, cannellini beans and basil.

3 In jar with tight-fitting lid, shake dressing ingredients. Pour over salad; toss to coat. Refrigerate at least 1 hour to blend flavors. Stir before serving.

1 Serving: Calories 110; Total Fat 6g (Saturated Fat 1g, Trans Fat 0g); Cholesterol 0mg; Sodium 220mg; Total Carbohydrate 12g (Dietary Fiber 3g, Sugars 2g); Protein 4g **Exchanges:** ½ Other Carbohydrate, ½ Vegetable, ½ Very Lean Meat, 1 Fat **Carbohydrate Choices:** 1

Northern Italian White Bean Salad   CALORIE SMART

PREP 15 min **TOTAL** 2 hr 15 min • 6 servings

- 2 cans (15 or 19 oz each) cannellini beans, drained, rinsed
- 1 large tomato, seeded, coarsely chopped (1 cup)
- 1 small red bell pepper, chopped (½ cup)
- ½ cup chopped red onion
- ¼ cup chopped fresh parsley
- ¼ cup olive or vegetable oil
- 2 tablespoons chopped fresh or 2 teaspoons dried basil leaves
- 2 tablespoons red wine vinegar
- ½ teaspoon salt
- ⅛ teaspoon pepper
- 12 leaves Bibb lettuce

1 In large glass or plastic bowl, gently mix all ingredients except lettuce.

2 Cover and refrigerate at least 2 hours to blend flavors. Use slotted spoon to spoon onto lettuce.

1 Serving: Calories 360; Total Fat 10g (Saturated Fat 1.5g, Trans Fat 0g); Cholesterol 0mg; Sodium 210mg; Total Carbohydrate 49g (Dietary Fiber 12g, Sugars 3g); Protein 18g **Exchanges:** 3 Starch, 1 Vegetable, 1 Very Lean Meat **Carbohydrate Choices:** 3

Green and Yellow Bean Salad

Betty's Staples
Canned Tuna or Salmon

It's easy to see why cans and pouches of tuna and salmon are pantry staples in many homes. They are versatile, inexpensive and convenient. Because the pouches do not contain extra water or oil, they may cost a little more. We all know about making tuna salad and sandwiches, but there are other creative ways to use tuna or salmon that you might like to try.

1. Mediterranean Tuna Salad: On individual salad plates, arrange 1 cup mixed salad greens, ½ cup drained canned cannellini beans, ½ cup chopped tomato, torn romaine, ½ cup sliced ripe olives and ½ can (3 ounces) drained tuna or salmon. Drizzle with Italian Dressing (page 137) and sprinkle with chopped fresh parsley.

2. Cheddar Tuna Melts: In small bowl, mix 1 can (6 ounces) drained tuna or salmon, ¼ cup chopped fresh chives and 1 to 2 tablespoons mayonnaise. Spread on 4 slices toasted hearty whole grain bread. Top each sandwich with 1 or 2 slices tomato and 1 or 2 slices sharp Cheddar cheese. Broil 2 to 3 minutes or until cheese is melted.

3. Chopped Summer Salad: In large bowl, toss 4 cups chopped lettuce, 1 can (6 ounces) drained tuna or salmon, 1 cup halved red grapes, 1 cup chopped carrots, 1 cup chopped honey-roasted peanuts and ½ cup Honey-Mustard Dressing (page 137). Sprinkle with 2 tablespoons sliced green onions.

4. Tuna Quesadillas: Toss 1 can (6 ounces) tuna or salmon with 2 tablespoons ranch dressing. Spread evenly on 2 (8-inch) flour tortillas. Sprinkle each with ½ cup shredded Monterey Jack cheese and ¼ cup corn salsa. Top each with another tortilla. Cook each in 1 tablespoon oil in skillet for 3 to 5 minutes or until golden brown, turning once.

5. Baked Potatoes with Tuna Topping: Bake potatoes and cut in half lengthwise. Mash in shell slightly with fork. Top each with 2 tablespoons chive and sour cream potato topper, ¼ cup drained canned tuna or salmon, ¼ cup cooked small broccoli florets and ½ cup shredded Cheddar cheese. Microwave on High 1 to 3 minutes or until cheese is melted.

6. Tuna-Lettuce Wraps: In medium bowl, mix 1 can (6 ounces) drained tuna or salmon, ¼ cup shredded carrots, ½ cup chopped cashews, 2 tablespoons chopped green or red onion and 2 tablespoons Asian Dressing (page 138). Spoon into Bibb lettuce leaves; roll up each one.

Mediterranean Tuna Salad, Tuna-Lettuce Wraps, Chopped Summer Salad

Chicken-Thyme Penne Salad

You'll need about 2 pounds of uncooked boneless skinless chicken breasts, which equals 4 cups cubed cooked chicken, to make this dish. Cook them however you want, or buy deli rotisserie chicken.

PREP 25 min **TOTAL** 4 hr 25 min • 8 servings

- 3 cups uncooked penne pasta (9 oz)
- 4 cups cubed cooked chicken
- 2 cups seedless red grapes, halved
- 2 medium stalks celery, sliced (1 cup)
- 1 small onion, chopped (⅓ cup)
- 3 tablespoons olive or vegetable oil
- 2 tablespoons chopped fresh or 2 teaspoons dried thyme leaves, crushed
- 1¼ cups mayonnaise or salad dressing (for homemade Mayonnaise, see page 460)
- 1 tablespoon milk
- 1 tablespoon honey
- 1 tablespoon coarse-grained mustard
- 1 teaspoon salt
- 1 cup chopped walnuts, toasted (page 23)

1 Cook and drain pasta as directed on package. Rinse with cold water to cool; drain.

2 In 4-quart bowl, mix pasta, chicken, grapes, celery and onion. In small bowl, mix oil and 1 tablespoon of the fresh thyme (or 1 teaspoon of the dried thyme). Pour over chicken mixture; toss until coated.

3 In small bowl, mix mayonnaise, milk, honey, mustard, salt and remaining thyme. Cover chicken mixture and mayonnaise mixture separately; refrigerate at least 4 hours but no longer than 24 hours.

4 Up to 2 hours before serving, toss chicken mixture and mayonnaise mixture. Cover and refrigerate. Just before serving, stir in ¾ cup of the toasted walnuts. Sprinkle salad with remaining ¼ cup walnuts.

1 Serving: Calories 690; Total Fat 46g (Saturated Fat 7g, Trans Fat 0g); Cholesterol 80mg; Sodium 600mg; Total Carbohydrate 41g (Dietary Fiber 4g, Sugars 10g); Protein 29g **Exchanges:** 2 Starch, 1 Fruit, 3 Medium-Fat Meat, 5½ Fat **Carbohydrate Choices:** 3

Turkey-Basil Penne Salad Substitute cooked turkey for the chicken and fresh basil for the thyme.

Sesame Noodle Salad

Sesame Noodle Salad

CALORIE SMART • FAST

Light-colored sesame oil has a delicate, nutty flavor, while dark sesame oil has a stronger, robust flavor.

PREP 15 min **TOTAL** 25 min • 12 servings

SESAME DRESSING

- 3 tablespoons vegetable oil
- 3 tablespoons soy sauce
- 1 tablespoon balsamic or rice vinegar
- 1 tablespoon dark sesame oil
- 4½ teaspoons sugar
- 1½ teaspoons grated gingerroot
- ½ teaspoon garlic powder
- ⅛ teaspoon ground red pepper (cayenne)

SALAD

- 8 oz uncooked soba (buckwheat) noodles or angel hair pasta
- 2 medium carrots, shredded (1 cup)
- 1 small cucumber, cut lengthwise in half, then cut crosswise into thin slices
- 2 medium green onions, thinly sliced (2 tablespoons)
- 1 tablespoon sesame seed, toasted (page 23)

1 In small bowl, stir all dressing ingredients until well mixed; set aside.

2 In 4-quart Dutch oven or saucepan, heat 2 quarts water to boiling. Cook noodles in boiling water 6 to 8 minutes or until tender (if using angel hair pasta, cook as directed on package); drain. Rinse with cold water to cool; drain.

3 In large bowl, toss noodles, remaining salad ingredients and dressing. Serve or cover and refrigerate.

1 Serving: Calories 120; Total Fat 5g (Saturated Fat 1g, Trans Fat 0g); Cholesterol 0mg; Sodium 230mg; Total Carbohydrate 16g (Dietary Fiber 2g, Sugars 2g); Protein 3g **Exchanges:** 1 Starch, 1 Fat **Carbohydrate Choices:** 1

DRESSING BASICS

Dressings can vary in ingredients, but usually some type of oil plus vinegar or another acidic ingredient make up the base. Oils, depending on the type used, provide body and may add flavor to the dressing or simply carry the flavor of the other ingredients. Traditionally, vinaigrettes are 3 parts oil to 1 part vinegar.

ABOUT OIL

Oils range in flavor from earthy and nutty to neutral or fruity and mildly sweet. Recipes often call for a specific oil designed to complement the ingredients, but feel free to experiment with a different oil or combination of oils.

ABOUT VINEGAR

There are many kinds of vinegar on the market, and they all add lively zest to salad dressings. Most recipes call for one type of vinegar, but you can try a little mixing and matching.

TYPE OF OIL	DESCRIPTION
Vegetable Oils (often generically labeled as vegetable oil; check label for oil source)	
Canola, Corn, Soybean, Sunflower	Delicate/neutral
Peanut	Mildly buttery
Safflower	Mildly nutty
Olive Oils	
Olive Oil and Light Olive Oil	Delicate/neutral; golden color and mild flavor
Extra-Virgin Olive Oil	Fruity olive flavor that is stronger than regular olive oil; golden to green or bright green color
Nut Oils (highly flavorful; start with a small amount, adding more as needed)	
Almond	Nutty, mildly sweet
Avocado	Nutty, sharp
Hazelnut	Nutty, rich
Walnut	Mildly nutty
Sesame Oil (highly flavorful; start with a small amount, adding more as needed)	
Light Sesame Oil	Nutty, light color
Dark Sesame Oil (also called Asian)	Strong toasted sesame seed flavor; amber color

TYPE OF VINEGAR	DESCRIPTION
Balsamic (white grapes)	Rich, sweet, dark brown or white
Cider (fermented apple cider)	Mild apple flavor, golden brown
Fruit (blueberries, raspberries or strawberries steeped in cider vinegar or white wine vinegar)	Flavor and color of berry used; mildly sweet
Herb (basil, chives, dill weed or tarragon steeped in white wine vinegar or cider vinegar)	Flavor of herb used
Rice (fermented rice)	Plain and sweetened forms; delicate, sweet flavor
White (distilled grain alcohol)	Strong, pungent and clear
Wine (champagne, sherry, red or white wine)	Flavor of wine used

Use a wire whisk to mix salad dressings.

Make-Ahead FRESH HERB VINAIGRETTE

CALORIE SMART • FAST

It's always nice to have vinaigrette on hand: It's super simple to make and not just for salads. Choose whatever herb or herbs you like best or have on hand. Vinaigrette stores well in the refrigerator, too, so make a double batch.

PREP 10 min **TOTAL** 10 min • About ¾ cup dressing

- ½ cup olive or vegetable oil
- 3 tablespoons red or white wine vinegar or your favorite vinegar
- 1 tablespoon chopped fresh herb leaves (basil, marjoram, oregano, rosemary, tarragon or thyme)
- 1 tablespoon chopped fresh parsley
- 1 tablespoon finely chopped shallot or green onion
- ¾ teaspoon salt
- ¼ teaspoon pepper

In tightly covered container, shake all ingredients. Shake before serving. Store tightly covered in refrigerator up to 1 week.

1 Tablespoon: Calories 80; Total Fat 9g (Saturated Fat 1g, Trans Fat 0g); Cholesterol 0mg; Sodium 150mg; Total Carbohydrate 0g (Dietary Fiber 0g, Sugars 0g); Protein 0g **Exchanges:** 2 Fat **Carbohydrate Choices:** 0

Blue Cheese Herb Vinaigrette Stir in ⅓ cup crumbled blue cheese.

Creamy Fresh Herb Vinaigrette In small bowl, add all vinaigrette ingredients and ⅓ cup mayonnaise. Beat with whisk until well blended. Stir before serving.

Ways to Use Vinaigrette

1. Dilled Potato Salad: Boil 2 pounds cubed small red potatoes 8 to 10 minutes or until fork-tender. Drain and rinse with cold water to cool. In medium bowl, stir potatoes with ½ cup vinaigrette made with fresh dill until coated.

2. Blue Cheese Chicken Salad: Toss 2 cups mixed baby greens, 1 cup shredded cooked chicken and ½ cup grape tomatoes in medium bowl. Drizzle with ¼ cup vinaigrette; sprinkle with ½ cup crumbled blue cheese.

3. Herbed Marinated Chicken: In shallow bowl, pour vinaigrette over 4 boneless skinless chicken breasts. Let stand in refrigerator 30 to 60 minutes. Grill or broil 11 to 15 minutes or until chicken is no longer pink in center, brushing with marinade occasionally. Discard marinating vinaigrette.

4. Niçoise Salmon Salad: On individual serving plates, arrange torn romaine, sliced hard-cooked egg, sliced tomato and cooked or smoked salmon. Drizzle with vinaigrette and sprinkle with garlic croutons.

5. Italian Beef Sandwiches: For each sandwich, spread Dijon mustard on crusty slice of bread. Layer with sliced cooked roast beef, provolone cheese, sliced roasted red bell pepper and shredded lettuce. Drizzle with 1 to 2 tablespoons vinaigrette and top with bread.

Fresh Herb Vinaigrette, Niçoise Salmon Salad

Raspberry Vinaigrette

CALORIE SMART • FAST • EASY

PREP 5 min TOTAL 5 min • 1 cup dressing

- ½ cup red wine vinegar
- ⅓ cup seedless red raspberry jam
- ¼ cup olive or vegetable oil
- ¼ teaspoon salt

In small glass or plastic bowl, beat all ingredients with whisk until well blended. Store tightly covered in refrigerator up to 1 week. Stir before serving.

1 Tablespoon: Calories 50; Total Fat 3.5g (Saturated Fat 0g, Trans Fat 0g); Cholesterol 0mg; Sodium 40mg; Total Carbohydrate 5g (Dietary Fiber 0g, Sugars 4g); Protein 0g **Exchanges:** ½ Fruit, ½ Fat **Carbohydrate Choices:** ½

Thousand Island Dressing

CALORIE SMART • FAST

PREP 10 min TOTAL 10 min • 1 cup dressing

- 1 cup mayonnaise or salad dressing (for homemade Mayonnaise, see page 460)
- 2 tablespoons chopped pimiento-stuffed green olives or sweet pickle relish
- 2 tablespoons chili sauce or ketchup
- 1 tablespoon chopped fresh parsley
- 1 teaspoon finely chopped onion
- 1 Hard-Cooked Egg (page 91), finely chopped
- ½ teaspoon paprika

In small bowl, mix all ingredients. Store tightly covered in refrigerator up to 5 days. Stir before serving.

1 Tablespoon: Calories 110; Total Fat 11g (Saturated Fat 2g, Trans Fat 0g); Cholesterol 20mg; Sodium 130mg; Total Carbohydrate 0g (Dietary Fiber 0g, Sugars 0g); Protein 0g **Exchanges:** 2 Fat **Carbohydrate Choices:** 0

LIGHTER **Directions** For 5 grams of fat and 55 calories per serving, use reduced-fat mayonnaise; substitute 2 hard-cooked egg whites for the hard-cooked whole egg.

Russian Dressing Omit olives, parsley and egg. Increase chili sauce to ¼ cup. Add 1 teaspoon prepared horseradish.

> ### Thousand Island Dressing
> This mayonnaise-based salad dressing, made with chili sauce and finely chopped stuffed green olives and a hard-cooked egg, also makes a yummy sandwich spread.

Italian Dressing

CALORIE SMART • FAST

PREP 10 min TOTAL 10 min • 1¼ cups dressing

- 1 cup olive or vegetable oil
- ¼ cup white or cider vinegar
- 2 tablespoons finely chopped onion
- 1 tablespoon chopped fresh or 1 teaspoon dried basil leaves
- 1 teaspoon sugar
- 1 teaspoon ground mustard
- ½ teaspoon salt
- ½ teaspoon dried oregano leaves
- ¼ teaspoon pepper
- 2 cloves garlic, finely chopped

In tightly covered container, shake all ingredients. Store tightly covered in refrigerator up to 1 week. Shake before serving.

1 Tablespoon: Calories 100; Total Fat 11g (Saturated Fat 1.5g, Trans Fat 0g); Cholesterol 0mg; Sodium 60mg; Total Carbohydrate 0g (Dietary Fiber 0g, Sugars 0g); Protein 0g **Exchanges:** 2 Fat **Carbohydrate Choices:** 0

LIGHTER **Directions** For 5 grams of fat and 50 calories per serving, substitute ½ cup apple juice for ½ cup of the oil.

Creamy Italian Dressing In small bowl, beat ½ cup Italian Dressing and ½ cup mayonnaise or salad dressing with whisk until smooth.

French Dressing Omit onion, sugar, oregano and garlic. Add ¼ cup fresh lemon juice and ½ teaspoon paprika; reduce mustard to ½ teaspoon.

Honey-Mustard Dressing

CALORIE SMART • FAST • EASY

PREP 5 min TOTAL 5 min • 1 cup dressing

- ½ cup vegetable oil
- ⅓ cup honey or real maple syrup
- ¼ cup fresh lemon juice
- 1 tablespoon Dijon mustard

In tightly covered container, shake all ingredients. Store tightly covered in refrigerator up to 1 week. Shake before serving.

1 Tablespoon: Calories 90; Total Fat 7g (Saturated Fat 1g, Trans Fat 0g); Cholesterol 0mg; Sodium 25mg; Total Carbohydrate 6g (Dietary Fiber 0g, Sugars 6g); Protein 0g **Exchanges:** ½ Fruit, 1 Fat **Carbohydrate Choices:** ½

Honey–Poppy Seed Dressing Omit mustard. Add 1 tablespoon poppy seed.

Blue Cheese Dressing

CALORIE SMART • EASY

PREP 10 min **TOTAL** 3 hr 10 min • 1⅔ cups dressing

- ¾ cup crumbled blue or Gorgonzola cheese (3 oz)
- 3 oz (from 8-oz package) cream cheese, softened
- ½ cup mayonnaise or salad dressing (for homemade mayonnaise, see page 460)
- ⅓ cup half-and-half
- 1 teaspoon cider vinegar
- ⅛ teaspoon pepper

1 Reserve ⅓ cup of the blue cheese. In small bowl, mix remaining blue cheese and the cream cheese until well blended. Stir in mayonnaise, half-and-half, vinegar and pepper until creamy. Stir in reserved ⅓ cup blue cheese.

2 Cover and refrigerate at least 3 hours to blend flavors. Stir before serving. Store tightly covered in refrigerator up to 5 days.

1 Tablespoon: Calories 50; Total Fat 5g (Saturated Fat 2g, Trans Fat 0g); Cholesterol 10mg; Sodium 80mg; Total Carbohydrate 0g (Dietary Fiber 0g, Sugars 0g); Protein 1g **Exchanges:** 1 Fat **Carbohydrate Choices:** 0

LIGHTER Directions For 3 grams of fat and 35 calories per serving, reduce blue cheese to ½ cup and use reduced-fat mayonnaise. Use 4 oz ⅓-less-fat cream cheese and ¼ cup fat-free (skim) milk.

Buttermilk Ranch Dressing   CALORIE SMART • EASY

PREP 10 min **TOTAL** 2 hr 10 min • 1¼ cups dressing

- ¾ cup mayonnaise or salad dressing (for homemade Mayonnaise, see page 460)
- 1 clove garlic, finely chopped
- ½ cup buttermilk
- 1 teaspoon parsley flakes
- ½ teaspoon dried minced onion
- ½ teaspoon salt
- Dash ground pepper

In small bowl, mix all ingredients. Cover and refrigerate at least 2 hours to blend flavors. Stir before serving. Store tightly covered in refrigerator up to 5 days.

1 Tablespoon: Calories 60; Total Fat 7g (Saturated Fat 1g, Trans Fat 0g); Cholesterol 0mg; Sodium 110mg; Total Carbohydrate 0g (Dietary Fiber 0g, Sugars 0g); Protein 0g **Exchanges:** 1½ Fat **Carbohydrate Choices:** 0

Miso Dressing

LIGHTER Directions For 4 grams of fat and 45 calories per serving, use reduced-fat mayonnaise.

Buttermilk Ranch–Parmesan Dressing Add ⅓ cup grated Parmesan cheese and ½ teaspoon paprika.

Miso Dressing   CALORIE SMART • FAST

Miso, also called bean paste, is a Japanese staple available in many flavors and colors. This salty, fermented soybean paste can be found in the refrigerated section of the grocery store with other international foods, often near the tofu, or in Asian food markets.

PREP 5 min **TOTAL** 5 min • ¾ cup dressing

- ¼ cup rice vinegar or cider vinegar
- ¼ cup vegetable oil
- ¼ cup white or yellow miso
- 1 teaspoon dark sesame oil
- 1 teaspoon grated gingerroot or ¼ teaspoon ground ginger
- ¼ teaspoon salt
- 1 clove garlic, finely chopped

In small bowl, beat all ingredients with whisk until well blended. Store tightly covered in refrigerator up to 1 week. Stir before serving.

1 Tablespoon: Calories 60; Total Fat 5g (Saturated Fat 1g, Trans Fat 0g); Cholesterol 0mg; Sodium 260mg; Total Carbohydrate 2g (Dietary Fiber 0g, Sugars 0g); Protein 0g **Exchanges:** 1 Fat **Carbohydrate Choices:** 0

Honey Miso Dressing Beat in 1 tablespoon honey.

Sriracha Miso Dressing Beat in 2 to 3 teaspoons Sriracha sauce.

Asian Dressing Omit miso, sesame oil and garlic. Add 2 tablespoons each dry sherry and soy sauce and 1 teaspoon sugar.

CHAPTER 6

Soups, Stews & Chilies

Heirloom Recipe and New Twist

It's hard to beat chicken noodle soup any time—it's warm, comforting and tasty and it fills the house with a wonderful aroma while it's cooking. This recipe has been a favorite of the test kitchens for many years and is truly a classic. The new twist, with a definite Italian flair, is hearty with cheesy chicken meatballs and orzo pasta.

HEIRLOOM

Chicken Noodle Soup

CALORIE SMART

PREP 15 min **TOTAL** 40 min • 6 servings

Chicken and Broth (page 143)
4 medium carrots, sliced (2 cups)
4 medium stalks celery, sliced (2 cups)
1 medium onion, chopped (½ cup)
1 cup uncooked medium egg noodles (2 oz)
Chopped fresh parsley, if desired

1 Refrigerate cut-up cooked chicken. Add enough water to broth to measure 5 cups.

2 In 4-quart Dutch oven or stockpot, heat broth, carrots, celery and onion to boiling; reduce heat. Cover and simmer about 15 minutes or until carrots are tender.

3 Stir in noodles and chicken. Heat to boiling; reduce heat. Simmer uncovered 7 to 10 minutes or until noodles are tender. Sprinkle with parsley.

1 Serving (1 Cup): Calories 240; Total Fat 8g (Saturated Fat 2g, Trans Fat 0g); Cholesterol 90mg; Sodium 990mg; Total Carbohydrate 14g (Dietary Fiber 3g, Sugars 5g); Protein 29g **Exchanges:** ½ Starch, 1 Vegetable, 3½ Very Lean Meat, 1 Fat **Carbohydrate Choices:** 1

Chicken Rice Soup Substitute ½ cup uncooked regular long-grain white rice for the noodles. Stir in rice with the vegetables. Cover and simmer about 15 minutes or until rice is tender. Stir in chicken; heat until chicken is hot.

Confetti Chicken Noodle Soup Add ½ cup each frozen sweet peas and corn with the noodles and chicken. Continue as directed.

Homestyle Chicken Noodle Soup Substitute 1½ cups frozen homestyle egg noodles (from a 12-oz bag) for the uncooked egg noodles. Add frozen noodles with the onion.

Chicken Noodle Soup

Chicken Meatball Soup

NEW TWIST

Chicken Meatball Soup

CALORIE SMART

PREP 35 min **TOTAL** 45 min • 6 servings

MEATBALLS

1 lb ground chicken

½ cup seasoned dry bread crumbs

1 egg

3 oz fontina cheese, cut in 18 (½-inch) cubes

SOUP

2 tablespoons olive oil

2 cloves garlic, finely chopped

1 medium onion, chopped (½ cup)

1 medium carrot, chopped (½ cup)

½ cup uncooked orzo or rosamarina pasta

⅓ cup chopped fresh basil leaves

1 can (14 oz) diced tomatoes with basil, oregano and garlic, undrained

1 carton (32 oz) chicken broth or 4 cups Chicken and Broth (at right)

¼ teaspoon pepper

1 Heat oven to 400°F. Line 13x9-inch pan with foil. In large bowl, mix chicken, bread crumbs and egg. Shape mixture into 18 (1½-inch) balls. Push 1 piece of cheese into center of each, pressing mixture around cheese and reshaping meatball. Place in pan.

2 Bake uncovered 12 to 15 minutes or until firm and no longer pink in center next to cheese.

3 Meanwhile, in 4-quart saucepan, heat oil over medium-low heat. Stir in garlic, onion and carrot. Cover and cook 10 minutes, stirring occasionally. Stir in remaining soup ingredients. Heat to boiling; reduce heat.

4 Add meatballs. Cover and simmer about 10 minutes or until pasta is tender. To serve, place 3 meatballs in each serving bowl; spoon 1 cup soup over meatballs.

1 Serving: Calories 300; Total Fat 16g (Saturated Fat 5g, Trans Fat 0g); Cholesterol 90mg; Sodium 900mg; Total Carbohydrate 21g (Dietary Fiber 2g, Sugars 2g); Protein 18g **Exchanges:** 1½ Other Carbohydrate, 2 Very Lean Meat, ½ Medium-Fat Meat, 2½ Fat **Carbohydrate Choices:** 1½

Chicken and Broth **CALORIE SMART**

PREP 25 min **TOTAL** 1 hr 25 min • 4 cups broth and 2½ to 3 cups cooked chicken

1 cut-up chicken or chicken parts (3 to 3½ lb)

1 teaspoon salt

½ teaspoon pepper

1 medium stalk celery with leaves, cut up

1 medium carrot, cut up

1 small onion, cut up

1 sprig fresh parsley

4½ cups cold water

1 In 4-quart Dutch oven or pot, place chicken and all remaining ingredients; heat to boiling. Skim foam from broth; reduce heat. Cover and simmer 40 to 45 minutes or until juice of chicken is clear when thickest part is cut to bone (at least 165°F).

2 Carefully remove chicken from broth with tongs. Cool chicken about 10 minutes or just until cool enough to handle. Strain broth through fine-mesh strainer; discard vegetables.

3 Remove skin and bones from chicken. Cut chicken into ½-inch pieces. Skim fat from broth. Use broth and chicken immediately, or cover and refrigerate broth and chicken in separate containers up to 24 hours or freeze up to 6 months.

1 Serving (1 Cup Broth and about ½ Cup Chicken): Calories 180; Total Fat 7g (Saturated Fat 2g, Trans Fat 0g); Cholesterol 85mg; Sodium 490mg; Total Carbohydrate 2g (Dietary Fiber 0g, Sugars 1g); Protein 27g **Exchanges:** 4 Very Lean Meat, 1 Fat **Carbohydrate Choices:** 0

Skimming Fat

With Fat Separator: Pour or ladle warm broth into fat separator; let stand a few minutes for fat to rise to surface. Pour out broth carefully, stopping when you get to the layer of fat.

With Spoon: Refrigerate broth 6 to 8 hours or overnight, until fat hardens on surface. Carefully scoop fat from surface with spoon.

Beef and Broth CALORIE SMART

PREP 30 min **TOTAL** 3 hr 45 min • 6 cups broth and 1 cup cooked beef

- 2 lb beef shank cross cuts or soup bones
- 2 tablespoons vegetable oil, if desired
- 6 cups cold water
- 1 medium carrot, chopped (½ cup)
- 1 medium stalk celery with leaves, chopped (½ cup)
- 1 small onion, chopped (⅓ cup)
- 1 teaspoon salt
- ¼ teaspoon dried thyme leaves
- 5 black peppercorns
- 3 whole cloves
- 3 sprigs fresh parsley
- 1 dried bay leaf

1 Remove marrow from centers of bones. In 4-quart Dutch oven or stockpot, melt marrow over medium heat until hot, or heat 2 tablespoons oil. Cook beef shanks in marrow or oil until brown on both sides.

2 Add water; heat to boiling. Skim foam from broth. Stir in remaining ingredients; heat to boiling. Skim foam from broth; reduce heat. Cover and simmer 3 hours.

3 Remove beef from broth. Cool beef about 10 minutes or just until cool enough to handle. Strain broth through fine-mesh strainer; discard vegetables and seasonings.

4 Remove beef from bones. Cut beef into ½-inch pieces. Skim fat from broth. Use broth and beef immediately, or cover and refrigerate broth and beef in separate containers up to 24 hours or freeze up to 6 months.

1 Cup: Calories 120; Total Fat 3g (Saturated Fat 1g, Trans Fat 0g); Cholesterol 50mg; Sodium 440mg; Total Carbohydrate 2g (Dietary Fiber 0g, Sugars 1g); Protein 20g **Exchanges:** ½ Vegetable, 2½ Very Lean Meat, ½ Fat **Carbohydrate Choices:** 0

SLOW-COOKER Directions Decrease water to 5 cups. Increase salt to 1¼ teaspoons. In 10-inch skillet, heat marrow or 2 tablespoons oil over medium heat. Cook beef in marrow or oil until brown on both sides. Spray 3½- to 6-quart slow cooker with cooking spray. In slow cooker, mix remaining ingredients; add beef. Cover; cook on Low heat setting 8 to 10 hours. Continue as directed in Step 3.

Borscht

Borscht CALORIE SMART

This recipe for a traditional favorite from Russia and Poland calls for mixed pickling spice, which is available at most grocery stores. It usually includes a fragrant combination of coarse pieces of allspice, bay leaves, cardamom, cinnamon, cloves, coriander, ginger, mustard seed and peppercorns.

PREP 30 min **TOTAL** 4 hr 10 min • 6 servings

- ¾ lb boneless beef chuck, tip or round roast, cut into ½-inch cubes
- 1 smoked pork hock
- 4 cups water
- 1 can (10.5 oz) condensed beef broth
- 1 teaspoon salt
- ¼ teaspoon pepper
- 4 medium beets, cooked (page 234), or 1 can (15 oz) sliced beets, drained
- 3 cups shredded green cabbage
- 2 medium potatoes, peeled, cut into cubes (2 cups)
- 1 large onion, sliced
- 2 cloves garlic, finely chopped
- 1 tablespoon mixed pickling spice
- 2 teaspoons dill seed or 1 sprig fresh dill weed
- ¼ cup red wine vinegar
- ¾ cup sour cream
  Chopped fresh dill weed, if desired

1 In 4-quart Dutch oven or stockpot, place beef, pork hock, water, broth, salt and pepper. Heat to boiling; reduce heat. Cover and simmer 1 hour to 1 hour 30 minutes or until beef is tender.

2 Shred beets, or cut into ¼-inch strips. Remove pork hock from soup; let stand until cool enough to handle. Remove pork from bone; cut pork into bite-size pieces.

3 Add pork, beets, cabbage, potatoes, onion and garlic to soup; stir. Tie pickling spice and dill seed in cheesecloth bag or place in tea ball; add to soup. Cover and simmer 2 hours.

4 Stir in vinegar. Simmer uncovered 10 minutes. Remove spice bag. Serve soup with sour cream. Sprinkle with fresh dill.

1 Serving: Calories 270; Total Fat 14g (Saturated Fat 7g, Trans Fat 0g); Cholesterol 60mg; Sodium 810mg; Total Carbohydrate 18g (Dietary Fiber 3g, Sugars 7g); Protein 18g **Exchanges:** 4 Vegetable, 2 Medium-Fat Meat, ½ Fat **Carbohydrate Choices:** 1

French Onion Soup CALORIE SMART

The long, slow cooking of the onions gives this soup its rich flavor and color. Gruyère cheese is a rich, nutty, buttery-tasting form of Swiss cheese with fewer and smaller holes.

PREP 30 min **TOTAL** 50 min • 4 servings

2	tablespoons butter
4	medium onions, sliced
2	cans (10½ oz each) condensed beef broth
1½	cups water
⅛	teaspoon pepper
⅛	teaspoon dried thyme leaves
1	dried bay leaf
4	slices (¾ to 1 inch thick) French bread, toasted
1	cup shredded Gruyère, Swiss or mozzarella cheese (4 oz)
¼	cup grated Parmesan cheese

1 In 4-quart nonstick Dutch oven or stockpot, melt butter over medium heat. Stir in onions to coat with butter. Cook uncovered 15 to 20 minutes, stirring frequently, until onions are deep golden brown (onions will shrink during cooking).

2 Stir in broth, water, pepper, thyme and bay leaf. Heat to boiling; reduce heat. Cover and simmer 15 minutes. Remove bay leaf.

3 Set oven control to broil. Place toasted bread in 4 ovenproof bowls or individual ceramic casseroles.* Spoon soup over bread; sprinkle with cheeses. Place bowls on cookie sheet or in pan with shallow sides.

4 Broil with tops about 5 inches from heat 1 to 2 minutes or just until cheese is melted and golden brown. (Watch carefully so cheese does not burn.) Serve with additional French bread, if desired.

*Do not use glass containers; they cannot withstand the heat from the broiler and may break.

1 Serving: Calories 360; Total Fat 18g (Saturated Fat 10g, Trans Fat 1g); Cholesterol 50mg; Sodium 1210mg; Total Carbohydrate 28g (Dietary Fiber 3g, Sugars 7g); Protein 22g **Exchanges:** 2 Starch, 2 High-Fat Meat **Carbohydrate Choices:** 2

Golden Onion Soup Omit French bread and cheeses; do not broil.

Caramelizing Onions

Cook onions 10 minutes, stirring every 3 to 4 minutes.

Continue cooking onions, stirring well every 5 minutes, until deep golden brown.

French Onion Soup

Beef Pho CALORIE SMART

Pho is a Vietnamese soup that features noodles, spicy broth and thinly sliced beef or chicken.

PREP 45 min **TOTAL** 1 hr 30 min • 6 servings

BEEF AND NOODLES

- 2 medium yellow onions, cut in half
- 1 piece (5 inches) gingerroot, peeled, cut lengthwise in half
- 6 whole cloves
- 5 whole star anise
- 1 cinnamon stick (3-inch)
- 1 carton (32 oz) beef broth (4 cups; for homemade broth, see page 146)
- 1 lb beef sirloin steak, 1 inch thick
- 7 oz Thai stir-fry rice noodles (from 14-oz box)
- 1 cup water
- ¼ cup fish sauce
- 2 tablespoons palm sugar or brown sugar

TOPPINGS, IF DESIRED

Sliced green onions
Sliced jalapeño chiles
Lime wedges
Thinly sliced fresh Thai basil leaves
Fresh cilantro leaves
Hoisin sauce
Sriracha sauce

1 Set oven control to broil. Spray broiler pan rack with cooking spray. Place onions and gingerroot on rack in pan. Broil with tops 4 to 6 inches from heat 10 to 15 minutes or until onions begin to char. Turn; broil 10 to 15 minutes longer or until onions begin to char. Remove from oven; set aside.

2 Heat 4-quart Dutch oven or stockpot over medium heat. Add cloves, star anise and cinnamon stick. Cook over medium heat 2 to 3 minutes, stirring frequently, until toasted. Add 2 cups of the broth, the onions and gingerroot. Heat to boiling; reduce heat to low. Cover and simmer 30 minutes, stirring occasionally.

3 Meanwhile, cut beef crosswise in half; place one half on plate. Freeze until partially frozen, 20 to 30 minutes (do not freeze solid). Cut remaining beef into 1-inch cubes; cover and refrigerate. Cook noodles as directed on package; keep warm. If noodles become sticky, rinse with hot water just before serving.

4 Strain simmered broth through fine-mesh strainer into bowl; discard spices, onions and gingerroot. Return broth to Dutch oven. Add remaining 2 cups broth, the water, fish sauce, sugar and cubed beef. Heat to boiling; reduce heat. Simmer 10 to 15 minutes or until beef is tender.

5 To serve, divide noodles among individual bowls. Cut partially frozen beef into paper-thin slices; place on noodles in each bowl. Immediately pour hot soup over beef to cover. Add desired toppings.

1 Serving: Calories 260; Total Fat 3.5g (Saturated Fat 1g, Trans Fat 0g); Cholesterol 50mg; Sodium 1690mg; Total Carbohydrate 33g (Dietary Fiber 1g, Sugars 5g); Protein 23g **Exchanges:** 1½ Starch, ½ Other Carbohydrate, 2½ Very Lean Meat, ½ Fat **Carbohydrate Choices:** 2

Vegetable Beef Soup CALORIE SMART

The prep time is long for this recipe, but if you already have the beef broth ready, you are almost there!

PREP 20 min **TOTAL** 1 hr 5 min • 7 servings

- Beef and Broth (page 146)
- 1 ear fresh sweet corn or ½ cup frozen whole kernel corn
- 2 medium potatoes, cut into pieces (2 cups)
- 2 medium tomatoes, chopped (1½ cups)
- 2 medium carrots, thinly sliced (1 cup)
- 2 medium stalks celery, sliced (1 cup)
- 1 medium onion, chopped (½ cup)
- 1 cup 1-inch pieces fresh green beans or frozen cut green beans
- 1 cup shelled green peas or frozen sweet peas
- ¼ teaspoon pepper

1 In 4-quart Dutch oven or stockpot, place strained beef and broth.

2 Cut kernels from ear of corn. Stir corn and remaining ingredients into broth. Heat to boiling; reduce heat. Cover and simmer about 30 minutes or until vegetables are tender.

1 Serving (1½ Cups): Calories 240; Total Fat 9g (Saturated Fat 3.5g, Trans Fat 0g); Cholesterol 45mg; Sodium 640mg; Total Carbohydrate 19g (Dietary Fiber 4g, Sugars 4g); Protein 20g **Exchanges:** 1 Starch, 1 Vegetable, 2 Lean Meat, ½ Fat **Carbohydrate Choices:** 1

Beef Pho

Family-Favorite Chili

Beef Stew

Family-Favorite Chili

CALORIE SMART • SLOW COOKER

PREP 20 min **TOTAL** 6 hr 35 min • 8 servings

- 2 lb lean (at least 80%) ground beef*
- 1 large onion, chopped (1 cup)
- 2 cloves garlic, finely chopped
- 1 can (28 oz) diced tomatoes, undrained
- 1 can (15 oz) tomato sauce
- 2 tablespoons chili powder
- 1½ teaspoons ground cumin
- ½ teaspoon salt
- ½ teaspoon pepper
- 1 can (15 to 16 oz) kidney or pinto beans, drained, rinsed
  Shredded Cheddar cheese, if desired

1 In 12-inch skillet, cook beef over medium heat 8 to 10 minutes, stirring occasionally, until thoroughly cooked; drain.

2 Spray 3½- to 6-quart slow cooker with cooking spray. In slow cooker, mix beef and remaining ingredients except beans and cheese. Cover; cook on Low heat setting 6 to 8 hours (or on High heat setting 3 to 4 hours).

3 Stir in beans. If using Low heat setting, increase to High. Cover; cook 15 to 20 minutes longer or until slightly thickened. Sprinkle individual servings with cheese.

1 Serving: Calories 300; Total Fat 12g (Saturated Fat 4.5g, Trans Fat 0.5g); Cholesterol 70mg; Sodium 800mg; Total Carbohydrate 22g (Dietary Fiber 6g, Sugars 6g); Protein 27g **Exchanges:** 1 Starch, 1 Vegetable, 3½ Lean Meat **Carbohydrate Choices:** 1½

*Always cook ground meat before adding to a slow cooker. Getting cold, uncooked ground beef to a safe temperature in a slow cooker takes too long to be safe.

Family-Favorite Turkey Chili with Brown Rice Substitute ground turkey breast for the ground beef, cooking until no longer pink in Step 1. Serve chili over cooked brown rice. Serve with reduced-fat Cheddar cheese.

Beef Stew CALORIE SMART

Look for beef stew meat, already trimmed and cut into ½- to 1-inch pieces, in the meat department.

PREP 15 min **TOTAL** 3 hr 45 min • 8 servings

- 1 lb beef stew meat, cut into ½-inch pieces
- 1 medium onion, cut into 8 wedges
- 1 bag (8 oz) ready-to-eat baby-cut carrots (about 30)
- 1 can (14.5 oz) diced tomatoes, undrained
- 1 can (10.5 oz) condensed beef broth
- 1 can (8 oz) tomato sauce
- ⅓ cup all-purpose flour
- 1 tablespoon Worcestershire sauce
- 1 teaspoon salt
- 1 teaspoon sugar
- 1 teaspoon dried marjoram leaves
- ¼ teaspoon pepper
- 12 small red potatoes (1½ lb), cut into quarters
- 2 cups sliced fresh mushrooms (about 5 oz) or 1 package (about 3.5 oz) fresh shiitake mushrooms, sliced

1 Heat oven to 325°F. In 4-quart ovenproof Dutch oven, mix all ingredients except potatoes and mushrooms. Cover and bake 2 hours, stirring once.

2 Stir in potatoes and mushrooms. Cover and bake 1 hour to 1 hour 30 minutes longer or until beef and vegetables are tender.

1 Serving: Calories 310; Total Fat 7g (Saturated Fat 2.5g, Trans Fat 0g); Cholesterol 35mg; Sodium 820mg; Total Carbohydrate 43g (Dietary Fiber 6g, Sugars 7g); Protein 18g **Exchanges:** 2 Starch, 2 Vegetable, 1 Medium-Fat Meat, ½ Fat **Carbohydrate Choices:** 3

Cheesy Potato-Bacon Soup

3 Stir in cheese until melted; stir in half of the bacon. Sprinkle individual servings with remaining bacon and the green onions.

1 Serving (1½ Cups): Calories 410; Total Fat 15g (Saturated Fat 9g, Trans Fat 0g); Cholesterol 45mg; Sodium 1210mg; Total Carbohydrate 50g (Dietary Fiber 5g, Sugars 5g); Protein 19g **Exchanges:** 3½ Starch, 1 High-Fat Meat, 1 Fat **Carbohydrate Choices:** 3

Minestrone with Italian Sausage CALORIE SMART

PREP 45 min **TOTAL** 45 min • 7 servings

- 1 tablespoon olive or vegetable oil
- 1 lb bulk sweet Italian pork sausage
- 2 medium carrots, coarsely chopped (1 cup)
- 1 medium onion, chopped (½ cup)
- 2 teaspoons dried basil leaves
- 2 teaspoons finely chopped garlic
- 5¼ cups beef broth (for homemade broth, see page 146)
- 1 can (14.5 oz) diced tomatoes, undrained
- 1 can (15.5 oz) great northern beans, drained, rinsed
- 1 cup uncooked small elbow macaroni (4 oz)
- 1 medium zucchini, cut in half lengthwise, then cut into ¼-inch slices (1 cup)
- 1 cup frozen cut green beans

1 In 5-quart Dutch oven or stockpot, heat oil over medium-high heat. Add sausage, carrots, onion, basil and garlic. Cook 5 to 7 minutes, stirring frequently, until sausage is no longer pink; drain.

2 Stir broth, tomatoes and great northern beans into sausage mixture. Heat to boiling; reduce heat to medium-low. Cover and cook 7 to 8 minutes, stirring occasionally.

3 Stir in macaroni, zucchini and green beans. Heat to boiling over medium high heat. Cook 5 to 6 minutes, stirring occasionally, until vegetables are hot and macaroni is tender.

1 Serving (1½ Cups): Calories 380; Total Fat 16g (Saturated Fat 5g, Trans Fat 0g); Cholesterol 25mg; Sodium 1400mg; Total Carbohydrate 38g (Dietary Fiber 6g, Sugars 5g); Protein 20g **Exchanges:** 2 Starch, 1 Vegetable, 1½ Medium-Fat Meat, 1½ Fat **Carbohydrate Choices:** 2½

Meatless Minestrone Use 1 additional can (15.5 oz) great northern beans (or your favorite canned beans) for the sausage, and substitute vegetable broth for the beef broth.

SLOW-COOKER Directions Chop onion (½ cup). Omit tomato sauce. Increase flour to ½ cup. Spray 3½- to 6-quart slow cooker with cooking spray. In slow cooker, mix all ingredients except beef. Add beef (do not stir). Cover; cook on Low heat setting 8 to 9 hours. Stir well before serving.

Cheesy Potato-Bacon Soup

SLOW COOKER

Look for bacon that is already cooked at the grocery store—it's a great time-saver. Or pick up a package of microwavable bacon instead.

PREP 15 min **TOTAL** 6 hr 35 min • 6 servings

- 1 bag (32 oz) frozen Southern-style diced hash brown potatoes, thawed
- 1 medium onion, chopped (½ cup)
- 1 medium stalk celery, diced (½ cup)
- 3½ cups chicken broth (for homemade broth, see page 143)
- 1 cup water
- 3 tablespoons all-purpose flour
- 1 cup half-and-half
- 2 cups shredded Cheddar cheese (8 oz)
- 12 slices bacon, crisply cooked, crumbled
- 4 medium green onions, thinly sliced (¼ cup)

1 Spray 3½- to 4-quart slow cooker with cooking spray. In slow cooker, mix potatoes, onion, celery, broth and water. Cover; cook on Low heat setting 6 to 8 hours.

2 In small bowl, mix flour and half-and-half; stir into potato mixture. Increase heat setting to High. Cover; cook 20 to 30 minutes or until mixture thickens.

Fish Broth   CALORIE SMART

Celery leaves add great flavor to broth. Try adding chopped celery leaves along with the celery stalks called for in soup recipes.

PREP 20 min **TOTAL** 1 hr • 6 cups broth

1½	lb fish bones and trimmings
4	cups cold water
2	cups dry white wine or clam juice
1	large stalk celery with leaves, chopped
1	small onion, sliced
3	medium fresh mushrooms, chopped
1	tablespoon lemon juice
1	teaspoon salt
½	teaspoon dried thyme leaves
3	sprigs fresh parsley
1	dried bay leaf

1 Rinse fish bones and trimmings with cold water; drain. In 4-quart Dutch oven or stockpot, mix bones, trimmings, 4 cups water and remaining ingredients; heat to boiling. Skim foam from broth; reduce heat. Cover and simmer 30 minutes.

2 Cool about 10 minutes. Strain broth through fine-mesh strainer; discard skin, bones, vegetables and seasonings. Use broth immediately, or cover and refrigerate up to 24 hours or freeze up to 6 months.

1 Cup: Calories 15; Total Fat 0g (Saturated Fat 0g, Trans Fat 0g); Cholesterol 0mg; Sodium 400mg; Total Carbohydrate 0g (Dietary Fiber 0g, Sugars 0g); Protein 0g **Exchanges:** Free **Carbohydrate Choices:** 0

Provençal Fish Soup

CALORIE SMART • FAST

Provençal refers to dishes prepared in Provence, France, where ingredients like olive oil, onions, garlic and tomatoes are commonly used.

PREP 25 min **TOTAL** 25 min • 8 servings

1	tablespoon olive oil
1	medium onion, chopped (½ cup)
4	cups fish or chicken broth (for homemade broth, see page 154 or page 143)
2	cans (14.5 oz each) diced tomatoes with basil, garlic and oregano, undrained
½	cup dry white wine or dry vermouth
¼	teaspoon pepper
1	lb halibut fillet, skinned, cut into 1-inch cubes*
	Toasted baguette slices, shaved Parmesan cheese and chopped fresh parsley, if desired

1 In 3-quart saucepan, heat oil over medium heat. Cook onion in oil 2 to 3 minutes, stirring occasionally, until crisp-tender.

2 Add broth, tomatoes, wine and pepper. Heat to boiling; reduce heat. Simmer uncovered 10 minutes, stirring occasionally.

3 Stir in fish. Heat to boiling; reduce heat. Simmer 5 minutes or until fish flakes easily with fork. Serve in shallow bowls topped with baguette slices and cheese; sprinkle with parsley.

*Cod or grouper can be substituted for the halibut.

1 Serving (1 Cup): Calories 100; Total Fat 2.5g (Saturated Fat 0g, Trans Fat 0g); Cholesterol 25mg; Sodium 640mg; Total Carbohydrate 6g (Dietary Fiber 1g, Sugars 0g); Protein 11g **Exchanges:** ½ Other Carbohydrate, 1½ Very Lean Meat, ½ Fat **Carbohydrate Choices:** ½

Provençal Fish Soup

New England Clam Chowder

CALORIE SMART

PREP 20 min **TOTAL** 35 min • 4 servings

    4 slices bacon, cut into ½-inch pieces
    1 medium onion, chopped (½ cup)
    1 medium stalk celery, sliced (½ cup)
    2 cans (6.5 oz each) minced or chopped clams,
       drained, ¼ cup liquid reserved*
  2¾ cups milk or half-and-half
    2 medium potatoes, peeled, diced (2 cups)
    ¼ teaspoon salt
       Dash pepper
    ¼ cup all-purpose flour
       Chopped fresh parsley, if desired

1 In 3-quart saucepan, cook bacon, onion and celery over medium heat, stirring occasionally, until bacon is crisp and onion is tender; drain.

2 Stir in clams, reserved clam liquid, ¾ cup of the milk, the potatoes, salt and pepper. Heat to boiling; reduce heat. Cover and simmer about 15 minutes or until potatoes are tender.

3 In medium bowl, mix remaining 2 cups milk and the flour with whisk until smooth and blended. Stir into clam mixture. Heat to boiling, stirring frequently. Boil and stir 1 minute or until thickened. Garnish with parsley.

*Or substitute 1 pint shucked fresh clams with their liquid for the canned clams. Chop the clams and stir in with the potatoes in Step 2.

1 Serving (1¼ Cups): Calories 240; Total Fat 5g (Saturated Fat 1.5g, Trans Fat 0g); Cholesterol 75mg; Sodium 490mg; Total Carbohydrate 19g (Dietary Fiber 1g, Sugars 8g); Protein 29g **Exchanges:** ½ Starch, ½ Low-Fat Milk, 1 Vegetable, 3 Very Lean Meat, 1 Fat **Carbohydrate Choices:** 1

Manhattan Clam Chowder

CALORIE SMART

Cooks in Rhode Island in the late 1800s liked to throw tomatoes into clam chowder. Sometime in the mid-20th century, their creation became known as Manhattan clam chowder. It resembles New England clam chowder but is made with the tomatoes instead of milk or cream.

PREP 20 min **TOTAL** 35 min • 4 servings

    ¼ cup chopped bacon or salt pork
    1 small onion, finely chopped (⅓ cup)
    2 cans (6.5 oz each) minced or chopped
       clams, undrained*
    2 medium potatoes, peeled, diced (2 cups)
    ⅓ cup chopped celery
    1 cup water
    1 can (14.5 oz) whole tomatoes, undrained
    2 teaspoons chopped fresh parsley
    1 teaspoon chopped fresh or ¼ teaspoon dried
       thyme leaves
    ¼ teaspoon salt
    ⅛ teaspoon pepper

1 In 2-quart saucepan, cook bacon and onion over medium heat 8 to 10 minutes, stirring occasionally, until bacon is crisp and onion is tender; drain.

2 Stir in clams, potatoes, celery and water. Heat to boiling; reduce heat. Cover and simmer about 15 minutes or until potatoes are tender.

3 Stir in remaining ingredients, breaking up tomatoes. Heat until hot, stirring occasionally.

*Or substitute 1 pint shucked fresh clams with their liquid for the canned clams. Chop the clams and stir in with the potatoes in Step 2.

1 Serving: Calories 230; Total Fat 3g (Saturated Fat 0.5g, Trans Fat 0g); Cholesterol 65mg; Sodium 450mg; Total Carbohydrate 23g (Dietary Fiber 3g, Sugars 4g); Protein 26g **Exchanges:** 1 Starch, 2 Vegetable, 3 Very Lean Meat **Carbohydrate Choices:** 1½

Oyster Stew   CALORIE SMART • FAST • EASY

PREP 15 min **TOTAL** 15 min • 4 servings

    ¼ cup butter
    1 pint shucked oysters, undrained, or fresh
       shucked oysters in their liquid
    2 cups milk
    ½ cup half-and-half
    ½ teaspoon salt
       Dash pepper
       Oyster crackers, if desired

1 In 1½-quart saucepan, melt butter over low heat. Stir in oysters. Cook 2 to 4 minutes, stirring occasionally, just until edges curl.

2 In 2-quart saucepan, heat milk and half-and-half over medium-low heat until hot. Stir in salt, pepper and oyster mixture; heat until hot. Serve with oyster crackers.

1 Serving (1 Cup): Calories 290; Total Fat 20g (Saturated Fat 10g, Trans Fat 1g); Cholesterol 115mg; Sodium 700mg; Total Carbohydrate 12g (Dietary Fiber 0g, Sugars 8g); Protein 14g **Exchanges:** 1 Low-Fat Milk, 1 Medium-Fat Meat, 3 Fat **Carbohydrate Choices:** 1

Vegetable Broth CALORIE SMART

Mild vegetables are preferred for a well-balanced neutral flavor. Broccoli, rutabaga, red cabbage or other strong-flavored vegetables would overpower the broth or give it a muddy, objectionable color.

PREP 20 min **TOTAL** 1 hr 30 min • 8 cups broth

- 8 cups cold water
- 6 cups coarsely chopped mild vegetables (bell peppers, carrots, celery, leeks, mushrooms,* potatoes, spinach or zucchini)
- 1 medium onion, coarsely chopped (½ cup)
- 4 cloves garlic, finely chopped
- ½ cup fresh parsley sprigs
- 2 tablespoons chopped fresh or 2 teaspoons dried basil leaves
- 2 tablespoons chopped fresh or 2 teaspoons dried thyme leaves
- 1 teaspoon salt
- ¼ teaspoon cracked black pepper
- 2 dried bay leaves

1 In 4-quart Dutch oven or stockpot, mix all ingredients. Heat to boiling; reduce heat. Cover and simmer 1 hour, stirring occasionally.

2 Cool about 10 minutes. Strain broth through fine-mesh strainer; discard vegetables and seasonings. Use broth immediately, or cover and refrigerate up to 24 hours or freeze up to 6 months. Stir before measuring.

*Some mushrooms have woody stems that cannot be eaten, but they can be used to flavor the broth and then discarded.

1 Cup: Calories 0; Total Fat 0g (Saturated Fat 0g, Trans Fat 0g); Cholesterol 0mg; Sodium 300mg; Total Carbohydrate 0g (Dietary Fiber 0g, Sugars 0g); Protein 0g **Exchanges:** Free **Carbohydrate Choices:** 0

Gazpacho

Gazpacho CALORIE SMART

PREP 15 min **TOTAL** 1 hr 15 min • 8 servings

- 1 can (28 oz) whole tomatoes, undrained
- 1 medium green bell pepper, finely chopped (1 cup)
- 1 cup finely chopped cucumber
- 1 cup croutons
- 1 medium onion, chopped (½ cup)
- 2 tablespoons dry white wine or chicken broth
- 2 tablespoons olive or vegetable oil
- 1 tablespoon ground cumin
- 1 tablespoon white vinegar
- ½ teaspoon salt
- ¼ teaspoon pepper

1 In blender or food processor, place tomatoes, ½ cup of the bell pepper, ½ cup of the cucumber, ½ cup of the croutons, ¼ cup of the onion and the remaining ingredients. Cover and blend on medium speed 30 to 60 seconds until smooth. Pour into large bowl.

2 Cover and refrigerate at least 1 hour. Serve remaining bell pepper, cucumber, onion and croutons as accompaniments.

1 Serving (½ Cup): Calories 80; Total Fat 4g (Saturated Fat 0.5g, Trans Fat 0g); Cholesterol 0mg; Sodium 320mg; Total Carbohydrate 10g (Dietary Fiber 2g, Sugars 4g); Protein 2g **Exchanges:** 2 Vegetable, ½ Fat **Carbohydrate Choices:** ½

Sriracha Gazpacho Add 1 to 2 teaspoons Sriracha sauce to the soup mixture. Just before serving, sprinkle with chopped fresh cilantro.

Green Gazpacho Use fresh green heirloom tomatoes (such as Green Zebra) instead of the canned tomatoes. Cut up to make about 4 cups. Add 1 avocado, pitted and peeled, to tomato mixture.

Storing Vegetable Broth

Freeze broth in ice-cube trays. Once frozen, put broth into freezer plastic bags and store in freezer.

Roasted Red Pepper Soup with Mozzarella

Roasted Red Pepper Soup with Mozzarella CALORIE SMART

PREP 40 min **TOTAL** 1 hr 10 min • 4 servings

- 4 red bell peppers
- 1 tablespoon olive oil
- 2 large onions, chopped (2 cups)
- 3 cloves garlic, sliced
- 2 cups vegetable broth or reduced-sodium chicken broth (for homemade broth, see page 156)
- 1 cup water
- ¼ teaspoon cracked black pepper
- 1 cup thinly sliced fresh basil leaves
- ½ yellow bell pepper, diced
- 8 bocconcini (small fresh mozzarella cheese balls), cut into quarters
- 4 slices crusty multigrain or whole wheat bread

1 Set oven control to broil. On rack in broiler pan, place red bell peppers. Broil with tops about 5 inches from heat, turning occasionally, until skin is blistered and evenly browned. Place roasted peppers in large bowl; cover with plastic wrap. Let stand 15 minutes.

2 In 4-quart saucepan, heat oil over medium-low heat. Cook onions and garlic in oil 7 to 9 minutes, stirring occasionally, until onions begin to turn brown; remove from heat.

3 Remove skin, stems, seeds and membranes from roasted peppers; cut peppers into strips. Stir bell pepper strips, broth, water and black pepper into onion mixture. Heat to boiling; reduce heat. Simmer uncovered 10 minutes, stirring occasionally. Stir in ½ cup of the basil. Remove from heat; cool slightly.

4 In blender or food processor, place about one-third of the soup mixture. Cover and blend on high speed until smooth, stopping blender to scrape side if necessary. Pour into large bowl. Repeat two times more with remaining soup mixture.

5 Top individual servings with yellow bell pepper and mozzarella; sprinkle evenly with remaining ½ cup basil. Serve with bread.

1 Serving (about 1½ Cups): Calories 200; Total Fat 6g (Saturated Fat 1.5g, Trans Fat 0g); Cholesterol 0mg; Sodium 620mg; Total Carbohydrate 29g (Dietary Fiber 6g, Sugars 13g); Protein 7g **Exchanges:** 1½ Starch, 1½ Vegetable, 1 Fat **Carbohydrate Choices:** 2

Tomato-Basil Soup CALORIE SMART

Fully ripe, juicy tomatoes provide the best flavor for this soup. If your tomatoes aren't completely ripe, you may need to increase the salt and sugar just a bit.

PREP 30 min **TOTAL** 1 hr • 4 servings

- 2 tablespoons olive or vegetable oil
- 1 medium carrot, finely chopped (½ cup)
- 1 medium onion, finely chopped (½ cup)
- 1 clove garlic, finely chopped
- 6 large tomatoes, peeled, seeded and chopped (6 cups)*
- 1 can (8 oz) tomato sauce
- ¼ cup thinly sliced fresh or 2 teaspoons dried basil leaves
- ½ teaspoon sugar
- ¼ teaspoon salt
- Dash pepper

1 In 3-quart saucepan, heat oil over medium heat. Cook carrot, onion and garlic in oil about 10 minutes, stirring occasionally, until tender but not browned.

2 Stir in tomatoes. Cook uncovered about 10 minutes, stirring occasionally, until thoroughly heated.

3 Stir in remaining ingredients. Cook uncovered about 10 minutes, stirring occasionally, until hot.

*Or substitute 3 cans (14.5 oz each) diced tomatoes, undrained, for the fresh tomatoes. Omit salt; increase sugar to 1 teaspoon.

1 Serving: Calories 170; Total Fat 8g (Saturated Fat 1g, Trans Fat 0g); Cholesterol 0mg; Sodium 550mg; Total Carbohydrate 22g (Dietary Fiber 6g, Sugars 10g); Protein 4g **Exchanges:** 4 Vegetable, 1 Fat **Carbohydrate Choices:** 1½

Learn to PUREE

The quick definition of puree is to mash or blend food until smooth, using a blender or food processor or by forcing food through a sieve. But there is more to this process than one might think. Pureed soups are likely the most famous foods prepared using this method. But you can also puree foods to feed babies, or foods like sweet potatoes can be pureed to serve as part of a meal.

Each appliance for pureeing works a little differently.

1. Blender: This provides the smoothest puree. Blend in small batches for the best results.

2. Food Processor: Because they tend to chop, not blend, food processors do not provide the smoothest mixture. The soup or vegetable mixture is often gritty with small bits of food left behind.

3. Immersion Blender: This tool will provide a smooth puree with the least work or cleanup. Immersion blenders are made to go right into pans of hot mixture, eliminating the need to puree soup in batches in a blender or food processor. To avoid damaging the motor, submerge the blender just to the top of the stem. Follow the manufacturer's directions before using or washing.

Tips for Great Results

- Food should be fully cooked before pureeing. If it is not, it is more difficult to get the puree really smooth. For the best flavor, don't overcook foods that will be pureed.

- Blend in a blender or process in a food processor in batches. Having too much food in either appliance will make it difficult to create a smooth puree. Adding the food with a ladle works well.

- Hot foods can release a lot of steam, so allow the soup to cool slightly before pureeing. Also, pureeing small amounts at a time allows for room in the appliance for the steam. Trapped steam can push the lid off, so for safety, leave the lid slightly cracked with a kitchen towel over the edge. If the lid has a vent, leave it open.

- If you have the option of more than one speed, start slow and increase the speed as you puree.

- For the smoothest soups, after pureeing, pass the soup through a strainer into the soup pot. The food pieces left behind can be re-pureed.

- For baby food, cook the food in a small amount of water. Drain the vegetables, but save the water. Add small amounts of the water while you process or blend the food until you have the consistency you like. Foods such as avocado or watermelon do not need to be cooked before pureeing.

Butternut Squash Soup

Sprinkle bowls of soup with pumpkin seeds or toasted walnuts.

PREP 30 min **TOTAL** 45 min • 6 servings

- 2 tablespoons butter
- 1 medium onion, chopped (½ cup)
- 1 butternut squash (2 lb), peeled, seeded and cut into pieces (page 237)*
- 2 cups chicken broth (for homemade broth, see page 143)
- ½ teaspoon dried marjoram leaves
- ¼ teaspoon black pepper
- ⅛ teaspoon ground red pepper (cayenne)
- 1 package (8 oz) cream cheese, cut into cubes
  Additional chicken broth or water, if desired

1 In 3-quart saucepan, melt butter over medium heat. Cook onion in butter, stirring occasionally, until crisp-tender.

2 Add squash, the 2 cups broth, the marjoram, black pepper and red pepper. Heat to boiling; reduce heat. Cover and simmer 12 to 15 minutes or until squash is tender.

3 In blender or food processor, place one-third each of the soup mixture and cream cheese. Cover and blend on high speed until smooth, scraping down side of blender if needed. Repeat twice with remaining soup mixture and cream cheese. Return mixture to saucepan. Heat over medium heat, stirring with whisk, until blended and hot (do not boil). Add additional broth if thinner consistency is desired.

*Squash will be easier to peel if you microwave it first. Pierce whole squash with knife in several places to allow steam to escape. Place on microwavable paper towel; microwave on High 4 to 6 minutes or until squash is hot and peel is firm but easy to cut. Cool slightly before peeling.

1 Serving: Calories 240; Total Fat 17g (Saturated Fat 10g, Trans Fat 0.5g); Cholesterol 50mg; Sodium 1220mg; Total Carbohydrate 15g (Dietary Fiber 2g, Sugars 6g); Protein 5g **Exchanges:** 1 Starch, 3½ Fat **Carbohydrate Choices:** 1

Butternut Squash Soup

Cream of Broccoli Soup

CALORIE SMART

PREP 35 min **TOTAL** 45 min • 8 servings

1½	lb fresh broccoli
2	cups water
1	large stalk celery, chopped (¾ cup)
1	medium onion, chopped (½ cup)
2	tablespoons butter
2	tablespoons all-purpose flour
2½	cups chicken broth (for homemade broth, see page 143)
½	teaspoon salt
⅛	teaspoon pepper
	Dash ground nutmeg
½	cup whipping cream
	Shredded Cheddar cheese, if desired

1 Remove florets from broccoli. Cut stalks into 1-inch pieces, discarding any leaves.

2 In 3-quart saucepan, heat water to boiling. Add broccoli florets and stalk pieces, celery and onion. Heat to boiling; reduce heat. Cover and simmer 7 to 10 minutes or until broccoli is tender (do not drain).

3 In blender, carefully place broccoli mixture. Cover and blend on medium speed 30 to 60 seconds or until smooth. Set aside.

4 In same saucepan, melt butter over medium heat. Stir in flour. Cook, stirring constantly, until mixture is smooth and bubbly; remove from heat. Stir in broth. Heat to boiling, stirring constantly. Boil and stir 1 minute.

5 Stir in broccoli mixture, salt, pepper and nutmeg; heat just to boiling. Stir in whipping cream; heat just until hot (do not boil or soup may curdle). Top individual servings with cheese.

1 Serving (1 Cup): Calories 110; Total Fat 8g (Saturated Fat 4.5g, Trans Fat 0g); Cholesterol 25mg; Sodium 510mg; Total Carbohydrate 6g (Dietary Fiber 2g, Sugars 2g); Protein 4g **Exchanges:** 2 Vegetable, 1 Fat **Carbohydrate Choices:** ½

Cream of Cauliflower Soup Substitute 1 medium head cauliflower (about 2 pounds), separated into florets, for the broccoli. Add 1≈tablespoon lemon juice with the vegetables in Step 2.

Wild Rice Soup   CALORIE SMART

PREP 35 min **TOTAL** 1 hr 10 min • 7 servings

¼	cup butter
4	medium stalks celery, sliced (2 cups)
2	medium carrots, coarsely shredded (2 cups)
1	large onion, chopped (1 cup)
1	medium green bell pepper, chopped (1 cup)
¼	cup plus 2 tablespoons all-purpose flour
1	teaspoon salt
½	teaspoon pepper
3	cups cooked wild rice (page 215)
2	cups water
2	cans (10.5 oz each) condensed chicken broth
3	cups half-and-half
⅔	cup slivered almonds, toasted if desired (page 23)
½	cup chopped fresh parsley

1 In 4-quart Dutch oven or stockpot, melt butter over medium-high heat. Cook celery, carrots, onion and bell pepper in butter about 10 minutes, stirring frequently, until crisp-tender.

2 Stir in flour, salt and pepper. Stir in wild rice, water and broth. Heat to boiling; reduce heat. Cover and simmer 15 minutes, stirring occasionally.

3 Stir in half-and-half, almonds and parsley. Heat just until hot (do not boil or soup may curdle).

1 Serving: Calories 360; Total Fat 20g (Saturated Fat 11g, Trans Fat 1g); Cholesterol 55mg; Sodium 1240mg; Total Carbohydrate 33g (Dietary Fiber 4g, Sugars 9g); Protein 12g **Exchanges:** 2 Starch, 1 Vegetable, ½ Very Lean Meat, 3½ Fat **Carbohydrate Choices:** 2

Chicken and Wild Rice Soup Stir in 4 cups cubed cooked chicken or turkey in Step 3.

Wild Rice Soup

The flavor of homemade cream of mushroom soup is amazing; it takes less than 30 minutes and has so many uses. Why not try it?

PREP 15 min **TOTAL** 30 min • 4 servings

1 lb fresh mushrooms, any type
¼ cup butter
3 tablespoons all-purpose flour
¼ teaspoon salt
1 cup whipping cream
1 can (14 oz) chicken broth (1⅔ cups)
1 tablespoon dry sherry, if desired
Freshly ground pepper, if desired

1 Slice only enough mushrooms to measure 1 cup. Coarsely chop remaining mushrooms.

2 In 3-quart saucepan, melt butter over medium heat. Cook sliced and chopped mushrooms in butter about 10 minutes, stirring occasionally, until golden brown. Sprinkle with flour and salt, stirring until well mixed.

3 Gradually stir in whipping cream and broth; heat to boiling. Cook 2 to 3 minutes, until thickened, stirring constantly. Stir in sherry. Sprinkle each serving with pepper.

1 Serving: Calories 350; Total Fat 31g (Saturated Fat 18g, Trans Fat 1g); Cholesterol 95mg; Sodium 840mg; Total Carbohydrate 11g (Dietary Fiber 2g, Sugars 3g); Protein 7g **Exchanges:** 3 Vegetable, 6 Fat **Carbohydrate Choices:** 1

LIGHTER **Directions** For 7 grams of fat and 145 calories per serving, decrease butter to 2 tablespoons and substitute fat-free half-and-half for the whipping cream.

Make-Ahead
CREAM OF
MUSHROOM SOUP

Ways to Use Cream of Mushroom Soup

1. Green Bean Casserole: Cook 2 lbs fresh beans, cut into 2-inch pieces, until crisp-tender (see page 234); drain. Mix beans with 1½ cups of the soup and ¼ teaspoon pepper. Spread in 2-quart baking dish; sprinkle with 1 can (2.8 oz) French-fried onions. Bake at 350°F 30 to 40 minutes or until heated through.

2. Chicken-Mushroom Soup: Make soup as directed. Stir in 1 cup chopped cooked chicken and ½ cup cooked peas. Heat over low heat until hot, stirring frequently.

3. Pork with Mushroom Sauce: Broil or grill pork chops. In small saucepan, heat soup (½ cup per serving) over low heat. Serve over pork chops; sprinkle with chopped fresh chives.

4. Vegetables with Mushroom Sauce: Cook 4 cups cauliflower florets and baby carrots until fork-tender. Heat 1 cup mushroom soup over low heat, stirring frequently. Spoon soup over vegetables. Sprinkle with chopped fresh chives.

Green Bean Casserole, Cream of Mushroom Soup

Slow Cooker Success

Use these tips to ensure great results from your slow cooker:

- Spray the inside of the insert or cooker with cooking spray for easy cleanup.
- Slow cookers work most efficiently when two-thirds to three-fourths full.
- Always keep the slow cooker covered for the specified cooking time. Each time the lid is removed, it allows heat to escape, adding 15 to 20 minutes to the cooking time. Exception: large cuts of meat should be rotated halfway through cooking for best results.
- Root vegetables take longer to cook than other vegetables, so cut them smaller and put them on the bottom of the cooker.
- Cover raw potatoes with liquid to prevent them from turning dark.

Slow Cooker Safety

Slow cookers heat up more slowly and cook at lower temperatures than other appliances. To keep food safe, follow these guidelines.

- Use ingredients that are completely thawed.
- Keep perishable foods refrigerated until you are ready to put them in the cooker.
- Always cook and drain ground meat just before placing in the cooker—not ahead of time.
- Brown poultry and meats just before placing in the cooker—not ahead of time.
- Whole chickens or meat loaf shouldn't be put in a cooker. The centers can't reach a safe temperature quickly enough.
- Follow recipes exactly for specific sizes when cutting ingredients and for layering so that the dish cooks properly.
- Place leftovers in shallow containers and refrigerate within 2 hours of cooking. Don't use the insert for storage.
- Always reheat foods with your microwave, conventional oven or stovetop before placing in the slow cooker to keep warm until serving. Don't use a slow cooker for heating up food.

Testing Bean Doneness

If you test just one bean when cooking dried beans, you might be fooled into thinking they are all tender. Choose about six beans from different spots in the pan to pierce with a fork. If they all aren't tender, cook them a bit longer.

Tortilla Green Chili

CALORIE SMART • FAST

PREP 15 min **TOTAL** 15 min • 4 servings

- 1 can (15 oz) black beans with cumin and chili, undrained
- 1 can (14.5 oz) diced tomatoes with green chiles, undrained
- 1 bag (12 oz) frozen whole kernel corn
- 1 jar (16 oz) mild green tomatillo salsa
- ½ cup coarsely crushed tortilla chips (about 1 oz)
- 1 avocado, pitted, peeled and cut into cubes
- 1 lime, sliced, then slices cut into quarters
- ¼ cup sour cream
  Additional tortilla chips, if desired.

1 In 4-quart saucepan, stir together beans, tomatoes, corn, salsa and tortilla chips. Heat to boiling; reduce heat to medium.

2 Cover and simmer 5 to 10 minutes, stirring occasionally, until slightly thickened. Top individual servings with avocado, lime, sour cream and if desired, additional tortilla chips.

1 Serving (1½ Cups): Calories 390; Total Fat 13g (Saturated Fat 3g, Trans Fat 0g); Cholesterol 10mg; Sodium 940mg; Total Carbohydrate 56g (Dietary Fiber 14g, Sugars 9g); Protein 12g **Exchanges:** 2 Starch, ½ Fruit, ½ Other Carbohydrate, 1½ Vegetable, ½ Very Lean Meat, 2½ Fat **Carbohydrate Choices:** 4

Tortilla Green Chili

CHAPTER 7

Pasta & Pizza

Spinach Fettuccine

Lasagnotte

Ditalini

Rigatoni

Ziti

Couscous

Gnocchi

Mini Gnocchi

Cellophane Noodles

Couscous (Israeli)

Cheese Ravioletti

Fusilli Bucati

Cheese Ravioli

Spinach Cheese Tortellini

Sausage Ravioli

Cheese Tortellini

Lasagna

Acini di Pepe

Long Ziti

Orzo

Mafalde

Vermicelli

Brown Rice Gluten-Free Spaghetti

Angel Hair

Spaghetti

Linguine

Elbow Macaroni

Gemelli

Tri-Color Rotini

Rotelle

Pappardelle

Radiatore

Campanelle

Fusilli Bucati

Trivelli

Angel Hair Nests

Tagliatelle

Wagon Wheels

Orecchiette

Farfalle (Bow Ties)

Egg Bows

Mezze Penne

Penne

Garganelli

Mostaccioli

Beet Rotini

Fine Egg Noodles

Conchiglioni

Gnocchi

Casarecci

Dumpling Egg Noodles

Torchio

Chiocciole

Manicotti

Lumache

Whole Wheat Elbow Macaroni

Whole Wheat Gobbetti

Whole Wheat Penne

Extra Wide Egg Noodles

Fettuccini

Bucatini

Tagliatelle

Rice Bran Pad Thai

Whole Wheat Linguine

Learn to MAKE PASTA

If you have never made homemade pasta, now is the opportunity to find out how simple it is. The flavor, texture and quality of really fresh pasta are unique and delicious. A pasta machine makes the process go quickly, but the dough can be rolled by hand, too.

Homemade Pasta CALORIE SMART

For hearty sauces, cut pasta wide like fettuccine. For lighter sauces, cut it into thinner strips.

PREP 30 min **TOTAL** 1 hr 55 min • 8 servings

- 2 cups all-purpose flour
- ½ teaspoon salt
- 2 eggs
- ¼ cup water
- 1 tablespoon olive or vegetable oil

1 In medium bowl, mix flour and salt. Make a well in center of flour mixture. Add eggs, water and oil to well; mix thoroughly. (If dough is too dry, mix in enough water to make dough easy to handle. If dough is too sticky, gradually add flour when kneading.)

2 Gather dough into a ball. On lightly floured surface, knead 5 to 10 minutes or until smooth and springy. Cover with plastic wrap or foil; let stand 15 minutes.

3 Divide dough into 4 equal parts. On lightly floured surface, roll one-fourth of dough at a time (keep remaining dough covered) into rectangle 1⁄16 to 1⁄8 inch thick (if using pasta machine*, pass dough through machine until 1⁄16 inch thick). Loosely fold rectangle crosswise into thirds. Cut crosswise into 2-inch strips for lasagna, ¼-inch strips for fettuccine or 1⁄8-inch strips for linguine. Unfold and gently shake out. Hang pasta on pasta drying rack or arrange in single layer on lightly floured towels; let stand 30 minutes or until dry.

4 In stockpot, heat 4 quarts water (salted if desired) to boiling; add pasta. Boil uncovered 2 to 5 minutes, stirring occasionally, until firm but tender. Begin testing for doneness when pasta rises to surface of water; drain.

1 Serving: Calories 150; Total Fat 3.5g (Saturated Fat 0.5g, Trans Fat 0g); Cholesterol 55mg; Sodium 160mg; Total Carbohydrate 24g (Dietary Fiber 0g, Sugars 0g); Protein 5g **Exchanges:** 1½ Starch, ½ Fat **Carbohydrate Choices:** 1½

*Our recipes were not developed for or tested in electric extrusion pasta machines. We recommend following manufacturer's directions.

Herb Pasta Add 1 tablespoon chopped fresh herbs to flour mixture before adding eggs.

Gluten-Free Pasta Substitute Betty Crocker Gluten Free all-purpose rice flour blend for the all-purpose flour and use ⅓ cup water instead of ¼ cup water. Make pasta as directed, except in Step 3, divide dough into 6 equal parts instead of 4. Gluten-free dough is more fragile than regular dough and can break easily, so smaller dough portions work best.

Ravioli To make homemade ravioli, see Four-Cheese Homemade Ravioli (page 172).

Whole Wheat Pasta Make as directed—except use 3 cups whole wheat or white whole wheat flour and 5 eggs, beaten. Omit water.

Cutting Homemade Pasta

On lightly floured surface, roll one-fourth of dough at a time into rectangle 1⁄16 to 1⁄8 inch thick (keep remaining dough covered).

Loosely fold rectangle crosswise into thirds.

Cut pasta crosswise into 2-inch strips for lasagna, ¼-inch strips for fettuccine or 1⁄8-inch strips for linguine.

Unfold and gently shake out strips. Hang strips on pasta drying rack or arrange in single layer on lightly floured towels.

Make a well in the center of the flour mixture. Add eggs, water and oil to well.

Pass the dough through pasta machine until dough is 1/16 to 1/8 inch thick.

To cut pasta with pasta machine, insert handle in hole for desired pasta shape; slowly pass dough through machine.

Arrange pasta in single layer on lightly floured towels, about 30 minutes or until dry.

Tips for Making Fresh Pasta

- If rolling the dough by hand, use a large wooden board or laminated counter. Avoid cold surfaces like granite, metal or marble because the dough tends to stick.

- Pasta dough that is dry will be fragile, so handle carefully. Keep dough covered with plastic wrap until ready to roll and cut.

- Be sure water is boiling before adding pasta. Do not rinse pasta after cooking. Drain carefully and toss with 1 to 2 teaspoons olive oil.

- Store fresh uncooked pasta, tightly wrapped, up to 2 days in the refrigerator or up to 2 weeks in the freezer.

Pasta can be cut into several widths: 2 inches (lasagna), 1/4 inch (fettuccine) or 1/8 inch (linguine).

Four-Cheese Homemade Ravioli   CALORIE SMART • EASY

*Homemade ravioli is easy and fun to make!
Serve with your favorite sauce or one of ours, such
as Italian Tomato Sauce (page 174), Bolognese
(page 180), Basil Pesto (page 456) or Creamy
Tomato-Vodka Sauce (page 174).*

PREP 1 hr **TOTAL** 1 hr 15 min • 5 servings

PASTA
Homemade Pasta (page 170)

FILLING
- ¾ cup ricotta cheese (from 15-oz container)
- ¼ cup shredded fontina cheese (1 oz)
- ¼ cup shredded Parmesan cheese (1 oz)
- ¼ cup shredded mozzarella cheese (1 oz)

1 Make pasta as directed through Step 2.
Divide dough into 4 equal parts. On lightly
floured surface, roll one-fourth of dough at
a time (keep remaining dough covered with
damp towel) into rectangle ¹⁄₁₆ to ⅛ inch thick
(if using hand-crank pasta machine, pass dough
through machine until ¹⁄₁₆ inch thick). Trim
dough into 4 (14x4-inch) rectangles. Cover with
damp towel until ready to fill.

2 In medium bowl, mix filling ingredients until
well blended. On 1 dough rectangle, place
10 mounds of filling (using slightly less than
1 measuring tablespoon for each mound) about
1½ inches apart in 2 rows. Moisten dough
lightly around mounds with water; top with
second rectangle of dough, lining up edges of
sheets. Press gently around edges to seal. Cut
between mounds, using pizza cutter, pastry

Four-Cheese Homemade Ravioli

wheel or knife, into 10 squares. Trim any
uneven edges and reseal if needed. Repeat with
remaining dough and filling.

3 In 8-quart Dutch oven or stockpot, heat
4 quarts water (salted if desired) to boiling; add
ravioli. Boil uncovered 7 to 10 minutes, stirring
occasionally, until tender (ravioli will rise to the
top during first few minutes). Remove ravioli
with large slotted spoon to colander to drain;
do not rinse. Do not dump pasta and water into
colander to drain or ravioli will break open.
Serve with your favorite sauce.

1 Serving (4 Ravioli): Calories 340; Total Fat 13g (Saturated
Fat 6g, Trans Fat 0g); Cholesterol 100mg; Sodium 480mg;
Total Carbohydrate 41g (Dietary Fiber 1g, Sugars 0g); Protein 16g
Exchanges: 2 Starch, ½ Other Carbohydrate, 1½ Medium-Fat Meat,
1 Fat **Carbohydrate Choices:** 3

Bacon, Chive and Parmesan Ravioli Make
pasta as directed. Omit filling ingredients. In
medium bowl, mix 1 container (8 oz) chives-
and-onion cream cheese, 6 slices bacon, crisply
cooked and crumbled, and ¼ cup grated
Parmesan cheese until well blended. Continue
as directed.

Making and Cutting Ravioli

Trim dough into 4
rectangles. Cover
with damp towel until
ready to fill.

Place 10 mounds of filling
(about 1½ inches apart) in 2
rows on each of two dough
rectangles.

Top with second rectangles
of dough, lining up edges of
sheets. Press gently between
mounds and dough edges to
seal filling inside each ravioli.

Cut between mounds,
using a pizza cutter, pastry
wheel or knife into 10
squares. Trim any uneven
edges and reseal if needed.

Potato Gnocchi

LIGHTER Directions For 2 grams of fat and 100 calories per serving, substitute ½ cup fat-free egg product for the eggs.

Potato Gnocchi

Potato gnocchi are small dumplings made from potatoes; their flavor and texture are similar to fresh pasta. Serve with your favorite pasta sauce or toss with melted butter.

PREP 20 min **TOTAL** 1 hr • 6 servings

- 2 medium russet potatoes (6 oz each)
- 1 teaspoon salt
- 2 eggs
- 2 to 2⅓ cups all-purpose flour
- 1 tablespoon salt

1 In 4-quart Dutch oven or saucepan, place potatoes and enough water to cover. Heat to boiling. Cover and boil about 30 minutes or until tender; drain and cool slightly. Peel potatoes; mash in large bowl until smooth. Cool.

2 Stir 1 teaspoon salt, the eggs and enough of the flour into mashed potatoes to make a stiff dough. Shape into 1-inch oval balls. To make the traditional ridges in gnocchi, use a gnocchi board or fork (see below).

3 In 6- to 8-quart Dutch oven or stockpot, heat about 4 quarts water and 1 tablespoon salt to boiling. Add about one-fourth of the gnocchi. After gnocchi rise to surface, boil uncovered 4 minutes. Remove with slotted spoon; drain. Repeat with remaining gnocchi.

1 Serving: Calories 220; Total Fat 2g (Saturated Fat 0.5g, Trans Fat 0g); Cholesterol 70mg; Sodium 470mg; Total Carbohydrate 43g (Dietary Fiber 2g, Sugars 0g); Protein 7g **Exchanges:** 3 Starch **Carbohydrate Choices:** 3

Spaetzle   CALORIE SMART • FAST

The word spaetzle *is German for "little sparrow," which is what these tiny noodles or dumplings look like. Serve them as a side dish tossed with a little melted butter—as you would serve potatoes or rice—or topped with a creamy sauce or gravy.*

PREP 25 min **TOTAL** 25 min • 6 servings

- 2 eggs, beaten
- ¼ cup milk or water
- 1 cup all-purpose flour
- ¼ teaspoon salt
  Dash pepper
- 1 tablespoon butter

1 Fill 4-quart Dutch oven or saucepan half full with water; heat to boiling. In medium bowl, mix eggs, milk, flour, salt and pepper with fork (batter will be thick).

2 Press a few tablespoons of the batter at a time through colander with ¼-inch holes, or spaetzle maker, into boiling water. Stir once or twice to prevent sticking. Cook 2 to 5 minutes or until spaetzle rise to surface and are tender; drain. Toss with butter.

1 Serving: Calories 120; Total Fat 4g (Saturated Fat 1.5g, Trans Fat 0g); Cholesterol 75mg; Sodium 135mg; Total Carbohydrate 17g (Dietary Fiber 0g, Sugars 0g); Protein 5g **Exchanges:** 1 Starch, 1 Fat **Carbohydrate Choices:** 1

Making Spaetzle

Press a few tablespoons batter at a time through spaetzle maker or colander with ¼-inch holes into boiling water.

Cook until spaetzle rise to surface and are tender.

Shaping Potato Gnocchi

To make traditional ridges in gnocchi, roll each 1-inch oval ball over gnocchi board.

Or make ridges by rolling each gnocchi over the tines of the back side of a table fork.

Cacio e Pepe FAST

Cacio e pepe translates to "cheese and pepper" and is a very simple, zesty pasta dish that can be made quickly.

PREP 25 min **TOTAL** 25 min ● 6 servings

 1 tablespoon salt
 1 package (16 oz) spaghetti
 ¼ cup olive oil
 2 teaspoons coarsely ground black pepper
 1½ cups finely shredded Pecorino Romano cheese (6 oz)
 Chopped fresh parsley, if desired

1 In 8-quart Dutch oven or stockpot, heat about 5 quarts water and salt to boiling. Add spaghetti; cook as directed on package. Remove 1 cup of the cooking water; set aside. Drain spaghetti but do not rinse; set aside.

2 In Dutch oven, heat oil over medium heat. Add pepper; cook 1 minute, stirring constantly. Add ¾ cup of the cooking water; heat until simmering. Add spaghetti; sprinkle with cheese. Toss with tongs until mixture clings to spaghetti. If mixture seems dry, add remaining ¼ cup reserved cooking water (pasta dish will not be saucy).

3 Sprinkle with parsley. Serve with additional cheese.

1 Serving: Calories 520; Total Fat 19g (Saturated Fat 6g, Trans Fat 0g); Cholesterol 30mg; Sodium 640mg; Total Carbohydrate 67g (Dietary Fiber 4g, Sugars 1g); Protein 21g **Exchanges:** 4 Starch, ½ Other Carbohydrate, 1 High-Fat Meat, 2 Fat **Carbohydrate Choices:** 4½

Angel Hair Pasta with Basil, Avocado and Tomatoes FAST

PREP 20 min **TOTAL** 20 min ● 6 servings

 8 oz uncooked angel hair (capellini) pasta
 2 tablespoons olive or vegetable oil
 2 cloves garlic, finely chopped
 ¾ cup chopped fresh basil leaves
 1 ripe small avocado, pitted, peeled and diced
 4 medium tomatoes, cut into small cubes
 ½ teaspoon salt
 ¼ teaspoon pepper

1 Cook and drain pasta as directed on package.

2 Meanwhile, in 3-quart saucepan, heat oil over medium heat. Cook garlic in oil about 5 minutes, stirring occasionally, until tender but not brown. Remove from heat; stir in basil, avocado and tomatoes.

3 In large bowl, gently toss vegetable mixture with pasta. Sprinkle with salt and pepper.

1 Serving: Calories 260; Total Fat 8g (Saturated Fat 1g, Trans Fat 0g); Cholesterol 0mg; Sodium 350mg; Total Carbohydrate 38g (Dietary Fiber 4g, Sugars 3g); Protein 7g **Exchanges:** 2 Starch, 1 Vegetable, 1½ Fat **Carbohydrate Choices:** 2½

Angel Hair Pasta with Chicken Stir 1 cup shredded cooked chicken into mixture with the tomatoes. Cook just until heated.

Angel Hair Pasta with Shrimp Stir ½ pound cooked medium shrimp into mixture with the tomatoes. Cook just until heated.

Cacio e Pepe

Chicken and Spaghetti Carbonara Add 2 cups cut-up cooked chicken in Step 4 before heating.

Fettuccine Alfredo FAST

Here's our version of the famous dish created in the early 1990s by restaurateur Alfredo di Lello in Rome. It is just as rich with butter and cheese as the original was then. The combination of whipping cream and Parmesan cheese is the secret to thickening this sauce.

PREP 25 min **TOTAL** 25 min • 4 servings

  8 oz uncooked fettuccine (for homemade fettuccine, see page 170)

    ALFREDO SAUCE

  ½ cup butter, cut into pieces

  ½ cup whipping cream

  ¾ cup grated Parmesan cheese

  ½ teaspoon salt

    Dash pepper

    Chopped fresh parsley, if desired

1 Cook and drain fettuccine as directed on package.

2 Meanwhile, in 10-inch skillet, heat butter and whipping cream over medium heat, stirring frequently, until butter is melted and mixture starts to bubble. Reduce heat to low; simmer uncovered 6 minutes, stirring frequently, until slightly thickened. Remove from heat. Stir in cheese, salt and pepper.

3 In large bowl, toss fettuccine with sauce until well coated. Sprinkle with parsley.

1 Serving: Calories 570; Total Fat 40g (Saturated Fat 21g, Trans Fat 2g); Cholesterol 155mg; Sodium 810mg; Total Carbohydrate 38g (Dietary Fiber 2g, Sugars 2g); Protein 15g **Exchanges:** 2½ Starch, 1 High-Fat Meat, 5½ Fat **Carbohydrate Choices:** 2½

LIGHTER Directions For 17 grams of fat and 370 calories per serving, reduce butter to ¼ cup and Parmesan cheese to ⅓ cup; substitute evaporated milk for the whipping cream.

Chicken Fettuccine Alfredo Stir in 1½ cups diced cooked chicken with the cheese, salt and pepper in Step 2.

Fettuccine Alfredo with Baby Spinach Omit parsley. Add 1 cup fresh baby spinach when tossing the fettuccine in Step 3. Toss until the spinach wilts.

Spaghetti Carbonara

Spaghetti Carbonara FAST

PREP 25 min **TOTAL** 25 min • 6 servings

  1 package (16 oz) spaghetti

  1 clove garlic, finely chopped

  6 slices bacon, cut into 1-inch pieces

  3 pasteurized eggs,* beaten, or ¾ cup fat-free egg product

  1 tablespoon olive or vegetable oil

  ½ cup freshly grated Parmesan cheese

  ½ cup freshly grated Romano cheese

  2 tablespoons chopped fresh parsley

  ¼ teaspoon pepper

    Additional grated Parmesan cheese, if desired

    Freshly ground pepper, if desired

1 In 4-quart Dutch oven or saucepan, cook spaghetti as directed on package; drain and return to Dutch oven.

2 Meanwhile, in 10-inch skillet, cook garlic and bacon over medium heat, stirring occasionally, until bacon is crisp; drain.

3 In small bowl, mix eggs, oil, Parmesan and Romano cheeses, parsley and ¼ teaspoon pepper.

4 Add bacon mixture and egg mixture to hot cooked spaghetti. Cook over low heat, tossing constantly, until egg mixture coats spaghetti. Serve with additional Parmesan cheese and freshly ground pepper.

*Pasteurized eggs are uncooked eggs that have been heat-treated to kill bacteria that can cause food poisoning and gastrointestinal distress. Because the eggs in this recipe are not cooked, be sure to use pasteurized eggs. They can be found in the dairy case at large supermarkets. Fat-free egg product is also pasteurized.

1 Serving: Calories 450; Total Fat 13g (Saturated Fat 5g, Trans Fat 0g); Cholesterol 25mg; Sodium 450mg; Total Carbohydrate 62g (Dietary Fiber 5g, Sugars 2g); Protein 22g **Exchanges:** 4 Starch, ½ Medium-Fat Meat **Carbohydrate Choices:** 4

Heirloom Recipe and New Twist

A staple of northern Italy, Bolognese is a hearty, thick and creamy tomato and meat sauce made with canned tomatoes, wine and milk or cream. In contrast, the Short Rib and Sausage Ragù is a very rich meat sauce that has very little tomato and no milk or cream. Make either recipe 1 to 2 days ahead and reheat before serving for the best flavor.

HEIRLOOM

Bolognese   CALORIE SMART

PREP 25 min **TOTAL** 1 hr 10 min • 6 cups

- 2 tablespoons olive or vegetable oil
- 1 tablespoon butter
- 2 medium carrots, finely chopped (1 cup)
- 1 medium stalk celery, finely chopped (½ cup)
- 1 medium onion, chopped (½ cup)
- 2 cloves garlic, finely chopped
- 1 lb lean (at least 80%) ground beef
- ¼ cup chopped pancetta or bacon
- ½ cup dry red wine, nonalcoholic red wine or beef broth
- 3 cans (28 oz each) whole tomatoes, drained, chopped
- 1 teaspoon dried oregano leaves
- ½ teaspoon pepper
- ½ cup milk or whipping cream

1 In 12-inch skillet, heat oil and butter over medium-high heat. Add carrots, celery, onion and garlic; cook, stirring frequently, until crisp-tender. Stir in beef and pancetta. Cook 8 to 10 minutes, stirring occasionally, until beef is thoroughly cooked; drain.

2 Stir in wine. Heat to boiling; reduce heat to low. Simmer uncovered until wine has evaporated. Stir in tomatoes, oregano and pepper. Heat to boiling; reduce heat to low. Cover and simmer 45 minutes, stirring occasionally. Remove from heat; stir in milk.

3 Use sauce immediately, or cover and refrigerate up to 48 hours or freeze up to 2 months.

½ **Cup:** Calories 100; Total Fat 4g (Saturated Fat 1g, Trans Fat 0g); Cholesterol 25mg; Sodium 360mg; Total Carbohydrate 8g (Dietary Fiber 2g, Sugars 4g); Protein 9g **Exchanges:** 1½ Vegetable, 1 Medium-Fat Meat **Carbohydrate Choices:** ½

Bolognese

Short Rib and Sausage Ragù

Short Rib and Sausage Ragù

PREP 45 min **TOTAL** 3 hr 45 min • 8 servings

- 3 lb boneless beef short ribs
- 1 teaspoon salt
- 2 tablespoons olive oil
- ¼ cup finely chopped carrot
- ¼ cup finely chopped celery
- ¼ cup finely chopped onion
- 2 cloves garlic, finely chopped
- ¼ lb mild bulk Italian sausage
- ½ cup dry red wine
- 2 tablespoons tomato paste
- 1 tablespoon all-purpose flour
- 3½ cups reduced-sodium beef broth (for homemade broth, see page 146)
- ¼ teaspoon pepper
- 2 slices bacon, crisply cooked, crumbled
- 2 sprigs (5 inch) fresh thyme
- 2 sprigs (5 inch) fresh rosemary
  Hot cooked pappardelle or rigatoni pasta, if desired
  Shredded Parmesan cheese, if desired

1 Rub all sides of ribs with salt. In 6-quart ovenproof Dutch oven or stockpot, heat oil over medium-high heat. Cook ribs in oil 6 to 8 minutes, turning frequently, until brown on all sides (brown in batches if necessary). Remove ribs; set aside.

2 Add carrot, celery, onion, garlic and sausage to Dutch oven. Cook over medium heat 6 to 8 minutes, stirring frequently and scraping up any browned bits, until sausage is brown; drain if necessary. Stir in wine. Heat to boiling; reduce heat. Simmer uncovered about 6 minutes or until wine is almost evaporated.

3 Heat oven to 350°F. Add tomato paste and flour to mixture in Dutch oven; stir until well blended. Gradually stir in 2½ cups of the broth. Add pepper and bacon. Tie herb sprigs together with kitchen string; place in broth. Place ribs in broth, turning to coat all sides (ribs may not fit in single layer).

4 Cover and bake 2 hours 30 minutes to 3 hours or until ribs begin to fall apart when tested with fork. Remove ribs. Skim fat from mixture in Dutch oven. Cut excess fat from ribs and discard. Pull ribs into 1-inch pieces; return to Dutch oven. (This type of ragù isn't meant to be saucy, but if desired, gently stir desired amount of remaining 1 cup broth into mixture to moisten without making it soupy, being careful not to break up meat pieces.) Heat until hot. Serve over pasta; sprinkle with cheese.

1 Serving: Calories 440; Total Fat 31g (Saturated Fat 11g, Trans Fat 1g); Cholesterol 125mg; Sodium 750mg; Total Carbohydrate 3g (Dietary Fiber 0g, Sugars 1g); Protein 35g **Exchanges:** 5 Medium-Fat Meat, 1 Fat **Carbohydrate Choices:** 0

Italian Sausage with Tomatoes and Penne CALORIE SMART • FAST

PREP 30 min **TOTAL** 30 min • 4 servings

- 3 cups uncooked penne pasta (9 oz)
- 1 lb Italian sausage links, cut crosswise into ¼-inch slices
- ½ cup beef broth (for homemade broth, see page 146)
- 1 medium yellow summer squash, cut in half lengthwise, then cut crosswise into ¼-inch slices
- 1 pint (2 cups) grape or cherry tomatoes, cut in half lengthwise
- ¼ cup chopped fresh or 1 tablespoon dried basil leaves
- 6 green onions, cut into ½-inch pieces
- 2 tablespoons olive oil
  Shaved Parmesan cheese, if desired

1 Cook and drain pasta as directed on package.

2 Meanwhile, spray 12-inch skillet with cooking spray; heat over medium-high heat. Add sausage; cook 4 to 6 minutes, stirring frequently, until brown. Stir in broth; reduce heat to medium. Cover and cook 5 minutes.

3 Stir in squash, tomatoes and 2 tablespoons of the basil. Heat to boiling; reduce heat to low. Cover and simmer 5 minutes, stirring occasionally. Stir in onions. Simmer uncovered 1 minute.

4 In large bowl, toss pasta, oil and remaining 2 tablespoons basil. Divide pasta among individual bowls; top evenly with sausage mixture. Serve with cheese.

1 Serving: Calories 490; Total Fat 31g (Saturated Fat 9g, Trans Fat 0g); Cholesterol 70mg; Sodium 1140mg; Total Carbohydrate 30g (Dietary Fiber 3g, Sugars 5g); Protein 21g **Exchanges:** 1 Starch, ½ Other Carbohydrate, 2 Vegetable, 2 High-Fat Meat, 3 Fat **Carbohydrate Choices:** 2

Spaghetti with White Clam Sauce FAST

PREP 20 min **TOTAL** 20 min • 4 servings

- 1 package (7 oz) spaghetti
- ¼ cup butter or olive oil
- 2 cloves garlic, finely chopped
- 2 tablespoons chopped fresh parsley
- 2 cans (6.5 oz each) minced clams, undrained
- ½ cup grated Parmesan cheese
  Additional chopped fresh parsley

1 Cook and drain spaghetti as directed on package.

2 Meanwhile, in 1½-quart saucepan, melt butter over medium heat. Cook garlic in butter about 3 minutes, stirring occasionally, until light golden. Stir in 2 tablespoons parsley and the clams. Heat to boiling; reduce heat. Simmer uncovered 3 to 5 minutes.

3 In large bowl, toss spaghetti and clam sauce. Sprinkle with cheese and additional parsley.

1 Serving: Calories 480; Total Fat 18g (Saturated Fat 8g, Trans Fat 1g); Cholesterol 100mg; Sodium 410mg; Total Carbohydrate 45g (Dietary Fiber 3g, Sugars 0g); Protein 36g **Exchanges:** 3 Starch, 3 Medium-Fat Meat, ½ Fat **Carbohydrate Choices:** 3

Linguine with White Clam Sauce and Basil

Substitute linguine for the spaghetti and chopped basil for the parsley.

Bucatini with Clam-Mushroom Sauce

Substitute bucatini or any other long-shaped pasta for the spaghetti. Cook 1 cup sliced mushrooms in butter 2 minutes before adding garlic. Stir in ½ teaspoon fresh thyme leaves just before serving.

Spaghetti with White Clam Sauce

Spanish Clams, Sausage and Linguine CALORIE SMART

PREP 25 min **TOTAL** 45 min • 6 servings

- ½ lb bulk spicy Italian pork sausage
- 3 medium onions, chopped (1½ cups)
- 2 medium carrots, chopped (1 cup)
- 3 cloves garlic, finely chopped
- 1 can (28 oz) crushed tomatoes, undrained
- 2 cans (14.5 oz each) diced tomatoes with roasted garlic, undrained
- ½ cup dry red wine or clam juice
- 1½ teaspoons ground cumin
- 1 teaspoon dried rosemary leaves, crushed
- ½ cup small pimiento-stuffed olives, coarsely chopped
- 12 oz uncooked linguine
- 24 littleneck clams (about 2 lb), scrubbed*
  Grated Pecorino Romano or Parmesan cheese, if desired

1 In 4-quart Dutch oven, cook sausage, onions, carrots and garlic over medium-high heat 5 to 7 minutes, stirring frequently, until sausage is no longer pink; drain.

2 Stir in remaining ingredients except linguine, clams, and cheese. Heat to boiling; reduce heat to medium-low. Partially cover and simmer 10 minutes. Meanwhile, cook and drain linguine as directed on package.

3 Add clams to sausage mixture. Cover and cook over medium-high heat 5 to 7 minutes or until clams open. Discard any unopened clams. Serve clam sauce over linguine, sprinkled with cheese.

*Or substitute 3 cans (10 oz each) drained whole clams for the fresh clams.

1 Serving: Calories 440; Total Fat 11g (Saturated Fat 3g, Trans Fat 0g); Cholesterol 35mg; Sodium 870mg; Total Carbohydrate 65g (Dietary Fiber 8g, Sugars 10g); Protein 21g **Exchanges:** 3 Starch, 4 Vegetable, ½ Medium-Fat Meat, 1 Fat **Carbohydrate Choices:** 4

Littleneck Clams

Littleneck clams are the smallest hardshell clam found on the East Coast. Their shell diameter is less than 2 inches. They are also known by their Indian name, quahog. Pacific littlenecks are usually slightly larger, with shells about 2½ inches in diameter.

Spanish Clams, Sausage and Linguine

Chicken- and Spinach-Stuffed Shells

PREP 30 min **TOTAL** 1 hr 10 min • 6 servings

- 18 uncooked jumbo pasta shells
- 1 container (15 oz) whole-milk ricotta cheese
- 1 egg, slightly beaten
- ¼ cup grated Parmesan cheese
- 2 cups frozen cut-leaf spinach, thawed, squeezed to drain
- 1 cup chopped cooked chicken
- 1 jar (26 oz) tomato pasta sauce (for homemade sauce, see page 174)
- 2 cups shredded Italian cheese blend (8 oz)

1 Heat oven to 350°F. Cook and drain pasta shells as directed on package, using minimum cook time. Rinse with cold water to cool; drain.

2 Meanwhile, in medium bowl, mix ricotta cheese, egg, Parmesan cheese, spinach and chicken.

3 Spread 1 cup of the pasta sauce in bottom of ungreased 13x9-inch (3-quart) glass baking dish. Spoon about 2 tablespoons ricotta mixture into each pasta shell. Arrange shells, filled sides up, on sauce in baking dish. Spoon remaining sauce over stuffed shells.

4 Cover and bake 30 minutes. Uncover; sprinkle with Italian cheese blend. Bake 5 to 10 minutes longer or until cheese is melted.

1 Serving: Calories 570; Total Fat 28g (Saturated Fat 15g, Trans Fat 0.5g); Cholesterol 120mg; Sodium 1330mg; Total Carbohydrate 48g (Dietary Fiber 4g, Sugars 12g); Protein 33g
Exchanges: 3 Starch, 1 Vegetable, 3 Medium-Fat Meat, 2 Fat
Carbohydrate Choices: 3

MAKE-AHEAD Directions Make as directed through Step 3. Cover tightly and refrigerate up to 24 hours. Add 5 to 10 minutes to the first bake time before topping with cheese.

Cheesy Rigatoni with Eggplant Sauce

PREP 20 min **TOTAL** 50 min • 4 servings

- 2½ cups uncooked rigatoni pasta (7½ oz)
- 2 tablespoons olive oil
- 1 medium onion, chopped (½ cup)
- 1 small unpeeled eggplant, cut into ½-inch cubes (3 cups)
- 1 medium zucchini, halved lengthwise, cut into ¼-inch slices (1½ cups)
- 1 can (14.5 oz) diced tomatoes with basil, garlic and oregano, undrained
- 1 can (8 oz) tomato sauce
- 1½ cups shredded mozzarella cheese (6 oz)

1 Heat oven to 350°F. Spray 12x8-inch (2-quart) glass baking dish with cooking spray. Cook and drain pasta as directed on package, using minimum cook time.

2 Meanwhile, in 12-inch nonstick skillet, heat oil over medium-high heat. Add onion, eggplant and zucchini; cook 5 to 7 minutes, stirring frequently, until crisp-tender. Stir in tomatoes and tomato sauce.

3 Spoon cooked pasta into baking dish. Spoon vegetable sauce over pasta.

4 Cover and bake 20 minutes. Uncover; sprinkle with mozzarella cheese. Bake 5 to 7 minutes longer or until cheese is melted.

1 Serving (2 Cups): Calories 540; Total Fat 17g (Saturated Fat 6g, Trans Fat 0g); Cholesterol 25mg; Sodium 1000mg; Total Carbohydrate 71g (Dietary Fiber 8g, Sugars 11g); Protein 25g
Exchanges: 4 Starch, 2 Vegetable, 1 Medium-Fat Meat, 2 Fat
Carbohydrate Choices: 5

MAKE-AHEAD Directions Make as directed through Step 3. Cover and refrigerate up to 24 hours. Bake about 10 minutes longer before topping with the cheese.

Chicken- and Spinach-Stuffed Shells

Cheesy Rigatoni with Eggplant Sauce

Macaroni and Cheese

Once you've tasted the depth of flavor in our homemade mac and cheese, you'll see why it's the perfect choice for the entire family. Don't even try to compare it to the box variety—it's in a league of its own.

PREP 25 min **TOTAL** 50 min • 4 servings

2½	cups elbow macaroni (7 oz)
¼	cup butter
¼	cup all-purpose flour
½	teaspoon salt
¼	teaspoon pepper
¼	teaspoon ground mustard
¼	teaspoon Worcestershire sauce
2	cups milk or half-and-half
2	cups shredded sharp Cheddar cheese (8 oz)

1 Heat oven to 350°F. Cook and drain macaroni as directed on package, using minimum cook time.

2 Meanwhile, in 3-quart saucepan, melt butter over low heat. Stir in flour, salt, pepper, mustard and Worcestershire sauce. Cook over low heat, stirring constantly, until mixture is smooth and bubbly; remove from heat.

3 Stir in milk. Heat to boiling, stirring constantly. Boil and stir 1 minute; remove from heat. Stir in cheese until melted. Gently stir macaroni into cheese sauce.

4 Pour into ungreased 2-quart casserole. Bake uncovered 20 to 25 minutes or until bubbly.

1 Serving (1 Cup): Calories 610; Total Fat 34g (Saturated Fat 19g, Trans Fat 1g); Cholesterol 100mg; Sodium 980mg; Total Carbohydrate 51g (Dietary Fiber 3g, Sugars 8g); Protein 26g **Exchanges:** 3 Starch, ½ Low-Fat Milk, 2 High-Fat Meat, 2½ Fat **Carbohydrate Choices:** 3½

STOVE-TOP Directions Cook and drain macaroni as directed on package. Continue as directed in Steps 2 and 3; omit Step 4.

LIGHTER Directions For 10 grams of fat and 390 calories per serving, reduce butter to 2 tablespoons. Use fat-free (skim) milk and 1½ cups reduced-fat Cheddar cheese (6 oz).

Bacon Macaroni and Cheese Stir in ⅔ cup crumbled crisply cooked bacon with macaroni in Step 3.

Caramelized Onion Macaroni and Cheese Stir in 1 cup Caramelized Onions (page 246) with macaroni in Step 3.

Fire-Roasted Tomato Macaroni and Cheese Stir in ½ teaspoon smoked paprika with flour in Step 2. Add 1 can (14.5 oz) fire-roasted diced tomatoes, drained, with macaroni in Step 3.

Bacon, Kale and Tomato Macaroni and Cheese In Step 3, stir in 4 slices cooked crumbled bacon, 1 cup finely chopped fresh kale (stems removed) and 1 can (14.5 oz) drained fire-roasted tomatoes with macaroni. Bake 15 minutes; stir. Mix 1 tablespoon melted butter with ½ cup panko bread crumbs; sprinkle over top. Bake 10 to 15 minutes longer or until topping is golden brown.

Lobster Macaroni and Cheese Add ⅛ teaspoon each ground red pepper (cayenne) and ground nutmeg with the flour in Step 2. Substitute ¾ cup each shredded fontina and Gruyère cheese for 1½ cups of the Cheddar. Stir in 2 cups cooked lobster pieces with macaroni in Step 3.

Southwest Macaroni and Cheese Omit ground mustard and Worcestershire sauce. Add 2 teaspoons ground ancho chile pepper or chili powder, ½ teaspoon ground cumin and ¼ teaspoon garlic powder with the flour in Step 2. Stir in 1 can (4.5 oz) diced green chiles, ¼ cup thinly sliced green onions, ¼ cup diced bell pepper and ¼ cup chopped fresh cilantro with macaroni in Step 3. Top with coarsely crushed corn chips before serving.

Bacon, Kale, and Tomato Macaroni and Cheese

Italian Sausage Lasagna

PREP 1 hr **TOTAL** 2 hr • 8 servings

- 1 lb bulk Italian pork sausage*
- 1 medium onion, chopped (½ cup)
- 1 clove garlic, finely chopped
- 3 tablespoons chopped fresh parsley
- 1 tablespoon chopped fresh or 1 teaspoon dried basil leaves
- 1 teaspoon sugar
- 1 can (15 oz) tomato sauce
- 1 can (14.5 oz) whole tomatoes, undrained
- 8 uncooked lasagna noodles
- 1 container (15 to 16 oz) ricotta cheese or small-curd cottage cheese
- ½ cup grated Parmesan cheese
- 1 tablespoon chopped fresh or 1½ teaspoons dried oregano leaves
- 2 cups shredded mozzarella cheese (8 oz)

1 In 10-inch skillet, cook sausage, onion and garlic over medium heat 8 to 10 minutes, stirring occasionally, until sausage is no longer pink; drain.

2 Stir in 2 tablespoons of the parsley, the basil, sugar, tomato sauce and tomatoes, breaking up tomatoes. Heat to boiling, stirring occasionally; reduce heat. Simmer uncovered about 45 minutes or until slightly thickened.

3 Heat oven to 350°F. Cook and drain noodles as directed on package, using minimum cook time. Meanwhile, in small bowl, mix ricotta cheese, ¼ cup of the Parmesan cheese, the oregano and remaining 1 tablespoon parsley.

4 In ungreased 13x9-inch (3-quart) glass baking dish, spread half of the sausage mixture (about 2 cups). Top with 4 noodles. Spread half of the ricotta cheese mixture (about 1 cup) over noodles. Sprinkle with half of the mozzarella cheese. Repeat layers, ending with mozzarella. Sprinkle with remaining ¼ cup Parmesan cheese.

5 Cover and bake 30 minutes. Uncover; bake about 15 minutes longer or until hot and bubbly. Let stand 15 minutes before cutting.

*Or substitute 1 pound lean (at least 90%) ground beef for the sausage.

1 Serving: Calories 430; Total Fat 23g (Saturated Fat 11g, Trans Fat 0g); Cholesterol 70mg; Sodium 1110mg; Total Carbohydrate 28g (Dietary Fiber 3g, Sugars 6g); Protein 28g **Exchanges:** 2 Starch, 3 Medium-Fat Meat, 1 Fat **Carbohydrate Choices:** 2

MAKE-AHEAD **Directions** Cover unbaked lasagna with foil; refrigerate no longer than 24 hours or freeze up to 2 months. Bake covered 45 minutes, then bake uncovered 15 to 20 minutes longer (35 to 45 minutes if frozen). Check the center and bake a little longer if necessary, until hot and bubbly.

Easy Italian Sausage Lasagna Substitute 4 cups (from two 26- to 28-oz jars) tomato pasta sauce with meat for the first 8 ingredients. Omit Steps 1 and 2.

Garden Vegetable Lasagna Substitute 1 jar (26 oz) chunky vegetable tomato pasta sauce for the first 8 ingredients. Heat 1 tablespoon olive oil in 10-inch skillet. Add 3 cups frozen broccoli cuts, 1½ cups sliced fresh mushrooms, 1 cup chopped bell pepper and ½ teaspoon garlic powder. Cook and stir 3 to 4 minutes, or until vegetables are crisp-tender. Stir in pasta sauce. Layer noodles, sauce, ricotta mixture and mozzarella cheese as directed in Step 4. Bake as directed.

Lasagna Noodles

There are a variety of brands of lasagna noodles. Cook the noodles in boiling water, following the directions on the package, just until tender or al dente. If the noodles are overcooked, they might fall apart while you are layering the lasagna. After cooking the noodles, place them in cold water until you're ready to layer. This keeps them from sticking together.

Italian Sausage Lasagna

Manicotti

Manicotti

PREP 40 min **TOTAL** 1 hr 35 min • 7 servings

- 14 uncooked manicotti pasta shells
- 1 lb lean (at least 80%) ground beef
- 1 cup sliced fresh mushrooms (3 oz)*
- 1 large onion, chopped (1 cup)
- 2 cloves garlic, finely chopped
- 1 jar (26 to 28 oz) tomato pasta sauce (for homemade sauce, see page 174)
- 2 boxes (9 oz each) frozen chopped spinach, thawed
- 2 cups small-curd cottage cheese
- ⅓ cup grated Parmesan cheese
- ¼ teaspoon ground nutmeg
- ¼ teaspoon pepper
- 2 cups shredded mozzarella cheese (8 oz)
- 2 tablespoons grated Parmesan cheese

1 Cook and drain pasta shells as directed on package, using minimum cook time.

2 Meanwhile, in 10-inch skillet, cook beef, mushrooms, onion and garlic over medium heat 8 to 10 minutes, stirring occasionally, until beef is thoroughly cooked; drain. Stir in pasta sauce.

3 Heat oven to 350°F. Spray 13x9-inch (3-quart) glass baking dish with cooking spray.

4 Squeeze thawed spinach to drain; spread on paper towels and pat dry. In medium bowl, mix spinach, cottage cheese, ⅓ cup Parmesan cheese, the nutmeg and pepper.

5 In baking dish, spread 1 cup of the beef mixture. Fill pasta shells with spinach mixture; place on beef mixture in dish. Pour remaining beef mixture evenly over shells, covering completely. Sprinkle with mozzarella cheese and 2 tablespoons Parmesan cheese.

6 Cover and bake 30 minutes. Uncover; bake 20 to 25 minutes longer or until hot and bubbly.

*Or substitute 1 can (4 oz) mushroom pieces and stems, drained, for the fresh mushrooms.

1 Serving: Calories 570; Total Fat 21g (Saturated Fat 10g, Trans Fat 0.5g); Cholesterol 70mg; Sodium 1360mg; Total Carbohydrate 55g (Dietary Fiber 6g, Sugars 12g); Protein 39g **Exchanges:** 2½ Starch, 1 Other Carbohydrate, 4½ Lean Meat, 1 Fat **Carbohydrate Choices:** 3½

Turkey Manicotti Substitute ground turkey for the ground beef and substitute chopped red or green bell pepper for the mushrooms.

Filling Manicotti Shells

Spoon filling into re-sealable food-storage plastic bag; seal bag.

With scissors, make ½-inch cut from one corner of bag.

Insert tip of bag into each manicotti shell; gently squeeze filling into each shell.

Or use teaspoon to carefully fill shells.

Fresh Tomato Pizza   CALORIE SMART

PREP 35 min **TOTAL** 3 hr 15 min • 1 pizza
(8 slices)

ITALIAN-STYLE CRUST

1 package (2¼ teaspoons) regular active or
fast-acting dry yeast

½ cup warm water (105°F to 115°F)

1¼ to 1½ cups all-purpose flour

½ teaspoon salt

½ teaspoon sugar

1 teaspoon olive oil

Cornmeal

TOPPINGS

4 oz fresh mozzarella cheese, well drained, cut
into ¼-inch-thick slices

2 plum (Roma) tomatoes, thinly sliced

¼ teaspoon salt

Freshly ground pepper to taste

¼ cup thin strips fresh basil leaves

1 tablespoon chopped fresh oregano leaves

1 tablespoon small capers, if desired

1 tablespoon olive oil

1 For crust, in large bowl, dissolve yeast in
warm water. Stir in ¾ cup of the flour, the salt,
sugar and oil. Stir in enough of the remaining
flour to make dough easy to handle. Place
dough on lightly floured surface; knead about
10 minutes or until smooth and springy. Grease
large bowl with shortening. Place dough in
bowl, turning dough to grease all sides. Cover
and let rise in warm place 20 minutes. Gently
push fist into dough to deflate. Cover and
refrigerate at least 2 hours but no longer than
48 hours. (If dough should double in size
during refrigeration, gently push fist into dough
to deflate.)

2 Move oven rack to lowest position. Heat oven
to 425°F. Grease cookie sheet or 12-inch pizza
pan with oil. Sprinkle with cornmeal. Pat dough
into 12-inch round on cookie sheet or pat in
pizza pan using floured fingers. Press dough
from center to edge so edge is slightly thicker
than center.

3 Place cheese slices on dough to within
½ inch of edge. Arrange tomatoes on cheese.
Sprinkle with salt, pepper, 2 tablespoons of the
basil, the oregano and capers. Drizzle with oil.

4 Bake about 20 minutes or until crust is
golden brown and cheese is melted. Sprinkle
with remaining 2 tablespoons basil. Cut into
slices to serve.

1 Slice: Calories 140; Total Fat 5g (Saturated Fat 2g, Trans Fat 0g);
Cholesterol 10mg; Sodium 300mg; Total Carbohydrate 17g
(Dietary Fiber 1g, Sugars 0g); Protein 6g **Exchanges:** 1 Starch, 1 Fat
Carbohydrate Choices: 1.

Calzone

PREP 45 min **TOTAL** 1 hr 40 min • 6 servings

Pizza Crust (page 192)

2 cups shredded mozzarella cheese (8 oz)

¼ lb salami, cut into thin strips

½ cup ricotta cheese

¼ cup chopped fresh basil leaves

2 plum (Roma) tomatoes, chopped

Freshly ground pepper to taste

1 egg, slightly beaten

1 Let pizza crust dough rest 30 minutes.

2 Heat oven to 375°F. Grease 2 cookie sheets
with shortening or cooking spray.

3 Divide dough into 6 equal parts. On lightly
floured surface, roll each part into 7-inch circle
with floured rolling pin.

4 On half of each dough circle, place equal
portions mozzarella cheese, salami, ricotta
cheese, basil and tomatoes to within 1 inch
of edge. Sprinkle with pepper. Carefully fold
dough over filling; pinch edges or press with
fork to seal securely.

5 Place calzones on cookie sheets. Brush
with egg. Bake about 25 minutes or until
golden brown.

1 Serving: Calories 490; Total Fat 24g (Saturated Fat 9g, Trans Fat 0g);
Cholesterol 75mg; Sodium 980mg; Total Carbohydrate 46g (Dietary
Fiber 2g, Sugars 4g); Protein 24g **Exchanges:** 3 Starch, 2 High-Fat Meat,
½ Fat **Carbohydrate Choices:** 3

LIGHTER **Directions** For 8 grams of fat and 350
calories per serving, use reduced-fat mozzarella
cheese and fat-free ricotta cheese; substitute
cooked chicken for the salami.

Stuffed-Crust Pizza CALORIE SMART

PREP 25 min **TOTAL** 1 hr 45 min • 1 pizza
(6 slices)

- 1 recipe Honey–Whole Wheat Bread (page 504) or 1 loaf (1 lb) frozen 100% whole-wheat bread dough, thawed
- 1 tablespoon yellow cornmeal
- 4 sticks (1 oz each) string cheese, cut lengthwise in half
- ¼ cup Italian-style tomato paste (from 6-oz can)
- 1 small onion, cut lengthwise in half, then thinly sliced
- 1 medium bell pepper, thinly sliced
- 1 can (4 oz) mushrooms pieces and stems, drained
- 1 oz sliced pepperoni, coarsely chopped (¼ cup)
- 12 pitted kalamata or Greek olives, coarsely chopped (⅓ cup)
- 2 cups shredded mozzarella cheese (8 oz)

1 Prepare Honey–Whole Wheat Bread as directed through Step 2, using honey.

2 Gently push fist into dough to deflate. Divide dough in half; save one half for another use.*

3 Heat oven to 400°F. Grease cookie sheet with shortening or cooking spray. Sprinkle cornmeal over cookie sheet. On cookie sheet, press or roll remaining dough half into 13-inch round. Arrange string cheese in circle around edge of dough. Carefully roll edge of dough up over string cheese; seal well.

4 Spread tomato paste evenly over dough. Top with onion, bell pepper, mushrooms, pepperoni and olives. Sprinkle with shredded cheese.

5 Bake 15 to 17 minutes or until crust is golden brown and cheese is melted. Cut into wedges to serve.

*Reserved dough can be shaped and baked as directed in Honey–Whole Wheat Bread recipe or used to make another pizza crust.

1 Serving: Calories 530; Total Fat 20g (Saturated Fat 9g, Trans Fat 0.5g); Cholesterol 40mg; Sodium 1270mg; Total Carbohydrate 64g (Dietary Fiber 6g, Sugars 12g); Protein 24g **Exchanges:** 3 Starch, 1 Other Carbohydrate, ½ Vegetable, 2 Medium Fat Meat, 1½ Fat **Carbohydrate Choices:** 4

Deluxe Stuffed-Crust Tomato Pizza Omit mushrooms. Thinly slice 2 plum (Roma) tomatoes. Layer tomatoes over olives. Sprinkle with ½ teaspoon dried basil leaves. Continue as directed.

Deluxe Stuffed-Crust Tomato Pizza

Chicken Sausage, Spinach and Swiss Pizza FAST

PREP 15 min **TOTAL** 25 min • 4 pizzas

- 4 baked flatbreads (from 11.2-oz package)
- 2 tablespoons olive oil
- 1 bag (6 oz) fresh baby spinach leaves
- ½ teaspoon garlic-pepper blend
- 3 fully cooked chicken sausage links (from 12-oz package), thinly sliced
- ¼ to ½ teaspoon crushed red pepper flakes
- ½ cup sliced green onions (8 medium)
- 2 cups shredded Gruyère or Swiss cheese (8 oz)

1 Heat oven to 400°F. Place flatbreads on 2 large ungreased cookie sheets. Brush flatbreads with 1 tablespoon of the oil. Bake 5 minutes.

2 Meanwhile, in large bowl, toss spinach with remaining 1 tablespoon oil and the garlic-pepper blend.

3 Top partially baked flatbreads evenly with spinach and sausage. Sprinkle with pepper flakes, onions and cheese. Bake 7 to 9 minutes or until cheese is melted.

1 Pizza: Calories 500; Total Fat 29g (Saturated Fat 12g, Trans Fat 0g); Cholesterol 95mg; Sodium 860mg; Total Carbohydrate 26g (Dietary Fiber 9g, Sugars 6g); Protein 33g **Exchanges:** 1½ Starch, ½ Vegetable, 4 Lean Meat, 3 Fat **Carbohydrate Choices:** 2

Making Stuffed Crust Pizza

Carefully roll edge of dough up over cheese; seal well.

CALORIE SMART = See Helpful Nutrition and Cooking Information, page 643   FAST = Ready in 30 minutes or less
EASY = Prep in 10 minutes or less **plus** five ingredients or less   LIGHTER = 25% fewer calories or grams of fat
MAKE AHEAD = Make-ahead directions   SLOW COOKER = Slow cooker directions

GRAIN AND RICE BASICS

Cultivated for centuries, grains are eaten by every culture in a variety of dishes. Whole grains are amazing foods. Not only are they budget-friendly, but they also have many nutritional benefits. In general, they are low in fat, have little or no cholesterol and are high in fiber.

JUST WHAT IS A WHOLE GRAIN?

- It is the entire seed of the plant containing all parts of the kernel, including the fiber-rich outer coating of bran, the energy-dense middle layer called the endosperm and the nutrient-packed germ. If any part of the grain is removed, it's not considered whole. Whole grains contain essential vitamins, minerals, antioxidants and phytonutrients plus healthy fats. Whole grains include barley, quinoa and brown rice.

- In contrast, a refined grain has been milled, which removes the bran and germ, giving the grain a finer texture, but also removing important fiber and vitamins. Most refined grains are labeled "enriched," meaning some nutrients have been added back in after processing. Refined grains include white rice and white flour.

STORAGE

- Because whole grains contain healthy fats, careful attention to storage of both whole grain and whole grain products is important, they won't keep as long as their refined counterparts. Whole grain flours can be kept 1 to 3 months in airtight containers on a cool, dry shelf or can be kept in the freezer 2 to 6 months.

Summer Quinoa-Tomato Salad (page 206)

COOKING HINTS

- In general, heat the water and grain to a boil and add the grain. Then reduce the heat. Water should be barely simmering when cooking grain so that it cooks slowly.

- Keep it covered—For most grains, simmer with the lid on and check occasionally to be sure the liquid is at a low simmer.

- Let it rest—When cooking is finished, remove pan from heat and let the grain stand covered for 5 to 10 minutes. Fluff with a fork just before serving.

- Cook extra—Make a little extra for other uses like stirring into soups, stews or salads. Store cooked grains tightly covered in the refrigerator up to 5 days or freeze for up to 3 months.

Whole Grains vs. Fiber

Whole grains naturally contain fiber in the outer coating of the grain kernel or bran. So fiber is a component of whole grains, but there are many other important nutrients and natural compounds found in whole grains that work together for health benefits. Eating whole grains can provide fiber, but not all grains are high in fiber.

Heirloom Recipe and New Twist

Tabbouleh, a traditional Middle Eastern whole-grain salad, has also become a favorite in the United States and is easy to make and serve. It typically uses bulgur, parsley, mint, olive oil, lemon and tomatoes in varying amounts and is always served chilled or at room temperature. The new twist features barley instead of bulgur, among other new flavors, but still uses plenty of the fresh herbs that are a signature of any tabbouleh. In fact, we love tabbouleh so much we've included a third featuring fresh fruit. Be sure to try them all!

HEIRLOOM

Classic Tabbouleh   CALORIE SMART

Serve this traditional version of tabbouleh with crisp bread.

PREP 10 min **TOTAL** 1 hr 40 min • 6 servings

- ¾   cup uncooked bulgur
- 1½ cups chopped fresh parsley
- 3   medium tomatoes, chopped (2¼ cups)
- 5   medium green onions, thinly sliced (⅓ cup)
- 2   tablespoons chopped fresh or 2 teaspoons crushed dried mint leaves
- ¼   cup olive or vegetable oil
- ¼   cup fresh lemon juice
- ¾   teaspoon salt
- ¼   teaspoon pepper
-     Whole ripe olives, if desired

1 In small bowl, cover bulgur with cold water. Let stand 30 minutes. Drain; press out as much water as possible.

2 In medium glass or plastic bowl, stir together bulgur, parsley, tomatoes, onions and mint.

3 In tightly covered container, shake oil, lemon juice, salt and pepper. Pour over bulgur mixture; toss until coated. Cover and refrigerate at least 1 hour to blend flavors. Garnish with olives.

1 Serving (¾ Cup): Calories 170; Total Fat 10g (Saturated Fat 1.5g, Trans Fat 0g); Cholesterol 0mg; Sodium 320mg; Total Carbohydrate 19g (Dietary Fiber 5g, Sugars 2g); Protein 3g **Exchanges:** 1 Starch, 1 Vegetable, 1 Fat **Carbohydrate Choices:** 1

Garbanzo Bean Tabbouleh Add 1 can (15 to 16 oz) garbanzo beans, drained and rinsed, and 1 cup chopped green bell pepper with the bulgur in Step 2.

Minty Tabbouleh Use ¾ cup each chopped fresh mint and parsley for the 1½ cups chopped fresh parsley. Omit the additional 2 tablespoons mint.

Southwestern Tabbouleh Substitute 1 cup chopped fresh cilantro for the parsley. Reduce lemon juice to 2 tablespoons; increase salt to 1 teaspoon. Add 2 teaspoons ground cumin with the salt and pepper in Step 3.

Classic Tabbouleh

Barley, Cauliflower and Red Lentil Tabbouleh

Barley, Cauliflower and Red Lentil Tabbouleh CALORIE SMART

PREP 10 min **TOTAL** 2 hr 10 min • 15 servings

SALAD

- ½ cup uncooked hulled (not pearl) barley (not quick-cooking)
- 2¼ cups water
- 1 cup dried red lentils, sorted, rinsed
- 2 cups fresh cauliflower florets (1 inch), separated into mini florets (about ¼ inch)
- 1 cup chopped fresh parsley
- ½ cup chopped fresh mint leaves
- 1 jar (12 oz) roasted red bell peppers, drained, patted dry and chopped
- 1 cup crumbled feta cheese (4 oz)

DRESSING

- ¼ cup olive oil
- 2 tablespoons fresh lemon juice
- 1¼ teaspoons Greek seasoning or salt

1 In 2-quart saucepan, heat barley and water to boiling. Reduce heat; cover and simmer 40 minutes. Add lentils; cook 10 to 15 minutes longer or until barley is chewy but tender and lentils are just tender. (Do not overcook or lentils will lose their shape and become mushy.) Let stand 5 minutes or until liquid is absorbed. Place in strainer; rinse with cold water. Drain well.

2 In medium glass or plastic bowl, place barley, lentils and remaining salad ingredients. In tightly covered container, shake dressing ingredients. Pour over barley mixture; gently toss to combine. Cover and refrigerate at least 1 hour to blend flavors.

1 Serving (½ Cup): Calories 130; Total Fat 6g (Saturated Fat 1.5g, Trans Fat 0g); Cholesterol 5mg; Sodium 170mg; Total Carbohydrate 15g (Dietary Fiber 4g, Sugars 2g); Protein 5g **Exchanges:** 1 Other Carbohydrate, ½ Vegetable, ½ Very Lean Meat, 1 Fat **Carbohydrate Choices:** 1

Types of Barley

Hulled barley is whole grain barley. Hulless barley is a variety of barley grown to lose its hulls during harvesting. **Pearl barley** has been polished to remove part or all of the outer bran layer, along with the hull. This is not a whole grain, but some of the bran may still be intact. **Quick-cooking barley** is made from pearl barley that's been partially cooked and dried. **Barley grits** are barley kernels cut into pieces.

Fruited Tabbouleh with Walnuts and Feta

Fruited Tabbouleh with Walnuts and Feta CALORIE SMART

PREP 20 min **TOTAL** 3 hr 20 min • 10 servings

- 1 cup uncooked bulgur
- 1 cup boiling water
- ¼ cup orange juice
- ¼ cup olive oil
- ½ medium unpeeled cucumber, seeded, chopped (about 1 cup)
- ½ cup chopped red onion
- ½ cup sweetened dried cranberries
- ⅓ cup loosely packed fresh parsley, finely chopped
- ⅓ cup loosely packed fresh mint leaves, finely chopped
- 1 tablespoon grated orange peel
- ½ teaspoon salt
- 1 orange, peeled, divided into sections and chopped
- ½ cup chopped walnuts, toasted (page 23)
- ½ cup crumbled feta cheese (2 oz)*

1 Place bulgur in large heatproof bowl. Pour boiling water over bulgur; stir. Let stand about 1 hour or until water is absorbed.

2 Stir in orange juice, oil, cucumber, onion, cranberries, parsley, mint, orange peel and salt; toss well. Cover and refrigerate 2 to 3 hours or until well chilled.

3 Just before serving, stir in chopped orange; sprinkle with walnuts and feta cheese.

*Crumbled chèvre (goat) cheese can be substituted for the feta cheese.

1 Serving (½ Cup): Calories 200; Total Fat 11g (Saturated Fat 2.5g, Trans Fat 0g); Cholesterol 5mg; Sodium 210mg; Total Carbohydrate 21g (Dietary Fiber 4g, Sugars 7g); Protein 4g **Exchanges:** 1 Starch, ½ Other Carbohydrate, 2 Fat **Carbohydrate Choices:** 1½

Balsamic Pork Chops with Quinoa

Balsamic Pork Chops with Quinoa CALORIE SMART

PREP 25 min **TOTAL** 45 min • 4 servings

- ½ cup uncooked quinoa
- 5 teaspoons vegetable oil
- 1 medium onion, cut into wedges
- 4 boneless pork loin chops, ½ to ¾ inch thick (6 oz each), trimmed of fat
- ¾ teaspoon seasoned salt
- ¼ teaspoon dried thyme leaves
- ¼ teaspoon pepper
- ¾ cup water
- ¼ cup white balsamic vinegar
- 2 tablespoons chopped fresh parsley
- 2 cups small fresh broccoli florets
- 1½ cups frozen peach slices

1 Rinse quinoa thoroughly by placing in a fine-mesh strainer and holding under cold running water until water runs clear; drain well. Set aside.

2 In 12-inch nonstick skillet, heat 2 teaspoons of the oil over medium-high heat. Cook onion in oil 5 minutes, stirring occasionally, until it begins to brown. Remove from skillet; set aside.

3 Sprinkle both sides of pork chops with ¼ teaspoon of the seasoned salt, the thyme and pepper. In skillet, heat remaining 3 teaspoons oil over medium heat. Add pork; cook 4 to 6 minutes, turning once, until browned. Remove from skillet to plate.

4 Add quinoa, onion, water, vinegar, parsley and remaining ½ teaspoon seasoned salt to skillet. Heat to boiling; reduce heat. Place pork and any juices on top of quinoa mixture. Cover and simmer 10 minutes.

5 Add broccoli and peaches. Cover and simmer about 10 minutes longer or until quinoa is tender and meat thermometer inserted in center of pork reads 145°F.

1 Serving: Calories 470; Total Fat 21g (Saturated Fat 6g, Trans Fat 0g); Cholesterol 115mg; Sodium 350mg; Total Carbohydrate 27g (Dietary Fiber 4g, Sugars 10g); Protein 44g **Exchanges:** 1 Starch, ½ Fruit, 1 Vegetable, 5½ Lean Meat, 1 Fat **Carbohydrate Choices:** 2

Summer Quinoa-Tomato Salad CALORIE SMART

PREP 15 min **TOTAL** 35 min • 8 servings

- ¾ cup uncooked quinoa
- 1½ cups water
- 2 large tomatoes, quartered, cut into chunks
- ¼ medium red onion, chopped
- 2 cloves garlic, finely chopped
- 3 tablespoons chopped fresh basil leaves
- 3 tablespoons chopped fresh parsley
- 4½ teaspoons olive oil
- 3 tablespoons balsamic vinegar
- ½ teaspoon salt
- ¼ teaspoon freshly ground pepper
- 2 teaspoons sugar
- ¼ cup grated Parmesan cheese

1 Rinse quinoa thoroughly by placing in a fine-mesh strainer and holding under cold running water until water runs clear; drain well.

2 In 2-quart saucepan, heat quinoa and water to boiling; reduce heat to low. Cover and simmer 15 to 20 minutes or until water is absorbed and quinoa is tender. Cool slightly.

3 In medium bowl, toss tomatoes, onion, garlic, basil, parsley, oil, vinegar, salt, pepper and sugar.

4 Spread quinoa in large serving bowl or on platter; spoon tomato mixture over top. Serve or cover and refrigerate up to 24 hours. Sprinkle with cheese just before serving.

1 Serving: Calories 110; Total Fat 4.5g (Saturated Fat 1g, Trans Fat 0g); Cholesterol 0mg; Sodium 210mg; Total Carbohydrate 14g (Dietary Fiber 1g, Sugars 4g); Protein 4g **Exchanges:** 1 Starch, 1 Fat **Carbohydrate Choices:** 1

Polenta CALORIE SMART • FAST

*Polenta is a staple in northern Italy and Eastern
European countries, but we know it as cornmeal
mush. It's very versatile, showing up for breakfast
with maple syrup, nestled next to a grilled pork
chop or topped with pasta sauce.*

PREP 20 min **TOTAL** 20 min • 6 servings

- 1 cup yellow cornmeal
- 4 cups water
- 1½ teaspoons salt
- 1 tablespoon butter or olive oil

1 In 2-quart saucepan, mix cornmeal and
¾ cup of the water (this helps to prevent
clumping). Stir in remaining 3¼ cups water
and the salt. Cook over medium heat 8 to
10 minutes, stirring constantly, until mixture
thickens and boils; reduce heat.

2 Cover and simmer about 10 minutes, stirring
occasionally, until very thick. Remove from
heat. Add butter; stir until polenta is smooth.

1 Serving (¾ Cup): Calories 110; Total Fat 2.5g (Saturated Fat 1.5g,
Trans Fat 0g); Cholesterol 5mg; Sodium 610mg; Total Carbohydrate 21g
(Dietary Fiber 1g, Sugars 0g); Protein 2g **Exchanges:** ½ Starch, 1 Other
Carbohydrate, ½ Fat **Carbohydrate Choices:** 1½

Fried Polenta Spray 9x5-inch loaf pan with
cooking spray. After simmering polenta 10
minutes in Step 2, spread in loaf pan. Cover and
refrigerate at least 12 hours or until firm. Turn
pan upside down to unmold. Cut into ½-inch
slices. Coat slices with flour. In 10-inch skillet,
melt 2 tablespoons butter over low heat. Cook
slices in butter about 5 minutes on each side or
until brown.

Fried Polenta

Faster Fried Polenta Use 13x9-in pan instead
of loaf pan; refrigerate polenta uncovered about
3 hours or until firm. Cut into 6 squares. (Cut
squares diagonally into triangles, if desired.)
Cook in butter as directed for Fried Polenta.

Parmesan Polenta Make Polenta or Rich and
Creamy Polenta as directed—except stir in
½ cup shredded Parmesan cheese with the
butter in Step 2.

Rich and Creamy Polenta Substitute half-
and-half for 1½ cups of the water. Continue
as directed.

Vegetable Polenta Simmer 5 minutes in Step
2, then stir in 1½ cups frozen mixed vegetables;
simmer 5 minutes longer or until polenta is
thick and vegetables are tender.

LEARN WITH BETTY Cooking Polenta

Perfect Polenta: This polenta is
smooth and creamy.

Undercooked Polenta: This polenta
mixture was not cooked long enough
and all of the water was added at
once.

Overcooked Polenta: This polenta
was cooked too long.

Apple-Rosemary Pork and Barley   CALORIE SMART • FAST

PREP 25 min **TOTAL** 25 min • 4 servings

- 1½ cups apple juice
- ¾ cup uncooked quick-cooking barley
- 2 tablespoons chopped fresh or 2 teaspoons dried rosemary leaves, crushed
- 2 teaspoons vegetable oil
- 1 pork tenderloin (¾ lb), cut into ¼-inch slices
- 1 medium onion, chopped (½ cup)
- 1 clove garlic, finely chopped
- ¼ cup apple jelly
- 1 large unpeeled red cooking apple, sliced (1½ cups)

1 In 2-quart saucepan, heat apple juice to boiling. Stir in barley and 1 tablespoon of the rosemary; reduce heat to low. Cover and simmer 10 to 12 minutes or until liquid is absorbed and barley is tender.

2 Meanwhile, in 10-inch nonstick skillet, heat oil over medium-high heat. Add pork, onion, garlic and remaining 1 tablespoon rosemary; cook about 5 minutes, stirring frequently, until pork is no longer pink in center. Stir in apple jelly and apple slices; cook until hot. Serve pork mixture over barley.

1 Serving: Calories 400; Total Fat 6g (Saturated Fat 1.5g, Trans Fat 0g); Cholesterol 55mg; Sodium 50mg; Total Carbohydrate 63g (Dietary Fiber 8g, Sugars 26g); Protein 23g **Exchanges:** 2 Starch, 2 Fruit, 2½ Very Lean Meat, 1 Fat **Carbohydrate Choices:** 4

Three-Grain Medley   CALORIE SMART • SLOW COOKER

PREP 10 min **TOTAL** 4 hr 10 min • 8 servings

- ⅔ cup uncooked wheat berries
- ½ cup uncooked hulled or pearl barley
- ½ cup uncooked wild rice
- ¼ cup chopped fresh parsley
- ¼ cup butter, melted
- 2 teaspoons finely shredded lemon peel
- 6 medium green onions, thinly sliced (6 tablespoons)
- 2 cloves garlic, finely chopped
- 3½ cups vegetable or chicken broth (for homemade broth, see page 156 or 143)
- 1 jar (2 oz) diced pimientos, undrained

1 Spray 3½- to 4-quart slow cooker with cooking spray. In slow cooker, mix all ingredients.

2 Cover; cook on Low heat setting 4 to 6 hours or until liquid is absorbed. Stir before serving.

1 Serving: Calories 200; Total Fat 6g (Saturated Fat 3.5g, Trans Fat 0g); Cholesterol 15mg; Sodium 190mg; Total Carbohydrate 30g (Dietary Fiber 5g, Sugars 0g); Protein 5g **Exchanges:** 2 Starch, 1 Fat **Carbohydrate Choices:** 2

Beef and Kasha Mexicana

CALORIE SMART • FAST

PREP 30 min **TOTAL** 30 min • 6 servings

- 1 lb extra-lean (at least 90%) ground beef
- 1 small onion, chopped (⅓ cup)
- 1 cup uncooked buckwheat kernels or groats (kasha)
- 1 can (14.5 oz) diced tomatoes, undrained
- 1 can (4.5 oz) chopped green chiles, undrained
- 1 package (1 oz) 40% less-sodium taco seasoning mix
- 2 cups frozen whole kernel corn, thawed
- 1½ cups water
- 1 cup shredded reduced-fat Cheddar cheese (4 oz)
- 2 tablespoons chopped fresh cilantro, if desired
- 2 tablespoons sliced pitted ripe olives, if desired

1 In 12-inch skillet, cook beef and onion over medium-high heat 5 to 7 minutes, stirring occasionally, until beef is thoroughly cooked; drain. Stir in kasha until kernels are moistened.

2 Stir in tomatoes, chiles, taco seasoning mix, corn and water. Heat to boiling; reduce heat to low. Cover and simmer 5 to 7 minutes, stirring occasionally, until kasha is tender.

3 Sprinkle cheese over kasha mixture. Cover and cook 2 to 3 minutes or until cheese is melted. Sprinkle with cilantro and olives.

1 Serving (1½ Cups): Calories 300; Total Fat 8g (Saturated Fat 3.5g, Trans Fat 0g); Cholesterol 50mg; Sodium 720mg; Total Carbohydrate 33g (Dietary Fiber 4g, Sugars 5g); Protein 23g **Exchanges:** 1½ Starch, ½ Other Carbohydrate, 2½ Lean Meat **Carbohydrate Choices:** 2

Beef and Kasha Tortillas Spoon mixture onto soft corn or flour tortillas; roll up.

Kasha and Bow-Tie Pilaf

Indian-Spiced Farro Salad

Kasha and Bow-Tie Pilaf

CALORIE SMART

Look for kasha, sometimes called roasted buckwheat kernels or groats, in the health-food, cereal or kosher-food area.

PREP 20 min **TOTAL** 35 min • 12 servings

- 3 tablespoons butter
- 1 large onion, coarsely chopped (1 cup)
- 1 medium red bell pepper, coarsely chopped
- 1 cup sliced fresh mushrooms (3 oz)
- 1 cup uncooked buckwheat kernels or groats (kasha)
- 1 egg, beaten
- 2 cups chicken broth (for homemade broth, see page 143)
- ½ teaspoon salt
- ¼ teaspoon pepper
- 1 cup uncooked bow-tie (farfalle) pasta (2 oz)
- ½ cup chopped fresh parsley

1 In 12-inch nonstick skillet, melt butter over medium heat. Cook onion, bell pepper and mushrooms in butter 3 to 4 minutes, stirring occasionally, until tender. Remove from skillet; set aside.

2 In small bowl, stir kasha and egg, coating well. In same skillet, cook kasha over medium heat about 3 minutes, stirring constantly, until browned and dry.

3 Return vegetables to skillet; stir in broth, salt and pepper. Heat to boiling; reduce heat to low. Cover and simmer 10 to 15 minutes or until broth is absorbed and kasha is tender.

4 Meanwhile, cook and drain pasta as directed on package. Stir pasta and parsley into kasha mixture.

1 Serving: Calories 100; Total Fat 4g (Saturated Fat 1.5g, Trans Fat 0g); Cholesterol 25mg; Sodium 300mg; Total Carbohydrate 13g (Dietary Fiber 2g, Sugars 2g); Protein 4g **Exchanges:** 1 Starch, ½ Fat **Carbohydrate Choices:** 1

Indian-Spiced Farro Salad

CALORIE SMART

Farro is an ancient Tuscan grain similar in taste and texture to pearl barley. Look for it in the grain aisle, specialty stores or Italian markets.

PREP 15 min **TOTAL** 1 hr 45 min • 12 servings

FARRO
- 1½ cups uncooked farro*
- 4 cups water

SALAD
- 1 medium red bell pepper, chopped
- ½ cup finely chopped red onion
- ⅓ cup finely chopped fresh cilantro leaves
- ⅓ cup finely chopped fresh mint leaves
- 2 tablespoons finely chopped seeded jalapeño chile
- ⅓ cup coarsely chopped dry-roasted peanuts

DRESSING
- 3 tablespoons vegetable oil
- 2 tablespoons fresh lime juice
- 2½ teaspoons ground cumin
- 1 teaspoon grated lime peel
- 1¼ teaspoons salt

1 In 2-quart saucepan, heat farro and water to boiling; reduce heat to low. Cover and simmer 25 to 30 minutes or until tender. Rinse with cold water; drain well.

2 In large bowl, mix all salad ingredients except peanuts; stir in farro. In small bowl, beat dressing ingredients with whisk until blended. Pour over salad; toss to coat. Cover and refrigerate 1 hour to blend flavors. Just before serving, stir in peanuts. Garnish with additional peanuts, cilantro and mint, if desired.

*Pearl barley can be substituted for the farro. Cook 45 to 50 minutes.

1 Serving (½ Cup): Calories 150; Total Fat 6g (Saturated Fat 1g, Trans Fat 0g); Cholesterol 0mg; Sodium 300mg; Total Carbohydrate 19g (Dietary Fiber 2g, Sugars 1g); Protein 4g **Exchanges:** 1½ Starch, 1 Fat **Carbohydrate Choices:** 1

Rice Pilaf FAST • EASY

Rice pilaf can be a new dish each time you make it just by adding different ingredients. The secret to the flavor is browning the rice in butter until it is golden brown before adding the liquid to the pan.

PREP 10 min **TOTAL** 30 min • 4 servings

    2 tablespoons butter
    1 small onion, chopped (⅓ cup)
    1 cup uncooked regular long-grain white rice
    2 cups chicken broth (for homemade broth, see page 143)
    ¼ teaspoon salt

1 In 3-quart saucepan, melt butter over medium heat. Cook onion in butter about 3 minutes, stirring occasionally, until tender.

2 Stir in rice. Cook 5 minutes, stirring frequently, until rice is golden brown. Stir in broth and salt.

3 Heat to boiling, stirring once or twice; reduce heat to low. Cover and simmer 15 minutes (do not lift cover or stir). Remove from heat; let stand covered 5 minutes.

1 Serving: Calories 260; Total Fat 7g (Saturated Fat 3g, Trans Fat 0g); Cholesterol 15mg; Sodium 700mg; Total Carbohydrate 42g (Dietary Fiber 0g, Sugars 0g); Protein 7g **Exchanges:** 2 Starch, 1 Other Carbohydrate, 1 Fat **Carbohydrate Choices:** 3

Brown Rice Pilaf Substitute uncooked regular brown rice for the white rice. Make as directed—except in Step 3, increase simmer time to 45 to 50 minutes.

Cashew Pilaf Stir ¼ cup coarsely chopped cashews and 2 tablespoons chopped fresh parsley into the cooked rice pilaf.

Curry Pilaf Stir in ½ cup diced dried fruit and raisin mixture, ¼ teaspoon ground allspice, ¼ teaspoon ground turmeric and ¼ teaspoon curry powder with the broth and salt in Step 2.

Mushroom Pilaf Cook 1 cup sliced fresh mushrooms or 1 can (4 oz) mushrooms pieces and stems, drained, with the onion in Step 1.

Orange and Cranberry Pilaf Add ½ teaspoon grated orange peel with the broth and salt in Step 2. Stir ¼ cup sweetened dried cranberries into the cooked rice pilaf.

Pine Nut and Green Onion Pilaf Cook ½ cup sliced green onions and ¼ cup pine nuts with the rice in Step 2.

Prosciutto, Parmesan and Pea Pilaf Cook 3 ounces prosciutto, chopped, with the rice in Step 2. Stir ¼ cup frozen sweet peas, thawed, and ¼ cup shredded Parmesan cheese into the cooked rice pilaf.

Cherry Pistachio Rice Pilaf Substitute uncooked wild and whole-grain brown rice blend for the white rice. Make as directed, except in Step 3, increase simmer time to 45 to 50 minutes. Stir ¼ cup each dried cherries and chopped pistachio nuts into the cooked rice pilaf.

Spanish Rice CALORIE SMART

PREP 15 min **TOTAL** 40 min • 10 servings

    2   tablespoons vegetable oil
    1   cup uncooked regular long-grain white rice
    1   medium onion, chopped (½ cup)
    2½   cups water
    1½   teaspoons salt
    ¾   teaspoon chili powder
    ⅛   teaspoon garlic powder
    1   small green bell pepper, chopped (½ cup)
    1   can (8 oz) tomato sauce
    1   large tomato, seeded, chopped (1 cup)

1 In 10-inch skillet, heat oil over medium heat. Cook rice and onion in oil about 5 minutes, stirring frequently, until rice is golden brown and onion is crisp-tender.

2 Stir in remaining ingredients except tomato. Heat to boiling; reduce heat. Cover and simmer 20 minutes, stirring occasionally. Stir in tomato. Cover and simmer about 5 minutes longer or until rice is tender.

1 Serving (½ Cup): Calories 120; Total Fat 3g (Saturated Fat 0g, Trans Fat 0g); Cholesterol 0mg; Sodium 500mg; Total Carbohydrate 20g (Dietary Fiber 1g, Sugars 2g); Protein 2g **Exchanges:** 1 Starch, ½ Fat **Carbohydrate Choices:** 1

Spanish Rice with Bacon Omit oil. Cut 6 slices bacon into 1-inch pieces. In 10-inch skillet, cook bacon over medium heat, stirring occasionally, until crisp. Remove from skillet with slotted spoon and drain on paper towels. Drain all but 2 tablespoons drippings from skillet. Cook rice and onion in bacon drippings over medium heat about 5 minutes, stirring frequently, until rice is golden brown and onion is crisp-tender. Continue as directed in Step 2. Stir in bacon just before serving.

Pork Fried Rice CALORIE SMART • FAST

Using cold cooked rice is best so the grains stay separated during frying.

PREP 25 min **TOTAL** 25 min • 4 servings

- 1 cup fresh bean sprouts
- 2 tablespoons vegetable oil
- 1 cup sliced fresh mushrooms (3 oz)
- 3 cups cold cooked regular long-grain white rice
- 1 cup cut-up cooked pork
- 2 medium green onions, sliced (2 tablespoons)
- 2 eggs, slightly beaten
- 3 tablespoons soy sauce
- Dash white pepper

1 Rinse bean sprouts with cold water; drain and set aside.

2 In 10-inch skillet, heat 1 tablespoon of the oil over medium heat; rotate skillet until oil covers bottom. Cook mushrooms in oil about 1 minute, stirring frequently, until coated.

3 Add bean sprouts, rice, pork and onions to skillet. Cook over medium heat about 5 minutes, stirring and breaking up rice, until sprouts are thoroughly cooked and no longer crisp and mixture is hot.

4 Move rice mixture to side of skillet. Add remaining 1 tablespoon oil to other side of skillet. Cook eggs in oil over medium heat, stirring constantly, until eggs are thickened throughout but still moist. Stir eggs into rice mixture. Stir in soy sauce and pepper.

1 Serving: Calories 360; Total Fat 14g (Saturated Fat 3.5g, Trans Fat 0g); Cholesterol 135mg; Sodium 1190mg; Total Carbohydrate 37g (Dietary Fiber 1g, Sugars 1g); Protein 20g **Exchanges:** 2½ Starch, 2 Lean Meat, 1 Fat **Carbohydrate Choices:** 2½

LIGHTER Directions For 3 grams of fat and 240 calories per serving, reduce pork to ½ cup and finely chop. Use a nonstick skillet and omit oil in Step 4. Substitute ½ cup fat-free egg product for the eggs.

Chicken Fried Rice Substitute 1 cup shredded cooked chicken for the pork and add 1 cup frozen sweet peas, cooked, in Step 3.

Shrimp Fried Rice Substitute 1 cup frozen cooked salad shrimp, thawed, for the pork.

Cherry Pistachio Rice Pilaf

Spanish Rice

Pork Fried Rice

Sticky Rice with Mango

Sticky Rice with Mango CALORIE SMART

Glutinous rice, also known as sweet or sticky rice, gets its sticky character from a high starch content. Garnish this classic Thai dessert with fresh, flaked or shredded coconut, either toasted or right out of the package.

PREP 15 min **TOTAL** 2 hr 5 min • 10 servings

STICKY RICE

1½ cups sweet rice (sticky or glutinous rice)*
1 can (13.66 oz) coconut milk (not reduced-fat and not cream of coconut)
½ cup sugar
¼ teaspoon salt
1 large mango, peeled, pitted and cut into ¼-inch slices

COCONUT SAUCE

2 tablespoons sugar
½ teaspoon cornstarch
Toasted flake coconut or sesame seed, if desired

1 Soak rice in cold water 1 hour; drain. Cook rice in rice cooker using the Sweet Rice setting according to manufacturer's directions. Or spray 2-quart saucepan with cooking spray. Add rice and 2 cups water. Heat to boiling; reduce heat to low. Cover and simmer 15 to 20 minutes or until water is absorbed. Spoon rice into large bowl and gently even top; set aside.

2 Meanwhile, in 2-quart saucepan, heat 1 cup of the coconut milk (reserve remaining coconut milk for sauce), ½ cup sugar and the salt over medium heat until hot. Simmer, stirring frequently, just until sugar is dissolved. Pour over rice; gently fold into rice. Let stand 30 to 35 minutes at room temperature or until almost all of milk mixture is absorbed.

3 In 1-quart saucepan, mix the reserved coconut milk, 2 tablespoons sugar and the cornstarch until cornstarch is dissolved. Heat to boiling; boil 1 minute, stirring constantly. Remove from heat. Spoon rice into individual bowls. Garnish with mango slices; drizzle each serving with 2 teaspoons coconut sauce. Sprinkle with sesame seed.

*One package (12 oz) Arborio rice can be substituted for the sweet rice. If making in rice cooker, follow manufacturer's directions. If making on stove top, make as directed on package for plain or basic white Arborio rice (not risotto), except omit any fat or salt called for on package. Continue as directed in Step 2.

1 Serving (½ Cup): Calories 190; Total Fat 7g (Saturated Fat 6g, Trans Fat 0g); Cholesterol 0mg; Sodium 65mg; Total Carbohydrate 30g (Dietary Fiber 1g, Sugars 19g); Protein 1g **Exchanges:** ½ Starch, 1½ Other Carbohydrate, 1½ Fat **Carbohydrate Choices: 2**

Making Sticky Rice

Pour cooked coconut mixture over cooked rice.   Drizzle each serving with coconut sauce.

Curried Veggie Brown Rice FAST

PREP 5 min **TOTAL** 20 min • 8 servings

2 cups chicken broth (for homemade broth, see page 143)
1½ teaspoons curry powder
½ teaspoon salt
2 cups uncooked instant brown rice
1½ cups frozen mixed vegetables
⅓ cup raisins
2 tablespoons chopped fresh parsley

1 In 2-quart saucepan, heat broth, curry powder and salt to boiling. Stir in rice; reduce heat to medium-low. Cover and cook 3 minutes.

2 Add vegetables. Cover and cook 4 to 6 minutes longer or until rice and vegetables are tender.

3 Remove from heat; let stand 3 to 4 minutes or until liquid is absorbed. Fluff rice with fork. Stir in raisins and parsley.

1 Serving (½ Cup): Calories 230; Total Fat 2g (Saturated Fat 0g, Trans Fat 0g); Cholesterol 0mg; Sodium 430mg; Total Carbohydrate 47g (Dietary Fiber 6g, Sugars 6g); Protein 6g **Exchanges:** 2 Starch, 1 Other Carbohydrate, ½ Vegetable **Carbohydrate Choices: 3**

Vegetables, Beans
& Legumes

Vegetables

Beans and Legumes

CALORIE SMART = See Helpful Nutrition and Cooking Information, page 643   FAST = Ready in 30 minutes or less
EASY = Prep in 10 minutes or less **plus** five ingredients or less   LIGHTER = 25% fewer calories or grams of fat
MAKE AHEAD = Make-ahead directions   SLOW COOKER = Slow cooker directions

VEGETABLE BASICS

Whether part of the main dish or served as a side, vegetables add texture, color, flavor and a bounty of healthful nutrients to any meal. Browse any farmers' market or grocery store, and you will see the array of choices available, from standards like carrots and broccoli to more exotic vegetables like golden beets and carnival squash. Among the varieties shown on the following pages, you'll find many treasures to brighten your table.

HEALTH BENEFITS

Eating vegetables provides health benefits. People who eat more vegetables as part of an overall healthy diet are likely to have a reduced risk of some chronic diseases. Vegetables provide nutrients vital for general wellness.

- Most vegetables are naturally low in fat and calories, and none have any cholesterol.

- Vegetables are important sources of many nutrients, including potassium, dietary fiber, folic acid, vitamin A and vitamin C.

- Dietary fiber from vegetables as part of an overall healthy diet can help reduce blood cholesterol levels and may lower risk of heart disease.

- To gain the most value from vegetables, choose a variety and plan for several servings every day. For specific amounts to eat daily, refer to the USDA's ChooseMyPlate.gov.

BUYING VEGETABLES

Look for the freshest vegetables possible—appearance is usually the best indication with good, bright color at the top of the list. Avoid any vegetable that looks withered or has soft spots. Leafy tops and vegetable greens should be crisp and fresh looking.

Organic vegetables are grown without synthetic fertilizers or pesticides. Look for organic produce at most grocery stores and specialty food stores.

STORING VEGETABLES

Storage varies for vegetables but in general, fresh vegetables should be used within a few days of purchase, as they do start to lose flavor quality and nutritional value if stored too long. See the vegetable listings, starting on page 225, for recommendations on individual vegetables.

American Eggplant

Asian Eggplant

Beefsteak Tomatoes

Heirloom Tomatoes

Yellow Pear Tomatoes

Campari Tomatoes

Cherry Tomatoes

Plum (Roma) Tomatoes

Grape Tomatoes

Tomatillos

Sweet Bell Peppers

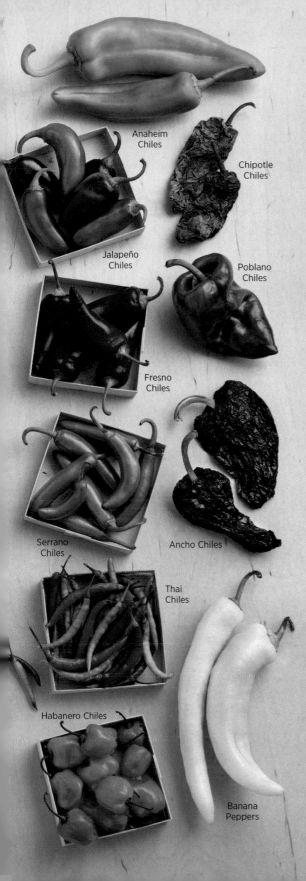

Anaheim Chiles

Chipotle Chiles

Jalapeño Chiles

Poblano Chiles

Fresno Chiles

Serrano Chiles

Ancho Chiles

Thai Chiles

Habanero Chiles

Banana Peppers

NIGHTSHADE VEGETABLES

This group also includes potatoes, page 231.

Eggplant: Choose firm, even-colored, unblemished eggplants heavy for their size. Caps and stems should be intact with no mold. Refrigerate in plastic bag up to 5 days.

> **Asian (Chinese, Japanese, Thai):** Colors include purple, green, white or striated. Longer, smaller than common eggplant.

Sweet Peppers: Choose shiny, brightly colored, unblemished peppers with firm sides. Refrigerate in plastic bag up to 5 days.

> **Banana:** Long, yellow, banana-shaped.

> **Bell:** Available in green, red, yellow, orange, purple, brown.

Tomatillos: Choose firm, unblemished fruit with tight-fitting husks. Store in paper bag in refrigerator up to 1 month. Remove husks; wash fruit before using.

Tomatoes: Choose firm, unblemished fruit heavy for their size. Store at room temperature (refrigerating will cause flavor loss); use within a few days.

> **Beefsteak:** Rich flavor, meaty texture. Good fresh or cooked.

> **Cherry:** Red or yellow; bite-size, great flavor. Use in salads, as garnish or cooked.

> **Heirloom:** Seeds are passed down through generations. Have distinct attributes like exceptional flavor or unusual coloring.

> **Plum (Roma):** Great flavor; fleshy, making them great for sauces and salads, as there is less juice than in a round tomato. **Grape** tomatoes are baby plum tomatoes.

CHILES

Choose firm chiles; avoid shriveled or soft spots. Store fresh chiles in refrigerator drawer; store dried ones in airtight container in a cool, dark place. Typically, the larger the chile, the milder the flavor.

Anaheim: Fresh, canned. Mild; frequently stuffed.

Fresno: Fresh. Medium-size. Similar in flavor to jalapeño. Usually red.

Habanero: Fresh or dried. Range from light green to bright orange. Distinctively hot.

Jalapeño: Fresh or canned. Dark green; hot to very hot. **Chipotle** is a dried, smoked jalapeño.

Poblano: Fresh or canned. Green: flavor ranges from mild to zippy. Reddish brown: sweeter than green. **Ancho** is a dried poblano.

Serrano: Fresh. Medium-size. Very hot and green at first, ripening to red or orange.

Thai: Fresh. Small; several colors. Very hot.

Yellow Onion

Red Onion

Sweet Onions

White Onion

Shallots

Cipollini Onions

Garlic

Elephant Garlic

Asparagus

Pearl Onions

White Asparagus

Green Onions (Scallions)

Leek

Shiitake

Dried Porcini

Portabella

Chanterelle

White
Button

Enoki

Oyster

Morel

Cremini/
Brown

ONIONS

The onion group of vegetables is often called the Lily family and includes not only onions but also garlic, leeks, shallots and asparagus. They all grow tubers, bulbs or rhizomes.

Asparagus: Spears are green, white or purple. Choose firm, brightly colored stalks with tight tips. Refrigerate in plastic bag up to 3 days.

Garlic: Made of papery-coated sections called cloves. Choose fresh, firm heads of garlic that have no green sprouts.

Leeks: Milder than onions. Look for crisp leaves and unblemished white bulb ends; avoid withered, yellow leaves. Refrigerate in a plastic bag up to 5 days. Cut lengthwise; wash thoroughly to remove dirt trapped between layers.

Onions: Choose firm, blemish-free onions with thin skins and no sign of mold or sprouting. Do not store near potatoes—onions will absorb moisture.

Green (Scallions): Look for bright green, fresh tops, white bulb ends. Refrigerate in plastic bag up to 1 week.

Red, Yellow, White: Store whole in cool (45°F to 60°F), dry, dark place with good ventilation up to 2 months. Once cut, cover with plastic wrap; refrigerate up to 4 days.

Sweet: Very juicy, mild sugary taste without the "burn" associated with other onions. Refrigerate whole in single layer 4 to 6 weeks.

Shallots: Papery skin; more like garlic than onions. Store in cool, dry place up to 2 weeks.

MUSHROOMS

Store unwashed, wrapped in paper towel in a plastic or paper bag. Refrigerate up to 4 days. For fresh, look for firm caps with good color and no soft spots or decay. Wash just before using.

Chanterelle: Fresh, dried. Delicate, nutty flavor; chewy texture. Cook as side dish, or add to soups, sauces, stir-fries.

Dried (Various): More concentrated flavor than fresh. Store in cool, dry place up to 1 year. Rehydrate as directed on package. One ounce dried (rehydrated) = 4 ounces fresh.

Morel: Fresh, dried. Smoky, earthy, nutty flavor. Sauté in butter.

Porcini: Often dried. Earthy flavor; firm texture. Popular in French and Italian cooking.

Portabella: Very large, with dense, meaty texture. Grill for sandwiches, sautés, slice for salads. **Cremini** is a young portabella.

Shiitake: Meaty texture; strong flavor. Choose plump ones with edges that curl under.

White (Button): Mild, earthy flavor. Small to quite large (for stuffing). Choose firm, white ones with no sign of decay.

Savoy Cabbage

Red Cabbage

Broccoli Rabe
(Rapini)

Kohlrabi

Green Cabbage

Brussels Sprouts

Broccoli

Kale

Cauliflower

Napa (Chinese)
Cabbage

Baby Bok Choy

Broccolini

Bok Choy

Mini Cucumbers

Cucumbers

Bi-color Corn

White Corn

Jerusalem Artichoke

Okra

English Cucumbers

Globe Artichokes

Celery

CABBAGE

These are all cruciferous vegetables, part of the cabbage family.

Bok Choy: Mild. Crunchy stalks; tender leaves. Use in salads and stir-fries; as side dish.

Broccoli: Florets and stalks edible. Use raw in salads, or cook. Florets should be tight and not flowering.

Broccolini: Cross between broccoli and Chinese kale. Mildly sweet, slightly peppery; crunchy. Refrigerate up to 10 days. Use raw in salads, crudités; cook crisp-tender as side dish.

Brussels Sprouts: Strong flavor similar to cabbage. Small sprouts will be milder than large ones. Look for those with compact heads. Cook for side dishes.

Cabbage: Choose cabbage with fresh, crisp leaves (firmly packed, if head variety). Refrigerate, tightly wrapped, up to 1 week.

Cauliflower: Mild and usually white. Florets should be firm and compact. Largest, toughest stalks usually not eaten. Use raw in salads, or cook.

Kale: Mild cabbage flavor; many varieties and colors. Store in coldest part of refrigerator 2 to 3 days (any longer, and flavor gets very strong). Remove and discard tough center stalk.

Kohlrabi (Cabbage Turnip): Bulbs have mild broccoli–celery root flavor. Leaves have flavor similar to collard greens. Use raw; add to soups, stews, stir-fries. Refrigerate leaves up to 4 days, bulbs up to 10 days.

OTHER VEGETABLES

Artichoke, Globe: Available fresh, canned (hearts and bottoms) in various sizes: jumbo for stuffing and steaming, baby in marinated salads. Or use sautéed or roasted. Refrigerate in plastic bag up to 1 week.

Artichoke, Jerusalem (Sunchoke): Available year-round (season peaks October to March). Choose hard artichokes with smooth skins and no soft spots. Use raw in salads, or boiled, steamed, fried. Refrigerate in plastic bag up to 1 week.

Celery: Crisp, mild and stringy stalks. Use raw in salads, or cook.

Corn: White, yellow, bicolored. Choose bright green, tight-fitting husks; fresh-looking silk; plump, consistently sized kernels. Wrap unhusked in damp paper towels; refrigerate up to 2 days.

English Cucumber: Available year-round (peak is May to August). Virtually seedless. Choose firm cucumbers with smooth skins; avoid shriveled or soft spots. Refrigerate in plastic bag up to 10 days.

Okra: Available fresh year-round in the South (May to October in rest of United States), canned, frozen. Choose tender, unblemished, bright green pods less than 4 inches long. Refrigerate in plastic bag up to 3 days.

Parsnips

Cassava (Yuca)

Rutabaga

Taro

Turnip

Carrots

Gingerroot

Beets

Celeriac

Radishes

Sweet
Potatoes

Fennel

Daikon Radish

Fingerling
Potatoes

Yukon Gold
Potatoes

Purple (or Blue)
Potatoes

New/Baby
Potatoes

Round Red
Potatoes

Russet/Idaho
Potatoes

ROOT VEGETABLES

Beets: Colors include reddish-purple, golden, rainbow and white. Choose brightly colored, firm beets with smooth skins. Remove greens as soon as possible; store separately. Greens and roots should be cooked. Refrigerate in plastic bag up to 1 week.

Carrots and Parsnips: Mild sweet flavor. Choose those with no signs of decay or cracking. Refrigerate in plastic bag up to 2 weeks.

Cassava (Yuca): Bland, starchy; absorbs other flavors. Two types: sweet and bitter (which must be cooked before eating). Choose hard, evenly shaped yuca; avoid blemishes, cracks, mold, stickiness. Store in cool, dark place up to 3 days. Use as side dish or in soups.

Fennel: Mild licorice flavor. Bulbs and greens can be eaten raw or cooked. Choose clean, firm bulbs with fresh looking greens. Refrigerate in plastic bag up to 1 week.

Jicama: A sweet vegetable that looks like a turnip and can be eaten raw; use in salads.

Gingerroot: Peppery, slightly sweet. Choose firm, smooth roots. Refrigerate fresh, unpeeled in plastic bag up to 3 weeks; freeze up to 6 months.

Radishes: Mild to peppery flavor. Great in salads, as snacks. Choose firm radishes with bright colors. **Daikon** are much larger; good in salads, stir-fries.

Refrigerate either variety in plastic bag up to 1 week.

Sweet Potatoes: Available in varieties ranging from pale skin with light yellow flesh to dark orange or red skin and flesh. Often mistakenly called yams but true yams are not sweet potatoes. Choose nicely shaped, smooth, firm potatoes with evenly colored skins. Store in cool (45°F to 60°F), dry, dark, well-ventilated place up to 2 weeks.

Turnips, Rutabagas, Celeriac: Good roasted, used in stews, baked dishes. Choose firm vegetables with no signs of decay or bruising. Refrigerate in plastic bag up to 2 weeks.

POTATOES

Store potatoes in a cool (45°F to 60°F) dry, dark, well-ventilated place as directed below.

All-Purpose Potatoes: Purple and **Yukon Gold** can be used with any cooking technique. Most of the color of purple potatoes will fade during cooking. Store 2 to 3 weeks.

Starchy Potatoes: Both **Russet** and **Idaho** are great for baking or frying. Store 3 to 5 weeks.

Waxy Potatoes: Fingerling, New and **Red** are great in soups or salads, as they hold their shape after cooking; also great for roasting and boiling. Store 2 to 3 weeks.

Hubbard Squash

Sweet
Dumpling
Squash

Buttercup
Squash

Sugar
Pie Pumpkin

Acorn
Squash

Delicata Squash

Turban Squash

Zucchini

Carnival
Squash

Pattypan Squash

Yellow
Crookneck Squash

Butternut
Squash

Spaghetti
Squash

Jack Be Little
Pumpkin

Yellow Summer Squash

Chayote Squash

Chinese
Long Beans

Mung Bean
Sprouts

Edamame

Yellow Wax
Beans

Green String Beans

Sugar Snap Peas

Snow Peas

Pea Shoots

SQUASH

Acorn: Green skin; acorn-shaped. Bake halves with filling or remove rind, cut up and roast.

Butternut: Yellow or gold; peanut-shaped. Cook as for acorn squash.

Carnival: Cream, orange or green. Flavor similar to sweet potatoes or butternut squash. Bake or steam.

Chayote: Mild flavor; requires bold seasoning. Refrigerate in plastic bag up to 1 month. Use raw in salads, or stuff and bake.

Delicata: Pale yellow skin with green stripes. Sweet, buttered-corn flavor. Seed cavity is small; lots of edible flesh. Bake or steam.

Pattypan: These small, flying saucer-shaped squash have thin, smooth to slightly bumpy skin that typically isn't removed for cooking or eating.

Summer: Thin, edible skin; soft, edible seeds. Choose firm squash with shiny, unblemished skin. Refrigerate in plastic bag up to 5 days.

Sweet Dumpling: Green, white stripes. Sweet; good stuffed with rice or stuffing.

Winter: Thick, hard skin, seeds. Choose squash heavy for its size and with dull-colored hard rind (no soft spots). Whole: store in cool (45°F to 60°F), dry, dark place with good ventilation up to 2 months. Cut and peeled: refrigerate in plastic wrap up to 5 days.

FRESH LEGUMES

Legumes are seed pods that split along both sides when ripe. Choose bright, smooth, crisp pods. Refrigerate in plastic bag up to 4 days.

Edamame (Fresh Soybeans): Often sold in their fuzzy green pods (avoid blemishes) or frozen. Serve as snack; add to rice, salads, scrambled eggs; mash into guacamole.

Long Beans (Asparagus Bean, Chinese Long Bean, Yard-Long Bean): Same family as black-eyed peas. Milder, less sweet than green beans. Usually cut in half or smaller pieces, then sautéed or stir fried. Mushy if overcooked.

Mung Bean Sprouts: Tender; great for salads or stir-fries. Refrigerate in plastic bag up to 3 days.

Pea Shoots: The best leaves and tendrils from pea plants. Choose fresh, crisp, young, tender shoots with top leaves. Remove coarse stems. Use raw in salads; steam as a side dish with lemon or sprinkled with ginger and sugar. Use within 2 days.

Peas (English, Sugar Snap, Snow): English peas must be removed from pods before cooking; sugar snaps and snow peas can be eaten in the pod. All can be eaten raw or cooked; great in salads or side dishes.

FRESH VEGETABLE COOKING CHART

Store vegetables in plastic bag in refrigerator or at room temperature if indicated in chart. Wash vegetables before using. Use fresh vegetables within a few days. For grilling direction, see page 422.

To Boil: In saucepan, heat 1 inch water to boiling. Add vegetables. Heat to boiling; reduce heat to low. Cook as directed and drain.

To Steam: In saucepan or skillet, place steamer basket in ½ inch water (water should not touch bottom of basket). Place vegetables in basket. Cover; heat to boiling; reduce heat to low. Steam as directed.

To Sauté: In skillet, cook in butter or oil over medium-high heat as directed.

To Bake: Heat oven to 350°F. Place vegetables in oven and bake as directed.

To Roast: Heat oven to 425°F. Toss cut (unless stated otherwise) vegetables with about 1 tablespoon olive oil and season as desired. Place vegetables in baking pan and roast as directed.

To Microwave: Use microwavable dish with cover or use plastic wrap to cover. Paper towels or plastic wrap used in the microwave should be microwave-safe. Add 2 tablespoons water to dish with vegetables. Microwave on High, unless stated otherwise, as directed; drain. Stir or rearrange vegetables once or twice during cooking. Let stand covered for 1 to 2 minutes to finish cooking.*

VEGETABLE WITH AMOUNT FOR 4 SERVINGS	PREPARATION	CONVENTIONAL DIRECTIONS	MICROWAVE DIRECTIONS*
Artichokes, Globe (4 medium)	Remove discolored leaves; trim stem even with base. Cut 1 inch off top. Snip tips off leaves. To retain color, dip in cold water mixed with lemon juice.	**Boil:** Covered with water, adding 2 tablespoons lemon juice to water, 20 to 30 minutes or until leaves pull out easily and bottom is tender when pierced with knife.	Place 1 or 2 artichokes in dish; add ¼ cup water. Microwave 5 to 7 minutes or until leaves pull out easily and bottom is tender when pierced with knife.
Artichokes, Jerusalem (1 lb)	Leave whole, or cut. To retain color, toss with cold water mixed with lemon juice.	**Boil:** Covered 7 to 9 minutes or until crisp-tender. **Steam:** 15 to 20 minutes or until crisp-tender.	Place in dish. Microwave 5 to 7 minutes or until crisp-tender.
Asparagus (1½ lb)	Break off ends of spears. Tie spears in bundles with string, or hold together with band of foil (do not use foil if microwaving). Or cut into 1-inch pieces.	**Boil:** Uncovered 6 to 8 minutes or until crisp-tender. **Steam:** 6 to 8 minutes or until crisp-tender. **Roast whole:** 10 to 12 minutes.	Place in dish. Microwave 4 to 6 minutes or until crisp-tender.
Beans, Green, Purple Wax and Yellow Wax (1 lb)	Remove ends. Leave beans whole, or cut into 1-inch pieces.	**Boil:** Uncovered 6 to 8 minutes or until crisp-tender. **Steam:** 10 to 12 minutes or until crisp-tender. **Roast (whole):** 6 to 8 minutes.	Place in dish. Microwave 8 to 10 minutes or until crisp-tender.
Beans, Lima (3 lb unshelled; 3 cups shelled)	To shell beans, remove thin outer edge of pod with sharp knife or scissors. Slip out beans.	**Boil:** Covered 15 to 20 minutes or until tender.	Place in dish; add ½ cup water. Microwave on High 4 to 5 minutes or until boiling; then Medium-Low 20 to 25 minutes or until tender.
Beets (5 medium)	Cut off all but 2 inches of tops. Leave whole with root ends attached. Peel after cooking.	**Boil:** Add water to cover and 1 tablespoon vinegar. Boil, covered, 20 to 30 minutes. **Steam:** 45 to 50 minutes or until tender. **Roast:** 35 to 40 minutes.	Place in dish with 2 tablespoons water. Microwave 12 to 16 minutes or until tender.

VEGETABLE WITH AMOUNT FOR 4 SERVINGS	PREPARATION	CONVENTIONAL DIRECTIONS	MICROWAVE DIRECTIONS*
Broccoli (1½ lb)	Trim off large leaves; remove tough ends of stems. Cut as desired.	**Boil:** Uncovered 4 to 6 minutes or until crisp-tender. **Steam:** 10 to 11 minutes or until crisp-tender.	Place in dish. Microwave 6 to 8 minutes or until crisp-tender.
Brussels Sprouts (1 lb)	Remove discolored leaves; cut off stem ends. Cut large sprouts in half.	**Boil:** Uncovered 8 to 12 minutes or until tender. **Steam:** 8 to 12 minutes or until tender. **Roast:** 12 to 15 minutes.	Place in dish. Microwave 5 to 6 minutes or until tender.
Carrots (6 or 7 medium)	Peel; cut off ends. Leave ready-to-eat baby-cut carrots whole or cut as desired.	**Boil:** Covered 7 to 10 minutes or until tender. **Steam:** 8 to 10 minutes or until tender. **Roast:** 25 to 30 minutes.	Place in dish. Microwave 5 to 9 minutes or until crisp-tender.
Cauliflower (1 medium head)	Remove outer leaves and stalk; cut off any discoloration. Leave whole or separate into florets.	**Boil:** Uncovered 8 to 12 minutes or until tender. **Steam:** 8 to 12 minutes or until tender. **Roast:** 15 to 20 minutes.	Place in dish. Microwave 8 to 10 minutes or until tender.
Corn (4 ears)	Husk ears and remove silk just before cooking.	**Boil:** Add water to cover and 1 tablespoon sugar. Boil, uncovered, 5 to 7 minutes. **Steam:** 5 to 7 minutes.	Wrap ears in waxed paper or place in dish. 1 ear: Microwave 2 to 3 minutes. 2 ears: Microwave 3 to 4 minutes.
Eggplant (1 medium)	Remove stems. Peel can be left on, or peel if desired. Cut as desired.	**Boil:** Covered 5 to 8 minutes or until tender. **Steam:** 5 to 7 minutes or until tender. **Sauté:** With 2 tablespoons butter, 5 to 10 minutes or until tender.	Place in dish. Microwave 7 to 9 minutes or until tender.
Fennel (3 to 4 medium)	Remove feathery tops and tough or discolored outer ribs; trim base. Cut bulbs into fourths.	**Boil:** Covered 8 to 11 minutes or until tender. **Steam:** 12 to 15 minutes or until tender. **Roast:** 20 to 25 minutes.	Place in dish. Microwave 4 to 5 minutes or until tender.
Greens: Beet, Chicory, Collards, Escarole, Kale, Mustard, Spinach, Swiss Chard and Turnip (1 lb)	Remove root ends and imperfect leaves.	**Steam:** 5 to 8 minutes or until tender.	Place in dish. Microwave beet, chicory or escarole 8 to 10 minutes or until tender. Microwave collards, kale, mustard, spinach, Swiss chard or turnips 4 to 6 minutes or until tender.
Kohlrabi (4 medium)	Cut off root ends and tops. Cut as desired.	**Boil:** Covered 15 to 20 minutes or until tender. **Steam:** 8 to 12 minutes or until tender.	Place in dish. Microwave 3 to 5 minutes or until tender.

VEGETABLE WITH AMOUNT FOR 4 SERVINGS	PREPARATION	CONVENTIONAL DIRECTIONS	MICROWAVE DIRECTIONS*
Leeks (6 medium)	Remove green tops to within 2 inches of white part. Peel outside layer of bulbs. Cut as desired.	**Boil:** Covered 10 to 12 minutes or until tender. **Steam:** 10 to 12 minutes or until tender. **Roast:** 12 to 15 minutes.	Place in dish. Microwave 4 to 5 minutes or until tender.
Mushrooms (1 lb)	Wipe each mushroom with damp paper towel to remove dirt. Trim off stem. Leave whole, or cut as desired.	**Sauté:** With 1 tablespoon butter, 4 to 6 minutes, stirring frequently, until tender. **Roast:** 5 to 10 minutes.	Place in dish; add 1 tablespoon butter. Microwave 3 to 4 minutes or until tender.
Okra (1 lb)	Remove ends. Leave whole or cut into slices.	**Boil:** Uncovered 8 to 10 minutes or until tender. **Steam:** 6 to 8 minutes or until tender.	Place in dish; add ¼ cup water. Microwave 5 to 6 minutes or until tender.
Onions, White, Yellow and Red (8 to 10 small)	Peel onions in cold water to prevent eyes from watering. Cut as desired.	**Boil:** Covered 15 to 20 minutes. **Steam:** 15 to 20 minutes. **Sauté:** With 2 tablespoons butter, 6 to 9 minutes or until tender. **Roast:** 30 to 40 minutes.	Place in dish; add ¼ cup water. Microwave 7 to 9 minutes or until tender.
Parsnips (6 to 8 medium)	Peel; cut off ends. Leave whole or cut as desired.	**Boil:** Covered 9 to 15 minutes or until tender. **Steam:** 9 to 15 minutes or until tender. **Roast:** 25 to 30 minutes.	Place in dish. Microwave 5 to 6 minutes or until tender.
Pea Pods, Snow or Chinese (1 lb)	Remove tips and strings.	**Boil:** Uncovered 2 to 3 minutes or until crisp-tender. **Steam:** 3 to 5 minutes or until crisp-tender.	Place in dish. Microwave 6 to 7 minutes or until crisp-tender.
Peas, Sweet (2 lb)	Shell just before cooking.	**Boil:** Uncovered 5 to 10 minutes or until tender. **Steam:** 8 to 10 minutes or until tender.	Place in dish. Microwave 4 to 6 minutes or until tender.
Peas, Sugar Snap (1 lb)	Snip off stem ends and remove strings.	**Boil:** Uncovered 4 to 5 minutes or until crisp-tender. **Steam:** 6 to 7 minutes or until crisp-tender.	Place in dish. Microwave 6 to 7 minutes or until crisp-tender.
Peppers, Bell (2 medium)	Remove stems, seeds and membranes. Leave whole to stuff and bake, or cut as desired.	**Steam:** 4 to 6 minutes or until crisp-tender. **Sauté:** With 1 tablespoon butter, 3 to 5 minutes or until crisp-tender. **Roast:** 15 to 20 minutes.	Place in dish. Microwave 3 to 4 minutes or until crisp-tender.
Potatoes, Fingerling (10 to 12) Small, Red and White (10 to 12)	Leave whole, or cut as desired.	**Boil:** Add water to cover. Boil, uncovered, 15 to 20 minutes or until tender. **Steam:** 18 to 22 minutes or until tender. **Roast:** 25 to 30 minutes.	Place in dish; add ¼ cup water. Microwave 9 to 11 minutes or until tender.

VEGETABLE WITH AMOUNT FOR 4 SERVINGS	PREPARATION	CONVENTIONAL DIRECTIONS	MICROWAVE DIRECTIONS*
Potatoes, Red and White (6 medium) Russet (4 medium) Yukon Gold (6 medium)	Leave whole, or peel and cut as desired.	**Boil:** Add water to cover. Boil, uncovered, 15 to 20 minutes or until tender. **Steam:** 15 to 20 minutes or until tender. **Bake:** Uncovered 1 hour or until tender. **Roast:** 40 to 45 minutes.	Pierce whole potatoes to allow steam to escape. Place on paper towel. 1 or 2 potatoes: Microwave 4 to 6 minutes or until tender. Cover; let stand 5 minutes. 3 or 4 potatoes: Microwave 8 to 12 minutes or until tender. Cover; let stand 5 minutes.
Potatoes, Sweet (4 medium)	Leave whole, or peel and cut as desired.	**Boil:** Add water to cover. Boil, uncovered, 10 to 15 minutes or until tender. **Steam:** 15 to 20 minutes or until tender. **Bake:** Uncovered 1 hour or until tender. **Roast:** 40 to 45 minutes.	Pierce whole potatoes to allow steam to escape. Place on paper towel. Microwave 9 to 11 minutes, or until tender. Cover; let stand 5 minutes.
Rutabagas (2 medium)	Peel; cut as desired.	**Boil:** Covered 20 to 25 minutes or until tender. **Steam:** 20 to 25 minutes or until tender. **Roast:** 40 to 45 minutes.	Place in dish; add ¼ cup water. Microwave 13 to 15 minutes or until tender.
Squash, Summer: Chayote, Crookneck, Zucchini, Pattypan, Straightneck (1½ lb)	Remove stem and blossom ends, but do not peel. Cut as desired.	**Boil:** Uncovered 5 to 10 minutes. **Steam:** 5 to 7 minutes or until tender. **Sauté:** With 1 tablespoon olive oil, 5 to 10 minutes or until tender.	Place in dish. Microwave 4 to 6 minutes or until almost tender.
Squash, Winter: Acorn, Buttercup, Butternut, Pumpkin, Spaghetti (2 lb)	Cook in halves or pieces with seeds removed.	**Boil:** Peeled and cut up, covered, 10 to 15 minutes or until tender. **Steam:** 10 to 15 minutes. **Bake:** Place squash halves cut side up in baking dish. Cover and bake 40 minutes or until tender.	Whole squash except spaghetti: Pierce with knife in several places to allow steam to escape. Place on paper towel. Microwave uncovered 5 minutes or until squash feels warm to the touch. Cut in half; remove seeds. Arrange halves in dish. Microwave 5 to 8 minutes or until tender. Whole spaghetti squash: Pierce with knife in several places to allow steam to escape. Place on paper towel. Microwave uncovered 18 to 23 minutes or until tender. Cut in half; remove seeds and fibers.
Turnips (4 medium)	Cut off tops. Leave whole, or cut as desired.	**Boil:** Covered 20 to 25 minutes. **Steam:** 15 to 20 minutes or until tender. **Roast:** 30 to 35 minutes.	Place in dish. Microwave 6 to 8 minutes or until tender.

*Vegetables continue to cook for a short time after being microwaved. Most vegetables require a stand time after cooking, which completes the cooking and equalizes the temperature throughout the food.

Artichokes with Rosemary Butter EASY

To eat a fresh artichoke, remove a leaf, dip it in the butter mixture and draw it between your teeth to scrape off the meaty part. Continue removing leaves until you see the center cone of light green leaves. Cut the leaves from the cone, then remove and discard the fuzzy choke to reveal the meaty heart in the center.

PREP 10 min **TOTAL** 45 min • 4 servings

- 4 **medium artichokes**
- ½ **cup butter**
- 1 **teaspoon chopped fresh or ¼ teaspoon dried rosemary leaves, crushed**
- 1 **teaspoon lemon juice**

1 Remove any discolored leaves and the small leaves at base of artichokes. Trim stems even with base of artichokes. Cutting straight across, slice 1 inch off tops and discard tops. Cut off points of remaining leaves with scissors. Rinse artichokes with cold water.

2 Place steamer basket in ½ inch water in 4-quart Dutch oven (water should not touch bottom of basket). Place artichokes in basket. Cover tightly. Heat to boiling; reduce heat. Steam 20 to 25 minutes or until bottoms are tender when pierced with knife.

3 In small microwavable bowl, microwave butter until melted; stir in rosemary and lemon juice. Pluck out artichoke leaves one at a time. Dip base of leaf into rosemary butter.

1 Serving: Calories 280; Total Fat 23g (Saturated Fat 15g, Trans Fat 1.5g); Cholesterol 60mg; Sodium 280mg; Total Carbohydrate 14g (Dietary Fiber 7g, Sugars 1g); Protein 4g **Exchanges:** 2 Vegetable, 5 Fat **Carbohydrate Choices:** 1

Asparagus with Parmesan

CALORIE SMART • FAST

PREP 10 min **TOTAL** 20 min • 4 servings

- 1½ **lb fresh asparagus**
- 1 **tablespoon olive oil**
- 1 **tablespoon butter**
- 1 **medium green onion, sliced (1 tablespoon)**
- 1 **clove garlic, finely chopped**
- ½ **teaspoon salt**
- ¼ **teaspoon freshly ground black pepper**
- ¼ **cup freshly grated or shredded Parmesan cheese**

1 Heat oven to 375°F. Snap off tough bottom ends of asparagus. In 3-quart saucepan, heat 1 inch water. Add asparagus. Return to boiling; reduce heat. Simmer uncovered 4 minutes.

2 Meanwhile, in ungreased 8-inch square pan, place oil, butter, onion and garlic. Heat uncovered in oven 5 minutes.

3 Drain asparagus; spread in oil mixture in pan. Sprinkle with salt, pepper and cheese. Bake uncovered about 10 minutes or until cheese is melted.

1 Serving: Calories 110; Total Fat 8g (Saturated Fat 3.5g, Trans Fat 0g); Cholesterol 10mg; Sodium 430mg; Total Carbohydrate 4g (Dietary Fiber 2g, Sugars 2g); Protein 4g **Exchanges:** 1 Vegetable, 1½ Fat **Carbohydrate Choices:** 0

Green Beans with Parmesan Substitute fresh whole green beans for the asparagus.

Asparagus with Goat Cheese Omit green onion. Substitute crumbled plain goat cheese. Sprinkle 2 tablespoons chopped walnuts and 1 teaspoon grated lemon peel with the goat cheese. Bake about 10 minutes or until cheese is warm.

Preparing Artichokes

Snapping Ends from Asparagus

Remove discolored leaves, leaves with thorns and small leaves at base of artichoke.

Trim stem even with base of artichoke; cut 1 inch from top of artichoke and discard top.

Using scissors, cut points from remaining leaves; rinse artichokes with cold water.

Snap off tough ends of asparagus where they break easily.

Green Beans with Glazed Shallots

Roasted Beets

Green Beans with Glazed Shallots CALORIE SMART • FAST

PREP 15 min **TOTAL** 15 min • 6 servings

- 1 lb fresh green beans, trimmed
- 2 tablespoons butter
- 2 shallots, finely chopped
- ½ teaspoon sugar
- 1 teaspoon lemon juice
- 1 tablespoon chopped fresh dill weed
- ¼ teaspoon salt

1 In 3-quart saucepan, place green beans in 1 inch water. Heat to boiling; boil uncovered 6 to 8 minutes or until crisp-tender. Drain; return to saucepan.

2 Meanwhile, in 10-inch skillet, melt butter over medium heat. Cook shallots in butter 2 to 3 minutes, stirring occasionally, until crisp-tender. Stir in sugar. Cook 2 to 3 minutes longer, stirring occasionally, until shallots are glazed and brown. Stir in lemon juice, dill weed and salt.

3 Add shallot mixture to green beans; toss to coat.

1 Serving: Calories 60; Total Fat 4g (Saturated Fat 2.5g, Trans Fat 0g); Cholesterol 10mg; Sodium 130mg; Total Carbohydrate 5g (Dietary Fiber 2g, Sugars 2g); Protein 1g **Exchanges:** 1 Vegetable, 1 Fat **Carbohydrate Choices:** ½

Cooking Beet Greens

If you are lucky enough to have fresh beet greens, here's how to cook them. Wash them well and cut the greens and stems into pieces. Heat 1 tablespoon olive oil in a skillet and cook 1 or 2 cloves chopped garlic until tender. Add the cooked greens; sprinkle with salt and pepper. Cook and stir 5 to 8 minutes or until wilted.

Roasted Beets CALORIE SMART • EASY

Beets are usually available year-round. If given a choice, pick smaller, young beets for the best flavor.

PREP 10 min **TOTAL** 1 hr 20 min • 6 servings

- 2 lb small beets (1½ to 2 inch)
- ½ teaspoon salt
- ¼ teaspoon coarsely ground black pepper
- 2 tablespoons olive oil
- 2 tablespoons chopped fresh basil leaves
- 1 tablespoon balsamic vinegar

1 Heat oven to 425°F. Cut off all but 2 inches of beet tops. Wash beets; leave whole with root ends attached. Place beets in ungreased 13x9-inch pan. Sprinkle with salt and pepper. Drizzle with oil.

2 Roast uncovered about 40 minutes or until beets are tender. Let beets cool until easy to handle, about 30 minutes. Peel beets and cut off root ends; cut beets into ½-inch slices.

3 In medium bowl, toss beets, basil and vinegar. Serve warm or at room temperature.

1 Serving: Calories 90; Total Fat 4.5g (Saturated Fat 0.5g, Trans Fat 0g); Cholesterol 0mg; Sodium 270mg; Total Carbohydrate 10g (Dietary Fiber 2g, Sugars 9g); Protein 2g **Exchanges:** 2 Vegetable, 1 Fat **Carbohydrate Choices:** ½

Preparing Beets

Before cooking, cut off all but 2 inches of stems. Wash beets; leave whole with root ends attached.

After cooking, peel beets with paring knife under cold water, removing stems, skins and roots.

Learn to ROAST

Roasting is a simple dry-heat cooking technique that is easy to master. "Dry heat" simply means that no liquid is added and it is the heat of the oven that cooks the food, rather than moisture being added to the food. Foods that are roasted are cooked uncovered. The primary difference between roasting and baking is based on the foods being cooked and the temperature used to cook the food. Crispy on the outside and tender on the inside, roasting makes meats and veggies look and taste fantastic. Sugars in vegetables are caramelized; heightening and sweetening their flavors. Meats develop a delicious, brown crust when roasted.

To roast, the oven temperature will usually be higher than for baked foods—above 400°F. It is important to use the correct oven temperature for roasting so that foods have a browned, slightly caramelized exterior and a tender interior.

Many vegetables, such as onions, carrots, potatoes and bell peppers, benefit from roasting. Each vegetable might cook at a different rate. For instance, if you want to add zucchini to the mix, you might add it after potatoes and carrots are partially cooked. Here are some guidelines for times for vegetables that can easily be roasted. For most vegetables, roast at 425°F unless a recipe indicates a different temperature. For roasting meats, see chart on page 314 for times.

- Cut vegetables into similar-size pieces so that they cook evenly.

- Use a large enough pan so that the vegetables can be in a single layer.

- Use a short-sided pan, such as a 15x10x1-inch or shallow roasting pan, to evaporate moisture from the foods, so they roast rather than steam.

- Toss vegetables with a small amount of olive oil and season as desired.

- Individual recipes will provide specific directions, but in general, cook until just slightly firm when pierced with a fork.

- Try roasting a single vegetable, then experiment with different combinations of vegetables that you like.

- Check the food pieces for color on the sides that touch the pan, as these sides will brown more quickly than the tops. Stir or turn pieces so that all sides brown.

> ## Vegetable Roasting
>
> While times differ based on factors such as how hot your oven runs or the size of the vegetables, here are some basic time guidelines for perfectly raosted vegetables:
>
> - **Carrots, parsnips, potatoes, sweet potatoes, Brussels sprouts, onions and fennel:** 35 to 45 minutes
> - **Bell peppers, cauliflower, green beans, butternut squash:** 20 to 25 minutes
> - **Zucchini, asparagus, leeks, pattypan squash, eggplant:** 15 to 20 minutes

Roasted Vegetables CALORIE SMART

Pick baby-cut carrots that are all about the same size so they cook evenly.

PREP 15 min **TOTAL** 40 min • 10 servings

> 3 tablespoons olive or vegetable oil
> ½ teaspoon salt
> ⅛ teaspoon pepper
> 1 clove garlic, finely chopped
> 1 cup ready-to-eat baby-cut carrots
> 6 small red potatoes, cut into quarters
> 2 small onions, cut into ½-inch wedges
> 1 small red bell pepper, cut into 1-inch pieces
> 1 medium zucchini, cut lengthwise in half, then cut crosswise into 1-inch slices
> 1 cup grape or cherry tomatoes

1 Heat oven to 425°F. In small bowl, stir oil, salt, pepper and garlic until well mixed. In ungreased 15x10x1-inch pan, toss carrots, potatoes, onions, bell pepper and zucchini with oil mixture until coated.

2 Roast uncovered 25 minutes, stirring once. Stir in tomatoes. Roast 5 to 10 minutes longer or until vegetables are tender and starting to brown.

1 Serving: Calories 110; Total Fat 4.5g (Saturated Fat 0.5g, Trans Fat 0g); Cholesterol 0mg; Sodium 130mg; Total Carbohydrate 16g (Dietary Fiber 3g, Sugars 3g); Protein 2g **Exchanges:** ½ Starch, 1 Vegetable, 1 Fat **Carbohydrate Choices:** 1

Roasted Root Vegetables Omit bell pepper, zucchini and tomatoes. Add 1½ cups each peeled, cubed parsnips and peeled, cubed turnips. Roast 35 to 40 minutes or until vegetables are fork-tender.

Broccoli with Roasted Red Peppers and Hazelnuts

CALORIE SMART • FAST

PREP 20 min TOTAL 20 min • 8 servings

- 5 cups fresh broccoli florets
- 1 tablespoon olive or vegetable oil
- 1 clove garlic, finely chopped
- ¼ cup chopped hazelnuts (filberts)
- ½ cup chopped drained roasted red bell peppers (from 7-oz jar) (to roast your own, see page 247)
- ¼ teaspoon salt

1 In 2-quart saucepan, heat 1 cup water to boiling. Add broccoli. Cover; cook about 1 minute or just until crisp. Drain and immediately place broccoli in ice water.

2 In 12-inch skillet, heat oil over medium heat. Cook garlic and hazelnuts in oil 1 to 2 minutes, stirring frequently, until nuts are lightly toasted.

3 Drain broccoli. Stir broccoli, roasted peppers and salt into nut mixture. Cook about 3 minutes, stirring occasionally, until broccoli is crisp-tender.

1 Serving (½ Cup): Calories 70; Total Fat 4g (Saturated Fat 0g, Trans Fat 0g); Cholesterol 0mg; Sodium 90mg; Total Carbohydrate 5g (Dietary Fiber 2g, Sugars 2g); Protein 2g **Exchanges:** 1 Vegetable, 1 Fat **Carbohydrate Choices:** ½

> ### Brussels Sprouts
> Part of the cruciferous vegetable family, Brussels sprouts look like tiny cabbages but deliver big on flavor. Choose fresh-looking sprouts and remove any discolored outer leaves before cooking.

Roasted Red Bell Peppers (page 247)

Cheesy Bacon Brussels Sprouts

Cheesy Bacon Brussels Sprouts CALORIE SMART

Brussels sprouts have gotten a bad rap over the years because they are often boiled to mushiness, which doesn't show them at their best. These spectacular sprouts, combined with bacon and cheese, may just convert even sworn Brussels sprouts haters.

PREP 35 min TOTAL 1 hr 15 min • 10 servings

- 1¼ lb fresh Brussels sprouts (1 to 1½ inch), cut in half (5 cups)
- 6 slices bacon, cut into 1-inch pieces
- 1 tablespoon butter
- 1 large onion, finely chopped (1 cup)
- 1 tablespoon all-purpose flour
- ¼ teaspoon dried thyme leaves
- ¼ teaspoon pepper
- ¾ cup half-and-half
- 2 teaspoons chicken bouillon granules
- ⅓ cup shredded Parmesan cheese
- ½ cup shredded Cheddar cheese (2 oz)

1 Heat oven to 350°F. In 3-quart saucepan, place Brussels sprouts and enough water just to cover. Heat to boiling; boil 6 to 8 minutes or until crisp-tender. Drain and return to saucepan; set aside.

2 In 10-inch skillet, cook bacon over medium heat 6 to 8 minutes, stirring occasionally, until crisp. Drain on paper towels; set aside. Reserve 1 tablespoon drippings in skillet.

3 Add butter to bacon drippings. Heat over medium-high heat until butter is melted. Add onion; cook 2 to 3 minutes, stirring frequently, until crisp-tender. Add flour, thyme and pepper; cook and stir until well blended. Gradually stir in half-and-half and bouillon granules. Heat to boiling, stirring constantly; boil and stir 1 minute.

4 Remove from heat; stir in Parmesan cheese. Pour sauce over Brussels sprouts in saucepan; mix gently. Spoon into ungreased 2-quart casserole.

5 Bake uncovered 15 minutes. Sprinkle with bacon and Cheddar cheese. Bake 10 to 15 minutes longer or until bubbly and cheese is melted.

1 Serving (½ Cup): Calories 130; Total Fat 8g (Saturated Fat 4g, Trans Fat 0g); Cholesterol 20mg; Sodium 330mg; Total Carbohydrate 8g (Dietary Fiber 3g, Sugars 3g); Protein 6g **Exchanges:** 1 Vegetable, ½ High-Fat Meat, 1 Fat **Carbohydrate Choices:** ½

Cheesy Bacon Broccoli Substitute 1¼ lb fresh broccoli, cut into 1½-inch pieces, for the Brussels sprouts.

Cheesy Bacon Green Beans Substitute 1 bag (1 lb) frozen cut green beans for the Brussels sprouts. In 2-quart microwavable casserole, place beans and 2 tablespoons water. Cover and microwave on High 5 minutes; drain. Continue as directed in Steps 2 through 5.

Cranberry-Pistachio Brussels Sprouts CALORIE SMART • FAST

PREP 25 min **TOTAL** 25 min • 6 servings

- 2 slices thick-sliced bacon
- 1 lb Brussels sprouts, trimmed, cut in half
- ¼ cup chicken broth
- ⅓ cup sweetened dried cranberries
- ¼ cup salted roasted pistachio nuts
- 1 tablespoon honey
- ¼ teaspoon cracked black pepper

1 In 10-inch skillet, cook bacon over medium-high heat until crisp. Drain on paper towels. Crumble bacon; set aside. Reserve 1 tablespoon drippings in skillet.

2 Cook Brussels sprouts in bacon drippings over medium heat 3 to 4 minutes, stirring frequently, until they just begin to brown. Add broth; reduce heat to medium-low. Cover and cook 5 to 6 minutes longer or until broth is evaporated and Brussels sprouts are tender.

3 Add cranberries, nuts, honey, pepper and bacon; toss to coat.

1 Serving: Calories 110; Total Fat 4.5g (Saturated Fat 1g, Trans Fat 0g); Cholesterol 0mg; Sodium 170mg; Total Carbohydrate 14g (Dietary Fiber 2g, Sugars 9g); Protein 4g **Exchanges:** ½ Starch, 1 Vegetable, 1 Fat **Carbohydrate Choices:** 1

Cranberry-Pistachio Brussels Sprouts

Sweet-Sour Red Cabbage CALORIE SMART

Some like this classic cabbage dish sweet, and some prefer it sour. For a sweeter touch, add another tablespoon of brown sugar; for a more sour taste, add an extra tablespoon of vinegar.

PREP 35 min **TOTAL** 50 min • 8 servings

- 1 medium head red cabbage (1½ lb), shredded
- 4 slices bacon, chopped
- 1 small onion, sliced
- ¼ cup packed brown sugar
- 2 tablespoons all-purpose flour
- ¼ cup water
- 3 tablespoons white vinegar
- ¼ teaspoon salt
- ⅛ teaspoon pepper

1 In 10-inch skillet, heat 1 inch water to boiling. Add cabbage; return to boiling. Boil uncovered about 15 minutes, stirring occasionally, until tender; drain and set aside. Wipe out skillet and dry with paper towel.

2 In same skillet, cook bacon over medium heat 4 minutes, stirring occasionally. Add onion. Cook 2 to 4 minutes, stirring occasionally, until bacon is crisp. Remove bacon and onion with slotted spoon; drain on paper towels. Reserve 1 tablespoon drippings in skillet.

3 Stir brown sugar and flour into bacon drippings. Stir in water, vinegar, salt and pepper until well mixed. Stir in cabbage, bacon and onion. Cook over medium heat 1 to 2 minutes, stirring occasionally, until hot.

1 Serving: Calories 100; Total Fat 4g (Saturated Fat 1.5g, Trans Fat 0g); Cholesterol 0mg; Sodium 160mg; Total Carbohydrate 13g (Dietary Fiber 2g, Sugars 10g); Protein 3g **Exchanges:** ½ Other Carbohydrate, 1 Vegetable, 1 Fat **Carbohydrate Choices:** 1

Caramelized Onions

CALORIE SMART • FAST

Sweet onions have more sugar than other onions, and it's the sugar that caramelizes, giving a deep golden brown color and rich flavor. If you can't find sweet onions, regular yellow onions can be used—just sprinkle about 1 tablespoon of brown sugar over the onions and cook as directed.

PREP 25 min **TOTAL** 25 min • 7 servings

- 2 **tablespoons butter***
- 3 **large sweet onions (Bermuda, Maui, Spanish or Walla Walla), sliced (8 cups)**
- ¼ **teaspoon salt**

In 12-inch nonstick skillet, melt butter over medium heat. Stir in onions and salt; cook uncovered 15 to 20 minutes, stirring frequently, until deep golden brown.

*Do not use margarine or vegetable oil spreads.

1 Serving: Calories 60; Total Fat 3.5g (Saturated Fat 1.5g, Trans Fat 0g); Cholesterol 10mg; Sodium 110mg; Total Carbohydrate 6g (Dietary Fiber 1g, Sugars 3g); Protein 0g **Exchanges:** 1 Vegetable, ½ Fat **Carbohydrate Choices:** ½

Cranberry Caramelized Onions Stir in ½ cup dried cranberries during last 5 to 10 minutes of cooking. Serve on turkey or chicken sandwiches.

Okra, Corn and Tomatoes

CALORIE SMART • FAST

PREP 30 min **TOTAL** 30 min • 8 servings

- 4 **slices bacon**
- 1 **cup coarsely chopped onion (1 large)**
- 2 **cups diced tomatoes (from 28-oz can), undrained**
- 2 **cans (15.25 oz each) whole kernel corn, drained**
- 2½ **cups frozen cut okra (from 1-lb bag)**
- 1 **teaspoon seasoned salt**
- ¼ **teaspoon garlic powder**
- ½ **teaspoon red pepper sauce**

1 In 12-inch skillet, cook bacon over low heat 8 to 10 minutes, turning occasionally, until crisp. Drain on paper towels. Crumble bacon; set aside. Reserve 1 tablespoon bacon drippings in skillet.

2 Cook onion in bacon drippings over medium heat 2 to 3 minutes, stirring occasionally, until tender. Stir in remaining ingredients except bacon. Heat to boiling; reduce heat to low. Cover and simmer 6 to 8 minutes, stirring occasionally, until okra is tender. Sprinkle with bacon.

1 Serving (¾ Cup): Calories 170; Total Fat 4.5g (Saturated Fat 1.5g, Trans Fat 0g); Cholesterol 5mg; Sodium 550mg; Total Carbohydrate 26g (Dietary Fiber 4g, Sugars 7g); Protein 6g **Exchanges:** 1 Starch, ½ Other Carbohydrate, 1 Vegetable, ½ Fat **Carbohydrate Choices:** 2

LEARN WITH BETTY Caramelized Onions

Perfect Onions: These onions are deep golden brown in color and will taste caramelized.

Undercooked Onions: These onions are too light in color and will not taste caramelized.

Overcooked Onions: These onions are too dark with charred edges and will taste burned.

Roasted Bell Peppers

CALORIE SMART • EASY

There is no reason to buy store-bought roasted peppers when making them at home is so, so easy! Give them a try.

PREP 10 min **TOTAL** 1 hr 20 min • 12 servings

- 6 large red, yellow or orange bell peppers (do not cut)
- 1 tablespoon olive oil

1 Heat oven to 400°F. Line 15x10x1-inch pan with foil. Arrange peppers in pan; brush with oil.

2 Roast 20 minutes; turn peppers over with tongs. Roast 20 minutes longer or until peppers are deep golden brown and charred in spots and slightly collapsed. Remove from oven. Wrap peppers in foil; let stand 15 minutes to steam and allow skins to loosen. Remove foil; let stand 15 minutes or until cool enough to handle. Reserve pan juices for another use, if desired.*

3 Remove stems. Cut peppers open; place, skin side down, on cutting board. Scrape off seeds with spoon. Turn peppers over; peel off skins, scraping off with edge of knife if necessary. Dice peppers or cut into strips. Cover and refrigerate up to 1 week or freeze up to 3 months.

*Use the reserved pan juices in soups, salad dressings or marinades, or brush on grilled chicken or add to a Bloody Mary.

1 Serving (¼ Cup): Calories 30; Total Fat 1.5g (Saturated Fat 0g, Trans Fat 0g); Cholesterol 0mg; Sodium 0mg; Total Carbohydrate 4g (Dietary Fiber 1g, Sugars 2g); Protein 0g **Exchanges:** 1 Vegetable, ½ Fat **Carbohydrate Choices:** 0

Preparing Roasted Peppers

Wrap peppers in foil; let stand 15 minutes to steam and allow skins to loosen.

Place cut peppers, skin side down, on cutting board. Scrape off seeds with spoon.

Mashed Potatoes   CALORIE SMART • EASY

Dot the mashed potatoes with small pieces of butter or sprinkle with paprika, chopped fresh parsley or chives, if you like.

PREP 10 min **TOTAL** 40 min • 6 servings

- 6 medium round red or white potatoes, Yukon Gold potatoes or russet potatoes (2 lb), peeled if desired, cut into quarters
- ⅓ to ½ cup milk, warmed
- ¼ cup butter, softened
- ½ teaspoon salt
- Dash pepper

1 In 2-quart saucepan, place potatoes and enough water just to cover potatoes. Heat to boiling; reduce heat. Cover and simmer 20 to 30 minutes or until potatoes are tender when pierced with fork; drain. Shake pan with potatoes over low heat to dry (this will help mashed potatoes be fluffier).

2 Mash potatoes in pan with potato masher until no lumps remain. Add milk in small amounts, mashing after each addition (amount of milk needed to make potatoes smooth and fluffy depends on type of potatoes used).

3 Add butter, salt and pepper. Mash vigorously until potatoes are light and fluffy and desired consistency.

1 Serving: Calories 200; Total Fat 8g (Saturated Fat 4g, Trans Fat 0g); Cholesterol 20mg; Sodium 260mg; Total Carbohydrate 28g (Dietary Fiber 3g, Sugars 1g); Protein 3g **Exchanges:** 1 Starch, 1 Other Carbohydrate, 1½ Fat **Carbohydrate Choices:** 2

LIGHTER Directions For 4 grams of fat and 145 calories per serving, use fat-free (skim) milk and reduce butter to 2 tablespoons.

Buttermilk Mashed Potatoes Substitute buttermilk for the milk.

Garlic Mashed Potatoes Cook 6 cloves garlic, peeled, with the potatoes. Mash garlic with potatoes.

Herbed Mashed Potatoes Stir in 2 tablespoons chopped fresh chives and ½ teaspoon each chopped fresh thyme leaves and rosemary leaves with the butter, salt and pepper in Step 3.

Horseradish Mashed Potatoes Add 2 tablespoons prepared mild or hot horseradish with the butter, salt and pepper in Step 3.

Potato Pancakes CALORIE SMART

Potato pancakes, or latkes, are eaten traditionally during Hanukkah, but they are great to serve any time. Serve them with sour cream or applesauce.

PREP 35 min **TOTAL** 35 min • 16 pancakes

- 4 medium russet potatoes (1½ lb), peeled
- 4 eggs, beaten
- 1 small onion, finely chopped (⅓ cup), if desired
- ¼ cup all-purpose flour
- 1 teaspoon salt
- ¼ cup vegetable oil

1 Shred enough potatoes to measure 4 cups. Rinse well; drain and pat dry.

2 In large bowl, mix potatoes, eggs, onion, flour and salt. In 12-inch skillet, heat 2 tablespoons of the oil over medium heat. Using ¼ cup potato mixture for each pancake, place 4 mounds into skillet. Flatten each with spatula to about 4 inches in diameter.

3 Cook pancakes about 4 minutes, turning once, or until golden brown. Remove from skillet; cover to keep warm. Repeat with remaining potato mixture; as mixture stands, liquid and potatoes will separate, so stir to mix as necessary. Add remaining oil to skillet as needed to prevent sticking.

1 Pancake: Calories 80; Total Fat 5g (Saturated Fat 1g, Trans Fat 0g); Cholesterol 55mg; Sodium 160mg; Total Carbohydrate 7g (Dietary Fiber 0g, Sugars 0g); Protein 2g **Exchanges:** ½ Starch, 1 Fat **Carbohydrate Choices:** ½

Candied Sweet Potatoes EASY

PREP 10 min **TOTAL** 35 min • 6 servings

- 6 medium unpeeled sweet potatoes (2 lb)*
- ⅓ cup packed brown sugar
- 3 tablespoons butter
- 3 tablespoons water
- ½ teaspoon salt

1 In 2-quart saucepan, place sweet potatoes and enough water just to cover sweet potatoes. Heat to boiling; reduce heat. Cover and simmer 20 to 25 minutes or until potatoes are tender when pierced with fork; drain. When potatoes are cool enough to handle, peel and cut into ¼-inch slices.

2 In 10-inch skillet, heat remaining ingredients over medium heat, stirring constantly, until smooth and bubbly. Add potatoes. Gently stir until glazed and hot.

*Or substitute 1 can (23 oz) sweet potatoes, drained and cut into 1/2-inch slices, for the fresh sweet potatoes; omit Step 1.

1 Serving: Calories 220; Total Fat 6g (Saturated Fat 3g, Trans Fat 0g); Cholesterol 15mg; Sodium 250mg; Total Carbohydrate 41g (Dietary Fiber 4g, Sugars 29g); Protein 2g **Exchanges:** ½ Starch, 2 Other Carbohydrate, 1 Fat **Carbohydrate Choices:** 3

Wilted Spinach CALORIE SMART • FAST

PREP 25 min **TOTAL** 25 min • 4 servings

- 2 tablespoons olive or vegetable oil
- 1 medium onion, chopped (½ cup)
- 1 slice bacon, chopped
- 1 clove garlic, finely chopped
- ½ teaspoon salt
- ¼ teaspoon pepper
- ¼ teaspoon ground nutmeg
- 1 lb fresh spinach, stems removed
- 2 tablespoons fresh lime juice

1 In 4-quart Dutch oven or saucepan, heat oil over medium heat. Cook onion, bacon and garlic in oil 8 to 10 minutes, stirring occasionally, until bacon is crisp; reduce heat to low.

2 Stir in salt, pepper and nutmeg. Gradually add spinach. Toss just until spinach is wilted. Drizzle with lime juice.

1 Serving (½ Cup): Calories 110; Total Fat 8g (Saturated Fat 1.5g, Trans Fat 0g); Cholesterol 0mg; Sodium 390mg; Total Carbohydrate 6g (Dietary Fiber 3g, Sugars 2g); Protein 3g **Exchanges:** 1 Vegetable, 1½ Fat **Carbohydrate Choices:** ½

Wilted Spinach and Kale Use ½ lb each fresh spinach and kale. Substitute ½ teaspoon dried oregano for the nutmeg.

Candied Sweet Potatoes

Spiral Summer Squash

Fried Green Tomatoes

Spiral Summer Squash

CALORIE SMART • FAST • EASY

If you love gadgets, try a vegetable spiralizer! Straight, even vegetables work best when using spiralizers. If you don't have a spiralizer, use a vegetable peeler. Pull the peeler down the sides of the squash, making long strips. The baking time may be shorter.

PREP 10 min **TOTAL** 20 min • 4 servings

- 1 zucchini (6 inches)
- 1 yellow summer squash (6 inches)
- 2 teaspoons olive oil
- ¼ teaspoon salt
  Freshly ground pepper, chopped parsley and grated Parmesan, if desired

1 Heat oven to 400°F. Line 15x10x1-inch pan with foil.

2 Cut off ends of squash. Cut squash with spiralizer according to manufacturer's directions. Place in pan. Drizzle with oil; sprinkle with salt. Toss to coat; spread squash in single layer.

3 Bake 8 to 10 minutes or just until tender. Sprinkle with pepper, parsley and Parmesan.

1 Serving: Calories 40; Total Fat 2.5g (Saturated Fat 0g, Trans Fat 0g); Cholesterol 0mg; Sodium 150mg; Total Carbohydrate 3g (Dietary Fiber 1g, Sugars 2g); Protein 1g **Exchanges:** ½ Vegetable, ½ Fat **Carbohydrate Choices:** 0

Fried Green Tomatoes **CALORIE SMART**

PREP 20 min **TOTAL** 40 min • 4 servings

- 2 medium firm green tomatoes, cut into ¼-inch slices
- 1 teaspoon salt
- ½ cup buttermilk
- ½ cup all-purpose flour
- ⅛ teaspoon pepper
- 2 cups vegetable oil
  Mayonnaise or Tartar Sauce (to make your own, see page 460 or 461)

1 Place tomato slices in colander; sprinkle with ½ teaspoon of the salt. Let stand 30 minutes. Pat tomatoes dry with paper towels.

2 Pour buttermilk into shallow bowl. In separate shallow bowl, mix flour and remaining salt and pepper. Dip tomatoes into buttermilk, coating both sides. Dip tomatoes into flour mixture, coating both sides; gently shake off excess.

3 In deep fryer or 10-inch skillet, heat ½ inch oil to 375°F. Fry 4 or 5 tomato slices at a time (do not let them touch) in oil 4 to 6 minutes, turning once, until golden brown. Drain on paper towels. Serve warm with Mayonnaise or Tartar Sauce.

1 Serving: Calories 130; Total Fat 5g (Saturated Fat 1g, Trans Fat 0g); Cholesterol 0mg; Sodium 630mg; Total Carbohydrate 17g (Dietary Fiber 1g, Sugars 4g); Protein 3g **Exchanges:** 1 Other Carbohydrate, 1 Vegetable, 1 Fat **Carbohydrate Choices:** 1

Making Spiral Summer Squash

Create veggie noodles by running firm, fresh veggies through spiralizer.

Place veggie spirals in pan; toss with oil and salt.

Making Fried Green Tomatoes

Dip tomatoes in buttermilk, coating both sides; shake off excess.

Fry tomatoes in oil, turning once, until golden brown.

Cannellini with Tomatoes and Sage   CALORIE SMART • FAST

PREP 15 min **TOTAL** 15 min • 4 servings

- 1 tablespoon olive or vegetable oil
- 2 cloves garlic, finely chopped
- 1 can (14.5 oz) diced tomatoes, undrained
- 1 can (15 or 19 oz) cannellini beans, drained, rinsed
- 1 tablespoon finely chopped fresh or ½ teaspoon dried sage leaves
- ¼ teaspoon coarse (kosher or sea) salt
- ⅛ teaspoon freshly ground pepper

1 In 10-inch skillet, heat oil over medium heat. Cook garlic in oil 1 to 2 minutes, stirring constantly, until light golden brown.

2 Stir in tomatoes, beans and sage. Heat to boiling; reduce heat. Simmer uncovered 5 to 7 minutes, stirring occasionally, until most of the liquid has evaporated. Stir in salt and pepper.

1 Serving: Calories 190; Total Fat 4g (Saturated Fat 0.5g, Trans Fat 0g); Cholesterol 0mg; Sodium 280mg; Total Carbohydrate 28g (Dietary Fiber 7g, Sugars 3g); Protein 10g **Exchanges:** 1½ Starch, 1 Vegetable, ½ Very Lean Meat, ½ Fat **Carbohydrate Choices:** 2

White Beans with Sun-Dried Tomatoes   SLOW COOKER • EASY

PREP 10 min **TOTAL** 4 hr 10 min • 5 servings

- 2 cups dried great northern beans (16 oz), sorted, rinsed
- 2 cloves garlic, crushed
- 6 cups water
- 1½ teaspoons dried basil leaves
- 1 teaspoon salt
- ¼ teaspoon pepper
- ¾ cup finely chopped sun-dried tomatoes in oil
- 1 can (2.25 oz) sliced ripe olives, drained

1 Spray 3½- to 6-quart slow cooker with cooking spray. In slow cooker, mix beans, garlic, water, basil, salt and pepper.

2 Cover; cook on High heat setting 4 to 5 hours. Before serving, stir in tomatoes and olives.

1 Serving: Calories 380; Total Fat 4g (Saturated Fat 0.5g, Trans Fat 0g); Cholesterol 0mg; Sodium 620mg; Total Carbohydrate 61g (Dietary Fiber 15g, Sugars 3g); Protein 23g **Exchanges:** 3½ Starch, 1½ Vegetable, 1½ Very Lean Meat, ½ Fat **Carbohydrate Choices:** 4

Cannellini with Tomatoes and Sage

Spicy Refried Black Beans

CALORIE SMART • FAST

For a tamer version of these refried beans, swap one 4.5-ounce can of diced green chiles for the fresh jalapeños and use just 1 teaspoon of the chipotle chiles.

PREP 5 min **TOTAL** 20 min • 6 servings

- 2 tablespoons vegetable oil
- 1 small onion, chopped (¼ cup)
- 2 jalapeño chiles, seeded, finely chopped
- 2 cloves garlic, finely chopped
- 2 cans (15 oz each) black beans, undrained
- 1 chipotle chile in adobo sauce (from 7-oz can), chopped*
- 1 teaspoon chili powder
- ½ teaspoon salt
  Sliced green onion and chopped tomato, if desired

1 In 10-inch skillet, heat oil over medium-high heat. Cook onion, jalapeño chiles and garlic in oil, stirring occasionally, until onion is tender, about 3 minutes. Stir in beans, chipotle chile, chili powder, and salt; mash beans.

2 Reduce heat. Simmer uncovered about 15 minutes, stirring occasionally, until desired consistency. Sprinkle with green onion and tomato.

*Freeze any unused chipotle chiles on cookie sheet lined with waxed paper, parchment paper or foil. Once frozen, place in resealable plastic food storage bag and store in freezer up to 6 months.

1 Serving: Calories 170; Total Fat 5g (Saturated Fat 0.5g, Trans Fat 0g); Cholesterol 0mg; Sodium 690mg; Total Carbohydrate 22g (Dietary Fiber 6g, Sugars 0g); Protein 7g **Exchanges:** 1½ Starch, ½ Very Lean Meat, 1 Fat **Carbohydrate Choices:** 1½

Red Beans and Rice CALORIE SMART

PREP 20 min **TOTAL** 2 hr • 8 servings

- 1 cup dried kidney beans (8 oz), sorted, rinsed*
- 3 cups water
- 2 oz salt pork (with rind) or 3 slices bacon, cut up
- 1 medium green bell pepper, chopped (1 cup)
- 1 medium onion, chopped (½ cup)
- 1 cup uncooked regular long-grain white rice
- 1 teaspoon salt

1 In 3-quart saucepan, heat beans and water to boiling. Boil uncovered 2 minutes; reduce heat. Cover and simmer 1 hour to 1 hour 15 minutes or until tender (do not boil or beans will fall apart). Drain, reserving liquid.

2 In 10-inch skillet, cook salt pork over medium heat, stirring occasionally, until crisp. Stir in bell pepper and onion. Cook, stirring occasionally, until onion is tender.

3 Add enough water to bean liquid, if necessary, to measure 2 cups. Add bean liquid, salt pork mixture, rice and salt to beans in saucepan. Heat to boiling, stirring once or twice; reduce heat. Cover and simmer 14 minutes (do not lift cover or stir). Remove from heat. Fluff with fork. Cover; let steam 5 to 10 minutes.

*One can (15 to 15.5 oz) red kidney beans, drained and liquid reserved, can be substituted for the dried beans. Omit water and skip Step 1.

1 Serving (¾ Cup): Calories 210; Total Fat 4.5g (Saturated Fat 1.5g, Trans Fat 0g); Cholesterol 0mg; Sodium 360mg; Total Carbohydrate 35g (Dietary Fiber 4g, Sugars 2g); Protein 7g **Exchanges:** 2 Starch, 1 Vegetable, ½ Fat **Carbohydrate Choices:** 2

SLOW-COOKER Directions Increase water to 3¼ cups. Use 1⅓ cups uncooked instant white rice. Spray 3½- to 6-quart slow cooker with cooking spray. In slow cooker, mix all ingredients except rice. Cover; cook on High heat setting 3 hours 30 minutes to 4 hours 30 minutes or until beans are tender. Stir in rice. Cover; cook 15 minutes longer. Stir well.

Hoppin' John Substitute 1 cup dried black-eyed peas for the kidney beans. Omit bell pepper.

Homemade Baked Beans

PREP 15 min **TOTAL** 8 hr 30 min • 10 servings

- 2 cups dried navy beans (16 oz), sorted, rinsed
- 13 cups water
- ½ cup packed brown sugar
- ¼ cup molasses
- 1 teaspoon salt
- 6 slices bacon, crisply cooked, crumbled
- 1 medium onion, chopped (½ cup)

1 Heat oven to 350°F. In 4-quart ovenproof Dutch oven, heat beans and 10 cups of the water to boiling. Boil uncovered 2 minutes.

2 Stir in brown sugar, molasses, salt, bacon and onion. Cover and bake 4 hours, stirring occasionally.

3 Stir in remaining 3 cups water. Bake uncovered 2 hours to 2 hours 15 minutes longer, stirring occasionally, until beans are tender and desired consistency.

1 Serving: Calories 240; Total Fat 2.5g (Saturated Fat 0.5g, Trans Fat 0g); Cholesterol 0mg; Sodium 340mg; Total Carbohydrate 45g (Dietary Fiber 11g, Sugars 16g); Protein 10g **Exchanges:** 1 Starch, 2 Other Carbohydrate, 1 Lean Meat **Carbohydrate Choices:** 3

SLOW-COOKER Directions Spray 3½- to 6-quart slow cooker with cooking spray. In slow cooker, place beans and 5 cups water. Cover; cook on High heat setting 2 hours. Turn off heat; let stand 8 to 24 hours. Stir in brown sugar, molasses, salt, bacon and onion. Cover; cook on Low heat setting 10 to 12 hours or until beans are very tender and most of liquid is absorbed.

Homemade Baked Beans

Spicy Black-Eyed Peas

CALORIE SMART • SLOW COOKER • EASY

PREP 5 min **TOTAL** 3 hr 15 min • 8 servings

- 2 cups dried black-eyed peas (16 oz), sorted, rinsed
- 1 medium onion, chopped (½ cup)
- 6 cups water
- 1 teaspoon salt
- ½ teaspoon pepper
- ¾ cup chunky-style salsa

1 Spray 3½- to 4-quart slow cooker with cooking spray. In slow cooker, mix all ingredients except salsa.

2 Cover; cook on High heat setting 3 to 4 hours.

3 Stir in salsa. Cover; cook about 10 minutes longer or until hot.

1 Serving: Calories 200; Total Fat 1g (Saturated Fat 0g, Trans Fat 0g); Cholesterol 0mg; Sodium 480mg; Total Carbohydrate 36g (Dietary Fiber 10g, Sugars 4g); Protein 12g **Exchanges:** 2 Starch, 1 Vegetable, ½ Very Lean Meat **Carbohydrate Choices:** 2½

Caribbean Black Beans

PREP 25 min **TOTAL** 1 hr 10 min • 5 servings

- 4½ cups water
- 1½ cups dried black beans (12 oz)*, sorted, rinsed
- 2 teaspoons vegetable oil
- 1 medium papaya or mango, peeled, seeded and diced (about 1½ cups)
- 1 medium red bell pepper, finely chopped
- ½ cup finely chopped red onion
- ½ cup orange juice
- ¼ cup lime juice
- 2 tablespoons chopped fresh cilantro
- ½ teaspoon ground red pepper (cayenne)
- 2 cloves garlic, finely chopped
- 5 cups hot cooked rice (page 215)

1 In 2-quart saucepan, heat water and beans to boiling. Boil uncovered 2 minutes; reduce heat. Cover; simmer 45 minutes, stirring occasionally, until beans are tender; drain.

2 In 10-inch skillet, heat oil over medium heat. Add remaining ingredients except rice; cook 5 minutes, stirring occasionally, until bell pepper is crisp-tender. Stir in beans. Cook 5 minutes or until hot. Serve over rice.

Caribbean Black Beans

*Or substitute 2 cans (15 oz each) black beans, drained and rinsed, for the dried beans. Omit water and Step 1.

1 Serving: Calories 450; Total Fat 3g (Saturated Fat 0.5g, Trans Fat 0g); Cholesterol 0mg; Sodium 10mg; Total Carbohydrate 89g (Dietary Fiber 14g, Sugars 12g); Protein 17g **Exchanges:** 4 Starch, 2 Fruit **Carbohydrate Choices:** 6

Garbanzo Beans with Vegetables **SLOW COOKER**

PREP 15 min **TOTAL** 4 hr 30 min • 8 servings

- 2 cups dried garbanzo beans (chickpeas; 16 oz), sorted, rinsed
- 5½ cups water
- 1 teaspoon salt
- ½ teaspoon pepper
- 2 tablespoons olive or vegetable oil
- 2 cups sliced fresh mushrooms (about 5 oz)
- 1 cup shredded carrots (1½ medium)
- 4 medium green onions, thinly sliced (¼ cup)
- 2 cloves garlic, finely chopped
- 2 tablespoons lemon juice
- 1 to 2 tablespoons prepared horseradish
- 2 teaspoons yellow mustard

1 Spray 4- to 5-quart slow cooker with cooking spray. In slow cooker, stir together beans, water, salt and pepper. Cover; cook on High heat setting 4 to 5 hours.

2 In 12-inch skillet, heat oil over medium heat. Add mushrooms, carrots, onions and garlic; cook about 5 minutes, stirring occasionally, until vegetables are tender. Stir vegetables, lemon juice, horseradish and mustard into beans. Cover; cook 15 minutes longer to blend flavors.

1 Serving: Calories 250; Total Fat 7g (Saturated Fat 1g, Trans Fat 0g); Cholesterol 0mg; Sodium 350mg; Total Carbohydrate 37g (Dietary Fiber 10g, Sugars 4g); Protein 11g **Exchanges:** 2 Starch, 1½ Vegetable, ½ Very Lean Meat, 1 Fat **Carbohydrate Choices:** 2½

CHAPTER 10

One-Dish Dinners

Betty's Staples
Shredded Cheeses

What isn't better with cheese? Shredded cheese is a handy go-to for quick meals and snacks. If you wish, freeze larger amounts to keep it fresh longer. When small amounts are lurking in your fridge, put them to use with these ideas. We've suggested cheeses to use in each dish, but feel free to use whatever you have on hand.

1. Cheesy Eggs: Make Scrambled Eggs (page 90) as directed, except beat ½ cup shredded Cheddar cheese into scrambled egg mixture before cooking. Sprinkle tops of scrambled eggs with additional cheese during final few minutes of cooking.

2. Simple Cheese Enchilada: Spoon about 2 tablespoons spicy chili beans and sauce in center of large flour tortilla; sprinkle with 2 tablespoons shredded Colby-Jack cheese. Roll up; place seam side down on microwave-safe plate. Sprinkle with additional cheese. Microwave 30 to 40 seconds or until hot.

3. Jacked-Up Rice: Stir ½ cup shredded pepper Jack cheese, ¼ cup chopped pickled jalapeño peppers and 2 tablespoons of the pickled jalapeño liquid into 2 cups hot cooked rice; cover and let stand a few minutes to melt cheese.

4. Bacon-Cheese Spread: In medium bowl, mix 2 tablespoons each shredded Cheddar cheese, chopped cooked bacon and chopped fresh chives with one 8-ounce package softened cream cheese. Serve with crackers.

5. Garlic-Cheese Crostini: Mix 1 tablespoon olive oil and 1 clove finely chopped garlic; brush lightly on eight ½-inch-thick slices baguette. Place on broiler pan; sprinkle with 2 tablespoons shredded Parmesan cheese. Broil with tops 4 to 6 inches from heat 1 to 2 minutes or until edges of bread are golden brown.

6. Easy Alfredo Sauce: Make White Sauce (page 459) as directed, except after boiling and stirring sauce 1 minute, stir in ½ cup shredded Romano cheese and a dash of grated nutmeg until melted.

7. Baked Jalapeño Poppers: In small bowl, mix 4 ounces softened cream cheese and 3 tablespoons shredded taco cheese blend. Cut 8 to 10 whole jalapeño chiles lengthwise and remove seeds. Fill chile halves with cheese mixture. Bake on cookie sheet at 350°F 10 to 15 minutes or until hot.

Garlic-Cheese Crostini, Jacked-Up Rice

Moroccan Chicken Pie

Phyllo means "leaf" in Greek. The paper-thin layers of phyllo don't contain much fat so they can dry out quickly. Sheets are usually brushed with melted butter (or in this case, sprayed with cooking oil) and layered to create a crisp, light and airy crust.

PREP 30 min **TOTAL** 1 hr 20 min • 6 servings

- 2 tablespoons butter
- 1 large onion, chopped (1 cup)
- ½ teaspoon ground cinnamon
- ½ teaspoon ground turmeric
- 2 tablespoons all-purpose flour
- 1 cup reduced-sodium chicken broth
- ⅓ cup raisins
- 3 cups shredded deli rotisserie chicken (from 2-lb chicken)
- ¼ cup chopped fresh cilantro
- ¼ teaspoon salt
- ¼ teaspoon freshly ground pepper
- 16 sheets frozen phyllo (filo) pastry (14x9 inch), thawed
  Cooking spray
- ½ cup slivered almonds, finely ground

1 Heat oven to 350°F. Lightly spray 9-inch glass pie plate with cooking spray.

2 In 10-inch nonstick skillet, melt butter over medium heat. Cook onion in butter 5 to 6 minutes, stirring occasionally, until softened and lightly browned. Stir in cinnamon and turmeric. Stir in flour; cook 1 minute, stirring constantly. Slowly stir in broth. Add raisins. Heat to boiling; boil gently 1 minute, stirring occasionally. In large bowl, stir together onion mixture, chicken, cilantro, salt and pepper.

3 Place phyllo sheets on work surface; cover with clean towel to keep from drying out. Place 1 phyllo sheet in bottom and up side of pie plate, allowing excess phyllo to extend over edge. Lightly spray with cooking spray; sprinkle with 1½ teaspoons of the ground almonds. Repeat layers, using 7 more phyllo sheets and alternating position of sheets to cover bottom and side of pie plate. (It does not matter if phyllo splits or creases when placed in the pan; it won't be noticeable after the pie is baked.)

4 Spoon chicken mixture into pastry-lined plate. Using kitchen scissors, cut excess phyllo from edges. Layer with remaining 8 phyllo sheets, spraying each with cooking spray and sprinkling with almonds. Fold excess phyllo under to form rustic crust edge.

5 Bake 30 to 40 minutes or until crust is golden brown. Let stand 10 minutes before serving.

1 Serving: Calories 440; Total Fat 15g (Saturated Fat 4.5g, Trans Fat 0g); Cholesterol 70mg; Sodium 760mg; Total Carbohydrate 49g (Dietary Fiber 3g, Sugars 6g); Protein 27g **Exchanges:** 3 Starch, ½ Other Carbohydrate, 2½ Lean Meat, 1 Fat **Carbohydrate Choices:** 3

Turkey and Butternut Squash Ragout   CALORIE SMART • SLOW COOKER

PREP 10 min **TOTAL** 7 hr 10 min • 4 servings

- 1½ lb turkey thighs (about 2 medium), skin removed
- 1 small butternut squash (about 2 lb), peeled, seeded and cut into 1½-inch pieces (3 cups)
- 1 medium onion, cut in half, sliced
- 1 can (16 oz) baked beans, undrained
- 1 can (14.5 oz) diced tomatoes with Italian-style herbs, undrained
- 2 tablespoons chopped fresh parsley

1 Spray 3½- to 4-quart slow cooker with cooking spray. In slow cooker, mix all ingredients except parsley.

2 Cover; cook on Low heat setting 7 to 8 hours.

3 Remove turkey from slow cooker to cutting board. Remove meat from bones; discard bones. Return turkey to slow cooker. Just before serving, sprinkle with parsley.

1 Serving: Calories 380; Total Fat 6g (Saturated Fat 2g, Trans Fat 0g); Cholesterol 115mg; Sodium 730mg; Total Carbohydrate 46g (Dietary Fiber 10g, Sugars 16g); Protein 36g **Exchanges:** 3 Starch, 1 Vegetable, 3 Very Lean Meat **Carbohydrate Choices:** 3

Moroccan Chicken Pie

Pasta Bolognese

Potato-Topped Meat Loaf Casserole CALORIE SMART

PREP 30 min **TOTAL** 1 hour 25 minutes • 6 servings

TOPPING

Mashed Potatoes (page 247)
- 1 egg
- 1½ cups frozen chopped broccoli, thawed
- ½ cup shredded sharp Cheddar cheese (2 oz)

MEAT LOAF

- 1 lb extra-lean (at least 90%) ground beef
- 3 tablespoons unseasoned dry bread crumbs
- 3 tablespoons steak sauce
- 1 tablespoon dried minced onion
- ½ teaspoon salt
- ¼ teaspoon pepper
- 1 egg

1 Heat oven to 350°F. Spray 8-inch square (2-quart) glass baking dish with cooking spray. Prepare Mashed Potatoes. Stir in egg. Stir in broccoli and cheese; set aside.

2 Meanwhile, in medium bowl, mix meat loaf ingredients. Press mixture in bottom and up sides of baking dish to within ½ inch of top.

3 Spoon potato mixture into meat shell, spreading evenly. Bake 25 to 30 minutes or until meat loaf is thoroughly cooked and meat thermometer inserted in center of loaf reads 160°F. Let stand 5 minutes before serving; drain liquid along edges.

1 Serving: Calories 330; Total Fat 15g (Saturated Fat 8g, Trans Fat 0.5g); Cholesterol 140mg; Sodium 610mg; Total Carbohydrate 26g (Dietary Fiber 2g, Sugars 4g); Protein 23g **Exchanges:** 1½ Starch, 2½ Medium-Fat Meat, ½ Fat **Carbohydrate Choices:** 2

Quick Potato-Topped Meat Loaf Casserole
Use 2½ to 3 cups leftover mashed potatoes. Place in medium microwavable bowl; cover with plastic wrap. Microwave 2 to 4 minutes on High, stirring occasionally, or until warm. Continue as directed.

Pasta Bolognese

PREP 30 min **TOTAL** 45 min • 6 servings

- 2 tablespoons olive oil
- 2 large onions, chopped (2 cups)
- 2 medium carrots, chopped (about 1 cup)
- 1 teaspoon salt
- 1 lb lean (at least 80%) ground beef
- ¼ cup tomato paste (from 6-oz can)
- 1 can (28 oz) fire-roasted diced tomatoes, undrained
- 1 carton (32 oz) beef broth (4 cups; for homemade broth, see page 146)
- ½ teaspoon crushed red pepper flakes
- 2 teaspoons Italian seasoning
- 1 lb uncooked spaghetti
- ½ cup shredded Parmesan cheese (2 oz)
- ¼ cup thinly sliced fresh basil leaves

1 In 4-quart Dutch oven or stockpot, heat oil over medium-high heat. Cook onions, carrots and salt in oil 5 to 8 minutes, stirring occasionally, until softened. Add beef; cook 5 to 8 minutes, stirring frequently, until no longer pink.

2 Stir in tomato paste and tomatoes. Stir in broth, pepper flakes and Italian seasoning; heat to simmering. Break spaghetti in half; rinse under cold water. Tuck spaghetti into simmering liquid, covering completely.

3 Reduce heat to medium-low; cook uncovered 13 to 15 minutes or until spaghetti is tender and sauce is reduced slightly. Top with cheese and basil.

1 Serving (1⅔ Cups): Calories 630; Total Fat 18g (Saturated Fat 6g, Trans Fat 0.5g); Cholesterol 55mg; Sodium 1520mg; Total Carbohydrate 86g (Dietary Fiber 7g, Sugars 7g); Protein 32g **Exchanges:** 2 Starch, 3 Other Carbohydrate, 2 Vegetable, 3 Lean Meat, 2 Fat **Carbohydrate Choices:** 6

Mashed or Smashed?

Mashed potatoes are typically prepared with peeled potatoes and mashed or beaten until silky smooth. Smashed potatoes are traditionally left lumpy on purpose and may or may not have the skins left on, for a dish with more texture, color and additional nutritional value. But there are no potatoe police: Feel free to prepare your potatoes however you like them.

Southwestern Steak with Corn and Chiles CALORIE SMART · FAST

Pumpkin seeds (pepitas) can usually be found near the packaged items in the produce section of your grocery store or near other prepackaged nuts.

PREP *30 min* **TOTAL** *30 min* • *4 servings*

- 2 tablespoons roasted salted hulled pumpkin seeds (pepitas), finely chopped
- 2 teaspoons Southwest seasoning
- ½ teaspoon pepper
- 1 boneless beef top sirloin steak, 1 inch thick (1 lb)
- 4 ears fresh sweet corn, husks removed, cut in half crosswise, or 8 frozen small pieces corn on the cob
- 2 large poblano chiles, cut in half lengthwise, stems and seeds removed
- 1 medium onion, cut into 8 wedges
- 4 teaspoons olive oil
- ¼ cup roasted salted hulled pumpkin seeds (pepitas)

1 In small bowl, mix chopped pumpkin seeds, 1 teaspoon of the seasoning blend and the pepper. Press mixture into all sides of beef; let stand at room temperature 15 minutes.

2 Meanwhile, set oven control to broil. Line 15x10x1-inch pan with heavy-duty foil; spray foil with cooking spray. Place corn, chiles and onion in pan. In same small bowl, mix oil and remaining 1 teaspoon seasoning blend. Drizzle mixture over vegetables; toss until evenly coated. Place vegetables in single layer on sides of pan. Place beef in center of pan.

3 Broil 4 to 6 inches from heat 10 to 15 minutes for medium doneness (150°F), turning beef and vegetables halfway through cooking time.

4 Slice beef; place on platter. Add vegetables to platter; sprinkle with ¼ cup pumpkin seeds.

1 Serving: Calories 410; Total Fat 16g (Saturated Fat 3.5g, Trans Fat 0g); Cholesterol 80mg; Sodium 170mg; Total Carbohydrate 27g (Dietary Fiber 4g, Sugars 7g); Protein 39g **Exchanges:** 2 Starch, 4 Lean Meat, ½ High-Fat Meat **Carbohydrate Choices:** 2

MAKE-AHEAD **Directions** Rub the beef and marinate the vegetables up to 24 hours in advance and refrigerate. Add a few extra minutes to the broiling time.

Cranberry-Chicken Pot Pie

Cranberry-Chicken Pot Pie CALORIE SMART

PREP 20 min **TOTAL** 55 min • 6 servings

- 1 cup chicken broth (for homemade broth, see page 143)
- 1½ cups cubed (½ inch) peeled dark orange sweet potatoes (about 9 oz)
- 1 cup chicken gravy (from 12-oz jar, or to make you own, see page 346)
- 2 cups fresh baby spinach leaves
- ½ cup sweetened dried cranberries
- 3 cups cut-up cooked chicken or turkey
- 1 box refrigerated pie crusts, softened as directed on box (or to make your own, see page 586)
- 1 teaspoon milk

1 Heat oven to 425°F. In 3-quart saucepan, heat broth and sweet potato to boiling; reduce heat. Cover and simmer about 6 minutes or until sweet potato is almost tender when pierced with fork. Gently stir in gravy, spinach and cranberries; fold in chicken. Remove from heat; cover and set aside.

2 On lightly floured surface, roll out 1 pie crust until 12 inches in diameter. Place crust in ungreased 9½- or 10-inch deep-dish glass pie plate or shallow 2-quart casserole; gently press in bottom and up side of pie plate. Do not stretch.

3 Spoon chicken mixture into crust-lined plate. Top with second crust; seal edge and flute. Brush top crust with milk. Cut several slits in top crust for steam to escape.

4 Bake 25 to 30 minutes or until crust is golden brown and filling is bubbly. Let stand 5 minutes before serving.

*Prepare as directed through Step 2.

1 Serving: Calories 500; Total Fat 24g (Saturated Fat 9g, Trans Fat 0g); Cholesterol 70mg; Sodium 740mg; Total Carbohydrate 50g (Dietary Fiber 2g, Sugars 8g); Protein 23g **Exchanges:** 2 Starch, 1 Other Carbohydrate, 1 Vegetable, 2 Lean Meat, 3½ Fat **Carbohydrate Choices:** 3

Learn to Make
FOIL PACKETS

This old campfire cooking technique is hands down one of the easiest ways to get dinner on the table quickly, easily and deliciously. With this method of cooking, you can prepare a whole meal or part of a meal in a tightly sealed foil packet, baking it in the oven. Or you can cook these packets over medium heat on your grill—adjusting cooking time as needed. Another benefit of cooking in packets is the easy cleanup!

Here are some tips for success:

- Use heavy-duty foil for the most secure packets.

- Cut the foil large enough that you can easily wrap food tightly with a good fold at top and sides. A general size for individual servings is 18x12 inches, but follow the recipe you're using for specific size.

- Spray the foil with cooking spray or use nonstick foil.

- Fill with foods that have similar cook times— cut foods that take longer to cook, like fresh carrots, into smaller or thinner pieces, so that they will be done with everything else.

- Use boneless meats such as patties, pork chops, chicken breasts, fish fillets or steaks.

- Place food centered on one half of foil, usually with meat pieces first, topped with other foods.

- Add a sprig of fresh herbs or sprinkle with dried herbs or seasoning.

- Use minimal liquid in packets—no more than 2 to 3 tablespoons. Use flavorful liquids such as fruit juice, soy sauce or marinades.

- To seal each packet, fold other side of foil over food so edges meet. Seal edges, making tight ½-inch fold; fold again, allowing a little space for heat circulation and expansion. Fold other sides to seal.

- Place packets on cookie sheet with sides. Bake at a high temperature to create steam in the packets, 425°F or 450°F. Depending on

the foods selected, bake time can range from 10 to 25 minutes.

- Open one packet to test for doneness. Carefully unwrap one fold (steam will be hot). Check doneness and carefully refold if more cooking time is needed.

- When done, remove from oven carefully. Cut large X across top of packets; carefully fold back foil.

Foil packets are easy to make ahead of time. Just prepare and refrigerate until ready to bake. If they are really cold, you may need to bake them a little extra longer.

Lemon and Herb Salmon Packets CALORIE SMART

PREP 15 min TOTAL 35 min • 2 servings

- 1¼ cups reduced-sodium chicken broth
- 1 cup uncooked instant brown rice
- ½ cup julienne carrots (see page 12)
- ½ to ¾ lb salmon fillet, cut into 2 pieces
- ½ teaspoon lemon-pepper seasoning
- 2 tablespoons chopped fresh chives
- 2 lemon slices (¼ inch thick)

1 Heat oven to 450°F. In 1-quart saucepan, heat broth to boiling over high heat. Stir in rice; reduce heat to low. Cover and simmer 5 minutes or until most of broth is absorbed. Stir in carrots.

2 Meanwhile, cut 2 (18x12-inch) sheets of heavy-duty foil; spray foil with cooking spray. Place salmon piece on one half of each sheet. Sprinkle with lemon-pepper seasoning; top with chives. Arrange lemon slices over fish.

3 Spoon rice mixture around salmon. Bring up other half of foil so edges meet. Seal edges, making tight ½-inch fold; fold again, allowing space for heat circulation and expansion. Fold other sides to seal. Place packets in ungreased 15x10x1-inch pan.

4 Bake 16 to 20 minutes or until fish flakes easily with fork. Place packets on plates. Cut large X across top of each packet; carefully fold back foil to allow steam to escape.

1 Serving: Calories 380; Total Fat 8g (Saturated Fat 2g, Trans Fat 0g); Cholesterol 75mg; Sodium 540mg; Total Carbohydrate 47g (Dietary Fiber 3g, Sugars 2g); Protein 31g **Exchanges:** 3 Starch, 3 Very Lean Meat, 1 Fat **Carbohydrate Choices:** 3

Lemon and Herb Salmon Packets

CALORIE SMART = See Helpful Nutrition and Cooking Information, page 643   FAST = Ready in 30 minutes or less
EASY = Prep in 10 minutes or less **plus** five ingredients or less   LIGHTER = 25% fewer calories or grams of fat
MAKE AHEAD = Make-ahead directions   SLOW COOKER = Slow cooker directions

< Broiled Boneless Top Sirloin, page 317, with Herb Butter, page 470

BEEF, PORK & LAMB BASICS

Choosing the right cut of meat will be just a little easier with the knowledge you will pick up in this chapter. From photos identifying a variety of cuts to detailed cooking times and delicious recipes, here's all you need to select and prepare meat perfectly.

TIPS FOR PURCHASING

- Choose packages without any tears, holes or leaks. There should be little or no liquid in the bottom of the tray.

- Packages should be cold and feel firm. Avoid packages that are stacked too high in the meat case, as they may not have been kept cold enough.

- Pay attention to the sell-by date and use or freeze within 2 days of the date.

- Choose meat that has good color. Don't purchase any that is gray or off-color.

- Purchasing meat from a butcher can ensure you are getting exactly what you want in terms of cut, preparation and amount. Evaluate the cost vs. prepackaged; it may save you time, money and waste.

- Place packages of meat in plastic bags so that the juices will not contaminate other food in your grocery cart.

- Refrigerate meat as soon as you get home from shopping. For longer commutes from the grocery store or on hot days, place meat in a small cooler with ice packs.

WHAT'S ON THE LABEL?

Organic: To be labeled organic, livestock must be raised in compliance with the National Organic Program. Regulations require that animals are able to graze in pastures, are fed with 100 percent organic feed and are not given antibiotics or hormones.

Grass-Fed vs. Grain-Fed: Grass-fed livestock feeds from a pasture. Livestock may have been "finished" on a diet of grains and supplements to gain weight rapidly. Most beef, lamb and goat is grain-fed, but grass-fed meats are becoming more accessible.

Natural: Many people think "natural" is the same as "organic"—it is not. If a meat package is labeled natural, it means that it doesn't contain artificial ingredients or added color or is minimally processed. Read on—the statement that follows the natural label will indicate what is natural about the product.

SERVINGS PER POUND

The number of servings per pound varies depending on the type of meat and the amount of bone and fat present.

TYPE OF MEAT	SERVINGS PER POUND
Boneless Cuts (ground, boneless chops, loin, tenderloin)	3 to 4
Bone-In Cuts (rib roasts, pot roasts, country-style ribs)	2 to 3
Very Bony Cuts (back ribs, spareribs, short ribs, shanks)	1 to 1½

Meatloaf (page 298)

RETAIL BEEF CUTS

A variety of cuts is available in the marketplace. The information and images here should help you choose the right cut for your recipe needs.

Diagram: **1** Chuck **2** Rib **3** Loin **4** Sirloin
5 Round **6** Brisket **7** Shank **8** Plate **9** Flank

Stew Meat

Beef Brisket Roast

Beef Chuck Shoulder
Pot Roast (boneless)

Beef Chuck Top Blade Steak

Beef Rib Roast
(bone-in; small end)

Beef
Short Ribs

Beef Rib-Eye
Roast (rolled)

Beef
Rib-Eye Steak

Beef Chuck 7-Bone
Pot Roast (bone-in)

Beef Tri-Tip
Roast

Beef Round Tip Roast

Beef Rump Roast or
Bottom Round
(boneless)

Beef Flank Steak

Beef Top Sirloin Steak (boneless)

Beef Top
Round Steak

Beef Skirt Steak

Beef Eye of
Round Steak

Porterhouse
Steak

Beef
T-Bone
Steak

Beef Tenderloin Steak

Beef Tenderloin Roast

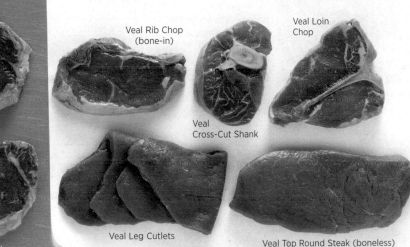

RETAIL VEAL CUTS

Here are some of the more commonly used cuts of
veal that you might find called for in recipes.

Veal Rib Chop
(bone-in)

Veal Loin
Chop

Veal
Cross-Cut Shank

Veal Leg Cutlets

Veal Top Round Steak (boneless)

Beef Top Loin Steak

STORING MEAT

- Meat wrapped in butcher paper should be repackaged tightly in plastic wrap, foil or freezer plastic bags.

- Meat packaged in clear plastic wrap on a plastic or Styrofoam tray doesn't need to be repackaged.

- Store meat in the meat compartment or coldest part of your refrigerator, or freeze it as soon as possible. Ground meat is more perishable than other cuts, so use it within 2 days.

- Cook or freeze meat within 2 days of the sell-by date.

- If meat was purchased frozen or was frozen right after purchasing, keep it in the refrigerator after thawing for the number of days listed in the Timetable for Storing Meat, below. If the meat was refrigerated several days before freezing, use it the same day you thaw it.

Handling Raw Meat

Cooking meat to the recommended doneness destroys any bacteria. To avoid any cross-contamination when preparing raw meat for cooking, follow the tips in Don't Cross-Contaminate, page 31.

Cutting Raw Meat

Need to cut raw meat into cubes, thin slices or strips? Put it in the freezer first. Leave the meat in the freezer until it's firm but not frozen, 30 to 60 minutes, depending on the size of the piece. It'll be easy to cube or slice—even paper thin.

Easily cut raw meat into cubes, thin slices or strips by partially freezing it first.

TIMETABLE FOR STORING MEAT

CUT OF MEAT	REFRIGERATOR (36°F TO 40°F)	FREEZER (0°F OR COLDER)
Ground Meat		
Beef	1 to 2 days	3 to 4 months
Veal	1 to 2 days	2 to 3 months
Pork	1 to 2 days	1 to 3 months
Steaks and Roasts		
Beef	3 to 4 days	6 to 12 months
Veal	1 to 2 days	6 to 9 months
Pork	2 to 4 days	3 to 6 months
Lamb	3 to 5 days	6 to 9 months
Cubes and Slices	2 to 3 days	6 to 12 months
Leftover Cooked Meats	3 to 4 days	2 to 3 months
Cured, Smoked and Ready-to-Serve Meat Products		
Corned Beef	1 week	2 weeks
Hot Dogs	3 to 5 days	1 month
Bacon	5 to 7 days	1 month

THAWING MEAT

Thaw meat slowly in the refrigerator in a dish or baking pan with sides or in a resealable food-storage plastic bag to catch any drips during thawing. Don't thaw meat on the countertop because bacteria thrive at room temperature.

AMOUNT OF FROZEN MEAT	THAWING TIME IN REFRIGERATOR*
Large Roast (4 pounds or larger)	4 to 7 hours per lb
Small Roast (under 4 pounds)	3 to 5 hours per lb
Steak or Chops (1 inch thick)	12 to 14 hours total
Ground Beef or Beef Pieces (1- to 1½-pound package)	24 hours total
Ground Beef Patties (½ to ¾ inch thick)	12 hours total

*To thaw meat in the microwave, follow manufacturer's directions.

Brandy-Herb Pan Steaks

uncovered 3 to 4 minutes or until slightly thickened. Serve with steaks.

1 Serving: Calories 200; Total Fat 5g (Saturated Fat 2g, Trans Fat 0g); Cholesterol 90mg; Sodium 110mg; Total Carbohydrate 0g (Dietary Fiber 0g, Sugars 0g); Protein 37g **Exchanges:** 5 Very Lean Meat, ½ Fat **Carbohydrate Choices:** 0

Mushroom Brandy-Herb Pan Steaks After removing steaks from skillet, add 1 teaspoon additional butter and 1 cup sliced fresh mushrooms. Cook 2 to 3 minutes, stirring frequently, until tender. Leave mushrooms in skillet and make sauce as directed in Step 3.

Peppered Flank Steak

CALORIE SMART

PREP 15 min **TOTAL** 4 hr 20 min • 6 servings

MARINADE
- ½ cup olive or vegetable oil
- ½ cup dry red wine
- 1 tablespoon honey
- ½ teaspoon dried thyme leaves
- ½ teaspoon dried marjoram leaves
- 1 clove garlic, finely chopped

STEAK
- 1 beef flank steak (about 1¼ lb)
- ¾ teaspoon coarse sea salt
- 1 tablespoon coarsely ground mixed peppercorns or black peppercorns*
- ½ cup chopped fresh parsley

1 In shallow glass or plastic dish or resealable food-storage plastic bag, mix all marinade ingredients. Add beef. Cover dish or seal bag; refrigerate at least 4 hours but no longer than 24 hours, turning occasionally.

2 Set oven control to broil. Spray broiler pan rack with cooking spray. Remove beef from marinade; discard marinade. Sprinkle both sides of beef with salt; rub into surface. Place beef on rack in pan.

3 Broil with top 4 to 6 inches from heat 5 minutes. Turn beef over; sprinkle with pepper. Broil 4 to 5 minutes longer or until desired doneness. Let stand 5 minutes. Cut beef across grain into thin slices. Sprinkle with parsley.

*Look for jars of peppercorns with a grinder top in your supermarket. The mixed peppercorns usually include black, white and green peppercorns.

1 Serving: Calories 190; Total Fat 8g (Saturated Fat 2g, Trans Fat 0g); Cholesterol 70mg; Sodium 330mg; Total Carbohydrate 2g (Dietary Fiber 0g, Sugars 0g); Protein 28g **Exchanges:** 4 Very Lean Meat, 1 Fat **Carbohydrate Choices:** 0

Brandy-Herb Pan Steaks CALORIE SMART • FAST

PREP 25 min **TOTAL** 25 min • 4 servings

- 1 teaspoon cracked or coarse ground black pepper
- ¾ teaspoon chopped fresh or ¼ teaspoon dried basil leaves
- ¾ teaspoon chopped fresh or ¼ teaspoon dried rosemary leaves
- ½ teaspoon coarse (kosher or sea) salt
- 4 boneless beef tenderloin steaks, 1 inch thick (1 to 1½ lb)
- 1 tablespoon butter
- ¼ cup beef broth (for homemade broth, see page 146)
- 2 tablespoons brandy or beef broth

1 In small bowl, mix pepper, basil, rosemary and salt. Rub mixture into both sides of each steak.

2 In 12-inch skillet, melt butter over medium heat. Cook steaks in butter 6 to 8 minutes, turning once, until medium-rare to medium (145°F to 160°F). Remove beef from skillet; cover to keep warm.

3 Add broth and brandy to skillet. Heat to boiling, stirring to loosen browned bits from bottom of skillet; reduce heat. Simmer

---

Making a Pan Sauce

Remove cooked meat from skillet; add liquid, stirring to loosen browned bits from bottom of skillet.

Simmer uncovered until mixture is slightly thickened.

Beef Stroganoff CALORIE SMART

PREP 25 min **TOTAL** 50 min • 6 servings

- 1½ lb beef tenderloin or boneless top loin steak
- 2 tablespoons butter
- 1½ cups beef broth (for homemade broth, see page 146)
- 2 tablespoons ketchup
- 1 teaspoon salt
- 1 clove garlic, finely chopped
- 1 package (8 oz) sliced fresh mushrooms (about 3 cups)
- 1 medium onion, chopped (½ cup)
- ¼ cup all-purpose flour
- 1 cup sour cream or plain yogurt
  Hot cooked noodles (page 167) or rice (page 215), if desired

1 Cut beef across grain into 1½x½-inch strips (beef is easier to cut if partially frozen). In 12-inch skillet, melt butter over medium-high heat. Cook beef in butter, stirring occasionally, until brown.

2 Reserve ⅓ cup of the broth. Stir remaining broth, the ketchup, salt and garlic into beef. Heat to boiling; reduce heat. Cover and simmer about 10 minutes or until beef is tender.

3 Stir in mushrooms and onion. Heat to boiling; reduce heat. Cover and simmer about 5 minutes longer or until onion is tender.

4 In tightly covered container, shake reserved ⅓ cup broth and the flour until mixed; gradually stir into beef mixture. Heat to boiling, stirring constantly. Boil and stir 1 minute; reduce heat to low. Stir in sour cream; heat until hot. Serve over noodles.

1 Serving: Calories 330; Total Fat 20g (Saturated Fat 10g, Trans Fat 1g); Cholesterol 100mg; Sodium 810mg; Total Carbohydrate 10g (Dietary Fiber 1g, Sugars 4g); Protein 28g **Exchanges:** 2 Vegetable, 3½ Lean Meat, 1 Fat **Carbohydrate Choices:** ½

Ground Beef Stroganoff Substitute 1 lb lean (at least 90%) ground beef for the tenderloin; omit butter. In 12-inch skillet, cook beef over medium heat, stirring occasionally, until thoroughly cooked; drain. Continue as directed.

Spiced Corned Beef Brisket with Horseradish Sour Cream

CALORIE SMART • SLOW COOKER

PREP 10 min **TOTAL** 8 hr 10 min • 8 servings

- 1 corned beef brisket (3 to 3½ lb)
- 1 large sweet onion (Bermuda, Maui or Spanish), sliced
- ¾ teaspoon crushed red pepper flakes
- 1 cup reduced-sodium chicken broth
- 1 tablespoon Worcestershire sauce
- ½ cup sour cream
- 1 tablespoon cream-style prepared horseradish
- 2 tablespoons chopped fresh parsley

1 Remove beef from package; discard liquid and seasoning packet. Trim fat from beef and thoroughly rinse.

2 Spray 5- to 6-quart slow cooker with cooking spray. Place onion in slow cooker. Top with beef; sprinkle with pepper flakes. In small bowl, mix broth and Worcestershire sauce; pour over beef.

3 Cover; cook on Low heat setting 8 to 9 hours or until beef is tender.

4 In small bowl, stir sour cream, horseradish and parsley until well mixed. Slice beef across the grain; serve with horseradish sour cream.

1 Serving: Calories 340; Total Fat 26g (Saturated Fat 9g, Trans Fat 1g); Cholesterol 125mg; Sodium 1480mg; Total Carbohydrate 4g (Dietary Fiber 0g, Sugars 2g); Protein 23g **Exchanges:** 3½ High-Fat Meat **Carbohydrate Choices:** 0

Beef Stroganoff

Reuben or Rachel Sandwich

For each Reuben sandwich, spread 1 tablespoon Thousand Island dressing on 1 slice marble rye or pumpernickel bread. Top with 1 slice Swiss cheese, ¼ cup sauerkraut, 2 ounces sliced corned beef and another bread slice. Spread outsides of bread with 1 to 2 tablespoons butter. Cook in covered skillet over low heat 8 to 10 minutes or until toasted and hot. Turn halfway through cooking. For a Rachel sandwich, substitute turkey or pastrami for the corned beef.

Beer-Braised Short Rib Dinner

Osso Buco

Beer-Braised Short Rib Dinner

PREP 15 min **TOTAL** 8 hr 15 min • 4 servings

- 4 beef short ribs (about 3¼ lb), cut in half
- 2 tablespoons applewood rub for meat
- 1 can (6 oz) tomato paste
- 1 bottle (12 oz) pale ale
- 6 medium carrots
- 1 medium leek, finely chopped
- 3 cloves garlic, finely chopped
- 1 teaspoon salt
- ¼ teaspoon pepper
- 3 medium Yukon Gold potatoes (about 1¼ lb), cut lengthwise into sixths
  Chopped fresh parsley, if desired

1 Line 15x10x1-inch pan with heavy-duty foil; spray foil with cooking spray. Rub ribs on all sides with applewood rub. Place ribs in pan.

2 In medium bowl, stir together tomato paste and ale with whisk until smooth. Finely chop 1 of the carrots. Stir chopped carrot, leek, garlic, salt and pepper into tomato mixture. Pour over ribs; turn to coat. Cover pan tightly with heavy-duty foil. Refrigerate at least 6 hours or up to 24 hours to marinate, turning ribs occasionally.

3 Heat oven to 400°F. Cut remaining 5 carrots into 2-inch pieces and place in pan with ribs, turning to coat. Arrange ribs, fat sides up, in marinade. Bake uncovered 1 hour.

4 Reduce oven temperature to 350°F. Turn ribs on side; add potatoes to pan, turning in marinade to coat. Bake 45 to 60 minutes longer, occasionally turning ribs, until ribs and potatoes are tender. (If too much ale mixture evaporates, add a little water to pan.) Sprinkle with parsley.

1 Serving: Calories 1090; Total Fat 78g (Saturated Fat 33g, Trans Fat 3.5g); Cholesterol 170mg; Sodium 1360mg; Total Carbohydrate 51g (Dietary Fiber 7g, Sugars 13g); Protein 46g **Exchanges:** 3 Starch, 1 Vegetable, 5 High-Fat Meat, 7 Fat **Carbohydrate Choices:** 3½

Osso Buco

These braised veal shanks, featuring white wine, beef broth and a touch of lemon peel, are very tender. Instead of serving with mashed potatoes or spaghetti, try Classic Risotto (make 1½ times the recipe, page 219).

PREP 40 min **TOTAL** 2 hr 40 min • 6 servings

- 6 veal or beef shank crosscuts, 2 to 2½ inches thick (3 to 3½ lb)
- ½ teaspoon salt
- ¼ teaspoon pepper
- ¼ cup all-purpose flour
- 2 tablespoons olive or vegetable oil
- ⅓ cup dry white wine or apple juice
- 1 can (10½ oz) condensed beef broth
- 1 clove garlic, finely chopped
- 1 dried bay leaf
- 2 tablespoons chopped fresh parsley
- 1 teaspoon grated lemon peel
  Shredded Parmesan or Asiago cheese, if desired
  Hot cooked mashed potatoes (page 247) or spaghetti (page 167)

1 Sprinkle veal with salt and pepper; coat with flour. In 4-quart Dutch oven, heat oil over medium heat. Cook veal in oil about 20 minutes, turning occasionally, until brown on all sides.

2 Stir in wine, broth, garlic and bay leaf. Heat to boiling; reduce heat. Cover and simmer 1 hour 30 minutes to 2 hours or until veal is tender.

3 Remove veal to serving platter. Skim fat from broth; remove and discard bay leaf. Pour broth over veal; sprinkle with parsley, lemon peel and cheese. Serve with mashed potatoes.

1 Serving: Calories 700; Total Fat 30g (Saturated Fat 9g, Trans Fat 4g); Cholesterol 255mg; Sodium 1090mg; Total Carbohydrate 41g (Dietary Fiber 4g, Sugars 3g); Protein 68g **Exchanges:** 2½ Starch, 7 Lean Meat, 1 Fat **Carbohydrate Choices:** 3

Meat Loaf CALORIE SMART

PREP 20 min **TOTAL** 1 hr 40 min • 6 servings

- 1½ lb lean (at least 80%) ground beef
- 1 cup milk
- 1 tablespoon Worcestershire sauce
- 1 teaspoon chopped fresh or ¼ teaspoon dried sage leaves
- ½ teaspoon salt
- ½ teaspoon ground mustard
- ¼ teaspoon pepper
- 1 clove garlic, finely chopped, or ⅛ teaspoon garlic powder
- 1 egg
- 3 slices bread, torn into small pieces*
- 1 small onion, finely chopped (⅓ cup)
- ½ cup ketchup, chili sauce or barbecue sauce

1 Heat oven to 350°F. In large bowl, mix all ingredients except ketchup. Spread mixture in ungreased 8x4- or 9x5-inch loaf pan, or shape into 9x5-inch loaf in ungreased 13x9-inch pan. Spread ketchup over top.

2 Insert ovenproof meat thermometer so tip is in center of loaf. Bake uncovered 1 hour to 1 hour 15 minutes or until beef is no longer pink in center and thermometer reads 160°F; drain. Let stand 5 minutes; remove from pan.

*½ cup dry bread crumbs or ¾ cup quick-cooking oats can be substituted for the bread.

1 Serving: Calories 290; Total Fat 15g (Saturated Fat 6g, Trans Fat 1g); Cholesterol 110mg; Sodium 610mg; Total Carbohydrate 15g (Dietary Fiber 0g, Sugars 3g); Protein 24g **Exchanges:** ½ Starch, ½ Other Carbohydrate, 3 Medium-Fat Meat **Carbohydrate Choices:** 1

LIGHTER Directions For 7 grams of fat and 240 calories per serving, substitute ground turkey breast for the ground beef and ¼ cup fat-free egg product for the egg. Use fat-free (skim) milk. Bake as directed until turkey is no longer pink in center and thermometer reads at least 165°F.

Mini Meat Loaves Spray 12 regular-size muffin cups with cooking spray. Divide beef mixture evenly among cups (cups will be very full). Brush tops with about ¼ cup ketchup. Place muffin pan on cookie sheet. Bake about 30 minutes or until loaves are no longer pink in center and thermometer reads 160°F when inserted in center of loaves in middle of muffin pan (outer loaves will be done sooner). Immediately remove from cups.

Horseradish Meat Loaf Omit sage. Stir in 1 to 2 tablespoons cream-style prepared horseradish in Step 1.

Sloppy Joes CALORIE SMART • FAST

PREP 30 min **TOTAL** 30 min • 6 sandwiches

- 1 lb lean (at least 80%) ground beef
- 1 medium onion, chopped (½ cup)
- ¼ cup chopped celery
- 1 cup ketchup
- 1 tablespoon Worcestershire sauce
- 1 teaspoon ground mustard
- ⅛ teaspoon pepper
- 6 burger buns, split

1 In 10-inch skillet, cook beef, onion and celery over medium heat 8 to 10 minutes, stirring occasionally, until beef is thoroughly cooked; drain.

2 Stir in ketchup, Worcestershire sauce, mustard and pepper. Heat to boiling; reduce heat. Simmer uncovered 10 to 15 minutes, stirring occasionally, until hot and bubbly. Spoon into buns.

1 Sandwich: Calories 320; Total Fat 11g (Saturated Fat 4g, Trans Fat 1.5g); Cholesterol 50mg; Sodium 630mg; Total Carbohydrate 35g (Dietary Fiber 1g, Sugars 12g); Protein 18g **Exchanges:** 1½ Starch, 1 Other Carbohydrate, 2 Medium-Fat Meat **Carbohydrate Choices:** 2

LIGHTER Directions For 3 grams of fat and 235 calories per serving, substitute ground turkey breast for the ground beef; spray skillet with cooking spray before heating.

Barbecue Beef Sandwiches CALORIE SMART • SLOW COOKER

PREP 15 min **TOTAL** 7 hr 35 min • 12 sandwiches

- 1 boneless beef chuck roast (3 lb), trimmed of excess fat
- 1 cup barbecue sauce (for homemade sauce, see page 411)
- ½ cup apricot or peach preserves
- 1 small onion, sliced
- ⅓ cup chopped green bell pepper
- 1 tablespoon Dijon mustard
- 2 teaspoons packed brown sugar
- 12 kaiser rolls or burger buns, split

1 Spray 4- to 5-quart slow cooker with cooking spray. Cut beef into 4 pieces; place in slow cooker. In medium bowl, mix remaining ingredients except rolls; pour over beef.

2 Cover; cook on Low heat setting 7 to 8 hours or until beef is tender.

3 Remove beef from slow cooker to cutting board; cut into thin slices. Return to slow cooker. Cover; cook 20 to 30 minutes longer or until hot. Spoon beef mixture into buns. If desired, serve juices in small bowls for dipping.

1 Sandwich: Calories 410; Total Fat 14g (Saturated Fat 5g, Trans Fat 1g); Cholesterol 60mg; Sodium 570mg; Total Carbohydrate 46g (Dietary Fiber 1g, Sugars 15g); Protein 26g **Exchanges:** 2 Starch, 1 Other Carbohydrate, 2½ Medium-Fat Meat **Carbohydrate Choices:** 3

Meat Loaf

French Dip Sandwiches

CALORIE SMART • SLOW COOKER

PREP 10 min **TOTAL** 7 hr 10 min • 10 sandwiches

1	boneless beef chuck roast (3 lb)
1½	cups water
⅓	cup soy sauce
1	teaspoon dried rosemary leaves
1	teaspoon dried thyme leaves
1	clove garlic, finely chopped
1	dried bay leaf
3	or 4 black peppercorns
2	loaves (1 lb each) French bread

1 Spray 3½- to 4-quart slow cooker with cooking spray. Place beef in slow cooker (if roast comes in netting or is tied, do not remove). In medium bowl, mix remaining ingredients except bread; pour over beef.

2 Cover; cook on Low heat setting 7 to 8 hours. Skim fat from surface of juices; discard bay leaf and peppercorns. Remove beef from slow cooker; place on cutting board (remove netting or strings). Cut beef into thin slices.

3 Cut each loaf of bread into 5 pieces, about 4 inches long; cut in half horizontally. Fill bread with beef. Serve cooking juices in small bowls for dipping.

1 Sandwich: Calories 400; Total Fat 13g (Saturated Fat 4.5g, Trans Fat 1g); Cholesterol 50mg; Sodium 1050mg; Total Carbohydrate 46g (Dietary Fiber 3g, Sugars 0g); Protein 25g **Exchanges:** 3 Starch, 2 Medium-Fat Meat **Carbohydrate Choices:** 3

Barbecue Beef Sandwiches

French Dip Sandwiches

RETAIL PORK CUTS

Here are many of the pork cuts available at the market. They will have different names in different regions of the country, but this should help you identify what you are purchasing.

Diagram: **1** Shoulder Butt **2** Loin **3** Picnic Shoulder **4** Side **5** Leg

Pork Center Cut Rib Chop (bone-in)

Pork Center Rib Roast (bone-in)

Pork Sirloin Chop (bone-in)

Pork Loin Boneless Rolled Roast (double)

Pork Crown Roast (bone-in)

Pork Loin Chop (bone-in)

Pork Tenderloin

Pork Loin Center Cut Boneless Roast and Chops

Pork Spareribs

Pork Loin Back Ribs

Pork Blade Steak (bone-in)

Pork Blade Roast (bone-in)

Pork Ham (bone-in/shank half)

Pork Center-Cut Ham Steak

Pork Loin Country-Style Ribs

Pork Smoked Picnic

RETAIL LAMB CUTS

These cuts of lamb show what is available at grocery stores. For specific cuts, ask a butcher to provide it for you, because lamb is not as readily available as pork or beef.

Diagram: **1** Shoulder **2** Rib **3** Loin and Sirloin **4** Leg and Hind Shank **5** Breast and Foreshank

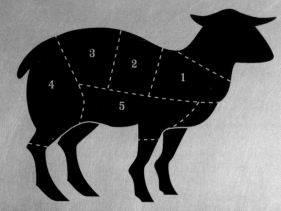

Lamb Stew Meat

Lamb Boneless Shoulder Roast

Lamb Loin Roast (bone-in)

Lamb Loin Chops

Lamb Foreshank

Lamb Arm Chop (bone-in)

Lamb Blade Chop (bone-in)

Lamb Loin Roast (boneless)

Lamb Spareribs

Lamb Sirloin Chop (bone-in)

Lamb Leg Sirloin (half of leg bone-in)

Lamb Rib Roast (bone-in)

Lamb Frenched Chops

Lamb Leg Roast (bone-in sirloin half of leg)

Lamb Leg Roast (boned and tied)

Lamb Rib Chops (bone-in)

Learn to
SEAR AND PANFRY

Searing and panfrying have similar techniques but are used for different purposes. Searing caramelizes the outsides of meat, which adds a wonderful color, builds flavor, and seals in juices by quickly cooking it. The meat is then finished cooking in another way—braising, roasting or simmering.

Panfrying involves cooking food in a small amount of oil, first by browning and then cooking it through. Panfrying requires less oil than deep frying. Often, foods are coated with flour or other ingredients before cooking to create a nice crust. Meats and vegetables or even tofu are candidates for this technique.

Tips for Searing or Panfrying

1. Choose the correct pan: Stainless steel or cast-iron skillets are the best pans for searing. These pans can be brought to a high enough heat to sear the meat evenly and quickly.

2. Prepare the meat: Searing can be done with small cubes of meat or steaks or chops; or sear larger cuts of meat before roasting. For panfrying, coat meat with seasonings, flour or crumbs just before cooking.

3. Add oil to the skillet: To sear, use no oil or heat a small amount—1 to 3 teaspoons swirled to cover the bottom of pan. To panfry, add ¼ inch oil to the pan.

4. Heat the skillet: Heat the pan over medium-high heat—the pan and/or oil should be hot when you add the meat.

5. Cook the meat: To sear, let the meat cook—when it's properly browned; it will start to come loose from the bottom of the pan. As it starts to loosen, turn the pieces and sear the other sides. For panfrying, allow meat to brown before turning—ideally, turn only one time to get a good sear on the surface—and continue cooking, uncovered, usually at a lower temperature, as directed in the recipe.

6. Deglaze the pan: After removing the meat, you can add liquid to create a sauce from the brown bits left in the pan (see page 466).

Panfried Pork Chops with Cider Sauce   CALORIE SMART • FAST

PREP 25 min **TOTAL** 25 min • 4 servings

- 4 boneless pork loin chops, ½ to ¾ inch thick (1 lb), trimmed of fat
- ¼ teaspoon seasoned salt
- ¼ teaspoon dried thyme leaves
- ⅛ teaspoon garlic powder
- ⅛ teaspoon pepper
- 1 tablespoon vegetable oil
- ½ cup apple cider
- ¼ cup brandy or apple cider
- 1 tablespoon butter

1 Sprinkle both sides of pork chops with seasoned salt, thyme, garlic powder and pepper. In 12-inch skillet, heat oil over medium-high heat. Add pork; cook about 5 minutes or until bottoms are browned.

2 Turn pork chops; reduce heat to medium-low. Cook uncovered 5 to 10 minutes longer or until pork is no longer pink in center. Remove from skillet to plate; cover to keep warm.

3 Add cider and brandy to skillet. Heat to boiling, stirring to loosen browned bits from bottom of skillet; reduce heat to low. Add butter; simmer 1 to 3 minutes, stirring frequently, until slightly thickened. Serve sauce over pork.

1 Serving: Calories 250; Total Fat 15g (Saturated Fat 5g, Trans Fat 0g); Cholesterol 75mg; Sodium 150mg; Total Carbohydrate 4g (Dietary Fiber 0g, Sugars 3g); Protein 24g **Exchanges:** ½ Starch, 3 Lean Meat, 1 Fat **Carbohydrate Choices:** 0

Pork Chops with Mustard-Chive Cream Sauce
Omit cider, brandy and butter. Prepare recipe through Step 2. Add ¼ cup dry sherry to skillet. Heat to boiling, stirring to loosen browned bits. Stir in ½ cup whipping cream, 1 tablespoon country-style Dijon mustard, 2 teaspoons chopped fresh chives, ⅛ teaspoon salt and ⅛ teaspoon pepper. Simmer 3 minutes, stirring frequently, until slightly thickened.

Spicy Southwestern Pork Chops
Omit all ingredients except pork chops. In small bowl, mix 1 teaspoon chili powder, 1 teaspoon chipotle chile pepper powder, ½ teaspoon ground cumin, ¼ teaspoon salt, ¼ teaspoon ground red pepper (cayenne), ¼ teaspoon garlic powder and ⅛ teaspoon black pepper. Rub on both sides of pork. Cook as directed through Step 2.

Cornbread and Bacon–Stuffed Pork Chops

PREP 30 min **TOTAL** 1 hr 30 min • 6 servings

- 6 bone-in pork rib or loin chops, 1 to 1¼ inches thick (about 4 lb)
- 4 slices bacon, cut into ½-inch pieces
- 1 medium onion, chopped (½ cup)
- 1 small green bell pepper, chopped (½ cup)
- 1 cup cornbread stuffing mix
- ½ cup water
- ½ cup shredded Cheddar cheese (2 oz)
- ½ teaspoon seasoned salt
- ½ teaspoon dried marjoram leaves
- ¼ teaspoon pepper

1 Heat oven to 350°F. Make a pocket in each pork chop by cutting into side of chop toward the bone.

2 In 12-inch skillet, cook bacon over medium heat, stirring occasionally, until crisp. Add onion and bell pepper. Cook 2 to 3 minutes, stirring occasionally, until vegetables are crisp-tender; drain. Remove from heat; stir in stuffing mix and water until well blended. Stir in cheese.

3 Sprinkle both sides of pork chops with seasoned salt, marjoram and pepper. Fill each pocket with about ⅓ cup stuffing. In same skillet, cook pork over medium heat until brown on both sides. Place pork in 13x9-inch pan.

4 Cover tightly with foil; bake 45 minutes. Uncover; bake about 15 minutes longer or until pork is no longer pink and meat thermometer inserted in center reads 145°F.

1 Serving: Calories 600; Total Fat 30g (Saturated Fat 11g, Trans Fat 0g); Cholesterol 210mg; Sodium 540mg; Total Carbohydrate 9g (Dietary Fiber 1g, Sugars 1g); Protein 73g **Exchanges:** ½ Starch, 9½ Very Lean Meat, ½ High-Fat Meat, 4 Fat **Carbohydrate Choices:** ½

Pecan-Crusted Pork Medallions FAST

PREP 20 min **TOTAL** 20 min • 4 servings

- 1 egg
- ¼ cup honey
- 1 pork tenderloin (1 lb), cut into ½-inch slices
- 1 cup chopped pecans
- ½ cup yellow cornmeal
- 1 teaspoon salt
- ½ teaspoon pepper
- 2 tablespoons vegetable oil

1 In large bowl, mix egg and honey. Add pork slices; toss to coat.

2 In food processor, place pecans, cornmeal, salt and pepper. Cover and process until finely chopped. Place pecan mixture in resealable plastic food-storage bag. Add pork slices; seal bag and shake to coat.

3 In 10-inch nonstick skillet, heat oil over medium-high heat. Cook pork in oil 6 to 8 minutes, turning once, until golden brown on outside and no longer pink in center.

1 Serving: Calories 530; Total Fat 32g (Saturated Fat 4.5g, Trans Fat 0g); Cholesterol 105mg; Sodium 640mg; Total Carbohydrate 35g (Dietary Fiber 3g, Sugars 19g); Protein 25g **Exchanges:** 2 Starch, 2 Lean Meat, 4 Fat **Carbohydrate Choices:** 2

Pumpkin Seed–Crusted Pork Medallions

Substitute 1 cup pepitas (pumpkin seeds) for the pecans. Add ½ teaspoon ancho chile powder with the pepper. Top each serving with 1 tablespoon each chopped fresh cilantro and crumbled cotija (Mexican) cheese.

Cutting a Pocket in a Pork Chop

With sharp knife, make pocket in side of pork chop, cutting toward bone.

Cornbread and Bacon–Stuffed Pork Chops

Pork Tenderloin with Roasted Vegetables CALORIE SMART

PREP 10 min **TOTAL** 50 min • 6 servings

- 2 pork tenderloins (about ¾ lb each)
- 1 bag (16 oz) ready-to-eat baby-cut carrots
- 2 lb small red potatoes (16 to 20), cut in half
- 1 medium onion, cut into wedges
- 6 cloves garlic, peeled
- 1 tablespoon olive or vegetable oil
- 2 teaspoons dried rosemary leaves, crushed
- 1 teaspoon dried sage leaves, crushed
- ¼ teaspoon salt
- ¼ teaspoon pepper

1 Heat oven to 450°F. Spray shallow roasting pan with cooking spray. Place pork in pan. Insert ovenproof meat thermometer so tip is in thickest part of pork.

2 Place carrots, potatoes, onion and garlic around pork. Drizzle with oil; sprinkle with rosemary, sage, salt and pepper.

3 Roast uncovered 25 to 30 minutes or until thermometer reads 145°F. Remove pork from pan. Stir vegetables; roast 5 to 10 minutes longer or until tender. Serve pork with vegetables and garlic.

1 Serving: Calories 320; Total Fat 7g (Saturated Fat 2g, Trans Fat 0g); Cholesterol 50mg; Sodium 220mg; Total Carbohydrate 38g (Dietary Fiber 5g, Sugars 6g); Protein 26g **Exchanges:** 2 Starch, 1½ Vegetable, 2½ Very Lean Meat, 1 Fat **Carbohydrate Choices:** 2½

Pork Tenderloin with Roasted Vegetables

Jerk Pulled Pork Sandwiches

Jerk Pulled Pork Sandwiches

SLOW COOKER

Pulled pork, a favorite style of Southern and some Southeastern barbecues, refers to the method of preparing the cooked pork by pulling it apart with your fingers or two forks.

PREP 10 min **TOTAL** 8 hr 40 min • 8 sandwiches

- 1 tablespoon Jamaican jerk seasoning (dry)
- 1 boneless pork shoulder (2½ lb)
- ¼ teaspoon dried thyme leaves
- 1 medium onion, chopped (½ cup)
- 1 cup cola carbonated beverage
- 2 cups barbecue sauce (for homemade sauce, see page 411)
- 8 burger buns, split, or flour tortillas (9 to 10 inch)
  Creamy coleslaw (from deli; for homemade coleslaw, see page 129), if desired

1 Rub jerk seasoning over pork (if pork comes in netting or is tied, do not remove); sprinkle with thyme. Spray 3½- to 6-quart slow cooker with cooking spray. In slow cooker, place pork and onion; pour cola over pork.

2 Cover; cook on Low heat setting 8 to 10 hours. Remove pork from slow cooker to cutting board or plate (remove netting or strings). Remove juices from slow cooker and reserve.

3 Using 2 forks or your fingers, shred pork into desired-size pieces; return to slow cooker. Stir in barbecue sauce and ½ cup reserved juices. Increase heat setting to High. Cover; cook 30 to 45 minutes or until thoroughly heated.

4 In 2-quart saucepan, heat remaining reserved juices to boiling. Spoon pork into buns; top with coleslaw. If desired, serve juices in small bowls for dipping.

1 Sandwich: Calories 420; Total Fat 14g (Saturated Fat 4.5g, Trans Fat 0g); Cholesterol 65mg; Sodium 900mg; Total Carbohydrate 49g (Dietary Fiber 2g, Sugars 21g); Protein 25g **Exchanges:** 2 Starch, 1 Other Carbohydrate, 3 Lean Meat, 1 Fat **Carbohydrate Choices:** 3

Pork Crown Roast with Fruited Stuffing Supreme

PREP 30 min **TOTAL** 4 hr 25 min • 16 servings

PORK ROAST

1 pork crown roast, about 16 to 18 ribs (8 to 10 lb)*
2 teaspoons salt
1 teaspoon pepper

STUFFING

1 lb bulk pork sausage
¼ cup butter
4 medium stalks celery, chopped (2 cups)
¾ cup chopped onion (about 1 large)
1 cup chicken broth (for homemade broth, see page 143)
1 teaspoon dried sage leaves, crushed
1 teaspoon poultry seasoning
6½ cups unseasoned stuffing cubes (16 oz)
1 can (8 oz) crushed pineapple in juice, undrained
1 cup applesauce
1 cup orange marmalade

1 Heat oven to 325°F. Sprinkle pork with salt and pepper. Place pork, bone ends up, on rack in shallow roasting pan. Wrap bone ends in foil to prevent excessive browning. Insert ovenproof meat thermometer so tip is in thickest part of pork and does not touch bone or rest in fat.

2 Place small heatproof bowl or crumpled foil in crown to hold shape of roast evenly. Do not add water. Roast uncovered 2 hours 40 minutes to 3 hours 20 minutes.

3 In 10-inch skillet, cook sausage over medium heat 8 to 10 minutes, stirring occasionally, until no longer pink; drain well and set aside. In same skillet, melt butter over medium-high heat. Cook celery and onion in butter about 5 minutes, stirring occasionally, until crisp-tender. Stir in broth, sage and poultry seasoning. In very large bowl, mix stuffing cubes, sausage, pineapple, applesauce and marmalade. Add vegetable mixture; stir until well blended.

4 About 1 hour before pork is done, remove bowl and fill center of crown with stuffing. (Remaining stuffing can be baked in 1½-quart covered casserole.) Cover stuffing with foil for first 30 minutes. Remove foil and finish roasting.

5 Remove pork from oven when thermometer reads 145°F. Cover loosely with foil; let stand at least 3 minutes. Remove foil from bone ends; place paper frills on bone ends, if desired. To serve, spoon stuffing into bowl and cut pork between ribs.

*A 4-lb boneless pork loin can be substituted for the crown roast. Place in roasting pan. Insert ovenproof meat thermometer so tip is in thickest part of pork and does not rest in fat. Bake uncovered about 1 hour 20 minutes. Remove pork from oven when thermometer reads 145°F. Cover loosely with foil; let stand at least 3 minutes. Make stuffing as directed and bake in covered casserole.

1 Serving: Calories 580; Total Fat 24g (Saturated Fat 9g, Trans Fat 0.5g); Cholesterol 135mg; Sodium 1020mg; Total Carbohydrate 44g (Dietary Fiber 2g, Sugars 19g); Protein 46g **Exchanges:** 2 Starch, 5 Lean Meat, 1 Fat **Carbohydrate Choices:** 3

Carving a Pork Crown Roast

Place roast on carving board or serving platter. Insert meat fork into roast to keep it from moving; cut slices between ribs.

Pork Crown Roast with Fruited Stuffing Supreme

Herbed Pork Loin Roast

Porketta Pot Roast

CALORIE SMART • SLOW COOKER

PREP 20 min **TOTAL** 9 hr 20 min • 8 servings

> 2 teaspoons Italian seasoning
> 1½ teaspoons fennel seed, crushed
> ¾ teaspoon salt
> ½ teaspoon celery seed
> 1 boneless pork shoulder (3 lb)
> 3 medium parsnips, peeled, cut into ¾-inch pieces (3 cups)
> 2 medium sweet potatoes, peeled, cut into ¾-inch pieces (3 cups)
> 12 cloves garlic, peeled, cut in half
> 1½ cups water

1 In small bowl, mix Italian seasoning, fennel seed, salt and celery seed. Pat seasoning mixture evenly onto pork (if pork comes in netting or is tied, do not remove). Heat 12-inch nonstick skillet over medium-high heat. Add pork; cook 5 to 10 minutes, turning several times, until brown on all sides.

2 Spray 4- to 5-quart slow cooker with cooking spray. In slow cooker, place parsnips, sweet potatoes and garlic; pour water over vegetables. Place pork on vegetables.

3 Cover; cook on Low heat setting 9 to 10 hours or until pork is tender. Remove pork from slow cooker to cutting board (remove netting or strings). Cut pork across grain into slices; serve with vegetables and cooking juices.

1 Serving: Calories 350; Total Fat 20g (Saturated Fat 7g, Trans Fat 0g); Cholesterol 90mg; Sodium 290mg; Total Carbohydrate 16g (Dietary Fiber 3g, Sugars 6g); Protein 26g **Exchanges:** 1 Starch, 3 Medium-Fat Meat, 1 Fat **Carbohydrate Choices:** 1

Herbed Pork Loin Roast **CALORIE SMART**

PREP 10 min **TOTAL** 1 hr 15 min • 6 servings

> 1 boneless pork loin roast (1½ lb), trimmed of fat
> ½ teaspoon olive oil
> 3 tablespoons chopped fresh sage leaves
> 2 tablespoons chopped fresh parsley
> 2 tablespoons chopped fresh oregano leaves
> 4½ teaspoons chopped fresh chives
> ½ teaspoon salt
> ½ teaspoon black pepper

1 Heat oven to 375°F. Spray broiler pan with cooking spray.

2 Rub pork with oil. In small bowl, mix remaining ingredients. Rub mixture over pork. Place pork on rack in pan. Insert ovenproof meat thermometer so tip is in thickest part of pork and does not rest in fat.

3 Roast uncovered 1 hour or until thermometer reads 145°F. Cover loosely with foil; let stand at least 3 minutes before slicing.

1 Serving: Calories 130; Total Fat 6g (Saturated Fat 2g, Trans Fat 0g); Cholesterol 0mg; Sodium 250mg; Total Carbohydrate 0g (Dietary Fiber 0g, Sugars 0g); Protein 10g **Exchanges:** 2 Lean Meat **Carbohydrate Choices:** 0

Dijon Herbed Pork Loin Roast In Step 2, omit olive oil. Mix 1 tablepoon Dijon mustard and 1 finely chopped clove garlic in small bowl; spread over pork. Continue as directed.

Pepper Garlic Pork Loin Roast Increase olive oil to 1 teaspoon; omit sage, oregano, chives and pepper. Mix parsley with 4 to 6 finely chopped cloves garlic and 1 teaspoon coarsely ground black pepper. Continue as directed.

Porketta Pot Roast

Make-Ahead
OVEN-ROASTED PULLED PORK

CALORIE SMART

This flavorful, tender pulled pork can be used for sandwiches (try topping with coleslaw!), tacos, burritos, quesadillas, salads or soup.

PREP 10 min **TOTAL** 5 hr 20 min • 10 servings

- 1 boneless pork shoulder blade roast (4 lb)
- ¼ cup packed brown sugar
- 2 teaspoons salt
- 1 teaspoon garlic powder
- 1 teaspoon onion powder
- 1 teaspoon paprika
- 1 teaspoon smoked paprika
- 1 teaspoon pepper

1 Heat oven to 325°F. In 13x9-inch (3-quart) glass baking dish, place pork, fat side up (if roast has netting, do not remove). In small bowl, mix remaining ingredients. Sprinkle mixture over all pork surfaces; rub and press into meat.

2 Cover with foil. Roast 4 hours to 4 hours 30 minutes or until very tender. Place roast on cutting board; remove excess fat from top of pork and discard. Cover roast loosely with foil; let stand 30 minutes or until cool enough to handle. Pull pork apart into bite-size pieces, discarding any fat or gristle.

3 Pour pan drippings into fat separator, or skim fat from drippings. Pour pan drippings into small bowl, leaving fat in separator. If desired, add some pan drippings to pulled pork. Reheat to use immediately, or cover and refrigerate 3 to 4 days or freeze 2 to 3 months.

1 Serving: Calories 270; Total Fat 15g (Saturated Fat 5g, Trans Fat 0g); Cholesterol 80mg; Sodium 520mg; Total Carbohydrate 6g (Dietary Fiber 0g, Sugars 5g); Protein 27g **Exchanges:** ½ Other Carbohydrate, 4 Lean Meat, ½ Fat **Carbohydrate Choices:** ½

The Origins of Pulled Pork

Pulled pork goes back to colonial days, when Southerners would roast less tender, fatty cuts of pork over low heat for long periods. The fat would keep the meat moist while the long cook time would make the pork ultra-tender, allowing it to be pulled apart.

Ways to Use Pulled Pork

Spend a little time on the weekend cooking this flavorful pulled pork, then plan to use it in a variety of ways during the week. The recipe makes about 5 cups of pulled pork to serve in sandwiches or to add to recipes. Check out these easy ideas for using the pork.

1. Pork and Coleslaw Sandwiches: Spread cut sides of buns with spicy mustard. Layer pulled pork and creamy coleslaw in buns.

2. Pulled Pork Pizza: Top purchased pizza crust with about 1 cup pulled pork, 1 cup chopped tomatoes and 1½ cups shredded Monterey Jack or Cheddar cheese. Bake as directed on pizza package.

3. Chopped Salad with Pork: In large bowl, mix 3 cups chopped romaine, 1 cup chopped red cabbage, 1 cup chopped red bell pepper, ½ cup sliced green onions, 1 cup corn salsa and 1½ cups pulled pork. Toss with ¼ cup Italian dressing.

4. Pulled Pork Nachos: On microwavable serving plate, layer 2 to 3 cups tortilla chips, 1 cup chopped tomatoes, 1 cup pulled pork and 1½ cups shredded Monterey Jack or Cheddar cheese. Microwave on High 1 to 2 minutes or until cheese is melted.

5. Pulled Pork Quesadillas: For each quesadilla, between 2 (8-inch) flour tortillas, layer ¾ cup pulled pork, ¼ cup chunky salsa, ½ cup coleslaw mix and ¾ cup shredded cheese. Brush outsides of tortillas with 1 to 2 teaspoons oil. Cook in skillet over medium heat 3 to 5 minutes or until browned on both sides. Cut into wedges.

6. Pork Burrito Bowls: For each serving, spoon 1 cup hot cooked rice in bowl. Top with ½ cup hot pulled pork, ¼ cup shredded Mexican blend cheese, ¼ cup shredded lettuce and 1 tablespoon salsa.

7. Skillet Pork Hash: In 10-inch skillet, cook ½ cup each chopped onion and bell pepper in 1 tablespoon oil over medium heat 3 to 5 minutes or until tender. Stir in 2 cups pulled pork, ½ cup cooked corn and 2 to 4 tablespoons chunky salsa. Cook and stir 8 to 10 minutes or until hot and flavors are blended.

8. Loaded Fries: Place about 1½ pounds prepared white potato or sweet potato fries on an ovenproof platter. Top with 1 to 1½ cups of the pulled pork, 1 cup shredded Colby-Jack cheese and finely chopped green onions. Return to the oven for 2 to 3 minutes or until cheese is melted.

Oven-Roasted Pulled Pork, Pulled Pork Quesadillas

Glazed Baked Ham CALORIE SMART

PREP 10 min **TOTAL** 1 hr 50 min • 10 servings

    1 cooked smoked bone-in ham (6 lb)
    1 cup packed brown sugar
    1 tablespoon cornstarch
    ¼ teaspoon salt
    1 can (8 oz) crushed pineapple, undrained
    2 tablespoons lemon juice
    1 tablespoon yellow or Dijon mustard

1 Heat oven to 325°F. Place ham on rack in shallow roasting pan. Insert ovenproof meat thermometer so tip is in center of thickest part of ham and does not touch bone or rest in fat. Bake uncovered 1 hour 30 minutes.

2 Meanwhile, in 1-quart saucepan, mix brown sugar, cornstarch and salt. Stir in pineapple, lemon juice and mustard. Cook and stir over medium heat until mixture thickens and boils. Boil and stir 1 minute. Brush glaze over ham during last 45 minutes of baking.

3 When thermometer reads at least 140°F, remove ham from oven. Cover loosely with foil; let stand 10 to 15 minutes before slicing.

1 Serving: Calories 140; Total Fat 3.5g (Saturated Fat 1g, Trans Fat 0g); Cholesterol 35mg; Sodium 830mg; Total Carbohydrate 14g (Dietary Fiber 0g, Sugars 14g); Protein 14g **Exchanges:** 1 Other Carbohydrate, 4 Lean Meat **Carbohydrate Choices:** 1

Ham with Brown Sugar–Orange Glaze

Omit all ingredients except ham. Bake ham as directed. In small bowl, mix ½ cup packed brown sugar, 2 tablespoons orange juice and ½ teaspoon ground mustard. Brush glaze over ham during last 45 minutes of baking.

All About Hams

Whatever kind of ham you choose, they all come from cured pork leg meat. Curing gives ham its distinctive sweet-smoky and salty flavor. Hams are usually either wet or dry cured. Most grocery store hams, including spiral-cut hams, are wet cured, meaning they have been processed with a brine of water, salt, sugar and spices. Brining keeps the meat moist and tender.

Dry-cured hams are rubbed with salt, sugar and spices, then aged anywhere from several weeks to more than a year. These hams, referred to as country hams, are often named for the city where they are processed. Dry-cured hams are slightly salty, so follow package directions for using.

Spicy Barbecue Pork Loin Ribs

PREP 15 min **TOTAL** 2 hr 45 min • 6 servings

    RIBS
    4½ lb pork loin back ribs
        Salt and pepper to taste

    SPICY BARBECUE SAUCE
    ⅓ cup butter
    2 tablespoons white or cider vinegar
    2 tablespoons water
    1 teaspoon sugar
    ½ teaspoon garlic powder
    ½ teaspoon onion powder
    ½ teaspoon black pepper
        Dash ground red pepper (cayenne)

Glazed Baked Ham

Carving Ham

Place ham on carving board or platter, fat side up, bone facing you. Cut in half next to bone.

Place boneless side of ham fat side up; cut slices. Cut slices from bone-in portion, cutting away from bone.

Spicy Barbecue Pork Loin Ribs with Molasses-Mustard Barbecue Sauce

1 Heat oven to 325°F. With knife or kitchen scissors, cut ribs into 6 serving pieces. Place ribs, meat side up, on rack in roasting pan or 13x9-inch pan. Sprinkle with salt and pepper. Cover and bake 1 hour 45 minutes.

2 In 1-quart saucepan, heat sauce ingredients over medium heat, stirring frequently, until butter is melted.

3 Brush some of the sauce over ribs. Bake uncovered about 45 minutes longer, brushing frequently with sauce, until meat is tender and no longer pink next to bones. Heat any remaining sauce to boiling; serve with ribs.

1 Serving: Calories 730; Total Fat 60g (Saturated Fat 23g, Trans Fat 0.5g); Cholesterol 225mg; Sodium 220mg; Total Carbohydrate 1g (Dietary Fiber 0g, Sugars 0g); Protein 48g **Exchanges:** 7 High-Fat Meat, 1 Fat **Carbohydrate Choices:** 0

SLOW-COOKER Directions Spray 5- to 6-quart slow cooker with cooking spray. Cut ribs into 2- or 3-rib portions; place in slow cooker. Sprinkle with ½ teaspoon salt and ¼ teaspoon pepper. Pour ½ cup water into slow cooker. Cover; cook on Low heat setting 8 to 9 hours. Remove ribs. Drain and discard liquid from slow cooker. Make sauce as directed; pour into bowl. Dip ribs into sauce to coat. Return ribs to slow cooker. Pour any remaining sauce over ribs. Cover; cook 1 hour.

Beef Short Ribs Substitute beef short ribs for the pork ribs. Heat oven to 350°F. Place ribs in 13x9-inch pan. Pour sauce over ribs. Cover and bake about 2 hours 30 minutes or until meat is tender.

Country-Style Pork Ribs Substitute 3 lbs country-style pork loin ribs for the back ribs. Heat oven to 350°F. Place ribs in 13x9-inch pan. Cover and bake about 2 hours; drain. Pour sauce over ribs. Bake uncovered 30 minutes longer or until meat is tender.

Pork Spareribs Substitute pork spareribs for the back ribs. Heat oven to 325°F. Cut ribs into 6 serving pieces. Place ribs, meat side up, on rack in roasting pan or 13x9-inch pan. Cover and bake 1 hour 15 minutes. Brush with sauce. Bake uncovered about 45 minutes longer, brushing frequently with sauce, until meat is tender and no longer pink next to bones.

Molasses-Mustard Barbecue Sauce In small bowl, mix ½ cup molasses and ⅓ cup Dijon mustard; stir in ⅓ cup cider or white vinegar.

Sweet-Savory Barbecue Sauce In 1-quart saucepan, mix 1 cup chili sauce, ¾ cup grape jelly, 1 tablespoon plus 1½ teaspoons dry red wine or beef broth and 1 teaspoon Dijon mustard. Heat over medium heat, stirring occasionally, until jelly is melted.

ROASTING MEAT

Roasting is a great method for cooking large, tender cuts of meat. Roast meat at 325°F or above. Lower temperatures can start bacterial growth before cooking is finished. See page 31 for more information.

Place meat fat side up on a rack in a shallow roasting pan. (Bone-in roasts don't need a rack.)

Insert ovenproof meat thermometer so tip is in center of thickest part of meat and does not touch bone or rest in fat. Don't add water or liquid; don't cover. Roast as directed in the chart below for desired final doneness, but removing from oven as directed in fourth column. Remove meat from oven; cover loosely with foil and let stand as directed below before carving.

TIMETABLE FOR ROASTING AND BAKING MEAT

CUT OF MEAT	WEIGHT IN POUNDS	APPROXIMATE TOTAL ROASTING TIME IN HOURS (UNLESS NOTED OTHERWISE)	REMOVE FROM OVEN WHEN INTERNAL TEMPERATURE REACHES	FINAL DONENESS TEMPERATURE (AFTER STANDING TIME)
Beef				
Rib-Eye Roast (small-end)*	3 to 4	1½ to 1¾	135°F	145°F medium-rare
Roast at 350°F.		1¾ to 2	150°F	160°F medium
Let stand 15 to 20 minutes.	4 to 6	1¾ to 2	135°F	145°F medium-rare
		2 to 2¼	150°F	160°F medium
	6 to 8	2½ to 2¾	135°F	145°F medium-rare
			150°F	160°F medium
Rib Roast (bone-in)	4 to 6 (2 ribs)	1¾ to 2¼	135°F	145°F medium-rare
Roast at 350°F.		2¼ to 2¾	150°F	160°F medium
Let stand 15 to 20 minutes.	6 to 8 (2 to 4 ribs)	2¼ to 2½	135°F	145°F medium-rare
		2¾ to 3	150°F	160°F medium
	8 to 10 (4 to 5 ribs)	2½ to 3	135°F	145°F medium-rare
		3 to 3½	150°F	160°F medium
Tenderloin Roast	2 to 3	35 to 40 minutes	135°F	145°F medium-rare
Roast at 425°F.		45 to 50 minutes	150°F	160°F medium
Let stand 15 to 20 minutes.	4 to 5	50 to 60 minutes	135°F	145°F medium-rare
		60 to 70 minutes	150°F	160°F medium
Tri-Tip Roast	1½ to 2	30 to 40 minutes	135°F	145°F medium-rare
Roast at 425°F.		40 to 45 minutes	150°F	160°F medium
Let stand 15 to 20 minutes.				
Round Tip Roast	3 to 4	1¾ to 2	140°F	145°F medium-rare
Roast at 325°F.		2¼ to 2½	155°F	160°F medium
Let stand 15 to 20 minutes.	4 to 6	2 to 2½	140°F	145°F medium-rare
		2½ to 3	155°F	160°F medium
	6 to 8	2½ to 3	140°F	145°F medium-rare
		3 to 3½	155°F	160°F medium
Rump Roast	3 to 4	1½ to 2	135°F	145°F medium-rare
Roast at 325°F.				
Let stand 15 to 20 minutes.				

*Large-end roasts add approximately 15 minutes to cooking time.

CUT OF MEAT	WEIGHT IN POUNDS	APPROXIMATE TOTAL ROASTING TIME IN HOURS (UNLESS NOTED OTHERWISE)	REMOVE FROM OVEN WHEN INTERNAL TEMPERATURE REACHES	FINAL DONENESS TEMPERATURE (AFTER STANDING TIME)
Bottom Round Roast Roast at 325°F. Let stand 15 to 20 minutes.	3 to 4	1½ to 2	135°F	145°F medium-rare
Eye Round Roast Roast at 325°F. Let stand 15 to 20 minutes.	2 to 3	1½ to 1¾	135°F	145°F medium-rare
Brisket, Fresh Bake at 325°F. Let stand 15 to 20 minutes.	2½ to 4	2½ to 3 (must be cooked with liquid to partially cover)	——	170°F well-done
Brisket, Corned Bake at 325°F. Let stand 15 to 20 minutes.	2½ to 3½ 3½ to 5	2½ to 3½ 3½ to 4½	Follow package directions.	170°F well-done; follow package directions
Veal				
Rump or Shoulder Roast (boneless) Roast at 325°F.	2 to 3	25 to 30 minutes per lb	145°F	Let stand at least 3 minutes.
Rib Roast (bone-in) Roast at 325°F.	2 to 4	30 to 34 minutes per lb	145°F	Let stand at least 3 minutes.
Pork*				
Loin Roast, bone-in boneless Roast at 325°F.	3 to 5 2 to 4	20 to 25 minutes per lb 23 to 33 minutes per lb	145°F 145°F	Let stand at least 3 minutes.
Crown Roast Roast at 325°F.	6 to 10	20 minutes per lb	145°F	Let stand at least 3 minutes.
Shoulder Roast/Butt Roast at 325°F.	3 to 6	20 minutes per lb	145°F	Let stand at least 3 minutes.
Ribs (back, spareribs) Bake at 325°F.	——	Cover and cook 1 hour 15 minutes, uncover and cook 45 minutes longer	Tender	No standing time
Ribs (country-style) Bake at 350°F.	——	Cover and cook 2 hours, uncover and cook 30 minutes longer.	Tender	No standing time
Tenderloin Roast at 425°F to450°F.	½ to 1½	20 to 30 minutes	145°F	Let stand at least 3 minutes.
Ham, Fully Cooked (bone-in or boneless) Roast at 325°F.	3 to 4 (boneless) 7 to 8 (bone-in) 14 to 16 (bone-in)	18 to 25 minutes per lb	140°F	No standing time

*The USDA recommends pork be cooked to 145°F with a 3-minute resting period. If you prefer pork more well-done, cook to 160°F.

Continued on next page.

Continued from previous page.

CUT OF MEAT	WEIGHT IN POUNDS	APPROXIMATE TOTAL ROASTING TIME IN HOURS (UNLESS NOTED OTHERWISE)	REMOVE FROM OVEN WHEN INTERNAL TEMPERATURE REACHES	FINAL DONENESS TEMPERATURE (AFTER STANDING TIME)
Fresh Leg/Uncured Ham, Cook Before Eating (bone-in) Roast at 325°F.	——	15 to 18 minutes per lb	145°F	Let stand at least 3 minutes.
Lamb				
Leg (bone-in) Roast at 325°F.	5 to 7	20 to 25 minutes per lb 25 to 30 minutes per lb	140°F 155°F	145°F medium-rare 160°F medium
Leg (rolled, boneless) Roast at 325°F.	4 to 7	20 to 25 minutes per lb 30 to 35 minutes	140°F 155°F	145°F medium-rare 160°F medium
Shoulder Roast or Shank Leg Half(bone-in) Roast at 325°F.	3 to 4	20 to 25 minutes 25 to 30 minutes	140°F 155°F	145°F medium-rare 160°F medium

BRAISING MEAT

Braising (or pot roasting) is great for large, less tender cuts of meat, such as those coming from the chuck, shank, brisket or round. These cuts are generally less expensive than more tender cuts. The meat is browned first to add depth of flavor, then covered and cooked slowly with a small amount of liquid to make the meat very tender.

See Learn to Braise, page 330.

PANFRYING MEAT

Panfrying (also known as pan broiling) is a great method for cooking tender cuts of meat without liquid and is faster than oven broiling, if you're in a hurry. It's important not to overcook meat with this method, or it can become tough and dry.

Use a nonstick skillet, or lightly coat a regular skillet with vegetable oil. Heat the skillet over medium heat (unless otherwise noted) for 5 minutes. Season meat as desired. Add the meat to the skillet. Don't add water, liquids or fats; don't cover. Cook for the minimum time listed or until the thermometer reaches the final doneness temperature, turning once. If the meat browns too quickly, reduce heat to medium-low.

See Learn to Sear and Panfry, page 302.

BROILING MEAT

Broiling is a great method for cooking smaller cuts of meat directly under the high heat of your oven quickly and without fat. Broiling enhances the flavor of smaller cuts by caramelizing the surface of the meat, creating a flavorful "crust" and sealing in the juices.

Set the oven control to broil; heat 10 minutes. Check the oven's use-and-care manual for whether the oven door should be partially opened or closed during broiling. Place the meat on a rack in the broiler pan; season to taste with salt and pepper. For cuts less than 1 inch thick, broil 2 to 3 inches from the heat. For cuts 1 to 1½ inches thick, broil 3 to 4 inches from the heat unless chart (right) gives a different distance. **Broil for the minimum time listed, turning once and adding additional time as needed.**

Cooking Ham

The most popular ham is fully cooked and ready to eat. Packaged cooked hams should be cooked to at least 140°F. If you are not sure what kind of ham you have, or the cooked ham has been repackaged, it must be heated to an internal temperature of 165°F. Raw fresh ham should be cooked to at least 145°F and allowed to stand or rest at least 3 minutes.

TIMETABLE FOR BROILING MEAT

CUT OF MEAT	THICKNESS IN INCHES	DISTANCE FROM HEAT	APPROXIMATE COOKING TIME IN MINUTES	FINAL DONENESS TEMPERATURE
Beef				
Steak: Rib Eye, Porterhouse, T-Bone, Top Loin (Strip) Steak	¾ / 1 / 1½	2 to 3 / 3 to 4 / 3 to 4	9 tp 13 / 13 to 20 / 24 to 32	145°F medium-rare to 160°F medium
Top Blade Chuck Steak	¾ / 1	2 to 3 / 3 to 4	8 to 11 / 12 to 15	145°F medium-rare to 160°F medium
Tenderloin Steak	1 / 1½	2 to 3 / 3 to 4	13 to 16 / 18 to 22	145°F medium-rare to160°F medium
Top Sirloin Steak (boneless)	¾ / 1 / 1½ / 2	2 to 3 / 3 to 4 / 3 to 4 / 3 to 4	9 to 12 / 16 to 21 / 26 to 31 / 34 to 39	145°F medium-rare to 160°F medium
Ground Patties (4-inch diameter) 4 per lb / 4 per 1½ lb	½ / ¾	2 to 3 / 3 to 4	12 to 13 / 12 to 14	160°F medium / 160°F medium
Veal				
Chop, Loin or Rib	1	4	14 to 16	145°F medium-rare
Pork				
Chop (bone-in or boneless)	¾ to 1 / 1½	4 to 5 / 4 to 5	8 to 12 / 12 to 22	Let stand at least 3 minutes. 145°F medium / 145°F medium
Ground Patties	½		8 to 12	160°F medium
Lamb				
Chop	1 to 1¼	4 to 5	9 to 12 minutes per lb	Let stand for at least 3 minutes. 145°F rare to 160°F medium.

TIMETABLE FOR PANFRYING MEAT

CUT OF MEAT	THICKNESS IN INCHES	APPROXIMATE COOKING TIME IN MINUTES	FINAL DONENESS TEMPERATURE
Beef			
Rib-Eye Steak	¾ / 1	9 to 11 / 12 to 15	145°F medium-rare to 160°F medium
Porterhouse/T-Bone Steak	¾ / 1	10 to 13 / 14 to 17	145°F medium-rare to 160°F medium

Continued on next page.

Continued from previous page.

CUT OF MEAT	THICKNESS IN INCHES	APPROXIMATE COOKING TIME IN MINUTES	FINAL DONENESS TEMPERATURE
Strip Steak (Boneless)	¾ 1	8 to 11 12 to 15	145°F medium-rare to 160°F medium
Ranch Steak (shoulder center)	¾ 1	8 to 11 12 to 15	145°F medium-rare to 160°F medium
Flatiron Steak (shoulder top blade)	8 oz each	11 to 14	145°F medium-rare to 160°F medium
Tenderloin Steak (use medium-high heat for ½-inch thickness)	½ ¾ 1	3 to 5 7 to 10 10 to 13	145°F medium-rare to 160°F medium
Top Sirloin Steak (boneless)	¾ 1	12 to 15 15 to 18	145°F medium-rare to 160°F medium
Top Round Steak (best when marinated before cooking)	¾ 1	12 to 15 15 to 17	145°F medium-rare to 160°F medium
Cubed Steak (use medium-high heat)	——	3 to 5	145°F medium-rare to 160°F medium

Ground Patties (4-inch diameter)
   4 per lb
   4 per 1½ lb
	
	½
	¾
		
		10 to 12
		14 to 16
			
			160°F medium
			160°F medium

Veal			
Chop, Loin or Rib (use medium-high heat)	¾	10 to 14	145°F medium-rare (let stand 3 minutes)
Cutlet (use medium-high heat)	⅛ ¼	3 to 4 5 to 6	145°F medium-rare (let stand 3 minutes)
Ground Patties (use medium-high heat)	½	9 to 12	160°F medium
Pork*			
Chop, Loin or Rib (bone-in or boneless)	¾ to 1	8 to 16	145°F medium-rare (let stand 3 minutes)
Cutlets (bone-in or boneless)	⅛ ¼	3 to 4 5 to 6	145°F medium-rare (let stand 3 minutes)
Tenderloin Medallions	¼ to ½	4 to 8	145°F (let stand 3 minutes)
Ground Patties	½	8 to 11	160°F medium
Ham Slice, Cooked Ham Steak, Cooked	½ 1 to 1	6 to 8 8 to 10	140°F medium 140°F medium
Lamb			
Chop, Loin or Rib	1 to 1¼	9 to 11	145°F medium-rare (let stand 3 minutes)
Ground Patties	½	9 to 12	160°F medium

*The USDA recommends pork be cooked to 145°F with a 3-minute resting period. If you prefer pork more well done, cook to 160°F.

Chicken & Turkey

CALORIE SMART = See Helpful Nutrition and Cooking Information, page 643   FAST = Ready in 30 minutes or less
EASY = Prep in 10 minutes or less plus five ingredients or less   LIGHTER = 25% fewer calories or grams of fat
MAKE AHEAD = Make-ahead directions   SLOW COOKER = Slow cooker directions

< Skillet-Fried Chicken, page 326

CHICKEN AND TURKEY BASICS

From fast-fix skillet meals and classic stews to roasted whole birds, chicken and turkey are ideal for everyday cooking and special occasions. Poultry works with many techniques and flavors, including many global dishes. Here are some useful guidelines for buying and storing poultry.

BUYING CHICKEN AND TURKEY

- Look for tightly wrapped packages without tears or leaks, and with little or no liquid.

- Check for a fresh odor; if it does not smell right, don't buy it.

- Choose cold packages; those stacked above the meat case might not be cold enough.

- Do not purchase any packages if the sell-by or use-by date has already passed.

- Whole birds and cut-up pieces should be plump and meaty, with smooth, moist-looking skin and no traces of feathers.

- Boneless skinless products should look plump and moist.

- Chicken skin color can vary from yellow to white and does not indicate quality. Turkey skin should be cream colored.

- Cut ends of bones should be pink to red.

- Place packages in plastic bags so juices don't drip and contaminate other foods.

- Place all poultry in the refrigerator as soon as you get home. If you're shopping on a hot day or are more than 30 minutes from home, place poultry in an ice-packed cooler until you can refrigerate it.

STORING CHICKEN AND TURKEY

- Poultry wrapped in butcher paper should be repackaged in plastic wrap, foil or resealable freezer plastic bags.

- Store poultry in the meat compartment or coldest part of the refrigerator, or freeze as soon as possible.

- Cook or freeze poultry within 2 days of the sell-by date.

- If poultry was purchased frozen or was frozen at home and thawed, use within 2 days.

THAWING CHICKEN AND TURKEY

- Thaw poultry completely before cooking.

- Thaw in the refrigerator, not at room temperature.

- Remove giblets as soon as possible during thawing, then wrap and refrigerate.

- Fully thawed poultry will have no ice crystals and will be soft, with flexible joints.

Herb-Roasted Chicken and Vegetables (page 322)

Herb-Garlic Butter Spatchcocked Chicken

CALORIE SMART

Similar to butterflying, spatchcocking refers to cutting poultry down the backbone and spreading it open like a book. Only poultry can be spatchcocked, but any boneless meat can be butterflied.

PREP 20 min **TOTAL** 1 hr 25 min • 4 servings

1	whole chicken (3½ to 4½ lb)
⅓	cup butter, softened
3	tablespoons chopped fresh or 1 tablespoon dried herb leaves (basil, chives, oregano, tarragon or thyme or combination)
5	teaspoons fresh lemon juice
½	teaspoon salt
2	cloves garlic, finely chopped

1 Heat oven to 375°F. Line 15x10x1-inch pan with foil.

2 Pat chicken dry with paper towels. Place chicken, breast side down, on cutting board. Using heavy-duty kitchen scissors or poultry shears, cut closely along one side of backbone from thigh end to neck. Repeat on other side. Remove backbone; save for making Chicken and Broth (page 143) or discard. Turn chicken over; flatten breast area by pressing firmly with heel of hand. Place chicken, breast side up, in pan. Tuck wings under breast.

3 In small bowl, beat remaining ingredients with electric mixer on medium speed until light and fluffy. Starting at leg end of chicken, gently

Herb-Garlic Butter Spatchcocked Chicken

separate skin (do not peel back) from chicken breast using fingers, being careful not to tear or puncture skin. Rub half of butter mixture under skin to cover entire breast area; gently replace skin. Rub remaining butter mixture on outside of chicken.

4 Roast uncovered 30 minutes. Brush chicken with pan juices. Roast 30 to 35 minutes longer or until thermometer inserted in thickest part of breast reads at least 165°F. Serve chicken with pan juices, if desired.

1 Serving: Calories 400; Total Fat 26g (Saturated Fat 13g, Trans Fat 1g); Cholesterol 165mg; Sodium 550mg; Total Carbohydrate 0g (Dietary Fiber 0g, Sugars 0g); Protein 40g **Exchanges:** 5½ Lean Meat, 2 Fat **Carbohydrate Choices:** 0

MAKE-AHEAD Directions The herb-garlic butter can be made 1 day ahead of time and refrigerated; soften at room temperature before preparing the chicken.

Spatchcocking a Chicken

With chicken breast-side down, using heavy-duty kitchen or poultry shears, cut chicken closely along one side of backbone from thigh end to neck.

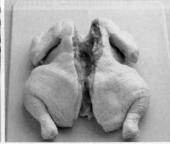

Cut along other side of backbone; remove bone.

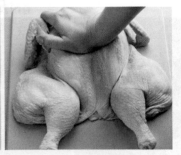

Turn chicken over. Flatten breast area by pressing firmly with heel of hand.

Cutting Up a Whole Chicken

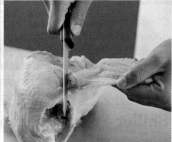

Cut off each leg by cutting skin between thigh and body; continue cutting through meat between tail and hip joint, cutting as closely as possible to backbone. Bend leg back until hip joint pops out as shown.

Separate thigh and drumstick by cutting about ⅛ inch from the fat line toward the drumstick as shown. (A thin white fat line runs crosswise at joint between drumstick and thigh.)

Remove each wing from body by cutting into wing joint with sharp knife, rolling knife to let the blade follow through at the curve of joint as shown.

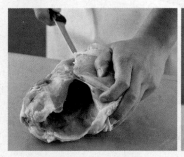

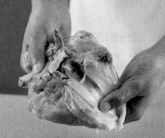

Separate back from breast by holding body, neck end down, and cutting downward along each side of backbone.

Bend breast halves back to pop out the keel bone. Remove keel bone as shown in Boning Chicken Breasts below.

Boning Chicken Breasts

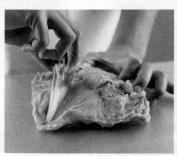

Loosen keel bone and white cartilage by running tip of index finger around both sides. Pull out bone in one or two pieces.

Insert tip of knife under long rib bone. Resting knife against bones, use steady, even pressure to gradually trim meat away from bones. Cut rib cage away from breast, cutting through shoulder joint to remove entire rib cage. Repeat on other side.

Slip knife under white tendons on either side of breast; loosen and pull out tendons (grasp end of tendons with paper towel if tendons are slippery). Remove skin if desired. Cut breast lengthwise in half.

Chicken and Dumplings

Chicken Cacciatore

Chicken and Dumplings

CALORIE SMART

PREP 20 min **TOTAL** 1 hr 10 min • 6 servings

BROTH

½ cup all-purpose flour

5 cups chicken broth (for homemade broth, see page 143)

1 cup frozen sweet peas

2 medium carrots, thinly sliced (1 cup)

1 large onion, chopped (1 cup)

¼ cup chopped fresh parsley or 1 tablespoon parsley flakes

⅛ teaspoon pepper

3 cups cubed cooked chicken

DUMPLINGS

1½ cups all-purpose flour

1 tablespoon chopped fresh parsley or dried parsley flakes

2 teaspoons baking powder

¼ teaspoon salt

3 tablespoons cold butter or shortening

¾ cup milk

1 In 4-quart Dutch oven, place ½ cup flour. Gradually whisk in 1 cup of the broth until smooth. Gradually stir in remaining broth. Add vegetables and pepper; heat to boiling. Reduce heat to low. Stir in chicken. Cook uncovered about 20 minutes or until carrots are tender.

2 In medium bowl, mix 1½ cups flour, parsley, baking powder and salt. Cut in butter, using pastry blender or fork, until mixture looks like fine crumbs. Stir in milk. Divide dough into six portions, about ⅓ cup each. Drop dough by heaping tablespoonsful onto hot chicken mixture. Cook uncovered over low heat 10 minutes. Cover; cook 10 minutes longer or until dumplings are completely cooked in center.

1 Serving: Calories 400; Total Fat 14g (Saturated Fat 6g, Trans Fat 0g); Cholesterol 110mg; Sodium 1190mg; Total Carbohydrate 42g

(Dietary Fiber 3g, Sugars 5g); Protein 26g **Exchanges:** 2 Starch, ½ Other Carbohydrate, ½ Vegetable, 2½ Lean Meat, 1 Fat **Carbohydrate Choices:** 3

Chicken Cacciatore **CALORIE SMART**

PREP 35 min **TOTAL** 1 hr 15 min • 6 servings

1 cut-up whole chicken (3 to 3½ lb)

½ cup all-purpose flour

¼ cup vegetable oil

2 medium onions

1 medium green bell pepper

1 can (14.5 oz) diced tomatoes, undrained

1 can (8 oz) tomato sauce

1 cup sliced fresh mushrooms (3 oz)

1½ teaspoons chopped fresh or ½ teaspoon dried oregano leaves

1 teaspoon chopped fresh or ¼ teaspoon dried basil leaves

½ teaspoon salt

2 cloves garlic, finely chopped

Hot cooked pasta (page 167), if desired

Grated Parmesan cheese, if desired

1 Coat chicken with flour. In 12-inch skillet, heat oil over medium-high heat. Cook chicken in oil 15 to 20 minutes or until brown on all sides; drain.

2 Cut onions and bell pepper in half; remove seeds. Cut each half crosswise into quarters.. Add onions, bell pepper and remaining ingredients except cheese to skillet with chicken; stir.

3 Heat to boiling; reduce heat. Cover and simmer 30 to 40 minutes or until juice of chicken is clear when thickest piece is cut to bone (at least 165°F). Serve over pasta with cheese.

1 Serving: Calories 400; Total Fat 23g (Saturated Fat 5g, Trans Fat 0g); Cholesterol 85mg; Sodium 630mg; Total Carbohydrate 19g (Dietary Fiber 3g, Sugars 6g); Protein 30g **Exchanges:** 3 Vegetable, 3 Medium-Fat Meat, 2 Fat **Carbohydrate Choices:** 1

SLOW-COOKER **Directions** Remove skin from chicken. Reduce flour to ⅓ cup and oil to 2 tablespoons; omit tomato sauce. Substitute 1 jar (4.5 oz) sliced mushrooms, drained, for the fresh mushrooms. Brown chicken as directed. Spray 3½- to 6-quart slow cooker with cooking spray. In slow cooker, place half of chicken. Mix raw onions, bell pepper and remaining ingredients except cheese; spoon half of mixture over chicken. Repeat with remaining chicken and vegetable mixture. Cover; cook on Low heat setting 4 to 6 hours. Serve with cheese.

Coq au Vin CALORIE SMART

A classic French dish of chicken simmered in red wine with mushrooms, onions, bacon or salt pork and various herbs.

PREP 45 min **TOTAL** 1 hr 20 min • 6 servings

- ½ cup all-purpose flour
- 1 teaspoon salt
- ¼ teaspoon pepper
- 1 cut-up whole chicken (3 to 3½ lb)
- 8 slices bacon
- ¾ cup frozen small whole onions
- 1 package (8 oz) sliced fresh mushrooms (about 3 cups)
- 1 cup chicken broth (for homemade broth, see page 143)
- 1 cup dry red wine or nonalcoholic red wine
- 4 medium carrots, cut into 2-inch pieces
- 1 clove garlic, finely chopped
- ½ teaspoon salt
  Bouquet garni*

1 In shallow dish, mix flour, 1 teaspoon salt and the pepper. Coat chicken with flour mixture; set aside.

2 In 12-inch skillet, cook bacon over medium heat 8 to 10 minutes, turning once, until crisp. Remove bacon with slotted spoon and drain on paper towels; set aside. Cook chicken in bacon drippings over medium heat about 15 minutes, turning occasionally, until brown on all sides.

3 Move chicken to one side of skillet; add onions and mushrooms to other side. Cook uncovered over medium-high heat about 6 minutes, stirring occasionally, until mushrooms are tender. Drain drippings from skillet.

4 Crumble bacon. Add bacon, broth, wine, carrots, garlic, ½ teaspoon salt and the bouquet garni to skillet; stir. Heat to boiling; reduce heat. Cover and simmer about 35 minutes or until juice of chicken is clear when thickest piece is cut to bone (at least 165°F). Remove bouquet garni; skim off excess fat.

*Tie ½ teaspoon dried thyme leaves, 2 large sprigs fresh parsley and 1 dried bay leaf in cheesecloth bag or place in tea ball.

1 Serving: Calories 350; Total Fat 19g (Saturated Fat 6g, Trans Fat 0g); Cholesterol 95mg; Sodium 1020mg; Total Carbohydrate 12g (Dietary Fiber 1g, Sugars 2g); Protein 33g **Exchanges:** 1 Starch, 2 Vegetable, 4 Lean Meat, ½ Fat **Carbohydrate Choices:** 1

Browning Chicken

Use medium-high heat to brown chicken. For the best browning, the skillet should be hot when you add the chicken. Let the chicken cook on one side without turning. When it is properly browned, it should release from the pan without sticking so the other side can be browned.

Coq au Vin

Learn to BRAISE

Braising cuts of meat or poultry involves first browning them in a small amount of oil, then cooking in a little liquid—either on the stovetop or in the oven. The long, slow cook time helps develop rich flavor while tenderizing the meat, making it a good choice for tougher, more economical cuts. Fish and vegetables can also be braised.

Most braising uses broth or water, but other liquids can be used to add flavor and color. Braising with wine or beer mellows the alcohol, but the flavor lingers with the meat. Try apple cider when braising pork, for a slightly sweet, subtle flavor.

For the best flavor, cook braised dishes the day before you want to serve them, and refrigerate the food overnight so the flavors can develop more fully. Spoon off any congealed fat from the top; reheat slowly and serve.

Braising Tips

- Use a pot or skillet with a tight cover. If you are braising in the oven, the pot should be ovenproof.

- Season the meat or poultry on all sides. Brown or sear (see page 302) the meat in a small amount of oil. Remove the meat from the pan and place on a plate.

- Add liquid to the pan to deglaze (¾ to 1 cup). Cook and stir, scraping any browned bits from the bottom of the pan.

- Return the meat or poultry to the pan with any accumulated liquid. There should be just enough liquid to come one-fourth to two-thirds of the way up the sides of the meat.

- Often other ingredients will be added, such as potatoes, carrots or other vegetables. For the best results, add these ingredients as directed in the recipe to prevent overcooking.

- Cover and simmer on the stovetop or in the oven until everything is tender.

Is Braising the Same as Stewing?

These are similar techniques, using different sizes of meat and amounts of liquid. Braising typically involves larger cuts of meat and less liquid. Stewing typically uses smaller pieces of meat with enough liquid to submerge it.

Chicken Tagine   CALORIE SMART

Tagines are Moroccan dishes of meat or poultry braised with vegetables, olives, spices and garlic. They are typically served over couscous.

PREP 30 min **TOTAL** 1 hr • 6 servings

1	tablespoon olive or vegetable oil
1	cut-up whole chicken (3 to 3½ lb)
1	medium onion, sliced
2	cloves garlic, finely chopped
¼	cup chopped fresh cilantro
1	teaspoon ground cumin
1	teaspoon ground turmeric
1	teaspoon ground ginger
1	teaspoon salt
1	cinnamon stick (2 inch)
1	cup chicken broth (for homemade broth, see page 143)
1	can (14.5 oz) diced tomatoes, undrained
1	cup pitted dried plums, cut into bite-size pieces
½	cup pitted green olives
1	small lemon, cut into quarters
	Hot cooked couscous or rice (page 215), if desired

1 In 4-quart Dutch oven, heat oil over medium-high heat. Add chicken, skin side down, onion and garlic. Cook uncovered 6 to 10 minutes, turning chicken occasionally, until chicken is brown on all sides.

2 Reduce heat to medium. Sprinkle cilantro, cumin, turmeric, ginger and salt over chicken. Add cinnamon stick; pour broth and tomatoes over chicken. Turn chicken several times to coat evenly. Add dried plums, olives and lemon, pressing into liquid around chicken. Reduce heat to low. Cover and simmer 30 minutes or until juice of chicken is clear when thickest piece is cut to bone (at least 165°F).

3 Place chicken on deep serving platter; cover to keep warm. Increase heat to high; boil sauce uncovered about 5 minutes, stirring occasionally, until thickened. Pour sauce over chicken. Garnish with additional chopped fresh cilantro, if desired. Serve over couscous.

1 Serving: Calories 370; Total Fat 18g (Saturated Fat 4.5g, Trans Fat 0g); Cholesterol 85mg; Sodium 920mg; Total Carbohydrate 23g (Dietary Fiber 4g, Sugars 13g); Protein 29g **Exchanges:** ½ Fruit, 2 Vegetable, 3½ Medium-Fat Meat, ½ Fat **Carbohydrate Choices:** 1½

Chicken Adobo

Spicy Chicken in Peanut Sauce

Chicken Adobo CALORIE SMART

PREP 30 min **TOTAL** 4 hr 50 min • 4 servings

MARINADE
- ½ cup cider vinegar
- ½ cup soy sauce
- ¼ cup packed brown sugar
- 1 teaspoon black peppercorns
- ⅛ teaspoon crushed red pepper flakes
- 4 cloves garlic, crushed
- 3 bay leaves

CHICKEN
- 4 chicken thighs
- 4 chicken drumsticks
  Hot cooked rice, if desired
  Diagonally sliced green onions, if desired

1 In shallow glass or plastic dish or resealable food-storage plastic bag, mix all marinade ingredients. Add chicken. Cover dish or seal bag; refrigerate at least 4 hours but no longer than 24 hours, turning occasionally.

2 Heat 12-inch nonstick skillet over medium-high heat. Remove chicken from marinade; reserve marinade. Place chicken, skin side down, in skillet. Cook 6 to 8 minutes, turning once, until deep golden brown. Pour marinade over chicken; heat to boiling. Cover and simmer 20 minutes, turning once, until juice of chicken is clear when thickest part is cut to bone (at least 165°F). Remove chicken to plate; cover to keep warm.

3 Heat marinade to boiling; reduce heat to medium. Cook 5 to 7 minutes or until reduced by half or to desired consistency. Pour into fat separator, or skim fat from marinade. Serve chicken and marinade with rice; sprinkle with onions.

1 Serving: Calories 280; Total Fat 8g (Saturated Fat 2g, Trans Fat 0g); Cholesterol 155mg; Sodium 1880mg; Total Carbohydrate 17g (Dietary Fiber 0g, Sugars 14g); Protein 36g **Exchanges:** 1 Other Carbohydrate, 5 Very Lean Meat, 1 Fat **Carbohydrate Choices:** 1

Spicy Chicken in Peanut Sauce SLOW COOKER

Pass small bowls of dry-roasted peanuts and chopped fresh cilantro to sprinkle over the chicken, and serve with wedges of warm pita bread.

PREP 15 min **TOTAL** 7 hr 15 min • 4 servings

- 1 tablespoon olive or vegetable oil
- 8 large bone-in chicken thighs (about 3 lb), skin removed
- 1 large onion, chopped (1 cup)
- 2 cans (14.5 oz each) diced tomatoes with green chiles, undrained
- 1 can (14.5 oz) crushed fire-roasted or regular diced tomatoes, undrained
- 2 tablespoons honey
- 1½ teaspoons ground cumin
- 1 teaspoon ground cinnamon
- ⅓ cup creamy peanut butter
- 2 cups hot cooked couscous or jasmine or basmati rice (page 215)

1 In 12-inch nonstick skillet, heat oil over medium-high heat. Cook chicken in oil about 4 minutes, turning once, until brown.

2 Spray 4- to 5-quart slow cooker with cooking spray. In slow cooker, mix onion, diced and crushed tomatoes, honey, cumin and cinnamon. Add chicken; spoon tomato mixture over chicken. Cover; cook on Low heat setting 7 to 8 hours.

3 Stir peanut butter into mixture in slow cooker until melted and well blended. Serve chicken and sauce over couscous.

1 Serving: Calories 740; Total Fat 33g (Saturated Fat 8g, Trans Fat 0.5g); Cholesterol 140mg; Sodium 1180mg; Total Carbohydrate 52g (Dietary Fiber 8g, Sugars 24g); Protein 60g **Exchanges:** 1 Starch, 1½ Other Carbohydrate, 3 Vegetable, 7½ Lean Meat, 2 Fat **Carbohydrate Choices:** 3½

Chicken Marsala

Chicken Piccata

Chicken Marsala CALORIE SMART

PREP 25 min **TOTAL** 35 min • 4 servings

- 4 boneless skinless chicken breasts (about 1¼ lb)
- ½ cup all-purpose flour
- ¼ teaspoon salt
- ¼ teaspoon pepper
- 2 tablespoons olive or vegetable oil
- 2 cloves garlic, finely chopped
- 1 cup sliced fresh mushrooms (3 oz)
- ¼ cup chopped fresh parsley or 1 tablespoon parsley flakes
- ½ cup Marsala wine or chicken broth
  Hot cooked pasta (page 167), if desired

1 Flatten chicken as directed below. In shallow dish, mix flour, salt and pepper. Coat chicken with flour mixture.

2 In 10-inch skillet, heat oil over medium-high heat. Cook garlic, mushrooms and parsley in oil 5 minutes, stirring frequently. Add chicken to skillet. Cook about 8 minutes, turning once, until brown.

3 Stir in wine. Cook 8 to 10 minutes longer or until chicken is no longer pink in center. Serve with pasta.

1 Serving: Calories 280; Total Fat 8g (Saturated Fat 2g, Trans Fat 0g); Cholesterol 85mg; Sodium 230mg; Total Carbohydrate 17g (Dietary Fiber 0g, Sugars 2g); Protein 34g **Exchanges:** 1 Starch, 4 Very Lean Meat, 1 Fat **Carbohydrate Choices:** 1

Flattening Chicken Breasts

Place chicken breast between pieces of plastic wrap or waxed paper. Using flat side of meat mallet or rolling pin, gently pound chicken breasts until ¼ inch thick.

Chicken Piccata CALORIE SMART • FAST

PREP 25 min **TOTAL** 25 min • 6 servings

- 6 boneless skinless chicken breasts (about 1½ lb)
- 1 egg, slightly beaten
- 1 tablespoon water
- ½ cup dry bread crumbs (any flavor)
- ½ teaspoon salt
- ¼ teaspoon pepper
- ⅛ teaspoon garlic powder
- ¼ cup all-purpose flour
- 2 tablespoons butter
- 2 tablespoons vegetable oil
- 2 tablespoons lemon juice
- 2 tablespoons dry white wine or chicken broth
  Chopped fresh parsley, if desired
  Lemon wedges, if desired

1 Between pieces of plastic wrap or waxed paper, place each chicken breast; gently pound with flat side of meat mallet or rolling pin until about ¼ inch thick. In small bowl, mix egg and water. In shallow dish, mix bread crumbs, salt, pepper and garlic powder. Coat chicken with flour. Dip into egg mixture; coat with bread crumb mixture.

2 In 12-inch skillet, heat butter and oil over medium heat. Add chicken; cook 8 to 10 minutes, turning once, until chicken is no longer pink in center. Remove chicken from skillet; cover to keep warm.

3 Stir lemon juice and wine into drippings in skillet; heat to boiling. Pour over chicken. Sprinkle with parsley; serve with lemon wedges.

1 Serving: Calories 290; Total Fat 14g (Saturated Fat 4.5g, Trans Fat 0g); Cholesterol 115mg; Sodium 370mg; Total Carbohydrate 11g (Dietary Fiber 0g, Sugars 0g); Protein 28g **Exchanges:** ½ Starch, 4 Very Lean Meat, 2½ Fat **Carbohydrate Choices:** 1

MEDITERRANEAN

Simple ingredients used in uncomplicated ways bring out the flavors of Mediterranean cooking.

Anchovies Tiny salt-cured fish fillets canned in oil. Used in tiny amounts to intensify and add depth of flavor to sauces, pasta and other dishes. **Anchovy Paste,** available in tubes near the other condiments, is a convenient substitution and keeps longer than anchovies in the refrigerator.

Capers Small flower buds from a bush native to the Mediterranean. Sun-dried and pickled or salt-cured, they add a pungent bite as garnishes or additions to sauces. **Caperberries** are the larger fruit from the same plant, with a similar but less intense flavor.

Chorizo Spicy paprika gives Spanish chorizo its signature ruddy red color and smoky flavor. It adds flavor to stews and other dishes when fried, or can be sliced and served as tapas.

Greek Cheese Cheese is the main protein source in the Greek diet—it's eaten all day long. **Kefalotiri,** one of the most popular hard cheeses, has a sharp, salty flavor, somewhat similar to Gruyère or Pecorino Romano. **Manouri** is a typically unsalted soft white cheese similar to cream cheese.

Honeycomb Greeks make and use a lot of honey in both sweet and savory dishes. Honey varies greatly in flavor, depending on where it's made. Both the comb and the honey in it are edible.

Marcona Almonds Spanish almonds long loved for being more tender, sweet and delicate than California almonds. Traditionally used in tapas and turrón—a Spanish nougat candy.

Phyllo (Filo) Similar to strudel dough, tissue-thin sheets of pastry used in Greek savory and sweet dishes—most commonly, baklava and spanakopita. Look for it near other frozen dough.

Seasonings Dukka Egyptian spice blend sprinkled over meats or vegetables or made into a dip. Typically it contains hazelnuts or chickpeas ground together with toasted nuts, sesame seed, coriander and cumin. **Saffron** Handpicked and dried stigmas from the purple crocus; available in threads or powdered. It adds color, aroma and flavor to many Mediterranean dishes. Very expensive—a little goes a long way. **Urfa Biber** Sun-dried Turkish chiles with chocolate and wine flavors, typically ground with a bit of salt. Adds heat, saltiness and acidity to dishes.

Panfried Chicken with Romesco Sauce CALORIE SMART

PREP 25 min **TOTAL** 45 min • 6 servings

ROMESCO SAUCE

- ½ cup slivered almonds
- 1 slice firm crusty white bread (about 5x5x½ inch)
- 1 medium tomato, cut in half, seeded
- 2 cloves garlic, peeled
- 1 jar (12 oz) roasted red bell peppers, rinsed, drained and patted dry
- ¼ cup olive oil
- 1 tablespoon sherry vinegar
- ½ teaspoon salt
- ¼ teaspoon smoked paprika

CHICKEN

- 2 tablespoons olive oil
- 6 boneless skinless chicken breasts (about 1¾ lb)
- 1 teaspoon garlic salt
  Chopped fresh parsley, if desired

1 Heat oven to 400°F. In 15x10x1-inch pan, place almonds, bread, tomato and garlic in single layer. Bake 5 to 6 minutes or until almonds and bread are lightly toasted. Break bread into bite-size pieces.

2 In food processor, place toasted almonds, bread, tomato and garlic. Cover and process, using quick on-and-off motions, until coarsely chopped. Add remaining sauce ingredients. Cover and process, using quick on-and-off motions, until almost smooth. Transfer sauce to small bowl; set aside. Sauce will thicken as it stands.

3 In 12-inch nonstick skillet, heat 2 tablespoons oil over medium heat. Sprinkle both sides of chicken with garlic salt; add to skillet. Cook 15 to 20 minutes, turning once, until juice of chicken is clear when center of thickest piece is cut (at least 165°F). Serve chicken with sauce; sprinkle with parsley.

1 Serving: Calories 400; Total Fat 23g (Saturated Fat 4g, Trans Fat 0g); Cholesterol 105mg; Sodium 630mg; Total Carbohydrate 8g (Dietary Fiber 1g, Sugars 3g); Protein 39g **Exchanges:** ½ Other Carbohydrate, 5½ Very Lean Meat, 4 Fat **Carbohydrate Choices:** ½

MAKE-AHEAD Directions The Romesco Sauce can be made up to 1 day ahead; cover and refrigerate. Let stand at room temperature 30 minutes before serving.

Basil

Rosemary

Thyme

Oregano

Orange

Kefalotiri

Olive Oil

Parmigiano
Reggiano

Garlic

Sundried
Tomatoes

Manouri

Kasseri

Roasted Red
Bell Peppers

Mixed Mediterranean Olives

Tomato
Paste

Honeycomb

Marcona
Almonds

Dukka

Prosciutto

Chorizo

Greek
Yogurt

Anchovies

Capers   Caperberries

Caraway
Seeds

Feta

Feta with Herbs

Saffron

Smoked
Paprika

Paprika

Anise Seed

Lemon

Phyllo (Filo)

Coffee Chicken with Quick Mole Sauce   CALORIE SMART

PREP 45 min **TOTAL** 2 hr 45 min • 6 servings

CHICKEN AND MARINADE

- 4 cups water
- ⅓ cup salt
- ⅓ cup packed dark brown sugar
- 1 tablespoon cumin seed
- 1 tablespoon chili powder
- 1 lime, thinly sliced
- 1 cup strong brewed coffee
- 6 boneless skinless chicken breasts (about 1¾ lb)
- 2 tablespoons vegetable oil

MOLE SAUCE

- 1 medium onion, thinly sliced
- 2 cloves garlic, finely chopped
- 1 can (28 oz) crushed tomatoes, undrained
- 1¼ cups chicken broth (for homemade broth, see page 143)
- 1 tablespoon creamy peanut butter
- 1 teaspoon granulated sugar
- ½ teaspoon ground cumin
  Dash ground cinnamon
- 1 oz unsweetened baking chocolate
- 2 chipotle chiles in adobo sauce (from 7-oz can), chopped
  *Corn tortillas, if desired.

1 In 2-quart saucepan, heat water, salt, brown sugar, cumin seed, chili powder and lime slices over medium heat, stirring occasionally, until salt and brown sugar are dissolved. Remove from heat; stir in coffee. Cool to room temperature.

2 Place chicken in 1-gallon resealable food-storage plastic bag or large bowl; pour cooled coffee mixture over chicken. Seal bag or cover bowl; refrigerate 2 to 3 hours to marinate, turning chicken occasionally.

3 Remove chicken from marinade; discard marinade. Pat chicken dry with paper towels. In 12-inch skillet, heat oil over medium heat. Cook chicken in oil 5 to 6 minutes, turning once, until golden brown. Remove from skillet; set aside.

4 Add onion to skillet; cook over medium heat 5 minutes, stirring occasionally, until soft and lightly browned. Add garlic; cook 30 seconds. Add remaining sauce ingredients, except corn tortillas. Cook uncovered 3 minutes, stirring

Coffee Chicken with Quick Mole Sauce

occasionally, until mixture simmers and peanut butter and chocolate are melted.

5 Reduce heat to medium-low; arrange chicken in sauce. Cook uncovered 15 to 20 minutes, stirring occasionally, until sauce thickens and juice of chicken is clear when center of thickest piece is cut (at least 165°F). Serve with corn tortillas.

*Warm corn tortillas as directed on package, if desired.

1 Serving: Calories 320; Total Fat 14g (Saturated Fat 4g, Trans Fat 0g); Cholesterol 80mg; Sodium 2130mg; Total Carbohydrate 15g (Dietary Fiber 3g, Sugars 8g); Protein 33g **Exchanges:** ½ Starch, ½ Other Carbohydrate, 4½ Lean Meat **Carbohydrate Choices:** 1

Tuscan Rosemary Chicken and White Beans   CALORIE SMART • FAST

PREP 15 min **TOTAL** 30 min • 4 servings

- ⅓ cup Italian dressing
- 4 boneless skinless chicken breasts (about 1¼ lb)
- ¼ cup water
- 2 medium carrots, sliced (1 cup)
- 2 medium stalks celery, sliced (1 cup)
- ¼ cup coarsely chopped drained sun-dried tomatoes in oil
- 1 teaspoon dried rosemary leaves, crushed
- 1 can (19 oz) cannellini beans, drained, rinsed

1 In 12-inch skillet, heat dressing over medium-high heat. Add chicken; cook 4 to 6 minutes, turning once, until lightly browned.

2 Reduce heat to medium-low. Add water, carrots, celery, tomatoes and rosemary. Cover and simmer about 10 minutes or until carrots are crisp-tender and juice of chicken is clear when center of thickest piece is cut (at least 165°F).

3 Stir in beans. Cover and cook 5 minutes or until beans are thoroughly heated.

1 Serving: Calories 390; Total Fat 9g (Saturated Fat 2g, Trans Fat 0g); Cholesterol 85mg; Sodium 340mg; Total Carbohydrate 33g (Dietary Fiber 8g, Sugars 5g); Protein 42g **Exchanges:** 1½ Starch, ½ Other Carbohydrate, 5½ Very Lean Meat, 1 Fat **Carbohydrate Choices:** 2

Thai-Style Coconut Chicken

Thai-Style Coconut Chicken

CALORIE SMART

PREP 35 min **TOTAL** 35 min • 4 servings

- 1 tablespoon vegetable oil
- 1 lb boneless skinless chicken breasts, cut into bite-size pieces
- 1 teaspoon grated lime peel
- 1 teaspoon grated gingerroot
- 1 clove garlic, finely chopped
- 2 serrano chiles or 1 jalapeño chile, seeded, finely chopped
- ¼ cup finely chopped fresh cilantro
- 1 can (14 oz) coconut milk (not cream of coconut)
- 1 teaspoon packed brown sugar
- ½ teaspoon salt
- 1 tablespoon soy sauce
- 1 cup fresh sugar snap peas
- 1 medium green bell pepper, cut into 1-inch pieces
- 1 medium tomato, seeded, chopped (¾ cup)
- 1 tablespoon chopped fresh basil leaves
  Hot cooked jasmine rice (page 215), if desired

1 In nonstick wok or 12-inch skillet, heat oil over medium-high heat. Add chicken; cook 2 to 3 minutes, stirring constantly, until chicken is no longer pink in center. Add lime peel, gingerroot, garlic, chiles and cilantro; cook and stir 1 minute.

2 Pour coconut milk over chicken. Stir in brown sugar, salt, soy sauce, peas and bell pepper. Reduce heat to medium. Simmer uncovered 3 to 5 minutes, stirring occasionally, until vegetables are crisp-tender. Stir in tomato.

3 Spoon into shallow serving bowls; top with basil. Serve with rice.

1 Serving: Calories 430; Total Fat 26g (Saturated Fat 17g, Trans Fat 0g); Cholesterol 85mg; Sodium 650mg; Total Carbohydrate 14g (Dietary Fiber 4g, Sugars 8g); Protein 35g **Exchanges:** ½ Starch, 1 Vegetable, 5 Lean Meat, 2 Fat **Carbohydrate Choices:** 1

Chicken Korma CALORIE SMART

PREP 20 min **TOTAL** 1 hr 30 min • 4 servings

- 1 lb boneless skinless chicken breasts, cut crosswise into ½-inch strips
- ¼ cup whipping cream
- 2 tablespoons finely chopped gingerroot
- 5 cloves garlic, finely chopped
- 1 tablespoon finely chopped fresh cilantro
- 1 teaspoon coriander seed, ground
- ½ teaspoon cumin seed, ground
- ½ teaspoon salt
- ¼ teaspoon ground red pepper (cayenne)
- 2 tablespoons Clarified Butter (page 469) or butter
- ½ cup tomato sauce
- ¼ cup finely chopped fresh or 2 tablespoons crumbled dried fenugreek leaves (méthi)*

1 In medium bowl, mix all ingredients except clarified butter, tomato sauce and fenugreek. Cover and refrigerate at least 1 hour but no longer than 24 hours.

2 In 10-inch skillet, heat clarified butter over medium heat. Add chicken mixture and tomato sauce. Cook about 5 minutes, stirring frequently, until chicken is partially cooked.

3 Stir in fenugreek; reduce heat. Cover and simmer about 10 minutes or until chicken is no longer pink in center. Serve with rice, if desired.

*Watercress leaves or fresh parsley can be substituted for the fenugreek, but the flavor will be milder.

1 Serving: Calories 270; Total Fat 15g (Saturated Fat 8g, Trans Fat 0g); Cholesterol 100mg; Sodium 570mg; Total Carbohydrate 7g (Dietary Fiber 2g, Sugars 2g); Protein 28g **Exchanges:** ½ Starch, 3½ Lean Meat, 1 Fat **Carbohydrate Choices:** ½

Chicken Korma

Caramel Chicken with Pickled Cucumber and Onion

PREP 25 min **TOTAL** 50 min • 4 servings

PICKLED CUCUMBER AND ONION

- ¼ cup cider vinegar
- 1 teaspoon granulated sugar
- ¼ teaspoon crushed red pepper flakes
- ¼ teaspoon salt
- ⅛ teaspoon pepper
- 1 medium cucumber
- 1 small red onion, cut in half, sliced (½ cup)

CHICKEN AND SAUCE

- ½ cup packed brown sugar
- ⅔ cup chicken broth (for homemade broth, see page 143)
- 3 tablespoons rice vinegar
- 2 tablespoons soy sauce
- 1 tablespoon vegetable oil
- 8 boneless skinless chicken thighs, cut into 1-inch pieces
- 1 teaspoon finely chopped gingerroot
- 2 cloves garlic, finely chopped
  Hot cooked rice (page 215), if desired
  Black sesame seed or toasted sesame seed, if desired

1 In medium glass or plastic bowl, mix cider vinegar, granulated sugar, pepper flakes, salt and pepper until sugar is dissolved. Cut cucumber in half lengthwise; remove seeds with spoon. Cut each half crosswise into ¼-inch slices. Add cucumber and onion to bowl; toss to coat. Set aside; stir occasionally.

2 In small bowl, mix brown sugar, broth, rice vinegar and soy sauce until sugar is almost dissolved; set aside. In 12-inch nonstick skillet, heat oil over medium-high heat. Add chicken, gingerroot and garlic; cook about 5 minutes, stirring occasionally, until chicken is lightly browned.

3 Add broth mixture to skillet. Heat to boiling; reduce heat to medium-low. Cook uncovered 20 to 25 minutes or until chicken is golden brown and sauce is thickened and reduced by half.

4 Serve chicken and sauce over rice. Top with pickled cucumber and onion; sprinkle with sesame seed.

Caramel Chicken with Pickled Cucumber and Onion

1 Serving: Calories 430; Total Fat 14g (Saturated Fat 3.5g, Trans Fat 0g); Cholesterol 120mg; Sodium 860mg; Total Carbohydrate 33g (Dietary Fiber 1g, Sugars 30g); Protein 42g **Exchanges:** 2 Other Carbohydrate, 6 Very Lean Meat, 2 Fat **Carbohydrate Choices:** 2

Skillet Chicken Nachos   FAST

PREP 20 min **TOTAL** 20 min • 6 servings

- 1 tablespoon olive or vegetable oil
- 1¼ lb boneless skinless chicken breasts, cut into ¼-inch pieces
- 1 package (1 oz) taco seasoning mix
- 1 can (8 oz) tomato sauce
- 1 medium red bell pepper, chopped (1 cup)
- 1 can (15 oz) black beans, drained, rinsed
- 1 can (7 oz) whole kernel sweet corn, drained
- 2 cups shredded Mexican cheese blend (8 oz)
- 6 oz tortilla chips (about 42 chips)
- ¼ cup chopped fresh cilantro

1 In 12-inch nonstick skillet, heat oil over medium-high heat. Cook chicken in oil 3 to 5 minutes, stirring occasionally, until no longer pink in center.

2 Stir in taco seasoning mix, tomato sauce, bell pepper, beans, corn and 1 cup of the cheese. Reduce heat to medium; cook 3 to 5 minutes, stirring occasionally, until thoroughly heated and cheese is melted.

3 Divide tortilla chips among 6 plates. Spoon chicken mixture evenly over chips. Sprinkle with remaining 1 cup cheese and the cilantro.

1 Serving: Calories 520; Total Fat 24g (Saturated Fat 9g, Trans Fat 0g); Cholesterol 95mg; Sodium 1320mg; Total Carbohydrate 38g (Dietary Fiber 5g, Sugars 4g); Protein 36g **Exchanges:** 2 Starch, ½ Other Carbohydrate, ½ Vegetable, 4 Very Lean Meat, 4 Fat **Carbohydrate Choices:** 2½

Skillet Beef Nachos Substitute 1¼ lb ground beef for the chicken. In Step 1, cook beef 5 to 7 minutes or until thoroughly cooked. Drain and continue as directed.

Chicken Salad
Sandwiches FAST · EASY

PREP 10 min **TOTAL** 10 min • 4 sandwiches

1½ cups chopped cooked chicken or turkey
1 medium stalk celery, chopped (½ cup)
1 small onion, finely chopped (⅓ cup)
½ cup mayonnaise or salad dressing
¼ teaspoon salt
¼ teaspoon pepper
8 slices bread

In medium bowl, mix chicken, celery, onion, mayonnaise, salt and pepper. Spread mixture on 4 of the bread slices. Top with remaining bread.

1 Sandwich: Calories 430; Total Fat 27g (Saturated Fat 4.5g, Trans Fat 0g); Cholesterol 60mg; Sodium 630mg; Total Carbohydrate 27g (Dietary Fiber 1g, Sugars 2g); Protein 19g **Exchanges:** 2 Starch, 2 Lean Meat, 4 Fat **Carbohydrate Choices:** 2

LIGHTER **Directions** For 260 calories and 6 grams of fat per serving, use fat-free mayonnaise.

Egg Salad Sandwiches Substitute 6 Hard-Cooked Eggs (page 91), chopped, for the chicken.

Ham Salad Sandwiches Substitute 1½ cups chopped cooked ham for the chicken. Omit salt and pepper. Stir in 1 teaspoon yellow mustard.

Tuna Salad Sandwiches Substitute 2 cans (5 oz each) tuna in water, drained, for the chicken. Stir in 1 teaspoon lemon juice.

Asian Chicken Roll-Ups

CALORIE SMART · FAST

PREP 15 min **TOTAL** 15 min • 4 roll-ups

2 tablespoons creamy peanut butter
2 tablespoons teriyaki baste and glaze (from 12-oz bottle) or stir-fry sauce
1 tablespoon packed brown sugar
1 tablespoon hot water
1 teaspoon sesame or vegetable oil
4 flour tortillas (8 to 10 inch)
½ lb thinly sliced roasted chicken or turkey breast (from deli)
1½ cups shredded iceberg lettuce
1½ cups shredded carrots
½ cup chopped fresh cilantro

1 In small bowl, beat peanut butter, teriyaki glaze, brown sugar, water and oil with whisk until blended.

2 Spread about 2 tablespoons peanut butter mixture over each tortilla. Top each with one-fourth of the chicken, about ⅓ cup lettuce, about ⅓ cup carrots and 2 tablespoons cilantro. Roll up tortillas.

1 Roll-Up: Calories 290; Total Fat 10g (Saturated Fat 2g, Trans Fat 0.5g); Cholesterol 25mg; Sodium 540mg; Total Carbohydrate 35g (Dietary Fiber 3g, Sugars 7g); Protein 16g **Exchanges:** 2 Starch, 1 Vegetable, 1 Lean Meat, 1 Fat **Carbohydrate Choices:** 2

Sage Chicken and Potatoes

CALORIE SMART

PREP 10 min **TOTAL** 1 hr 10 min • 4 servings

4 boneless skinless chicken breasts (about 1¼ lb)
3 medium unpeeled russet potatoes, cut into ¾-inch pieces (3 cups)
1½ cups ready-to-eat baby-cut carrots
1½ cups Pan Gravy (page 346) or 1 jar (12 oz) home-style gravy
2 tablespoons Worcestershire sauce
1 teaspoon dried sage leaves
½ teaspoon garlic-pepper blend

1 Heat oven to 400°F. Spray 13x9-inch (3-quart) glass baking dish with cooking spray.

2 In baking dish, arrange chicken, potatoes and carrots. In small bowl, mix remaining ingredients; pour over chicken and vegetables.

3 Spray sheet of foil with cooking spray; place sprayed side down over baking dish. Bake 50 to 60 minutes or until vegetables are tender and juice of chicken is clear when center of thickest piece is cut (at least 165°F).

1 Serving: Calories 320; Total Fat 9g (Saturated Fat 2.5g, Trans Fat 0g); Cholesterol 75mg; Sodium 680mg; Total Carbohydrate 30g (Dietary Fiber 4g, Sugars 5g); Protein 31g **Exchanges:** 2 Starch, 3½ Very Lean Meat, 1 Fat **Carbohydrate Choices:** 2

Sage Chicken and Potatoes

Crunchy Cornmeal Chicken with Mango-Peach Salsa

Dijon Chicken Smothered in Mushrooms

Crunchy Cornmeal Chicken with Mango-Peach Salsa FAST

PREP 30 min **TOTAL** 30 min • 4 servings

CHICKEN

- ½ cup yellow cornmeal
- ½ teaspoon salt
- ¼ teaspoon pepper
- 4 boneless skinless chicken breasts (about 1¼ lb)
- 2 tablespoons vegetable oil
  Hot cooked rice (page 215), if desired

MANGO-PEACH SALSA

- 3 medium peaches, peeled, chopped (1½ cups)*
- 1 ripe large mango, peeled, seeded and chopped (1½ cups)**
- 1 large tomato, seeded, chopped (1 cup)
- ¼ cup chopped fresh cilantro
- 3 tablespoons vegetable oil
- 2 tablespoons white vinegar
- ¼ teaspoon salt

1 In shallow dish, mix cornmeal, ½ teaspoon salt and the pepper. Coat chicken with cornmeal mixture.

2 In 10-inch skillet, heat 2 tablespoons oil over medium-high heat. Cook chicken in oil 15 to 20 minutes, turning once, until juice of chicken is clear when center of thickest piece is cut (at least 165°F).

3 Meanwhile, in large bowl, mix all salsa ingredients. Serve chicken with salsa over rice.

*About 1½ cups chopped frozen (thawed) sliced peaches can be substituted for the fresh peaches.

**Refrigerated mango slices (from a jar), well drained and chopped, can be substituted for the fresh mango.

1 Serving: Calories 450; Total Fat 22g (Saturated Fat 4g, Trans Fat 0g); Cholesterol 85mg; Sodium 520mg; Total Carbohydrate 30g (Dietary Fiber 5g, Sugars 12g); Protein 34g **Exchanges:** 2 Fruit, 5 Lean Meat, 1 Fat **Carbohydrate Choices:** 2

Dijon Chicken Smothered in Mushrooms CALORIE SMART • FAST

PREP 25 min **TOTAL** 25 min • 4 servings

- 4 boneless skinless chicken breasts (about 1¼ lb)
- ¼ cup all-purpose flour
- ½ teaspoon salt
- ¼ teaspoon pepper
- 2 tablespoons olive or vegetable oil
- ½ cup chicken broth (for homemade broth, see page 143)
- 1 jar (4.5 oz) sliced mushrooms, drained
- 4½ teaspoons Dijon mustard
  Fresh thyme sprigs, if desired

1 Between pieces of plastic wrap or waxed paper, place each chicken breast; gently pound with flat side of meat mallet or rolling pin until about ¼ inch thick. In shallow dish, mix flour, salt and pepper. Coat chicken with flour mixture.

2 In 12-inch nonstick skillet, heat oil over medium-high heat. Cook chicken in oil 6 to 8 minutes, turning once, until no longer pink in center. Remove chicken from skillet to serving plate; cover to keep warm.

3 Stir broth into skillet. Heat to boiling over medium-high heat. Stir in mushrooms and mustard. Cook 2 to 3 minutes, stirring frequently, until slightly thickened. Spoon sauce over chicken. Garnish with thyme.

1 Serving: Calories 240; Total Fat 11g (Saturated Fat 2g, Trans Fat 0g); Cholesterol 70mg; Sodium 750mg; Total Carbohydrate 8g (Dietary Fiber 1g, Sugars 0g); Protein 27g **Exchanges:** ½ Starch, 3½ Lean Meat **Carbohydrate Choices:** ½

Dijon Pork Smothered in Mushrooms

Substitute pork tenderloin for the chicken. Cut into 1-inch slices, and flatten as directed in Step 1. Continue as directed, cooking until pork is no longer pink in center.

Country French Chicken and Rice

Oven Chicken Cordon Bleu

CALORIE SMART

PREP 20 min TOTAL 50 min • 4 servings

- 4 boneless skinless chicken breasts (about 1¼ lb)
- 2 teaspoons Dijon mustard
- 4 teaspoons chopped fresh chives
- 4 very thin slices (about ¾ oz each) lean cooked ham
- 4 very thin slices (about ¾ oz each) reduced-fat Swiss cheese
- 1 egg white
- 1 tablespoon water
- ⅓ cup finely crushed cornflakes or bran flakes cereal
- ¼ teaspoon paprika

1 Heat oven to 375°F. Spray 8-inch square (2-quart) glass baking dish with cooking spray. Between pieces of plastic wrap or waxed paper, place each chicken breast; gently pound with flat side of meat mallet or rolling pin until about ¼ inch thick.

2 Spread each chicken breast with ½ teaspoon mustard; sprinkle with 1 teaspoon chives. Cut ham and cheese slices to fit chicken. Place ham and cheese on chicken; roll up, tucking ends inside.

3 In shallow dish, slightly beat egg white and water. Place cereal crumbs in another shallow dish. Coat chicken rolls with egg white mixture; roll in crumbs. Place in baking dish; sprinkle with paprika.

4 Bake uncovered 25 to 30 minutes or until chicken is no longer pink in center.

1 Serving: Calories 150; Total Fat 4g (Saturated Fat 1.5g, Trans Fat 0g); Cholesterol 60mg; Sodium 440mg; Total Carbohydrate 2g (Dietary Fiber 0g, Sugars 1g); Protein 25g **Exchanges:** 3 Lean Meat **Carbohydrate Choices:** 0

Country French Chicken and Rice   CALORIE SMART

PREP 25 min TOTAL 3 hr 25 min • 8 servings

- ¼ cup chopped sun-dried tomatoes in oil, drained
- 2 tablespoons herbes de Provence*
- 2 tablespoons olive oil
- 2 tablespoons lemon juice
- 1 tablespoon finely chopped garlic
- 1 teaspoon salt
- 8 bone-in chicken thighs (about 2 lb), skin and fat removed
- 1½ cups sliced fresh mushrooms (4 oz)
- 1 cup uncooked regular long-grain white rice
- 1 medium carrot, shredded (½ cup)
- 2 cups boiling water
- 1 tablespoon chopped fresh parsley
- 2 teaspoons grated lemon peel

1 In 1-gallon resealable food-storage plastic bag, mix tomatoes, herbes de Provence, oil, lemon juice, garlic and ½ teaspoon of the salt. Add chicken and mushrooms; seal bag. Turn to coat chicken and mushrooms in marinade. Refrigerate at least 2 hours but no longer than 24 hours.

2 Heat oven to 375°F. Spray 13x9-inch (3-quart) glass baking dish with cooking spray. In baking dish, stir together rice, carrot and remaining ½ teaspoon salt; stir in boiling water. Pour chicken, mushrooms and marinade evenly over rice mixture.

3 Cover with foil. Bake 50 to 60 minutes or until liquid is absorbed and juice of chicken is clear when thickest piece is cut to bone (at least 165°F). Sprinkle with parsley and lemon peel.

*Any combination of dried basil, fennel seed, lavender, marjoram, rosemary, sage, summer savory, tarragon or thyme can be substituted for the herbes de Provence.

1 Serving: Calories 260; Total Fat 10g (Saturated Fat 2.5g, Trans Fat 0g); Cholesterol 45mg; Sodium 360mg; Total Carbohydrate 23g (Dietary Fiber 1g, Sugars 1g); Protein 18g **Exchanges:** 1½ Starch, 2 Lean Meat, ½ Fat **Carbohydrate Choices:** 1½

Oven Chicken Cordon Bleu

Pan Gravy CALORIE SMART • FAST • EASY

PREP 10 min **TOTAL** 10 min • 1 cup gravy

 Drippings from roast turkey or other
 cooked meat
2 tablespoons all-purpose flour
1 cup liquid (turkey or meat juices,
 broth, water)
 Few drops browning sauce, if desired
 Salt and pepper to taste

1 After removing turkey from roasting pan, pour drippings (turkey juices and fat) into fat separator or glass measuring cup, leaving browned bits in pan. The fat will rise to the top. With spoon, return 2 tablespoons of the fat to the pan. Pour or spoon off and discard any remaining fat; reserve remaining drippings.

2 Stir flour into fat in roasting pan. Cook over low heat, stirring constantly and scraping up browned bits, until mixture is smooth and bubbly; remove from heat.

3 Gradually stir in reserved drippings plus enough broth or water to equal 1 cup. Heat to boiling, stirring constantly. Boil and stir 1 minute. Stir in browning sauce if a darker color is desired. Stir in salt and pepper.

1 Tablespoon: Calories 20; Total Fat 1.5g (Saturated Fat 0.5g, Trans Fat 0g); Cholesterol 0mg; Sodium 65mg; Total Carbohydrate 0g (Dietary Fiber 0g, Sugars 0g); Protein 0g **Exchanges:** Free **Carbohydrate Choices:** 0

Pan Cream Gravy Substitute half-and-half or whole milk for the liquid.

Thin Gravy Reduce fat from meat drippings and flour to 1 tablespoon each.

Bread Stuffing

PREP 15 min **TOTAL** 55 min • 10 servings

¾ cup butter
2 large stalks celery (with leaves), chopped
 (1½ cups)
1 large onion, chopped (1 cup)
9 cups soft bread cubes (about 15 slices bread)
1½ teaspoons chopped fresh or ½ teaspoon dried
 thyme leaves
1½ teaspoons chopped fresh or ½ teaspoon dried
 sage leaves or ¼ teaspoon ground sage
1 teaspoon salt
¼ teaspoon pepper

1 Heat oven to 350°F. Spray 13x9-inch (3-quart) glass baking dish with cooking spray.

2 In 4-quart Dutch oven or saucepan, melt butter over medium-high heat. Cook celery and onion in butter 4 to 6 minutes, stirring occasionally, until tender. Add remaining ingredients; stir gently to mix well. Spoon into baking dish.

Making Bread Stuffing

Cook celery and onion in butter until tender.

Spoon stuffing into baking dish. Bake until center is hot and edges are beginning to brown.

Making Pan Gravy

Pour turkey drippings into fat separator or glass measuring cup, leaving browned particles in pan.

Stir flour into fat in cooking pan, stirring constantly and scraping up browned bits.

Gradually stir in reserved drippings plus enough broth to equal 1 cup.

3 Cover with foil; bake 25 minutes. Remove foil; bake 10 to 15 minutes longer or until center is hot and edges are beginning to brown.

1 Serving (½ Cup): Calories 230; Total Fat 15g (Saturated Fat 7g, Trans Fat 1g); Cholesterol 35mg; Sodium 530mg; Total Carbohydrate 19g (Dietary Fiber 1g, Sugars 2g); Protein 3g **Exchanges:** 1 Starch, 3 Fat **Carbohydrate Choices:** 1

Cornbread Stuffing Substitute cornbread cubes for the soft bread cubes. For Cornbread-Sausage Stuffing, omit salt; add ½ lb cooked crumbled bulk pork or chorizo sausage (see Sausage Stuffing below) and 1 cup chopped toasted pecans with the remaining stuffing ingredients.

Oyster Stuffing Add 2 cans (8 oz each) whole oysters, drained and chopped, with the remaining stuffing ingredients.

Sausage Stuffing Omit salt. In 10-inch skillet, cook 1 lb bulk pork sausage or fresh chorizo sausage over medium heat, stirring occasionally, until no longer pink; drain, reserving drippings. Substitute drippings for part of the butter. Add cooked sausage with the remaining stuffing ingredients.

Wild Rice Stuffing In ungreased 2-quart casserole, mix 3 cups cooked wild rice, ¼ cup melted butter, 1 cup orange juice, 1 medium apple, peeled and cut into chunks, 1 cup dry bread crumbs and ½ cup each raisins and walnuts. Cover and bake at 325°F for 55 to 60 minutes or until apple is tender.

Apple-Maple Brined Turkey Breast

PREP 30 min **TOTAL** 14 hr 30 min • 8 servings

BRINE AND TURKEY

- ½ gallon (64 oz) apple cider
- 1 cup real maple syrup or maple-flavored syrup
- ½ cup coarse kosher salt
- ¼ cup chopped fresh or 1 tablespoon rubbed sage leaves
- 1 tablespoon dried marjoram leaves
- 5 cloves garlic, finely chopped
- 1 bone-in whole turkey breast (5 to 6 lb), thawed if frozen

BASTING SAUCE AND GRAVY

- ¼ cup butter, cut into pieces
- 1½ teaspoons chopped fresh or ½ teaspoon rubbed sage leaves

- ½ teaspoon salt
- ¼ teaspoon dried marjoram leaves
- ¼ teaspoon coarsely ground black pepper
- ¼ cup all-purpose flour

1 Reserve 1 cup apple cider for basting; cover and refrigerate. In 6-quart nonreactive bowl (glass or stainless steel) or stockpot (stainless steel), stir remaining cider, the syrup, kosher salt, ¼ cup fresh sage, 1 tablespoon marjoram and the garlic until salt is dissolved. Add turkey breast. Cover and refrigerate 12 hours. Do not brine turkey for more than 12 hours or it will become too salty.

2 Heat oven to 325°F. Remove turkey from brine; discard brine. Thoroughly rinse turkey under cool running water, gently rubbing outside and inside of turkey to release salt. Pat skin and cavity dry with paper towels.

3 Place turkey, skin side up, on rack in large shallow roasting pan. Insert ovenproof meat thermometer so tip is in thickest part of breast and does not touch bone. Roast uncovered 1 hour.

4 In 1-quart saucepan, heat reserved cider, the butter, 1½ teaspoons fresh sage, ½ teaspoon salt, ¼ teaspoon marjoram and the pepper over medium heat until butter is melted and mixture is hot. Roast turkey about 1 hour longer or until thermometer reads at least 165°F, basting generously with cider mixture and pan juices every 15 minutes.

5 Remove turkey from oven. Cover loosely with foil; let stand 15 to 20 minutes. Meanwhile, pour pan drippings and browned bits into measuring cup; let stand 5 minutes. Skim 4 tablespoons fat from top of drippings and pour into 2-quart saucepan; skim and discard any remaining fat. Add enough water to remaining drippings to measure 2 cups; set aside.

6 Stir flour into fat in saucepan with whisk. Cook and stir over medium heat until mixture is smooth and bubbly; remove from heat. Gradually stir in reserved 2 cups drippings. Heat to boiling, stirring constantly. Boil and stir about 1 minute or until gravy thickens. Serve with turkey.

1 Serving: Calories 470; Total Fat 21g (Saturated Fat 8g, Trans Fat 0.5g); Cholesterol 165mg; Sodium 2080mg; Total Carbohydrate 17g (Dietary Fiber 0g, Sugars 12g); Protein 55g **Exchanges:** 1 Other Carbohydrate, 7½ Lean Meat **Carbohydrate Choices:** 1

Roast Goose with Apple Stuffing

PREP 30 min **TOTAL** 4 hr 20 min • 8 servings

  1 whole goose (8 to 10 lb), thawed if frozen
  ¼ cup butter
  2 medium stalks celery (with leaves), chopped (1 cup)
  1 medium onion, chopped (½ cup)
  6 cups soft bread crumbs (about 9 slices bread)
  3 medium unpeeled tart apples, chopped (3 cups)
  1½ teaspoons chopped fresh sage leaves or ½ teaspoon rubbed sage or ground sage
  ¾ teaspoon chopped fresh or ¼ teaspoon dried thyme leaves
  ½ teaspoon salt
  ¼ teaspoon pepper
     Pan Gravy (page 346)*, if desired

1 Heat oven to 350°F. Discard giblets and neck or reserve for another use. Remove excess fat from goose.

2 Place goose, breast side up, on rack in shallow roasting pan. Fasten neck skin to back of goose with skewer. Fold wings across back of goose so tips are touching. Pierce skin all over with fork so fat can drain. Insert ovenproof meat thermometer so tip is in thickest part of inside thigh and does not touch bone. (Do not add water or cover goose.)

3 Roast goose uncovered 3 hours to 3 hours 30 minutes, removing excess fat from pan occasionally. If necessary, place tent of foil loosely over goose during last hour to prevent excessive browning. Meanwhile, spray 2-quart casserole with cooking spray. In 3-quart saucepan, melt butter over medium-high heat. Cook celery and onion in butter, stirring occasionally, until tender; remove from heat. Stir in remaining ingredients except gravy. Spoon into casserole. Cover with foil and refrigerate until baking time.

4 Bake stuffing covered alongside goose for last 35 to 45 minutes of roasting time, removing foil from stuffing during last 10 minutes of baking, until center is hot and edges are beginning to brown. Goose is done when thermometer reads at least 165°F and legs move easily when lifted or twisted. Reserve drippings if making gravy. Let stand 15 to 20 minutes for easiest carving.

*Pan Gravy recipe makes 1 cup. Increase, if needed, for desired amount.

1 Serving: Calories 820; Total Fat 54g (Saturated Fat 18g, Trans Fat 1.5g); Cholesterol 210mg; Sodium 630mg; Total Carbohydrate 26g (Dietary Fiber 2g, Sugars 7g); Protein 57g **Exchanges:** 1 Starch, ½ Fruit, 8 Medium-Fat Meat, 2 Fat **Carbohydrate Choices:**2

Roast Goose with Apple Stuffing

TIMETABLE FOR ROASTING POULTRY

Roasting times are general guidelines. Also check turkey labels for timing recommendations.

Begin checking turkey doneness about 1 hour before end of recommended roasting time. For purchased stuffed turkeys, follow package directions instead of this timetable.

TYPE OF POULTRY	WEIGHT IN POUNDS	OVEN TEMPERATURE	ROASTING TIME IN HOURS
Chicken			
Whole Chicken (Not Stuffed)*	3 to 3½	375°F	1¾ to 2
Turkey			
Whole Turkey (Not Stuffed)*	8 to 12	325°F	2¾ to 3
	12 to 14	325°F	3 to 3¾
	14 to 18	325°F	3¾ to 4¼
	18 to 20	325°F	4¼ to 4½
	20 to 24	325°F	4½ to 5
Whole Turkey Breast (Bone-In)	4 to 6	325°F	1½ to 2¼
	6 to 8	325°F	2¼ to 3¼
Game			
Whole Duck			
(domestic)		375°F	20 minutes per lb
(wild)		350°F	18 to 20 minutes per lb
Whole Goose	7 to 9	325°F	2¼ to 3¾
	9 to 11	325°F	3¾ to 4½
	11 to 13	325°F	4½ to 5½
Whole Pheasant	2 to 3	350°F	1 to 1½
Whole Rock Cornish Hen	1½ to 2	350°F	1¼ to 1½

*For optimal food safety and even doneness, the USDA recommends cooking stuffing separately. However, if you choose to stuff poultry or game birds, it's necessary to use an accurate food thermometer to make sure the center of the stuffing reaches a safe minimum temperature of 165°F. Cooking home-stuffed poultry or game birds is riskier than cooking those that are not stuffed. Even if the poultry or game bird itself has reached the safe minimum internal temperature of 165°F, the stuffing may not have reached same temperature. Bacteria can survive in stuffing that has not reached 165°F, possibly resulting in food-borne illness. Do not stuff poultry or game birds that will be grilled, smoked, fried or microwaved, because the stuffing will never get hot enough in the center to be safe.

TIMETABLE FOR BROILING POULTRY

Cook poultry right from the refrigerator. Set oven control to broil. Check the owner's manual for whether the oven door should be partially opened or closed during broiling. Place poultry on rack in broiler pan. Broil for the time listed, turning once, until thermometer reaches at least 165°F or until juice is clear when centers of thickest pieces are cut.

CUT OF POULTRY	WEIGHT IN POUNDS	BROILING TIME
Chicken		
Cut-Up	3 to 3½	Skin side down 30 minutes; turn. Broil 15 to 25 minutes longer (7 to 9 inches from heat)
Bone-In Split Breasts	2½ to 3	25 to 35 minutes (7 to 9 inches from heat)
Boneless Skinless Breasts	1¼	15 to 20 minutes (4 to 6 inches from heat)
Wings	2 to 2½	10 minutes (5 to 7 inches from heat)
Turkey		
Tenderloins	1 to 1½	8 to 12 minutes (4 to 6 inches from heat)
Breast Slices	1 to 1½	7 minutes (4 to 6 inches from heat)

CALORIE SMART = See Helpful Nutrition and Cooking Information, page 643   FAST = Ready in 30 minutes or less
EASY = Prep in 10 minutes or less **plus** five ingredients or less   LIGHTER = 25% fewer calories or grams of fat
MAKE AHEAD = Make-ahead directions   SLOW COOKER = Slow cooker directions

FISH BASICS

Fish is delicious, healthful and available in a multitude of varieties, both fresh and freshly frozen. As you find out just how easy it is to select great fish and terrific ways to prepare it, you'll want to have fish more often. Here's what you need to know about buying, storing and cooking fish.

BUYING FISH

- Flesh should be shiny, firm and spring back when touched. Avoid fish with dark edges or brown or yellowish discoloration.

- Contents of the package should smell fresh and mild, not fishy or like ammonia.

- Buy and use the fish by the sell-by date.

- For whole fish, eyes should be bright, clear and just slightly bulging. Only a few fish, like walleye, have naturally cloudy eyes.

- Gills should be bright pink to red and scales should be bright and shiny.

- Frozen fish should be tightly wrapped and not have any freezer burn (dry or dark spots).

STORING FISH

- Keep fresh or thawed fish in the original packaging in the coldest part of your refrigerator. Use within 2 days.

- Fish that is packaged in clear plastic wrap on a tray can be frozen as it is. Other fish should be tightly wrapped in freezer bags or foil. Freeze for up to 6 months. Thaw overnight in the refrigerator.

CHOOSING FISH BY FLAVOR AND TEXTURE

Fish can be categorized by flavor and texture, making it easy to substitute one fish for another within a category.

MILD FLAVOR	MODERATE FLAVOR	FULL FLAVOR
Delicate to Medium Texture		
Alaskan Pollock	Atlantic Salmon	Herring/Sardines
Barramundi	Branzino	Smelt
Flounder	Chinook Salmon	
Sole	Walleye	
	Whitefish	
Medium-Firm Texture		
Butterfish/Sablefish	Catfish	Bluefish
Cod	Char	Mackerel
Haddock	Coho Salmon	Salmon (Alaskan, Sockeye)
Lingcod	Drum	Shad
Snapper/Red Snapper	Hake/Whiting	Wahoo/Ono
Tilapia	Lake Perch	
Tilefish	Mahi Mahi	
	Pompano	
	Porgy/Scup	
	Rainbow Trout	
	Redfish	
	Rockfish/Ocean Perch	
	Sea Bass	
Firm Texture		
Grouper	Shark	Cobia
Halibut	Tuna (Albacore, Skipjack, Yellowfin/Ahi)	Marlin
Monkfish		Swordfish
Pompano		Tuna (Bluefin, Bonito)
Striped Bass		
Sturgeon		

Red Snapper   Tuna   Tilapia   Salmon

THE BEST COOKING METHODS FOR FISH

Instead of shopping for a specific fish, scan the seafood counter for what's freshest and on sale. You can decide what to buy based on the cooking method you wish to use or the type of fish that appeals to you most that day. Look to this chart to match the fish to the best cooking methods and you're on your way to cooking fish successfully!

COOKING METHODS	FISH TYPE
Panfrying	Flounder, Halibut, Salmon or Sole (with skin on) or medium-firm fish such as char, perch or snapper
Oven-Frying	Medium-firm, mild flavored skinless fish such as cod or haddock
Broiling	Fillets or steaks of any texture fish such as shark or swordfish (thin or delicate-textured fish should not be turned or it can fall apart)
Grilling	Fillets with skins or steaks of medium-firm texture, steaks or whole firm-textured fish such as mahi mahi, red fish or ono
Baking	Delicate or medium-firm fillets or steaks, such as tilapia, rockfish or red snapper. (If fish has skin, it can be removed either before or after cooking.)
Steaming (packets made with parchment or foil*)	Skinless fillets or steaks of any texture fish such as flounder, grouper or tuna
Roasting	Whole fish or large fillets or steaks such as snapper, trout, sea bass
Deep-Frying	Mild-flavored delicate or medium-firm textured skinless fillets such as cod, halibut or catfish or whole fish such as sea ball, a small grouper or red snapper

*See Learn to Make Foil Packets, page 278.

COOKING FISH

Fish is naturally delicate and tender so over-cooking makes it dry. Use the "10-minute rule" for moist, flaky fish—here's how to do it.

- Measure the fish at its thickest point. If it will be stuffed or rolled, measure it before stuffing or rolling.

- Fish fillets will often have skin on one side. Cook the fish skin side down. The skin helps to hold the fish together and is easy to remove after cooking.

- Cook the fish 10 minutes per inch of thickness. Turn over halfway through cooking time only if specified. Fillets less than ½ inch thick generally need no turning. Cook frozen fish (not thawed) 20 minutes per inch. Add 5 minutes to the total cooking time if the fish is cooked in foil or in a sauce.

- Cook just until the fish flakes easily with a fork. Insert the tines of a fork gently into the thickest part of the fish and twist slightly. The flesh should begin to separate along the natural lines.

- Baking, broiling or grilling fish with the skin on helps to hold the delicate flesh together. To remove skin after cooking, carefully insert a metal spatula between the skin and the flesh, starting at the tail end if present (if no tail end, start at any edge). Hold on to a small piece of the skin and slide the fish off.

FISH POUNDS PER SERVING

The number of servings per pound varies depending on the form of fish.

TYPE OF FISH	POUNDS PER SERVING
Fillets or Steaks	⅓ to ½
Pan-Dressed (often scaled with internal organs, head, tail and fins removed)	½
Drawn (whole with head and tail; only internal organs removed)	½ to ¾
Whole (right from the water)	¾ to 1

Seafood Sustainability

Many chefs, restaurateurs and consumers ask for sustainable seafood. It's sustainable when the population of a fish species is managed to provide for today's needs without damaging the ability of the species to reproduce. If you buy fish managed under a U.S. fishery management plan, it considers social and economic outcomes for fishing communities; prevents overfishing; rebuilds depleted stocks; minimizes bycatch and interactions with protected species; and identifies and conserves essential fish habitat.

For more information, go to www.fishwatch.gov.

Panfried Fish CALORIE SMART • FAST

PREP 20 min **TOTAL** 20 min • 6 servings

- 1½ lb perch, red snapper or other medium-firm fish fillets (½ to ¾ inch thick), skin removed
- ¾ teaspoon salt
- ¼ teaspoon pepper
- 1 egg
- 1 tablespoon water
- ⅔ cup all-purpose flour, cornmeal or dry bread crumbs
  Vegetable oil or shortening

1 Cut fish into 6 serving pieces. Sprinkle both sides with salt and pepper. In small bowl, beat egg and water with fork or whisk until blended. Place flour in shallow dish. Dip fish into egg, then coat with flour.

2 In 12-inch skillet, heat about ⅛ inch oil over medium heat. Fry fish in oil 6 to 8 minutes, turning once, until fish flakes easily with fork and is brown on both sides. (Fish cooks very quickly, especially the thinner tail sections; be careful not to overcook.) Remove with slotted spatula; drain on paper towels.

1 Serving: Calories 200; Total Fat 7g (Saturated Fat 1.5g, Trans Fat 0g); Cholesterol 95mg; Sodium 230mg; Total Carbohydrate 11g (Dietary Fiber 0g, Sugars 0g); Protein 24g **Exchanges:** 1 Starch, 3 Very Lean Meat, ½ Fat **Carbohydrate Choices:** 1

Browned-Butter Panfried Fish Omit oil. In skillet, heat ¼ cup butter over medium heat 3 to 4 minutes, stirring constantly, until light brown. Coat fish as directed in Step 1; cook in butter as directed in Step 2.

Garlic-Butter Panfried Fish Omit salt. Substitute crushed garlic butter–flavored croutons for the flour. (Place croutons in resealable food-storage plastic bag and crush with rolling pin.) Continue as directed.

Parmesan, Herb and Lemon Panfried Fish
Omit salt and pepper. Substitute ⅓ cup Italian-style panko bread crumbs for the ⅔ cup flour. In shallow dish, mix bread crumbs, ⅓ cup grated Parmesan cheese and 1 teaspoon grated lemon peel. Continue as directed.

Oven-Fried Fish CALORIE SMART • FAST

PREP 10 min **TOTAL** 25 min • 4 servings

- 1 lb cod, haddock or other medium-firm fish fillets (about ¾ inch thick), skin removed
- ¼ cup cornmeal
- ¼ cup unseasoned dry bread crumbs
- ¾ teaspoon chopped fresh or ¼ teaspoon dried dill weed
- ½ teaspoon paprika
- ¼ teaspoon salt
- ⅛ teaspoon pepper
- ¼ cup milk
- 3 tablespoons butter, melted

1 Move oven rack to position slightly above middle of oven. Heat oven to 450°F.

2 Cut fish into 4 serving pieces. In shallow dish, mix cornmeal, bread crumbs, dill, paprika, salt and pepper. Pour milk into another shallow dish. Dip fish into milk, then coat with cornmeal mixture.

3 Place fish in ungreased 13x9-inch pan. Drizzle butter over fish. Bake uncovered about 12 minutes or until fish flakes easily with fork.

1 Serving: Calories 240; Total Fat 11g (Saturated Fat 5g, Trans Fat 0.5g); Cholesterol 85mg; Sodium 360mg; Total Carbohydrate 12g (Dietary Fiber 0g, Sugars 1g); Protein 24g **Exchanges:** 1 Starch, 3 Lean Meat **Carbohydrate Choices:** 1

Panfrying Fish

Dip fish in egg.

Coat both sides with flour.

Fry fish in oil, turning once.

Fish is done when brown on both sides and flakes easily with a fork.

Learn to BROIL

Broiling is a high-heat method where food is cooked a short distance from a direct heat source above—usually a flame in a gas oven or hot coil in an electric oven. The broiler will be located in the oven or sometimes in a compartment under the oven. Some think of broiling as a cousin to grilling because the surfaces of food are well-browned, creating a wonderful caramelized taste. Advantages of broiling include quickly cooked foods with great flavor, plus minimal cleanup.

To check the distance between the food and the pan, place the broiler pan in a cold oven. Then measure the distance from where the food will be to the broiler element. Use the distance recommended in the recipe or refer to the oven manufacturer's recommendations. Always watch food carefully while broiling to prevent burning.

Broiling Tips

- Turn the broiler on 5 to 10 minutes ahead of time so that it can heat up.

- For easy cleanup, line the broiler pan with foil and poke holes to let the juices drain. The bottom pan can also be lined with foil.

- Place the food in the center of the pan and place the pan under the broiler at the distance indicated in the recipe (see above).

- On most ovens, you can leave the oven door open slightly to allow air to circulate. This also helps to keep steam from forming—too much steam and the food will not crisp. Check the oven manufacturer's guidelines to be sure this is recommended.

- Remove the pan from the oven to turn the food as indicated in the recipe directions.

- Follow recipe times carefully. If food is not quite cooked, you can place it under the broiler for a bit longer.

Best Foods for Broiling

- **Beef and Pork:** Meats less than 1½ inches thick, such as steaks and chops, are good candidates for broiling. Use tender cuts or marinate for tenderness. Ground meat patties and sausages are also great.

- **Chicken and Turkey:** Most pieces work well under the broiler. Items such as chicken quarters, legs and bone-in or boneless breasts are ideal, as are turkey cutlets and tenderloins. Try to broil the same thickness or size of pieces for even cooking.

- **Fish and Shellfish:** Fillets and steaks are ideal to cook under the broiler. They cook quickly and evenly. Shrimp and scallops also perform well under the broiler.

- **Vegetables:** Many vegetables are great under the broiler. Good candidates include asparagus spears, bell pepper halves or strips and onion wedges.

- **Fruits:** Many fruits can be broiled, such as peach or nectarine halves, grapefruit halves, pineapple slices and bananas.

Buttery Broiled Fish Steaks CALORIE SMART • FAST

PREP 20 min **TOTAL** 20 min • 4 servings

    4 salmon, tuna, halibut or other medium-firm
       to firm fish steaks, about ¾ inch thick
       (6 oz each)
       Salt and pepper to taste
    2 tablespoons butter, melted
       Lemon wedges, if desired

1 Set oven control to broil. Sprinkle both sides of fish with salt and pepper. Place fish on rack in broiler pan. Brush with 1 tablespoon of the butter.

2 Broil with tops about 4 inches from heat 5 minutes. Carefully turn fish; brush with remaining 1 tablespoon butter. Broil 4 to 6 minutes longer or until fish flakes easily with fork. Serve with lemon wedges.

1 Serving: Calories 280; Total Fat 15g (Saturated Fat 6g, Trans Fat 0g); Cholesterol 125mg; Sodium 340mg; Total Carbohydrate 0g (Dietary Fiber 0g, Sugars 0g); Protein 36g **Exchanges:** 5 Lean Meat **Carbohydrate Choices:** 0

Broiled Fish Fillets Substitute 1 lb fish fillets, cut into 4 serving pieces, for the fish steaks. Broil with tops about 4 inches from heat 5 to 6 minutes or until fish flakes easily with fork (do not turn).

Buttery Broiled Fish Steaks

Sole Amandine

Roasted Tilapia and Vegetables

Sole Amandine CALORIE SMART • FAST

A French term, amandine *means "garnished with almonds" and is often misspelled as "almondine." If you own a gratin dish (a shallow oval-shaped ovenproof baking dish), use it to bake this classic.*

PREP 10 min **TOTAL** 30 min • 6 servings

1½ lb sole, orange roughy or other delicate- to medium-texture fish fillets (½ to ¾ inch thick), skin removed

½ cup sliced almonds

¼ cup butter, softened

2 tablespoons grated lemon peel

½ teaspoon salt

½ teaspoon paprika

2 tablespoons fresh lemon juice

1 Heat oven to 375°F. Spray 11x7-inch (2-quart) glass baking dish with cooking spray. Cut fish into 6 serving pieces. Place in baking dish, tucking under any thin ends for more even cooking.

2 In small bowl, mix almonds, butter, lemon peel, salt and paprika; spoon evenly over fish. Sprinkle with lemon juice.

3 Bake uncovered 15 to 20 minutes or until fish flakes easily with fork.

1 Serving: Calories 210; Total Fat 13g (Saturated Fat 4.5g, Trans Fat 0g); Cholesterol 75mg; Sodium 330mg; Total Carbohydrate 2g (Dietary Fiber 1g, Sugars 0g); Protein 21g **Exchanges:** 3 Very Lean Meat, 2½ Fat **Carbohydrate Choices:** 0

LIGHTER Directions For 140 calories and 6 grams of fat per serving, reduce both the almonds and butter to 2 tablespoons.

Orange Sole Amandine Substitute orange peel for the lemon peel and orange juice for the lemon juice. Garnish with fresh basil leaves if desired.

Roasted Tilapia and Vegetables CALORIE SMART

PREP 15 min **TOTAL** 40 min • 4 servings

½ lb fresh asparagus spears

2 small zucchini, cut in half lengthwise, then cut into ½-inch pieces

1 medium bell pepper, cut into ½-inch strips

1 large onion, cut into ½-inch wedges, separated

2 tablespoons olive oil

2 teaspoons Montreal steak grill seasoning

4 tilapia fillets (about 1½ lb)

1 tablespoon butter, melted

½ teaspoon paprika

1 Heat oven to 450°F. Snap off tough ends of asparagus; cut each spear in half. In large bowl, mix asparagus, zucchini, bell pepper, onion and oil. Sprinkle with 1 teaspoon of the grill seasoning; toss to coat. Spread vegetables in ungreased 15x10x1-inch pan. Roast 5 minutes on lowest oven rack.

2 Meanwhile, spray 13x9-inch (3-quart) glass baking dish with cooking spray. Pat fish dry with paper towels. Brush fish with butter; sprinkle with paprika and remaining 1 teaspoon grill seasoning. Place in baking dish.

3 Place baking dish on middle oven rack. Roast fish and vegetables uncovered 17 to 18 minutes or until fish flakes easily with fork and vegetables are tender.

1 Serving: Calories 290; Total Fat 12g (Saturated Fat 3.5g, Trans Fat 0g); Cholesterol 100mg; Sodium 520mg; Total Carbohydrate 10g (Dietary Fiber 3g, Sugars 5g); Protein 34g **Exchanges:** 2 Vegetable, 4 Lean Meat, ½ Fat **Carbohydrate Choices:** ½

Snapper with Tomato-Pepper Sauce CALORIE SMART • FAST

PREP 20 min **TOTAL** 20 min • 4 servings

- 1 lb red snapper, cod or other medium-firm fish fillets (½ inch thick)
- 1 large tomato, chopped (1 cup)
- 1 small green bell pepper, chopped (½ cup)*
- 1 small onion, sliced
- 2 tablespoons finely chopped fresh cilantro or parsley
- ¼ teaspoon salt
- ¼ cup dry white wine or chicken broth
- 2 cups hot cooked rice (page 215), if desired

1 Heat 12-inch nonstick skillet over medium heat. If fish fillets are large, cut into 4 serving pieces. Arrange fish, skin side down, in single layer in skillet. Cook uncovered 4 to 6 minutes, turning once, until fish flakes easily with fork. Remove fish to warm platter; keep warm.

2 Add tomato, bell pepper, onion, cilantro and salt to skillet. Cook over medium heat 3 to 5 minutes, stirring frequently, until bell pepper and onion are crisp-tender. Stir in wine; cook about 1 minute or until hot. Spoon sauce over fish. Serve with rice.

*For a slightly sweeter-tasting sauce, use a red, yellow or orange bell pepper instead of green.

1 Serving: Calories 120; Total Fat 1.5g (Saturated Fat 0g, Trans Fat 0g); Cholesterol 60mg; Sodium 250mg; Total Carbohydrate 5g (Dietary Fiber 1g, Sugars 2g); Protein 22g **Exchanges:** 1 Vegetable, 3 Very Lean Meat **Carbohydrate Choices:** ½

Snapper with Tomato-Pepper Sauce

Asian Tuna with Wasabi Aioli

CALORIE SMART

PREP 25 min **TOTAL** 2 hr 25 min • 8 servings

TUNA
- 2 lb tuna steaks (¾ to 1 inch thick)
- ½ cup vegetable oil
- ⅓ cup soy sauce
- 2 tablespoons packed brown sugar
- 2 teaspoons sesame oil
- 2 teaspoons grated gingerroot
- 2 cloves garlic, finely chopped

WASABI AIOLI
- ½ cup mayonnaise or salad dressing
- 1 teaspoon wasabi powder*

GARNISH
- 2 teaspoons sesame seed, toasted (page 23) if desired

1 If tuna steaks are large, cut into 8 serving pieces. In shallow glass or plastic dish or resealable food-storage plastic bag, mix vegetable oil, soy sauce, brown sugar, sesame oil, gingerroot and garlic. Add tuna; turn to coat with marinade. Cover dish or seal bag; refrigerate at least 2 hours but no longer than 4 hours to marinate, turning once.

2 Meanwhile, in small bowl, mix aioli ingredients. Cover and refrigerate until serving time.

3 Set oven control to broil. Remove tuna from marinade; reserve marinade. Place tuna on rack in broiler pan. Broil with tops 4 to 6 inches from heat 10 to 15 minutes, brushing 2 or 3 times with marinade and turning once, until fish flakes easily with fork and is slightly pink in center. Discard any remaining marinade. Sprinkle sesame seed over tuna. Serve with aioli.

*Prepared horseradish can be substituted for the wasabi powder.

1 Serving: Calories 350; Total Fat 27g (Saturated Fat 4.5g, Trans Fat 0g); Cholesterol 75mg; Sodium 600mg; Total Carbohydrate 4g (Dietary Fiber 0g, Sugars 3g); Protein 22g **Exchanges:** 3 Medium-Fat Meat, 2½ Fat **Carbohydrate Choices:** 0

Common Types of Tuna

Albacore is also know as "white tuna" because of its light flesh. Mild-flavored, albacore is the most expensive canned tuna. Young bluefin tuna are lighter in flesh with a milder flavor than mature bluefin, which has dark-red flesh and a strong flavor.

Cornmeal-Crusted Catfish

Lemon- and Parmesan-Crusted Salmon

Cornmeal-Crusted Catfish CALORIE SMART • FAST

You can substitute regular ranch dressing for the fat-free variety, if that's what you have on hand. Or feel free to make your own, see page 138.

PREP 10 min **TOTAL** 25 min • 4 servings

- 1 lb catfish fillets (about ¾ inch thick)
- ¼ cup fat-free ranch dressing
- ¼ cup yellow cornmeal
- ¼ cup unseasoned dry bread crumbs
- 1 teaspoon chili powder
- ½ teaspoon paprika
- ½ teaspoon garlic salt
- ¼ teaspoon pepper
  Chopped fresh parsley, if desired

1 Heat oven to 450°F. Spray rack in broiler pan with cooking spray. Cut fish into 4 serving pieces. Lightly brush dressing on both sides of fish.

2 In shallow dish, mix remaining ingredients except parsley. Coat fish with cornmeal mixture. Place fish on rack in pan.

3 Bake about 15 minutes or until fish flakes easily with fork. Sprinkle with parsley.

1 Serving: Calories 230; Total Fat 8g (Saturated Fat 2g, Trans Fat 0g); Cholesterol 70mg; Sodium 440mg; Total Carbohydrate 17g (Dietary Fiber 1g, Sugars 1g); Protein 20g **Exchanges:** 1 Starch, 2½ Lean Meat **Carbohydrate Choices:** 1

Cornmeal-Crusted Cod Substitute 1 pound cod fillets, cut into serving size pieces, for the catfish.

Lemon- and Parmesan-Crusted Salmon CALORIE SMART

PREP 10 min **TOTAL** 35 min • 4 servings

- 1 salmon fillet (1¼ lb)
- 2 tablespoons butter, melted
- ¼ teaspoon salt
- ¾ cup medium- to firm-textured bread crumbs (about 1 slice bread)*
- ¼ cup grated Parmesan cheese
- 2 medium green onions, thinly sliced (2 tablespoons)
- 2 teaspoons grated lemon peel
- ¼ teaspoon dried thyme leaves

1 Heat oven to 375°F. Spray shallow baking pan with cooking spray. Pat salmon dry with paper towels. Place salmon, skin side down, in pan. Brush with 1 tablespoon of the butter. Sprinkle with salt.

2 In small bowl, mix bread crumbs, cheese, onions, lemon peel and thyme. Stir in remaining 1 tablespoon butter. Press bread crumb mixture evenly on salmon.

3 Bake uncovered 15 to 25 minutes or until fish flakes easily with fork. Cut into 4 serving pieces. Serve immediately.

*Soft-textured bread is not recommended because it's too moist and won't create a crisp crumb topping.

1 Serving: Calories 290; Total Fat 16g (Saturated Fat 6g, Trans Fat 0g); Cholesterol 115mg; Sodium 420mg; Total Carbohydrate 4g (Dietary Fiber 0g, Sugars 0g); Protein 33g **Exchanges:** 5 Lean Meat, ½ Fat **Carbohydrate Choices:** 0

Salmon Burgers with Sour Cream–Dill Sauce

1 Serving: Calories 230; Total Fat 11g (Saturated Fat 3.5g, Trans Fat 0g); Cholesterol 80mg; Sodium 320mg; Total Carbohydrate 7g (Dietary Fiber 0g, Sugars 6g); Protein 24g **Exchanges:** ½ Starch, 3 Lean Meat **Carbohydrate Choices:** ½

Salmon Patties with Sour Cream–Dill Sauce   CALORIE SMART • FAST

Serve these patties as burgers by placing in buns with lettuce leaves.

PREP 30 min **TOTAL** 30 min • 4 servings

- ⅓ cup sour cream
- 3 tablespoons mayonnaise or salad dressing
- ¾ teaspoon dried dill weed
- 1 egg
- 2 tablespoons milk
- 1 can (14¾ oz) salmon, drained, skin and bones removed, flaked
- 2 medium green onions, chopped (2 tablespoons)
- 1 cup soft bread crumbs (about 1½ slices bread)
- ¼ teaspoon salt
- 1 tablespoon vegetable oil

1 In small bowl, stir sour cream, mayonnaise and dill until well mixed. Cover and refrigerate until serving time.

2 In medium bowl, beat egg and milk with fork or whisk. Stir in salmon, onions, bread crumbs and salt. Shape mixture into 4 patties about 4 inches in diameter.

3 In 10-inch nonstick skillet, heat oil over medium heat. Cook patties in oil about 8 minutes, turning once, until golden brown. Serve with sauce.

1 Serving: Calories 300; Total Fat 22g (Saturated Fat 6g, Trans Fat 0g); Cholesterol 120mg; Sodium 750mg; Total Carbohydrate 6g (Dietary Fiber 0g, Sugars 2g); Protein 20g **Exchanges:** ½ Starch, 2½ Lean Meat, 3 Fat **Carbohydrate Choices:** ½

Honey-Mustard Glazed Salmon   CALORIE SMART

PREP 20 min **TOTAL** 35 min • 4 servings

- 1 salmon fillet (1 lb)
- 1 tablespoon packed brown sugar
- 1 tablespoon butter, melted
- 1 tablespoon olive or vegetable oil
- 1 tablespoon honey
- 1 tablespoon soy sauce
- 1 tablespoon Dijon mustard
- 1 clove garlic, finely chopped

1 Place salmon, skin side down, in shallow glass or plastic dish. In small bowl, mix remaining ingredients; pour over salmon. Cover and refrigerate at least 15 minutes but no longer than 1 hour.

2 Set oven control to broil. Remove salmon from marinade; reserve marinade. Place salmon, skin side down, on rack in broiler pan. Broil with top 4 to 6 inches from heat 10 to 15 minutes, brushing 2 or 3 times with marinade, until fish flakes easily with fork. Discard any remaining marinade. Cut into 4 pieces to serve.

LEARN WITH BETTY Salmon Doneness

Perfectly Done: Salmon is pink and cloudy-looking and flakes easily with a fork.

Underdone: Salmon is translucent and does not flake easily with a fork.

Overdone: Salmon is dry and tough.

Heirloom Recipe and New Twist

This classic Beer-Batter Fried Fish is often requested because the light flavor of the batter gets crispy while the fish inside is tender and flavorful. The secret is in the temperature of the oil and the consistency of the batter. For the Cajun Fish Soft Tacos, we use a flavorful coating so the fish is cooked in a skillet with equally delicious results. If you enjoy a bit of spice, this recipe will soon be one of your favorites too.

HEIRLOOM

Beer-Batter Fried Fish

CALORIE SMART • FAST

PREP 25 min **TOTAL** 25 min • 4 servings

- 1 lb walleye, sole or other delicate- to medium-texture fish fillets (about ½ inch thick), skin removed
- 3 to 4 tablespoons all-purpose flour
- 1 cup all-purpose flour
- ½ cup regular or nonalcoholic beer
- 1 egg
- ½ teaspoon salt
  Vegetable oil for frying
  Tartar Sauce (page 461), if desired

1 Cut fish into 8 serving pieces. Lightly coat with 3 to 4 tablespoons flour. In medium bowl, mix 1 cup flour, the beer, egg and salt with wooden spoon until smooth. (If batter is too thick, stir in additional beer, 1 tablespoon at a time, until desired consistency.)

2 In deep fryer or 4-quart Dutch oven, heat oil (1½ inches) to 350°F. Dip fish into batter, letting excess drip into bowl. Fry fish in batches in oil about 4 minutes, turning once, until golden brown (tail sections may cook more quickly). Remove with slotted spoon; drain on paper towels. Serve hot with tartar sauce.

1 Serving: Calories 390; Total Fat 17g (Saturated Fat 3g, Trans Fat 0g); Cholesterol 115mg; Sodium 410mg; Total Carbohydrate 30g (Dietary Fiber 1g, Sugars 0g); Protein 27g **Exchanges:** 2 Starch, 3 Very Lean Meat, 3 Fat **Carbohydrate Choices:** 2

NEW TWIST

Cajun Fish Soft Tacos FAST

PREP 30 min **TOTAL** 30 min • 4 servings

PICKLED CABBAGE
- 1½ cups thinly sliced green cabbage
- ½ cup thinly sliced red cabbage
- 2 tablespoons chopped fresh chives
- 3 tablespoons cider vinegar
- 1 tablespoon sugar
- ¼ teaspoon salt

FISH
- 1 lb tilapia or other medium-firm fish fillets (about ½ inch thick), skin removed
- 1½ teaspoons Cajun seasoning
- 1 egg
- 1 tablespoon red pepper sauce
- ½ cup cornmeal
- 2 tablespoons vegetable oil
- 8 flour tortillas (6 inch), heated as directed on package

Beer-Batter Fried Fish | Cajun Fish Soft Tacos

SEASONED SOUR CREAM

½ cup sour cream

2 teaspoons chopped fresh chives

¼ teaspoon Cajun seasoning*

TOPPINGS, IF DESIRED

Chopped seeded tomato

Cubed avocado

1 In medium bowl, mix cabbages and 2 tablespoons chives. In tightly covered container, shake vinegar, sugar and salt until sugar is dissolved. Pour over cabbage mixture; toss to coat. Set aside; stir before serving.

2 Sprinkle fish with 1½ teaspoons Cajun seasoning and press into flesh. In small bowl, beat egg and pepper sauce with fork or whisk until blended. Place cornmeal in shallow dish. Dip fish into egg mixture, then coat with cornmeal.

3 In 12-inch nonstick skillet, heat oil over medium heat. Cook fish in oil 6 to 8 minutes, turning once, until fish flakes easily with fork and is brown on both sides. (Fish cooks very quickly, especially the thinner tail sections; be careful not to overcook.)

4 Meanwhile, in small bowl, mix seasoned sour cream ingredients. Gently break fish into bite-size pieces; divide fish among tortillas, placing 4 or 5 pieces down center of each. Top with pickled cabbage, seasoned sour cream, tomato and avocado.

*Or substitute 2 teaspoons red pepper sauce for the Cajun seasoning.

1 Serving (2 Tacos): Calories 510; Total Fat 20g (Saturated Fat 7g, Trans Fat 1g); Cholesterol 110mg; Sodium 1200mg; Total Carbohydrate 51g (Dietary Fiber 3g, Sugars 8g); Protein 31g **Exchanges:** 3 Starch, ½ Vegetable, 3 Very Lean Meat, 3½ Fat **Carbohydrate Choices:** 3½

Toasted Spice Seared Mackerel FAST

PREP 15 min **TOTAL** 25 min • 4 servings

GREMOLATA MAYONNAISE

½ cup mayonnaise

2 tablespoons chopped fresh parsley

1 teaspoon grated orange peel

1 teaspoon grated lemon peel

TOASTED SPICE RUB

1 tablespoon coriander seed

2 teaspoons cumin seed

1 teaspoon fennel seed

1 tablespoon sugar

1 teaspoon salt

¼ teaspoon pepper

FISH

1¼ lb mackerel, snapper, tilapia or other medium-firm fish fillets (about ½ inch thick)

2 tablespoons vegetable oil

1 In small bowl, mix gremolata mayonnaise ingredients until well blended. Cover and refrigerate until serving time.

2 Heat 8-inch skillet over medium-high heat. Add coriander, cumin and fennel seed; toast 2 to 3 minutes, stirring constantly, until coriander seed turns golden brown and mixture becomes fragrant. Place toasted spices in spice grinder. Grind until mixture looks like finely ground pepper. Transfer to small bowl; stir in sugar, salt and pepper.

3 Heat oven to 400°F. Rub tops of fish fillets with spice mixture; let stand 5 minutes. In 12-inch ovenproof skillet, heat oil over medium-high heat. Place fish, skin side down, in skillet; sear 2 minutes or until deep golden brown. Remove from heat. Carefully turn fish fillets over.

4 Bake 2 to 4 minutes or until fish flakes easily with fork. Serve with gremolata mayonnaise.

1 Serving: Calories 560; Total Fat 48g (Saturated Fat 9g, Trans Fat 0g); Cholesterol 95mg; Sodium 860mg; Total Carbohydrate 5g (Dietary Fiber 0g, Sugars 4g); Protein 27g **Exchanges:** ½ Other Carbohydrate, 4 Lean Meat, 7 Fat **Carbohydrate Choices:** ½

Toasted Spice Seared Mackerel

SHELLFISH BASICS

Because shellfish are easy to prepare plus taste delicious, their popularity is no surprise. Shellfish are grouped into two main categories: crustaceans and mollusks. Crustaceans have long bodies with soft, jointed shells and include crab, crayfish, lobsters and shrimp. Mollusks have soft bodies, may or may not be covered by a shell and have no spinal column. Types include clams, mussels, scallops, oysters, abalone, octopus and squid (calamari).

BUYING AND USING SHELLFISH

- **Clams, Mussels and Oysters (in the shell):** Clam varieties include **hard shell** (cherrystone and littleneck) and **soft-shell** (razor and steamers). Clams, mussels and oysters in shells should be purchased alive. Look for tightly closed shells that are not cracked, chipped or broken. They should have a very mild aroma. Shells may open naturally but will close if lightly tapped, indicating they are still alive. If shells do not close, throw them out.

- **Shucked Clams, Mussels and Oysters (no shells):** These shellfish should be plump and surrounded by a clear, slightly milky or light gray liquid. They should have a mild aroma.

- **Scallops:** Varieties include **sea scallops** (1½ to 2 inches wide) and tiny **bay scallops** (½ inch wide). Scallops should look moist and have a mild, sweet aroma. They should not be standing in liquid or stored on ice. These shellfish are creamy white and may have a light orange, light tan or pink tint.

- **Crabs and Lobsters:** Live crabs and lobsters will show some leg movement and lobsters will curl their tails under when picked up. These shellfish must be cooked live or killed immediately before cooking; throw out any that are dead. Crabmeat is available fresh, and both crab and lobster meat are available canned and frozen.

- **Shrimp:** Varieties include raw ("green") with the heads on; raw in the shell without the heads; raw, peeled and deveined; cooked in the shell; or cooked, peeled and deveined.

Shrimp should have a clean sea aroma. If they have an ammonia smell, they are spoiled and should be discarded.

- **Squid (Calamari):** Color of squid ranges from cream with reddish brown spots to light pink. Buy fresh squid that's whole with clear eyes and a fresh sea aroma. Cleaned squid is also available in juices and the meat should be firm.

Imitation Seafood Products

Imitation seafood products, shaped into pieces to resemble crab or lobster, are usually made from pollock and are less expensive than shellfish but are similar in taste and texture to the real thing. Because some of these products, often labeled surimi, contain a shellfish extract, check labels carefully if you have a seafood allergy.

Lobster

Snow Crab

King Crab

Tiger Shrimp

Brown Shrimp

Salad Shrimp

Laughing Bird Shrimp

Crayfish

Soft-Shell Crab

Hard-Shell Blue Crab

Cherrystone Clams

Sea Scallops

Countneck Clams

Littleneck Clams

Lantern Bay Scallops

Blue Point Oysters

Squid (Calamari)

Prince Edward Island (P. E. I.) Mussels

Manila Clams

STORING SHELLFISH

- Live crabs (hard shell or soft-shell) and lobsters should be cooked the same day they're purchased. Put them on a tray with sides, cover with a damp cloth and refrigerate until ready to cook.

- Raw scallops, shrimp, squid and shucked shellfish should be stored in a leak-proof bag or plastic container with a lid. Cook scallops, shrimp and squid within 2 days. Shucked shellfish should be used within 7 days.

- Live clams, mussels and oysters should be refrigerated in a container covered with a clean, damp cloth, not with an airtight lid or in a plastic bag, which will cause suffocation. Live clams, mussels and oysters may open their shells even when refrigerated. Give the shells a tap—they will close if alive; if not, throw them out. Cook within 2 days.

SHELLFISH PER SERVING

The amount of shellfish you need per person depends on the type you're preparing.

TYPE OF SHELLFISH	AMOUNT PER SERVING
Clams, Mussels or Oysters	
In shell	3 large hard-shell clams
	6 small hard-shell clams
	18 soft-shell clams
	18 mussels
	6 oysters
Shucked	¼ lb
Crab (hard shell) or Lobster	1¼ lb live or ¼ lb cooked
Crab (soft-shell)	2 crabs
Shrimp	
With head, unpeeled	1 lb
Without head, unpeeled	½ lb
Without head, peeled	¼ lb
Squid	
Whole	½ lb
Cleaned	¼ lb

SUCCESSFULLY COOKING SHELLFISH

Cooked shellfish should be moist and slightly chewy; overcooking makes it tough and rubbery. Follow these guidelines to determine when shellfish is done:

- Crabs and lobsters turn bright red.

- Scallops turn milky white or opaque and get firm.

- Raw shrimp turns pink and gets firm.

- Live clams, oysters and mussels open their shells.

- Shucked clams, oysters and mussels get plump and opaque. Oyster edges start to curl.

- **To cook in a skillet (panfry),** heat about 1 tablespoon oil over medium-high heat. Cook the shellfish as directed below.

- **To boil,** bring water to a boil in large saucepan. Add shellfish and cook as directed below.

- **To broil,** place shellfish on broiler rack. Broil 7 to 9 inches from heat as directed below.

TIMETABLE FOR COOKING SHELLFISH

Shellfish can be cooked in a variety of ways. Keep in mind the cooking time varies depending on the method of preparation.

TYPE OF SHELLFISH	AMOUNT IN POUNDS	METHOD AND COOK TIME
Scallops (bay or sea)	1	Panfry 3 to 6 minutes
		Boil 2 to 3 minutes
		Broil 3 to 5 minutes
Shrimp (peeled and deveined)	1	Panfry 3 to 6 minutes
		Boil 2 to 3 minutes
		Broil 3 to 5 minutes
Shrimp (in shell)	1	Boil 4 to 6 minutes
Clams or Oysters (in shell)	4	Boil or steam 5 to 7 minutes
Mussels (in shell)	2	Boil or steam 5 to 7 minutes
Squid	1	Panfry 2 to 3 minutes

REHEATING COOKED CRAB LEGS

Most crab legs available for purchase are already cooked. Follow these steps to reheat them before serving.

1. Cut crab legs to fit 8-inch square microwavable dish.

2. Cover with plastic wrap, folding one edge or corner back about ¼ inch to vent steam.

3. Microwave on Medium-High (70%), rotating dish once if the microwave has no turntable, until hot. Let stand as directed before serving.

TYPE OF SHELLFISH	APPROXIMATE WEIGHT IN POUNDS	MICROWAVE TIME IN MINUTES	STAND TIME IN MINUTES
Cooked Crab Legs (thawed if frozen)	2	5 to 6	5

UNDERSTANDING SHRIMP COUNT

Fresh and frozen shrimp are sold by a descriptive size name like *jumbo* or *large*, and by "count," or number per pound. The larger the shrimp, the lower the count. Size and count vary throughout the United States.

COMMON SHRIMP SIZE MARKET NAME	COUNT (APPROXIMATE NUMBER) PER POUND
Colossal	Fewer than 10
Jumbo	11 to 15
Extra Large	16 to 20
Large	21 to 30
Medium	31 to 35
Small	36 to 45
Miniature or Tiny	About 100

Soft-Shell Crabs

Soft-shell crabs are the same species as Atlantic hard-shell blue crabs, except soft-shell crabs have been caught immediately after shedding their old hard shells. They stay soft for only a couple of hours before their shells harden again. Like all live crabs, they should be cooked the same day they're purchased.

Note: For more information about shellfish handling, safety and nutrition, call the FDA's Center for Food Safety and Applied Nutrition, 1-888-SAFEFOOD (723-3366). Recorded information is available 24 hours a day, or you can speak to an information specialist by calling Monday through Friday, 10 a.m. to 4 p.m. Eastern Standard Time. Or check the FDA's website at www.fda.gov.

Shucking Fresh Oysters | Deveining Shrimp

Slip tip of oyster knife between top and bottom shells, next to hinge. Carefully run knife around oyster to other side of hinge, using twisting motion, to pry top and bottom shells apart.

Cut muscle attached in middle of oyster to both top and bottom shells to spread apart and separate. Remove top shell from bottom, being careful to not spill oyster juice in bottom shell.

Remove meat from bottom shell by sliding knife inward, under meat, close against surface of bottom shell, to keep meat intact.

Using a small, pointed knife or shrimp deveiner, make a shallow cut along the center back of each shrimp; wash out vein.

Deep-Fried Shrimp

Shrimp Creole

Deep-Fried Shrimp CALORIE SMART

Watch the temperature of the oil carefully during frying. If it starts to smoke, turn down the heat and wait until the temperature returns to 350°F before putting in the next batch of shrimp.

PREP 40 min **TOTAL** 40 min • 4 servings

- ½ cup all-purpose flour
- 1 teaspoon salt
- ½ teaspoon pepper
- 2 eggs
- ¾ cup dry bread crumbs
- 1 lb uncooked medium shrimp, thawed if frozen, peeled (with tail shells left on), deveined
  Vegetable oil for frying

1 In shallow dish, mix flour, salt and pepper. In another shallow dish, beat eggs slightly with fork or whisk. In third shallow dish, place bread crumbs. Pat shrimp dry with paper towels. Coat shrimp with flour mixture; dip into egg, then coat with bread crumbs.

2 In deep fryer or 4-quart Dutch oven, heat oil (2 to 3 inches) to 350°F. Fry 4 or 5 shrimp at a time in oil about 1 minute, turning once, until golden brown. Drain on paper towels.

1 Serving: Calories 300; Total Fat 14g (Saturated Fat 2.5g, Trans Fat 0g); Cholesterol 215mg; Sodium 920mg; Total Carbohydrate 27g (Dietary Fiber 0g, Sugars 2g); Protein 19g **Exchanges:** 2 Starch, 2 Lean Meat, 1 Fat **Carbohydrate Choices:** 2

Deep-Fried Oysters or Clams Substitute ¾ pound shucked oysters or clams, drained, for the shrimp.

Deep-Fried Sea Scallops Substitute ¾ pound sea scallops, drained, for the shrimp. Fry 3 to 4 minutes or until golden brown on outside and white and opaque inside. Bay scallops, which are smaller, will cook more quickly.

Shrimp Creole CALORIE SMART

This traditional dish from Louisiana is a slightly spicy mixture of spices with tomatoes and shrimp. It's similar to gumbo but thicker.

PREP 30 min **TOTAL** 1 hr • 6 servings

- ¼ cup butter
- 3 medium onions, chopped (1½ cups)
- 2 medium green bell peppers, finely chopped (2 cups)
- 2 medium stalks celery, finely chopped (1 cup)
- 2 cloves garlic, finely chopped
- 1 can (15 oz) tomato sauce
- 1 cup water
- 2 teaspoons chopped fresh parsley
- 1½ teaspoons salt
- ¼ teaspoon ground red pepper (cayenne)
- 2 dried bay leaves
- 2 lb uncooked medium shrimp, thawed if frozen, peeled, deveined
- 6 cups hot cooked rice (page 215)

1 In 3-quart saucepan, melt butter over medium heat. Cook onions, bell peppers, celery and garlic in butter about 10 minutes, stirring occasionally, until onions are tender. Stir in remaining ingredients except shrimp and rice. Heat to boiling; reduce heat to low. Simmer uncovered 10 minutes.

2 Stir in shrimp. Heat to boiling; reduce heat to medium. Cover and cook 4 to 6 minutes, stirring occasionally, until shrimp are pink. Remove and discard bay leaves. Serve shrimp mixture over rice.

1 Serving: Calories 400; Total Fat 9g (Saturated Fat 4.5g, Trans Fat 0g); Cholesterol 160mg; Sodium 1860mg; Total Carbohydrate 57g (Dietary Fiber 3g, Sugars 6g); Protein 22g **Exchanges:** 3½ Starch, 1 Vegetable, 1½ Very Lean Meat, 1 Fat **Carbohydrate Choices:** 4

LIGHTER Directions For 335 calories and 3 grams of fat per serving, reduce butter to 1 tablespoon and use a nonstick saucepan.

Shrimp Scampi   CALORIE SMART • FAST

Serve these succulent shrimp over a bed of hot angel hair pasta or fettuccine and sprinkle with extra chopped fresh parsley.

PREP 20 min **TOTAL** 20 min • 6 servings

- 2 tablespoons olive or vegetable oil
- 1½ lb uncooked medium shrimp, thawed if frozen, peeled, deveined
- 2 medium green onions, thinly sliced (2 tablespoons)
- 2 tablespoons fresh lemon juice
- 1 tablespoon chopped fresh parsley
- 2 cloves garlic, finely chopped
- ¼ teaspoon salt
   Grated or shredded Parmesan cheese, if desired

In 10-inch skillet, heat oil over medium heat. Add shrimp, onions, lemon juice, parsley, garlic and salt to skillet; cook 2 to 3 minutes, stirring frequently, until shrimp are pink. Remove from heat; sprinkle with cheese.

1 Serving: Calories 90; Total Fat 4g (Saturated Fat 0.5g, Trans Fat 0g); Cholesterol 105mg; Sodium 220mg; Total Carbohydrate 1g (Dietary Fiber 0g, Sugars 0g); Protein 12g **Exchanges:** 2 Very Lean Meat, ½ Fat **Carbohydrate Choices:** 0

Shrimp Gumbo   CALORIE SMART

PREP 45 min **TOTAL** 45 min • 6 servings

- ¼ cup butter, divided
- 2 medium onions, sliced
- 1 medium green bell pepper, cut into thin strips
- 2 cloves garlic, finely chopped
- 2 tablespoons all-purpose flour
- 3 cups beef broth (for homemade broth, see page 146)
- ½ teaspoon red pepper sauce
- ¼ teaspoon salt
- ¼ teaspoon pepper
- 1 dried bay leaf
- 1 package (12 oz) frozen cut okra, thawed and drained
- 1 can (14.5 oz) whole tomatoes, undrained
- 1 can (6 oz) tomato paste
- 1 lb uncooked medium shrimp, thawed if frozen, peeled, deveined
- 3 cups hot cooked rice (page 215)
- ¼ cup chopped fresh parsley

1 In 4-quart Dutch oven, melt 1 tablespoon of the butter over medium heat. Cook onions, bell pepper and garlic in butter 5 minutes, stirring occasionally. Remove and set aside. Melt remaining butter in Dutch oven over medium heat. Stir in flour. Cook and stir over medium heat until bubbly and medium golden brown, 2 to 3 minutes; remove from heat.

2 Stir in onions, peppers and remaining ingredients except shrimp, rice and parsley, breaking up tomatoes. Heat to boiling; reduce heat. Simmer uncovered 10 minutes, stirring occasionally.

3 Stir in shrimp. Cover and simmer about 5 minutes or until shrimp turn pink. Discard bay leaf. Serve gumbo over rice. Sprinkle with parsley.

1 Serving: Calories 320; Total Fat 9g (Saturated Fat 5g, Trans Fat 0g); Cholesterol 125mg; Sodium 1310mg; Total Carbohydrate 41g (Dietary Fiber 4g, Sugars 9g); Protein 20g **Exchanges:** 1½ Starch, 1 Other Carbohydrate, ½ Vegetable, 2 Very Lean Meat, 1½ Fat **Carbohydrate Choices:** 3

Scallops with Artichokes and Tomatoes   CALORIE SMART • FAST

PREP 20 min **TOTAL** 20 min • 4 servings

- 1 lb bay scallops
- 4 medium green onions, sliced (¼ cup)
- ¼ teaspoon salt
- ⅛ teaspoon white pepper
- 1 clove garlic, finely chopped
- 1 box (9 oz) frozen artichoke hearts, thawed, drained*
- 1 cup cherry tomatoes, cut into quarters
- 1 cup shredded fresh spinach leaves
- 1 tablespoon lemon juice
   Hot cooked linguine or angel hair pasta, if desired

1 In 10-inch nonstick skillet, cook scallops, onions, salt, pepper and garlic over medium-high heat 4 minutes, stirring frequently, until scallops are white and opaque.

2 Stir in artichokes, tomatoes and spinach. Cook, stirring occasionally, until tomatoes are hot and spinach is wilted, drain. Sprinkle with lemon juice. Serve over linguine.

*A 14-ounce can of artichoke hearts, drained and cut into quarters, can be substituted for the frozen artichoke hearts.

1 Serving: Calories 110; Total Fat 1g (Saturated Fat 0g, Trans Fat 0g); Cholesterol 25mg; Sodium 580mg; Total Carbohydrate 12g (Dietary Fiber 5g, Sugars 2g); Protein 14g **Exchanges:** 2½ Vegetable, 1 Very Lean Meat **Carbohydrate Choices:** 1

Betty's Staples
Cooked Shrimp

With cooked shrimp on hand, a quick, delicious meal is minutes away. Buy them precooked or cook them yourself; refrigerate up to 2 days or freeze up to 2 months.

1. Shrimp and Melon Salad: On individual salad plates, arrange 3 or 4 Bibb lettuce leaves and top with 1 cup each cubed cantaloupe and watermelon and ½ to ¾ cup cooked shrimp. Drizzle with balsamic vinaigrette.

2. Tomato-Basil Shrimp and Pasta: In skillet, heat 1 can diced tomatoes with garlic, basil and oregano with 1 chopped bell pepper over medium-low heat until pepper is fork-tender. Stir in 1½ cups cooked shrimp and 2 tablespoons chopped fresh basil; heat through. Serve over pasta.

3. Shrimp Tacos: For each taco, in taco shell, layer about ¼ cup each shredded lettuce and chopped fresh tomato, ½ cup heated cooked shrimp and a few slices avocado. Drizzle with 1 to 2 tablespoons each salsa and French dressing.

4. Scrambled Eggs and Shrimp: Make scrambled eggs, page 90. Just before eggs are cooked, stir in 1½ cups cooked shrimp and 2 tablespoons chopped fresh parsley.

5. Shrimp and Egg Salad Wraps: In medium bowl, mix 4 chopped hard-cooked eggs, 1 cup chopped cooked shrimp, 1 tablespoon chopped fresh dill and 3 tablespoons creamy mustard-mayonnaise sauce. Spoon ¼ of mixture down center of flour tortilla; top with ½ cup shredded lettuce. Roll up tortilla.

Shrimp Tacos

Citrus Seafood Skillet

Citrus Seafood Skillet

CALORIE SMART • FAST

"Fresh and light" best describes this seafood trio. If you love the flavors of ceviche, you'll find them all here in this quickly cooked dinner.

PREP 20 min **TOTAL** 20 min • 4 servings

- 1 tablespoon olive oil
- 1 orange bell pepper, cut into ¼-inch strips
- ½ medium red onion (halved lengthwise), sliced
- 1 tablespoon finely chopped seeded jalapeño chile
- ½ lb bay scallops
- ½ lb uncooked deveined peeled medium shrimp, thawed if frozen
- ½ lb uncooked squid (calamari) tubes, thawed if frozen and cut into rings
- ½ teaspoon salt
- 3 tablespoons fresh lime juice
- 2 teaspoons grated lime peel
- 2 tablespoons chopped fresh cilantro
  Hot cooked rice, if desired

1 In 12-inch skillet, heat oil over medium-high heat. Cook bell pepper, onion and chile in oil 2 to 3 minutes, stirring occasionally, until crisp-tender.

2 Pat seafood dry with paper towels. Add scallops and shrimp to skillet; sprinkle seafood and vegetables with salt. Cook 3 to 4 minutes, adding calamari during last 1 minute of cooking, until shrimp turn pink and scallops and calamari turn white and opaque. Add lime juice and lime peel; cook and stir just until thoroughly heated. Sprinkle with cilantro. Serve with rice.

1 Serving: Calories 170; Total Fat 4.5g (Saturated Fat 1g, Trans Fat 0g); Cholesterol 210mg; Sodium 550mg; Total Carbohydrate 7g (Dietary Fiber 1g, Sugars 2g); Protein 24g **Exchanges:** ½ Other Carbohydrate, 3½ Very Lean Meat, ½ Fat **Carbohydrate Choices:** ½

Steamed Clams CALORIE SMART

PREP 20 min **TOTAL** 50 min • 4 servings

- 4 lb cherrystone, littleneck or steamer clams in shells
- 6 cups water
- ⅓ cup white vinegar
- ½ cup boiling water, chicken broth or white wine Melted butter or Clarified Butter (page 469), if desired

1 Discard any broken-shell or open (dead) clams that do not close when tapped. Place remaining clams in large container. Cover with 6 cups water and the vinegar. Let stand 30 minutes; drain. Scrub clams in cold water.

2 In steamer*, place clams and boiling water. Cover and steam 5 to 8 minutes or until clam shells open at least 1 inch, removing clams as they open. Discard any unopened clams. Serve hot clams in shells with butter.

*If steamer is not available, place clams in 6-quart Dutch oven. Add 1 inch boiling water; cover tightly.

1 Serving: Calories 50; Total Fat 0.5g (Saturated Fat 0g, Trans Fat 0g); Cholesterol 25mg; Sodium 40mg; Total Carbohydrate 2g (Dietary Fiber 0g, Sugars 0g); Protein 9g **Exchanges:** 1 Lean Meat **Carbohydrate Choices:** 0

Buying Clams

In the fish market, you might find a variety of clams and names for them. Littleneck (topnecks) are the smallest hard-shell clams, with cherrystone (quahogs or chowder clams) being a little bigger. Steamer clams are soft-shell clams but can be cooked in the same way as hard-shell clams.

Steamed Mussels in Wine Sauce CALORIE SMART • FAST

Serve the mussels with crusty Italian bread for sopping up the garlic-flavored wine sauce.

PREP 30 min **TOTAL** 30 min • 4 servings

- 24 large fresh mussels in shells (about 2 lb)
- 2 tablespoons olive oil
- ½ cup chopped fresh parsley
- 4 cloves garlic, finely chopped
- 2 plum (Roma) tomatoes, chopped
- 1 cup dry white wine or chicken broth
- ½ teaspoon salt
- ½ teaspoon freshly ground pepper

1 Discard any broken-shell or open (dead) mussels that do not close when tapped. Scrub remaining mussels, removing any barnacles with a dull paring knife. If there are beards, remove them by tugging them away from shells.

2 Place mussels in large container. Cover with cool water. Agitate water with hand, then drain and discard water. Repeat several times until water runs clear; drain.

3 In 12-inch skillet, heat oil over medium-high heat. Cook parsley and garlic in oil, stirring frequently, until garlic is lightly golden. Add tomatoes, mussels, wine, salt and pepper. Cover and cook about 10 minutes or until mussel shells open.

4 Discard any unopened mussels. Spoon sauce from skillet over each serving.

1 Serving: Calories 170; Total Fat 8g (Saturated Fat 1g, Trans Fat 0g); Cholesterol 40mg; Sodium 640mg; Total Carbohydrate 6g (Dietary Fiber 0g, Sugars 0g); Protein 16g **Exchanges:** 1 Vegetable, 2 Lean Meat, ½ Fat **Carbohydrate Choices:** ½

Opening Raw Clams

Hold clam with hinged side against heavy cloth or oven mitt. Insert oyster knife or blunt-tipped knife between shell halves.

Gently twist knife to pry open the shell and release juices. Be sure to work over bowl or plate to catch juices.

Holding clam firmly, move sharp knife around clam, cutting muscle at hinge. Gently twist knife to pry open shell. Cut clam meat from shell.

Determining Spoiled Mussels

After cooking mussels, discard those that do not open; they are spoiled.

VEGETARIAN BASICS

FEATURES

MAIN DISHES

SIDE DISHES

BONUS RECIPES

CALORIE SMART = See Helpful Nutrition and Cooking Information, page 643   FAST = Ready in 30 minutes or less
EASY = Prep in 10 minutes or less **plus** five ingredients or less   LIGHTER = 25% fewer calories or grams of fat
MAKE AHEAD = Make-ahead directions   SLOW COOKER = Slow cooker directions

< Portabello Muffuletta Sandwiches, page 400

VEGETARIAN BASICS

Welcome to the colorful, nutrition-packed, tasty world of vegetarian cooking. Whether you are looking for occasional meatless meals; are increasing the amount of grains, legumes, and vegetables your family eats; or you have health, ethical or environmental reasons for eating meatless, this is the chapter for you.

PLANT-BASED DIETS

What we eat can make a difference in our lives. Plant-based diets, which emphasize fruits, vegetables, grains, soy, beans, legumes and nuts, are generally rich in fiber, vitamins and other important nutrients. If you are new to eating meatless, start with one or two meals a week. Use protein-rich foods containing beans and legumes, tofu, soy or cheese. Add plenty of vegetables and fruits for taste and eye appeal.

Meatless diets vary based on the types of foods allowed. Below are the most common plant-based diets, although there might be some variation within each eating style.

FOOD ALLOWED	DIET				
	Vegan	Semi-Vegetarian (Flexitarian)	Lacto-Ovo-Vegetarian	Lacto-Vegetarian	Ovo-Vegetarian
Fruit	✓	✓	✓	✓	✓
Vegetables	✓	✓	✓	✓	✓
Grains	✓	✓	✓	✓	✓
Legumes	✓	✓	✓	✓	✓
Nuts & Seeds	✓	✓	✓	✓	✓
Tofu & Soy	✓	✓	✓	✓	✓
Eggs		✓	✓		✓
Dairy Products		✓	✓	✓	
Fish & Seafood		may include occasionally			
Meat		may include occasionally			
Poultry		may include occasionally			

California Black Bean Burgers (page 399)

Moussaka

5 Bake uncovered about 1 hour or until firm. Let stand 10 minutes before serving.

1 Serving: Calories 330; Total Fat 6g (Saturated Fat 2.5g, Trans Fat 0g); Cholesterol 15mg; Sodium 1560mg; Total Carbohydrate 40g (Dietary Fiber 7g, Sugars 21g); Protein 29g **Exchanges:** 2 Starch, 2 Vegetable, 2½ Very Lean Meat, 1 Fat **Carbohydrate Choices:** 2½

Asian Stuffed Portabellas

CALORIE SMART

PREP 20 min **TOTAL** 1 hr 25 min • 4 servings

- ¾ cup uncooked regular brown rice
- 1½ cups water
- 4 large portabella mushrooms (4 to 5 inches in diameter), stems removed
- 1 tablespoon vegetable oil
- 1½ cups coleslaw mix (shredded cabbage and carrots)
- ½ cup cut-up fresh snow pea pods
- ¼ cup sliced green onions (4 medium)
- 1 tablespoon finely chopped gingerroot
- 1 clove garlic, finely chopped
- ¼ cup reduced-sodium soy sauce
- 2 teaspoons sesame oil
- 4 teaspoons sesame seed

1 In 1½-quart saucepan, heat brown rice and water to boiling; reduce heat. Cover and simmer 45 to 50 minutes or until water is absorbed.

2 Heat oven to 400°F. Spray 15x10x1-inch pan with cooking spray. Place mushrooms, gill sides down, in pan. Bake 5 minutes or until tender and beginning to brown.

3 Meanwhile, in 10-inch nonstick skillet, heat vegetable oil over medium-high heat. Add coleslaw mix, pea pods, onions, gingerroot and garlic. Cook 2 to 3 minutes, stirring frequently, until coleslaw mix is wilted and vegetables are crisp-tender. Stir in cooked rice; sprinkle with soy sauce and sesame oil. Cook, tossing gently with soy sauce and oil, until thoroughly heated; remove from heat.

4 Turn mushrooms gill sides up. Spoon about ¾ cup rice mixture onto each mushroom; sprinkle each with 1 teaspoon sesame seed. Bake 13 to 15 minutes or until sesame seed begins to turn brown.

1 Serving: Calories 250; Total Fat 9g (Saturated Fat 1g, Trans Fat 0g); Cholesterol 0mg; Sodium 560mg; Total Carbohydrate 35g (Dietary Fiber 6g, Sugars 3g); Protein 7g **Exchanges:** 1½ Starch, ½ Other Carbohydrate, 1½ Vegetable, 1½ Fat **Carbohydrate Choices:** 2

Moussaka CALORIE SMART

Our version of moussaka uses soy-protein burgers in the flavorful eggplant "lasagna." You'll love the protein but won't miss the meat!

PREP 30 min **TOTAL** 1 hr 40 min • 4 servings

- 4 frozen soy-protein burgers or soy-protein vegetable burgers
- 1 medium unpeeled eggplant (about 1½ lb), cut into ¼-inch slices
- ¼ cup all-purpose flour
- ½ teaspoon salt
- ½ teaspoon pepper
- ¼ teaspoon ground nutmeg
- ¼ teaspoon ground cinnamon
- 3 cups milk
- 4 oz (half of 8-oz package) cream cheese, cut into cubes
- 1 can (15 oz) tomato sauce
- 2 eggs, beaten

1 Heat oven to 375°F. Spray 3-quart casserole with cooking spray. On large microwavable plate, microwave burgers uncovered on High 2 to 3 minutes, turning once, until thawed. Cut into 1-inch pieces; set aside.

2 In 2-quart saucepan, place eggplant and enough water to cover. Heat to boiling; cook 5 to 8 minutes or until tender. Drain in colander; set aside.

3 In same saucepan, mix flour, salt, pepper, nutmeg, cinnamon and milk. Heat to boiling, stirring constantly. Boil 1 minute, stirring constantly. Remove from heat. Stir in cream cheese until melted and smooth.

4 In casserole, layer half of the eggplant, the burger pieces, tomato sauce, 1½ cups of the white sauce and the remaining eggplant. Stir eggs into remaining white sauce; pour over eggplant.

Betty's Staples
Canned Tomatoes

If you have a can of diced or whole tomatoes in your pantry, an easy meal has a great start. With just a few ingredients and some imagination, it's simple to take that can of tomatoes and turn it into a delicious dinner.

1. Quick Skillet Pasta Sauce: Heat 1 tablespoon olive oil in skillet over medium heat. Add 2 sliced garlic cloves; cook 30 seconds. Add a 28-ounce can tomatoes (breaking any large pieces with a spoon), 1 teaspoon dried basil leaves and ¼ teaspoon crushed red pepper flakes. Heat to boiling; reduce heat. Simmer uncovered about 10 minutes or until thickened. Stir in ½ teaspoon salt and ¼ teaspoon pepper. Serve over hot cooked pasta.

2. Cajun Tomatoes with Black-Eyed Peas: Cook chopped onion, garlic and bell pepper in small amount of oil until tender. Stir in a 14-ounce can of tomatoes, a 16-ounce can drained black-eyed peas and sprinkle with a little ground red pepper (cayenne) and thyme. Simmer until hot and desired consistency. If desired, serve with rice.

3. Easy Pizza: Heat a 14-ounce can of tomatoes in a saucepan until slightly thickened. Spoon onto a purchased pizza crust and top with pepperoni slices and shredded mozzarella cheese. Bake as directed on the pizza package.

4. Shrimp with Tomatoes: Heat a 14-ounce can of tomatoes (breaking any large pieces with a spoon) in skillet with chopped green bell pepper, a sprinkle of garlic powder, a few drops of sriracha sauce and chopped fresh or dried oregano. Stir in 1 to 2 cups cooked shrimp (any size) and heat until very hot and desired consistency.

5. Italian Meatballs with Tomato Sauce: Mix 15 to 20 frozen Italian meatballs with a 28-ounce can of tomatoes in a skillet. Cover and cook, stirring occasionally, until meatballs are thawed and mixture is very hot. Serve with mashed potatoes or over pasta.

6. Chicken Tortilla Soup: Heat tomatoes with 4 cups of chicken broth, about 1 cup shredded rotisserie chicken and a 4-ounce can diced green chiles until boiling. Reduce heat and simmer for about 5 minutes and sprinkle with baked corn chips and chopped fresh cilantro.

7. Thyme Tomatoes with Chicken: Brown 4 chicken breast halves (seasoned with salt, pepper and garlic powder) in skillet and pour a 14-ounce can of tomatoes over them. Sprinkle with chopped fresh or dried thyme and cover. Simmer 10 to 15 minutes or until chicken is no longer pink in the center and sauce is desired consistency.

8. Tomatoes with Ravioli: Heat a 20-ounce package of refrigerated ravioli with a 28-ounce can of tomatoes, sliced zucchini and chopped red onion until ravioli are tender. Sprinkle with a little crumbled goat cheese.

Cajun Tomatoes with Black-Eyed Peas

Learn to
PREPARE TOFU

Sometimes called bean curd, tofu is made from soybeans and processed into a solid form. This versatile food absorbs flavors easily and can be used as a healthful source of protein in meals. Tofu is readily available in grocery stores—look for it in the refrigerated section, as it needs to be kept cold. Cooking tofu is not difficult, but there are some tips that will help make the process easy and result in great-tasting tofu dishes.

Tofu Storage

- Tofu is perishable, so check the sell-by date on the package. If unopened, it will keep in the refrigerator up to 5 days. Once opened, use within 2 days. Store covered with water and change the water daily.

- Tofu can be frozen up to 5 months. Freeze in original container or wrap tightly in plastic wrap.

Cooking Tips

Stir-frying and baking are easy ways to cook tofu. Choose the method depending on the texture you want and what you are cooking with it. For use in most cooking, extra-firm and firm tofu will be the best types to use.

- Most tofu is packaged in water and is like a sponge, so it needs to be drained well before cooking. On a plate or other surface, press the tofu between layers of paper towels or kitchen towels; top with a weight such as a heavy skillet or plate. Let it stand for at least 1 hour.

- Determine how to cut the tofu according to what you are making or the recipe used. Cubes will work well in stir-fries, soups and stews; cut into larger pieces or slices for frying, baking or grilling.

- To marinate and add flavor, place the tofu pieces in a container and pour the marinade mixture over it. Cover and marinate in the refrigerator at least 1 hour or overnight. The tofu in the marinade can also be frozen. When ready to cook, just thaw in the refrigerator and cook as desired. Tofu becomes a bit firmer after freezing.

- **Stir-Frying Tofu:** Results in tofu with dry, firm texture and crispy edges.

  - Heat a nonstick pan over medium heat and add 1 tablespoon vegetable or olive oil. Season tofu with salt and pepper or other desired seasonings.

  - Cook 4 to 5 minutes or until light golden brown on both sides, turning once.

- **Baking Tofu:** Results in tofu with denser, firmer texture.

  - Heat oven to 350°F. Lightly spray a shallow pan with cooking spray or grease lightly.

  - Place tofu in the pan. It can be seasoned with salt and pepper, soy sauce or other desired seasonings, or it can be marinated.

  - Bake 30 to 35 minutes or until thoroughly heated and slightly golden brown.

Tofu Stir-Fry with Black Bean Sauce CALORIE SMART • FAST

Black bean sauce is robust in flavor, thin and salty. It is made from fermented black beans, garlic and often star anise. Look for it with other Asian ingredients.

PREP 25 min **TOTAL** 25 min • 5 servings

- 1 tablespoon olive oil
- 1 large onion, thinly sliced (1 cup)
- 4 cups chopped fresh broccoli
- 1 medium red bell pepper, cut into ½-inch slices, then cut in half (1 cup)
- ⅓ cup black bean garlic sauce (from 7-oz jar)
- 2 tablespoons soy sauce
- 1 tablespoon chili-garlic sauce (from 8-oz jar)
- 1 package (12 to 14 oz) firm lite tofu, drained if needed, cut into ¾-inch cubes
- ⅓ cup chopped fresh cilantro
- 5 cups hot cooked brown basmati rice (page 215)
- ¼ cup honey-roasted or regular sunflower seeds

1 In wok or 12-inch skillet, heat oil over medium-high heat. Cook onion in oil about 2 minutes, stirring occasionally, until crisp-tender. Add broccoli and bell pepper; stir-fry about 2 minutes or until almost crisp-tender.

2 In small bowl, mix black bean sauce, soy sauce and chili-garlic sauce. Stir into vegetable

Tofu Stir-Fry with Black Bean Sauce

mixture. Add tofu; stir-fry 2 to 3 minutes or until thoroughly heated. Stir in cilantro. Serve over rice. Sprinkle with sunflower seeds.

1 Serving (1 Cup Tofu Mixture and 1 Cup Rice): Calories 340; Total Fat 10g (Saturated Fat 1.5g, Trans Fat 0g); Cholesterol 0mg; Sodium 540mg; Total Carbohydrate 48g (Dietary Fiber 9g, Sugars 4g); Protein 14g **Exchanges:** 3 Starch, 1 Vegetable, ½ Medium-Fat Meat, 1 Fat **Carbohydrate Choices:** 3

Tofu-cation

If you're new to the tofus scene, here's the skinny on how to purchase tofu: Look for tofu packed in clear liquid with no gelatinous or discolored areas. If the liquid is cloudy, it may be spoiled. When opened, fresh tofu shouldn't smell or taste sour.

Preparing Tofu

Press tofu between layers of paper towels; top with a weight, such as a heavy skillet or plate, to remove moisture.

To stir-fry tofu, cook 4 to 5 minutes or until light golden brown on both sides, turning once.

To bake tofu, place on pan; season and bake until thoroughly heated and slightly golden brown.

When Are Coals Ready?

After lighting briquettes with either method, leave them in a mounded shape until they are glowing red (10 to 20 minutes) and mostly covered in gray ash. (After dark, you'll know coals are ready when they have an even red glow.) Spread the coals into a single layer for grilling.

Determine the temperature of the coals by holding the palm of your hand near the grill rack and timing how long you can comfortably keep it there:

- 2 seconds = high heat
- 3 seconds = medium-high heat
- 4 seconds = medium heat
- 5 seconds = low heat

CONTROLLING THE HEAT

Below are ways adjust the grill temperature—but also consider moving your food to hotter or cooler parts of the grill to get the right heat under the food you are grilling as an alternative method if needed. (Also see Direct and Indirect Heat, right.)

- **Gas/Electric Grill:** If the heat is too hot, use a lower burner setting. If heat is too low, use a higher heat setting.
- **Charcoal Grill:** If the coals are too hot, spread them out or close the air vents halfway. If too cool, move the coals closer together or knock off the ashes by tapping them with long-handled tongs or open the air vents.

PREVENTING AND TAMING FLARE-UPS

Fats and sugary sauces dripping through the grill rack can cause flare-ups that burn the food and can cause a fire hazard. Use these tricks to prevent flare-ups:

- Trim excess fat from meats.
- Keep the bottom of the grill uncovered so that the grease can drain easily into the grease catch pan.

- Keep the grill bottom and catch pan clean and debris-free.
- Brush sugary or tomato-based sauces on food only during the last 10 to 15 minutes to prevent them from burning.
- Clean off residue from the grill rack after each use. For a gas grill, turn the heat setting on high for 10 to 15 minutes with the grill cover closed to burn off residue from the grill rack and lava rock or ceramic briquettes. For a charcoal grill, use a brass bristle brush (or crumble a large sheet of aluminum foil and use long-handled tongs) to scrape residue off the grill rack while the grill is still warm.

When a Flare-Up Happens

- Move food to a different area of the grill rack; cover the grill to extinguish the flames.
- For a charcoal grill, spread the coals farther apart or move food and spritz the flames with water from a spray bottle. When the flames are extinguished, move food back to the desired area.
- For a gas or electric grill, turn all burners off. NEVER USE WATER TO EXTINGUISH FLAMES ON A GAS OR ELECTRIC GRILL. When the flames are gone, light the grill again.

FOOD SAFETY WHEN GRILLING

- If you've brushed raw meat or poultry with a marinade or sauce, wash the brush with hot, soapy water before using on cooked meat.
- Use a clean plate to place the grilled food on, not the same plate that carried the raw food.
- Set aside some of the marinade or sauce for serving before any of it is brushed on raw meat. If the marinade has been brushed on raw meat and the brush has been dipped again into the marinade, you can boil the remaining portion for 1 minute before serving.

DIRECT AND INDIRECT HEAT

For best results, follow the grill manufacturer's directions for both methods.

- **Direct-Heat Grilling:** Food is cooked on the grill rack directly over heat. Best for foods that cook in less than 25 minutes: burgers, chicken pieces, chops, steaks.

- **Indirect-Heat Grilling:** Food is cooked on the grill rack next to, not directly over, the heat source. Best for foods that take longer than 25 minutes: ribs, whole chickens or turkeys, roasts. For best results, place large cuts of meat or whole turkeys or chickens on a roasting rack set inside a disposable heavy-duty foil pan on grill rack. If necessary, add water to foil pan to keep meat drippings from burning.

Setting Up Grill for Direct Heat

For charcoal grill, evenly spread hot, white coals over firebox of grill.

For gas grill, heat all burners on high for 10 to 15 minutes; then reduce heat as needed.

Setting Up Grill for Indirect Heat

For charcoal grill, move hot, white coals to edge of firebox, leaving area in middle free of coals; place drip pan in open area. Grill food over drip pan.

For gas grill, heat all burners on high for 10 to 15 minutes. Turn off center burner. Grill food over center burner. Adjust temperature of ignited burners as needed. If grill only has two burners, turn off one and grill over that burner.

Southwestern Rub

CALORIE SMART • FAST • EASY

Rubs are simple ways to season meats—just sprinkle on the seasoning mixture and rub it into the meat with your fingers. Because this rub has oil in it, it's known as a wet rub rather than a dry rub.

PREP 10 min **TOTAL** 25 min • 3 tablespoons

- 1 tablespoon chili powder
- 1 teaspoon ground cumin
- ¼ teaspoon salt
- ¼ teaspoon ground red pepper (cayenne)
- 1 clove garlic, finely chopped
- 1 tablespoon vegetable oil

1 In small bowl, mix all ingredients.

2 Spread rub evenly on 1 pound boneless meat (chicken, pork or beef) or 2½ pounds ½-inch-thick pork chops (about 8). Cover and refrigerate at least 15 minutes but no longer than 24 hours. Cook meat as desired.

1 Teaspoon: Calories 15; Total Fat 1.5g (Saturated Fat 0g, Trans Fat 0g); Cholesterol 0mg; Sodium 75mg; Total Carbohydrate 0g (Dietary Fiber 0g, Sugars 0g); Protein 0g **Exchanges:** Free **Carbohydrate Choices:** 0

Jamaican Jerk Seasoning

CALORIE SMART • FAST • EASY

PREP 10 min **TOTAL** 25 min • 3 tablespoons

- 1 tablespoon dried minced onion
- 2 teaspoons dried thyme leaves
- 1 teaspoon ground allspice
- 1 teaspoon pepper
- ½ teaspoon salt
- ½ teaspoon ground cinnamon
- ¼ teaspoon ground red pepper (cayenne)

1 In small bowl, mix all ingredients.

2 Spread rub evenly on 1 pound boneless meat (chicken, pork or beef). Cover and refrigerate at least 15 minutes but no longer than 24 hours. Cook meat as desired.

1 Teaspoon: Calories 0; Total Fat 0g (Saturated Fat 0g, Trans Fat 0g); Cholesterol 0mg; Sodium 130mg; Total Carbohydrate 0g (Dietary Fiber 0g, Sugars 0g); Protein 0g **Exchanges:** Free **Carbohydrate Choices:** 0

Beer Can Chicken

CALORIE SMART • EASY

The steam from the beer and the savory rub make this chicken very moist and flavorful.

PREP 10 min **TOTAL** 1 hr 55 min • 6 servings

BASIC BARBECUE RUB

- 1 tablespoon paprika
- 2 teaspoons salt
- ½ teaspoon garlic powder
- ½ teaspoon onion powder
- ½ teaspoon pepper

CHICKEN

- 1 whole chicken (4 to 4½ lb)
- 1 can (12 oz) regular or nonalcoholic beer

Beer Can Chicken

1 In small bowl, mix rub ingredients. Fold wings of chicken across back with tips touching. Sprinkle rub inside cavity and all over outside of chicken; rub with fingers. If desired, tie legs together with kitchen string.

2 Pour out ½ cup of beer from can for another use. Holding chicken upright with larger opening of body cavity downward; insert beer can into larger cavity. Insert ovenproof meat, grilling or digital thermometer so tip is in thickest part of inside thigh and does not touch bone.

3 Heat gas or charcoal grill for indirect cooking. For two-burner gas grill, heat one burner to medium; place chicken with beer can upright on unheated side. For one-burner gas grill, place chicken on grill over low heat. For charcoal grill, move medium coals to edge of firebox; place chicken with beer can upright on grill rack over drip pan.

4 Cover grill; cook 1 hour 15 minutes to 1 hour 30 minutes or until thermometer reads at least 165°F and legs move easily when lifted or twisted. Using tongs, carefully lift chicken to 13x9-inch pan, holding large metal spatula under beer can for support. Let stand 15 minutes before carving. Remove beer can; discard.

1 Serving: Calories 300; Total Fat 18g (Saturated Fat 5g, Trans Fat 0.5g); Cholesterol 115mg; Sodium 700mg; Total Carbohydrate 0g (Dietary Fiber 0g, Sugars 0g); Protein 36g **Exchanges:** 5 Lean Meat, 1 Fat **Carbohydrate Choices:** 0

Making Beer Can Chicken

Sprinkle seasoning inside cavity of chicken and rub all over outside.

Insert open beer can into cavity of chicken.

Using tongs, carefully lift finished chicken to pan, holding metal spatula under beer can for support.

Grilled Barbecue Chicken CALORIE SMART

PREP 50 min **TOTAL** 50 min • 6 servings

BARBECUE SAUCE

1 medium onion, finely chopped (½ cup)
1 cup ketchup or 1 can (8 oz) tomato sauce
½ cup hot water
⅓ cup lemon juice
1 tablespoon Worcestershire sauce
2 teaspoons paprika
1 teaspoon sugar
1 teaspoon salt
½ teaspoon pepper

CHICKEN

1 teaspoon salt
1 teaspoon paprika
¼ teaspoon pepper
1 cut-up whole chicken (3 to 3½ lb)

1 Heat gas or charcoal grill. In 1-quart saucepan, stir together all sauce ingredients. Heat over medium heat until boiling, stirring occasionally. Remove from heat.

2 In small bowl, mix 1 teaspoon salt, 1 teaspoon paprika and ¼ teaspoon pepper. Sprinkle mixture over both sides of chicken.

3 Carefully brush oil on grill rack. Place chicken, skin side up, on grill over medium heat. Cover grill; cook 15 minutes. Turn chicken; brush with barbecue sauce. Cover grill; cook 20 to 25 minutes longer, turning and brushing with sauce, until juice of chicken is clear when thickest pieces are cut to bone (at least 165°F).

1 Serving: Calories 380; Total Fat 13g (Saturated Fat 3.5g, Trans Fat 0g); Cholesterol 155mg; Sodium 1410mg; Total Carbohydrate 14g (Dietary Fiber 1g, Sugars 11g); Protein 51g **Exchanges:** 1 Other Carbohydrate, 7 Very Lean Meat, 2 Fat **Carbohydrate Choices:** 1

Grilled Barbecue Chicken Breasts Substitute 6 bone-in chicken breasts for the cut-up whole chicken. Place chicken, skin side up, on grill over medium heat. Cover grill; cook 10 minutes. Turn chicken; brush with barbecue sauce. Cover grill; cook 10 to 15 minutes longer or until juice of chicken is clear when thickest part is cut to bone (at least 165°F).

Turkey Breast with Chili-Cumin Rub CALORIE SMART

Whole turkey breasts grill beautifully. Because they're available in different sizes, adjust the grilling time as needed and check the meat thermometer for doneness.

PREP 10 min **TOTAL** 2 hr 50 min • 8 servings

CHILI-CUMIN RUB

2 tablespoons packed brown sugar
2 teaspoons paprika
1 teaspoon chili powder
1 teaspoon ground cumin
½ teaspoon ground mustard
½ teaspoon ground ginger
½ teaspoon garlic-pepper blend
½ teaspoon salt

TURKEY

1 bone-in whole turkey breast (5 to 6 lb), thawed if frozen
2 tablespoons cold butter

1 In small bowl, mix rub ingredients. Loosen skin on turkey breast in 4 or 5 places. Cut butter into small slices; place randomly under skin of turkey. Sprinkle rub mixture over entire outside of turkey; rub with fingers. Insert ovenproof meat, grilling or digital thermometer so tip is in thickest part of breast and does not touch bone.

2 Heat gas or charcoal grill for indirect cooking. For two-burner gas grill, heat one burner to medium; place turkey, breast side up, on unheated side. For one-burner gas grill, place turkey, breast side up, on grill over low heat. For charcoal grill, move medium coals to edge of firebox; place turkey, breast side up, on grill rack over drip pan filled with ½ inch water.

3 Cover grill; cook 30 minutes. Turn turkey. Cover grill; cook 1 hour 30 minutes to 2 hours longer or until thermometer reads at least 165°F. Remove turkey from grill; cover with foil. Let stand 10 minutes before slicing.

1 Serving: Calories 390; Total Fat 18g (Saturated Fat 6g, Trans Fat 0g); Cholesterol 155mg; Sodium 290mg; Total Carbohydrate 4g (Dietary Fiber 0g, Sugars 3g); Protein 54g **Exchanges:** 7½ Very Lean Meat, 3 Fat **Carbohydrate Choices:** 0

Preparing Steaks for the Grill

Trim fat from steaks to ¼-inch thickness to cut down on flare-ups while grilling.

Rub seasonings such as garlic and pepper into beef. Let beef stand for 30 minutes for best flavor and texture when grilled.

Texas T-Bones CALORIE SMART

PREP 25 min **TOTAL** 55 min • 8 servings

STEAKS

- 4 beef T-bone steaks, about ¾ inch thick (10 to 12 oz each)
- 2 cloves garlic, cut in half
- 4 teaspoons black peppercorns, crushed Salt and pepper to taste, if desired

MUSTARD BUTTER

- ¼ cup butter, softened
- 1 tablespoon Dijon mustard
- ½ teaspoon Worcestershire sauce
- ¼ teaspoon lime juice

1 Heat gas or charcoal grill. Trim fat from steaks to ¼-inch thickness. Rub garlic on beef. Press peppercorns into beef. Let stand for 30 minutes to reach room temperature. In small bowl, mix mustard butter ingredients; set aside.

2 Place beef on grill over medium heat. Cover grill; cook 10 to 12 minutes for medium doneness (160°F), turning once. Sprinkle with salt and pepper. Serve with mustard butter.

1 Serving: Calories 310; Total Fat 12g (Saturated Fat 4.5g, Trans Fat 0.5g); Cholesterol 95mg; Sodium 240mg; Total Carbohydrate 14g (Dietary Fiber 0g, Sugars 10g); Protein 37g **Exchanges:** 1 Fruit, 5 Lean Meat **Carbohydrate Choices:** 1

Grilled Balsamic- and Roasted Garlic–Marinated Steak CALORIE SMART

PREP 30 min **TOTAL** 8 hr 30 min • 6 servings

- ½ cup balsamic vinegar
- ¼ cup chili sauce
- 2 tablespoons packed brown sugar
- 2 tablespoons olive or vegetable oil
- 2 teaspoons chopped roasted garlic (from 4-oz jar)
- ½ teaspoon Italian seasoning
- ¼ teaspoon salt
- ¼ teaspoon coarsely ground black pepper
- 1 boneless beef top round steak, 1 to 1½ inches thick (1½ lb)

1 In shallow glass dish or resealable food-storage plastic bag, mix all ingredients except beef. Add beef; turn to coat. Cover dish or seal bag. Refrigerate 8 hours or overnight, turning beef occasionally.

2 Heat gas or charcoal grill. Remove beef from marinade; reserve marinade.

3 Place beef on grill over medium heat. Cover grill; cook 16 to 18 minutes, turning and brushing with marinade once or twice, until beef is of desired doneness. Discard any remaining marinade. Cut beef across grain into thin slices.

1 Serving: Calories 140; Total Fat 4.5g (Saturated Fat 1.5g, Trans Fat 0g); Cholesterol 60mg; Sodium 105mg; Total Carbohydrate 2g (Dietary Fiber 0g, Sugars 1g); Protein 23g **Exchanges:** 3 Very Lean Meat, ½ Fat **Carbohydrate Choices:** 0

LEARN WITH BETTY Beef Steak Doneness

Medium-Rare (145°F): Steak is very pink in the center and slightly brown toward the exterior.

Medium (160°F): Steak is light pink in the center and brown toward the exterior.

Well-Done (170°F): Steak is uniformly brown throughout.

Beef Fajitas

PREP 1 hr **TOTAL** 9 hr • 6 servings

- 1 boneless beef top sirloin steak, 1½ inches thick (1½ lb), trimmed of excess fat
  Fajita Marinade (page 476)
- 2 large onions, sliced
- 2 medium green or red bell peppers, cut into ¼-inch strips
- 2 tablespoons vegetable oil
- 12 flour tortillas (9 or 10 inch)
- 1 cup picante sauce
- 1 cup shredded Cheddar or Monterey Jack cheese (4 oz)
- 1½ cups guacamole (for homemade Guacamole, see page 41)
- ¾ cup sour cream

1 Pierce beef with fork in several places. Place in resealable food-storage plastic bag or shallow glass or plastic dish. Pour marinade over beef; turn to coat. Cover and refrigerate at least 8 hours but no longer than 24 hours, turning occasionally.

2 Heat gas or charcoal grill. In large bowl, toss onions and bell peppers with oil; place in grill basket (grill "wok"). Set aside.

3 Remove beef from marinade; reserve marinade. Place beef on grill over medium heat. Cover grill; cook 22 to 26 minutes for medium-rare (145°F) to medium doneness (160°F), turning once and brushing occasionally with reserved marinade. Add vegetables to grill for last 6 to 8 minutes of cooking, shaking basket or stirring vegetables once or twice, until crisp-tender.

4 Meanwhile, heat oven to 325°F. Wrap tortillas in foil. Heat in oven about 15 minutes or until warm. Remove tortillas from oven; keep wrapped.

5 Discard any remaining marinade. Cut beef across grain into very thin slices. For each fajita, place a few slices of beef, some of the onion mixture, 1 heaping tablespoonful each picante sauce and cheese, 2 tablespoons guacamole and 1 tablespoon sour cream on center of tortilla. Fold 1 end of tortilla up about 1 inch over filling; fold right and left sides over folded end, overlapping. Fold remaining end down.

1 Serving: Calories 710; Total Fat 33g (Saturated Fat 12g, Trans Fat 1.5g); Cholesterol 100mg; Sodium 910mg; Total Carbohydrate 63g (Dietary Fiber 7g, Sugars 8g); Protein 38g **Exchanges:** 3½ Starch, ½ Other Carbohydrate, 4 Medium-Fat Meat, 2 Fat **Carbohydrate Choices:** 4

LIGHTER Directions For 11 grams of fat and 520 calories per serving, omit oil; spray onions and bell peppers with cooking spray and toss before placing in grill basket. Use fat-free tortillas and reduced-fat cheese and sour cream. Omit guacamole.

Chicken Fajitas Substitute 1 pound boneless skinless chicken breasts for the beef. Marinate 2 hours. Cook chicken on grill over medium heat 15 to 20 minutes, turning occasionally, until juice of chicken is clear when center of thickest part is cut (at least 165°F). Cut chicken into thin slices.

Shrimp Fajitas Substitute 1 pound uncooked medium shrimp, peeled and deveined, for the beef. Marinate 1 hour. Cook shrimp in grill basket (grill "wok") over medium heat 4 to 6 minutes, until pink, turning occasionally.

Heirloom Recipe and New Twist

Flank steak is a great recipe to have in your repertoire. With these easy-to-follow directions, it will be a success every time. Use any leftovers to make quick Mexican-inspired meals. For a flavor twist, try our jerk version. You'll be surprised how a few common herbs and spices, combined in a new way, make a great new flavor.

HEIRLOOM

Flank Steak with Smoky Honey-Mustard Sauce CALORIE SMART

PREP 30 min **TOTAL** 35 min • 6 servings

HONEY-MUSTARD SAUCE

- ¼ cup Honey-Mustard Dressing (see page 137)
- 1 tablespoon frozen (thawed) orange juice concentrate
- 1 tablespoon water
- 1 clove garlic, finely chopped
- 1 chipotle chile in adobo sauce (from 7-oz can), finely chopped

STEAK

- 1 beef flank steak (about 1½ lb)
- 6 flour tortillas (8 to 10 inch), heated as directed on package
  Sliced tomato and avocado, if desired

1 Heat gas or charcoal grill. In small bowl, mix sauce ingredients. In both sides of beef, make cuts about ½ inch apart and ⅛ inch deep in diamond pattern. Brush 2 tablespoons of the sauce on both sides of beef.

2 Place beef on grill over medium heat. Cover grill; cook 17 to 21 minutes, turning once, until beef is of desired doneness. Remove beef from grill to cutting board or plate; cover and let stand 5 minutes. Cut beef across grain into thin slices. Serve with remaining sauce, tortillas, tomato and avocado.

1 Serving: Calories 360; Total Fat 16g (Saturated Fat 4.5g, Trans Fat 1.5g); Cholesterol 55mg; Sodium 460mg; Total Carbohydrate 22g (Dietary Fiber 0g, Sugars 2g); Protein 31g **Exchanges:** 1½ Starch, 4 Lean Meat, ½ Fat **Carbohydrate Choices:** 1½

Sirloin Steak with Smoky Honey-Mustard Sauce Substitute 1½-pound boneless beef top sirloin steak (1 inch thick) for the flank steak.

Flank Steak with Smoky Honey-Mustard Sauce

Grilled Jerk Flank Steak

Easy Grilled Steak Kabobs

Grilled Jerk Flank Steak CALORIE SMART

PREP 30 min **TOTAL** 4 hr 35 min • 6 servings

- 3 tablespoons teriyaki marinade and sauce (from 10-oz bottle)
- 1 tablespoon vegetable oil
- 2 teaspoons pumpkin pie spice
- ½ teaspoon dried thyme leaves
- ½ teaspoon salt
- ¼ teaspoon pepper
- 2 cloves garlic, finely chopped
- 1 jalapeño chile, finely chopped (not seeded)
- 1 beef flank steak (1½ lb)

1 In shallow glass dish or resealable food-storage plastic bag, mix all ingredients except beef. Add beef; turn to coat. Cover dish or seal bag. Refrigerate at least 4 hours but no longer than 24 hours.

2 Heat gas or charcoal grill. Remove beef from marinade; discard marinade.

3 Place beef on grill over medium heat. Cover grill; cook 17 to 21 minutes, turning once, until beef is of desired doneness. Remove beef from grill to cutting board or plate; cover and let stand 5 minutes. Cut beef across grain into thin slices.

1 Serving: Calories 180; Total Fat 8g (Saturated Fat 3g, Trans Fat 0g); Cholesterol 50mg; Sodium 170mg; Total Carbohydrate 0g (Dietary Fiber 0g, Sugars 0g); Protein 26g **Exchanges:** 3½ Lean Meat **Carbohydrate Choices:** 0

BROILER Directions

Marinate beef as directed in Step 1. Place beef on rack in broiler pan. Broil with top 4 to 5 inches from heat about 10 minutes, turning once, until beef is of desired doneness.

Slicing Flank Steak

Using sharp knife, cut steak across grain, cutting at a slight angle.

Easy Grilled Steak Kabobs CALORIE SMART

PREP 35 min **TOTAL** 35 min • 4 servings

- 1 boneless beef top sirloin steak, 1 inch thick (1 lb)
- 1 large bell pepper (any color), cut into 16 pieces
- 16 medium fresh mushrooms
- 1 tablespoon chopped fresh or 1 teaspoon dried dill weed
- 1 tablespoon lemon juice
- 1 tablespoon olive or vegetable oil
- 1 tablespoon honey mustard
- ¼ teaspoon salt
- ¼ teaspoon pepper

1 Heat gas or charcoal grill. Cut beef into 24 (1-inch) cubes.

2 On each of 8 (10- to 12-inch) metal skewers, alternately thread beef, bell pepper and mushrooms, leaving about ¼ inch space between each piece. In small bowl, mix remaining ingredients.

3 Place kabobs on grill over medium heat. Cover grill; cook 15 to 18 minutes, turning and brushing 3 or 4 times with oil mixture, until beef is desired doneness and vegetables are tender.

1 Serving: Calories 220; Total Fat 8g (Saturated Fat 2g, Trans Fat 0g); Cholesterol 75mg; Sodium 200mg; Total Carbohydrate 4g (Dietary Fiber 1g, Sugars 2g); Protein 32g **Exchanges:** 1 Vegetable, 4 Very Lean Meat, 1 Fat **Carbohydrate Choices:** 0

Easy Grilled Chicken Kabobs Substitute boneless skinless chicken breasts or chicken thighs, cut into 1-inch pieces, for the steak. Cook until chicken is no longer pink in center.

Caramelized Beer-Onion and Bacon Burgers

Caramelized Beer-Onion and Bacon Burgers

PREP 1 hour 15 min **TOTAL** 1 hour 15 min • 4 burgers

- 8 slices bacon, crisply cooked, drippings reserved
- 2 large sweet onions, thinly sliced (about 1 ½ lb)
- 1 bottle (12 oz) pilsner-style beer
- 1½ lb lean (at least 80%) ground beef
- ½ teaspoon salt
- ¼ teaspoon pepper
- 4 slices (about ¾ oz each) Cheddar cheese
- 8 leaves red leaf lettuce or red romaine lettuce
- 4 slices tomato
- 4 kaiser rolls or crusty rolls, split

1 In 10-inch skillet, heat 1 tablespoon bacon drippings over medium-high heat. Add onions; cook about 15 minutes, stirring frequently.

2 Reserve ½ cup beer. Stir remaining beer into onions. Heat to boiling; reduce heat to medium and simmer uncovered, stirring occasionally, until onions are golden and liquid has evaporated, about 30 minutes. Cool. Coarsely chop 4 slices of the cooked bacon; set aside.

3 Heat charcoal or gas grill. Chop half of the onion mixture. In medium bowl, stir chopped onion mixture and bacon into beef. Add salt and pepper. Shape beef mixture into 4 large patties, thinner at center and thicker at edges.

4 Place patties on grill over medium heat. Cover grill; cook 11 to 13 minutes, turning once, until meat thermometer inserted in center of patties reads 160°F. After turning, brush reserved ½ cup beer on burgers, then top burgers with cheese. Cover grill; cook about 1 minute longer or until cheese is melted.

Grilled Corn on the Cob

Grilled corn is an easy and delicious side dish for any summer meal. Start with four ears of fresh corn (with husks) and butter and add your choice of toppings below. Grill and enjoy!

Heat gas or charcoal grill. In small bowl, mix ¼ cup softened butter with desired topping ingredients. Remove large outer husks from each ear of corn; gently pull back inner husks and remove silk. Spread each ear of corn with about 2 teaspoons topping; reserve any remaining topping. Pull husks up over ears.

Place corn on grill. Cook uncovered over medium heat 10 to 15 minutes, turning frequently, until tender. Let stand 5 minutes. Pull back or remove husks; spread corn with remaining topping.

1. Buffalo: 1 ounce crumbled blue cheese, 2 teaspoons red pepper sauce, 2 teaspoons finely chopped green onion.

2. Chili-Lime: ¼ teaspoon grated lime peel, 4 teaspoons lime juice, 1 to 2 teaspoons ground red chiles or chili powder.

3. Parmesan-Pepper: ¼ cup grated Parmesan cheese, ¼ teaspoon freshly ground black pepper.

4. Garlic-Cilantro: 2 teaspoons each finely chopped garlic and fresh cilantro leaves, ¼ teaspoon salt.

5. Fresh Herb: 2 tablespoons chopped fresh basil leaves, 1 tablespoon chopped fresh chives, ½ teaspoon garlic salt.

6. Lemon-Dill: 1½ teaspoons grated lemon peel, 1 tablespoon fresh lemon juice, 1 teaspoon chopped fresh dill weed, pinch of salt.

5 Place burgers on bun bottoms; top with lettuce leaves, tomato slices, and remaining caramelized onions. Cut remaining 4 slices bacon in half; crisscross 2 pieces on top of onions on each burger, and cover with bun tops.

1 Burger: Calories 620; Total Fat 35g (Saturated Fat 14g, Trans Fat 2g); Cholesterol 145 mg, Sodium 1090mg; Total Carbohydrate 30g (Dietary Fiber 2g, Sugars 5g); Protein 46g **Exchanges:** 1 Starch, ½ Other Carbohydrate, 2 Vegetable, 3 Medium-Fat Meat, 2½ Fat **Carbohydrate Choices:**2

Patty Melts with Smothered Onions CALORIE SMART

Although patty melts are usually made with ground beef, you could also make them with ground turkey or a mixture of ground pork and beef. Varying the cheese is also a nice option.

PREP 35 min **TOTAL** 35 min • 4 sandwiches

- 1 lb lean (at least 80%) ground beef
- ½ teaspoon salt
- ¼ teaspoon dried thyme leaves
- ¼ teaspoon dried oregano leaves
- ⅛ teaspoon pepper
- 2 teaspoons Dijon mustard
- 1 clove garlic, finely chopped
- 1 teaspoon olive or vegetable oil
- 2 medium red onions, thinly sliced, separated into rings
- ⅛ teaspoon salt
- Dash pepper
- 8 slices rye bread
- 4 slices (¾ oz each) Swiss cheese

1 Heat gas or charcoal grill. In medium bowl, mix beef, ½ teaspoon salt, the thyme, oregano, ⅛ teaspoon pepper, the mustard and garlic. Shape mixture into 4 patties, about ¾ inch thick.

2 In 8-inch skillet, heat oil over medium-high heat. Cook onions in oil 8 to 10 minutes, stirring frequently, until tender. Stir in ⅛ teaspoon salt and dash pepper; keep warm.

3 Place patties on grill over medium heat. Cover grill; cook 13 to 15 minutes, turning once, until meat thermometer inserted in center of patties reads 160°F. Add bread slices to side of

Patty Melts with Smothered Onions

grill for last 5 minutes of cooking, turning once, until lightly toasted.

4 Top patties with cheese. Cover grill; cook about 1 minute longer or until cheese is melted. Place each patty on 1 bread slice; top with onions and remaining bread.

1 Sandwich: Calories 440; Total Fat 22g (Saturated Fat 9g, Trans Fat 1g); Cholesterol 90mg; Sodium 880mg; Total Carbohydrate 31g (Dietary Fiber 3g, Sugars 5g); Protein 31g **Exchanges:** 2 Starch, 4 Medium-Fat Meat, 1 Fat **Carbohydrate Choices:** 2

Grilling Sausage and Bratwurst

Place uncooked sausage or bratwurst on heated grill over medium-low heat. Cover grill; cook 15 to 20 minutes, turning occasionally, until no longer pink in center. If flare-ups occur, move links to another part of grill.

Or, to cut down on flare-ups and to prevent overbrowning, cook bratwurst first in cider, beer or water and then brown them on the grill. For 4 bratwurst, heat 1½ cups cider, beer or water to boiling in 2-quart saucepan. Add links; reduce heat to low. Cover and simmer 15 minutes. Drain meat; grill over medium heat 6 minutes, turning once, until brown.

Grill fully cooked bratwurst or sausage over medium-low heat 7 to 10 minutes, turning frequently, until golden brown and heated through.

LEARN WITH BETTY Hamburgers

Perfect Hamburger: The center of this hamburger has reached a safe 160°F and is no longer pink.

Undercooked Hamburger: The center of this hamburger has not reached a safe temperature of 160°F and is too pink.

Overcooked Hamburger: This burger has been cooked over 160°F and is hard and dry.

Pork Ribs with Smoky Barbecue Sauce

PREP 30 min **TOTAL** 1 hr 40 min • 4 servings

RIBS

2 racks (2 lb each) pork back ribs (not cut into serving pieces)

1 tablespoon vegetable oil

4 teaspoons chopped fresh or 1½ teaspoons dried thyme leaves

SMOKY BARBECUE SAUCE

½ cup ketchup

¼ cup water

3 tablespoons packed brown sugar

2 tablespoons white vinegar

2 teaspoons celery seed

¼ teaspoon liquid smoke

¼ teaspoon red pepper sauce

1 Brush meaty side of ribs with oil; sprinkle with thyme. Heat gas or charcoal grill for indirect cooking. For two-burner gas grill, heat one burner to medium; place ribs, meaty side up, on unheated side. For one-burner gas grill, place ribs, meaty side up, on grill over low heat. For charcoal grill, move medium coals to edge of firebox; place ribs, meaty side up, on grill rack over drip pan.

2 Cover grill; cook 1 hour to 1 hour 10 minutes or until meat is tender and no longer pink next to bones. Meanwhile, in 1-quart saucepan, mix sauce ingredients; heat to boiling. Reduce heat; simmer uncovered 15 minutes, stirring occasionally. Brush sauce over pork 2 or 3 times during last 15 minutes of grilling. Heat any remaining sauce to boiling; boil and stir

1 minute. Cut ribs into 4 serving pieces. Serve with sauce.

1 Serving: Calories 960; Total Fat 70g (Saturated Fat 25g, Trans Fat 0g); Cholesterol 265mg; Sodium 550mg; Total Carbohydrate 18g (Dietary Fiber 0g, Sugars 17g); Protein 64g **Exchanges:** 1 Other Carbohydrate, 9 Medium-Fat Meat, 5 Fat **Carbohydrate Choices:** 1

SLOW-COOKER Directions Spray 5- to 6-quart slow cooker with cooking spray. Cut ribs into 4 serving pieces. Omit oil and thyme. Place ribs in slow cooker. Cover; cook on Low heat setting 6 hours. Place ribs on grill over medium heat. Brush with sauce. Cover grill; cook about 15 minutes.

Southwest Pork Ribs with Smoky Barbecue Sauce Omit oil and thyme. In small bowl, mix 2 tablespoons each regular chili powder or ancho chile pepper powder, ground cumin, smoked or regular paprika, garlic powder, salt and packed brown sugar. Rub desired amount of mixture into meaty side of ribs. Continue as directed. Store any remaining rub in airtight container in cool, dark location for up to 6 months.

Grilled Rosemary Lamb Chops CALORIE SMART • FAST

French-cut lamb chops are small and very tender. If these chops are not available, the recipe can also be made with lamb loin or sirloin chops. Both of these cuts will be a little meatier, so allow 1 or 2 chops per serving.

PREP 20 min **TOTAL** 20 min • 2 servings

1 tablespoon country-style Dijon mustard

1 tablespoon chopped fresh rosemary leaves

2 teaspoons honey

1 clove garlic, finely chopped

½ teaspoon salt

¼ teaspoon coarsely ground black pepper

6 French-cut baby lamb chops (1 to 1¼ inches thick)

1 Heat gas or charcoal grill. In small bowl, mix all ingredients except lamb. Spread mixture on one side of each lamb chop.

2 Place lamb, coated side up, on grill over medium heat. Cover grill; cook 12 to 15 minutes for medium doneness (160°F).

1 Serving (3 Chops): Calories 330; Total Fat 14g (Saturated Fat 5g, Trans Fat 0.5g); Cholesterol 140mg; Sodium 880mg; Total Carbohydrate 7g (Dietary Fiber 0g, Sugars 6g); Protein 43g **Exchanges:** ½ Other Carbohydrate, 6 Very Lean Meat, 2 Fat **Carbohydrate Choices:** ½

Pork Ribs with Smoky Barbecue Sauce

Grilled Rosemary Lamb Chops

Spicy Coconut-Curry Grilled Shrimp

Grilled Fish CALORIE SMART • FAST

PREP 20 min **TOTAL** 20 min • 4 servings

- 1½ lb fish steaks or 1 lb fish fillets (halibut, lake trout, mahimahi, marlin, red snapper, salmon, swordfish or tuna), about ¾ inch thick
- 2 tablespoons butter, melted
- 1 teaspoon salt
- ¼ teaspoon pepper
- 1 lemon, cut into 4 wedges

1 Heat gas or charcoal grill. Cut fish into 4 serving pieces if necessary. Brush fish with 1 tablespoon of the butter; sprinkle with salt and pepper.

2 Carefully brush oil on grill rack. Place fish on grill over medium heat (if fish fillets have skin, place skin side down). Cover grill; cook 10 to 14 minutes, brushing 2 or 3 times with remaining 1 tablespoon butter, until fish flakes easily with fork. Serve with lemon.

1 Serving: Calories 210; Total Fat 8g (Saturated Fat 4g, Trans Fat 0g); Cholesterol 105mg; Sodium 770mg; Total Carbohydrate 1g (Dietary Fiber 0g, Sugars 0g); Protein 32g **Exchanges:** 4½ Very Lean Meat, 1 Fat **Carbohydrate Choices:** 0

Herbed Grilled Fish Sprinkle fish with 1 teaspoon Italian seasoning with the salt and pepper. Substitute olive oil for butter.

Honey-Dijon Grilled Fish Mix 2 tablespoons each honey and Dijon mustard. Brush mixture on fish before grilling. Omit butter and salt.

Grilled Fish Tacos Wrap 4 flour tortillas (6 inch) in foil; place on grill during last 3 minutes the fish is cooking. Cook tortillas,

Removing Skin from Cooked Fish

Grab skin from tail end with tongs or fingers and gently peel off.

turning once, until warm. Cut grilled fish into serving-size pieces. Place fish on tortillas. Top each with 2 tablespoons Sweet-and-Sour Coleslaw (page 129) or desired coleslaw and 1 tablespoon chopped fresh mango or desired salsa. Fold tortillas over filling.

Spicy Coconut-Curry Grilled Shrimp CALORIE SMART

PREP 25 min **TOTAL** 55 min • 6 servings

- 18 bamboo skewers (6 inch)
- ¾ cup canned coconut milk (not cream of coconut)
- 2 teaspoons curry powder
- 2 teaspoons cornstarch
- 1 teaspoon honey
- ¼ teaspoon salt
- 54 uncooked medium shrimp (about 2 lb), thawed if frozen, peeled, deveined
- 2 tablespoons olive or vegetable oil
- 1 teaspoon red pepper sauce

1 Soak skewers in water at least 30 minutes before using to prevent burning. Meanwhile, heat gas or charcoal grill. In small microwavable bowl, mix coconut milk, curry powder, cornstarch, honey and salt. Microwave uncovered on High about 2 minutes, stirring every 30 seconds, until mixture bubbles and thickens; set aside.

2 In large bowl, place shrimp. Drizzle with oil and pepper sauce; toss to coat. Thread 3 shrimp on each skewer, leaving space between each.

3 Place kabobs on grill over medium heat. Cover grill; cook 4 to 6 minutes, turning once, until shrimp are pink. Serve with coconut-curry sauce.

1 Serving (3 Kabobs and 4 Teaspoons Sauce): Calories 210; Total Fat 11g (Saturated Fat 5g, Trans Fat 0g); Cholesterol 215mg; Sodium 370mg; Total Carbohydrate 5g (Dietary Fiber 1g, Sugars 2g); Protein 24g **Exchanges:** ½ Other Carbohydrate, 3½ Lean Meat **Carbohydrate Choices:** ½

SMOKING BASICS

To traditionalists, smoking is the original BBQ. Smoking is an unfussy form of outdoor cooking that uses low heat and hardwoods to impart smoky flavor to meat, poultry and fish. Smoking foods at home is easy with these tips.

TYPES OF SMOKERS

Smokers come in a variety of shapes and sizes. Regardless of the style, all smokers contain a firebox, water pan and grill racks.

To smoke, the food is placed on a grill rack, which is high above or next to the heat. A pan of water or other liquid (beer, fruit juice, wine, soda) rests between the heat source and the food. Water-soaked aromatic wood chunks, chips or shreds are added to the smoker. Foods are cooked very slowly in a dense fog created from the damp wood chips, infusing the characteristic flavor, moistness and tenderness smoked meats are known for. Foods best for smoking include ribs, beef brisket, roasts, poultry and fish.

SAFETY TIPS FOR SMOKING

Follow the manufacturer's directions for specific safety tips for your smoker and use these basic tips to ensure successful results:

- Keep the smoker away from buildings and from where people will frequently walk by, since the smoky aromas can last for hours.

- Use only completely thawed meats, poultry, fish or seafood. The heat inside the smoker is too low to thaw and cook the food safely.

- It's best to smoke foods when the outside temperature is 65°F or higher and there is little or no wind. Below 55°F, the smoker and food will not get hot enough to cook properly and may result in an additional 2 to 3 hours of cooking.

- Use long tongs and barbecue mitts to avoid burns when doing anything in the hot smoker.

- It's important throughout the cooking process to monitor the temperature inside the smoker (to ensure that the smoker stays between 225°F and 300°F) and of the meat; smoked meat can have a reddish appearance even when fully cooked. A digital oven-probe thermometer can stay in the food in the smoker and sound an alarm when the food has reached the correct temperature. This prevents you from having to open the smoker to check the temperature. If using an ovenproof meat thermometer, you'll have to open the smoker to check it, which can let heat out and increase the cook time. See Thermometers, page 17, for more information.

Wood chips for smoking, clockwise from top left: Hickory chips, mesquite chips, apple chips and cedar chips

Smoking on a Grill

Here's how to get smoked flavor on a grill.

- Cover 1 to 2 cups wood chips or shreds or 2 to 3 wood chunks with water, and soak at least 30 minutes; drain.

- Put soaked wood onto a piece of heavy-duty foil; seal tightly to form a pouch. Poke 6 to 8 slits in top of pouch with a sharp knife.

- Put pouch on grill rack or follow manufacturer's directions for adding wood chips. Cover grill and let pouch get hot enough to start smoking, about 10 minutes. Add food, leaving the pouch in the grill during cooking.

Smoked Beef Brisket

Smoked Hot and Spicy Ribs

Smoked Beef Brisket

CALORIE SMART

PREP 10 min **TOTAL** 5 hr 50 min • 12 servings

- 2 cups hickory wood chips

  BRISKET RUB
- 1 tablespoon coarse sea salt
- 1 tablespoon coarsely ground black pepper
- 1 tablespoon packed brown sugar
- 2 teaspoons onion powder
- 2 teaspoons garlic powder
- 1 teaspoon ground mustard
- 1 teaspoon smoked paprika
- 1 teaspoon chili powder

  BRISKET
- 1 fresh beef brisket (not corned beef), 3 lb

1 In large bowl, cover wood chips with water; soak 30 minutes. Drain. Prepare and heat smoker using wood chips and adding water to pan following manufacturer's directions.

2 In small bowl, mix all rub ingredients. Rub mixture onto all surfaces of beef.

3 Carefully brush oil on smoker rack. Place beef on rack in smoker. Cover and smoke 4 to 5 hours or until tender. If smoking stops, add additional wood chips through side door of smoker. Remove beef from smoker to cutting board or plate; cover and let stand 10 minutes. Cut beef across grain into thin slices.

1 Serving: Calories 170; Total Fat 7g (Saturated Fat 2.5g, Trans Fat 0g); Cholesterol 70mg; Sodium 1210mg; Total Carbohydrate 2g (Dietary Fiber 0g, Sugars 1g); Protein 24g **Exchanges:** 3½ Very Lean Meat, 1 Fat **Carbohydrate Choices:** 0

Oven-Baked Beef Brisket Heat oven to 325°F. Omit wood chips. Rub mix on beef. Place beef in 4-quart ovenproof Dutch oven or 3-quart casserole. Cover and bake 3 hours, turning beef over halfway through baking, until tender. Let stand 10 minutes before slicing.

Smoked Hot and Spicy Ribs

PREP 15 min **TOTAL** 5 hr 15 min • 6 servings

- 4 cups hickory wood chips

  HOT AND SPICY RUB
- 1 tablespoon garlic powder
- 1 tablespoon paprika
- 2 teaspoons ground red pepper (cayenne)
- 2 teaspoons dried thyme leaves, crushed
- 1 teaspoon salt
- 1 teaspoon black pepper

  RIBS
- 5 lb pork spareribs (not cut into serving pieces)
  Barbecue sauce, if desired (for homemade, see page 411)

1 In large bowl, cover wood chips with water; soak 30 minutes. Drain. Prepare and heat smoker using wood chips and adding water to water pan following manufacturer's directions.

2 In small bowl, mix rub ingredients. Cut rack of ribs in half to fit on smoker rack if necessary. Rub spice mixture into pork.

3 Place pork on rack in smoker. Cover smoker; cook 4 hours 30 minutes to 5 hours or until meat is tender and no longer pink next to bones. If smoking stops, add additional wood chips through side door of smoker. Cut ribs into serving pieces; serve with barbecue sauce.

1 Serving: Calories 580; Total Fat 45g (Saturated Fat 16g, Trans Fat 0g); Cholesterol 180mg; Sodium 530mg; Total Carbohydrate 2g (Dietary Fiber 0g, Sugars 0g); Protein 43g **Exchanges:** 6 Medium-Fat Meat, 3 Fat **Carbohydrate Choices:** 0

Removing Silverskin from Pork Ribs

Slide knife under silverskin; lift and loosen until you can grab it with a paper towel. Pull it off in one piece if possible.

CALORIE SMART = See Helpful Nutrition and Cooking Information, page 643   FAST = Ready in 30 minutes or less
EASY = Prep in 10 minutes or less **plus** five ingredients or less   LIGHTER = 25% fewer calories or grams of fat
MAKE AHEAD = Make-ahead directions   SLOW COOKER = Slow cooker directions

< Strawberry Freezer Jam, page 432

DO-IT-YOURSELF BASICS

DIY has come full circle, when you talk about food. Past generations made their own pickles, jellies and jams and canned vegetables because they had to. Today, the make-it-yourself movement in the kitchen has become, "We want to." While there are many options to choose from in our grocery stores, people are making their own versions of these foods for many reasons. Whether it's avoiding preservatives, controlling seasoning and salt levels, taking advantage of fresh, locally grown produce at its peak or making foods to share as gifts from your kitchen—nothing beats homemade.

CHOOSING CONTAINERS

When making your own food, choosing the right container is important so the food will be delicious when you are ready to enjoy it. Follow these general guidelines, or see individual recipes for specific requirements.

Freezer Jam/Chutney: Choose plastic freezer containers or glass preserving jars without curves under the neck of the jars. Be sure to choose a size that will leave enough room for the food to expand.

Fruit Butter: Choose wide-mouth glass preserving jars or plastic containers with tight-fitting lids.

Canned Jelly: Choose glass preserving jars (regular or wide mouth) with lids and bands.

Pickles: Choose glass preserving jars (regular or wide mouth) with lids and bands. For whole pickles, choose wide-mouth jars.

Pickled Vegetables: Choose nonreactive covered containers.

Vinegar: Choose glass bottles with a narrow neck and screw top, cork or two-piece canning lids. Sterilize bottles before using. See page 431.

Dried Vegetables: Choose containers with tight-fitting lids.

Seasoning Mixes/Dried Herbs: Choose small containers with tight-fitting lids.

Dessert/Beverage Mixes: Choose food-safe glass jars with screw-on lids to show off the layers or plastic containers with tight-fitting lids.

EATING LOCAL

Options for eating local may be all around you— it's knowing where to look and understanding what the offerings are that can help you make the best choices for yourself..

Farmers' Markets: Farmers from the area all bring their produce to sell at nearby markets.

U-Picks: Farms where you are allowed to come in and pick your own produce.

Farm Stands: Farmers set up stands along the side of the road or in store parking lots where their produce is brought in daily for purchase.

Food Co-ops: Grocery stores owned and controlled by their members, although you typically don't need to be a member to shop there. They usually specialize in natural foods and often offer local and organic foods.

Community-Supported Agriculture (CSA): You buy a "share" of the local farmer's produce in advance and then receive a weekly portion of fresh produce or other items.

Grocery Stores: Many grocery stores are getting on the fresh bandwagon, offering in-season locally grown produce.

Apple Butter CALORIE SMART

PREP 20 min **TOTAL** 4 hr 20 min • 4 cups

12	medium Granny Smith or other cooking apples (4 lb), peeled, cut into quarters
1½	cups packed brown sugar
1	tablespoon ground cinnamon
1	teaspoon ground allspice
1	teaspoon ground nutmeg
½	teaspoon ground cloves
1¼	cups apple juice
1	tablespoon lemon juice

1 In 4-quart Dutch oven or saucepan, mix all ingredients. Heat to boiling, stirring occasionally; reduce heat. Cover and simmer 1 hour.

2 Mash apples with potato masher or large fork. Simmer uncovered about 1 hour longer, stirring occasionally, until mixture is very thick. Cool about 2 hours.

3 Spoon into glass or plastic containers. Cover and store in refrigerator up to 3 weeks.

1 Tablespoon: Calories 40; Total Fat 0g (Saturated Fat 0g, Trans Fat 0g); Cholesterol 0mg; Sodium 0mg; Total Carbohydrate 9g (Dietary Fiber 0g, Sugars 8g); Protein 0g **Exchanges:** ½ Fruit **Carbohydrate Choices:** ½

SLOW-COOKER Directions Reduce apple juice to ½ cup. Spray 5- to 6-quart slow cooker with cooking spray. In slow cooker, mix all ingredients. Cover; cook on Low heat setting 8 to 10 hours or until apples are very tender. Mash apples with potato masher or large fork. Cook uncovered 1 to 2 hours longer, stirring occasionally, until very thick.

Apple-Cranberry Chutney

CALORIE SMART

Serve the chutney with roast turkey, ham or pork. Or for a quick appetizer, spoon chutney over a block of cream cheese and serve with crackers.

PREP 15 min **TOTAL** 3 hr • 2 cups

2	medium cooking apples, chopped (2 cups)
2	cups fresh or frozen cranberries
1	medium red bell pepper, chopped (1 cup)
1	small onion, finely chopped (⅓ cup)
¾	cup packed brown sugar
½	cup golden raisins, dried cranberries or dried cherries
½	cup white vinegar
1½	teaspoons finely chopped gingerroot
1	clove garlic, finely chopped

1 In 2-quart saucepan, mix all ingredients. Heat to boiling, stirring occasionally; reduce heat. Cover and simmer 30 minutes.

2 Uncover; simmer about 15 minutes longer, stirring occasionally, until mixture has thickened and fruit is tender. Cool about 2 hours.

3 Spoon into glass or plastic containers; cover. Store in refrigerator up to 2 weeks or in freezer up to 2 months.

¼ Cup: Calories 150; Total Fat 0g (Saturated Fat 0g, Trans Fat 0g); Cholesterol 0mg; Sodium 10mg; Total Carbohydrate 36g (Dietary Fiber 2g, Sugars 31g); Protein 0g **Exchanges:** 1 Fruit, 1½ Other Carbohydrate **Carbohydrate Choices:** 2½

Pear-Cranberry Chutney Substitute 2 medium firm, ripe pears, chopped (2 cups), for the apples.

Apple Butter

Apple-Cranberry Chutney

Peach-Jalapeño Jam (see page 436)

CALORIE SMART

PREP 1 hr 10 min **TOTAL** 25 hr 55 min • 6 half-pints

- 6 (½ pint) glass preserving jars with lids and bands
- 4 cups finely chopped, peeled peaches (about 3 pounds)
- ¼ cup fresh lemon juice
- ½ teaspoon butter
- 1 package (1¾ oz) powdered fruit pectin
- 3 cups regular granulated sugar
- ⅓ cup diced jalapeño chiles*

1 Fill boiling water canner half full with water; heat until water is simmering. Wash jars as directed in Preparing Jars for Canning, page 431.

2 In 4-quart saucepan, mix peaches, lemon juice, butter (helps prevent foaming) and pectin, stirring until pectin is dissolved. Heat to boiling, stirring frequently. Add sugar all at once; mix well. Stir in chiles. Heat to a full rolling boil that covers the entire surface, not just the edges of the pan, stirring constantly. Boil and stir 1 minute; remove from heat.

3 Quickly skim off any foam. Immediately ladle or pour into jars, leaving ½ inch headspace. Drain flat lids well. Wipe rims and threads of jars. Place flat lids on jars and screw bands on tightly to seal. Place jars on elevated rack in canner; lower rack into canner. To process jam safely, water must cover jars by 1 to 2 inches; add additional boiling water if necessary. Cover. Heat to boiling; continue boiling 10 minutes. Turn off heat. Remove canner lid. Let jars stand in canner 5 minutes.

4 Carefully remove jars with canning jar lifter or heavy duty tongs and place upright on dry towel. Cool completely. After 24 hours, check seal on cooled jars by pressing middle of lids with finger. If the lids spring back, jars are not sealed and must be stored in the refrigerator. Store completely sealed, unopened jars in a cool, dry place up to 1 year. Once opened, store in refrigerator up to 3 weeks.

*If chiles are very hot try using ¼ cup.

1 Tablespoon: Calories 30; Total Fat 0g (Saturated Fat 0g, Trans Fat 0g); Cholesterol: 0mg; Sodium 0mg; Total Carbohydrate 7g (Dietary Fiber 0g, Sugars 7g); Protein 0g **Exchanges:** ½ Other Carbohydrate **Carbohydrate Choices:** ½

Rosemary Peach Jam Omit jalapeño chiles. Add three 5-inch sprigs fresh rosemary with sugar in Step 2. Discard rosemary before ladling jam into jars.

Spiced Peach Jam Omit jalapeño chiles. Add 2 cinnamon sticks and 6 whole cloves with pectin in Step 2. Discard cinnamon sticks and cloves before ladling jam into jars.

Sweet Tomato Jam   CALORIE SMART

Try this sweet jam made with fresh tomatoes on crostini or grilled cheese, with hummus and pita chips or sandwiched between shortbread cookies.

PREP 20 min **TOTAL** 1 hr 50 min • 2 cups

- 12 medium ripe tomatoes, seeded, chopped (6 cups)
- ½ cup sugar
- ¼ cup cider vinegar*
- ¼ cup olive oil
- 1 teaspoon salt
- ½ teaspoon coarsely ground black pepper

1 In 12-inch skillet, heat all ingredients to boiling. Reduce heat to medium-low. Simmer uncovered 45 to 60 minutes, stirring occasionally, until thickened and almost all liquid is absorbed. Remove from heat; cool 30 minutes.

2 Spoon into clean jars or nonmetal containers; cover with tight-fitting lids. Refrigerate up to 1 week or freeze up to 3 months.

* Red or white wine vinegar or balsamic vinegar can be substituted for the cider vinegar.

1 Tablespoon: Calories 40; Total Fat 2g (Saturated Fat 0g, Trans Fat 0g); Cholesterol 0mg; Sodium 75mg; Total Carbohydrate 5g (Dietary Fiber 0g, Sugars 4g); Protein 0g **Exchanges:** ½ Other Carbohydrate, ½ Fat **Carbohydrate Choices:** ½

Sweet Tomato Jam

Learn to CAN PEACH-JALAPEÑO JAM

Making homemade jam isn't difficult, but it does require close attention to directions from trusted recipes, so that the end results are safe to store and eat. Food canning techniques have changed over the years, so it is best be up to date with the latest techniques and recipes, rather than processing Grandma's famous jam using her outdated instructions. If done incorrectly, you can put your family and friends at risk of ingesting dangerous bacteria in the food you processed. Follow the general guidelines on page 431 and specific directions in recipes (see page 435 for Peach-Jalapeño Jam recipe).

How to "Put Up" Jam Successfully

- Use the proper canning techniques. See page 431 for more information.

- Inspect and wash jars; keep warm until ready to fill. Repurpose jars that have defects.

- Skim foam from jam mixture. Foam forms when cooking jam mixture; skim and discard it for the best-looking jam and so it won't affect headspace.

- Fill jars as directed in recipe; do not over-fill. Proper amount of headspace is necessary to ensure no mold growth.

- Wipe rims and threads. Prevent spoilage during storage by wiping off any jam that might be on the rim of jar or on the threads.

Jelly, Jam or Preserves?

Jelly is the clear, bright condiment made with fruit juice, sugar and possibly pectin to help it gel. It will hold its shape when turned out of its container. **Jam** uses crushed or chopped fruits and is usually less thick than jelly. **Conserves** are jams made with a variety of fruit and nuts. **Preserves** are like jam only usually with larger pieces of fruit left intact. **Marmalade** is preserves with the addition of fruit rind.

- Cover with new lids. New lids have fresh seals, which are necessary for proper processing to get a vacuum seal. Do not reuse lids.

- Screw on bands securely. Bands can be reused. Tighten enough to secure lid well but do not over-tighten. Bands may loosen during processing but can be retightened after the processed jam has cooled.

- Place jars on rack in canner. Do not put jars directly on bottom of pan. Jars need water boiling all around them to process properly and could potentially break if processed directly on the bottom of the pan.

- Have enough water in the canner. There should be enough water to cover the jars 1 inch above the tops. Add additional boiling water, if necessary.

- Cover and boil for the full time given. Follow directions exactly, making sure water is fully boiling, pan is covered and jars are being processed the full time called for in the recipe. This kills organisms that could grow in the food and/or on the jar when stored.

- Remove and cool jars carefully. Jars can slip and break if not taken out of boiling water with large canning or heavy-duty tongs. To prevent jars from cracking, let them cool on a towel rather than directly on a cold countertop.

- Check seals after 24 hours. Press on center of each lid with finger. If lid springs back, it didn't seal properly. Reprocess any that didn't seal well or refrigerate and use within 1 month. Tighten any bands that have loosened.

- Store jars properly. Properly sealed, unopened jars can be stored in a cool, dry place up to 1 year. Once jars are opened, they should be stored in the refrigerator and used within 1 month.

Creative Uses for Peach-Jalapeño Jam (page 435)

Now that you've got fresh jam on hand, here are some terrific ways to use it:

Meat Glaze Brush it on chicken, turkey, pork or beef during cooking for a flavorful glaze. Brush it on during the last 15 to 20 minutes of cooking to prevent burning.

Quick Spread Spoon it over a block of softened cream cheese to serve with crackers as a quick appetizer or snack.

Zesty BBQ Sauce Heat 1 cup barbecue sauce in a small saucepan over medium-low heat, stirring occasionally. Stir in 3 to 4 tablespoons jam until melted. Add more if desired.

Sweet-and-Savory Yogurt Top plain yogurt with a spoonful of jam and roasted pumpkin seeds for a breakfast or snack with kick.

Savory Bread Sidekick Offer the jam with corn muffins or any bread or rolls instead of butter for an unexpected side dish.

Spicy Peach Vinaigrette Prepare Raspberry Vinaigrette (page 137), except use white wine vinegar and Peach-Jalapeño Jam.

Seafood Sauce Serve with crab cakes or coconut shrimp or in place of cocktail sauce with cold cooked shrimp.

Easy Quesadillas Place 4 (8-inch) tortillas on cookie sheet; spread with about 1 tablespoon jam. Top each with 2 tablespoons shredded Monterey Jack cheese and 1 tablespoon chopped walnuts; top with another tortilla and press lightly. Bake at 375°F 8 to 10 minutes or until cheese begins to melt and tortillas begin to brown.

Add sugar and pectin and bring to a full rolling boil.

Quickly ladle into sterilized jars.

After processing, carefully remove jars from water.

Check seals after 24 hours.

Heirloom Recipe and New Twist

It may be strange to call pickles fresh, but try our Easy Refrigerator Pickles, and you'll quickly see why homemade pickles are so special. Our twist recipe is geared for those who love foods with kicked-up flavor—but we didn't stop with pickles. While we were at it, we pickled a variety of veggies just for fun.

HEIRLOOM	**NEW TWIST**

Easy Refrigerator Pickles

CALORIE SMART

When choosing cucumbers for pickles, pick out the smaller ones, and pickle them soon after buying or harvesting.

PREP 10 min **TOTAL** 24 hr 10 min • 6 cups

  6 cups thinly sliced unpeeled unwaxed cucumbers

  2 small onions, sliced

  1 medium carrot, thinly sliced (½ cup)

1¾ cups sugar

  2 tablespoons salt

  1 tablespoon chopped fresh or 1 teaspoon dried dill weed

  1 cup white or cider vinegar

1 In 2½- or 3-quart glass container, layer cucumbers, onions and carrot.

2 In medium bowl, stir remaining ingredients until sugar is dissolved; pour over vegetables. Cover and refrigerate at least 24 hours before serving. Store covered in refrigerator up to 2 weeks.

¼ **Cup:** Calories 70; Total Fat 0g (Saturated Fat 0g, Trans Fat 0g); Cholesterol 0mg; Sodium 590mg; Total Carbohydrate 16g (Dietary Fiber 0g, Sugars 16g); Protein 0g **Exchanges:** 1 Other Carbohydrate **Carbohydrate Choices:** 1

Spicy Pickled Vegetables

CALORIE SMART

PREP 15 min **TOTAL** 24 hr 15 min • 6 cups

  3 cups white wine vinegar

1½ cups sugar

  2 cloves garlic, finely chopped

  1 medium head cauliflower (1½ lb), separated into small florets (6 cups)

  ½ lb fresh green beans, trimmed

  2 medium carrots, cut into 3x¼x¼-inch pieces (1½ cups)

  2 jalapeño chiles, cut lengthwise into quarters, seeded

1 In 1-quart saucepan, heat vinegar, sugar and garlic over medium heat just until mixture begins to simmer and sugar is dissolved. Remove from heat; cool 5 minutes.

2 Meanwhile, in 2 (1-quart) jars or glass containers, layer cauliflower, beans, carrots and chiles, dividing evenly between jars. Pour vinegar mixture over vegetables. Cover and refrigerate at least 24 hours before serving but no longer than 2 weeks.

¼ **Cup:** Calories 70; Total Fat 0g (Saturated Fat 0g, Trans Fat 0g); Cholesterol 0mg; Sodium 15mg; Total Carbohydrate 16g (Dietary Fiber 1g, Sugars 14g); Protein 1g **Exchanges:** 1 Other Carbohydrate, ½ Vegetable **Carbohydrate Choices:** 1

Easy Refrigerator Pickles

Spicy Pickled Vegetables

Garlic Dill Pickles CALORIE SMART

PREP 1 hr 20 min **TOTAL** 1 week 2 hr • 4 quarts

- 4 (1-quart) canning jars with lids
- 7 pints unwaxed pickling cucumbers, 24 to 30 (3-inch) cucumbers
- 12 to 16 sprigs fresh dill weed
- 12 cloves garlic, peeled
- 4 slices (½ inch thick) onion
- 4 teaspoons mustard seed
- 4 cups water
- 2 cups cider or white vinegar
- 2 tablespoons pickling or canning salt*

1 Fill boiling water canner half full with water; heat until water is simmering. Wash jars as directed in Preparing Jars for Canning (page 431).

2 Wash cucumbers; cut off stems and blossom ends. Pack cucumbers loosely in jars. To each jar, add 3 or 4 dill weed sprigs, 3 garlic cloves, 1 onion slice and 1 teaspoon mustard seed. In large saucepan, heat water, vinegar and salt to boiling. Pour into jars, leaving ½ inch headspace.

3 Drain flat lids well. Wipe rims and threads of jars. Place flat lids on jars and screw bands on tightly to seal. Place jars on elevated rack in canner; lower rack into canner. To process pickles safely, water must cover jars by 1 to 2 inches; add additional boiling water if necessary. Cover. Heat to boiling; continue boiling 10 minutes. Carefully remove jars with canning jar lifter or heavy-duty tongs and place upright on towel. Cool completely.

4 After 24 hours, check seal on cooled jars by pressing middles of lids with finger. If the lids spring back, jars are not sealed and must be stored in refrigerator. Store completely sealed, unopened jars in a cool, dry place up to 1 year (let stand at least 1 week to blend flavors before serving). Once opened, store in refrigerator up to 3 weeks.

* Pickling or canning salt, available in most grocery stores, is preferred for making pickles. Table salt can cause the brine to become cloudy and darken the pickles.

1 Pickle: Calories 5; Total Fat 0g (Saturated Fat 0g, Trans Fat 0g); Cholesterol 0mg; Sodium 220mg; Total Carbohydrate 1g (Dietary Fiber 0g, Sugars 0g); Protein 0g **Exchanges:** Free **Carbohydrate Choices:** 0

Pickled Tarragon Baby Carrots CALORIE SMART • EASY

PREP 10 min **TOTAL** 24 hr 10 min • 3½ cups

- 1 bag (1 lb) ready-to-eat baby-cut carrots
- ½ cup tarragon vinegar
- 1 tablespoon chopped fresh or 1 teaspoon dried tarragon leaves
- 1 tablespoon olive or vegetable oil
- ¼ teaspoon coarsely ground black pepper

1 In 3-quart saucepan, heat 2 quarts water to boiling. Add carrots; cook 3 minutes. Meanwhile, in 1- to 1½-quart heatproof glass or plastic container, mix remaining ingredients. Drain carrots; immediately stir into mixture in container.

2 Cover and refrigerate 24 hours to blend flavors, stirring once, before serving. Store covered in refrigerator up to 3 months.

¼ Cup: Calories 25; Total Fat 1g (Saturated Fat 0g, Trans Fat 0g); Cholesterol 0mg; Sodium 25mg; Total Carbohydrate 3g (Dietary Fiber 1g, Sugars 2g); Protein 0g **Exchanges:** ½ Vegetable **Carbohydrate Choices:** 0

Spicy Pickled Carrots Cook 1 sliced jalapeño chile with the carrots. Substitute distilled white vinegar for the tarragon vinegar and cilantro for the fresh tarragon.

Pickled Green Beans Substitute 1 pound trimmed fresh green beans for the carrots. Add 1 clove finely chopped garlic with the beans. Substitute white wine vinegar for the tarragon vinegar and thyme for the fresh tarragon.

Packing Cucumbers

Wash cucumbers; cut off stems and blossom ends.

Pack cucumbers loosely in jars. Add dill, garlic, onion and mustard seed to jars.

Why Use Unwaxed Cucumbers?

It's important to use unwaxed cucumbers because the brine can't get through the wax to pickle the flesh. Waxing cucumbers preserves them for transportation to the grocery store. Unwaxed cucumbers can be found at farmers' markets and roadside stands.

Pickled Beets

Jalapeño-Garlic Pickled Green Beans

Pickled Beets CALORIE SMART

Classic pickled beets got a bit of an update with less sugar in the brine. They are still sweetly delicious. Try them on a salad with toasted walnuts and crumbles of a creamy Gorgonzola or blue cheese.

PREP 1 hr 10 min **TOTAL** 25 hr 10 min • 4 pints (8 cups)

- 3 lb small to medium beets (1½ to 2½ inch)
- 1¼ cups cider vinegar
- ¾ cup water
- ¾ cup sugar
- ½ teaspoon whole cloves
- ½ teaspoon salt
- 2 (3-inch) cinnamon sticks

1 Cut off all but 2 inches of beet tops. Wash beets; leave whole with root ends attached. Place in 4-quart saucepan. Add water to cover. Heat to boiling; boil uncovered, 20 to 30 minutes or just until beets are tender. Check smaller beets for doneness first. Let beets cool until easy to handle, about 30 minutes. Peel beets and cut off root ends. Cut beets into wedges, 1½-inch chunks or ¼-inch slices.

2 In 3-quart stainless steel saucepan, heat vinegar, water, sugar, cloves, salt and cinnamon sticks to boiling. Reduce heat; simmer 5 minutes. Add beets; heat to boiling. Remove from heat; discard cinnamon sticks.

3 Spoon hot beets and liquid into 4 (1-pint) glass preserving jars, leaving ½ inch headspace. Place flat lids on jars and screw bands on tightly to seal. Let stand at room temperature to cool completely. Refrigerate at least 24 hours or up to 3 months. Flavor will intensify the longer they are refrigerated. Or, to process for canning, see Garlic Dill Pickles (page 441).

¼ **Cup:** Calories 25; Total Fat 0g(Saturated Fat 0g, Trans Fat 0g); Cholesterol 0mg; Sodium 45mg; Total Carbohydrate 5g (Dietary Fiber 1g, Sugars 4g); Protein 0g **Exchanges:** ½ Vegetable **Carbohydrate Choices:** ½

Jalapeño-Garlic Pickled Green Beans CALORIE SMART

PREP 30 min **TOTAL** 24 hr 30 min • 4 pints (8 cups)

- 2 lb fresh green or yellow wax beans, trimmed
- 2¾ cups white vinegar
- 1½ cups water
- ¼ cup sugar
- 1 teaspoon canning and pickling salt
- 12 slices (¼inch) red or green jalapeño chiles
- 8 cloves garlic, peeled

1 Cut beans into 4-inch lengths to fit into jars. In 4-quart stainless steel saucepan, heat vinegar, water, sugar and salt to boiling. Add beans, pushing them into liquid; heat to boiling. Boil 1 minute. Place strainer over large glass bowl. Drain beans in strainer over bowl, reserving liquid.

2 Pack beans upright into 4 (1-pint) glass preserving jars. To each jar, add 3 slices jalapeño and 2 cloves garlic. Pour hot liquid into jars, leaving ½ inch headspace. Make sure all beans are submerged in liquid. Place flat lids on jars and screw bands on tightly to seal. Let stand at room temperature to cool completely. Refrigerate at least 24 hours up to 3 months. Flavor will intensify the longer the beans are refrigerated. Or, to process for canning, see Garlic Dill Pickles (page 441).

¼ **Cup:** Calories 15; Total Fat 0g (Saturated Fat 0g, Trans Fat 0g); Cholesterol 0mg; Sodium 30mg; Total Carbohydrate 2g (Dietary Fiber 0g, Sugars 1g); Protein 0g **Exchanges:** Free **Carbohydrate Choices:** 0

Lemon-Dill Pickled Green Beans Make as directed, except omit jalapeño and garlic. To each jar, add 2 (⅛-inch) strips lemon peel and 4 sprigs fresh dill weed. Continue as directed.

Kimchi CALORIE SMART

A daikon radish is a large, long, Asian radish with a fresh, sweet flavor and moist, crunchy texture. The flesh is white; the skin is white or black. Look for firm, unwrinkled radishes.

PREP 20 min **TOTAL** 5 days • 3 cups

- 1 large head Chinese (napa) cabbage (2 lb)
- ¼ cup non-iodized coarse sea salt or kosher salt*
- 1 tablespoon red pepper flakes
- 1 teaspoon finely chopped gingerroot
- 1 teaspoon sugar
- 4 cloves garlic, finely chopped
- 2 tablespoons fish sauce or water
- ½ lb daikon radish, peeled, cut into 2x¼-inch strips (2¼ cups)
- 2 medium carrots, peeled, cut into 2x¼-inch strips (1 cup)
- 4 medium green onions, cut into ¼-inch slices

1 Cut cabbage lengthwise into quarters; remove core pieces. Cut quarters crosswise into 1-inch strips. Place cabbage in large bowl. Sprinkle with salt. Gently rub salt into cabbage until cabbage starts to soften just a little. Cover cabbage with water. Place plate on top and weight with something heavy so it doesn't float. Let stand 1 hour.

2 Place the cabbage in large colander to drain. Rinse very thoroughly for several minutes, turning the cabbage over so you are rinsing all of the cabbage leaves to remove excess salt. Drain. Rinse out and dry the bowl used for the soaking the cabbage. Place cabbage in bowl; set aside.

3 In small bowl, mix pepper flakes, gingerroot, sugar, garlic and fish sauce. Stir until sugar

is dissolved. Working in batches, lift cabbage above bowl and squeeze cabbage over the bowl to catch the juices. Return cabbage to bowl with juices. Add radish, carrots and onions. Add pepper flake mixture; toss to coat, making sure mixture is thoroughly coated (gloved hands may work more easily).

4 Spoon into glass or plastic container with tight-fitting lid, leaving 1 inch headspace. Press the kimchi into the container with the back of a spoon, allowing the brine to rise to the top covering the vegetables. Cover. Let stand at room temperature 3 to 5 days to ferment and develop flavor. You may see bubbles develop inside the container. Check the kimchi every day to make sure the vegetables are submerged in the brine. If not, push the vegetable mixture down with the back of a spoon.

5 The kimchi can be tasted during this period, and if you like the level of fermentation, place the jar in the refrigerator. Store kimchi tightly covered in the refrigerator up to 3 months.

* Iodized salt can interfere with fermentation; non-iodized salt is readily available.

1 Tablespoon: Calories 5; Total Fat 0g (Saturated Fat 0g, Trans Fat 0g); Cholesterol 0mg; Sodium 220mg; Total Carbohydrate 1g (Dietary Fiber 0g, Sugars 0g); Protein 0g **Exchanges:** Free **Carbohydrate Choices:** 0

Making Kimchi

Place a plate with something heavy on top to keep cabbage submerged in water.

Use a spoon to press kimchi ingredients into container with tight-fitting lid, leaving 1 inch of headspace.

Fermenting Vegetables

Until a few generations ago, fermenting was a common practice for food preservation. Now both home cooks and small restaurateurs are getting interested in fermenting their own vegetables. Why? Fermented vegetables take on new flavors, adding interest—they are usually tarter in flavor than their raw predecessors. They also are easier to digest than raw and may be helpful for overall digestive health.

Just about any raw vegetable can be safely fermented at home, if done properly. They can actually be safer to eat than raw vegetables because the fermentation process hunts down and kills any harmful bacteria that may be present in the raw vegetables.

While there's no veggie you can't ferment, green tomatoes, string beans, cucumbers, cabbage, daikon radishes, parsnips and okra are the most flavorful choices for fermenting. Some vegetables, due to their biological makeup, end up with an undesirable flavor when fermented. Kale, for example, has a high chlorophyll content that gives the fermented version a flavor most people won't enjoy.

Ketchup CALORIE SMART

Choose fleshy, ripe tomatoes for best flavor and consistency. Beefsteak varieties are an excellent choice for this iconic condiment.

PREP 40 min **TOTAL** 2 hr 10 min • 5¼ cups

- 2 tablespoons vegetable oil
- 1 large onion, chopped (1 cup)
- 3 stalks celery, chopped (1 cup)
- 8 lb ripe tomatoes, coarsely chopped
- 1 cup cider vinegar
- 4 teaspoons salt
- 2 teaspoons pepper
- 1 teaspoon chili powder
- ½ teaspoon ground coriander
- ½ teaspoon ground cloves
- ½ cup sugar

1 In 8-quart Dutch oven or stockpot, heat oil over medium heat. Cook onion and celery in oil until tender, stirring occasionally. Add remaining ingredients except sugar. Heat to boiling; reduce heat. Cook uncovered until tomatoes are completely softened, stirring occasionally, about 20 minutes.

2 Working in batches, place tomato mixture in blender or food processor. Cover and blend until smooth. Strain through fine-mesh strainer, pressing firmly with back of spoon until only seeds remain. Return each pureed batch to Dutch oven.

3 Add sugar to tomato mixture. Heat to boiling; reduce heat to medium-low. Cook uncovered 1 hour to 1 hour 30 minutes or until desired thickness. Cool to room temperature. Spoon into half-pint jars or plastic containers; cover with lids. Refrigerate up to 6 months or freeze up to 1 year.

1 Tablespoon: Calories 20; Total Fat 0g (Saturated Fat 0g, Trans Fat 0g); Cholesterol 0mg; Sodium 115mg; Total Carbohydrate 3g (Dietary Fiber 0g, Sugars 2g); Protein 0g **Exchanges:** Free **Carbohydrate Choices:** 0

Straining Ketchup Mixture

Strain pureed mixture in fine-mesh strainer, pressing with back of spoon until only the seeds remain.

Drying Fresh Herbs

Drying herbs while in the peak of growing season is a way to save money and enjoy their flavors throughout the year. For best flavor, pick herbs in the morning, after the dew has dried. Dry the herbs until the leaves are crisp enough that they will crumble in your hands. Store dried herbs as whole leaves in small containers with tight-fitting lids in a cool, dry place. For the best flavor, crumble the leaves when you are ready to use them. Dried herbs are stronger in flavor than fresh, so use about half the amount of the fresh herb called for; if recipe calls for a tablespoon of a fresh herb, substitute 1 teaspoon dried.

Sturdy Herbs

Parsley, rosemary, sage, summer savory and thyme

Pick herbs on the stems for easy drying. Bundle the stems and secure the bottoms with a rubber band. Hang and let dry indoors for best color and flavor. Remove leaves from stems; discard stems.

Tender Herbs

Basil, lemon balm, mint, oregano and tarragon

These herbs have a high moisture content and will mold if not dried quickly. Prepare as directed above for sturdy herbs, except put small bunches inside paper lunch bags; tie stems and bag with rubber band. Cut holes in bags to allow air to circulate. Hang in place where there are air currents, so they can dry quickly. The bags will catch any leaves or seeds that fall. In humid areas, dry mint and bay leaves only (remove stems) in a single layer, with no leaves touching each other, on paper towel–lined trays. Cover with another layer of paper towel. To dry a large quantity, stack layers of leaves in this manner with paper towels in between the layers.

Freezing Fresh Herbs

Another way to preserve herbs is to freeze them while at their peak freshness to use whenever you like.

Sturdy Herbs

Place the chopped leaves of sturdy herbs (see above) in ice cube trays or mini muffin cups. Cover with water, broth or olive or vegetable oil. Cover and freeze until firm. Place frozen cubes in a resealable freezer plastic bag (pressing all the air out) to add to simmering soups, stews or sauces.

Tender Herbs

Freeze leaves in a single layer on a cookie sheet and then transfer to a freezer bag, as directed above. Alternatively for basil or cilantro leaves, you could make pesto (see page 456) and freeze it in ice cube trays or mini muffin cups, as for sturdy herbs.

Crystallized Ginger CALORIE SMART

Homemade crystallized ginger (candied ginger) is as easy to make as boiling water and is significantly cheaper than store-bought. It's delicious in scones, cookies and cakes, to name a few uses, and is perfect for gift giving.

PREP 20 min **TOTAL** 25 hr 10 min • 2½ cups

- 1¼ cups water
- 1¼ cups sugar
- 1 lb gingerroot, peeled, cut into ⅛-inch slices (about 2½ cups)
- ½ to ⅔ cup sugar

1 In 2-quart saucepan, heat water and 1¼ cups sugar to boiling. Stir constantly until sugar is dissolved. Add gingerroot; return to boiling. Reduce heat; simmer uncovered 25 to 30 minutes, stirring occasionally, until gingerroot is tender.

2 Place waxed paper, plastic wrap or foil under cooling rack. With slotted spoon, remove gingerroot from liquid and place in single layer on cooling rack.* Let stand 20 minutes or until completely cool.

3 Line 15x10x1-inch pan with paper towels. Place ½ cup sugar in 1-gallon resealable food-storage plastic bag. Using tongs, place ginger pieces in bag. Seal and toss until ginger is thoroughly coated with sugar, adding remaining sugar if needed. Arrange ginger pieces in single layer in pan. Let stand uncovered at room temperature 24 hours to dry. Store in tightly covered container at room temperature up to 2 weeks, or refrigerate up to 3 months or freeze up to 6 months.

* After removing the gingerroot, you can continue to cook the liquid until it thickens and becomes syrupy. Mix the syrup with chilled club soda or seltzer for homemade ginger ale, add to cold or hot tea or drizzle over ice cream.

1 Teaspoon: Calories 10; Total Fat 0g (Saturated Fat 0g, Trans Fat 0g); Cholesterol 0mg; Sodium 0mg; Total Carbohydrate 2g (Dietary Fiber 0g, Sugars 1g); Protein 0g **Exchanges:** Free **Carbohydrate Choices:** 0

Oven-Dried Tomatoes

CALORIE SMART • EASY

Plum tomatoes work best for drying because they are thick-fleshed with few seeds. Regular tomatoes can be used but may take longer to dry.

PREP 10 min **TOTAL** 12 hr 10 min • 12 servings

- 24 plum (Roma) tomatoes

1 Heat oven to 200°F. Rinse tomatoes under cold running water and remove stems; drain on paper towels. Cut each tomato lengthwise in half. Using small spoon, scoop out and discard seeds.

2 Place tomato halves, cut sides down, in single layer on broiler rack. Place larger halves on outer edges of rack for even drying.

3 Dry in oven 6 to 12 hours, turning once after 4 hours, or until tomatoes are shriveled, dry to the touch and very chewy in texture. Edges may be crisp, but tomatoes should not be crisp in center; they should be somewhat pliable. Check after 6 hours and remove any smaller tomatoes that have dried. Tomatoes will be dark red and some pieces may have brown or dark spots.

4 Remove from oven and cool completely. Store in tightly covered container in cool, dark location. To rehydrate, place tomatoes in small bowl. Cover with hot or boiling water. Let stand 15 to 30 minutes or until softened.

1 Serving (2 Tomatoes): Calories 20; Total Fat 0g (Saturated Fat 0g, Trans Fat 0g); Cholesterol 0mg; Sodium 5mg; Total Carbohydrate 4g (Dietary Fiber 1g, Sugars 3g); Protein 1g **Exchanges:** Free **Carbohydrate Choices:** 0

Making Crystallized Ginger

Place sugar mixture–soaked ginger slices on cooling rack until cool.

Toss cooled ginger with sugar in sealed bag until ginger is thoroughly coated.

Drying Tomatoes

Cut each tomato in half lengthwise; remove seeds with small spoon.

Place tomato halves, cut side down, on broiler rack.

Natural Homemade Food Color

Making homemade natural food color is as easy as turning to the produce, juice and vegetable aisle in your grocery store. The colors are more muted and subtle, and it takes a bit of trial and error to get the look you want, but it's a fun experiment along the way!

FRESH BERRY-BASED (MAUVE, PINK, PURPLE)

1 cup blackberries, raspberries or strawberries

FRESH VEGETABLE-BASED (GREEN)

1 cup firmly packed fresh curly parsley or small spinach leaves

3 to 4 tablespoons water

FRESH VEGETABLE-BASED (GREEN, MAUVE, PURPLE)

3 cups shredded or chopped red cabbage

4 cups water

½ teaspoon baking soda

JUICE-BASED (ORANGE, PALE YELLOW, PEACH, PINK, PURPLE)

Frozen (thawed) grape juice concentrate (use desired amount)

1 cup carrot juice

1 cup canned beet juice

1 To use the coloring for frosting, start with 1 teaspoon color for each cup of Creamy Vanilla Frosting (page 579; omit vanilla for best color or substitute clear vanilla). If using canned frosting, colors will be much more muted.

2 To make Fresh Berry-Based color: Place desired type of berry in food processor or blender. Cover and process to puree. Place in fine-mesh strainer over bowl, stirring and pressing through with back of spoon to remove seeds. For muted, lighter color, use uncooked puree. For more intense color, place berry puree in 1-quart saucepan. Heat to boiling. Reduce heat to medium-low. Simmer until puree has been reduced to 1 tablespoon for most intense color, stirring occasionally. Cool completely before use. Blackberries make mauve to purple; raspberries make light to deep pink; strawberries make light to medium pink.

3 To make Fresh Vegetable-Based color (green only): Place parsley or spinach and water in food processor or blender. Cover and process to finely chop. Place in fine-mesh strainer over

bowl and press with back of spoon to extract as much green liquid as possible from vegetable pulp. For muted, lighter color, use uncooked liquid. For more intense color, place liquid in 1-quart saucepan. Heat to boiling. Reduce heat to medium-low. Simmer until liquid has been reduced to 1 tablespoon for most intense color, stirring occasionally. Cool completely before use. Uncooked makes pale, light green; cooked makes medium sage green.

4 To make Fresh Vegetable-Based color: In 3-quart saucepan, heat cabbage and water to boiling. Reduce heat; simmer 20 minutes to extract as much color as possible. Remove from heat. Place strainer over large bowl. Drain cabbage in strainer over bowl, reserving liquid. Divide liquid in half in two 2-quart saucepans for two colors; one purple and one that will become sage green. To create the sage green, add the baking soda to the liquid in one of the saucepans. Heat to boiling. Reduce heat to medium-low. Simmer until liquid has been reduced to 1 tablespoon for most intense color, stirring occasionally. Cool completely before use. The two-way cooked cabbage coloring method gives you mauve and purple shades without baking soda and sage green shades with the addition of baking soda.

5 To make Juice-Based color: Use thawed frozen grape juice concentrate as is for mauve to purple colors; it does not need to be cooked and reduced for intense color. For muted, light color, use uncooked beet and carrot juice. For more intense color, place liquid in 1-quart saucepan. Heat to boiling. Reduce heat to medium-low. Simmer until liquid has been reduced to 1 tablespoon for most intense color, stirring occasionally. Cool completely before use. Uncooked makes pale, light yellow to peach and pink; cooked makes orange to deep orange, deep pink, purple.

Use It or Lose It

It's best to make and use your natural food colors as soon as you make them or within a day or two, since they don't have any preservatives to keep them longer. If you won't be using them immediately, cover and refrigerate up to 2 days.

Salt-Free Herb Mix

CALORIE SMART • FAST

This super-versatile salt-free seasoning is great to sprinkle on meats, poultry, fish and vegetables. Or, toss hot cooked pasta with olive oil or melted butter and some of this blend, then sprinkle with shredded cheese.

PREP 5 min **TOTAL** 5 min • ¼ cup

- 1 tablespoon onion powder
- 1 tablespoon garlic powder
- 1 tablespoon parsley flakes
- 1 teaspoon dried basil leaves
- 1 teaspoon dried thyme leaves
- 1 teaspoon dried marjoram leaves
- 1 teaspoon coarsely ground black pepper

In small container with tight-fitting lid, mix all ingredients until well blended; cover. Store in cool, dry place up to 6 months. Stir or shake well before each use.

1 Teaspoon: Calories 5; Total Fat 0g (Saturated Fat 0g, Trans Fat 0g); Cholesterol 0mg; Sodium 0mg; Total Carbohydrate 1g (Dietary Fiber 0g, Sugars 0g); Protein 0g **Exchanges:** Free **Carbohydrate Choices:** 0

Salt-Free Taco Seasoning Mix

CALORIE SMART • FAST

Use this homemade taco seasoning in any recipe calling for the store-bought version. The beauty of this mix is you can add your own salt to taste. Twelve teaspoons of this mix is equal to a 1-ounce package of purchased taco seasoning mix.

PREP 5 min **TOTAL** 5 min • ½ cup

- 2 tablespoons chili powder
- 1 tablespoon onion powder
- 5 teaspoons ground cumin
- 5 teaspoons paprika
- 2½ teaspoons garlic powder
- ⅛ to ¼ teaspoon ground red pepper (cayenne)

In small container with tight-fitting lid, mix all ingredients until well blended; cover. Store in cool, dry place up to 6 months. Stir or shake well before each use.

1 Teaspoon: Calories 10; Total Fat 0g (Saturated Fat 0g, Trans Fat 0g); Cholesterol 0mg; Sodium 10mg; Total Carbohydrate 1g (Dietary Fiber 0g, Sugars 0g); Protein 0g **Exchanges:** Free **Carbohydrate Choices:** 0

Smoky Salt-Free Taco Seasoning Mix

Substitute 2 teaspoons smoked paprika for 2 teaspoons of the regular paprika.

Confetti Cookie Mix CALORIE SMART

PREP 50 min **TOTAL** 50 min • 1 jar mix (3 dozen cookies)

DRY COOKIE MIX

- 1 cup sugar
- ¾ cup all-purpose flour
- ⅓ cup unsweetened baking cocoa
- ½ teaspoon baking soda
- ¼ teaspoon salt
- 1½ cups quick-cooking or old-fashioned oats
- 1 cup miniature candy-coated milk chocolate candies

TO COMPLETE COOKIES

- ½ cup butter, softened
- 2 tablespoons water
- ½ teaspoon vanilla
- 3 eggs

1 In medium bowl, mix sugar, flour, cocoa, baking soda and salt. Transfer mixture to 1-quart jar with tight-fitting lid; tap lightly to pack. Top with oats and candies; cover.

2 To make cookies, heat oven to 350°F. In large bowl, place contents of jar, butter, water, vanilla and eggs. Stir with spoon 30 seconds or until combined. On ungreased cookie sheets, spoon dough by rounded teaspoonfuls 2 inches apart. Bake 10 to 12 minutes or until edges are set. Cool 5 minutes; remove from cookie sheets to cooling racks.

1 Cookie: Calories 100; Total Fat 4.5g (Saturated Fat 2.5g, Trans Fat 0g); Cholesterol 15mg; Sodium 60mg; Total Carbohydrate 14g (Dietary Fiber 1g, Sugars 9g); Protein 1g **Exchanges:** ½ Starch, ½ Other Carbohydrate, 1 Fat **Carbohydrate Choices:** 1

Confetti Cookie Mix

Sauces

Seasonings

CALORIE SMART = See Helpful Nutrition and Cooking Information, page 643   FAST = Ready in 30 minutes or less
EASY = Prep in 10 minutes or less **plus** five ingredients or less   LIGHTER = 25% fewer calories or grams of fat
MAKE AHEAD = Make-ahead directions   SLOW COOKER = Slow cooker directions

SAUCE BASICS

Whether a plain white sauce or the flavor punch of a mole poblano, sauces can transform a meal from ordinary to extraordinary. Learn how easy it is to masterfully create delicious sauces, worthy of putting you in the "great cook" category!

THICKENING SAUCES

Sauces can be thickened in different ways, depending on what they are used for and the ingredients used. Here are the four classic thickening methods:

Roux: A mixture of flour and fat (usually butter) is cooked over low to medium heat until smooth and bubbly, cooking the flour to remove the floury taste before liquid is added. Some recipes call for cooking the roux until it turns golden to deep brown, which adds color and flavor. See White Sauce and Roux, page 459.

Cornstarch: Often stirred into cold water or other liquid to thoroughly blend before being added to a hot mixture. Sauces thickened with cornstarch become clear and almost shiny.

Emulsion: An egg-based sauce cooked over low heat. If the temperature is too hot, the mixture will overcook and curdle. These sauces must be cooked thoroughly to kill any potential salmonella bacteria. See Hollandaise Sauce, page 461.

Reduction: A liquid such as broth, wine or a sauce mixture is boiled or simmered to evaporate some of the water in it until the volume is reduced and the mixture thickens, which concentrates the flavor. To speed this process, use a skillet (which has a large surface area) instead of a saucepan. See Peppery Red Wine Sauce, page 466.

TIPS FOR PERFECT SAUCES

It's easy to make an ultra-smooth, lump-free sauce if you follow these tips. Take your time —if you rush it, the sauce could curdle or separate. If it doesn't turn out the way you wanted, try our kitchen secrets for fixing sauces:

Making Sauce

- Gather all of the ingredients before beginning to give full attention to cooking the sauce.

- Use the heat specified in the recipe.

- Use a whisk to mix sauces and stir constantly to avoid lumps.

- Finish savory sauces with a pat of butter to enhance the flavor and give the sauce a velvety texture. Season with salt and pepper to taste before serving.

Fixing Sauces

Lumpy Sauce: Strain through a tightly woven mesh strainer; pushing liquid through the strainer with the back of a spoon. Discard what is left in the strainer.

Too-Thin Sauce: For a gravy or other sauce thickened with flour, stir a little plain-flavored instant mashed potato flakes into the hot sauce until desired consistency. (The sauce will continue to thicken as it cools, so make the consistency slightly thinner than you would like it.)

Curdled Egg-Based Sauce: Strain out the lumps and try whisking the sauce into another gently heated egg yolk in a clean bowl; heat until hot.

Curdled Cream Sauce: Add one-third more of the original cream volume; slowly stir into the hot, curdled sauce, 1 tablespoon at a time.

Salsa Verde (page 458)

Heirloom Recipe and New Twist

Basil pesto is a classic recipe you'll want to make often and have on hand. Few dishes pack as much flavor punch as fresh pesto. It's a natural to make when fresh basil is abundant. See the next page to learn how to freeze small amounts to have on hand whenever you want it. Toss pesto with hot cooked pasta, dollop it on pizza or use it as a sandwich spread. Our twist recipe is a great example of how adaptable pesto can be. With broccoli as the base instead of herbs, the pesto takes on a completely different flavor.

HEIRLOOM

Basil Pesto   CALORIE SMART • FAST • EASY

PREP 10 min **TOTAL** 10 min • 1¼ cups

>   2   cups firmly packed fresh basil leaves
> ¾   cup grated Parmesan cheese
> ¼   cup pine nuts, toasted if desired (page 23)
> ½   cup olive or vegetable oil
>   3   cloves garlic, peeled

1 In food processor or blender, place all ingredients. Cover and process on medium speed about 3 minutes, stopping occasionally to scrape down sides with rubber spatula, until smooth.

2 Use immediately, or cover tightly and refrigerate up to 5 days or freeze up to 1 month (color of pesto will darken as it stands).

1 Tablespoon: Calories 80; Total Fat 8g (Saturated Fat 1.5g, Trans Fat 0g); Cholesterol 0mg; Sodium 70mg; Total Carbohydrate 0g (Dietary Fiber 0g, Sugars 0g); Protein 2g **Exchanges:** 1½ Fat **Carbohydrate Choices:** 0

Basil, Roasted Red Pepper and Walnut Pesto
Use food processor. Reduce basil to 1 cup and oil to ⅓ cup. Add ½ cup drained roasted red or yellow bell peppers (from a jar). Substitute walnuts for the pine nuts.

Cilantro Pesto Substitute 1½ cups firmly packed fresh cilantro and ½ cup firmly packed fresh parsley for the basil.

Spinach Pesto Substitute 2 cups firmly packed fresh spinach leaves for the basil.

Sun-Dried Tomato Pesto Use food processor. Omit basil. Reduce oil to ⅓ cup. Add ½ cup sun-dried tomatoes in oil, undrained.

Basil Pesto

Broccoli-Walnut Pesto and Beet-Dill Pesto

Blending Pesto

Place all ingredients in food processor or blender.

Cover and process, stopping occasionally to scrape down side.

Broccoli-Walnut Pesto

CALORIE SMART • FAST

Pesto doesn't have to be "herb-centric." In fact, vegetable-based pestos are varied, come in beautiful hues and are absolutely delicious! Try these four amazing beauties with pasta, as a crostini topper, with cheese and crackers or, as we did in the Test Kitchens, eaten right out of the jar with a spoon!

PREP 15 min **TOTAL** 15 min • 1½ cups

- 2 **cups small fresh broccoli florets**
- ½ **cup lightly packed fresh basil leaves**
- ½ **cup chopped walnuts, toasted (page 23)**
- 1 **clove garlic, peeled**
- ⅓ **cup shredded Parmesan cheese**
- ¼ **teaspoon salt**
- ¼ **teaspoon pepper**
- ½ **cup olive oil**

1 In 2-quart saucepan, heat 2 cups water to boiling. Add broccoli; boil uncovered 1 to 2 minutes or just until bright green. Remove broccoli from boiling water; immediately place in ice water until cold. Drain well.

2 In food processor, place broccoli and remaining ingredients. Cover and process until smooth, stopping occasionally to scrape down sides with rubber spatula, until smooth.

3 Use pesto immediately, or press and smooth plastic wrap directly on surface of pesto and refrigerate up to 3 days or freeze up to 1 month.

2 Tablespoons: Calories 130; Total Fat 13g (Saturated Fat 2g, Trans Fat 0g); Cholesterol 0mg; Sodium 105mg; Total Carbohydrate 2g (Dietary Fiber 0g, Sugars 0g); Protein 2g **Exchanges:** ½ Vegetable, 2½ Fat **Carbohydrate Choices:** 0

Beet-Dill Pesto

Substitute 1 pound fresh red beets (cooked as directed in Roasted Beets, page 239), cooled and peeled, or 1 can (15 ounces) whole beets, well drained, for the broccoli. Substitute 3 tablespoons fresh dill weed for the basil and reduce oil to 2 tablespoons. Continue as directed in Step 2.

Brussels Sprouts–Cashew Pesto Make as directed, except substitute 2 cups halved fresh Brussels sprouts for the broccoli and boil 3 minutes, omit basil, substitute ½ cup cashew halves and pieces for the walnuts (not toasted) and add 2 tablespoons water.

Roasted Carrot–Almond Pesto Omit broccoli and basil. Substitute slivered almonds for the walnuts. Heat oven to 350°F. Spray 15x10x1-inch pan with cooking spray. Spread 1 bag (12 ounces) ready-to-eat petite baby-cut carrots in pan. Drizzle with 1 tablespoon of the oil; toss to coat. Bake uncovered 35 to 45 minutes, stirring occasionally, until tender. Cool completely. Continue as directed in Step 2. Add 1 to 2 tablespoons water if necessary.

Chimichurri Sauce

CALORIE SMART • EASY

Chimichurri is a common condiment in Argentina. Either curly- or flat-leaf (Italian) parsley can be used in this recipe. Flat-leaf parsley has a stronger peppery flavor. Use this sauce to perk up the flavor of grilled meat or poultry.

PREP 10 min **TOTAL** 2 hr 10 min • 1 cup

- 1 **bunch fresh parsley, stems removed**
- 2 **cloves garlic, peeled**
- ¾ **cup olive or vegetable oil**
- ¼ **cup white vinegar**
- ½ **teaspoon salt**
- ⅛ **teaspoon pepper**

In food processor, place parsley. Cover and process until chopped. Add remaining ingredients. Cover and process until well blended. Transfer to small bowl; cover and refrigerate 2 hours to blend flavors. Store covered in refrigerator up to 1 week.

1 Tablespoon: Calories 90; Total Fat 10g (Saturated Fat 1.5g, Trans Fat 0g); Cholesterol 0mg; Sodium 75mg; Total Carbohydrate 0g (Dietary Fiber 0g, Sugars 0g); Protein 0g **Exchanges:** 2 Fat **Carbohydrate Choices:** 0

Making Pesto Cubes

For homemade pesto any-time, freeze pesto in ice cube trays. Once frozen, move pesto cubes to a resealable plastic freezer bag and store in freezer up to 6 months.

Mole Poblano CALORIE SMART

This thick, dark, lush version of mole poblano is accented by chocolate, which is common to this classic Mexican sauce. There are hundreds of moles, depending on the region and the cook. Our version is easy and delicious. It's great to use with chicken, pork and beef.

PREP 45 min **TOTAL** 1 hr 15 min • 3 cups

- 3 oz dried ancho chiles*
  Boiling water
- ¼ cup slivered almonds
- ¼ cup pumpkin seeds (pepitas)
- 1 tablespoon sesame seed
- ½ cup chopped white or Spanish onion
- 3 tablespoons raisins
- 3 tablespoons creamy peanut butter
- 3 tablespoons sugar
- 1 oz semisweet baking chocolate, finely chopped
- ½ teaspoon ground cinnamon
- ½ teaspoon salt
- 2⅓ cups chicken broth (for homemade broth, see page 143)
- 1 tablespoon vegetable oil

1 In medium bowl, cover dried chiles with boiling water. Place plate or bowl over chiles, weighted if necessary to keep chiles submerged. Let stand 30 minutes to soften completely. Drain. Remove stems. Cut chiles open; place, skin side down, on cutting board. Scrape off seeds with spoon; set chiles aside.

2 Heat 8-inch skillet over medium heat. Add almonds, pepitas and sesame seed. Cook 5 to 7 minutes, stirring frequently, until nuts and seed begin to brown, then stirring constantly until nuts are golden brown.

3 In food processor, place chiles, almonds, pepitas, sesame seed, onion, raisins, peanut butter, sugar, chocolate, cinnamon, salt and ½ cup of the broth. Cover and process until smooth (mixture will be thick).

4 In 10-inch skillet, heat oil over medium heat. Add mole. Cook 3 minutes, stirring frequently. Gradually add remaining broth. Heat to boiling, stirring constantly; reduce heat. Simmer uncovered 15 minutes, stirring frequently. Cool. Transfer to tightly covered container. Refrigerate up to 1 week or freeze up to 3 months.

Mole Poblano

*Ancho chiles are dried fresh poblanos. If you can't find them in your area, check online sources.

¼ Cup: Calories 140; Total Fat 8g (Saturated Fat 2g, Trans Fat 0g); Cholesterol 0mg; Sodium 190mg; Total Carbohydrate 12g (Dietary Fiber 3g, Sugars 7g); Protein 4g **Exchanges:** 1 Other Carbohydrate, ½ High-Fat Meat, 1 Fat **Carbohydrate Choices:** 1

Peanut Sauce CALORIE SMART • FAST • EASY

Peanut sauce goes hand in hand with chicken satay, but it also tastes great with grilled poultry or meats or tossed with noodles and vegetables. Try it as a salad dressing for Asian-inspired combinations.

PREP 10 min **TOTAL** 10 min • 1 cup

- ½ cup creamy peanut butter
- ½ cup water
- 2 tablespoons fresh lime juice
- ½ teaspoon ground coriander
- ½ teaspoon ground cumin
- ⅛ teaspoon salt
- ⅛ teaspoon ground red pepper (cayenne), if desired
- 2 cloves garlic, finely chopped

1 Place peanut butter in medium bowl. Gradually stir in water and lime juice with whisk until smooth and creamy; stir in remaining ingredients.

2 Use immediately, or to make a warm sauce, place all ingredients in 1-quart saucepan. Heat over medium heat, stirring with whisk frequently, until smooth and warm.

3 Or cover and refrigerate up to 3 days or freeze up to 2 months.

1 Tablespoon: Calories 50; Total Fat 4g (Saturated Fat 1g, Trans Fat 0g); Cholesterol 0mg; Sodium 55mg; Total Carbohydrate 2g (Dietary Fiber 0g, Sugars 0g); Protein 2g **Exchanges:** ½ High-Fat Meat **Carbohydrate Choices:** 0

Sriracha Sauce CALORIE SMART

Sriracha is a fiery fermented sauce that adds a huge punch of flavor. Our homemade version is so easy to make, so flavorful and so beautifully red that you may never get store-bought again! Make sure to look for completely red jalapeños for best flavor and color.

PREP 25 min **TOTAL** 8 days • 1¼ cups

 1 lb red jalapeño chiles (12 to 14 medium)
 3 tablespoons sugar
 4 cloves garlic, peeled
 2½ teaspoons salt
 ⅓ cup cider vinegar

1 Remove stems from chiles but do not remove seeds; cut chiles in half.* In food processor, place chiles, sugar, garlic and salt. Cover and process about 20 seconds, using short on-and-off motions, until chiles are very finely chopped. Be aware that the chile fumes may be strong.

2 Transfer mixture to glass jar. Cover and let stand at room temperature 5 to 8 days, stirring every day, until mixture begins to ferment when small bubbles form on bottom and sides of jar. Mixture may rise in volume in jar.

3 In blender, place chile mixture and vinegar. Cover and blend until smooth. Place fine-mesh strainer over 2-quart saucepan. Pour chile mixture into strainer, pressing firmly with back of spoon until only seeds remain. Discard seeds. Heat sauce to boiling; reduce heat to low. Simmer uncovered 10 minutes or until sauce thickens and clings to metal spoon. Cool. Transfer to tightly covered container. Store in refrigerator up to 6 months.

*Use plastic or rubber gloves when handling chiles. Wash knives and cutting boards thoroughly. The fumes from fresh chiles can also be irritating to some people.

1 Teaspoon: Calories 5; Total Fat 0g (Saturated Fat 0g, Trans Fat 0g); Cholesterol 0mg; Sodium 100mg; Total Carbohydrate 1g (Dietary Fiber 0g, Sugars 0g); Protein 0g **Exchanges:** Free **Carbohydrate Choices:** 0

Thai Red Curry Paste CALORIE SMART

PREP 50 min **TOTAL** 50 min • ½ cup

 10 dried chiles de árbol or red spur chiles
    boiling water
 4 fresh red Fresno or serrano chiles
 ½ cup coarsely chopped shallots
 ¼ cup coarsely chopped garlic
 2 tablespoons chopped fresh cilantro stems*
 1 tablespoon finely chopped gingerroot
 1 tablespoon ground coriander
 2 teaspoons finely chopped lemongrass**
 1 teaspoon ground cumin
 1 strip fresh lime peel, 1½ x ½ inches
 ½ teaspoon salt
 4 to 6 teaspoons water

1 Soak dried chiles in boiling water 30 minutes (place plate on top and weight with can to keep chiles submerged). Cut tops off fresh chiles. Cut in half lengthwise, remove seeds and coarsely chop.

2 Place all ingredients except water in small food processor or blender. Cover and process until finely chopped, scraping down sides as needed. Add just enough water until a paste forms, scraping down sides as needed. Store in tightly covered jar in refrigerator up to 6 months.

* Only the cilantro stems are used in this Thai curry paste. For the most flavor, avoid the woody portions of the stem and select the tender bright green portions.

** Resembling a green reed, lemongrass is an ancient herb of Southeast Asia. The flavor is reminiscent of citrus, bay leaves and pepper. Peel away the tough outer layers and use only the tender inner core.

1 Tablespoon: Calories 25; Total Fat 0g (Saturated Fat 0g, Trans Fat 0g); Sodium 150mg; Total Carbohydrate 4g (Dietary Fiber 1g); Protein 0g **Exchanges:** ½ Other Carbohydrate **Carbohydrate Choices:** 0

Thai Red Curry Paste

White Wine–Garlic Sauce

PREP 15 min **TOTAL** 35 min • 1 cup

- ¼ cup olive oil
- 4 cloves garlic, finely chopped
- 2 cups dry white wine (such as Chardonnay or Sauvignon Blanc) or nonalcoholic white wine
- ¼ cup white wine vinegar
- ½ cup whipping cream
- ¼ cup chopped fresh parsley
- ½ teaspoon salt
- ½ teaspoon pepper

1 In 10-inch skillet, heat oil over medium-high heat. Add garlic; cook 1 minute, stirring constantly. Add wine and vinegar; heat to boiling over high heat. Reduce heat to medium-high; simmer until mixture coats back of metal spoon, 10 to 12 minutes.

2 Stir in whipping cream; simmer until mixture coats back of metal spoon and is slightly reduced, 3 to 4 minutes longer, stirring constantly. Remove from heat. Stir in parsley, salt and pepper.

¼ **Cup:** Calories 260; Total Fat 25g (Saturated Fat 9g, Trans Fat 0g); Cholesterol 40mg; Sodium 310mg; Total Carbohydrate 3g (Dietary Fiber 0g, Sugars 0g); Protein 1g **Exchanges:** ½ Other Carbohydrate, 5 Fat **Carbohydrate Choices:** 0

Wine

Leftover wine can be used in a variety of ways to heighten the flavor of dishes. When wine is heated, the alcohol is burned off, leaving the essence to add complexity to the flavors of the dish. Use dry white wines for savory poultry dishes, dry red wines for savory beef or pork dishes. Sweet wines can be used in desserts. Try one of these ideas next time you find yourself with an opened bottle:

1. **Gravy:** Try substituting dry white wine (up to half) as part of the liquid for turkey or chicken gravy. Or use a dry red wine (in the same manner) in a beef or pork gravy.

2. **Stew:** Use leftover red wine to replace some of the broth (up to half) in your favorite stew recipe.

3. **Pasta Sauce:** When heating pasta sauce, add a little leftover red wine (about ½ cup wine to 2 cups pasta sauce). For a thicker sauce, bring it to a boil and reduce heat. Simmer uncovered until desired consistency.

4. **Mulled Wine:** Pour leftover red wine into a freezer container and freeze. Each time you have leftover wine, add to the container. When you have collected approximately 2 bottles worth, empty the frozen wine into a 3-quart saucepan and continue as directed for Mulled Wine (page 468).

5. **Wine Cubes:** Pour leftover wine into an ice cube tray; freeze. Use white wine cubes to keep glasses of white wine chilled on hot days without diluting it, or use white or red cubes for white or red sangria, respectively.

6. **White Wine Sauce:** Prepare White Sauce (page 459), substituting ½ cup of dry white wine for ½ cup of the milk.

7. **Port Cranberry Sauce:** Prepare Cranberry Sauce (page 641), substituting 1 cup sweet red wine, such as Port, for 1 cup of the water.

White Wine–Garlic Sauce

Herbed Butter

Herbed Butter

CALORIE SMART • FAST • EASY

This simple sauce is sensational drizzled over fish, seafood, poultry or vegetables or tossed with pasta.

PREP 5 min **TOTAL** 5 min • ½ cup

- ½ cup butter, cut into pieces*
- 2 tablespoons chopped fresh or 2 teaspoons dried herb leaves (basil, chives, oregano, savory, tarragon or thyme or a mix of these varieties)
- 2 teaspoons fresh lemon juice

In 1-quart saucepan or 8-inch skillet, melt butter over medium heat. Stir in herbs and lemon juice. Use immediately.

*Do not use margarine or vegetable oil spread.

1 Tablespoon: Calories 100; Total Fat 12g (Saturated Fat 6g, Trans Fat 0.5g); Cholesterol 30mg; Sodium 75mg; Total Carbohydrate 0g (Dietary Fiber 0g, Sugars 0g); Protein 0g **Exchanges:** 2½ Fat **Carbohydrate Choices:** 0

Herbed Browned Butter Sauce In 1-quart saucepan, heat butter over medium heat just until light brown. Watch carefully because butter can brown and then burn quickly. Continue as directed.

Clarified Butter FAST

Think you've never heard of clarified butter? Many seafood restaurants serve it hot with lobster and crab. A staple in Indian cuisine, it's known as ghee (see page 256). Aside from serving it with seafood, it's great brushed over warm Naan (page 516) or pita bread, or drizzled over hot cooked basmati rice.

PREP 20 min **TOTAL** 30 min • ¾ cup

- 1 lb unsalted butter, cut into 1-inch pieces

1 In 1-quart saucepan, melt butter over low heat. Continue simmering over low heat 15 to 20 minutes, occasionally skimming off milk solids that rise to surface, until butter is clear and deep yellow in color. Do not stir (some of the milk solids will turn brown and sink to bottom of pan).

2 Remove from heat. Cool 5 to 10 minutes; do not stir. Gently pour clarified butter into airtight container, leaving milk solids in saucepan. Discard milk solids. Store covered in refrigerator up to 1 month.

1 Tablespoon: Calories 280; Total Fat 31g (Saturated Fat 19g, Trans Fat 1g); Cholesterol 80mg; Sodium 0mg; Total Carbohydrate 0g (Dietary Fiber 0g, Sugars 0g); Protein 0g **Exchanges:** 6 Fat **Carbohydrate Choices:** 0

Garlic Clarified Butter Stir 1 or 2 finely chopped cloves garlic into butter after removing from heat. After cooling, use fine-mesh strainer to gently pour clarified butter into container so that garlic pieces will be removed before storage.

Clarifying Butter

Simmer butter over low heat, occasionally skimming off milk solids that rise to surface.

Continue until butter is clear and deep yellow in color.

Carefully pour warm clarified butter into airtight container, leaving any milk solids in saucepan.

HERBS

Basil: Sweet and spicy, fragrant. Chop leaves just before using. Use with eggs, meat, pesto, salads, soups, stews, tomato dishes or herb butters.

Bay Leaves: Earthy, grassy, slightly piney (fresh leaves are more potent than dried). Use in Greek dishes, soups, stews or under chicken skin or to top fish while cooking. Discard leaves before eating.

Chervil: Mild, parsley-like. Use with eggs, fish, in salads, sauces, soups or stuffing.

Chives: Mild green onion flavor. Use with potatoes, eggs or fish, in appetizers or as a garnish.

Cilantro: Looks similar to Italian parsley but with a lively, pungent smell and taste. Chop leaves; discard stems. Use in salsas and other Mexican, Indian, Indonesian dishes, marinades, pasta salads, soups or stews.

Dill Weed: Fresh, peppery, tangy. Chop leaves and tender stems; discard woody stems. Use in bread, dips, fish, pickles, herb butters, salads (sparingly) or sauces.

Fennel: Anise flavor. Chop leaves and stems. Use in soups, salads, stuffing or tossed with cooked vegetables. Seeds are used as spice.

Horseradish: Pungent, peppery. Choose firm roots without blemishes; peel and grate before using. Use in sauces or condiments for fish or meat.

Italian Parsley: Also known as flat-leaf parsley, it is more fragrant, less bitter than regular (curly) parsley. Chop leaves; discard stems. Use in Italian, European and Middle Eastern dishes for stronger parsley flavor.

Lemongrass: Sour lemon flavor; extremely fibrous and stringy. Cut off and discard bulb; remove tough or outer leaves. Cut yellow (lower section) into thin slices. Bend, bruise pieces to release flavor (discard after cooking) or process in food processor; cook thoroughly to soften enough to eat. Use in Asian dishes or soups.

Marjoram: Sweet, slightly oregano-like yet delicate flavor; add at the end of cooking. Use with vegetables such as carrots, zucchini, mushrooms, peas, spinach and tomatoes, with fish, lamb, poultry or in soups, stews or stuffing.

Mint: Strong, cool, fresh and sweet flavor. Many varieties, with a range of flavors. Use in Greek or Italian dishes, in beverages or desserts or with cucumbers, peas, potatoes, carrots or lamb.

Oregano: Pungent—use sparingly. Use in Italian dishes, meat, poultry, sauces, soups or vegetables.

Parsley: Helps the fresh flavor of a dish to come through. Works well with garlic to temper its flavor. Chop curly leaves; discard stems. Use in sauces, eggs, stuffing, herb butters or with corn or potatoes.

Rosemary: Strong flavor with hints of pine and lemon—use sparingly. Remove and chop leaves; discard stems. Use in soups, breads, fish, lamb, salads, seafood, tomato dishes or vegetables.

Sage: Slightly bitter with subtle musty mint flavor—use sparingly. Many varieties, with range of colors and flavors. Use in Mediterranean foods, particularly Italian dishes, stuffing, marinades or with peas, eggplant, lima beans, carrots or poultry.

Savory: Mint-thyme flavor; combines well with other herbs. Use in poultry, fish, meat, vegetables, any kind of beans or in herb butters.

Tarragon: Delicate, anise-like flavor—use sparingly. Use in salads, salad dressings, egg dishes, sauces or with poultry, fish or cheese.

Thyme: Peppery, minty, mild lemon flavor—use sparingly. Many varieties, with range of colors and flavors. Chop leaves and soft stems; discard woody stems. Use in stews, dressings or with vegetables, poultry, fish, pork, beef or lamb.

Adjusting for Flavor Preferences

Our recipes are tasted by several people with a wide range of taste preferences. You'll find the seasoning levels to be in the "average" category, in terms of salt level and spiciness, unless otherwise indicated by the recipe title. Sometimes we call for an ingredient with a range of amount—typically done where hotness of a dish can be varied. Use the lesser amount if you like things milder or more if you like foods with more kick.

Lemon Thyme

Thyme

Dill Weed

Cilantro

Sage

Parsley

Mint

Rosemary

Purple Sage

Italian (Flat-leaf) Parsley

Oregano

Bay Leaves

Basil

Chives

Lemongrass

Tarragon

Marjoram

SPICES/SEASONINGS

Many dried spices and seasonings can be toasted to enhance their flavors before being added to a dish. To toast spices and seasonings, heat in small, heavy skillet over medium heat, stirring constantly, until fragrant. Watch closely—they can go from toasted to burnt very quickly.

Allspice: Available whole, ground. Cinnamon-clove-nutmeg flavor. Use in baked goods, jerk seasoning, pickling, pies or with fruit.

Anise Seed: Available whole, ground. Sweet licorice flavor. Use in cakes, cookies, breads or fruit dishes.

Caraway Seed: Available whole. Delicate, nutty anise flavor. Use in breads, stews, with vegetables or meats.

Cardamom: Available as whole or split pods, whole or ground seeds. The flavor has hints of eucalyptus, camphor and lemon. Use in Indian and Middle Eastern dishes and to flavor coffee or tea. Dominant flavor in chai.

Celery Seed: Available whole, ground. Strong flavor—use sparingly. Use in soups, salads, salad dressings, meat dishes or pickling.

Cinnamon: Available in sticks, ground. Sweet, woodsy flavor. Use in baked goods, hot drinks, pickling or savory dishes.

Cloves: Available whole, ground. Sweet, peppery flavor. Use in baked goods, pickling, sauces, tea or with fruit, ham or other meat.

Coriander: Available whole, ground. Lemon-sage flavor. Seeds of the cilantro plant—but not to be substituted for cilantro, which has a different flavor. Use in soups, stews, sausages, ratatouille, pickling or curries.

Cumin: Available whole, ground. Nutty, earthy, with a peppery bite. Use in Mexican, Thai, Mediterranean dishes, dry rubs, chilies, stews or with beans or lentils.

Dill Seed: Available whole, ground. Caraway-dill flavor. Not to be substituted for dill weed, which has a different flavor. Use in pickling, breads or salad dressings.

Dill Weed (Dried): Dried dill leaves. Not to be substituted for dill seed, which has a different flavor. Use in breads, dips, pickling, salads, sauces or with vegetables or fish.

Fennel Seed: Available whole, ground. Sweet anise flavor. Use in breads, cakes or sweet sausages.

Garlic: Available minced, powdered (finely ground), dehydrated, flaked, fresh or as paste or juice. Slightly musty flavor. Use in appetizers, bread, salads, soups or with vegetables, fish, poultry or meat.

Ginger: Available ground, crystallized, fresh. Spicy-hot, sweet flavor. Use in beverages, baked goods, sauces, soup, Asian dishes, tea or with fruit, vegetables, fish, poultry or meat.

Mustard Seed: Available whole, ground, powdered (finely ground), or as oil. Use seeds in pickling or with vegetables, cooked meats, ground or powdered in sauces, main dishes, pasta salads or salad dressings; oil for stir-fries, salad dressings or marinades.

Nutmeg: Available whole, ground (**Mace** is the covering of the nutmeg seed, so it can be used the same way). Sweet, spicy flavor. Use in baked goods, eggnog and other beverages, custards, sauces or with vegetables.

Paprika: Available ground. Ranges from sweet to hot in flavor; slightly bitter. Use in casseroles, eggs, salads, soups or with vegetables, fish or meat.

Peppercorns: Available in black, white and green varieties; whole, ground, cracked (green sold packed in brine or dried). Slightly hot flavor with a hint of sweetness (black is the strongest, green the mildest). Use in savory foods of all kinds. Pink peppercorns are not true peppercorns but rather dried berries of the Baies rose plant.

Red Pepper (Cayenne): Available ground. Very hot, peppery flavor. Use in savory foods of all kinds.

Saffron: Available in threads, powdered. Distinctive flavor; mildly bitter. Use in Indian and Spanish dishes.

Sesame Seed: Seeds available in a variety of colors or as oil. Light, nutty flavor (white seeds milder than black). Use to add flavor and crunch to breads, salads, stir-fries or other Asian dishes.

Star Anise: Available whole, ground. Bitter, more pungent flavor than anise. Key ingredient in five-spice powder. Use in Asian dishes.

Turmeric: Available ground and increasingly available fresh. Fragrant, woodsy flavor. Key ingredient in prepackaged curry powder, food color. Use in eggs, pickling, rice, Indian dishes, poultry or seafood.

Sesame Seed

Star Anise

Allspice

Black Sesame Seed

Cumin

Anise Seed

Cardamom

Mace

Dill Seed

Minced Garlic

Ginger

Turmeric

Nutmeg

Celery Seed

Cinnamon

Dill Weed

Coriander

Paprika

Cloves

Mustard Seed

Caraway Seed

Saffron

Poppy Seed

Fennel Seed

Teriyaki Marinade

CALORIE SMART • EASY

PREP 5 min **TOTAL** 1 hr 5 min • ½ cup

- ¼ cup water
- 3 tablespoons soy sauce
- 1 tablespoon fresh lemon juice
- 1 tablespoon vegetable oil
- 1 tablespoon packed brown sugar
- ⅛ teaspoon coarsely ground black pepper
- 1 clove garlic, finely chopped

1 In shallow glass or plastic dish or resealable food-storage plastic bag, mix all ingredients.

2 Add about 1 pound boneless or 2 to 3 pounds bone-in beef, pork or chicken, turning to coat with marinade. Cover dish or seal bag; refrigerate at least 1 hour but no longer than 24 hours, turning meat occasionally.

3 Remove meat from marinade; reserve marinade. Cook meat as desired, brushing occasionally with marinade. Remaining marinade must be boiled to be served as a sauce (if not boiled, discard marinade). In 1-quart saucepan, heat marinade to boiling, stirring constantly; boil and stir 1 minute.

1 Tablespoon: Calories 25; Total Fat 1.5g (Saturated Fat 0g, Trans Fat 0g); Cholesterol 0mg; Sodium 340mg; Total Carbohydrate 2g (Dietary Fiber 0g, Sugars 2g); Protein 0g **Exchanges:** ½ Fat **Carbohydrate Choices:** 0

Fajita Marinade   CALORIE SMART

PREP 5 min **TOTAL** 1 hr 5 min • ½ cup

- ¼ cup vegetable oil
- ¼ cup red wine vinegar
- 1 teaspoon sugar
- 1 teaspoon dried oregano leaves
- 1 teaspoon chili powder
- ½ teaspoon garlic powder
- ½ teaspoon salt
- ¼ teaspoon pepper

1 In shallow glass or plastic dish or resealable food-storage plastic bag, mix all ingredients.

2 Add about 1 pound boneless or 2 to 3 pounds bone-in beef, pork or chicken, turning to coat with marinade. Cover dish or seal bag; refrigerate at least 1 hour but no longer than 24 hours, turning meat occasionally.

3 Remove meat from marinade; reserve marinade. Cook meat as desired, brushing occasionally with marinade. Remaining marinade must be boiled to be served as a sauce (if not boiled, discard marinade). In 1-quart saucepan, heat marinade to boiling, stirring constantly; boil and stir 1 minute.

1 Tablespoon: Calories 70; Total Fat 7g (Saturated Fat 1g, Trans Fat 0g); Cholesterol 0mg; Sodium 150mg; Total Carbohydrate 0g (Dietary Fiber 0g, Sugars 0g); Protein 0g **Exchanges:** 1½ Fat **Carbohydrate Choices:** 0

Fajita Marinade

Seasoned Brine

Seasoned Brine CALORIE SMART • EASY

Brining is a great way to impart flavor into meat or poultry but also is a sure-fire way to ensure it will cook up incredibly tender and juicy. You may find that brined meat and poultry takes a little longer to cook, due to the added moisture.

PREP 5 min **TOTAL** 24 hr 5 min • 4 cups

- 4 cups water
- ½ cup packed brown sugar
- 2 tablespoons salt
- 2 cloves garlic, crushed
- 1 teaspoon cracked black pepper*

1 In medium bowl, mix all ingredients until brown sugar and salt are dissolved.

2 Place up to 5 pounds meat or poultry in 2-gallon heavy-duty resealable food-storage plastic bag. Add brine; seal bag. Refrigerate 24 hours, turning occasionally.

3 Remove meat or poultry from brine; discard brine. Grill or cook as desired.

* If you can't find cracked pepper, use whole peppercorns. To crack peppercorns, place in small resealable food-storage plastic bag. Seal bag; pound with meat mallet or rolling pin just to crack open. Or, use mortar and pestle.

1 Tablespoon: Calories 110; Total Fat 0g (Saturated Fat 0g, Trans Fat 0g); Cholesterol 0mg; Sodium 3550mg; Total Carbohydrate 28g (Dietary Fiber 0g, Sugars 27g); Protein 0g **Exchanges:** Free **Carbohydrate Choices:** 2

CUT OF MEAT OR POULTRY	WEIGHT IN POUNDS	BRINING TIME IN HOURS
Turkey		
Whole	8 to 12	6 to 12
	12 to 14	9 to 14
	14 to 20	10 to 20
	20 to 24	15 to 24
Breast (bone-in)	5 to 7	3½ to 5½
Chicken		
Whole	3 to 3½	8 to 24
Pieces		1 to 3
Cornish Game Hens		8 to 24
Pork		
Chops		3 to 8
Tenderloin	¾ to 1	8 to 12
Pork Loin Roast (bone-in or boneless)	2 to 5	12 to 24

Garlic Marinade CALORIE SMART

PREP 10 min **TOTAL** 1 hr 15 min • ¾ cup

- ¼ cup vegetable oil
- 4 cloves garlic, finely chopped
- 1 tablespoon chopped fresh or 1 teaspoon dried rosemary leaves, crushed
- ½ teaspoon ground mustard
- 2 teaspoons soy sauce
- ¼ cup red or white wine vinegar
- ¼ cup dry sherry or apple juice

1 In 10-inch skillet, heat oil over medium-high heat. Cook garlic in oil, stirring frequently, until golden. Stir in rosemary, mustard and soy sauce; remove from heat. Stir in vinegar and sherry; cool.

2 In shallow glass or plastic dish or resealable food-storage plastic bag, place 2 to 2½ pounds boneless or 3 to 4 pounds bone-in beef, pork or lamb. Pour marinade over meat. Cover dish or seal bag; refrigerate at least 1 hour but no longer than 24 hours, turning meat occasionally.

3 Remove meat from marinade; reserve marinade. Cook meat as desired, brushing occasionally with marinade. Remaining marinade must be boiled to be served as a sauce (if not boiled, discard marinade). In 1-quart saucepan, heat marinade to boiling, stirring constantly; boil and stir 1 minute.

1 Tablespoon: Calories 45; Total Fat 4.5g (Saturated Fat 0.5g, Trans Fat 0g); Cholesterol 0mg; Sodium 50mg; Total Carbohydrate 0g (Dietary Fiber 0g, Sugars 0g); Protein 0g **Exchanges:** 1 Fat **Carbohydrate Choices:** 0

Balsamic Garlic Marinade Substitute ½ cup balsamic vinegar for the wine vinegar and sherry.

Onion and Garlic Marinade Cook ¼ cup finely chopped onion with the garlic until tender. Substitute thyme for the rosemary.

Marinade Success

- Use glass or plastic containers or food-storage plastic bags to mix and marinate in. They won't react with acidic ingredients like wine, lemon juice or vinegar.
- Use ½ cup marinade for each 1 pound of meat, poultry, fish or vegetables.
- Marinate all foods except fish in the refrigerator up to 24 hours—any longer and food can become mushy. Marinate fish only 15 to 30 minutes.

CALORIE SMART = See Helpful Nutrition and Cooking Information, page 643   FAST = Ready in 30 minutes or less
EASY = Prep in 10 minutes or less **plus** five ingredients or less   LIGHTER = 25% fewer calories or grams of fat
MAKE AHEAD = Make-ahead directions   SLOW COOKER = Slow cooker directions

< Dried Cherry and Walnut Bread, page 510

QUICK BREAD BASICS

Breads that use baking powder or baking soda as the leavening to make them rise are called quick breads. Unlike yeast breads, which require rising time, quick breads usually can be baked as soon as they are mixed. Muffins, scones and biscuits are a few common types of quick breads that you can make, no matter what your skill level, as they offer fresh-from-the oven results, easily.

SELECTING PANS

- Use only the pan size indicated in the recipe.

- For golden-brown color and tender crusts, use shiny pans and cookie sheets rather than pans with dark finishes, to reflect the heat.

- If using dark or nonstick pans, reduce oven temperature by 25°F. These pans absorb heat more easily than shiny pans, causing baked goods to brown more quickly.

- Insulated pans often require slightly longer baking times and result in baked goods that may be less brown.

PREPPING INGREDIENTS

- Check expiration dates on leavening packages for freshness. Old products may inhibit quick breads from rising properly.

- Chop, mash or shred fruits, vegetables and nuts in advance so they are ready to be added to the batter.

- Measure flour by spooning into a dry measuring cup and leveling off with the straight edge of a knife or metal spatula.

- Use liquid measuring cups to measure liquids by filling and placing on the counter to read amount accurately at eye level.

- In recipes calling for butter, it's best to use real butter. If you use margarine, be sure the product has at least 65 percent fat. Don't use reduced-fat butter or whipped products.

Tips for Perfect Quick Breads

- Mix most batters for quick breads with a spoon, not an electric mixer, just until the dry ingredients are moistened, as overmixing can result in tough quick breads with peaked tops.

- For those recipes that require a mixer, we tested with handheld electric mixers. If you have a stand mixer, follow the manufacturer's directions for speed settings.

- To prevent gummy, soggy or heavy loaves, don't use more fruit or vegetables than called for in the recipe.

- Grease bottom only of loaf or muffin pans, unless otherwise specified; this prevents a lip and a hard, dry edge from forming.

- Allow at least 2 inches of space around pans in the oven for heat circulation.

- Quick bread loaves normally form cracks on top; this is due to the leavening action and is perfectly fine.

- Cool loaves completely, about 2 hours, to prevent crumbling when sliced.

- Cut loaves with a serrated knife, using a light sawing motion. Flavor improves and slicing is easier if loaves have been refrigerated for 24 hours.

- Wrap completely cooled loaves tightly in plastic wrap or foil and refrigerate up to 1 week. To freeze, place tightly wrapped loaves in freezer bags and freeze up to 3 months.

Cake Doughnuts (page 492)

Blueberry Muffins CALORIE SMART

Homemade blueberry muffins burst with fresh flavor that store-bought can never duplicate—and it doesn't take rocket science to make them great. Overmixing leads to peaked tops, tough interiors and dry muffins, so follow these simple steps and your muffins will be beautiful and delicious!

PREP 10 min **TOTAL** 40 min • 12 muffins

- ¾ cup milk
- ¼ cup vegetable oil or melted butter
- 1 egg
- 2 cups all-purpose flour
- ½ cup granulated sugar
- 2 teaspoons baking powder
- ½ teaspoon salt
- 1 cup fresh, canned (drained) or frozen (do not thaw) blueberries
- 2 tablespoons coarse sugar or additional granulated sugar, if desired

1 Heat oven to 400°F. Grease bottoms only of 12 regular-size muffin cups with shortening or cooking spray, or place paper baking cup in each muffin cup.

2 In large bowl, beat milk, oil and egg with fork or whisk until well mixed. Stir in flour, granulated sugar, baking powder and salt all at once just until flour is moistened (batter will be lumpy). Fold in blueberries. Divide batter evenly among muffin cups; sprinkle each with ½ teaspoon coarse sugar.

3 Bake 20 to 25 minutes or until golden brown and toothpick inserted in center comes out clean. If baked in greased pan, let stand about 5 minutes in pan, then remove from pan to cooling rack; if baked in paper baking cups, immediately remove from pan to cooling rack. Serve warm if desired.

1 Muffin: Calories 170; Total Fat 6g (Saturated Fat 1g, Trans Fat 0g); Cholesterol 20mg; Sodium 190mg; Total Carbohydrate 27g (Dietary Fiber 0g, Sugars 10g); Protein 3g **Exchanges:** 1 Starch, 1 Fruit, 1 Fat **Carbohydrate Choices:** 2

Apple-Cinnamon Muffins Omit blueberries. Stir in 1 cup chopped peeled apple (about 1 medium) and ½ teaspoon ground cinnamon with the flour. Bake 25 to 30 minutes.

Banana Muffins Omit blueberries. Reduce milk to ⅓ cup. Beat in 1 cup mashed very ripe bananas (2 medium) with the milk. Use packed brown sugar instead of granulated sugar in the muffins.

Chocolate Chip Muffins Omit blueberries. Fold 1 cup miniature semisweet chocolate chips into batter.

Cranberry-Orange Muffins Omit blueberries. Beat in 1 tablespoon grated orange peel with the milk. Fold 1 cup coarsely chopped sweetened dried cranberries into batter.

Streusel-Topped Blueberry Muffins Omit coarse sugar. Make batter as directed; divide evenly among muffin cups. In medium bowl, mix ¼ cup all-purpose flour, ¼ cup packed brown sugar and ¼ teaspoon ground cinnamon. Cut in 2 tablespoons cold butter, using pastry blender or fork, until crumbly. Sprinkle about 1 tablespoon streusel over batter in each muffin cup. Bake as directed.

Preparing Muffins

Stir dry ingredients in all at once just until flour is moistened.

Divide batter evenly among muffin cups.

Blueberry Muffins

Bran Muffins

Bran Muffins CALORIE SMART

PREP 15 min **TOTAL** 50 min • 12 muffins

- 1¼ cups original bran cereal shreds or 2 cups bran cereal flakes, crushed
- 1⅓ cups milk
- ½ cup raisins, dried cherries or sweetened dried cranberries, if desired
- ½ teaspoon vanilla
- ¼ cup vegetable oil
- 1 egg
- 1¼ cups all-purpose or whole wheat flour
- ½ cup packed brown sugar
- 1 tablespoon baking powder
- ¼ teaspoon salt
- ¼ teaspoon ground cinnamon, if desired

1 Heat oven to 400°F. Grease bottoms only of 12 regular-size muffin cups with shortening or cooking spray, or place paper baking cup in each muffin cup.

2 In medium bowl, stir cereal, milk, raisins and vanilla until well mixed. Let stand about 5 minutes or until cereal has softened. Beat in oil and egg with fork.

3 In another medium bowl, stir remaining ingredients until well mixed; stir into cereal mixture just until moistened. Divide batter evenly among muffin cups.

4 Bake 18 to 25 minutes or until toothpick inserted in center comes out clean. If baked in greased pan, let stand about 5 minutes in pan, then remove from pan to cooling rack; if baked in paper baking cups, immediately remove from pan to cooling rack. Serve warm if desired.

1 Muffin: Calories 170; Total Fat 6g (Saturated Fat 1g, Trans Fat 0g); Cholesterol 20mg; Sodium 220mg; Total Carbohydrate 26g (Dietary Fiber 3g, Sugars 10g); Protein 3g **Exchanges:** 1½ Starch, 1 Fat **Carbohydrate Choices:** 2

MAKE-AHEAD Directions Bake muffins as directed; cool completely. Place in freezer containers or resealable freezer plastic bags. Freeze up to 3 months. Reheat in the microwave.

Date-Bran Muffins Stir in 1 cup chopped dates with remaining ingredients in Step 3.

Jumbo Upside-Down Muffins Grease bottoms only of 6 jumbo muffin cups with shortening or cooking spray (do not use paper baking cups). Mix 3 tablespoons packed brown sugar, 2 tablespoons melted butter and 1 tablespoon light corn syrup in small bowl until well mixed. Spoon about 2 teaspoons into the bottom of each muffin cup. Prepare batter as directed, except substitute ¾ cup chopped dates for the raisins. Bake 18 to 25 minutes. Run metal spatula around muffins to loosen. Immediately place cookie sheet upside down on muffin pan; turn cookie sheet and pan over to remove muffins.

LEARN WITH BETTY Muffins

Perfect Muffin: This muffin is slightly rounded, with a bumpy top.

Overmixed Muffin: This muffin has a peaked, smooth top.

Overbaked Muffin: This muffin is dry with a rough top and is too brown.

Golden Harvest Muffins

PREP 20 min **TOTAL** 50 min • 18 muffins

- 2 eggs
- ¾ cup vegetable oil
- ¼ cup milk
- 2 teaspoons vanilla
- 2 cups all-purpose flour
- 1 cup packed brown sugar
- 2 teaspoons baking soda
- 2 teaspoons ground cinnamon
- ½ teaspoon salt
- 1½ cups shredded carrots (2 or 3 medium)
- 1 cup shredded peeled apple (1 medium)
- ½ cup coconut
- ½ cup raisins
- ¾ cup sliced almonds

1 Heat oven to 350°F. Grease bottoms only of 18 regular-size muffin cups with shortening or cooking spray, or place paper baking cup in each muffin cup.

2 In large bowl, beat eggs, oil, milk and vanilla with whisk until well blended. Add flour, brown sugar, baking soda, cinnamon and salt; stir just until dry ingredients are moistened. Stir in carrots, apple, coconut, raisins and ½ cup of the almonds. Divide batter evenly among muffin cups. Sprinkle remaining ¼ cup almonds over batter.

3 Bake 20 to 25 minutes or until toothpick inserted in center comes out clean. If baked in greased pan, let stand about 5 minutes in pan, then remove from pan to cooling rack; if baked in paper baking cups, immediately remove from pan to cooling rack. Serve warm if desired.

Banana Bread

1 Muffin: Calories 250; Total Fat 13g (Saturated Fat 2.5g, Trans Fat 0g); Cholesterol 25mg; Sodium 230mg; Total Carbohydrate 29g (Dietary Fiber 2g, Sugars 17g); Protein 3g **Exchanges:** 1 Starch, 1 Other Carbohydrate, 2½ Fat **Carbohydrate Choices:** 2

Banana Bread   CALORIE SMART

Although the true origin of banana bread is not known, this enduring favorite has been around at least since the 1930s. Our version of banana bread has appeared in all editions of the Betty Crocker Cookbook. It's a great way to use those bananas that are turning brown and soft.

PREP 15 min **TOTAL** 3 hr 40 min • 2 loaves (12 slices each)

- 1¼ cups sugar
- ½ cup butter, softened
- 2 eggs
- 1½ cups mashed very ripe bananas (3 medium)
- ½ cup buttermilk
- 1 teaspoon vanilla
- 2½ cups all-purpose flour
- 1 teaspoon baking soda
- 1 teaspoon salt
- 1 cup chopped nuts, if desired

1 Heat oven to 350°F. Grease bottoms only of 2 (8x4- or 9x5-inch) loaf pans with shortening or cooking spray.

2 In large bowl, stir sugar and butter until well mixed. Stir in eggs until well mixed. Stir in bananas, buttermilk and vanilla; beat with spoon until smooth. Stir in flour, baking soda and salt just until moistened. Stir in nuts. Divide batter evenly between pans.

3 Bake 8-inch loaves about 1 hour, 9-inch loaves about 1 hour 15 minutes, or until toothpick inserted in center comes out clean. Cool 10 minutes in pans on cooling rack.

4 Loosen sides of loaves from pans; remove from pans and place top side up on cooling rack. Cool completely, about 2 hours, before slicing. Wrap tightly and store at room temperature up to 4 days, or refrigerate.

1 Slice: Calories 150; Total Fat 4.5g (Saturated Fat 2.5g, Trans Fat 0g); Cholesterol 30mg; Sodium 190mg; Total Carbohydrate 24g (Dietary Fiber 0g, Sugars 12g); Protein 2g **Exchanges:** ½ Starch, 1 Other Carbohydrate, 1 Fat **Carbohydrate Choices:** 1½

Blueberry-Banana Bread Omit nuts. Stir in 1 cup fresh or frozen (do not thaw) blueberries into batter.

Zucchini Bread CALORIE SMART

You don't need to peel the zucchini if it is very fresh and green. Older, larger zucchini may require peeling before shredding. The peel adds little green flecks to the bread.

PREP 20 min **TOTAL** 3 hr 50 min • 2 loaves (12 slices each)

3	cups shredded zucchini (2 or 3 medium)
1⅔	cups sugar
⅔	cup vegetable oil
2	teaspoons vanilla
4	eggs
3	cups all-purpose or whole wheat flour
2	teaspoons baking soda
1	teaspoon salt
1	teaspoon ground cinnamon
½	teaspoon baking powder
½	teaspoon ground cloves
½	cup chopped nuts
½	cup raisins, if desired

1 Heat oven to 350°F. Grease bottoms only of 2 (8x4- or 9x5-inch) loaf pans with shortening or cooking spray.

2 In large bowl, stir zucchini, sugar, oil, vanilla and eggs until well mixed. Stir in flour, baking soda, salt, cinnamon, baking powder and cloves. Stir in nuts and raisins. Divide batter evenly between pans.

3 Bake 8-inch loaves 50 to 60 minutes, 9-inch loaves 1 hour 10 minutes to 1 hour 20 minutes, or until toothpick inserted in center comes out clean. Cool 10 minutes in pans on cooling rack.

4 Loosen sides of loaves from pans; remove from pans and place top side up on cooling rack. Cool completely, about 2 hours, before slicing. Wrap tightly and store at room temperature up to 4 days, or refrigerate up to 10 days.

1 Slice: Calories 200; Total Fat 9g (Saturated Fat 1.5g, Trans Fat 0g); Cholesterol 35mg; Sodium 230mg; Total Carbohydrate 27g (Dietary Fiber 1g, Sugars 14g); Protein 3g **Exchanges:** 1 Starch, 1 Other Carbohydrate, 1½ Fat **Carbohydrate Choices:** 2

Cranberry Bread Omit zucchini, cinnamon, cloves and raisins. Add ½ cup milk and 2 teaspoons grated orange peel with the oil. Stir 3 cups fresh or frozen (thawed and drained) cranberries into batter. Bake 1 hour to 1 hour 10 minutes.

Orange-Zucchini Bread Stir in 2 teaspoons grated orange peel with the flour mixture. When loaf is cooled, drizzle with Orange Glaze (page 581). Let stand until set.

Pumpkin Bread Substitute 1 can (15 ounces) pureed pumpkin (not pumpkin pie mix) for the zucchini.

Cranberry Bread

Cranberry–Sweet Potato Bread

PREP 25 min **TOTAL** 3 hr 35 min • 2 loaves
(12 slices each)

- 2⅓ cups sugar
- ⅔ cup water
- ⅔ cup vegetable oil
- 1 teaspoon vanilla
- 2 cups mashed cooked dark-orange sweet potatoes (about 1¼ lb)*
- 4 eggs
- 3⅓ cups all-purpose flour
- 2 teaspoons baking soda
- 1½ teaspoons salt
- 1 teaspoon ground cinnamon
- ½ teaspoon baking powder
- ½ teaspoon ground nutmeg
- 1 cup sweetened dried cranberries
- 1 cup chopped pecans, if desired

1 Heat oven to 350°F. Grease 2 loaf pans (8x4- or 9x5-inch) with shortening or cooking spray; lightly flour.

2 In large bowl, mix sugar, water, oil, vanilla, sweet potatoes and eggs until well blended. In medium bowl, mix flour, baking soda, salt, cinnamon, baking powder and nutmeg. Add to sweet potato mixture; stir just until dry ingredients are moistened. Stir in cranberries and pecans. Divide batter evenly between pans.

3 Bake 8-inch loaves about 1 hour, 9-inch loaves about 1 hour 10 minutes, or until toothpick inserted in center comes out clean. Cool 15 minutes in pans on cooling rack.

4 Loosen sides of loaves from pans; remove from pans and place top side up on cooling rack. Cool completely, about 2 hours, before slicing. Wrap tightly and store at room temperature up to 4 days, or refrigerate.

*Or substitute 1 can (23 ounces) sweet potatoes in syrup, drained and mashed, for the cooked sweet potatoes.

1 Slice: Calories 240; Total Fat 7g (Saturated Fat 1.5g, Trans Fat 0g); Cholesterol 35mg; Sodium 280mg; Total Carbohydrate 41g (Dietary Fiber 1g, Sugars 25g); Protein 3g **Exchanges:** 1 Starch, 1½ Other Carbohydrate, 1½ Fat **Carbohydrate Choices:** 3

Cornbread   CALORIE SMART

PREP 10 min **TOTAL** 35 min • 12 servings

- 1 cup milk
- ¼ cup butter, melted
- 1 egg
- 1¼ cups yellow, white or blue cornmeal
- 1 cup all-purpose flour
- ½ cup sugar
- 1 tablespoon baking powder
- ½ teaspoon salt

1 Heat oven to 400°F. Grease bottom and side of 9-inch round pan, 8-inch square pan or 8-inch cast-iron skillet with shortening.

2 In large bowl, beat milk, butter and egg with whisk. Stir in remaining ingredients all at once just until flour is moistened (batter will be lumpy). Pour into pan.

3 Bake 20 to 25 minutes or until golden brown and toothpick inserted in center comes out clean. Serve warm if desired.

1 Serving: Calories 170; Total Fat 5g (Saturated Fat 2.5g, Trans Fat 0g); Cholesterol 30mg; Sodium 260mg; Total Carbohydrate 29g (Dietary Fiber 0g, Sugars 10g); Protein 4g **Exchanges:** 1 Starch, 1 Other Carbohydrate, 1 Fat **Carbohydrate Choices:** 2

Corn Muffins Grease bottoms only of 12 regular-size muffin cups with shortening or cooking spray. Divide batter evenly among muffin cups. Bake as directed.

Cranberry–Sweet Potato Bread

Oatmeal Streusel Bread

PREP 25 min **TOTAL** 3 hr 30 min • 1 loaf
(12 slices)

STREUSEL

- ¼ cup packed brown sugar
- ¼ cup chopped walnuts, toasted (page 23)
- 2 teaspoons ground cinnamon

BREAD

- 1 cup all-purpose flour
- ½ cup whole wheat flour
- ½ cup old-fashioned oats
- 2 tablespoons ground flaxseed or flaxseed meal
- 1 teaspoon baking powder
- ½ teaspoon salt
- ¼ teaspoon baking soda
- ¾ cup packed brown sugar
- ⅔ cup vegetable oil
- 2 eggs
- ¼ cup sour cream
- 2 teaspoons vanilla
- ½ cup milk

ICING

- ¾ to 1 cup powdered sugar
- 1 tablespoon milk
- 2 teaspoons light corn syrup

1 Heat oven to 350°F. Spray bottom only of 9x5-inch loaf pan with cooking spray. In small bowl, stir together streusel ingredients; set aside.

2 In medium bowl, stir all-purpose flour, whole wheat flour, oats, flaxseed, baking powder, salt and baking soda with whisk until blended.

3 In large bowl, beat brown sugar and oil with electric mixer on medium speed 1 minute or until blended. Add eggs, one at a time, beating well after each addition. Beat in sour cream and vanilla. Add flour mixture alternately with milk, beating on low speed after each addition until smooth.

4 Spoon one-third of batter in pan (about 1 cup); sprinkle with half of the streusel (about ⅓ cup). Top with half of remaining batter (about 1 cup), spreading gently. Sprinkle with remaining streusel. Top with remaining batter. Gently run knife through batter to swirl.

5 Bake 50 to 55 minutes or until toothpick inserted in center comes out clean. Cool on cooling rack 10 minutes. Loosen sides of loaf from pan; remove from pan and place top side up on cooling rack. Cool completely, about 2 hours.

6 In small bowl, beat icing ingredients, adding enough of the powdered sugar for desired drizzling consistency. Drizzle icing over bread. Let stand until set. Wrap tightly and store at room temperature up to 4 days, or refrigerate.

1 Slice: Calories 320; Total Fat 16g (Saturated Fat 2g, Trans Fat 0g); Cholesterol 40mg; Sodium 190mg; Total Carbohydrate 40g (Dietary Fiber 1g, Sugars 27g); Protein 4g **Exchanges:** 1½ Starch, 1 Other Carbohydrate, 3 Fat **Carbohydrate Choices:** 2½

Cornbread

Oatmeal Streusel Bread

Heirloom Recipe and New Twist

There's nothing like hot, homemade biscuits when you're craving comfort food. Our heirloom recipe, made with all-purpose flour, makes the classic biscuits the South is known for. The light, fluffy texture is perfect for holding a pat of butter or a drizzle of honey. When made with whole wheat flour, they'll take on a heartier texture and nutty flavor. Our twist recipe amplifies the Southern appeal by using sweet potatoes and bacon.

HEIRLOOM

Baking Powder Biscuits

CALORIE SMART • FAST • EASY

PREP 10 min **TOTAL** 25 min • 12 biscuits

- 2 cups all-purpose or whole wheat flour
- 1 tablespoon sugar
- 1 tablespoon baking powder
- 1 teaspoon salt
- ½ cup shortening or cold butter, cut into 8 pieces
- ¾ cup milk

1 Heat oven to 450°F. In medium bowl, mix flour, sugar, baking powder and salt. Cut in shortening, using pastry blender or fork, until mixture looks like fine crumbs. Stir in milk until dough leaves side of bowl (dough will be soft and sticky).

2 Place dough on lightly floured surface. Knead lightly 10 times. Roll or pat until ½ inch thick. Cut with floured 2- to 2¼-inch biscuit cutter. On ungreased cookie sheet, place biscuits about 1 inch apart for crusty sides, touching for soft sides.

3 Bake 10 to 12 minutes or until golden brown. Immediately remove from cookie sheet to cooling rack. Serve warm.

1 Biscuit: Calories 160; Total Fat 9g (Saturated Fat 2.5g, Trans Fat 1.5g); Cholesterol 0mg; Sodium 330mg; Total Carbohydrate 18g (Dietary Fiber 0g, Sugars 2g); Protein 3g **Exchanges:** 1 Starch, 2 Fat **Carbohydrate Choices:** 1

Buttermilk Biscuits Reduce baking powder to 2 teaspoons; add ¼ teaspoon baking soda with the sugar. Substitute buttermilk for the milk. (If buttermilk is thick, use slightly more than ¾ cup.)

Drop Biscuits Increase milk to 1 cup. Grease cookie sheet with shortening. Drop dough by 12 spoonfuls about 2 inches apart onto cookie sheet.

Ham 'n Egg Biscuit Sandwiches Make biscuits as directed—except use 3-inch cutter (yield will be 6 biscuits). Split biscuits in half while still warm. Spread with mayonnaise and mustard if desired. On each biscuit bottom, place 1 slice American cheese, 1 fried or poached egg (see pages 90 and 91) and 1 slice deli ham; cover with biscuit tops. Serve immediately.

Making Baking Powder Biscuits

Cut shortening into flour mixture until the mixture looks like fine crumbs.

Drop Biscuits

Sweet Potato–Bacon Biscuits

NEW TWIST
....

Sweet Potato–Bacon Biscuits

CALORIE SMART

PREP 20 min **TOTAL** 35 min • 8 biscuits

- 1½ cups all-purpose flour
- 1 tablespoon baking powder
- ¼ teaspoon salt
- 8 slices bacon, crisply cooked, crumbled
- ½ teaspoon chopped fresh thyme leaves
- ¼ cup butter, frozen
- ⅔ cup mashed canned sweet potatoes (from 15-oz can)
- 2 tablespoons buttermilk
- 2 tablespoons butter, melted

1 Heat oven to 450°F. In large bowl, mix flour, baking powder and salt; stir in bacon and thyme. Shred frozen butter, using large holes of grater; add to flour mixture and toss to coat. Stir in sweet potatoes and buttermilk just until soft dough forms.

2 Place dough on lightly floured surface; gently roll in flour to coat. Knead lightly 4 or 5 times. Press or roll dough until ¾ inch thick. Cut with floured 2½-inch biscuit cutter. On ungreased cookie sheet, place biscuits about 1 inch apart.

3 Bake 12 to 15 minutes or until light golden brown. Brush with melted butter. Serve warm.

1 Biscuit: Calories 180; Total Fat 7g (Saturated Fat 3g, Trans Fat 0g); Cholesterol 15mg; Sodium 480mg; Total Carbohydrate 24g (Dietary Fiber 1g, Sugars 4g); Protein 6g **Exchanges:** 1½ Starch, 1½ Fat **Carbohydrate Choices:** 1½

Easy Cream Biscuits

CALORIE SMART • EASY

Whipping cream replaces shortening or butter, making these biscuits rich and super tender.

PREP 10 min **TOTAL** 35 min • 12 biscuits

- 1¾ cups all-purpose flour
- 2½ teaspoons baking powder
- ½ teaspoon salt
- About 1¼ cups whipping cream

1 Heat oven to 450°F. In large bowl, mix flour, baking powder and salt. Stir in just enough whipping cream so dough leaves side of bowl and forms a ball. (If dough is too dry, mix in 1 to 2 teaspoons more whipping cream.)

2 Place dough on lightly floured surface; gently roll in flour to coat. Knead lightly 10 times, sprinkling with flour if dough is too sticky. Roll or pat until ½ inch thick. Cut with floured 2- to 2¼-inch biscuit cutter. On ungreased cookie sheet, place biscuits about 1 inch apart.

3 Bake 10 to 12 minutes or until golden brown. Immediately remove from cookie sheet to cooling rack. Serve warm.

1 Biscuit: Calories 140; Total Fat 8g (Saturated Fat 5g, Trans Fat 0g); Cholesterol 30mg; Sodium 210mg; Total Carbohydrate 15g (Dietary Fiber 0g, Sugars 0g); Protein 2g **Exchanges:** 1 Other Carbohydrate, 1½ Fat **Carbohydrate Choices:** 1

Chocolate Chip Cream Biscuits Stir in 1 tablespoon sugar and ¼ cup miniature semisweet chocolate chips with the flour. Drizzle with Chocolate Glaze (page 582) if desired.

Herbed Cream Biscuits Stir in ½ teaspoon Italian seasoning with the flour.

LEARN WITH BETTY Biscuits

Perfect Biscuit: This biscuit is light golden brown and high, with fairly smooth sides. It will be tender and light.

Underleavened Biscuit: This biscuit did not have enough leavening and was mixed too much. It will be tough and not flaky.

Overbaked Biscuit: This biscuit was overbaked and the oven was too hot. It will be hard and crumbly.

Scones

PREP 15 min **TOTAL** 35 min • 8 scones

- 1¾ cups all-purpose flour
- 3 tablespoons granulated sugar
- 2½ teaspoons baking powder
- ½ teaspoon salt
- ⅓ cup cold butter, cut into 8 pieces
- 1 egg, beaten
- ½ teaspoon vanilla
- 4 to 6 tablespoons whipping cream
- Additional whipping cream
- Coarse sugar or additional granulated sugar

1 Heat oven to 400°F. In large bowl, mix flour, granulated sugar, baking powder and salt. Cut in butter, using pastry blender or fork, until mixture looks like fine crumbs. Stir in egg, vanilla and just enough of the 4 to 6 tablespoons whipping cream so dough leaves side of bowl.

2 Place dough on lightly floured surface; gently roll in flour to coat. Knead lightly 10 times. On ungreased cookie sheet, roll or pat dough into 8-inch round. Cut into 8 wedges with sharp knife that has been dipped in flour, but do not separate wedges. Brush with additional whipping cream; sprinkle with coarse sugar.

3 Bake 14 to 16 minutes or until light golden brown. Immediately remove from cookie sheet; carefully separate wedges. Serve warm.

1 Scone: Calories 240; Total Fat 11g (Saturated Fat 6g, Trans Fat 0.5g); Cholesterol 55mg; Sodium 360mg; Total Carbohydrate 31g (Dietary Fiber 0g, Sugars 10g); Protein 4g **Exchanges:** 1 Starch, 1 Other Carbohydrate, 2 Fat **Carbohydrate Choices:** 2

Cherry–Chocolate Chip Scones Stir in ½ cup each dried cherries and miniature semisweet chocolate chips with the egg, vanilla and whipping cream.

Chocolate Chip Scones Stir in ½ cup miniature semisweet chocolate chips with the egg, vanilla and whipping cream.

Currant Scones Stir in ½ cup dried currants or raisins with the egg, vanilla and whipping cream.

Lemon-Cherry Scones Stir in ½ cup dried cherries and 2 teaspoons grated lemon peel with the egg, vanilla and whipping cream.

Raspberry-White Chocolate Scones Substitute almond extract for the vanilla; increase whipping cream to ½ cup. Stir in ¾ cup frozen unsweetened raspberries (do not thaw) and ⅔ cup white vanilla baking chips with the egg, almond extract and whipping cream. Omit kneading step. On ungreased cookie sheet, pat dough into 8-inch round. Continue as directed, except bake 18 to 23 minutes. Raspberries will color the dough a little bit.

Making Scones

Roll or pat dough into 8-inch round on un-greased cookie sheet.

Cut into 8 wedges with sharp knife or pizza cutter dipped in flour; do not separate.

Cherry–Chocolate Chip Scones

Cheddar-Chile Cornbread Scones

Popovers

Cheddar-Chile Cornbread Scones

PREP 20 min **TOTAL** 45 min • 8 scones'

- 1¼ cups white whole wheat flour
- 1 cup cornmeal
- 1 tablespoon sugar
- 2 teaspoons baking powder
- ½ teaspoon salt
- ½ cup cold butter, cut into 8 pieces
- ¼ cup milk
- 1 egg, beaten
- ¾ cup shredded Cheddar cheese (3 oz)
- 1 can (4.5 oz) chopped green chiles, undrained
- ⅔ cup crumbled crisply cooked bacon, if desired
  Honey, if desired

1 Heat oven to 425°F. Grease cookie sheet with shortening or cooking spray. In large bowl, mix flour, cornmeal, sugar, baking powder and salt. Cut in butter, using pastry blender or fork, until mixture looks like coarse crumbs. Stir in milk, egg, cheese, chiles and bacon.

2 Place dough on lightly floured surface; knead lightly 10 times. On cookie sheet, roll or pat dough into 8-inch round. Cut into 8 wedges, but do not separate wedges.

3 Bake 18 to 23 minutes or until golden brown. Immediately remove from cookie sheet; carefully separate wedges. Serve warm with honey.

1 Scone: Calories 310; Total Fat 17g (Saturated Fat 10g, Trans Fat 0.5g); Cholesterol 65mg; Sodium 510mg; Total Carbohydrate 33g (Dietary Fiber 2g, Sugars 3g); Protein 7g **Exchanges:** 1 Starch, 1 Other Carbohydrate, ½ High-Fat Meat, 2½ Fat **Carbohydrate Choices:** 2

Popovers CALORIE SMART • EASY

Popovers get their name because they pop up high out of their baking cups in the oven. Serve them hot with butter or try one of the sweet or savory butters on page 470.

PREP 10 min **TOTAL** 45 min • 6 popovers

- 2 eggs
- 1 cup all-purpose flour
- 1 cup milk
- ½ teaspoon salt

1 Heat oven to 450°F. Generously grease 6-cup popover pan with shortening. Heat popover pan in oven 5 minutes.

2 Meanwhile, in medium bowl, beat eggs slightly with fork or whisk. Beat in remaining ingredients just until smooth (do not overbeat or popovers may not puff as high). Fill cups about half full.

3 Bake 20 minutes. Reduce oven temperature to 325°F. Bake 10 to 15 minutes longer or until deep golden brown. Immediately remove from cups. Serve hot.

1 Popover: Calories 120; Total Fat 3g (Saturated Fat 1g, Trans Fat 0g); Cholesterol 75mg; Sodium 240mg; Total Carbohydrate 18g (Dietary Fiber 0g, Sugars 2g); Protein 6g **Exchanges:** 1 Starch, 1 Fat **Carbohydrate Choices:** 1

Yorkshire Pudding Heat oven to 350°F. Place ¼ cup vegetable oil or meat drippings in 9-inch square pan; place pan in oven and heat until hot. Increase oven temperature to 450°F. Prepare popover batter; carefully pour into hot oil. Bake 18 to 23 minutes or until puffy and golden brown (pudding will puff during baking but will deflate shortly after being removed from oven). Cut pudding into squares; serve immediately.

Cake Doughnuts   CALORIE SMART

Don't forget to also fry the holes—no one can resist bite-size treats.

PREP 45 min **TOTAL** 45 min • 24 doughnuts

      Vegetable oil
3⅓ cups all-purpose flour
  1 cup sugar
  ¾ cup milk
  1 tablespoon baking powder
  ½ teaspoon salt
  ½ teaspoon ground cinnamon
  ¼ teaspoon ground nutmeg
  2 tablespoons shortening
  2 eggs
      Additional sugar, if desired

1 In deep fryer or 3-quart saucepan, heat 3 to 4 inches oil to 375°F.

2 In large bowl, beat 1½ cups of the flour and the remaining ingredients except additional sugar with electric mixer on low speed 30 seconds, scraping bowl constantly. Beat on medium speed 2 minutes, scraping bowl occasionally. Stir in remaining flour.

3 On generously floured surface, roll dough lightly to coat. Gently roll to ⅜-inch thickness. Cut dough with floured 2½-inch doughnut cutter.

4 Slide doughnuts into hot oil, using wide spatula. Turn doughnuts as they rise to the surface. Fry 2 to 3 minutes or until golden brown on both sides. Remove from oil with long fork; do not prick doughnuts. Drain on paper towels. While warm, roll in powdered or granulated sugar, if desired.

1 Doughnut: Calories 190; Total Fat 5g (Saturated Fat 1g, Trans Fat 0g); Cholesterol 20mg; Sodium 120mg; Total Carbohydrate 35g (Dietary Fiber 0g, Sugars 21g); Protein 3g **Exchanges:** 1 Starch, 1 Other Carbohydrate, 1 Fat **Carbohydrate Choices:** 2

Applesauce Doughnuts Reduce sugar to ¾ cup. Add 1 cup applesauce. Increase cinnamon to 1 teaspoon; omit nutmeg. Cover and refrigerate about 1 hour or until dough stiffens. Divide dough in half; roll half of the dough; cut doughnuts. Repeat with remaining dough. Sprinkle hot doughnuts with cinnamon-sugar if desired.

Glazed Doughnuts Frost doughnuts with Chocolate or Vanilla Glaze (page 582 or 581). Sprinkle with candy sprinkles, if desired.

Baked Blueberry-Orange Doughnuts

PREP 25 min **TOTAL** 40 min • 12 doughnuts

      STREUSEL
  3 tablespoons all-purpose flour
  3 tablespoons sugar
  1 tablespoon butter
  3 tablespoons sliced almonds
  ½ teaspoon grated orange peel

      DOUGHNUTS
  ½ cup butter, softened
  ⅔ cup sugar
  2 eggs
  ¼ cup milk
  ¼ cup fresh orange juice
  2 cups all-purpose flour
  2 teaspoons grated orange peel
1½ teaspoons baking powder
  ½ teaspoon salt
  ¾ cup fresh blueberries

1 Heat oven to 425°F. Lightly spray 2 regular-size doughnut pans (6 doughnuts per pan) with cooking spray.

2 In small bowl, mix 3 tablespoons flour and 3 tablespoons sugar. Cut in 1 tablespoon butter, using pastry blender or fork, until mixture is crumbly. Stir in almonds and ½ teaspoon orange peel; set streusel aside.

3 In medium bowl, beat ½ cup butter, ⅔ cup sugar and the eggs with electric mixer on medium speed until smooth. Add milk and orange juice; beat on low speed until well mixed. Stir in 2 cups flour, 2 teaspoons orange peel, the baking powder and salt just until flour is moistened. Fold in blueberries.

4 Spoon batter evenly into doughnut pans, filling wells about ¼ inch from top of pan; sprinkle evenly with streusel. Bake 6 to 8 minutes or until toothpick inserted in center comes out clean. Cool 5 minutes; remove from pan to cooling rack. Serve warm if desired.

1 Doughnut: Calories 250; Total Fat 11g (Saturated Fat 6g, Trans Fat 0g); Cholesterol 55mg; Sodium 250mg; Total Carbohydrate 34g (Dietary Fiber 1g, Sugars 16g); Protein 4g **Exchanges:** 1 Starch, 1½ Other Carbohydrate, 2 Fat **Carbohydrate Choices:** 2

Beignets with Espresso Sugar CALORIE SMART

PREP 50 min **TOTAL** 3 hr 30 min • 30 beignets

ESPRESSO SUGAR

⅔ cup sugar

1 to 1¼ teaspoons espresso coffee powder

BEIGNETS

2¾ cups all-purpose flour

¼ cup sugar

¼ teaspoon salt

1 package regular active or fast-acting dry yeast (2¼ teaspoons)

¾ cup very warm milk (120°F to 130°F)

¼ cup butter, melted

1 teaspoon vanilla

2 eggs

Vegetable oil for frying

GLAZE

⅓ cup dark, semisweet or milk chocolate chips

1 teaspoon vegetable oil

1 In small bowl, stir together ⅔ cup sugar and the espresso powder; set aside. Grease large bowl with shortening or cooking spray; set aside.

2 Insert paddle attachment in electric stand mixer. In another large bowl, mix 2 cups of the flour, ¼ cup sugar, the salt and yeast. Add warm milk and butter. Beat on low speed 1 minute, scraping bowl and paddle frequently. Remove paddle attachment and insert dough hook. Add vanilla and eggs; beat until smooth. Beat on low speed 1 minute, scraping bowl and dough hook frequently. Stir in enough remaining flour to make dough easy to handle (dough will be slightly sticky).

3 Place dough in greased bowl, turning dough to grease all sides. Cover bowl with plastic wrap and let rise in warm place about 2 hours or until dough has doubled in size.

4 Sprinkle cookie sheet with flour; set aside. Place dough on surface generously sprinkled with flour. Roll dough in flour to coat. With floured rolling pin, roll dough to ½-inch thickness. Using 2-inch round cookie cutter, cut 30 rounds, gently pressing together and rerolling dough scraps as necessary. On lightly floured surface, sprinkle both sides of each round with flour; place about 2 inches apart on cookie sheet. Cover loosely with plastic wrap sprayed with cooking spray; let rise in warm place 30 to 40 minutes or until slightly risen.

5 In deep fryer or 4-quart Dutch oven, heat 2 inches oil to 325°F over medium heat. Cover cooling rack with paper towels. Fry 4 or 5 beignets at a time in hot oil until golden brown on both sides, about 1 minute on each side. Remove from oil with slotted spoon to cooling rack. Immediately roll in espresso sugar.

6 In small microwavable bowl, microwave chocolate chips on High 30 to 60 seconds, stirring once, until chips are softened and can be stirred smooth. Stir in 1 teaspoon oil until smooth. Spoon into small resealable food-storage plastic bag; seal bag. Cut off tiny corner of bag; squeeze bag to drizzle chocolate over beignets.

1 Beignet: Calories 150; Total Fat 9g (Saturated Fat 2.5g, Trans Fat 0g); Cholesterol 15mg; Sodium 40mg; Total Carbohydrate 17g (Dietary Fiber 0g, Sugars 8g); Protein 2g **Exchanges:** 1 Starch, 1½ Fat **Carbohydrate Choices:** 1

Making Beignets

Cut rounds using 2-inch cookie cutter, gently pressing together and rerolling dough scraps as necessary.

Fry 4 or 5 beignets at a time until golden brown on both sides. Remove from oil; immediately roll in espresso sugar.

Beignets with Espresso Sugar

Strawberry Cream Brunch Cake

PREP 20 min **TOTAL** 1 hr 35 min ● 16 servings

CREAM CHEESE FILLING

 1 package (8 oz) cream cheese, softened
¼ cup sugar
 2 tablespoons all-purpose flour
 1 egg

CAKE

2¼ cups all-purpose flour
¾ cup sugar
¾ cup cold butter
½ teaspoon baking powder
½ teaspoon baking soda
¼ teaspoon salt
¾ cup sour cream
 1 teaspoon almond extract
 1 egg
½ cup strawberry or raspberry preserves
½ cup sliced almonds

1 Heat oven to 350°F. Grease bottom and side of 10-inch springform pan or 11x7-inch (2-quart) glass baking dish with shortening; lightly flour.

2 In small bowl, mix filling ingredients until smooth; set aside.

3 In large bowl, mix 2¼ cups flour and ¾ cup sugar. Cut in butter, using pastry blender or fork, until mixture looks like coarse crumbs. Reserve 1 cup of the crumb mixture. Stir baking powder, baking soda, salt, sour cream, almond extract and 1 egg into remaining crumb mixture. Spread batter over bottom and 2 inches up side (about ¼ inch thick) of pan.

4 Spoon filling over batter. Carefully spoon preserves evenly over filling. Mix almonds and reserved crumb mixture; sprinkle over preserves.

5 Bake springform pan 50 to 60 minutes, 11x7-inch dish 35 to 45 minutes, or until filling is set and crust is deep golden brown. Cool 15 minutes; remove side of springform pan. Serve warm if desired. Store covered in refrigerator.

1 Serving: Calories 320; Total Fat 18g (Saturated Fat 10g, Trans Fat 0.5g); Cholesterol 70mg; Sodium 220mg; Total Carbohydrate 35g (Dietary Fiber 1g, Sugars 18g); Protein 4g **Exchanges:** 1½ Starch, 1 Other Carbohydrate, 3½ Fat **Carbohydrate Choices:** 2

Strawberry Cream Brunch Cake

MAKE-AHEAD Directions Bake Strawberry Cream Brunch Cake as directed. Cool cake completely, then wrap tightly and freeze up to 1 month. To thaw, let stand at room temperature several hours before serving.

Sour Cream Coffee Cake

PREP 30 min **TOTAL** 2 hr ● 16 servings

BROWN SUGAR FILLING

½ cup packed brown sugar
½ cup finely chopped nuts
1½ teaspoons ground cinnamon

COFFEE CAKE

 3 cups all-purpose or whole wheat flour
1½ teaspoons baking powder
1½ teaspoons baking soda
¾ teaspoon salt
1½ cups granulated sugar
¾ cup butter, softened
1½ teaspoons vanilla
 3 eggs
1½ cups sour cream

GLAZE

½ cup powdered sugar
¼ teaspoon vanilla
 2 to 3 teaspoons milk

1 Heat oven to 350°F. Grease bottom, side and tube of 10-inch angel food (tube) cake pan or 12-cup fluted tube cake pan or bottoms and sides of 2 (9x5-inch) loaf pans with shortening or cooking spray.

2 In small bowl, stir filling ingredients until well mixed; set aside. In large bowl, stir flour, baking powder, baking soda and salt until well mixed; set aside.

3 In another large bowl, beat granulated sugar, butter, 1½ teaspoons vanilla and the eggs with electric mixer on medium speed 2 minutes, scraping bowl occasionally. Alternately add flour mixture and sour cream, beating on low speed until blended.

4 For angel food or fluted tube cake pan, spread one-third of the batter (about 2 cups) in pan, then sprinkle with one-third of the filling; repeat twice. For loaf pans, spread one-fourth of the batter (about 1½ cups) in each pan, then sprinkle each with one-fourth of the filling; repeat once.

5 Bake angel food or fluted tube cake pan about 1 hour, loaf pans about 45 minutes, or until toothpick inserted near center comes out clean. Cool 10 minutes; remove cake from pan to cooling rack. Cool 20 minutes.

6 In small bowl, stir glaze ingredients until smooth and thin enough to drizzle. Drizzle glaze over coffee cake. Serve warm if desired.

1 Serving: Calories 360; Total Fat 16g (Saturated Fat 8g, Trans Fat 0.5g); Cholesterol 75mg; Sodium 360mg; Total Carbohydrate 49g (Dietary Fiber 1g, Sugars 30g); Protein 5g **Exchanges:** 2 Starch, 1 Other Carbohydrate, 3 Fat **Carbohydrate Choices:** 3

Lemon Curd–Filled Butter Cake

A classic lemon curd is the filling in this buttery-rich dense yellow cake. To save time, you can substitute a jar of purchased lemon curd.

PREP 30 min **TOTAL** 2 hr 45 min • 12 servings

LEMON CURD

- ¼ cup granulated sugar
- 2 tablespoons cornstarch
- ¾ cup cold water
- 3 egg yolks
- 1 tablespoon grated lemon peel
- 3 tablespoons fresh lemon juice

CAKE

- 1 cup butter, softened
- 1 cup granulated sugar
- 5 eggs
- 1¾ cups all-purpose flour
- 2 teaspoons grated lemon peel
- 1½ teaspoons baking powder
- 1 teaspoon vanilla
- ⅓ cup slivered almonds, toasted (page 23)
- ½ teaspoon powdered sugar, if desired

1 In 1-quart saucepan, mix ¼ cup granulated sugar and the cornstarch. Stir in water and egg yolks with whisk until well mixed and no lumps remain. Heat to boiling over medium heat, stirring constantly, until mixture begins to thicken. Cook and stir 1 minute; remove from heat. Stir in 1 tablespoon lemon peel and the lemon juice. Refrigerate uncovered 20 minutes, stirring once, until room temperature.

2 Heat oven to 350°F. Grease bottom and side of 9-inch springform pan with shortening; lightly flour.

3 In large bowl, beat butter and 1 cup granulated sugar with electric mixer on medium speed about 1 minute or until smooth. Beat in eggs, one at a time, just until blended, then continue beating on medium speed 2 minutes, scraping bowl once. On low speed, beat in flour, 2 teaspoons lemon peel, the baking powder and vanilla about 30 seconds or just until blended.

4 Spread half of the batter (about 2 cups) in bottom of pan. Spoon lemon curd evenly onto batter, spreading to ½ inch of edge. Drop remaining batter by tablespoonfuls around edge of curd and pan; spread batter evenly and toward center to cover curd. Sprinkle almonds over top.

5 Bake 45 to 55 minutes or until center is set, cake is firm to the touch and top is golden brown. Cool in pan on cooling rack at least 1 hour (center will sink slightly). Run thin knife around side of cake; remove side of pan. Sprinkle with powdered sugar before serving. Store covered in refrigerator.

1 Serving: Calories 360; Total Fat 20g (Saturated Fat 9g, Trans Fat 1g); Cholesterol 180mg; Sodium 190mg; Total Carbohydrate 37g (Dietary Fiber 0g, Sugars 21g); Protein 6g **Exchanges:** 1 Starch, 1½ Other Carbohydrate, 4 Fat **Carbohydrate Choices:** 2½

Lemon Curd–Filled Butter Cake

YEAST BREAD BASICS

Making yeast breads is a lot easier than you would think when you know all the tips and tricks. And with our kitchen-tested recipes, you can turn out beautiful, delicious breads every time.

YEAST BREAD INGREDIENTS

Flour: All-purpose and bread flours both have enough gluten-forming protein to develop the gluten necessary to work for yeast bread recipes. (See Learn to Knead Yeast Dough, page 498.)

Whole wheat flour has a high level of protein but won't make the same lofty loaves that all-purpose or bread flour can because the shards of bran in the flour tear the gluten strands, inhibiting its development. **Rye flour** doesn't have enough gluten-forming protein to be used on its own—it is used in combination with all-purpose or bread flour so it develops enough gluten to make desirable loaves.

Yeast: Yeast is temperature sensitive—proper yeast growth is necessary for dough to rise the way it should. If the liquid in the dough recipe is added too hot, it can kill the yeast. If liquid is too cool when added, it can prevent growth. Always check the package expiration date before use.

Dry yeast is the most commonly available form and comes in active dry yeast and instant (fast-acting) yeast varieties, which may shorten rising times. **Bread machine yeast** is a type of instant yeast that can also be used in traditional baking methods. Be sure to use the type of yeast called for in a recipe, as not all yeasts work well in all types of dough-preparation methods.

Yeast can be dissolved using the traditional mixing method. Before combining with other ingredients, the yeast is dissolved in warm water with a small amount of sugar; the sugar acts as food for the yeast. The quick-mix method mixes yeast with the other dry ingredients before adding very warm liquid.

Liquid: Water gives bread a crisp crust, while milk results in a softer crust and bread with added nutrients. Use a thermometer to accurately determine the liquid's temperature before adding.

Sweetener: Sugar, honey and molasses feed the yeast to help it grow, add flavor and help brown the crust. Don't use artificial sweeteners because they won't feed the yeast.

Salt: Salt adds flavor and keeps yeast growth in check. Never omit salt if specified in recipe.

Fat: Butter, shortening and vegetable or olive oil make bread tender and moist and add flavor.

Eggs: Eggs add richness and color and structure.

STORING AND SERVING YEAST BREADS

- See Refrigerator and Freezer Storage Chart, page 33.

- If breads are to be frozen, frost or glaze after they are thawed.

- Store soft-crust breads and rolls in resealable food-storage plastic bags or airtight containers in a cool, dry place up to 7 days.

- Store unsliced crisp-crust breads unwrapped at room temperature up to 3 days. Once sliced, keep in a closed paper bag or tightly wrapped in foil and use within 1 day or freeze.

- To freeze, wrap loaves tightly in plastic wrap and place in freezer bags. Freeze up to 3 months.

- To reheat thawed breads or rolls, wrap in foil and bake at 350°F (10 to 15 minutes for rolls or 15 to 20 minutes for loaves). For a crisper crust, unwrap during the last 5 minutes.

Bread Machine Tips

Follow these tips for bread machine techniques:

- Follow the directions in your manual for the order ingredients should be placed in your bread machine.

- Carefully measure the ingredients, using dry measuring cups for flour and sugar and liquid measuring cups for liquids and measuring, not serving spoons.

- Use bread machine yeast: It has a fine granulation that disperses more evenly during the mixing and kneading cycles.

- Don't open the machine during rising or baking cycles, as it can cause the dough to collapse. If you need to check the progress of your dough, only check during mixing or kneading cycles.

- When using the delay cycle, be sure the yeast does not come in contact with the liquid. Don't use the delay cycle with recipes using eggs, fresh dairy products (except butter), honey, meats or fresh fruits or vegetables, because bacteria can grow during this cycle.

- Keep the area around the bread machine open for good ventilation.

Why Use a Bread Machine?

Here are some reasons why a bread machine might be a great tool for your family:

- It's a quick and easy way to mix, raise and bake homemade bread to have fresh bread any time, saving time and money.

- It's a great way to control what goes into your bread, without added preservatives or other ingredients. (But homemade bread won't stay fresh as long as store-bought, for this very reason. So purchase the machine that will make the size of loaf your family can consume in a day or two.)

- It's also a super-simple way to get yeast doughs that are all ready to shape and bake. French bread, pizza dough and pretzel and yeast roll dough can be made in the bread machine on the dough setting, skipping a lot of time and attention from making them by hand. Then you take it from there—shaping the dough and baking it.

- All the ingredients get dumped into the machine at once; no dissolving yeast separately or using a lot of bowls and utensils.

- Since you don't have to knead the dough by hand, it only takes a few minutes to put everything into the machine and let it do its thing.

Making Bread Dough

After the first addition of flour has been beaten in, dough will be very soft and fall in "sheets" off rubber spatula.

To knead, fold dough toward you. Push dough away from you with short rocking motion. Rotate dough a quarter turn; repeat. Dough will feel springy and smooth.

Dough should rise until doubled in size. Press fingertips about ½ inch into dough. If indentations remain, dough has risen enough.

Shaping Traditional Bread Loaves   ## Making Free-Form Loaves

Flatten dough with hands or rolling pin into 18x9-inch rectangle.

Tightly roll dough up toward you, beginning at 9-inch side.

Shape dough into smooth ball by stretching surface of dough around to bottom on all four sides; pinch bottom to seal.

Place on cookie sheet; carefully slash tic-tac-toe pattern on each loaf top with serrated knife.

Focaccia CALORIE SMART

PREP 30 min **TOTAL** 1 hr 50 min • 2 loaves
(12 slices each)

- 2½ to 3 cups all-purpose or bread flour
- 2 tablespoons chopped fresh or 1 tablespoon dried rosemary leaves, crumbled
- 1 tablespoon sugar
- 1 teaspoon salt
- 1 package regular active or fast-acting dry yeast (2¼ teaspoons)
- 5 tablespoons olive or vegetable oil
- 1 cup very warm water (120°F to 130°F)
- ¼ cup grated Parmesan cheese

1 In large bowl, mix 1 cup of the flour, the rosemary, sugar, salt and yeast. Add 3 tablespoons of the oil and the warm water. Beat with electric mixer on medium speed 3 minutes, scraping bowl frequently. Stir in enough remaining flour until dough is soft and leaves side of bowl.

2 Place dough on lightly floured surface. Knead 5 to 8 minutes or until smooth and springy. Grease large bowl with shortening. Place dough in bowl, turning dough to grease all sides. Cover bowl loosely with plastic wrap and let rise in warm place about 30 minutes or until dough has almost doubled in size. Dough is ready if indentation remains when touched.

3 Grease 2 cookie sheets or 12-inch pizza pans with small amount of oil or spray with cooking spray. Gently push fist into dough to deflate. Divide dough in half. Shape each half into a flattened 10-inch round on cookie sheet. Cover loosely with plastic wrap lightly sprayed with cooking spray and let rise in warm place about 30 minutes or until dough has doubled in size.

4 Heat oven to 400°F. Gently make ½-inch-deep depressions about 2 inches apart in dough with fingers. Carefully brush with remaining 2 tablespoons oil; sprinkle with cheese. Bake 15 to 20 minutes or until golden brown. Cut into wedges; serve warm if desired.

1 Slice: Calories 80; Total Fat 3.5g (Saturated Fat 0.5g, Trans Fat 0g); Cholesterol 0mg; Sodium 120mg; Total Carbohydrate 12g (Dietary Fiber 0g, Sugars 0g); Protein 2g **Exchanges:** 1 Starch **Carbohydrate Choices:** 1

Focaccia Breadsticks Make dough as directed. After kneading, cover loosely with plastic wrap; let rest 30 minutes. Grease 2 cookie sheets with shortening or cooking spray; sprinkle with cornmeal. Divide dough into 12 pieces. Roll and shape each piece into 12-inch rope, sprinkling with flour if dough is too sticky. Place ½ inch apart on cookie sheets. Brush with oil and sprinkle with Parmesan cheese or coarse (kosher or sea) salt if desired. Cover loosely with plastic wrap and let rise in warm place about 20 minutes or until dough has almost doubled in size. Heat oven to 425°F. Uncover breadsticks. Bake 10 to 12 minutes or until golden brown. Makes 12 breadsticks.

Onion Focaccia Make dough as directed, except omit rosemary. In 10-inch skillet, heat ⅓ cup olive oil over medium heat. Stir in 4 cups thinly sliced onions and 4 cloves garlic, finely chopped. Cook uncovered 10 minutes, stirring every 3 to 4 minutes. Reduce heat to medium-low. Cook 30 to 40 minutes longer, stirring well every 5 minutes, until onions are light golden brown. Continue and bake as directed, except do not brush dough with oil or sprinkle with Parmesan cheese; after second rising, carefully spread onion mixture over loaves.

Making Impressions in Focaccia Dough

Gently make ½-inch-deep depressions about 2 inches apart with fingertips.

Focaccia

Black Pepper and Parmesan Grissini CALORIE SMART

Grissini is Italian for "breadsticks"; they are thin and crisp.

PREP 30 min **TOTAL** 2 hr 30 min • 32 grissini

BREADSTICKS
- ¾ cup warm water (105°F to 115°F)
- 1 teaspoon regular active dry yeast
- ½ teaspoon sugar
- 2 tablespoons olive oil
- ½ cup whole wheat flour
- 1¼ to 1¾ cups all-purpose flour
- ⅓ cup grated Parmesan cheese
- 1 teaspoon salt
- ½ teaspoon coarsely ground black pepper

TOPPING
- 2 to 3 teaspoons olive oil
- ¼ cup grated Parmesan cheese
- 1 teaspoon coarsely ground black pepper

1 In large bowl, stir together warm water, yeast and sugar until yeast is dissolved. Add 2 tablespoons oil. Stir in whole wheat flour and ½ cup of the all-purpose flour with whisk until mixture is smooth. Cover and let stand in warm place 35 to 45 minutes or until mixture is light and bubbly.

2 Stir in ⅓ cup cheese, the salt and ½ teaspoon pepper. Add ¾ cup of the all-purpose flour, slowly adding additional flour as necessary to make dough easy to handle.

3 Place dough on lightly floured surface. Knead 10 minutes or until dough is smooth and springy. Place dough in large bowl greased with oil, turning dough to grease all sides. Cover bowl loosely with plastic wrap and let rise in warm place about 1 hour or until dough is doubled in size. Dough is ready if indentation remains when touched.

4 Position one oven rack in lower third of oven and second oven rack in upper third of oven. Heat oven to 425°F. Line 2 cookie sheets with cooking parchment paper.

5 Gently push fist into dough to deflate. On lightly oiled surface, pat dough to 8-inch square. Using pizza cutter or sharp knife, cut square in half. Cut each half crosswise into 16 strips. Roll each strip to 10- to 12-inch length; place on cookie sheet. Brush with 2 to 3 teaspoons oil; sprinkle with ¼ cup cheese and 1 teaspoon pepper.

6 Bake 12 to 15 minutes or until golden brown and crisp, moving cookie sheets to other rack position halfway through baking. Cool completely on cooling rack.

1 Grissini: Calories 45; Total Fat 2g (Saturated Fat 0.5g, Trans Fat 0g); Cholesterol 0mg; Sodium 100mg; Total Carbohydrate 5g (Dietary Fiber 0g, Sugars 0g); Protein 1g **Exchanges:** ½ Starch, ½ Fat **Carbohydrate Choices:** ½

MAKE-AHEAD **Directions** After kneading, the bread can rise overnight (covered) in the refrigerator. When ready to bake, bring to room temperature, deflate dough and continue as directed.

Black Pepper and Parmesan Grissini

Classic White Bread CALORIE SMART

PREP 35 min **TOTAL** 3 hr • 2 loaves (16 slices each)

- 6 to 7 cups all-purpose or bread flour
- 3 tablespoons sugar
- 1 tablespoon salt
- 2 tablespoons shortening or softened butter
- 2 packages regular active or fast-acting dry yeast (4½ teaspoons)
- 2¼ cups very warm water (120°F to 130°F)
- 2 tablespoons butter, melted, if desired

1 In large bowl, stir 3½ cups of the flour, the sugar, salt, shortening and yeast until well mixed. Add warm water. Beat with electric mixer on low speed 1 minute, scraping bowl frequently. Beat on medium speed 1 minute, scraping bowl frequently. Stir in enough remaining flour, 1 cup at a time, to make dough easy to handle.

2 Place dough on lightly floured surface. Knead about 10 minutes or until dough is smooth and springy. Grease large bowl with shortening. Place dough in bowl, turning dough to grease all sides. Cover bowl loosely with plastic wrap and let rise in warm place 40 to 60 minutes or until dough has doubled in size. Dough is ready if indentation remains when touched.

3 Grease bottoms and sides of 2 (8x4- or 9x5-inch) loaf pans with shortening or cooking spray. Gently push fist into dough to deflate. Divide dough in half. On lightly floured surface, flatten each half with hands or rolling pin into 18x9-inch rectangle. Roll dough up tightly, beginning at 9-inch side. Press with thumbs to seal after each turn. Pinch edge of dough into roll to seal. Pinch each end of roll to seal. Fold ends under loaf. Place loaves, seam sides down, in pans. Brush loaves lightly with 1 tablespoon of the melted butter. Cover loosely with plastic wrap and let rise in warm place 35 to 50 minutes or until dough has doubled in size.

4 Move oven rack to low position so that tops of pans will be in center of oven. Heat oven to 425°F. Bake 25 to 30 minutes or until loaves are deep golden brown and sound hollow when tapped. Remove from pans to cooling rack. Brush loaves with remaining 1 tablespoon melted butter. Cool completely.

1 Slice: Calories 100; Total Fat 1g (Saturated Fat 0g, Trans Fat 0g); Cholesterol 0mg; Sodium 220mg; Total Carbohydrate 21g (Dietary Fiber 0g, Sugars 1g); Protein 3g **Exchanges:** 1 Starch **Carbohydrate Choices:** 1½

Honey–Whole Wheat Bread

CALORIE SMART

PREP 35 min **TOTAL** 3 hr 10 min • 2 loaves (16 slices each)

- 3 cups whole wheat flour
- ⅓ cup honey or real maple syrup
- ¼ cup shortening or softened butter
- 3 teaspoons salt
- 2 packages regular active or fast-acting dry yeast (4½ teaspoons)
- 2¼ cups very warm water (120°F to 130°F)
- 3 to 4 cups all-purpose or bread flour
- 2 tablespoons butter, melted, if desired

1 In large bowl, beat whole wheat flour, honey, shortening, salt and yeast with electric mixer on low speed until well mixed. Add warm water. Beat on low speed 1 minute, scraping bowl frequently. Beat on medium speed 1 minute,

LEARN WITH BETTY Yeast Bread

Perfect Yeast Bread: This loaf is high and evenly shaped and golden brown, with an even texture.

Underrisen Yeast Bread: This loaf did not rise because yeast got too hot and dough was not kneaded enough.

Overrisen Yeast Bread: This loaf was kneaded too much and contained too much flour.

Four-Grain Batter Bread

scraping bowl frequently. Stir in enough all-purpose flour, 1 cup at a time, to make dough easy to handle.

2 Place dough on lightly floured surface. Knead about 10 minutes or until dough is smooth and springy. Grease large bowl with shortening. Place dough in bowl, turning dough to grease all sides. Cover bowl loosely with plastic wrap and let rise in warm place 40 to 60 minutes or until dough has doubled in size. Dough is ready if indentation remains when touched.

3 Gently push fist into dough to deflate. Divide dough in half. On lightly floured surface, flatten each half with hands or rolling pin into 18x9-inch rectangle. Roll dough up tightly, beginning at 9-inch side. Press with thumbs to seal after each turn. Pinch edge of dough into roll to seal. Pinch each end of roll to seal. Fold ends under loaf.

4 Grease bottoms and sides of 2 (8x4- or 9x5-inch) loaf pans with shortening or cooking spray. Place loaves, seam sides down, in pans. Brush loaves with 1 tablespoon of the melted butter. Cover loosely with plastic wrap and let rise in warm place 35 to 50 minutes or until dough has doubled in size.

5 Move oven rack to low position so that tops of pans will be in center of oven. Heat oven to 375°F. Uncover loaves. Bake 40 to 45 minutes or until loaves are deep golden brown and sound hollow when tapped. Remove from pans to cooling rack. Brush loaves with remaining 1 tablespoon melted butter; cool.

1 Slice: Calories 120; Total Fat 2g (Saturated Fat 0g, Trans Fat 0g); Cholesterol 0mg; Sodium 220mg; Total Carbohydrate 22g (Dietary Fiber 2g, Sugars 3g); Protein 3g **Exchanges:** 1½ Starch **Carbohydrate Choices:** 1½

Sunflower-Herb Whole Wheat Bread Add
1 tablespoon dried basil leaves and 2 teaspoons dried thyme leaves with the salt. Stir in 1 cup unsalted sunflower nuts with the all-purpose flour.

Four-Grain Batter Bread

CALORIE SMART

Homemade bread doesn't get much easier than this! It's called batter bread because the dough is soft and doesn't require kneading. Just mix it, put it in the pan, let it rise and bake.

PREP 15 min **TOTAL** 1 hr 10 min • 2 loaves (16 slices each)

Cornmeal
4½ to 4¾ cups all-purpose or bread flour
2 tablespoons sugar
1 teaspoon salt
¼ teaspoon baking soda
2 packages regular active or fast-acting dry yeast (4½ teaspoons)
2 cups milk
½ cup water
½ cup whole wheat flour
½ cup wheat germ
½ cup quick-cooking oats

1 Grease bottoms and sides of 2 (8x4-inch) loaf pans with shortening or cooking spray; sprinkle with cornmeal.

2 In large bowl, mix 3½ cups of the all-purpose flour, the sugar, salt, baking soda and yeast. In 1-quart saucepan, heat milk and water over medium heat, stirring occasionally, until very warm (120°F to 130°F). Add milk mixture to flour mixture. Beat with electric mixer on low speed until moistened. Beat on medium speed 3 minutes, scraping bowl occasionally.

3 Stir in whole wheat flour, wheat germ, oats and enough remaining all-purpose flour to make a stiff batter. Divide batter evenly between pans. Round tops of loaves by patting with floured hands. Sprinkle with cornmeal. Cover loosely with plastic wrap and let rise in warm place about 30 minutes or until batter is about 1 inch below tops of pans.

4 Heat oven to 400°F. Bake about 25 minutes or until tops of loaves are light brown. Remove from pans to cooling rack; cool.

1 Slice: Calories 100; Total Fat 1g (Saturated Fat 0g, Trans Fat 0g); Cholesterol 0mg; Sodium 90mg; Total Carbohydrate 19g (Dietary Fiber 1g, Sugars 2g); Protein 4g **Exchanges:** 1 Starch **Carbohydrate Choices:** 1

Whole Wheat–Raisin Batter Bread Increase
whole wheat flour to 2 cups. Omit wheat germ and oats. Stir in 1 cup raisins with the second addition of all-purpose flour.

Sourdough Bread CALORIE SMART

PREP 30 min **TOTAL** 11 hr 45 min • 2 loaves
(16 slices each)

- 1 cup Sourdough Starter
- 2½ cups all-purpose or bread flour
- 2 cups warm water (105°F to 115°F)
- 3¾ to 4¼ cups all-purpose or bread flour
- 3 tablespoons sugar
- 1 teaspoon salt
- 3 tablespoons vegetable oil

1 In 3-quart glass bowl, mix sourdough starter, 2½ cups flour and the warm water with wooden spoon until smooth. Cover and let stand in warm, draft-free place 8 hours.

2 Add 3¾ cups flour, the sugar, salt and oil to mixture in bowl. Stir with wooden spoon until dough is smooth and flour is completely absorbed. (Dough should be just firm enough to gather into ball. If necessary, add remaining ½ cup flour gradually, stirring until all flour is absorbed.)

3 On heavily floured surface, knead dough about 10 minutes or until smooth and springy. Grease large bowl with shortening. Place dough in bowl, turning to grease all sides. Cover and let rise in warm place about 1 hour 30 minutes or until dough has doubled in size. Dough is ready if indentation remains when touched.

4 Grease large cookie sheet with shortening. Gently push fist into dough several times to remove air bubbles. Divide dough in half. Shape each half into a round, slightly flat loaf. Do not tear dough by pulling. Place loaves on opposite corners on cookie sheet. With sharp serrated knife, make three ¼-inch-deep slashes in top of each loaf. Cover and let rise about 45 minutes or until dough has doubled in size.

5 Heat oven to 375°F. Brush loaves with cold water. Place in middle of oven. Bake 35 to 45 minutes, brushing occasionally with water, until loaves sound hollow when tapped. Remove from cookie sheet to cooling rack. Cool completely, about 1 hour.

1 Slice: Calories 110; Total Fat 2.5g (Saturated Fat 0g, Trans Fat 0g); Cholesterol 0mg; Sodium 220mg; Total Carbohydrate 20g (Dietary Fiber 0g, Sugars 2g); Protein 3g **Exchanges:** 1½ Starch **Carbohydrate Choices:** 1

Sourdough Bread

Sourdough Starter

- 1 teaspoon regular active dry yeast
- ¼ cup warm water (105°F to 115°F)
- ¾ cup milk
- 1 cup all-purpose flour

1 In 3-quart glass bowl, dissolve yeast in warm water. Stir in milk. Gradually stir in flour; beat until smooth. Cover with towel or cheesecloth; let stand in warm, draft-free place (80°F to 85°F) about 24 hours or until starter begins to ferment (bubbles will appear on surface of starter). If starter has not begun fermentation after 24 hours, discard and begin again. If fermentation has begun, stir well; cover tightly with plastic wrap and return to warm, draft-free place. Let starter stand 2 to 3 days or until foamy.

2 When starter has become foamy, stir well; pour into 1-quart crock or glass jar with tight-fitting cover. Store in refrigerator. Starter is ready to use when a clear liquid has risen to top. Stir before using. Use 1 cup starter in Sourdough Bread recipe; reserve remaining starter. To remaining starter, add ¾ cup milk and ¾ cup flour. Store covered at room temperature about 12 hours or until bubbles appear; refrigerate.

3 Use starter regularly, every week or so. If the volume of the breads you bake begins to decrease, dissolve 1 teaspoon active dry yeast in ¼ cup warm water. Stir in ½ cup milk, ¾ cup flour and the remaining starter.

Rich Egg Bread   CALORIE SMART

PREP 30 min **TOTAL** 3 hr 5 min • 1 loaf
(16 slices)

- 3 to 3¼ cups all-purpose or bread flour
- ¼ cup sugar
- 1½ teaspoons salt
- 1 package regular active or fast-acting dry yeast (2¼ teaspoons)
- 1 cup very warm water (120°F to 130°F)
- 2 tablespoons vegetable oil
- 1 egg
- Melted butter, if desired

1 In large bowl, mix 1½ cups of the flour, the sugar, salt and yeast. Add warm water and oil. Beat with electric mixer on low speed 1 minute, scraping bowl frequently. Beat on medium speed 1 minute, scraping bowl frequently. Add egg; beat until smooth. Stir in enough remaining flour, ¼ cup at a time, to make dough easy to handle.

2 Place dough on lightly floured surface. Knead about 10 minutes or until dough is smooth and springy. Grease large bowl with shortening. Place dough in bowl, turning dough to grease all sides. Cover bowl loosely with plastic wrap and let rise in warm place about 1 hour or until dough has doubled in size. (At this point, dough can be refrigerated up to 24 hours.) Dough is ready if indentation remains when touched.

3 Grease bottom and sides of 9x5- or 8x4-inch loaf pan with shortening or cooking spray. Gently push fist into dough to deflate. On lightly floured surface, flatten dough with hands or rolling pin into 18x9-inch rectangle. Roll up tightly, beginning at 9-inch side. Pinch edge of dough into roll to seal. Pinch each end of roll to seal. Fold ends under loaf. Place loaf, seam side down, in pan. Cover loosely with plastic wrap lightly sprayed with cooking spray and let rise in warm place about 1 hour or until dough has doubled in size.

4 Move oven rack to low position so that top of pan will be in center of oven. Heat oven to 375°F. Bake 30 to 35 minutes or until loaf is deep golden brown and sounds hollow when tapped. Remove from pan to cooling rack. Brush loaf with melted butter. Cool completely.

1 Slice: Calories 120; Total Fat 2.5g (Saturated Fat 0g, Trans Fat 0g); Cholesterol 15mg; Sodium 230mg; Total Carbohydrate 21g (Dietary Fiber 0g, Sugars 3g); Protein 3g **Exchanges:** 1½ Starch **Carbohydrate Choices:** 1½

Challah Braid Make dough as directed. Lightly grease cookie sheet with shortening or cooking spray. After pushing fist into dough, divide into 3 equal parts. Roll each part into 14-inch rope. Place ropes close together on cookie sheet. Braid ropes gently and loosely, starting in middle; do not stretch. Pinch ends; tuck ends under braid securely. Brush with vegetable oil. Cover loosely with plastic wrap and let rise in warm place 40 to 50 minutes or until dough has doubled in size. Heat oven to 375°F. In small bowl, beat 1 egg yolk and 2 tablespoons water; brush over braid. Sprinkle with poppy seed. Bake 25 to 30 minutes or until golden brown.

Braiding Challah

Braid ropes gently and loosely, starting at middle; do not stretch.

Cinnamon Swirl Raisin Bread Knead ½ cup raisins into dough after deflating in Step 3. Before rolling up dough, brush with 2 teaspoons softened butter. Mix ¼ cup sugar with 1½ teaspoons ground cinnamon; sprinkle over butter.

Challah Braid

Dried Cherry and Walnut Bread

PREP 25 min **TOTAL** 3 hr 30 min • 1 loaf
(16 slices)

- 3¼ to 3¾ cups bread flour
- 2 tablespoons sugar
- 1 package fast-acting dry yeast (2¼ teaspoons)
- 1¼ cups very warm water (120°F to 130°F)
- 2 tablespoons vegetable oil
- 1 cup coarsely chopped walnuts
- 1 cup dried cherries
- 1 tablespoon grated orange peel
- 1 teaspoon salt
- 1 tablespoon cornmeal
- 1 teaspoon milk

1 In large bowl, mix 1½ cups of the flour, the sugar and yeast. Add warm water and oil. Beat with electric mixer on low speed 1 minute, scraping bowl frequently. Beat on medium speed 1 minute, scraping bowl frequently. Stir in 1¾ cups flour, the walnuts, cherries, orange peel and salt with wooden spoon until dough pulls away from side of bowl and forms a sticky ball.

2 Place dough on lightly floured surface. Knead 2 to 3 minutes or until dough is smooth and springy, using enough of the remaining ½ cup flour as necessary to form into smooth ball. Grease large bowl with oil. Place dough in bowl, turning to grease all sides. Cover bowl loosely with plastic wrap and let rise in warm place 1 hour or until dough has doubled in size.

3 Lightly grease large cookie sheet with shortening or cooking spray; sprinkle with cornmeal. Gently push fist into dough to deflate. Place dough on lightly floured surface. Gently shape into smooth ball by stretching surface of dough around to bottom on all sides; pinch bottom to seal. Place on cookie sheet. Cover dough loosely with plastic wrap sprayed with cooking spray and let rise in warm place 30 to 40 minutes or until doubled in size.

4 Heat oven to 350°F. Brush top of loaf with milk. With serrated knife, cut 3 (¼-inch-deep) slashes across top of dough. Bake 35 to 40 minutes or until loaf is deep golden brown and sounds hollow when tapped. Cool completely on cooling rack, about 1 hour.

1 Slice: Calories 210; Total Fat 7g (Saturated Fat 1g, Trans Fat 0g); Cholesterol 0mg; Sodium 150mg; Total Carbohydrate 32g (Dietary Fiber 2g, Sugars 9g); Protein 5g **Exchanges:** 1½ Starch, ½ Other Carbohydrate, 1½ Fat **Carbohydrate Choices:** 2

Dinner Rolls CALORIE SMART

PREP 30 min **TOTAL** 2 hr 15 min • 15 rolls

- 3½ to 3¾ cups all-purpose or bread flour
- ¼ cup sugar
- ¼ cup butter, softened
- 1 teaspoon salt
- 1 package regular active or fast-acting dry yeast (2¼ teaspoons)
- ½ cup very warm water (120°F to 130°F)
- ½ cup very warm milk (120°F to 130°F)
- 1 egg
  Melted butter, if desired

1 In large bowl, stir 2 cups of the flour, the sugar, ¼ cup butter, the salt and yeast until well mixed. Add warm water, warm milk and egg. Beat with electric mixer on low speed 1 minute, scraping bowl frequently. Beat on medium speed 1 minute, scraping bowl frequently. Stir in enough remaining flour, ¼ cup at a time, to make dough easy to handle.

2 Place dough on lightly floured surface. Knead about 5 minutes or until dough is smooth and springy. Grease large bowl with shortening. Place dough in bowl, turning dough to grease all sides. Cover bowl loosely with plastic wrap and let rise in warm place about 1 hour or until dough has doubled in size. Dough is ready if indentation remains when touched.

3 Grease bottom and sides of 13x9-inch pan with shortening or cooking spray. Gently push fist into dough to deflate. Divide dough into 15 equal pieces. Shape each piece into a ball; place in pan. Brush with melted butter. Cover loosely with plastic wrap and let rise in warm place about 30 minutes or until dough has doubled in size.

4 Heat oven to 375°F. Uncover rolls. Bake 12 to 15 minutes or until golden brown. Serve warm if desired.

1 Roll: Calories 160; Total Fat 4g (Saturated Fat 2g, Trans Fat 0g); Cholesterol 25mg; Sodium 190mg; Total Carbohydrate 26g (Dietary Fiber 1g, Sugars 4g); Protein 4g **Exchanges:** 2 Starch **Carbohydrate Choices:** 2

MAKE-AHEAD Directions After placing rolls in pan, cover tightly with foil and refrigerate 4 to 24 hours. About 2 hours before baking, remove from refrigerator; remove foil and cover loosely with plastic wrap. Let rise in warm place until dough has doubled in size. If some rising has occurred in the refrigerator, rising time may be less than 2 hours. Bake as directed.

Cloverleaf Rolls Grease 24 regular-size muffin cups with shortening or cooking spray. Make dough as directed, except after pushing fist into dough, divide dough into 72 equal pieces. (To divide, cut dough in half, then continue cutting pieces in half until there are 72 pieces.) Shape each piece into a ball. Place 3 balls in each muffin cup. Brush with melted butter. Cover loosely with plastic wrap and let rise in warm place about 30 minutes or until dough has doubled in size. Bake as directed. Makes 24 rolls.

Crescent Rolls Grease cookie sheet with shortening or cooking spray. Make dough as directed, except after pushing fist into dough, cut dough in half. Roll each half into 12-inch round on floured surface. Spread with softened butter. Cut each circle into 16 wedges. Roll up each wedge, beginning at rounded edge. Place rolls, with points underneath, on cookie sheet and curve slightly. Brush with melted butter. Cover loosely with plastic wrap and let rise in warm place about 30 minutes or until dough has doubled in size. Bake as directed. Makes 32 rolls.

Roll Top Treatments

Brush unbaked rolls with melted butter (about 1 tablespoon for each 12 rolls). Then sprinkle with one of the following before baking:

Rosemary Sea Salt: Mix 3 tablespoons coarsely chopped fresh rosemary leaves and 1 teaspoon sea salt.

Garlic-Parmesan: Mix 2 tablespoons grated Parmesan and a dash of garlic powder.

Two-Seed: Mix 2 tablespoons each sesame seed and poppy seed.

Making Dinner Rolls

Place dough balls slightly apart in pan so they have room to double in size.

Making Cloverleaf Rolls

Place 3 dough balls next to each other in each muffin cup.

Making Crescent Rolls

Cut dough circles into wedges. Roll up each wedge, beginning at rounded edge.

Soft Pretzels CALORIE SMART

PREP 45 min **TOTAL** 2 hr • 16 pretzels

- 3¾ to 4¼ cups all-purpose flour
- 1 tablespoon sugar
- 1½ teaspoons salt
- 1 package regular active or fast-acting dry yeast (2¼ teaspoons)
- 1½ cups warm water (120°F to 130°F)
- 2 tablespoons vegetable oil
- 1 cup water
- 2 teaspoons baking soda
- 2 teaspoons coarse (kosher or sea) salt

1 In large bowl, stir 2 cups of the flour, the sugar, table salt and yeast with wooden spoon until well mixed. Add warm water and oil. Beat with electric mixer on low speed 1 minute, scraping bowl frequently. Beat on medium speed 1 minute, scraping bowl frequently. With wooden spoon, stir in enough of the remaining flour, about ½ cup at time, until dough is soft, leaves side of bowl and is easy to handle (dough may be slightly sticky).

2 Place dough on lightly floured surface. Knead 5 to 10 minutes or until dough is smooth and springy. Cover loosely with plastic wrap sprayed with cooking spray and let rest 10 minutes.

3 Heat oven to 425°F. Spray cookie sheets with cooking spray. In shallow bowl, stir 1 cup water and baking soda to make pretzel "wash."

4 Divide dough into 16 equal pieces. Roll each piece into 24-inch rope (dip hands in pretzel wash to make rolling dough easier). To make pretzel shape, form rope into a circle, crossing ends at top. Fold dough so crossed ends rest on bottom of circle. Stir pretzel wash; brush over both sides of pretzel, using pastry brush. Place pretzel on cookie sheet. Repeat with remaining dough. Reserve remaining pretzel wash.

5 Cover pretzels loosely with plastic wrap. To make thin pretzels, let rest about 5 minutes or until very slightly puffed. To make thicker pretzels, let rise in warm place 15 to 20 minutes or until puffed.

6 Just before baking, brush pretzels with reserved wash; sprinkle with coarse salt. Bake 1 cookie sheet at a time 10 to 13 minutes or until golden brown. Remove from cookie sheets to cooling rack; cool at least 15 minutes before serving.

1 Pretzel: Calories 120; Total Fat 2g (Saturated Fat 0g, Trans Fat 0g); Cholesterol 0mg; Sodium 670mg; Total Carbohydrate 23g (Dietary Fiber 0g, Sugars 0g); Protein 3g **Exchanges:** 1 Starch, ½ Other Carbohydrate **Carbohydrate Choices:** 1½

Parmesan-Herb Soft Pretzels In small bowl, mix 2 tablespoons grated Parmesan cheese, ½ teaspoon dried basil leaves and ¼ teaspoon garlic powder. Brush hot baked pretzels with melted butter; sprinkle with cheese mixture.

Bakery-Style Pumpernickel Rolls CALORIE SMART

PREP 30 min **TOTAL** 4 hr 30 min • 12 rolls

- 2½ cups all-purpose flour
- ¾ cup rye flour
- 1 tablespoon regular active dry yeast
- 2 tablespoons unsweetened baking cocoa
- 1½ teaspoons coarse (kosher or sea) salt
- 1⅓ cups warm water (105°F to 115°F)
- 3 tablespoons full-flavored (dark) molasses
- 1 tablespoon cornmeal
- 1 egg
- 1 tablespoon water
- 1 teaspoon caraway seed, if desired

1 In large bowl, mix all-purpose flour, rye flour, yeast, cocoa and salt. In small bowl, mix warm water and molasses. Add water mixture to flour mixture; stir with wooden spoon until dough is thoroughly mixed and no dry spots remain, 1 to 2 minutes. Cover loosely with plastic wrap. Let rise at room temperature 2 hours; refrigerate at least 1 hour but no longer than 24 hours.

Shaping Soft Pretzels

Roll each dough piece into 24-inch rope.

Form rope into a circle, crossing ends at top. Fold dough so crossed ends rest on bottom of circle.

2 Line large cookie sheet with cooking parchment paper; sprinkle with cornmeal. Place dough on generously floured surface; turn dough to lightly coat with flour. Shape dough into a ball; cut in half. Cut each half into 6 equal pieces, coating with flour as needed to prevent sticking. Shape each piece into a ball by stretching surface of dough around to bottom on all sides; pinch bottom to seal. Place about 2 inches apart on cookie sheet. Cover loosely with plastic wrap sprayed with cooking spray; let rise in warm place 40 minutes or until doubled in size.

3 Place empty broiler tray or cast-iron skillet on bottom oven rack. Heat oven to 400°F. In small bowl, beat egg and 1 tablespoon water. Brush buns with egg mixture; sprinkle with caraway seed. Place cookie sheet on middle oven rack. Gently pull out bottom rack and pour 1 cup hot water into broiler tray; gently slide rack back and quickly shut oven door.

4 Bake 12 to 15 minutes or until buns begin to slightly brown and sound hollow when tapped. Cool 5 minutes on cooling rack. Serve warm or at room temperature.

1 Roll: Calories 150; Total Fat 1g (Saturated Fat 0g, Trans Fat 0g); Cholesterol 20mg; Sodium 300mg; Total Carbohydrate 30g (Dietary Fiber 2g, Sugars 3g); Protein 4g **Exchanges:** 1½ Starch, ½ Other Carbohydrate **Carbohydrate Choices:** 2

Bakery-Style Pumpernickel Loaf Shape dough into 7x5-inch oval and place on cookie sheet. Cover loosely with plastic wrap sprayed with cooking spray; let rise in warm place 1 hour or until doubled in size. Continue as directed in Steps 3 and 4, brushing top and sides of loaf with egg mixture; sprinkle top with caraway seed. Bake 25 to 30 minutes or until loaf sounds hollow when tapped. Cool completely.

Making English Muffins

Cook rounds 6 to 8 minutes, turning once, until deep golden brown.

Bake rounds 5 to 10 minutes or until center is completely cooked.

English Muffins CALORIE SMART

PREP 35 min **TOTAL** 3 hr • 9 muffins

- 2 to 2½ cups all-purpose flour
- 1 tablespoon sugar
- 1 teaspoon salt
- 2 tablespoons shortening
- 1 package regular active or fast-acting dry yeast (2¼ teaspoons)
- 1 cup very warm milk (120°F to 130°F)
- Cornmeal

1 In large bowl, mix 2 cups of the flour, the sugar, salt, shortening and yeast. Add milk; stir until dough forms. If necessary, stir in enough remaining flour, 2 tablespoons at a time, until dough is no longer sticky. Dough should be soft.

2 Place dough on lightly floured surface. Knead 4 to 5 minutes or until smooth and springy. Grease large bowl with shortening. Place dough in bowl, turning dough to grease all sides. Cover bowl loosely with plastic wrap and let rise in warm place 40 minutes to 1 hour or until doubled in size. Dough is ready if indentation remains when touched.

3 Gently push fist into dough to deflate. On lightly floured surface, roll dough into 13-inch round ¼ inch thick. Cut dough into 9 (3½-inch) rounds, rerolling dough as necessary. Generously sprinkle ungreased cookie sheet with cornmeal. Carefully transfer rounds to cookie sheet, placing about 1 inch apart. Sprinkle tops of rounds with cornmeal. Cover and let rise about 1 hour or until almost doubled in size.

4 Heat oven to 350°F. Heat nonstick griddle or 12-inch skillet over medium heat (350°F). Carefully transfer rounds to hot griddle. Cook 6 to 8 minutes, turning once, until deep golden brown. Return to cookie sheet. Bake 5 to 10 minutes or until center is completely cooked. Cool 10 to 15 minutes. To serve, split with fork.

1 Muffin: Calories 150; Total Fat 3.5(Saturated Fat 1, Trans Fat 0); Cholesterol 0mg; Sodium 280mg; Total Carbohydrate 24g(Dietary Fiber 1g, Sugars 3g); Protein 4g **Exchanges:** 1 Starch, ½ Other Carbohydrate, ½ Fat **Carbohydrate Choices:** 1½

Easy Naan

If you have never seen the way naan breads are made, take a peek the next time you are at an Indian restaurant: The chef slaps a piece of dough between his hands, stretching it into that familiar teardrop shape. Working quickly, he reaches into the tandoor (clay-lined oven) and slaps the dough against its inner wall. Within seconds, the dough puffs up and forms brown spots. He peels the bread away from the wall with a flat-edged skewer and brushes it with clarified butter.

PREP 20 min **TOTAL** 1 hr 20 min • 4 breads

    3 cups all-purpose flour
    1 tablespoon sugar
    1 teaspoon salt
    ½ cup milk
    2 tablespoons vegetable oil
    ½ cup plain yogurt
½ to ¾ cup water
    1 tablespoon butter, melted*

1 In large bowl, mix together flour, sugar and salt. Stir in milk and oil. Stir in yogurt. Stir in water, 2 tablespoons at a time, until dough forms. The dough should not be sticky or dry.

2 Knead dough in bowl or on lightly floured surface 2 to 3 minutes or until dough becomes smooth and elastic. Brush dough lightly with some of the melted butter and cover with plastic wrap; set aside 30 minutes. (At this point, dough can be covered and refrigerated up to 24 hours. When ready to roll, let dough stand at room temperature 30 minutes so it becomes soft and easy to handle.)

3 Heat oven to 450°F. Place pizza stone in oven to heat. Divide dough into 4 equal pieces. Shape each into a ball; brush each lightly with some of the butter.

4 Roll one piece of dough into 8-inch round or teardrop shape, about ¼ inch thick, on lightly floured surface, taking care not to tear dough. Repeat with remaining dough.

5 Place one piece of dough on hot pizza stone. Bake 3 to 4 minutes or until brown spots form and bubbles start to appear on surface. Turn; bake 7 to 8 minutes longer. Remove bread with spatula; brush lightly with melted butter. Wrap bread in foil to keep warm while baking remaining dough. Cut breads in half to serve.

*Clarified butter (page 469) can be substituted for the melted butter.

1 Serving (½ Bread): Calories 240; Total Fat 7g (Saturated Fat 2.5g, Trans Fat 0g); Cholesterol 10mg; Sodium 520mg; Total Carbohydrate 38g (Dietary Fiber 1g, Sugars 2g); Protein 5g **Exchanges:** 2 Starch, ½ Other Carbohydrate, 1 Fat **Carbohydrate Choices:** 2½

Delicious Uses for Naan

Traditionally, Indian food is eaten with your right hand, not with utensils. Pieces of naan would be ripped off and used to scoop up food to be eaten or used to dip into saucy foods to enjoy the sauce.

Today, in addition to being a tasty scoop, naan is being used in creative new ways. Any way flatbread is used, naan can be used as well. Turn it into a pizza by topping it with your favorite pizza toppings before baking. Spoon your favorite sandwich fillings on it and roll it up, like a wrap. Or serve it with soups and stews in place of bread or with dips, in place of chips.

Easy Naan

Making Naan

Roll 1 piece of dough at a time into circle or teardrop shape about ¼ inch thick.

Bake dough on hot pizza stone until brown spots or bubbles begin to appear on surface. Turn; bake other side.

CHAPTER 19

Cookies, Bars & Candies

CHOOSING THE RIGHT INGREDIENTS

Flour: For cookies and bars, all-purpose flour is recommended. Whole wheat flour can also be used, but only substitute it for one-third to one-half the amount of all-purpose flour to keep cookies from becoming too dry. White whole wheat flour is also available. It is has the same nutritional benefits as whole wheat flour but with a lighter color and milder flavor than regular whole wheat. Experiment with substituting some or all whole wheat flour for all-purpose flour in your cookie and bar recipes. For more information on flour and how to measure it correctly, see Flour, page 6, and Measuring Correctly, page 16.

Sweeteners: In addition to adding sweetness, sugar also helps to brown and add tenderness to baked goods.

Leavenings: Cookies usually call for baking powder or baking soda, which are not interchangeable. For more information, see Baking Ingredients, page 4.

Fats and Oils: Fats add tenderness and flavor to cookies and bars, but they are not all equal. For best results, use butter or, if the recipe calls for it, shortening. If you choose to use margarine, use only products with at least 65 percent fat. Any other spreads or reduced-fat products contain more water, resulting in cookies that are soft, tough and puffy.

Eggs: Eggs give richness, moisture and structure to cookies and bars. All the recipes in this book have been tested with large eggs. Egg product substitutes, made of egg whites, can be substituted for whole eggs, but the cookies and bars may come out drier.

Liquids: Water, fruit juice, cream or milk tends to make cookies crisper by causing them to spread more. Add only as much liquid as the recipe calls for.

Oats: Quick-cooking and old-fashioned oats are interchangeable unless a recipe calls for a specific type. Instant oatmeal products are not the same as quick-cooking oats and should not be used for baking.

Bake a Test Cookie

If you're new to cookie baking or are trying a new recipe, bake just one cookie as directed in the recipe to see how it performs. This is a great way to make adjustments before baking an entire batch. If the cookie spreads too much, add 1 to 2 tablespoons flour to the dough, or refrigerate the dough 1 to 2 hours before baking. If the cookie is too round or hard, add 1 to 2 tablespoons milk to the dough.

Softening Butter

Let butter soften at room temperature for 30 to 40 minutes. You can also soften it in the microwave; see Microwave Cooking and Heating chart, pages 29 and 30. If the butter is too soft, the dough will be too soft, causing the cookies to spread too much.

Nuts, Peanuts and Almond Brickle Chips: When a recipe calls for nuts, feel free to substitute any variety of nut or peanuts. Nuts and almond brickle chips can easily become rancid, giving them an unpleasant, strong flavor that can ruin the taste of cookies. To prevent rancidity, store nuts and peanuts tightly covered in the refrigerator or freezer up to 2 years. Do not freeze cashews, as they will become soggy. Store almond brickle chips in the refrigerator or freezer up to 6 months. Always taste items that tend to turn rancid before adding them to a recipe. If they don't taste fresh, compost or throw them out.

MIXING

For most recipes in this book, you can use an electric mixer or a spoon when mixing cookie or bar dough. The sugars, fats and liquids are usually beaten together first until well mixed. Flour and other ingredients are almost always stirred in by hand to avoid overmixing the dough, which can result in tough cookies.

Beating Butter and Sugar

Butter and sugar have been beaten long enough when mixture is light and fluffy and light in color.

TIPS FOR PERFECT COOKIES AND BARS

- Use completely cooled cookie sheets, as cookies will spread too much if placed and baked on a warm or hot cookie sheet.

- Make cookies all the same size so they bake evenly. Small ice cream–type scoops measure the same amount of cookie dough. The spring-loaded handles release the dough easily onto the cookie sheet. See Dropping Dough onto Pan, page 524. In general, a #16 scoop yields ¼ cup and a #70 scoop equals 1 level tablespoon, but scoops can vary by manufacturer. To ensure the scoop is the size you want to use, measure the volume by filling the scoop with water and measuring the amount of water.

- Bake pans of cookies and bars in the middle of the oven. For even baking, bake one sheet at a time. If you do bake two sheets at once, position oven racks as close to the middle as possible and rotate the position of the sheets halfway through baking.

- Check cookies and bars at the minimum bake time, baking longer if needed.

- Cool cookies as directed. Use a flat, thin metal spatula to remove them from the baking sheet to a cooling rack.

- Cool bars and brownies in the pan on a cooling rack.

- Use a plastic knife to cut brownies and soft, sticky bars such as Lemon Bars, page 542.

It cuts bars with the nicest edges and also prevents pans from getting scratched from a metal knife.

STORING COOKIES AND BARS

- Store crisp cookies at room temperature in loosely covered containers.

- Keep chewy and soft cookies at room temperature in resealable food-storage plastic bags or tightly covered containers.

- Let frosted or decorated cookies set or harden before storing; then store by placing them between layers of parchment or waxed paper, plastic wrap or foil.

- Store only one type of cookie in a container to keep the texture and flavor intact. If different types of cookies are stored in the same container, they can transfer moisture to one another, making crisp cookies soft, and they can also pick up flavors from each other.

- Most bars can be stored tightly covered, but follow specific recipe directions, as some may need to be stored loosely covered or may need to be refrigerated.

- For general directions on freezing and thawing cookies and bars, see Food Storage, page 33, and Refrigerator and Freezer Food Storage Chart, page 33. Do not freeze meringue, custard-filled or cream-filled cookies.

Removing Stuck Cookies

If cookies are difficult to remove from the cookie sheet because they were left to cool too long, put the cookies back into the oven for 1 to 2 minutes, and then remove them from the sheet. They should then come off easily.

Quick Pan Cleanup

Line baking pans for bars with foil for super-easy cleanup and ease in cutting. Turn pan upside down. Tear off a piece of foil longer than the pan. Smooth the foil over the bottom and sides of pan; then remove foil. Flip the pan over and gently fit the shaped foil into the pan. When the bars are cool, lift them out of the pan using the edges of the foil as handles. Peel back the foil and cut bars as directed.

Baking Cocoa

When a recipe calls for cocoa, it means unsweetened baking cocoa, not hot chocolate products, which are sweetened and have additional ingredients in them. Three types of baking cocoa are available: **Regular** (nonalkalized) is most commonly available and used for most recipes calling for cocoa. **Dutch or European** (alkalized) goes through a "Dutching" process to neutralize the natural acids found in cocoa, resulting in a darker cocoa with a more mellow chocolate flavor. Regular cocoa can be substituted for Dutch, but don't substitute Dutch in recipes calling for regular cocoa because the leavening in the recipe may not work well with it, affecting rising. **Dark** is a blend of both regular and Dutch cocoas. It can be substituted for regular baking cocoa in recipes, but the baked good will have a darker color and more intense flavor than if made with regular baking cocoa.

LEARN WITH BETTY Chocolate Chip Cookies

Perfect Cookie: It is slightly rounded on top and evenly golden brown.

Flat Cookie: The butter was too soft or partially melted, the flour was under-measured or the cookie sheet was too hot.

Round or Hard Cookie: Too much flour was used and cookie was over-baked.

Chocolate Chip Cookies

CALORIE SMART

The secret to great chocolate chip cookies is the combination of fresh ingredients, correct measuring and a good baking technique.

PREP 1 hr **TOTAL** 1 hr • 4 dozen cookies

- ¾ cup granulated sugar
- ¾ cup packed brown sugar
- 1 cup butter, softened
- 1 teaspoon vanilla
- 1 egg
- 2¼ cups all-purpose flour
- 1 teaspoon baking soda
- ½ teaspoon salt
- 2 cups semisweet or dark chocolate chips (about 12 oz)
- 1 cup coarsely chopped nuts, if desired

1 Heat oven to 375°F. In large bowl, beat granulated sugar, brown sugar, butter, vanilla and egg with electric mixer on medium speed, or mix with spoon, until well blended. Stir in flour, baking soda and salt (dough will be stiff). Stir in chocolate chips and nuts.

2 Onto ungreased cookie sheets, drop dough by rounded tablespoonfuls about 2 inches apart. For perfectly sized and shaped cookies, use a #70 (1 level tablespoon) cookie scoop.

3 Bake 8 to 10 minutes or until light brown (centers will be soft). Cool 1 to 2 minutes; remove from cookie sheets to cooling racks.

1 Cookie: Calories 140; Total Fat 8g (Saturated Fat 3.5g, Trans Fat 0g); Cholesterol 15mg; Sodium 80mg; Total Carbohydrate 16g (Dietary Fiber 0g, Sugars 10g); Protein 1g **Exchanges:** 1 Other Carbohydrate, 1½ Fat **Carbohydrate Choices:** 1

LIGHTER Directions For 5 grams of fat and 90 calories per serving, reduce butter to ¾ cup and omit nuts. Substitute 1 cup miniature semisweet chocolate chips for the chocolate chips.

Candy Cookies Substitute 2 cups candy-coated chocolate candies for the chocolate chips.

Chocolate Chip Bars Press dough in ungreased 13x9-inch pan. Bake 15 to 20 minutes or until golden brown. Cool in pan on cooling rack. Cut into 8 rows by 6 rows. Makes 48 bars.

Jumbo Chocolate Chip Cookies Onto ungreased cookie sheets, drop dough by ¼ cupfuls or #16 cookie scoop about 3 inches apart. Bake 12 to 15 minutes or until edges are set (centers will be soft). Cool 1 to 2 minutes; remove from cookie sheets to cooling racks. Makes 1½ dozen cookies.

Dropping Dough onto Pan

Scoop dough with one spoon and use another spoon to push dough onto cookie sheet.

Or use a spring-handle cookie scoop to quickly make evenly sized and shaped cookies.

For jumbo cookies, use a measuring cup or a large spring-handle ice cream scoop.

Dulce de Leche Chocolate Chip Cookies

PREP 1 hr **TOTAL** 1 hr 45 min • 3 dozen cookies

- 1 can (13.4 oz) dulce de leche (caramelized sweetened condensed milk)*
- 1½ cups butter, softened
- 1¼ cups granulated sugar
- 1¼ cups packed brown sugar
- 1 tablespoon vanilla
- 2 eggs
- 4 cups all-purpose flour
- 2 teaspoons baking soda
- 1 teaspoon salt
- 4 cups semisweet chocolate chips (about 24 oz)
- 1 cup chopped pecans, toasted (page 23)

1 Line cookie sheet with waxed paper or foil. Spoon 36 measuring teaspoonfuls dulce de leche onto cookie sheet. Freeze 1 hour or until slightly firm (dollops will not freeze solid).

2 Heat oven to 350°F. Line cookie sheets with cooking parchment paper. In large bowl, beat butter, granulated sugar, brown sugar, vanilla and eggs with electric mixer on medium speed, or mix with spoon, until well blended. Stir in flour, baking soda and salt. Using heavy-duty wooden spoon, stir in chocolate chips and pecans; dough will be stiff and chunky (you may need to use your hands).

3 Onto cookie sheets, drop dough by ¼ cupfuls or #16 ice cream scoop about 3 inches apart. Press thumb into center of each cookie to make deep indentation, but do not press all the way to cookie sheet. Place 1 dollop dulce de leche into center of each cookie, forming dough around dollop to enclose. (If dulce de leche dollops become too warm to work with, return to freezer.)

4 Bake 12 to 15 minutes or until light brown (centers will be soft). Cool 1 to 2 minutes. Remove from cookie sheets to cooling racks.

*See page 7. If you can't find dulce de leche, substitute 42 round chewy caramels in milk chocolate (from 12-ounce bag), unwrapped. No need to freeze these, just unwrap from the gold foil and insert in the indentation as directed in Step 3. Continue as directed.

1 Cookie: Calories 340; Total Fat 17g (Saturated Fat 9g, Trans Fat 0g); Cholesterol 35mg; Sodium 220mg Total Carbohydrate 43g (Dietary Fiber 2g, Sugars 30g); Protein 3g **Exchanges:** 1 Starch, 2 Other Carbohydrate 3½ Fat **Carbohydrate Choices: 3**

Chocolate Crinkles

Chocolate Crinkles CALORIE SMART

PREP 1 hr **TOTAL** 4 hr • 6 dozen cookies

- 2 cups granulated sugar
- ½ cup vegetable oil
- 2 teaspoons vanilla
- 4 oz unsweetened baking chocolate, melted, cooled
- 4 eggs
- 2 cups all-purpose flour
- 2 teaspoons baking powder
- ½ teaspoon salt
- 1 cup powdered sugar

1 In large bowl, stir granulated sugar, oil, vanilla and chocolate until well mixed. Stir in eggs, one at a time. Stir in flour, baking powder and salt. Cover and refrigerate at least 3 hours.

2 Heat oven to 350°F. Grease cookie sheets with shortening or cooking spray, or line with cooking parchment paper or silicone baking mats.

3 In small bowl, place powdered sugar. Drop dough by teaspoonfuls into powdered sugar; roll around to coat. Shape into balls. On cookie sheets, place balls about 2 inches apart.

4 Bake 10 to 12 minutes or until almost no indentation remains when touched in center. Immediately remove from cookie sheets to cooling racks.

1 Cookie: Calories 70; Total Fat 2.5g (Saturated Fat 1g, Trans Fat 0g); Cholesterol 10mg; Sodium 35mg; Total Carbohydrate 10g (Dietary Fiber 0g, Sugars 7g); Protein 0g **Exchanges:** ½ Starch, ½ Fat **Carbohydrate Choices: ½**

Chocolate-Filled Orange-Rosemary Butter Balls

Gingersnaps

Chocolate-Filled Orange-Rosemary Butter Balls CALORIE SMART

PREP 1 hr **TOTAL** 1 hr 30 min • 30 sandwich cookies

COOKIES

1 cup butter, softened
½ cup powdered sugar
1 tablespoon grated orange peel
1 tablespoon finely chopped fresh rosemary leaves
¼ teaspoon salt
1 teaspoon vanilla
2 cups all-purpose flour
½ teaspoon baking powder
¼ cup white decorator sugar crystals, if desired

FILLING

½ cup dark chocolate chips
2 tablespoons whipping cream

1 Heat oven to 400°F. In large bowl, beat butter, powdered sugar, orange peel, rosemary, salt and vanilla with electric mixer on medium speed until creamy. On low speed, beat in flour and baking powder until dough forms.

2 In small bowl, place sugar crystals. Shape dough into 1-inch balls. Roll in sugar. On ungreased cookie sheets, place balls 2 inches apart. Press lightly with tines of fork to flatten slightly.

3 Bake 6 to 8 minutes or until set. Remove from cookie sheets to cooling racks. Cool completely, about 30 minutes.

4 In small microwavable bowl, microwave chocolate chips and whipping cream uncovered on High in 15-second intervals until chips can be stirred smooth. Refrigerate until cooled and mixture starts to set, about 10 minutes.

5 For each sandwich cookie, spread ½ teaspoon filling on bottom of 1 cookie. Top with second cookie, bottom side down; gently press together. Let stand until set.

1 Sandwich Cookie: Calories 110; Total Fat 7g (Saturated Fat 4.5g, Trans Fat 0g); Cholesterol 20mg; Sodium 75mg; Total Carbohydrate 10g (Dietary Fiber 0g, Sugars 3g); Protein 1g **Exchanges:** ½ Other Carbohydrate, 1½ Fat **Carbohydrate Choices:** ½

Gingersnaps CALORIE SMART

PREP 45 min **TOTAL** 45 min • 4 dozen cookies

1 cup packed brown sugar
¾ cup shortening
¼ cup molasses
1 egg
2¼ cups all-purpose flour
2 teaspoons baking soda
1 teaspoon ground cinnamon
1 teaspoon ground ginger
½ teaspoon ground cloves
¼ teaspoon salt
Granulated sugar

1 Heat oven to 375°F. Lightly grease cookie sheets with shortening or cooking spray, or line with cooking parchment paper or silicone baking mats.

2 In large bowl, beat brown sugar, shortening, molasses and egg with electric mixer on medium speed, or mix with spoon, until well blended. Stir in remaining ingredients except granulated sugar.

3 Shape dough by rounded teaspoonfuls into balls. Dip tops into granulated sugar. On cookie sheets, place balls, sugared sides up, about 3 inches apart.

4 Bake 10 to 12 minutes or just until set. Immediately remove from cookie sheets to cooling racks.

1 Cookie: Calories 80; Total Fat 3.5g (Saturated Fat 1g, Trans Fat 0.5g); Cholesterol 0mg; Sodium 70mg; Total Carbohydrate 11g (Dietary Fiber 0g, Sugars 6g); Protein 0g **Exchanges:** 1 Other Carbohydrate, ½ Fat **Carbohydrate Choices:** 1

Soft No-Roll Sugar Cookies

Snickerdoodles

Soft No-Roll Sugar Cookies

CALORIE SMART

PREP 50 min **TOTAL** 2 hr 50 min • 3½ dozen cookies

- 1½ cups granulated sugar
- 1 cup powdered sugar
- 1 cup butter, softened
- ¾ cup vegetable oil
- 2 tablespoons milk
- 1 tablespoon vanilla
- 2 eggs
- 4¼ cups all-purpose flour
- 1 teaspoon baking soda
- 1 teaspoon cream of tartar
- ½ teaspoon salt

1 In large bowl, beat 1 cup of the granulated sugar, the powdered sugar, butter, oil, milk, vanilla and eggs with electric mixer on medium speed, or mix with spoon, until well blended. Stir in flour, baking soda, cream of tartar and salt. Cover and refrigerate about 2 hours or until firm.

2 Heat oven to 350°F. Shape dough into 1½-inch balls. In small bowl, place remaining ½ cup granulated sugar. Roll balls in sugar. On ungreased cookie sheets, place balls about 3 inches apart. Press bottom of drinking glass on each ball until about ¼ inch thick. Sprinkle each cookie with a little additional granulated sugar.

3 Bake 13 to 15 minutes or until set and edges just begin to turn brown. Immediately remove from cookie sheets to cooling racks.

1 Cookie: Calories 160; Total Fat 9g (Saturated Fat 3g, Trans Fat 0g); Cholesterol 20mg; Sodium 90mg; Total Carbohydrate 20g (Dietary Fiber 0g, Sugars 10g); Protein 2g **Exchanges:** 1 Starch, ½ Other Carbohydrate, 1½ Fat **Carbohydrate Choices:** 1

Chocolate Chip, Cherry and Pistachio Soft No-Roll Sugar Cookies Stir in 1 cup semisweet chocolate chips, ½ cup dried cherries and ½ cup pistachio nuts before refrigerating.

Glazed Soft No-Roll Sugar Cookies After cooling, drizzle cookies with Chocolate Glaze (page 582). Let stand until set.

Snickerdoodles   CALORIE SMART

This favorite, whimsically named cookie originated in New England in the 1800s. It's traditionally rolled in cinnamon-sugar before baking.

PREP 40 min **TOTAL** 40 min • 4 dozen cookies

- 1¾ cups sugar
- ½ cup butter, softened
- ½ cup shortening
- 2 eggs
- 2¾ cups all-purpose flour
- 2 teaspoons cream of tartar
- 1 teaspoon baking soda
- ¼ teaspoon salt
- 1 tablespoon ground cinnamon

1 Heat oven to 400°F. In large bowl, beat 1½ cups of the sugar, the butter, shortening and eggs with electric mixer on medium speed, or mix with spoon, until well blended. Stir in flour, cream of tartar, baking soda and salt.

2 Shape dough into 1¼-inch balls. In small bowl, mix remaining ¼ cup sugar and the cinnamon. Roll balls in cinnamon-sugar mixture. On ungreased cookie sheets, place balls 2 inches apart.

3 Bake 8 to 10 minutes or just until set. Immediately remove from cookie sheets to cooling racks.

1 Cookie: Calories 90; Total Fat 4.5g (Saturated Fat 1.5g, Trans Fat 0g); Cholesterol 15mg; Sodium 55mg; Total Carbohydrate 13g (Dietary Fiber 0g, Sugars 7g); Protein 1g **Exchanges:** 1 Other Carbohydrate, 1 Fat **Carbohydrate Choices:** 1

Learn to DECORATE

The options for decorating cookies can range from ridiculously easy to over-the-top elaborate. How you wish to decorate your cookies might depend on the time you have, the purpose for the cookies and your skill level. Look here for some basic tips to help you create beautiful cookies that will entice people to grab them and take a bite.

Cookies can be decorated before baking or after they are baked and cooled. See Storing Cookies and Bars, page 521, and Refrigerator and Freezer Storage Chart, page 33, for how to store them.

Decorate Before Baking

- Sprinkle unbaked cookies on cookie sheet with coarse clear or colored sugar. To make your own, see Colored Sugar, right. To keep the sugar on top of the cookie, place the cookie cutter used to cut the cookie back over it on the cookie sheet before sprinkling. Or roll unbaked balls of cookie dough in the sugar before placing on the cookie sheet.

- Make an Egg Yolk Paint to brush on sugar cookies before baking (see Paintbrush Sugar Cookies, right).

- Make a Baked-On Decorating Mixture: Mix ½ cup softened butter, ½ cup all-purpose flour and 3 teaspoons milk in a small bowl until well mixed. Divide mixture in half; tint each half with 4 drops food color. Place the mixtures in decorating bags fitted with a small writing tip. Pipe colors onto unbaked sugar cookies.

Decorating Baked Cookies

- Always cool cookies completely before frosting.

- Spread cookies with Vanilla Glaze (page 581) or Chocolate Glaze (page 582) on a cooling rack so that drips can fall away from the cookies and the glaze can dry. Place a jelly roll pan or piece of parchment or waxed paper under the cooling rack to catch the drips for easy cleanup.

- Sprinkle the glaze while wet with finely chopped nuts, colored sugars or candy sprinkles.

- Once glaze is dry, frost or drizzle dots of colored frosting or gel; pull through the dots with a toothpick to make designs.

- Pipe designs onto cookies using icing in a decorating bag with various tips or by placing the icing into small, resealable food-storage plastic bags (cutting a tiny corner off one end) or food-safe plastic squeeze bottles.

Rolling Cookies

On lightly floured surface, shape refrigerated dough (half at a time) into flattened round without cracks.

Using ruler or sticks as guide, roll dough ¼ inch thick.

Using cookie cutters dipped in flour, cut desired shapes.

Using a Decorating Bag

Insert coupler inside disposable pastry bag. (Cut end if necessary so coupler will reach tip of bag.)

Attach tip with ring; open bag, pulling opening far over hand, and fill with frosting.

Squeeze and twist with even pressure to pipe frosting onto cookies.

Sugar Cookies CALORIE SMART

PREP 1 hr TOTAL 3 hr • 5 dozen cookies

- 1½ cups powdered sugar
- 1 cup butter, softened
- 1 teaspoon vanilla
- ½ teaspoon almond extract
- 1 egg
- 2½ cups all-purpose flour
- 1 teaspoon baking soda
- 1 teaspoon cream of tartar
- Granulated sugar or Colored Sugar (right)

Sugar Cookies and variations

1 In large bowl, beat powdered sugar, butter, vanilla, almond extract and egg with electric mixer on medium speed, or mix with spoon, until well blended. Stir in flour, baking soda and cream of tartar. Cover and refrigerate at least 2 hours.

2 Heat oven to 375°F. Lightly grease cookie sheets with shortening or cooking spray, or line with cooking parchment paper or silicone baking mats.

3 Divide dough in half. Roll each half on lightly floured surface until ¼ inch thick. Cut with floured 2-inch cookie cutters. Sprinkle with granulated sugar. On cookie sheets, place cutouts about 2 inches apart.

4 Bake 7 to 8 minutes or until edges are light brown. Remove from cookie sheets to cooling racks.

1 Cookie: Calories 60; Total Fat 3g (Saturated Fat 1.5g, Trans Fat 0g); Cholesterol 10mg; Sodium 45mg; Total Carbohydrate 8g (Dietary Fiber 0g, Sugars 4g); Protein 0g **Exchanges:** ½ Starch, ½ Fat **Carbohydrate Choices:** ½

Colored Sugar Place ½ cup granulated sugar in resealable food-storage plastic bag. Add liquid food color to tint as desired. Seal bag. Squeeze and rub sugar in bag until it becomes evenly colored. Homemade colored sugar might clump; if it does, just break apart until clumps are gone.

Frosted and Decorated Sugar Cookies Omit granulated sugar. Frost cooled cookies with Creamy Vanilla Frosting (page 579), tinted with food color if desired. Decorate with colored sugar, small candies, candied fruit or nuts if desired.

Paintbrush Sugar Cookies Omit granulated sugar. Cut rolled dough into desired shapes with cookie cutters. (Cut no more than 12 cookies at a time to keep dough from drying out.) Mix 1 egg yolk and ¼ teaspoon water. Divide mixture among several custard cups. Tint each with different food color to make bright colors. (If paint thickens while standing, stir in a few drops water.) Paint designs on cookies with small new paintbrushes. Bake as directed.

Decorating Cookies

Colored Sugar: Sprinkle cookies with decorating sugar or decors before baking.

Frosted: Frost cookies and top with nuts, decorating sugar or sprinkles. Or frost and top with dots of colored frosting or gel food color; use a toothpick to make designs.

Painted: Make egg yolk paints and paint cookies before baking.

Gingerbread Cookies

Gingerbread Cookies CALORIE SMART

PREP 1 hr 40 min **TOTAL** 3 hr 40 min • 5 dozen cookies

COOKIES

½ cup packed brown sugar
½ cup butter, softened
½ cup molasses
⅓ cup cold water
3½ cups all-purpose flour
2 teaspoons baking soda
2 teaspoons ground ginger
½ teaspoon ground allspice
½ teaspoon ground cinnamon
¼ teaspoon ground cloves
¼ teaspoon salt

DECORATOR'S FROSTING

2 cups powdered sugar
2 tablespoons water or milk
½ teaspoon vanilla
Food color, colored sugars and small candies, if desired

1 In large bowl, beat brown sugar, butter, molasses and water with electric mixer on medium speed, or mix with spoon, until well blended. Stir in remaining cookie ingredients until mixed. Cover and refrigerate at least 2 hours.

2 Heat oven to 350°F. Grease cookie sheets with shortening or cooking spray, or line with cooking parchment paper or silicone baking mats.

3 Divide dough in half. Roll each half on lightly floured surface until ¼ inch thick. Cut with floured 2½-inch gingerbread boy or girl cookie cutter. On cookie sheets, place cutouts about 2 inches apart. After cutting as many cookies as possible, lightly press scraps of dough together; reroll dough and cut additional cookies.

4 Bake 10 to 12 minutes or until no indentation remains when touched in center. Immediately remove from cookie sheets to cooling racks. Cool completely, about 30 minutes. Cool cookie sheets 10 minutes between batches.

5 Meanwhile, in medium bowl, mix powdered sugar, water and vanilla with spoon until smooth and spreadable. Stir in liquid food color, one drop at a time, until frosting is desired color. (For intense, vivid color, use paste food color. You would have to use too much liquid food color to get a vivid color, and the frosting will begin to separate and look curdled.) Cover and set aside.

LEARN WITH BETTY Melting Chocolate

Perfectly Melted: This chocolate was melted perfectly; it is smooth and creamy.

Too Melted or Seized: This chocolate has either been melted over too high a heat or has come in contact with a small amount of liquid, causing it to seize.

Correcting Seized Chocolate: To make chocolate smooth again, use a whisk to beat in at least 1 tablespoon melted butter, vegetable oil or melted vegetable shortening. Heat over very low heat, if necessary, stirring constantly.

6 When ready to decorate, spoon frosting into small resealable food-storage plastic bag. Seal bag; push frosting down in one corner. Cut off tiny corner of bag. Squeeze bag to pipe frosting onto cookies and make desired design. Or spread over cookies with small metal spatula. Decorate with colored sugars and candies.

1 Cookie: Calories 60; Total Fat 1.5g (Saturated Fat 1g, Trans Fat 0g); Cholesterol 0mg; Sodium 65mg; Total Carbohydrate 10g (Dietary Fiber 0g, Sugars 3g); Protein 0g **Exchanges:** ½ Other Carbohydrate, ½ Fat **Carbohydrate Choices:** ½

Shortbread Cookies CALORIE SMART

PREP 40 min **TOTAL** 40 min • 2 dozen cookies

- ¾ cup butter, softened
- 5 tablespoons sugar
- 2 cups all-purpose flour

1 Heat oven to 350°F. In large bowl, stir butter and 4 tablespoons of the sugar until well mixed. Stir in flour. (If dough is crumbly, mix in 1 to 2 tablespoons more softened butter.)

2 Roll dough on lightly floured surface until ½ inch thick. Cut with floured 1½-inch cookie cutters. On ungreased cookie sheet, place cutouts ½ inch apart. Sprinkle evenly with remaining 1 tablespoon sugar.

3 Bake 15 to 20 minutes or until set. Immediately remove from cookie sheet to cooling rack.

1 Cookie: Calories 100; Total Fat 6g (Saturated Fat 3g, Trans Fat 0g); Cholesterol 15mg; Sodium 40mg; Total Carbohydrate 10g (Dietary Fiber 0g, Sugars 2g); Protein 1g **Exchanges:** ½ Starch, 1 Fat **Carbohydrate Choices:** ½

Shortbread Cookie Wedges Make dough as directed. On ungreased cookie sheet, pat dough into 8-inch round. Sprinkle with 1 tablespoon sugar. Bake 20 to 24 minutes or until set. Cool 10 minutes on cookie sheet on cooling rack. Using sharp knife, cut into 24 wedges.

Cherry Shortbread Cookies Stir in ½ cup chopped dried cherries, cranberries or blueberries with the flour.

Chocolate-Dipped Shortbread Cookies Make and bake cookies as directed; cool completely. In small microwavable bowl, microwave 1 cup chocolate chips and 1 teaspoon vegetable oil on High 30 to 60 seconds or until mixture can be stirred smooth.

Dip cookies in chocolate; wipe excess on edge of bowl. Place on waxed paper to set.

Ginger Shortbread Cookies Stir in 3 tablespoons chopped crystallized ginger with the flour.

Shortbread Nut Cookies Stir in ½ cup finely chopped hazelnuts (filberts), macadamia nuts, pecans, pistachio nuts or slivered almonds, toasted if desired, with the flour.

Toffee Shortbread Cookies Stir in ½ cup toffee bits with the flour.

Whole Wheat Shortbread Cookies Substitute 1¼ cups whole wheat flour for the all-purpose flour. Continue as directed.

Dipping Cookies in Chocolate

Heat 1 cup chocolate chips and 1 teaspoon oil until mixture can be stirred smooth.

Dip cookies; wipe excess on edge of bowl. Place on waxed paper to set.

Shortbread Cookies and variations

Brown Sugar Refrigerator Cookies and variations

Brown Sugar Refrigerator Cookies CALORIE SMART

PREP 50 min **TOTAL** 2 hr 50 min • 6 dozen cookies

1	cup packed brown sugar
1	cup butter, softened
1	teaspoon vanilla
1	egg
3	cups all-purpose flour
1½	teaspoons ground cinnamon
½	teaspoon baking soda
½	teaspoon salt
⅓	cup finely chopped nuts

1 In large bowl, beat brown sugar, butter, vanilla and egg with electric mixer on medium speed, or mix with spoon, until well blended. Stir in flour, cinnamon, baking soda and salt. Stir in nuts.

2 On plastic wrap, shape dough into 10x3-inch rectangle. Wrap and refrigerate about 2 hours or until firm but no longer than 24 hours.

3 Heat oven to 375°F. Unwrap dough; cut into ⅛-inch slices. On ungreased cookie sheets, place slices 2 inches apart.

4 Bake 6 to 8 minutes or until light brown. Cool 1 to 2 minutes; remove from cookie sheets to cooling racks.

1 Cookie: Calories 60; Total Fat 3g (Saturated Fat 1.5g, Trans Fat 0g); Cholesterol 10mg; Sodium 45mg; Total Carbohydrate 7g (Dietary Fiber 0g, Sugars 3g); Protein 0g **Exchanges:** ½ Starch, ½ Fat **Carbohydrate Choices:** ½

Citrus–Brown Sugar Refrigerator Cookies
Add 1 tablespoon grated lemon or orange peel with the flour. Frost cookies with **Vanilla Glaze**. For glaze, mix 2 cups powdered sugar, ⅓ cup melted butter and 1 teaspoon vanilla. Stir in 2 to 4 tablespoons hot water, 1 tablespoon at a time, until glaze is smooth and has the consistency of thick syrup. Drizzle over cookies, sprinkle with grated lemon peel.

Maple–Brown Sugar Refrigerator Cookies
Substitute 2 teaspoons maple flavor for the vanilla.

Toasted Coconut–Brown Sugar Refrigerator Cookies
Add 1 cup toasted coconut (page 23) with the flour. Frost cookies with Vanilla Glaze (page 581) and sprinkle with additional toasted coconut.

Thumbprint Cookies CALORIE SMART

PREP 50 min **TOTAL** 50 min • 3 dozen cookies

¼	cup packed brown sugar
¼	cup shortening
¼	cup butter, softened
½	teaspoon vanilla

Making Refrigerator Cookies

Beat cookie mixture with electric mixer or with spoon; stir in nuts.

Shape dough on plastic wrap into 10x3-inch rectangle.

Wrap; refrigerate about 2 hours or until firm.

Unwrap; cut rectangle into ⅛-inch slices.

Left to right: Lemon-Almond Thumbprint Cookies, Thumbprint Cookies, Hazelnut Thumbprint Cookies

Spritz Cookies

1 egg, separated
1 cup all-purpose flour
¼ teaspoon salt
1 cup finely chopped nuts
About 6 tablespoons jelly or jam (any flavor)

1 Heat oven to 350°F. In medium bowl, beat brown sugar, shortening, butter, vanilla and egg yolk with electric mixer on medium speed, or mix with spoon. Stir in flour and salt.

2 Shape dough into 1-inch balls. In small bowl, beat egg white slightly with fork. Place nuts in another small bowl. Dip each ball into egg white, then roll in nuts. On ungreased cookie sheets, place balls about 1 inch apart. Press thumb into center of each cookie to make indentation, but do not press all the way to the cookie sheet.

3 Bake about 10 minutes or until light brown. Quickly remake indentations with end of wooden spoon handle if necessary. Immediately remove from cookie sheets to cooling racks. Fill each with about ½ teaspoon jelly.

1 Cookie: Calories 80; Total Fat 5g (Saturated Fat 1.5g, Trans Fat 0g); Cholesterol 10mg; Sodium 55mg; Total Carbohydrate 7g (Dietary Fiber 0g, Sugars 3g); Protein 1g **Exchanges:** ½ Starch, 1 Fat **Carbohydrate Choices:** ½

Hazelnut-Chocolate Thumbprint Cookies
Roll balls of dough in finely chopped hazelnuts (filberts). Instead of jelly, fill indentations with hazelnut spread with cocoa.

Lemon-Almond Thumbprint Cookies
Roll balls of dough in finely chopped slivered almonds. Fill indentations with lemon curd.

Peanut-Fudge Thumbprint Cookies
Roll balls of dough in finely chopped dry-roasted peanuts. Instead of jelly, fill indentations with hot fudge topping (look for the thick topping, not pourable or syrup varieties).

Spritz Cookies CALORIE SMART
PREP 45 min **TOTAL** 45 min • 5 dozen cookies

1 cup butter, softened*
½ cup sugar
2¼ cups all-purpose flour
1 egg
1 teaspoon almond extract or vanilla
½ teaspoon salt
Few drops red or green food color, if desired
Sugar, colored sugar or multi-colored candy sprinkles, if desired

1 Heat oven to 400°F. In large bowl, beat butter and ½ sugar with electric mixer on medium speed, or mix with spoon, until well blended. Stir in remaining ingredients.

2 Place dough in cookie press. On ungreased cookie sheets, form desired shapes. Sprinkle with sugar.

3 Bake 6 to 9 minutes or until set but not brown. Immediately remove from cookie sheets to cooling racks.

*Do not use margarine or vegetable oil spreads.

1 Cookie: Calories 50; Total Fat 3g (Saturated Fat 1.5g, Trans Fat 0g); Cholesterol 10mg; Sodium 40mg; Total Carbohydrate 5g (Dietary Fiber 0g, Sugars 2g); Protein 0g **Exchanges:** ½ Other Carbohydrate, ½ Fat **Carbohydrate Choices:** ½

Chocolate Buttery Spritz Cookies
Stir 2 ounces unsweetened baking chocolate, melted and cooled, into butter-sugar mixture.

Making Spritz Cookies

Place desired design disk in cookie press. Place dough in press; press dough through press onto cookie sheet.

French Macarons with Bittersweet Chocolate Ganache CALORIE SMART

In France, these popular cookies are sold in patisseries in a wide variety of colors and flavors.

PREP 55 min **TOTAL** 3 hr 10 min • 20 sandwich cookies

French Macarons with Bittersweet Chocolate Ganache

COOKIES

- 1¼ cups blanched whole almonds (about 7 oz)
- 1½ cups powdered sugar
- 3 egg whites, at room temperature*
- ¼ teaspoon salt
- ½ teaspoon red paste or gel food color
- 3 tablespoons granulated sugar

GANACHE

- ¼ cup whipping cream
- 1 teaspoon light corn syrup
- 2 oz bittersweet or semisweet baking chocolate, finely chopped
- 1 tablespoon butter, softened

1 In food processor or blender, place almonds and ½ cup of the powdered sugar. Cover and process, scraping sides occasionally, until almonds are very finely ground. Place strainer over medium bowl. Using rubber spatula, press almond mixture through strainer into bowl. Return any almonds left in strainer to blender; add remaining 1 cup powdered sugar. Cover and process, scraping sides occasionally, until well blended.

2 In large bowl, beat egg whites, salt and food color with electric mixer on high speed just until foamy. Gradually add granulated sugar, 1 tablespoon at a time, beating on high speed 1 to 2 minutes or just until stiff peaks form. Using rubber spatula, fold about half of the almond mixture into egg white mixture until completely incorporated. Fold in remaining almond mixture.

3 Line 2 large cookie sheets with cooking parchment paper or silicone baking mats. Spoon half of the batter into decorating bag fitted with ½-inch round tip. Onto one cookie sheet, pipe batter in 20 (1½-inch) rounds about 1½ inches apart. Repeat with remaining batter and second cookie sheet. If tops have a peak, wet fingertips lightly on damp paper towel and press down to flatten. Tap bottom of cookie sheet on counter a few times to flatten cookies. Let stand uncovered at room temperature 30 minutes to allow a light crust to form on tops.

4 Heat oven to 300°F. Bake one cookie sheet at a time 17 to 18 minutes or until tops look set.

Making Macarons

Gradually add sugar to egg whites, 1 tablespoon at a time, beating on high speed just until stiff peaks form.

Pipe batter in 20 (1½-inch) rounds about 1½ inches apart on parchment-lined cookie sheet.

Spread ganache on bottom of 1 cookie. Top with second cookie, bottom side down; gently press together.

Cool 10 minutes. With metal pancake turner, remove cookies from cookie sheets to cooling racks; cool completely.

5 Meanwhile, in 2-cup microwavable measuring cup, microwave whipping cream and corn syrup uncovered on High 1 minute. Stir in chocolate and butter until chocolate is melted. Let stand about 30 minutes. Cover and refrigerate about 30 minutes or until spreading consistency.

6 For each sandwich cookie, spread slightly less than 1 teaspoon ganache on bottom of 1 cookie. Top with second cookie, bottom side down; gently press together. Store in tightly covered container.

*To quickly bring the whites to room temperature, soak whole eggs in a bowl of hot water for about 10 minutes before cracking and separating.

1 Sandwich Cookie: Calories 140; Total Fat 7g (Saturated Fat 2g, Trans Fat 0g); Cholesterol 0mg; Sodium 45mg; Total Carbohydrate 15g (Dietary Fiber 1g, Sugars 13g); Protein 3g **Exchanges:** 1 Other Carbohydrate, ½ High-Fat Meat, ½ Fat **Carbohydrate Choices:** 1

Lemon Macarons Tint egg white mixture with desired amount of yellow food color in Step 2. Omit ganache. Fill with Lemon Frosting (page 579) or Lemon Curd (page 581).

Mint Macarons Tint egg white mixture with desired amount of green food color in Step 2. In Step 5, add 1 tablespoon finely chopped fresh mint leaves to heated cream mixture; let stand 30 minutes. Place fine-mesh strainer over medium bowl. Using back of wooden spoon, press mint mixture through strainer into bowl; discard mint. Return cream mixture to

measuring cup. Microwave on High 1 minute. Continue with ganache as directed.

Orange Macarons Tint egg white mixture orange with desired food color in Step 2. Use ganache if desired, or fill with Orange Frosting (page 579).

Hazelnut Biscotti CALORIE SMART

PREP 25 min **TOTAL** 1 hr 30 min • 40 cookies

  1 **cup hazelnuts (filberts), coarsely chopped**
  1 **cup sugar**
  ½ **cup butter, softened**
  1 **teaspoon almond extract**
  1 **teaspoon vanilla**
  2 **eggs**
3½ **cups all-purpose flour**
  1 **teaspoon baking powder**
  ½ **teaspoon baking soda**

1 Heat oven to 350°F. Spread hazelnuts in ungreased shallow pan. Bake uncovered about 10 minutes, stirring occasionally, until golden brown; cool.

2 In large bowl, beat sugar, butter, almond extract, vanilla and eggs with electric mixer on medium speed, or mix with spoon, until well blended. Stir in flour, baking powder and baking soda. Stir in hazelnuts.

3 Place dough on lightly floured surface. Gently knead 2 to 3 minutes or until dough holds together and hazelnuts are evenly distributed. Divide dough in half. On large ungreased cookie sheet, shape each half into 10x3-inch rectangle, rounding edges slightly.

4 Bake about 25 minutes or until center is firm to the touch. Cool on cookie sheet 15 minutes; move to cutting board. Using sharp knife, cut each rectangle crosswise into ½-inch slices.

5 Place slices, cut sides down, on ungreased cookie sheet. Bake about 15 minutes or until crisp and light brown. Immediately remove from cookie sheet to cooling rack.

1 Cookie: Calories 100; Total Fat 4.5g (Saturated Fat 1.5g, Trans Fat 0g); Cholesterol 15mg; Sodium 45mg; Total Carbohydrate 14g (Dietary Fiber 0g, Sugars 5g); Protein 2g **Exchanges:** 1 Starch, ½ Fat **Carbohydrate Choices:** 1

Almond Biscotti Substitute 1 cup slivered almonds for the hazelnuts.

Making Biscotti

On cookie sheet, shape each dough half into 10x3-inch rectangle, rounding edges slightly.

Cool baked rectangles 15 minutes; cut into ½-inch slices. Place cut side down on same cookie sheet. Bake until crisp and golden brown.

Lemon Bars

Triple-Nut Bars

Lemon Bars CALORIE SMART

PREP 10 min **TOTAL** 2 hr • 25 bars

- 1 cup all-purpose flour
- ½ cup butter, softened
- ¼ cup powdered sugar
- 2 eggs
- 1 cup granulated sugar
- 2 teaspoons grated lemon peel
- 2 tablespoons fresh lemon juice
- ½ teaspoon baking powder
- ¼ teaspoon salt
  Additional powdered sugar

1 Heat oven to 350°F. In medium bowl, mix flour, butter and ¼ cup powdered sugar with spoon until well mixed. Press in ungreased 8- or 9-inch square pan, building up ½-inch edges.

2 Bake crust 20 minutes; remove from oven. In medium bowl, beat remaining ingredients except additional powdered sugar with electric mixer on high speed about 3 minutes or until light and fluffy. Pour over hot crust.

3 Bake 25 to 30 minutes or until no indentation remains when touched lightly in center. Cool completely in pan on cooling rack, about 1 hour. Sprinkle with powdered sugar. Cut into 5 rows by 5 rows.

1 Bar: Calories 100; Total Fat 4g (Saturated Fat 2g, Trans Fat 0g); Cholesterol 25mg; Sodium 65mg; Total Carbohydrate 14g (Dietary Fiber 0g, Sugars 10g); Protein 1g **Exchanges:** 1 Other Carbohydrate, 1 Fat **Carbohydrate Choices:** 1

Pressing Crust in Pan

Using fingertips, press dough in pan; build up ½-inch edges.

Triple-Nut Bars

PREP 35 min **TOTAL** 1 hr 50 min • 36 bars

CRUST
- ¾ cup butter, softened
- ½ cup packed brown sugar
- ½ teaspoon almond extract
- 1½ cups all-purpose flour

TOPPING
- 1 cup butter
- 1½ cups packed brown sugar
- ¼ cup honey
- ¼ cup light corn syrup
- ½ teaspoon vanilla
- 1 cup walnut pieces
- 1 cup unblanched or blanched whole almonds
- 1 cup pecan halves

1 Heat oven to 350°F. In medium bowl, beat ¾ cup butter, ½ cup brown sugar and the almond extract with electric mixer on medium-low speed until blended. On low speed, beat in flour until soft dough forms. Press dough in bottom of ungreased 13x9-inch pan. Bake 17 to 20 minutes or until golden brown.

2 Meanwhile, in 2-quart saucepan, cook all topping ingredients except nuts over medium-high heat 12 to 15 minutes, stirring frequently, until mixture comes to a full rolling boil. Boil 1 to 2 minutes, stirring frequently. Remove from heat.

3 Sprinkle walnuts, almonds and pecans over crust. Pour brown sugar mixture over nuts. Bake 13 to 15 minutes or until top of mixture is bubbly. Cool completely in pan on cooling rack, about 1 hour. Cut into 6 rows by 6 rows.

1 Bar: Calories 230; Total Fat 15g (Saturated Fat 6g, Trans Fat 0g); Cholesterol 25mg; Sodium 70mg; Total Carbohydrate 21g (Dietary Fiber 1g, Sugars 15g); Protein 2g **Exchanges:** 1½ Other Carbohydrate, 3 Fat **Carbohydrate Choices:** 1½

Dried Fruit

Does dried fruit get passed over in your cupboard? If you are looking for ways to use dried fruit other than eating it out of your hand, try the ideas below. If you don't have the exact dried fruit called for, feel free to improvise with what you do have.

1. On-the-Go Mix: In medium bowl, mix 1 cup bite-size pretzels, ½ cup each toasted oat cereal and dried fruit (any variety) and ¼ cup each dry-roasted whole almonds or peanuts and roasted pumpkin seeds. Place in small resealable plastic bags or plastic containers.

2. Fruit 'n Nuts Salad: For each serving, top 1 cup baby spinach leaves with 2 tablespoons each dried cherries, crumbled feta cheese and toasted pecan halves. Drizzle with your favorite vinaigrette dressing.

3. Pomegranate Oatmeal: Make oatmeal as directed on package, except—stir in 2 tablespoons dried pomegranate seeds with the water.

4. Fruity Couscous: Make 10-ounce box of couscous as directed on package, except—add ¼ cup each dried cranberries and chopped dried apricots with the water.

5. Lemon-Fig Muffins: Prepare Blueberry Muffins (page 482) as directed, except—stir in 2 teaspoons grated lemon peel with the milk and substitute chopped dried figs for the blueberries.

6. Fruitcake-Inspired Brownies: Toss ¼ cup each chopped dried apricots, dates and cherries with 1 tablespoon all-purpose flour; set aside. Prepare Chocolate Brownies (page 540) as directed, except—add apricots, dates and cherries with the walnuts.

Date Bars CALORIE SMART

PREP 20 min **TOTAL** 1 hr • 36 bars

FILLING
- 3 cups chopped pitted dates (1 lb)
- 1½ cups water
- ¼ cup granulated sugar

BARS
- 1 cup packed brown sugar
- 1 cup butter, softened
- 1¾ cups all-purpose or whole wheat flour
- 1½ cups quick-cooking oats
- ½ teaspoon baking soda
- ½ teaspoon salt

1 In 2-quart saucepan, cook filling ingredients over low heat about 10 minutes, stirring constantly, until thickened. Cool 5 minutes.

2 Heat oven to 400°F. Grease bottom and sides of 13x9-inch pan with shortening.

3 In large bowl, stir brown sugar and butter until well mixed. Stir in flour, oats, baking soda and salt until crumbly. Press half of the crumb mixture evenly in bottom of pan. Spread with filling. Top with remaining crumb mixture; press lightly.

4 Bake 25 to 30 minutes or until light brown. Cool 5 minutes in pan on cooling rack. Cut into 6 rows by 6 rows while warm.

1 Bar: Calories 160; Total Fat 5g (Saturated Fat 2.5g, Trans Fat 0g); Cholesterol 15mg; Sodium 85mg; Total Carbohydrate 25g (Dietary Fiber 2g, Sugars 17g); Protein 2g **Exchanges:** 1 Starch, ½ Other Carbohydrate, 1 Fat **Carbohydrate Choices:** 1½

Fig Bars Substitute 3 cups chopped dried figs for the dates.

Fruitcake-Inspired Brownies

Date Bars

Luscious Chocolate Truffles

Luscious Chocolate Truffles CALORIE SMART

PREP 35 min **TOTAL** 1 hr 15 min • 24 truffles

- 2 **cups semisweet, dark or milk chocolate chips (about 12 oz)**
- 2 **tablespoons butter, softened**
- ¼ **cup whipping cream**
- 2 **tablespoons liqueur (almond, cherry, coffee, hazelnut, Irish cream, orange, raspberry or other flavor), if desired**
- 1 **tablespoon shortening**
  Finely chopped nuts, if desired
- ¼ **cup powdered sugar, if desired**
- ½ **teaspoon milk, if desired**

1 In 2-quart saucepan, melt 1 cup of the chocolate chips over low heat, stirring constantly; remove from heat. Stir in butter. Stir in whipping cream and liqueur. Refrigerate 10 to 15 minutes, stirring frequently, just until thick enough to hold a shape.

2 Line cookie sheet with foil. Onto cookie sheet, drop chocolate mixture by teaspoonfuls; shape into balls. (If mixture is too sticky, refrigerate until firm enough to shape.) Freeze 30 minutes.

3 In 1-quart saucepan, heat shortening and remaining 1 cup chocolate chips over low heat, stirring constantly, until chocolate is melted and mixture is smooth; remove from heat. Using fork, dip truffles, one at a time,

into chocolate, tapping fork on side of pan to remove excess chocolate . Return to cookie sheet. Immediately sprinkle some of the truffles with nuts. Refrigerate about 10 minutes or until coating is set.

4 In small bowl, stir powdered sugar and milk until smooth; drizzle over some of the truffles. Refrigerate just until set. Store in tightly covered container in refrigerator. Remove from refrigerator about 30 minutes before serving.

1 Truffle: Calories 160; Total Fat 10g (Saturated Fat 6g, Trans Fat 0g); Cholesterol 10mg; Sodium 15mg; Total Carbohydrate 14g (Dietary Fiber 1g, Sugars 12g); Protein 1g **Exchanges:** ½ Other Carbohydrate, 1½ Fat **Carbohydrate Choices:** 1

Toffee Truffles Stir in 3 tablespoons chopped toffee bits with the whipping cream.

White Chocolate–Chocolate Truffles Stir in 3 tablespoons chopped white chocolate with the whipping cream.

Making Truffles

Refrigerate truffle mixture just until thick enough to hold a shape.

Using fork, dip truffles into chocolate, covering completely; tap off excess

Pralines

Pistachio-Cranberry Divinity

Pralines CALORIE SMART

Pronounced prah-LEEN *or* PRAY-leen, *this confection originated in Louisiana, where brown sugar and pecans are abundant.*

PREP 25 min **TOTAL** 1 hr 15 min • 36 candies

- 1½ cups granulated sugar
- 1½ cups packed light brown sugar
- 1 cup half-and-half
- 2 tablespoons light corn syrup
- ⅛ teaspoon salt
- 2 tablespoons butter
- 1 teaspoon vanilla
- 1¾ cups pecan halves

1 Check the accuracy of your candy thermometer before starting (see Using a Candy Thermometer, page 544). In 3-quart saucepan, mix granulated sugar, brown sugar, half-and-half, corn syrup and salt. Heat to boiling, stirring constantly. Reduce heat to medium. Cook uncovered about 6 minutes, without stirring, to 236°F on candy thermometer or until small amount of mixture dropped into cup of very cold water forms a soft ball that flattens when removed from water; remove from heat. Drop butter into hot mixture (do not stir in). Cool uncovered 10 minutes without stirring.

2 Add vanilla and pecans. Beat with spoon about 2 minutes or until mixture is thickened and just begins to lose its gloss. On waxed paper, quickly drop mixture by heaping tablespoonfuls, dividing pecans equally; spread slightly. Let stand uncovered 30 minutes or until candies are firm.

3 Wrap candies individually in waxed paper or plastic wrap. Store in tightly covered container.

1 Candy: Calories 120; Total Fat 5g (Saturated Fat 1g, Trans Fat 0g); Cholesterol 0mg; Sodium 20mg; Total Carbohydrate 19g (Dietary Fiber 0g, Sugars 18g); Protein 0g **Exchanges:** 1½ Other Carbohydrate, 1 Fat **Carbohydrate Choices:** 1

Pistachio-Cranberry Divinity CALORIE SMART

PREP 30 min **TOTAL** 1 hr • 20 candies

- 1 egg white
- ¼ cup water
- ¼ cup light corn syrup
- 1½ cups sugar
- ½ teaspoon vanilla
- ½ cup chopped pistachio nuts
- ¼ cup sweetened dried cranberries, coarsely chopped

1 Check the accuracy of your candy thermometer before starting (see Using a Candy Thermometer, page 544). Line large cookie sheet with waxed paper. In medium bowl, beat egg white with electric mixer on high speed until soft peaks form; set aside.

2 In 2-quart saucepan, mix water, corn syrup and sugar. Cook over medium heat, stirring constantly, until sugar is dissolved. Without stirring, cook over medium heat 8 to 10 minutes or until syrup reaches 250°F on candy thermometer.

3 When syrup is 250°F, continue beating egg white on high speed while slowly pouring syrup into egg white. Beat 2 to 3 minutes or until mixture holds a soft peak and does not flatten when dropped from a spoon.

4 Fold in vanilla, nuts and cranberries. Quickly spoon mixture by rounded teaspoonfuls onto cookie sheet. Let stand about 30 minutes or until completely set.

1 Candy: Calories 100; Total Fat 1.5g (Saturated Fat 0g, Trans Fat 0g); Cholesterol 0mg; Sodium 20mg; Total Carbohydrate 20g (Dietary Fiber 0g, Sugars 17g); Protein 0g **Exchanges:** 1½ Other Carbohydrate, ½ Fat **Carbohydrate Choices:** 1

Marshmallows CALORIE SMART

PREP 55 min **TOTAL** 9 hr • 77 marshmallows

- ⅓ cup powdered sugar
- 2½ tablespoons unflavored gelatin
- ½ cup cold water
- 1½ cups granulated sugar
- 1 cup corn syrup
- ¼ teaspoon salt
- ½ cup water

1 Check the accuracy of your candy thermometer before starting (see Using a Candy Thermometer, page 544). Generously grease bottom and sides of 11x7-inch (2-quart) glass baking dish with butter; sprinkle with 1 tablespoon of the powdered sugar. In bowl of stand electric mixer, sprinkle gelatin over ½ cup cold water to soften; set aside.

2 In 2-quart saucepan, heat granulated sugar, corn syrup, salt and ½ cup water over medium heat, stirring constantly, until sugar is dissolved. Heat to boiling; cook uncovered about 25 minutes, without stirring, to 240°F on candy thermometer or until small amount of mixture dropped into cup of very cold water forms a ball that flattens between fingers (see Testing Candy Temperatures, page 545).

3 Remove from heat; slowly pour syrup into softened gelatin while beating on low speed. Increase speed to high; beat 6 to 8 minutes or until mixture is white and has almost tripled in volume. Pour into baking dish, patting lightly with wet hands. Let stand uncovered at least 8 hours or overnight.

4 Sprinkle cutting board with about 1 tablespoon powdered sugar. Place remaining powdered sugar in small bowl. To remove marshmallow mixture, loosen sides from dish and gently lift in one piece onto cutting board. Using sharp knife greased with butter, cut into 1-inch squares (11 rows by 7 rows). Dip bottom and sides of each marshmallow into bowl of powdered sugar. Store in tightly covered container at room temperature up to 3 weeks.

1 **Marshmallow:** Calories 35; Total Fat 0g (Saturated Fat 0g, Trans Fat 0g); Cholesterol 0mg; Sodium 10mg; Total Carbohydrate 8g (Dietary Fiber 0g, Sugars 6g); Protein 0g**Exchanges:** ½ Other Carbohydrate **Carbohydrate Choices:** ½

Cocoa Marshmallows In small bowl, mix ¼ cup powdered sugar and 1 tablespoon unsweetened baking cocoa. Sprinkle 1 tablespoon of the mixture in greased baking dish; set remaining powdered sugar mixture aside. In Step 3, after increasing mixer speed to high, gradually add ¼ cup unsweetened baking cocoa and 1 teaspoon vanilla, beating 6 to 8 minutes or until mixture is light brown in color and has almost tripled in volume. Continue as directed, using remaining powdered sugar mixture for sprinkling on the cutting board and dipping the marshmallows.

Peppermint Marshmallows In Step 3, after beating mixture 6 to 8 minutes, add 1 teaspoon peppermint extract; beat 1 minute longer. Pour into baking dish, patting lightly with wet hands. Drop 8 to 10 drops red food color randomly onto top of marshmallow mixture. Pull table knife through food color to create swirl pattern over top. Continue as directed.

Making Marshmallows

Beat syrup-gelatin mixture until almost tripled in volume; beat in peppermint extract.

Drop food color randomly onto marshmallow mixture; pull table knife through to swirl pattern.

Peppermint Marshmallows

CHAPTER 20
Cakes & Cupcakes

• ABOUT BUTTER CAKES

Sometimes called shortening cakes, these are cakes made with butter or shortening, flour, eggs, liquid and baking powder or soda.

- Avoid overmixing batter, which can cause tunnels or a sunken center.

- Bake cakes on center oven rack, arranging pans so that there is at least 1 inch of space between the pans and the sides of the oven.

- If not all pans will fit on one rack, refrigerate one pan of batter until the others are baked, and then bake remaining layer separately.

- Grease pans with solid shortening, not butter or margarine. Use cooking spray if recipe calls for it.

- To remove cake from pan, insert knife between cake and pan, then slide around edge to loosen it. Place wire rack upside down over cake. Invert carefully so cake is on rack and remove the pan. Invert onto another rack to flip cake right side up.

- Cut cake with thin, sharp knife in gentle sawing motion.

Removing Cakes from Pans

Place wire rack upside down over loosened cake. Invert cake carefully onto rack; remove pan.

Invert cake and rack onto another rack and flip cake right side up. Remove first rack.

Foolproof Foam Cakes

The best foam cakes are high, golden brown with cracks in the surface, soft, moist and delicate. Here are some things that can happen, with solutions to help.

- Low and compact — underbeaten, overmixed or overfolded batter, incorrect cooling or underbaking.

- Coarse and not tender — underbeaten egg whites or underfolded batter.

ABOUT FOAM CAKES

Angel food, sponge and chiffon cakes are types of foam cakes, which depend on beaten egg whites for their light and airy texture.

Angel food cakes contain no added leavening, fat or egg yolks. They have a high proportion of beaten egg whites to flour.

Sponge cakes use both egg whites and yolks and sometimes a little leavening, but do not contain other added fat.

Chiffon cakes are a cross between foam and butter cakes, made with some leavening, vegetable oil or shortening and egg yolks, as well as beaten egg whites.

- Use a clean, dry bowl and beaters to beat egg whites so they will whip properly. Even a speck of fat from an egg yolk can keep whites from whipping up properly.

- Do not grease and flour pans unless directed in a recipe. During baking, batter needs to cling and climb up the sides of the pans.

- For any tube pan cake, move oven rack to the lowest position in oven so the cake will bake completely without browning too much.

LEARN WITH BETTY Foam Cakes

Perfect Cake: This cake is high and golden brown, with feathery, light texture.

Underrisen Cake: This cake is compact because of underbeaten or very overbeaten egg whites, overfolded batter or underbaking.

Overbaked Cake: This cake is too brown and crumbly from batter not being properly folded or underbeaten egg whites and overbaking.

German Chocolate Cake

Samuel German, an employee of the Baker's Chocolate Company, developed a sweet chocolate in 1852. Over a hundred years later, in 1957, a reader of a Dallas newspaper submitted her recipe for this now-famous three-tiered cake with coconut-pecan frosting. Sales of sweet chocolate soared, and the rest is delicious history!

PREP 30 min **TOTAL** 2 hr 20 min • 12 servings

CAKE

- 4 oz sweet baking chocolate, chopped
- ½ cup water
- 2¼ cups all-purpose flour or 2½ cups cake flour
- 1 teaspoon baking soda
- 1 teaspoon salt
- 2 cups granulated sugar
- 1 cup butter, softened
- 4 whole eggs, separated
- 1 teaspoon vanilla
- 1 cup buttermilk

COCONUT-PECAN FROSTING

- 1 cup granulated sugar or packed brown sugar
- ½ cup butter, cut into pieces
- 1 cup evaporated milk or half-and-half
- 1 teaspoon vanilla
- 3 egg yolks
- 1⅓ cups coconut
- 1 cup chopped pecans, toasted if desired (page 23)

1 Heat oven to 350°F. Grease bottoms and sides of 3 (8- or 9-inch) round cake pans with shortening. Line pan bottoms with waxed paper or cooking parchment paper; grease paper.

2 In 1-quart saucepan, heat chocolate and water over low heat, stirring frequently, until chocolate is completely melted; cool.

3 In medium bowl, mix flour, baking soda and salt; set aside. In another medium bowl, beat 2 cups granulated sugar and 1 cup butter with electric mixer on high speed until light and fluffy. Beat in 4 egg yolks, one at a time. Beat in chocolate and 1 teaspoon vanilla on low speed. Add flour mixture alternately with buttermilk, beating on low speed after each addition just until smooth.

German Chocolate Cake

4 Wash and dry mixer beaters. In small bowl, beat 4 egg whites on high speed until stiff; fold into batter. Pour into pans. If all pans won't fit in oven at one time, refrigerate batter in third pan and bake separately.

5 Bake 8-inch pans 35 to 40 minutes, 9-inch pans 30 to 35 minutes, or until toothpick inserted in center comes out clean. Cool 10 minutes; remove from pans to cooling racks. Remove waxed paper. Cool completely, about 1 hour.

6 Meanwhile, in 2-quart saucepan, stir together 1 cup granulated sugar, ½ cup butter, the milk, 1 teaspoon vanilla and 3 egg yolks until well mixed. Cook over medium heat about 12 minutes, stirring frequently, until thickened and bubbly. Stir in coconut and pecans. Cool about 30 minutes, beating occasionally with spoon, until spreadable.

7 Spread frosting between layers and on top of cake, leaving side of cake unfrosted. Store covered in refrigerator.

1 Serving: Calories 670; Total Fat 33g (Saturated Fat 21g, Trans Fat 1g); Cholesterol 175mg; Sodium 600mg; Total Carbohydrate 82g (Dietary Fiber 2g, Sugars 63g); Protein 8g **Exchanges:** 2½ Starch, 3 Other Carbohydrate, 6½ Fat **Carbohydrate Choices:** 5½

Chocolate Layer Cake

Homemade chocolate cake is impressive but certainly not hard to achieve. To make great cakes, use the right pans, measure ingredients accurately and follow directions carefully.

PREP 20 min **TOTAL** 2 hr 5 min • 12 servings

- 2¼ cups all-purpose flour or 2½ cups cake flour
- 1⅔ cups sugar
- ⅔ cup unsweetened baking cocoa
- 1¼ teaspoons baking soda
- 1 teaspoon salt
- ¼ teaspoon baking powder
- 1¼ cups water
- ¾ cup butter, softened
- 2 eggs
- 1 teaspoon vanilla
  Fudge Frosting (page 578) or Fluffy White Frosting (page 581), if desired

1 Heat oven to 350°F. Grease bottoms and sides of 2 (9-inch) or 3 (8-inch) round cake pans with shortening; lightly flour.

2 In large bowl, beat all ingredients except frosting with electric mixer on low speed 30 seconds, scraping bowl constantly. Beat on high speed 3 minutes, scraping bowl occasionally. Pour batter into pans.

3 Bake 30 to 35 minutes or until toothpick inserted in center comes out clean. Cool 10 minutes; remove from pans to cooling racks. Cool completely, about 1 hour.

Chocolate Layer Cake

4 Fill and frost layers with frosting.

1 Serving: Calories 330; Total Fat 13g (Saturated Fat 6g, Trans Fat 0.5g); Cholesterol 65mg; Sodium 430mg; Total Carbohydrate 48g (Dietary Fiber 2g, Sugars 28g); Protein 5g **Exchanges:** 2 Starch, 1 Other Carbohydrate, 2½ Fat **Carbohydrate Choices:** 3

Turtle Layer Cake Substitute Caramel Frosting (page 580) for Fudge Frosting. After frosting first layer, press ½ cup coarsely chopped pecans gently into frosting on top of cake before topping with second layer. Sprinkle top of frosted cake with an additional ½ cup coarsely chopped pecans; press lightly into frosting.

Chocolate Sheet Cake Grease bottom and sides of 13x9-inch pan with shortening; lightly flour. Make batter as directed; pour into pan. Bake 40 to 45 minutes or until toothpick inserted in center comes out clean. Cool completely in pan on cooling rack. Frost top of cake with frosting. Decorate cake, if desired. See Easy Chocolate Dessert Garnishes, page 611.

Frosting a Layer Cake

Brush any loose crumbs from cooled cake layer. Place 4 strips of waxed paper around edge of plate. Place layer, rounded side down, on plate.

Spread ⅓ to ½ cup frosting over top of first layer to within about ¼ inch of edge.

Place second cake layer, rounded side up, on frosted first layer. Coat side of cake with a very thin layer of frosting to seal in crumbs.

Frost side of cake in swirls, making a rim about ¼ inch high above top of cake. Spread remaining frosting on top, just to the built-up rim. Carefully remove waxed paper strips.

Red Velvet Cake

PREP 25 min **TOTAL** 2 hr • 12 servings

CAKE

- 2½ cups all-purpose flour
- 1½ cups sugar
- 2 tablespoons unsweetened baking cocoa
- 1 tablespoon baking powder
- 1 teaspoon salt
- 1½ cups vegetable oil
- 1 cup buttermilk
- 1 teaspoon vanilla
- 1 bottle (1 oz) red food color
- 2 eggs

FROSTING

- ½ cup all-purpose flour
- 1½ cups milk
- 1½ cups sugar
- 1½ cups butter, softened
- 1 tablespoon vanilla

1 Heat oven to 350°F. Grease bottoms and sides of 3 (8- or 9-inch) round cake pans with shortening; lightly flour.

2 In large bowl, beat all cake ingredients with electric mixer on low speed 30 seconds, scraping bowl constantly. Beat 2 minutes on medium speed, scraping bowl occasionally. Pour batter into pans.

3 Bake 25 to 35 minutes or until toothpick inserted in center comes out clean. Cool 10 minutes; remove from pans to cooling rack. Cool completely, about 1 hour.

4 Meanwhile, in 2-quart saucepan, mix ½ cup flour and 1½ cups milk with whisk until

Red Velvet Cake

smooth. Cook over medium heat until mixture is very thick, stirring constantly. Remove from heat; cool 10 minutes. In large bowl, beat 1½ cups sugar and the butter with electric mixer on medium speed until light and fluffy. Gradually add flour mixture by tablespoonfuls, beating on high speed until smooth. Beat in 1 tablespoon vanilla.

5 Fill and frost cake, using 1 cup frosting between layers. Store covered in refrigerator.

1 Serving: Calories 800; Total Fat 52g (Saturated Fat 20g, Trans Fat 1g); Cholesterol 100mg; Sodium 510mg; Total Carbohydrate 76g (Dietary Fiber 1g, Sugars 52g); Protein 5g **Exchanges:** 1½ Starch, 3½ Other Carbohydrate, 10½ Fat **Carbohydrate Choices:** 5

Red Velvet Cupcakes Place paper baking cup in each of 24 regular-size muffin cups. Heat oven and make cake batter as directed in recipe. Divide batter among muffin cups, filling each about two-thirds full. Bake 20 to 22 minutes or until toothpick inserted in center comes out clean. Remove cupcakes from pan to cooling rack. Cool completely, about 30 minutes. Frost with red velvet cake frosting (above) or Fluffy White Frosting (page 581).

Flouring Pan	Scraping Bowl	Making Red Velvet Cake Frosting	

Place 1 to 2 tablespoons flour in greased pan. Rotate pan until all sides and bottom are coated; tap pan and shake out excess flour.	Beat cake ingredients on low speed 30 seconds, scraping bowl constantly. Beat on high speed 3 minutes, scraping bowl occasionally.	Cook frosting in sauce-pan over medium heat, stirring constantly, until very thick.	Gradually add flour mix-ture by tablespoonfuls, beating on high speed until smooth and thick.

Chocolate-Fig Cake

PREP 30 min **TOTAL** 3 hr 30 min • 16 servings

CAKE

- 6 oz dried Calimyrna figs, stems removed, chopped (1 cup)
- 1 cup dry red wine (such as Merlot or Cabernet Sauvignon) or water
- 1 cup butter, softened
- 1 cup granulated sugar
- 2 eggs
- 1 teaspoon vanilla
- 1¾ cups all-purpose flour
- 2 tablespoons unsweetened regular baking cocoa
- 1 teaspoon baking soda
- 4 oz semisweet baking chocolate, melted, cooled

FROSTING AND GARNISH

- 1 container (8 oz) mascarpone cheese
- 2½ cups powdered sugar
- ½ teaspoon vanilla
- 1 bar (1.55 oz) milk chocolate, if desired

1 Heat oven to 350°F. Grease bottom and side of 9- or 10-inch springform pan with shortening; lightly flour. In 1½-quart saucepan, heat figs and wine to boiling over medium-high heat. Remove from heat; cool.

2 In large bowl, beat butter and granulated sugar with electric mixer on medium speed until creamy. Add eggs and 1 teaspoon vanilla. Beat until thick and creamy, scraping bowl occasionally. Add flour, cocoa and baking soda. Beat on low speed until moistened, scraping bowl occasionally. Add melted chocolate and fig mixture. Beat until blended. Spread batter in pan.

3 Bake 55 to 60 minutes or until toothpick inserted in center comes out clean. Cool completely in pan on cooling rack, about 2 hours. Remove side of pan.

4 In medium bowl, beat cheese, powdered sugar and ½ teaspoon vanilla with electric mixer on low speed until blended. Beat on medium speed until thick and creamy. Frost side and top of cake.

5 To make garnish, see Chocolate Curls, page 611. Arrange curls on cake. Garnish cake with chocolate curls. Store in refrigerator.

Chocolate-Fig Cake

1 Serving: Calories 380; Total Fat 19g (Saturated Fat 12g, Trans Fat 0g); Cholesterol 65mg; Sodium 190mg; Total Carbohydrate 47g (Dietary Fiber 2g, Sugars 32g); Protein 3g **Exchanges:** 3 Other Carbohydrate, ½ Medium-Fat Meat, 3½ Fat **Carbohydrate Choices:** 3

Double-Chocolate Hot Fudge Sundae Cake

PREP 15 min **TOTAL** 1 hr 5 min • 9 servings

- 1 cup all-purpose flour
- ¾ cup granulated sugar
- 2 tablespoons unsweetened baking cocoa
- 2 teaspoons baking powder
- ¼ teaspoon salt
- ½ cup chocolate or regular milk
- 2 tablespoons butter, melted, or vegetable oil
- 1 teaspoon vanilla
- ½ cup semisweet chocolate chips
- ½ cup chopped walnuts or pecans, toasted (page 23), if desired
- 1 cup packed brown sugar
- ¼ cup unsweetened baking cocoa
- 1¾ cups hot strong brewed coffee or hot water
  Ice cream, if desired

1 Heat oven to 350°F. In ungreased 9-inch square pan, mix flour, granulated sugar, 2 tablespoons cocoa, the baking powder and salt. Mix in milk, butter and vanilla with fork until smooth. Stir in chocolate chips and nuts.

2 Spread batter in pan. Sprinkle with brown sugar and ¼ cup cocoa. Pour hot coffee evenly over batter.

3 Bake about 40 minutes or until top is dry. Cool 10 minutes. Spoon warm cake into dessert dishes. Top with ice cream. Spoon sauce from pan onto each serving.

1 Serving: Calories 260; Total Fat 4g (Saturated Fat 1g, Trans Fat 0g); Cholesterol 0mg; Sodium 190mg; Total Carbohydrate 54g (Dietary Fiber 2g, Sugars 41g); Protein 3g **Exchanges:** 2 Starch, 1 Fat **Carbohydrate Choices:** 3½

Starlight Yellow Cake

PREP 20 min **TOTAL** 2 hr 10 min • 12 servings

- 2¼ cups all-purpose flour
- 1½ cups sugar
- 3½ teaspoons baking powder
- 1 teaspoon salt
- ½ cup butter, softened
- 1¼ cups milk
- 1 teaspoon vanilla
- 3 eggs

  Creamy Chocolate Frosting (page 579) or Peanut Butter Frosting (page 579), if desired

Starlight Yellow Cake

1 Heat oven to 350°F. Grease bottoms and sides of 2 (9-inch) round cake pans, 3 (8-inch) round cake pans or 13x9-inch pan with shortening; lightly flour.

2 In large bowl, beat all ingredients except frosting with electric mixer on low speed 30 seconds, scraping bowl constantly. Beat on high speed 3 minutes, scraping bowl occasionally. Pour batter into pan(s).

3 Bake 9-inch pans 25 to 30 minutes, 8-inch pans 30 to 35 minutes, 13x9-inch pan 35 to 40 minutes, or until toothpick inserted in center comes out clean or cake springs back when touched lightly in center. Cool rounds 10 minutes; remove from pans to cooling racks. Cool 13x9-inch cake in pan on cooling rack. Cool completely, about 1 hour.

4 Fill and frost round layers or frost top of 13x9-inch cake with frosting.

1 Serving: Calories 290; Total Fat 10g (Saturated Fat 4.5g, Trans Fat 0g); Cholesterol 75mg; Sodium 420mg; Total Carbohydrate 45g (Dietary Fiber 0g, Sugars 27g); Protein 5g **Exchanges:** 2 Starch, 1 Other Carbohydrate, 1½ Fat **Carbohydrate Choices:** 3

Boston Cream Pie While cake layers are baking, in 2-quart heavy saucepan, stir 1¼ cups whole milk, ¼ cup sugar, 2 egg yolks, 2 tablespoons cornstarch and ¼ teaspoon salt. Heat to boiling over medium heat, stirring constantly; boil 1 minute or until thickened and mixture coats back of spoon. Remove from heat; stir in 1 tablespoon butter and 1 teaspoon vanilla. Cover surface of custard with plastic wrap. Refrigerate until set, about 2 hours. Omit Creamy Chocolate Frosting. Fill cooled cake layers with custard. Top cake with Chocolate Glaze (page 582).

Testing Cakes for Doneness

Insert wooden cake tester or toothpick into center of cake.

When you remove cake tester, it should be clean, maybe with some dry crumbs on it. If there is wet batter, the cake is not done.

LEARN WITH BETTY Butter Cakes

Perfect Cake: This cake is high and golden brown, with a slightly rounded top. The texture is soft, velvety and tender.

Underrisen Cake: This cake did not rise and is pale in color because of too much liquid or fat, not enough leavening or pan was too large.

Overbaked Cake: This cake is too brown and sunk in the middle because of too much leavening, too much liquid or too long in the oven.

Silver White Cake

PREP 20 min **TOTAL** 2 hr 15 min • 12 servings

- 2¼ cups all-purpose flour
- 1⅔ cups sugar
- ⅔ cup shortening
- 1¼ cups milk
- 3½ teaspoons baking powder
- 1 teaspoon salt
- 1 teaspoon vanilla or almond extract
- 5 egg whites
  Fluffy White Frosting (page 581) or Creamy Chocolate Frosting (page 579), if desired

1 Heat oven to 350°F. Grease 2 (9-inch) round cake pans, 3 (8-inch) round cake pans or 13x9-inch pan with shortening; lightly flour.

2 In large bowl, beat all ingredients except egg whites and frosting with electric mixer on low speed 30 seconds, scraping bowl constantly. Beat on high speed 2 minutes, scraping bowl occasionally. Beat in egg whites on high speed 2 minutes, scraping bowl occasionally. Pour batter into pan(s).

3 Bake 9-inch rounds 30 to 35 minutes, 8-inch rounds 23 to 28 minutes, 13x9-inch pan 40 to 45 minutes, or until toothpick inserted in center comes out clean or cake springs back when touched lightly in center. Cool rounds 10 minutes; remove from pans to cooling racks. Cool 13x9-inch cake in pan on cooling rack. Cool completely, about 1 hour.

4 Fill and frost round layers or frost top of 13x9-inch cake with frosting.

1 Serving: Calories 320; Total Fat 12g (Saturated Fat 3g, Trans Fat 0g); Cholesterol 0mg; Sodium 370mg; Total Carbohydrate 47g (Dietary Fiber 0g, Sugars 29g); Protein 4g **Exchanges:** 1 Starch, 2 Other Carbohydrate, 2½ Fat **Carbohydrate Choices:** 3

Chocolate Chip Cake Fold ½ cup miniature or finely chopped regular semisweet chocolate chips into batter after beating in egg whites.

Cookies 'n Creme Cake Stir 1 cup crushed creme-filled chocolate sandwich cookies into batter after beating in egg whites. Bake and cool as directed. Frost with Fluffy White Frosting; garnish with whole or coarsely crushed creme-filled chocolate sandwich cookies.

Marble Cake Reserve 1¾ cups of the batter. Pour remaining batter into pan(s). Stir 3 tablespoons unsweetened baking cocoa and ⅛ teaspoon baking soda into reserved batter. Drop chocolate batter by tablespoonfuls randomly onto white batter. Cut through batters with knife for marbled design. Bake as directed.

Strawberry Cake Use 9-inch round cake pans and Fluffy White Frosting. After frosting first layer, top with 1 cup sliced fresh strawberries, overlapping as needed. Add second layer; frost cake. Garnish cake with whole or sliced strawberries.

Marbling Batter

Drop chocolate batter by tablespoonfuls randomly over white batter. Cut through batters with knife.

Marble Cake with Fluffy White Frosting (page 581)

Coconut Cake

Coconut Cake

PREP 50 min **TOTAL** 2 hr 20 min • 16 servings

CAKE

- 2¾ cups all-purpose flour
- 2 teaspoons baking powder
- 1 teaspoon salt
- 1 cup butter, softened
- 2 cups sugar
- 4 whole eggs
- 1½ teaspoons vanilla
- 1½ teaspoons almond extract
- 1 cup milk

BOILED FROSTING

- 1½ cups sugar
- ½ cup water
- 4 egg whites
- ½ teaspoon cream of tartar
- ⅛ teaspoon salt
- 6 large marshmallows, cut into small pieces

FILLING

- 2 tablespoons sugar
- ¼ cup reduced-fat (lite) coconut milk (not cream of coconut)
- 2 to 3 cups sweetened flaked coconut

1 Heat oven to 350°F. Grease 3 (9-inch) round cake pans with shortening; lightly flour. In medium bowl, mix flour, baking powder and 1 teaspoon salt; set aside.

2 In large bowl, beat butter with electric mixer on medium speed 30 seconds. Gradually add 2 cups sugar, ¼ cup at a time, beating well after each addition. Beat 2 minutes longer. Add whole eggs, one at a time, beating well after each addition. Beat in vanilla and almond extract. Add flour mixture alternately with milk, beating on low speed just until blended. Pour batter into pans.

3 Bake 18 to 20 minutes or until toothpick inserted in center comes out clean. Cool 10 minutes; remove from pans to cooling racks. Cool completely, about 1 hour.

4 In 2-quart saucepan, mix 1½ cups sugar and the water. Cook over medium heat, stirring constantly, until mixture is clear. Cook, without stirring, to 240°F on candy thermometer, about 10 minutes. Meanwhile, in large bowl, beat egg whites with electric mixer on low speed until foamy. Add cream of tartar and ⅛ teaspoon salt; beat on medium speed until soft peaks form. Increase speed to high; pour hot syrup into egg white mixture. Add marshmallows, a few pieces at a time, beating until stiff peaks form and frosting is thick enough to spread.

5 In small microwavable bowl, microwave 2 tablespoons sugar and the coconut milk on High 1 minute; stir until sugar is dissolved. Brush half of the coconut milk mixture over one cake layer to within ½ inch of edge. Frost with 1 cup of the frosting; sprinkle with ½ cup of the coconut. Top with second cake layer; brush with remaining coconut milk mixture. Frost with 1 cup frosting; sprinkle with ½ cup coconut. Top with remaining cake layer. Spread remaining frosting on top and side of cake; sprinkle with remaining coconut.

1 Serving: Calories 460; Total Fat 17g (Saturated Fat 11g, Trans Fat 0g); Cholesterol 80mg; Sodium 400mg; Total Carbohydrate 70g (Dietary Fiber 1g, Sugars 52g); Protein 5g **Exchanges:** ½ Starch, 4 Other Carbohydrate, ½ Lean Meat, 3 Fat **Carbohydrate Choices:** 4½

Tres Leches Cake

Carrot Cake

Tres Leches Cake

In Spanish, tres leches *means "three milks."*

PREP 25 min **TOTAL** 4 hr 15 min • 15 servings

> Batter for Starlight Yellow Cake (page 559) or Silver White Cake (page 560)
> 2 cups whipping cream
> 1 cup whole milk
> 1 can (14 oz) sweetened condensed milk (not evaporated)
> ⅓ cup rum or 1 tablespoon rum extract plus enough water to measure ⅓ cup
> 2 tablespoons rum or 1 teaspoon rum extract
> ½ teaspoon vanilla
> ½ cup chopped pecans, toasted (page 23)

1 Heat oven to 350°F. Grease bottom only of 13x9-inch pan with shortening. Make batter as directed in recipe; pour into pan. Bake 35 to 40 minutes for yellow cake, 40 to 45 minutes for white cake, or until toothpick inserted in center comes out clean or cake springs back when touched lightly in center. Let stand 5 minutes.

2 Pierce top of hot cake every ½ inch with long-tined fork, wiping fork occasionally to reduce sticking. In large bowl, stir 1 cup of the whipping cream, the whole milk, condensed milk and ⅓ cup rum until well mixed. Carefully pour milk mixture evenly over top of cake. Cover and refrigerate about 3 hours or until chilled and most of milk mixture has been absorbed into cake (when cutting cake to serve, you may notice some of the milk mixture on the bottom of the pan).

3 In chilled large deep bowl, beat remaining 1 cup whipping cream, 2 tablespoons rum and the vanilla with electric mixer on low speed until mixture begins to thicken. Gradually increase speed to high and beat just until soft peaks form, lifting beaters occasionally to check thickness. Frost cake with whipped cream mixture. Sprinkle with pecans. Store covered in refrigerator.

1 Serving: Calories 480; Total Fat 24g (Saturated Fat 12g, Trans Fat 1g); Cholesterol 110mg; Sodium 400mg; Total Carbohydrate 57g (Dietary Fiber 0g, Sugars 42g); Protein 8g **Exchanges:** 2 Starch, 2 Other Carbohydrate, 4½ Fat **Carbohydrate Choices:** 4

Tropical Tres Leches Cake Make cake through Step 3, except omit pecans. Sprinkle with 1 cup coconut, toasted (page 23), and ½ cup chopped macadamia nuts, toasted (page 23).

Carrot Cake

PREP 20 min **TOTAL** 2 hr 5 min • 12 servings

> 1½ cups sugar
> 1 cup vegetable oil
> 3 eggs
> 2 cups all-purpose flour
> 2 teaspoons ground cinnamon
> 1 teaspoon baking soda
> ½ teaspoon salt
> 1 teaspoon vanilla
> 3 cups shredded carrots (4 medium)
> 1 can (8 oz) crushed pineapple in juice, drained (½ cup)
> 1 cup chopped nuts
> ½ cup coconut
> Cream Cheese Frosting (page 580), if desired

1 Heat oven to 350°F. Grease bottom and sides of 13x9-inch pan or 2 (8- or 9-inch) round cake pans with shortening; lightly flour.

2 In large bowl, beat sugar, oil and eggs with electric mixer on low speed about 30 seconds or until blended. Add flour, cinnamon, baking soda, salt and vanilla; beat on medium speed 1 minute. Stir in carrots, pineapple, nuts and coconut (batter will be thick). Pour into pan(s).

3 Bake 13x9-inch pan 40 to 45 minutes, round pans 30 to 35 minutes, or until toothpick inserted in center comes out clean. Cool 13x9-inch cake in pan on cooling rack. Cool rounds 10 minutes; remove from pans to cooling racks. Cool completely, about 1 hour.

4 Frost top of 13x9-inch cake or fill and frost round layers with frosting. Store covered in refrigerator.

1 Serving: Calories 470; Total Fat 28g (Saturated Fat 6g, Trans Fat 0g); Cholesterol 55mg; Sodium 240mg; Total Carbohydrate 47g (Dietary Fiber 3g, Sugars 28g); Protein 5g **Exchanges:** 1 Starch, 2 Other Carbohydrate, ½ Vegetable, 5½ Fat **Carbohydrate Choices:** 3

LIGHTER **Directions** For 10 grams of fat and 280 calories per serving, substitute ½ cup unsweetened applesauce for ½ cup of the oil, and 1 egg plus 4 egg whites for the eggs. Omit nuts.

Carrot Cupcakes Place paper baking cup in each of 24 regular-size muffin cups. Divide batter evenly among muffin cups. Bake 30 to 35 minutes or until toothpick inserted in center comes out clean. Cool 10 minutes; remove from pans to cooling racks. Cool completely, 30 minutes.

Zucchini Cake Substitute 3 cups shredded zucchini (2 or 3 medium) for the carrots.

Pear-Ginger Upside-Down Cake

PREP 30 min **TOTAL** 1 hr 50 min • 8 servings

TOPPING
- ¼ cup butter
- ⅔ cup packed brown sugar
- ½ teaspoon ground ginger
- 3 pears, peeled, cut into ½-inch wedges
- ¼ cup finely chopped crystallized ginger

CAKE
- 1 tablespoon all-purpose flour
- ¼ cup finely chopped crystallized ginger
- 1⅓ cups all-purpose flour
- 1 teaspoon baking powder
- ¼ teaspoon salt
- 1 cup packed brown sugar
- 6 tablespoons butter, softened
- 2 eggs
- ½ teaspoon vanilla
- ¼ cup milk

GINGER WHIPPED CREAM
- 1 cup whipping cream
- 2 tablespoons granulated sugar
- ¼ teaspoon ground ginger
- 1 tablespoon chopped crystallized ginger (to make your own, see page 447)

Pear-Ginger Upside-Down Cake

1 Heat oven to 325°F. Grease bottom and sides of 8- or 9-inch square pan with shortening.

2 In 1-quart saucepan, melt ¼ cup butter over medium heat, stirring occasionally. Stir in ⅔ cup brown sugar. Heat to boiling; remove from heat. Stir in ½ teaspoon ground ginger. Pour into pan; spread evenly. Arrange pear wedges on sugar mixture, overlapping tightly and making 2 layers if necessary. Sprinkle ¼ cup crystallized ginger over pears.

3 In small bowl, toss 1 tablespoon flour and ¼ cup crystallized ginger; set aside. In another small bowl, mix 1⅓ cups flour, the baking powder and salt; set aside.

4 In large bowl, beat 1 cup brown sugar and 6 tablespoons butter with electric mixer on medium speed, scraping bowl occasionally, until fluffy. Beat in eggs, one at a time, until smooth. Add vanilla. Alternately add flour mixture with milk, beating on low speed after each addition until smooth. Stir in ginger-flour mixture. Spread batter over pears in pan.

5 Bake 55 to 65 minutes or until toothpick inserted in center of cake comes out clean. Cool 15 minutes on cooling rack.

6 Meanwhile, in chilled medium bowl, beat whipping cream on high speed until it begins to thicken. Gradually add granulated sugar and ¼ teaspoon ground ginger, beating until soft peaks form. Sprinkle with crystallized ginger. Loosen edges of cake with small knife. Place serving plate upside down over pan; turn plate and pan over. Serve cake warm with ginger whipped cream.

1 Serving: Calories 600; Total Fat 27g (Saturated Fat 15g, Trans Fat 1g); Cholesterol 135mg; Sodium 290mg; Total Carbohydrate 84g (Dietary Fiber 3g, Sugars 62g); Protein 5g **Exchanges:** 1½ Starch, 4 Other Carbohydrate, 5½ Fat **Carbohydrate Choices:** 5½

Heirloom Recipe and New Twist

Just the right combination of sweet, spicy and tangy, our heirloom recipe conjures up visions of a can't-wait-to-sink-my-teeth-into-it cake showcased on grandmother's sideboard or in a bakery display. Our twist version combines spice cake with apples and then adds a lighter, fresh maple glaze. Either way, you can't go wrong and aren't likely to see leftovers!

HEIRLOOM

Sour Cream Spice Cake

PREP 30 min **TOTAL** 2 hr 25 min • 16 servings

CAKE

2¼ cups all-purpose flour
1½ cups packed brown sugar
1 cup raisins, chopped
1 cup sour cream
½ cup chopped walnuts
¼ cup butter, softened
¼ cup shortening
½ cup water
2 teaspoons ground cinnamon
1¼ teaspoons baking soda
1 teaspoon baking powder
¾ teaspoon ground cloves
½ teaspoon salt
½ teaspoon ground nutmeg
2 eggs

BROWNED BUTTER CREAM FROSTING

⅓ cup butter*
3 cups powdered sugar
1½ teaspoons vanilla
1 to 2 tablespoons milk

Walnut halves, broken, if desired

1 Heat oven to 350°F. Grease bottom and sides of 13x9-inch pan or 2 (8- or 9-inch) round cake pans with shortening; lightly flour.

2 In large bowl, beat all cake ingredients with electric mixer on low speed 30 seconds, scraping bowl constantly. Beat on high speed 3 minutes, scraping bowl occasionally. Pour batter into pan(s).

3 Bake 13x9-inch pan 40 to 45 minutes, round pans 30 to 35 minutes, or until toothpick inserted in center comes out clean. Cool 13x9-inch cake in pan on cooling rack. Cool rounds 10 minutes; remove from pans to cooling racks. Cool completely, about 1 hour.

4 Meanwhile, in 1-quart saucepan, heat ⅓ cup butter over medium heat just until light brown, stirring constantly. Watch carefully, because butter can brown and then burn quickly. Remove from heat; cool. In medium bowl, mix powdered sugar and browned butter until well blended. Add vanilla and milk; beat until frosting is smooth and spreadable. Frost top of 13x9-inch cake or fill and frost round layers with frosting. Garnish with broken walnut halves.

* Do not use margarine or vegetable oil spreads in the frosting.

1 Serving: Calories 420; Total Fat 16g (Saturated Fat 7g, Trans Fat 0g); Cholesterol 50 mg; Sodium 290mg; Total Carbohydrate 65g (Dietary Fiber 1g, Sugars 48g); Protein 4g **Exchanges:** 1 Starch, 3½ Other Carbohydrate, 3 Fat **Carbohydrate Choices:** 4

Sour Cream Spice Cake

Spiced Apple Cake with Maple Glaze

Spiced Apple Cake with Maple Glaze

PREP 30 min **TOTAL** 2 hr 35 min • 16 servings

CAKE

3 cups chopped peeled apples (3 medium)
3 cups all-purpose flour
1 teaspoon baking powder
½ teaspoon baking soda
½ teaspoon salt
2 teaspoons ground cinnamon
½ teaspoon ground nutmeg
¼ teaspoon ground cloves
2 cups packed brown sugar
1 cup vegetable oil
4 eggs
1 teaspoon vanilla

GLAZE

1½ cups powdered sugar
3 to 4 tablespoons whipping cream
¼ teaspoon maple flavor

1 Heat oven to 350°F. Generously grease 12-cup fluted tube cake pan with shortening; lightly flour.

2 In medium bowl, toss apples with 2 tablespoons of the flour. In another medium bowl, mix baking powder, baking soda, salt, cinnamon, nutmeg, cloves and remaining flour. In large bowl, beat brown sugar, oil, eggs and vanilla with electric mixer on medium speed until mixed. On low speed, beat in flour mixture just until blended. Stir in apples. Spoon batter into pan.

3 Bake 55 minutes or until toothpick inserted in center comes out clean. Cool 10 minutes; remove from pan to cooling rack. Cool completely, about 1 hour.

4 In medium bowl, mix glaze ingredients until smooth. Drizzle glaze over cake.

1 Serving: Calories 400; Total Fat 16g (Saturated Fat 3g, Trans Fat 0g); Cholesterol 50mg; Sodium 170mg; Total Carbohydrate 60g (Dietary Fiber 1g, Sugars 40g); Protein 4g **Exchanges:** 1½ Starch, 2½ Other Carbohydrate, 3 Fat **Carbohydrate Choices:** 4

Caramel Snickerdoodle Cake

Caramel Snickerdoodle Cake

PREP 20 min **TOTAL** 2 hr 40 min • 16 servings

2 tablespoons sugar
2 teaspoons ground cinnamon
2½ cups all-purpose flour
1¾ cups sugar
2 teaspoons baking soda
1 teaspoon salt
1 can (5 oz) evaporated milk
1 cup sour cream
½ cup butter, melted
1 teaspoon vanilla
2 eggs, beaten
10 caramels, unwrapped

1 Heat oven to 350°F. Grease 12-cup fluted tube cake pan with shortening. In small bowl, mix 2 tablespoons sugar and 1 teaspoon of the cinnamon. Sprinkle mixture over inside of pan, turning to evenly coat. Shake out any excess.

2 In large bowl, mix flour, 1¾ cups sugar, the baking soda, salt and remaining 1 teaspoon cinnamon. Reserve 1 tablespoon of the milk for topping. Add remaining milk, the sour cream, butter, vanilla and eggs to dry ingredients; stir until well blended. Pour batter into pan.

3 Bake 40 to 50 minutes or until toothpick inserted in center comes out clean. Cool 30 minutes, remove from pan to cooling rack. Cool completely, about 1 hour.

4 In small microwavable bowl, microwave caramels with reserved milk uncovered on High 1 to 2 minutes, stirring every 30 seconds, until caramels are melted and mixture is smooth. Drizzle over cake.

1 Serving: Calories 340; Total Fat 11g (Saturated Fat 6g, Trans Fat 0g); Cholesterol 50mg; Sodium 420mg; Total Carbohydrate 54g (Dietary Fiber 0g, Sugars 33g); Protein 4g **Exchanges:** 1½ Starch, 2 Other Carbohydrate, 2 Fat **Carbohydrate Choices:** 3½

Molten Chocolate Cakes

Molten cakes or lava cakes, made popular by restaurants, are easy to make at home. The batter can be made a day ahead of time—perfect for entertaining. Be sure to follow the recipe steps exactly and bake at the correct oven temperature. If the centers are too cake-like in texture, bake a few minutes less the next time; if they're too soft, bake a minute or two longer.

PREP 20 min **TOTAL** 40 min • 6 servings

- Unsweetened baking cocoa
- 6 oz semisweet baking chocolate, chopped
- ½ cup plus 2 tablespoons butter
- 3 whole eggs
- 3 egg yolks
- 1½ cups powdered sugar
- ½ cup all-purpose flour
- Additional powdered sugar, if desired

1 Heat oven to 450°F. Grease bottoms and sides of 6 (6-oz) custard cups with shortening; sprinkle with cocoa.

2 In 2-quart saucepan, melt chocolate and butter over low heat, stirring frequently. Cool slightly.

3 In large bowl, beat whole eggs and egg yolks with whisk or hand beater until well blended. Beat in 1½ cups powdered sugar. Beat in melted chocolate mixture and flour. Divide batter evenly among custard cups. Place cups on cookie sheet with sides.

4 Bake 12 to 14 minutes or until sides are set and centers are still soft (tops will be puffed and cracked). Let stand 3 minutes. Run small knife or metal spatula around side of each cake to loosen. Immediately place heatproof serving plate upside down over each cup; turn plate and cup over and remove cup. Sprinkle cakes with additional powdered sugar. Serve warm.

1 Serving: Calories 550; Total Fat 33g (Saturated Fat 16g, Trans Fat 1g); Cholesterol 265mg; Sodium 170mg; Total Carbohydrate 56g (Dietary Fiber 2g, Sugars 44g); Protein 7g **Exchanges:** 2 Starch, 2 Other Carbohydrate, 6 Fat **Carbohydrate Choices:** 4

MAKE-AHEAD **Directions** After pouring batter into custard cups, cover tightly with plastic wrap and refrigerate up to 24 hours. Remove plastic wrap before baking. You may need to bake the cakes 1 to 2 minutes longer.

Molten Chocolate Cakes

Espresso Cake with Mocha Streusel Ribbon

PREP 30 min **TOTAL** 4 hr 30 min • 16 servings

STREUSEL

- 2 tablespoons all-purpose flour
- 2 tablespoons packed brown sugar
- 1 tablespoon instant espresso coffee powder or granules
- 1 tablespoon cold butter
- ½ cup miniature semisweet chocolate chips
- ¼ cup chopped pecans

CAKE

- 3 cups all-purpose flour
- 1 teaspoon baking powder
- ¼ teaspoon salt
- 1 cup milk
- ¼ cup instant espresso coffee powder or granules
- 2½ cups granulated sugar
- 1 cup butter, softened
- 1 teaspoon vanilla
- 5 eggs

GLAZE

- 3 tablespoons whipping cream
- ⅔ cup miniature semisweet chocolate chips
- 2 teaspoons instant espresso coffee powder or granules

1 Heat oven to 325°F. Grease 12-cup fluted tube cake pan with shortening; lightly flour. In small bowl, mix 2 tablespoons flour, the brown sugar and 1 tablespoon espresso powder. Cut in 1 tablespoon butter, using pastry blender or fork, until crumbly. Stir in ½ cup chocolate chips and the pecans; set aside.

Espresso Cake with Mocha Streusel Ribbon

2 In medium bowl, mix 3 cups flour, the baking powder and salt; set aside. In 1-cup glass measuring cup, stir milk and ¼ cup espresso powder; set aside.

3 In large bowl, beat granulated sugar, 1 cup butter, the vanilla and eggs with electric mixer on low speed 30 seconds. Beat on high speed 5 minutes, scraping bowl occasionally. Add flour mixture alternately with milk mixture, beating on low speed just until smooth after each addition. Spread 3 cups batter into pan. Sprinkle streusel over batter. Carefully spread remaining batter over streusel.

4 Bake 1 hour 30 minutes to 1 hour 40 minutes or until toothpick inserted in center comes out clean and crack at the center top of cake no longer looks moist. Cool 20 minutes; remove from pan to cooling rack. Cool completely, about 2 hours.

5 In small microwavable bowl, mix glaze ingredients. Microwave uncovered on High 30 seconds; stir until smooth. Spoon over cake, allowing some to drip down side of cake.

1 Serving: Calories 450; Total Fat 20g (Saturated Fat 11g, Trans Fat 0.5g); Cholesterol 95mg; Sodium 210mg; Total Carbohydrate 61g (Dietary Fiber 2g, Sugars 41g); Protein 6g **Exchanges:** 2 Starch, 2 Other Carbohydrate, 4 Fat **Carbohydrate Choices:** 4

LEARN WITH BETTY Molten Chocolate Cake

Perfect Cake: This cake has a flowing chocolate center. There are no problems.

Underbaked Cake: This cake is too runny because it was not baked long enough.

Overbaked Cake: This cake is completely cooked through because it was baked too long.

Italian Cream Cake

PREP 40 min **TOTAL** 2 hr • 16 servings

CAKE

½ cup butter, softened
2 cups granulated sugar
5 eggs
2 cups all-purpose flour
1 teaspoon baking soda
1 cup buttermilk
½ cup vegetable oil
1 teaspoon vanilla
1 cup sweetened coconut

FROSTING AND GARNISH

12 oz cream cheese, softened
¼ cup butter, softened
1 teaspoon vanilla
5 cups powdered sugar
1 to 2 tablespoons milk
½ cup chopped pecans
16 whole pecans

1 Heat oven to 350°F. Grease bottoms and sides of 3 (8- or 9-inch) round cake pans with shortening. Line pan bottoms with waxed paper or cooking parchment paper; grease paper and lightly flour.

2 In large bowl, beat ½ cup butter and the granulated sugar with electric mixer on low speed until creamy. Add eggs; beat on medium speed until creamy. Add flour and baking soda; beat on low speed until combined. Beat on medium speed until smooth. Add buttermilk, oil and 1 teaspoon vanilla; beat on low speed until combined. Beat on medium speed 2 minutes or until smooth. Fold in coconut. Pour batter into pans.

3 Bake 20 to 25 minutes or until toothpick inserted in center comes out clean. Cool 10 minutes; remove from pans to cooling racks. Remove waxed paper. Cool completely, about 45 minutes.

4 In large bowl, beat cream cheese, ¼ cup butter, 1 teaspoon vanilla, the powdered sugar and 1 tablespoon of the milk with electric mixer on low speed until blended. Gradually beat in enough remaining milk to make frosting smooth and spreadable. Reserve ¾ cup of the frosting for top of cake.

5 On cake plate, place one cake layer, top side up. Spread with ⅔ cup frosting. Top with another layer, top side down; spread with ⅔ cup frosting. Top with remaining layer, top side up. Spread side and top of cake with remaining frosting. Press chopped pecans into side of cake. Arrange pecan halves on top of cake. Store in refrigerator.

1 Serving: Calories 630; Total Fat 31g (Saturated Fat 13g, Trans Fat 0.5g); Cholesterol 105mg; Sodium 270mg; Total Carbohydrate 80g (Dietary Fiber 1g, Sugars 65g); Protein 6g **Exchanges:** 2 Starch, 3½ Other Carbohydrate, 6 Fat **Carbohydrate Choices:** 5

Italian Cream Cake

Jelly Roll

If you tried to roll a regular layer cake, it would crack. This special kind of cake, called a sponge cake, is soft and flexible so it can be rolled up.

Jelly Roll

PREP 30 min **TOTAL** 1 hr 15 min • 10 servings

    3   eggs
    1   cup granulated sugar
   ⅓   cup water
    1   teaspoon vanilla
   ¾   cup all-purpose flour
    1   teaspoon baking powder
   ¼   teaspoon salt
        Powdered sugar
        About ⅔ cup jelly or jam (any flavor)

1 Heat oven to 375°F. Line 15x10x1-inch pan with waxed paper, foil or cooking parchment paper; generously grease paper or foil with shortening.

2 In medium bowl, beat eggs with electric mixer on high speed about 5 minutes or until very thick and lemon colored. Gradually beat in granulated sugar. Beat in water and vanilla on low speed. Gradually add flour, baking powder and salt, beating on low speed just until smooth. Pour batter into pan, spreading to corners.

3 Bake 12 to 15 minutes or until toothpick inserted in center comes out clean. Immediately loosen cake from sides of pan and turn upside down onto towel generously sprinkled with powdered sugar. Carefully remove paper. Trim off stiff edges of cake if necessary. While cake is hot, carefully roll cake and towel from narrow end. Cool on cooling rack at least 30 minutes.

4 Unroll cake and remove towel. Beat jelly slightly with fork to soften; spread over cake. Roll up cake again; place seam side down on serving plate. Sprinkle with powdered sugar.

1 Serving: Calories 200; Total Fat 1.5g (Saturated Fat 0.5g, Trans Fat 0g); Cholesterol 65mg; Sodium 135mg; Total Carbohydrate 42g (Dietary Fiber 0g, Sugars 31g); Protein 3g **Exchanges:** 1 Starch, 2 Other Carbohydrate **Carbohydrate Choices:** 3

Chocolate Cake Roll Increase eggs to 4. Beat in ¼ cup unsweetened baking cocoa with the flour. If desired, fill cake with ice cream instead of jelly or jam. Spread 1 to 1½ pints (2 to 3 cups) slightly softened ice cream over cooled cake. Roll up cake; wrap in plastic wrap. Freeze about 4 hours or until firm. Serve slices drizzled with hot fudge sauce.

Lemon Curd Jelly Roll Make cake as directed, except add 2 teaspoons grated lemon peel with the flour. Omit jelly; spread cake with ⅔ cup Lemon Curd (page 602) or purchased lemon curd. Roll up as directed. Store covered in refrigerator.

Making Jelly Roll

Pour batter into 15x10x1-inch pan, spreading batter to the corners.

While cake is hot, carefully roll up with towel from narrow end.

Unroll cake, remove towel and spread jelly over the cake.

CUPCAKE AND FROSTING BASICS

Frosted cupcakes are sure to bring smiles, so choose from the Frosting recipes, starting on page 578, to top your creations. If you like heavily frosted, bakery-style cupcakes, consider doubling the recipe you choose.

Mini Cupcakes

To make mini cupcakes, place mini paper baking cup in each of 24 mini muffin cups. Make batter as directed in recipe. Fill each cup until about two-thirds full. (Cover and refrigerate remaining batter until ready to bake; cool pan before reusing.) Bake 12 to 16 minutes or until toothpick inserted in center comes out clean. Cool in pan 5 minutes. Remove cupcakes from pans; place on cooling racks to cool. Repeat with remaining batter to make an additional 48 mini cupcakes. Frost with desired frosting. Makes 72 mini cupcakes.

Chocolate Cupcakes CALORIE SMART

PREP 20 min **TOTAL** 1 hr 15 min • 24 cupcakes

     2 cups all-purpose flour
    1¼ teaspoons baking soda
     1 teaspoon salt
     ¼ teaspoon baking powder
     1 cup hot water
     ⅔ cup unsweetened baking cocoa
     ¾ cup shortening
    1½ cups sugar
     2 eggs
     1 teaspoon vanilla

1 Heat oven to 350°F. Place paper baking cup in each of 24 regular-size muffin cups.

2 In medium bowl, mix flour, baking soda, salt and baking powder; set aside. In small bowl, mix hot water and cocoa until dissolved; set aside.

3 In large bowl, beat shortening with electric mixer on medium speed 30 seconds. Gradually add sugar, about ¼ cup at a time, beating well after each addition and scraping bowl occasionally. Beat 2 minutes longer. Add eggs, one at a time, beating well after each addition. Beat in vanilla. On low speed, alternately add flour mixture, about one-third of mixture at a

time, and cocoa mixture, about one-half at a time, beating just until blended.

4 Divide batter evenly among muffin cups, filling each about two-thirds full.

5 Bake 20 to 25 minutes or until toothpick inserted in center comes out clean. Cool in pans 5 minutes. Remove cupcakes from pans; place on cooling racks to cool. Frost with desired frosting.

1 Cupcake: Calories 160; Total Fat 7g (Saturated Fat 2g, Trans Fat 1g); Cholesterol 20mg; Sodium 180mg; Total Carbohydrate 22g (Dietary Fiber 1g, Sugars 13g); Protein 2g **Exchanges:** ½ Starch, 1 Other Carbohydrate, 1½ Fat **Carbohydrate Choices:** 1½

Yellow Cupcakes CALORIE SMART

PREP 15 min **TOTAL** 1 hr 15 min • 24 cupcakes

    2⅓ cups all-purpose flour
    2½ teaspoons baking powder
     ½ teaspoon salt
     1 cup butter or margarine, softened
    1¼ cups sugar
     3 eggs
     1 teaspoon vanilla
     ⅔ cup milk

1 Heat oven to 350°F. Place paper baking cup in each of 24 regular-size muffin cups. Grease and flour muffin cups, or spray with baking spray with flour.

2 In medium bowl, mix flour, baking powder and salt; set aside.

3 In large bowl, beat butter with electric mixer on medium speed 30 seconds. Gradually add sugar, about ¼ cup at a time, beating well after each addition and scraping bowl occasionally. Beat 2 minutes longer. Add eggs, one at a time, beating well after each addition. Beat in vanilla. On low speed, alternately add flour mixture, about one-third of mixture at a time,

Chocolate, Yellow and White Cupcakes with Creamy Chocolate Frosting (page 579)

and milk, about one-half at a time, beating just until blended.

4 Divide batter evenly among muffin cups, filling each with about 3 tablespoons batter or until two-thirds full.

5 Bake 20 to 25 minutes or until golden brown and toothpick inserted in center comes out clean. Cool in pans 5 minutes. Remove cupcakes from pans; place on cooling racks to cool. Frost with desired frosting.

1 Cupcake: Calories 170; Total Fat 9g (Saturated Fat 5g, Trans Fat 0g); Cholesterol 45mg; Sodium 190mg; Total Carbohydrate 20g (Dietary Fiber 0g, Sugars 11g); Protein 2g **Exchanges:** 1 Starch, ½ Other Carbohydrate, 1½ Fat **Carbohydrate Choices:** 1

White Cupcakes CALORIE SMART

PREP 15 min **TOTAL** 1 hr 15 min • 24 cupcakes

  2¾ cups all-purpose flour
   3 teaspoons baking powder
   ½ teaspoon salt
   ¾ cup shortening or butter
  1⅔ cups sugar
   5 egg whites
  2½ teaspoons vanilla
  1¼ cups milk

1 Heat oven to 350°F. Place paper baking cup in each of 24 regular-size muffin cups.

2 In medium bowl, mix flour, baking powder and salt; set aside.

3 In large bowl, beat shortening with electric mixer on medium speed 30 seconds. Gradually add sugar, about ⅓ cup at a time, beating well after each addition and scraping bowl occasionally. Beat 2 minutes longer. Add egg whites, one at a time, beating well after each addition. Beat in vanilla. On low speed, alternately add flour mixture, about one-third of mixture at a time, and milk, about one-half at a time, beating just until blended.

4 Divide batter evenly among muffin cups, filling each about two-thirds full.

5 Bake 18 to 20 minutes or until toothpick inserted in center comes out clean. Cool in pans 5 minutes. Remove cupcakes from pans; place on cooling racks to cool. Frost with desired frosting.

1 Cupcake: Calories 180; Total Fat 7g (Saturated Fat 2g, Trans Fat 1g); Cholesterol 0mg; Sodium 125mg; Total Carbohydrate 26g (Dietary Fiber 0g, Sugars 15g); Protein 2g **Exchanges:** ½ Starch, 1 Other Carbohydrate, 1½ Fat **Carbohydrate Choices:** 2

Maple-Cornmeal Cupcakes with Maple-Butter Frosting

PREP 45 min **TOTAL** 1 hr 45 min • 18 cupcakes

CUPCAKES

1½	cups all-purpose flour
⅓	cup yellow cornmeal
2	teaspoons baking powder
½	teaspoon salt
½	cup butter, softened
1	cup granulated sugar
1	teaspoon maple flavor
2	eggs
¾	cup milk

FROSTING

4	cups powdered sugar
2	tablespoons butter, softened
2	teaspoons maple flavor
3	to 4 tablespoons milk

GARNISH

18	maple leaf candies or pecan halves, if desired

1 Heat oven to 350°F. Place paper baking cup in each of 18 regular-size muffin cups. In medium bowl, mix flour, cornmeal, baking powder and salt; set aside.

2 In large bowl, beat ½ cup butter with electric mixer on medium speed 30 seconds. Gradually add granulated sugar, about ¼ cup at a time, beating well after each addition. Beat 2 minutes longer. Beat in 1 teaspoon maple flavor and the eggs. Add flour mixture alternately with ¾ cup milk, beating on low speed just until blended. Divide batter evenly among muffin cups, filling each about two-thirds full.

3 Bake 20 to 25 minutes or until golden brown and toothpick inserted in center comes out clean. Cool 5 minutes; remove from pans to cooling racks. Cool completely, about 30 minutes.

4 In medium bowl, beat frosting ingredients, adding enough milk, until frosting is smooth and spreadable. Frost cupcakes. Garnish each with candy or pecan half.

1 Cupcake: Calories 280; Total Fat 7g (Saturated Fat 4.5g, Trans Fat 0g); Cholesterol 40mg; Sodium 180mg; Total Carbohydrate 50g (Dietary Fiber 0g, Sugars 38g); Protein 2g **Exchanges:** 1½ Starch, 2 Other Carbohydrate, 1 Fat **Carbohydrate Choices:** 3

Maple-Cornmeal Cupcakes with Maple-Butter Frosting

Banana Split–Chocolate Mug Cake

PREP 10 min **TOTAL** 15 min • 1 serving

¼	cup all-purpose flour
2	tablespoons sugar
2	tablespoons unsweetened baking cocoa
½	teaspoon baking powder
⅛	teaspoon salt
⅓	cup mashed banana (about 1 small)
3	tablespoons milk
1	tablespoon butter, melted
⅓	cup vanilla or favorite flavor ice cream
1	tablespoon hot fudge topping
1	fresh strawberry

1 In small bowl, mix flour, sugar, cocoa, baking powder and salt with wooden spoon until well blended. Beat in banana, milk and butter with whisk until smooth. Pour into 10-ounce microwavable mug.

Making Chocolate Mug Cake

Mix cake ingredients as directed in recipe; pour into 10-ounce microwavable mug.

Microwave on High 1 to 2 minutes or until set and cake rises (center will have a slightly wet appearance).

2 Microwave uncovered on High 1 to 2 minutes or until set and cake rises (center will have a slightly wet appearance). Cool 5 minutes. Top with ice cream, hot fudge and strawberry.

1 Serving: Calories 620; Total Fat 21g (Saturated Fat 13g, Trans Fat 0.5g); Cholesterol 55mg; Sodium 770mg; Total Carbohydrate 98g (Dietary Fiber 7g, Sugars 56g); Protein 10g **Exchanges:** ½ Starch, ½ Fruit, 4½ Other Carbohydrate, 1 Milk, 2½ Fat **Carbohydrate Choices:** 6½

Lemon Meringue Cupcakes

PREP 1 hr **TOTAL** 2 hr • 24 cupcakes

CUPCAKES

- 2⅓ cups all-purpose flour
- 2½ teaspoons baking powder
- ½ teaspoon salt
- 1 cup butter, softened
- 1¼ cups sugar
- 3 whole eggs
- 2 tablespoons grated lemon peel
- 1 teaspoon vanilla
- ⅔ cup milk
- 1 jar (10 to 12 oz) lemon curd

MERINGUE

- 4 egg whites
- ¼ teaspoon cream of tartar
- 1½ teaspoons vanilla
- ⅔ cup sugar

1 Heat oven to 350°F. Place paper baking cup in each of 24 regular-size muffin cups; spray paper cups with baking spray with flour. In medium bowl, mix flour, baking powder and salt; set aside.

2 In large bowl, beat butter with electric mixer on medium speed 30 seconds. Gradually add 1¼ cups sugar, about ¼ cup at a time, beating well after each addition. Beat 2 minutes longer. Add eggs, one at a time, beating well after each addition. Beat in lemon peel and 1 teaspoon vanilla. Alternately add flour mixture and milk, beating on low speed just until blended. Divide batter evenly among muffin cups, filling each about two-thirds full.

3 Bake 20 to 25 minutes or until toothpick inserted in center comes out clean. Cool 5 minutes; remove from pans to cooling racks. Cool completely, about 30 minutes.

4 By slowly spinning end of round handle of wooden spoon back and forth, make deep, ¾-inch-wide indentation in center of top of each cupcake, not quite to bottom. (Wiggle end of spoon in cupcake to make opening large enough.) Spoon lemon curd into small resealable food-storage plastic bag; seal bag. Cut ⅜-inch tip off bottom corner of bag. Insert tip of bag into opening in each cupcake; squeeze bag to fill opening.

5 Increase oven temperature to 450°F. In medium bowl, beat egg whites, cream of tartar and 1½ teaspoons vanilla with electric mixer on high speed until soft peaks form. Gradually add ⅔ cup sugar, 1 tablespoon at a time, beating until stiff peaks form and mixture is glossy. Frost cupcakes with meringue; place on cookie sheet. Bake 2 to 3 minutes or until lightly browned.

1 Cupcake: Calories 230; Total Fat 9g (Saturated Fat 6g, Trans Fat 0g); Cholesterol 60mg; Sodium 210mg; Total Carbohydrate 34g (Dietary Fiber 0g, Sugars 24g); Protein 3g **Exchanges:** 1 Starch, 1½ Other Carbohydrate, 1½ Fat **Carbohydrate Choices:** 2

Lemon Meringue Cupcakes

Cream Cheese Frosting FAST·EASY

This is the perfect frosting for carrot cake and spice or applesauce cakes. Be sure to refrigerate the frosted cake, since cream cheese is perishable.

PREP 10 min **TOTAL** 10 min • 2½ cups

- 1 package (8 oz) cream cheese, softened
- ¼ cup butter, softened
- 2 to 3 teaspoons milk
- 1 teaspoon vanilla
- 4 cups powdered sugar

1 In large bowl, beat cream cheese, butter, milk and vanilla with electric mixer on low speed until smooth.

2 Gradually beat in powdered sugar, 1 cup at a time, on low speed until frosting is smooth and spreadable.

3 Frost 13x9-inch cake, or fill and frost 8- or 9-inch two-layer cake. Leftover frosting can be tightly covered and refrigerated up to 5 days or frozen up to 1 month. Let stand 30 minutes at room temperature to soften; stir before using.

About 3 Tablespoons: Calories 260; Total Fat 10g (Saturated Fat 6g, Trans Fat 0g); Cholesterol 30mg; Sodium 80mg; Total Carbohydrate 40g (Dietary Fiber 0g, Sugars 39g); Protein 2g **Exchanges:** 1 Starch, 1½ Other Carbohydrate, 2 Fat **Carbohydrate Choices:** 2½

Chocolate Cream Cheese Frosting Add 2 ounces unsweetened baking chocolate, melted and cooled 10 minutes, with the butter.

Cinnamon Cream Cheese Frosting Stir in ½ teaspoon ground cinnamon with the vanilla.

Caramel Frosting EASY

For a richer frosting, use whole milk or half-and-half.

PREP 10 min **TOTAL** 40 min • 2 cups

- ½ cup butter
- 1 cup packed brown sugar
- ¼ cup milk
- 2 cups powdered sugar

1 In 2-quart saucepan, melt butter over medium heat. Stir in brown sugar. Heat to boiling, stirring constantly; reduce heat to low. Boil and stir 2 minutes. Stir in milk. Heat to boiling; remove from heat. Cool to lukewarm, about 30 minutes.

2 Gradually stir in powdered sugar. Place saucepan of frosting in bowl of cold water. Beat with spoon until frosting is smooth and spreadable. If frosting becomes too stiff, stir in additional milk, 1 teaspoon at a time, or heat over low heat, stirring constantly.

3 Frost 13x9-inch cake, or fill and frost 8- or 9-inch two-layer cake. Leftover frosting can be tightly covered and refrigerated up to 5 days or frozen up to 1 month. Let stand 30 minutes at room temperature to soften; stir before using.

About 3 Tablespoons: Calories 220; Total Fat 8g (Saturated Fat 4g, Trans Fat 0g); Cholesterol 20mg; Sodium 60mg; Total Carbohydrate 38g (Dietary Fiber 0g, Sugars 37g); Protein 0g **Exchanges:** 2½ Other Carbohydrate, 1½ Fat **Carbohydrate Choices:** 2½

Salty Caramel Frosting Sprinkle ½ teaspoon kosher (coarse) salt over frosted cupcakes or cake.

LEARN WITH BETTY Browned Butter

Perfectly browned butter: This butter is golden brown.

Underbrowned butter: This butter is not browned enough.

Overbrowned butter: This butter is scorched and too brown.

Fluffy White Frosting

CALORIE SMART

This frosting got its name because its large white peaks hold up long after it's beaten. It's sometimes called White Mountain Frosting.

PREP 25 min **TOTAL** 55 min • 3 cups

- 2 egg whites
- ½ cup sugar
- ¼ cup light corn syrup
- 2 tablespoons water
- 1 teaspoon vanilla

1 Let egg whites stand at room temperature for 30 minutes. Room temperature egg whites will have more volume when beaten than cold egg whites. In medium bowl, beat egg whites with electric mixer on high speed just until stiff peaks form.

2 In 1-quart saucepan, stir sugar, corn syrup and water until well mixed. Cover and heat to rolling boil over medium heat. Uncover and boil 4 to 8 minutes, without stirring, to 242°F on candy thermometer or until small amount of mixture dropped into cup of very cold water forms a firm ball that holds its shape until pressed (see Testing Candy Temperatures, page 545). For an accurate temperature reading, tilt the saucepan slightly so mixture is deep enough for thermometer.

3 Pour hot syrup very slowly in thin stream into egg whites, beating constantly on medium speed. Add vanilla. Beat on high speed about 10 minutes or until stiff peaks form.

4 Frost 13x9-inch cake, or fill and frost 8- or 9-inch two-layer cake. Leftover frosting can be tightly covered and refrigerated up to 2 days; do not freeze. Let stand 30 minutes at room temperature to soften; do not stir.

¼ **Cup:** Calories 60; Total Fat 0g (Saturated Fat 0g, Trans Fat 0g); Cholesterol 0mg; Sodium 15mg; Total Carbohydrate 14g (Dietary Fiber 0g, Sugars 11g); Protein 0g **Exchanges:** 1 Other Carbohydrate **Carbohydrate Choices:** 1

Butterscotch Frosting Substitute packed brown sugar for the sugar. Reduce vanilla to ½ teaspoon.

Cherry-Nut Frosting Stir in ¼ cup chopped candied cherries, ¼ cup chopped nuts and, if desired, 6 to 8 drops red food color.

Peppermint Frosting Stir in ⅓ cup coarsely crushed hard peppermint candies or ½ teaspoon peppermint extract.

Vanilla Glaze FAST • EASY

PREP 5 min **TOTAL** 5 min • 1 cup

- ⅓ cup butter
- 2 cups powdered sugar
- 1½ teaspoons vanilla
- 2 to 4 tablespoons hot water

1 In 1½-quart saucepan, melt butter over low heat; remove from heat. Stir in powdered sugar and vanilla.

2 Stir in hot water, 1 tablespoon at a time, until glaze is smooth and has the consistency of thick syrup.

3 Glaze 12-cup fluted tube cake, 10-inch angel food or chiffon cake or top of 8- or 9-inch layer cake.

4 Teaspoons: Calories 130; Total Fat 5g (Saturated Fat 3g, Trans Fat 0g); Cholesterol 15mg; Sodium 35mg; Total Carbohydrate 20g (Dietary Fiber 0g, Sugars 19g); Protein 0g **Exchanges:** 1½ Other Carbohydrate, 1 Fat **Carbohydrate Choices:** 1

Browned Butter Glaze Brown the butter as directed in Browned Butter Frosting (page 579; see Learn with Betty on left page). Continue as directed.

Lemon Glaze Stir 1 teaspoon grated lemon peel into melted butter. Omit vanilla. Substitute lemon juice, heated, for the hot water.

Orange Glaze Stir 1 teaspoon grated orange peel into melted butter. Omit vanilla. Substitute orange juice, heated, for the hot water.

Fluffy White Frosting

CALORIE SMART = See Helpful Nutrition and Cooking Information, page 643   FAST = Ready in 30 minutes or less
EASY = Prep in 10 minutes or less **plus** five ingredients or less   LIGHTER = 25% fewer calories or grams of fat
MAKE AHEAD = Make-ahead directions   SLOW COOKER = Slow cooker directions

< Blueberry Pie, page 592

PIE BASICS

What makes a pie stand out from the crowd? It's the crust. When you bite into a really flaky, tender crust, you immediately know that the pie is special. When you know how to work with it, it's not hard to turn out a beautiful pie. We'll show you all the tricks and tips you need to become a legendary pie maker.

PICKING PIE PANS

The best pans to use for making pies are actually heat-resistant glass pie plates. The next best alternative would be a dull aluminum pie pan. Shiny or disposable pie pans reflect the heat and prevent crusts from browning. Dark pans absorb heat, causing overbrowning. Nonstick pans can cause a filled crust that isn't well anchored to the edge of the pan or an unfilled pie crust to shrink excessively. Use the size pie plate or pan called for in the recipe. Because pastry is high in fat, there is no need to grease the pie plate.

FREEZING PIE PASTRY

You can make pastry ahead and freeze it to have on hand for when you are ready to make a pie. Better yet, freeze the pastry in a freezer-to-oven glass pie plate so you are even closer to homemade pie. Unbaked and baked pie pastry (without filling) can be frozen up to 2 months.

- For rounds of pastry dough (see Pie Pastry, page 586, for how to make pastry rounds), wrap tightly in plastic wrap and freeze. Thaw in refrigerator before rolling and filling.

- For unbaked pastry crust in a pie plate, wrap tightly in foil or place in a freezer plastic bag. Fill crust while frozen and bake so that the crust won't be soggy.

- For baked pastry crust in a pie plate, wrap tightly (when completely cooled) in foil or place in a freezer plastic bag. Thaw before using.

FREEZING FILLED PIES

See and Refrigerator and Freezer Food Storage Chart, page 33, for freezing pies.

- Completely cool baked pies before freezing.

- Freeze pies with room around them so that the pastry edge won't get broken or misshapen during freezing. Once they are

Tips for Perfect Pie Pastry

- Using a pastry blender is the fastest way to get the pastry ingredients to pea-size crumbs. If you don't have one, using a potato masher is a great alternative. Finish mixing with a fork if the crumbs are larger than pea size. Alternately, a fork can be used for all the mixing, but it will take longer to do.

- Overworking the pastry dough will make it tough—handle it as little as possible.

- Another easy method for rolling the pastry is to do so between two sheets of waxed paper (anchor the bottom sheet to the counter by sprinkling counter with a few drops of water first). Flip pastry with both sheets of waxed paper over; carefully peel off the top piece of waxed paper. Flip pastry so remaining piece of waxed paper is on top; center over the pie plate and set on pie plate. Gently peel off waxed paper and ease pastry into plate.

frozen, other items can touch up against the pies.

- Do not freeze cream, custard and meringue-topped pies. The filling and the meringue will break down and become watery.

- Fruit pies can be frozen baked or unbaked. Pecan and pumpkin pies need to be baked before freezing.

Baked One-Crust Pie (page 587)

Pie Pastry

This pastry is perfect for making any pie or tart. Follow individual recipes for which amount of pastry to make. Make your pies extra special; see Pastry Edge Treatments (right) and Learn to Make a Lattice Crust (page 596).

PREP 20 min **TOTAL** 1 hr 5 min • 8 servings

ONE-CRUST PASTRY
1 cup plus 1 tablespoon all-purpose flour
½ teaspoon salt
⅓ cup cold shortening
3 to 5 tablespoons ice-cold water

TWO-CRUST PASTRY
2 cups plus 2 tablespoons all-purpose flour
1 teaspoon salt
⅔ cup cold shortening
6 to 8 tablespoons ice-cold water

1 In medium bowl, mix flour and salt. Cut in shortening, using pastry blender or fork, until mixture forms coarse crumbs the size of small peas. Sprinkle with water, 1 tablespoon at a time, tossing with fork until all flour is moistened and pastry almost leaves side of bowl (1 to 2 teaspoons more water can be added if necessary).

2 Gather pastry into a ball. For one-crust pastry, shape into flattened round on lightly floured surface. For two-crust pastry, divide pastry in half and shape into 2 rounds on lightly floured surface. Wrap flattened round or rounds in plastic wrap and refrigerate 45 minutes or until dough is firm and cold, yet pliable. This allows the shortening to become slightly firm, which helps make the baked pastry flaky. If refrigerated longer, let pastry soften slightly at room temperature before rolling.

3 Using floured rolling pin, roll one round of pastry on lightly floured surface (or pastry board with floured pastry cloth) into round 2 inches larger than upside-down 9-inch glass pie plate or 3 inches larger than 10- or 11-inch tart pan. Fold pastry into fourths and place in pie plate or tart pan, or roll pastry loosely around rolling pin and transfer to pie plate or tart pan. Unfold or unroll pastry and ease into plate or pan, pressing firmly against bottom and side and being careful not to stretch pastry, which will cause it to shrink when baked.

Making Pastry

Cut in shortening, using a pastry blender, until mixture forms coarse, pea-sized crumbs.

Alternatively, use a fork to cut in the shortening.

Roll pastry loosely around rolling pin and transfer to pie plate or tart pan.

Ease pastry into pie plate, pressing firmly against bottom and side. Trim overhanging edge 1 inch from rim of pie plate.

4 For one-crust pie, trim overhanging edge of pastry 1 inch from rim of pie plate. Fold edge under to form standing rim; flute edges (see Pastry Edge Treatments, right). For tart, trim overhanging edge of pastry even with top of tart pan. Fill and bake as directed in pie or tart recipe.

5 For two-crust pie, roll out second pastry round. Fold into fourths and place over filling, or roll loosely around rolling pin and place over filling. Unfold or unroll pastry over filling. Cut slits in pastry so steam can escape. Trim overhanging edge of top pastry 1 inch from rim of plate. Fold edge of top crust under bottom crust, forming a stand-up rim of pastry that is even thickness on edge of pie plate, pressing on rim to seal; flute edges (see Pastry Edge Treatments, right). Bake as directed in pie recipe.

1 Serving One-Crust Pastry: Calories 140; Total Fat 9g (Saturated Fat 2g, Trans Fat 0g); Cholesterol 0mg; Sodium 150mg; Total Carbohydrate 13g (Dietary Fiber 0g, Sugars 0g); Protein 1g **Exchanges:** 1 Starch, 1½ Fat **Carbohydrate Choices:** 1

1 Serving Two-Crust Pastry: Calories 290; Total Fat 20g (Saturated Fat 5g, Trans Fat 0g); Cholesterol 0mg; Sodium 300mg; Total Carbohydrate 25g (Dietary Fiber 1g, Sugars 0g); Protein 3g **Exchanges:** 1 Starch, ½ Other Carbohydrate, 4 Fat **Carbohydrate Choices:** 1½

BAKING METHODS FOR PIE CRUST

For many pies, such as apple or pecan pie, the filling is added to the unbaked pastry so that the crust and filling bake together at the same time. For other pies, such as pumpkin or banana cream pie, the crust is either partially baked or completely baked before the filling is added. This method is used to prevent the crust from becoming soggy from liquid fillings or when the filling doesn't need to be baked.

Partially Baked One-Crust Pie

Use this when indicated in recipe to prevent bottom crust from becoming soggy.

1 Heat oven to 425°F. Prepare One-Crust Pastry (left). Carefully line pastry with a double thickness of foil, gently pressing foil to bottom of and side of pastry. Let foil extend over edge to prevent excessive browning.

2 Bake 10 minutes; carefully remove foil and bake 2 to 4 minutes longer or until pasty just begins to brown and has become set. If crust bubbles, gently push bubbles down with back of spoon.

3 Fill and bake as directed in pie or tart recipe, changing oven temperature if necessary.

Partially Baked One-Crust Pie

Carefully line pastry with foil, gently pressing foil to bottom and side of pastry and bake in oven as directed.

Fill partially baked pastry; bake pie as directed.

Decorative Cutouts

For an extra-pretty pie, make decorative cutouts on the top of a two-crust pie. Use a small cookie cutter or paring knife and cut shapes from the top crust before placing it on the filling. Once top crust is on filling, attach cutouts on top of crust with a little cold water. Sprinkle with coarse sugar.

Baked One-Crust Pie

Use this for one-crust pies and tarts baked completely before filling is added, such as banana cream or lemon meringue pie.

1 Heat oven to 475°F. Prepare One-Crust Pastry (left), except for pie, trim overhanging edge of pastry 1 inch from rim of pie plate. For tart, trim overhanging edge of pastry even with top of tart pan. Prick bottom and side of pastry thoroughly with fork to prevent puffing.

2 Bake 8 to 10 minutes or until light brown; cool on cooling rack.

3 Fill cooled crust as directed in pie or tart recipe.

Pastry Edge Treatments

It's important that the bottom and top crusts are well sealed to prevent the filling from escaping through it while baking. Seal edge as directed for Two-Crust Pastry (left). Then make the edge attractive by using one of these treatments:

Scalloped Edge

Place thumb and index finger about 1 inch apart on outside of raised edge. With other index finger, push pastry toward outside, continuing around edge, repeating motion, to form scalloped edge.

Rope or Pinched Edge

Place side of thumb on pastry rim at angle. Pinch pastry by pressing knuckle of index finger down into pastry toward thumb. Continue around edge, repeating motion, to form rope edge.

Fork or Herringbone Edge

Dip fork tines in flour; press fork diagonally onto edge without pressing through pastry. Rotate tines 90 degrees and press again next to first set of marks. Continue around edge of pastry, rotating tines back and forth.

Heirloom Recipe and New Twist

What makes homemade apple pie so special? You can use local apples for the freshest, juiciest pie—mix two or three varieties for best taste and texture. Sweetly wrapped in a tender, flaky crust, it's drool-worthy. Our twist Apple Slab Pie makes it easy to serve pie to a crowd. This one-crust version gets topped with a powdered sugar glaze . . . mmm!

HEIRLOOM

Classic Apple Pie

PREP 30 min **TOTAL** 3 hr 20 min • 8 servings

Two-Crust Pastry (page 586)
½ cup sugar
¼ cup all-purpose flour
¾ teaspoon ground cinnamon
¼ teaspoon ground nutmeg
Dash salt
6 cups thinly sliced (⅛ inch thick) peeled tart apples (6 medium)
2 tablespoons cold butter, if desired
2 teaspoons water
1 tablespoon sugar

1 Heat oven to 425°F. Place pastry in 9-inch glass pie plate.

2 In large bowl, mix ½ cup sugar, the flour, cinnamon, nutmeg and salt. Stir in apples. Spoon into pastry-lined pie plate. Cut butter into small pieces; sprinkle over apples. Cover with top pastry; cut slits in pastry. Seal and flute (see Pastry Edge Treatments, page 587).

3 Brush top crust with 2 teaspoons water; sprinkle with 1 tablespoon sugar. Cover edge with 2- to 3-inch-wide strip of foil to prevent excessive browning; remove foil during last 15 minutes of baking.

4 Bake 40 to 50 minutes or until crust is golden brown and juice begins to bubble through slits in crust. Cool on cooling rack at least 2 hours.

1 Serving: Calories 420; Total Fat 21g (Saturated Fat 7g, Trans Fat 2g); Cholesterol 10mg; Sodium 330mg; Total Carbohydrate 53g (Dietary Fiber 3g, Sugars 23g); Protein 4g **Exchanges:** 1½ Starch, 2 Fruit, 4 Fat **Carbohydrate Choices:** 3½

French Apple Pie Heat oven to 400°F. Make One-Crust Pastry (page 586). Spoon apple mixture into pastry-lined pie plate. Omit butter, 2 teaspoons water and 1 tablespoon sugar. In small bowl, mix 1 cup all-purpose flour and ½ cup packed brown sugar. Cut in ½ cup cold butter with fork until crumbly. Sprinkle over apple mixture. Bake 35 to 40 minutes or until golden brown. Cover top with foil during last 10 to 15 minutes of baking, if necessary, to prevent excessive browning. Serve warm.

Classic Peach Pie Prepare Classic Apple Pie as directed, except use ⅔ cup sugar and ⅓ cup flour. Decrease cinnamon to ¼ teaspoon and omit nutmeg. Substitute sliced peeled fresh peaches (6 to 8) for the sliced apples. Stir in 1 teaspoon lemon juice with the peaches. Decrease butter to 1 tablespoon. Bake pie about 45 minutes.

Making Classic Apple Pie

Spoon apple mixture into pastry. Cut butter into small pieces; sprinkle over apples.

Cover pastry edge with pie crust shield to prevent excess browning.

Or cover pastry edge with 2- to 3-inch-wide strip of foil to prevent excess browning.

Cool baked pie on cooling rack at least 2 hours.

Apple Slab Pie CALORIE SMART

PREP 30 min **TOTAL** 2 hr 25 min • 24 servings

Two-Crust Pastry (page 586) or Easy
Buttermilk Pastry (page 588)
- 1 cup granulated sugar
- 3 tablespoons all-purpose flour
- 1 teaspoon ground cinnamon
- ¼ teaspoon ground nutmeg
- ¼ teaspoon salt
- 4½ teaspoons lemon juice
- 9 cups thinly sliced (⅛ inch thick) peeled apples (9 medium)
- 1 cup powdered sugar
- 2 tablespoons milk

1 Heat oven to 450°F. Stack pastry rounds on top of each other on lightly floured surface. Roll to 17x12-inch rectangle. Fit crust into 15x10x1-inch pan, pressing into corners. Fold extra pastry crust under, even with edges of pan; seal edges.

2 In large bowl, mix granulated sugar, flour, cinnamon, nutmeg, salt and lemon juice. Add apples; toss to coat. Spoon into pastry-lined pan.

3 Bake 33 to 38 minutes or until crust is golden brown and filling is bubbly. Cool on cooling rack 45 minutes.

4 In small bowl, mix powdered sugar and milk until well blended. Drizzle over pie. Allow glaze to set before serving, about 30 minutes.

1 Serving: Calories 150; Total Fat 4g (Saturated Fat 1.5g, Trans Fat 0g); Cholesterol 0mg; Sodium 110mg; Total Carbohydrate 28g (Dietary Fiber 0g, Sugars 17g); Protein 0g **Exchanges:** 2 Other Carbohydrate, 1 Fat **Carbohydrate Choices:** 2

Classic Apple Pie

Apple Slab Pie

Making Apple Slab Pie

Stack pastry rounds on top of each other on lightly floured surface. Roll into rectangle.

Fit crust into pan, pressing into corners. Fold extra pastry crust under, even with edges of pan; seal edges.

Spoon apple mixture into pastry-lined pan.

In small bowl, mix powdered sugar and milk. Drizzle over baked pie. Allow glaze to set before serving.

Learn to Make
LATTICE CRUST

A lattice top crust is a gorgeous way to decorate a two-crust pie, allowing the filling to show through for an easy "wow." Make Two-Crust Pastry (page 586), except trim overhanging edge of bottom crust 1 inch from rim of plate. Place filling in crust. After rolling pastry for top crust, cut into ½- to 1-inch wide strips using a pastry wheel or pizza cutter with a straight edge, such as a ruler, to even strips.

CLASSIC LATTICE TOP

Place half of the strips equal distance apart on filling, using shorter strips toward edge of pie. Weave remaining strips over and under first strips. Trim strips evenly with edge of overhanging bottom crust. Fold edge up, forming high stand-up rim; flute as desired (see Pastry Edge Treatments, page 587).

Making a Lattice Top

Place strips about ½ inch apart across the pie vertically, then weave strips horizontally over and under the strips.

Making Pastry in the Food Processor

Use One-Crust Pastry or Two-Crust Pastry recipe on page 586, except make these changes when using your food processor to mix the dough:

1 Measure 2 tablespoons ice-cold water for One-Crust Pastry or 4 tablespoons ice-cold water for Two-Crust Pastry into a liquid measuring cup; set aside.

2 Place flour, salt and shortening in food processor. Cover and process, using quick on-and-off motions, until particles are the size of small peas.

3 With food processor running, pour water all at once through feed tube just until dough leaves side of bowl (dough should not form a ball). Continue as directed in Step 2 of pastry recipe.

Cherry Pie

Sour cherries—also called pie cherries, tart cherries or tart red cherries—make wonderful pies. In fact, this is the pie featured on the cover. Take advantage of their short season by making a homemade pie. If fresh aren't available, use our variation below, which uses bags of frozen pitted sweet cherries.

PREP 30 min **TOTAL** 3 hr 15 min • 8 servings

> Two-Crust Pastry (page 586) or Easy Buttermilk Pastry (page 588)

1⅓ cups sugar

½ cup all-purpose flour

6 cups fresh sour cherries, pitted

2 tablespoons cold butter, if desired

1 Heat oven to 425°F. Place pastry in 9-inch glass pie plate.

2 In large bowl, mix sugar and flour. Stir in cherries. Spoon into pastry-lined pie plate. Cut butter into small pieces; sprinkle over cherries.

3 Make Classic Lattice Top (left) or cover with top pastry; cut slits in pastry if covering with top pastry. Seal and flute (see Pastry Edge Treatments, page 587). Cover edge with pie crust shield ring or 2- to 3-inch-wide strip of foil to prevent excessive browning; remove shield or foil during last 15 minutes of baking.

4 Bake 35 to 45 minutes or until crust is golden brown and juice begins to bubble through slits in crust. Cool on cooling rack at least 2 hours.

1 Serving: Calories 540; Total Fat 22g (Saturated Fat 5g, Trans Fat 3.5g); Cholesterol 0mg; Sodium 300mg; Total Carbohydrate 81g (Dietary Fiber 4g, Sugars 49g); Protein 5g **Exchanges:** 2 Starch, 1 Fruit, 2 Other Carbohydrate, 4 Fat **Carbohydrate Choices:** 5½

Quick Cherry Pie Decrease sugar to ⅔ cup and substitute 2 bags (1 pound each) frozen (thawed) pitted dark sweet cherries for the fresh sour cherries.

Butter Pastry

We prefer pies made with shortening because of the tender, ultra-flaky texture and the way the flavor (or lack of it) lets the flavors of the fillings shine. If you're a fan of butter pastry, use the Pie Pastry recipe on page 586, substituting butter (cut into ½-inch pieces) for half of the shortening.

Stone Fruit

Stone fruit are eaten plain or can be used in so many types of dishes. Blanch them about 30 seconds and the peels will pull right off (see Blanching, page 19).

1. Easy Bellini Cocktails: Puree sliced peeled ripe nectarines or peaches in food processor or blender until smooth. For each Bellini, spoon 2 to 3 tablespoons puree into a champagne flute. Fill glass with chilled sparkling white wine. Stir and serve immediately.

2. Grilled Pluot Dessert: Place 4 ripe pluot or peach halves cut sides down on hot, oiled grill over medium heat. Grill 3 minutes. Turn cut sides up; brush with 1 tablespoon butter; sprinkle with mixture of 1½ teaspoons sugar and ⅛ teaspoon each ground cinnamon and ground ginger. Grill 3 minutes longer or until softened. Serve with ice cream.

3. Cherry BBQ Sauce: Stir ¼ cup pureed or finely chopped pitted ripe cherries into ⅔ cup prepared barbecue sauce. Brush on chicken or pork while grilling.

4. Peachy Lemonade: Make Lemonade (page 72), except—mix 1 cup water, 2 medium peeled, sliced peaches or nectarines and 1 cup sugar in 2-quart saucepan. Heat to boiling; reduce heat. Simmer uncovered 5 to 7 minutes or until peaches are fork-tender. Remove from heat; cool. Place mixture in blender container. Cover and blend on medium speed until smooth; pour into large pitcher. Stir in remaining water and lemon juice. Serve over ice with slices of fresh peaches.

5. Summery Salad: For 4 servings, toss 4 cups desired salad greens with purchased balsamic vinaigrette. Arrange on salad plates. Top each with sliced (peeled if desired) fresh peaches, blue cheese crumbles and Cinnamon-Sugared Nuts (page 41) or purchased candied pecans.

6. Strawberry-Peach Salsa: Mix ¼ cup lime juice, 1 tablespoon honey and ¼ teaspoon salt in medium bowl. Toss with 1 cup chopped fresh strawberries, 2 cups chopped fresh peaches (peeled if desired), ¼ cup chopped fresh cilantro and 1 jalapeño chile, seeded and chopped. Cover and refrigerate 1 hour to blend flavors. Serve with chicken or fish.

7. Berry-Plum Pops: Place 1 cup almond milk (any variety), 3 medium peeled, sliced fresh plums, 1 container (6 ounces) berry yogurt (any variety) and 2 tablespoons agave or honey in blender; blend until smooth. Pour about ¼ cup into 3-ounce paper cups. Insert flat wooden sticks with rounded ends in cups. Freeze until firm, about 1 hour 30 minutes. Remove cups to serve.

8. Sour Cream–Nectarine Pancakes: Heat skillet over medium-high heat. Beat 2 cups original baking mix, 1 cup sour cream, ½ cup milk, 2 eggs and 2 teaspoons poppy seed in large bowl with whisk until smooth. For each pancake, pour about 3 tablespoons batter onto hot skillet. Immediately press 3 or 4 thin slices nectarine into batter. Cook about 3 minutes or until edges are dry. Turn; cook about 3 minutes or until golden brown.

Strawberry-Peach Salsa

Raspberry-Almond Pie

Mixed Berry Crumble Tart

Raspberry-Almond Pie

PREP 50 min **TOTAL** 4 hr 45 min • 8 servings

  Two-Crust Pastry (page 586)
½ cup whole blanched almonds
2 tablespoons butter
¼ cup granulated sugar
2 teaspoons all-purpose flour
1 egg
½ teaspoon almond extract
1 cup granulated sugar
5 tablespoons cornstarch
1 tablespoon grated orange peel
5 cups fresh or frozen (thawed) raspberries
1 egg
1 tablespoon whipping cream
2 tablespoons coarse sugar or sanding sugar

1 Heat oven to 400°F. Place 1 pastry round in 9-inch glass pie plate; flute edges. On lightly floured surface, roll second pastry to 13-inch round. With 1½-inch star cookie cutter, cut out 45 stars; set aside.

2 Place almonds in food processor. Cover and process until finely chopped. Add butter, ¼ cup granulated sugar and the flour; process until blended. Add 1 egg and the almond extract; process until blended. Spread mixture evenly in pastry-lined pie plate.

3 In large bowl, mix 1 cup granulated sugar, the cornstarch and orange peel. Add raspberries; toss gently. Spoon berry mixture evenly over almond layer. Arrange stars on top of filling, covering entire surface. In small bowl, beat 1 egg and the whipping cream. Brush mixture over stars and edge of crust; sprinkle with coarse sugar.

4 Place cookie sheet on rack below pie in case of spillover. Bake 10 minutes. Cover crust edge with pie crust shield ring or 2- to 3-inch-wide strip of foil to prevent excessive browning. Bake 40 to 45 minutes longer or until crust is golden brown and juices are bubbly. (If crust becomes too brown, cover entire crust loosely with foil.) Cool on cooling rack at least 3 hours.

1 Serving: Calories 580; Total Fat 28g (Saturated Fat 7g, Trans Fat 0g); Cholesterol 55mg; Sodium 340mg; Total Carbohydrate 76g (Dietary Fiber 7g, Sugars 38g); Protein 8g **Exchanges:** 2½ Starch, 1 Fruit, 1½ Other Carbohydrate, 5½ Fat **Carbohydrate Choices:** 5

Mixed Berry Crumble Tart

PREP 30 min **TOTAL** 1 hr 15 min • 8 servings

  One-Crust Pastry (page 586)
1½ cups sliced fresh strawberries
1½ cups fresh blueberries
1 cup fresh raspberries
⅔ cup sugar
2 tablespoons cornstarch
¾ cup all-purpose flour
½ cup sugar
1 teaspoon grated orange peel
⅓ cup butter, melted

1 Heat oven to 425°F. Make pastry as directed, except roll into 13-inch round. Place pastry in 10- or 11-inch tart pan with removable bottom; press against bottom and side of pan. Trim overhanging edge of pastry even with top of pan.

2 In large bowl, gently toss berries with ⅔ cup sugar and the cornstarch. Spoon into pastry-lined pan.

3 In small bowl, stir flour, ½ cup sugar, the orange peel and butter with fork until crumbly. Sprinkle evenly over berries.

4 Bake 35 to 45 minutes or until fruit bubbles in center. Remove tart from side of pan. Serve warm.

1 Serving: Calories 420; Total Fat 18g (Saturated Fat 6g, Trans Fat 2g); Cholesterol 20mg; Sodium 200mg; Total Carbohydrate 60g (Dietary Fiber 3g, Sugars 35g); Protein 3g **Exchanges:** 1 Starch, 3 Fruit, 3½ Fat **Carbohydrate Choices:** 4

Strawberries and Cream Tart

PREP 25 min **TOTAL** 1 hr 40 min • 10 servings

CRUST

One-Crust Pastry (page 586) or Press-in-the-Pan Tart Pastry (page 589)

FILLING

1 package (8 oz) cream cheese, softened
⅓ cup sugar
¼ to ½ teaspoon almond extract
1 cup whipping cream, whipped

TOPPING

4 cups fresh strawberries, cut in half
½ cup semisweet chocolate chips
1 tablespoon shortening

1 Heat oven to 450°F. Place pastry in 10-inch tart pan with removable bottom. Bake as directed for Baked One-Crust Pie (page 587). Cool completely.

2 In large bowl, beat cream cheese with electric mixer on medium speed until fluffy. Gradually add sugar and almond extract; beat well. Fold in whipped cream. Spread filling into cooled baked crust. Arrange strawberry halves over filling. Refrigerate while making drizzle.

3 In 1-quart saucepan, melt chocolate chips and shortening over low heat, stirring constantly, until smooth. Drizzle over strawberries and filling. Refrigerate until set, about 30 minutes. Remove tart from side of pan. Cover and refrigerate any remaining tart.

1 Serving: Calories 340; Total Fat 24g (Saturated Fat 13g, Trans Fat 0.5g); Cholesterol 55mg; Sodium 190mg; Total Carbohydrate 28g (Dietary Fiber 1g, Sugars 16g); Protein 3g **Exchanges:** 1 Fruit, 1 Other Carbohydrate, ½ High-Fat Meat, 4 Fat **Carbohydrate Choices:** 2

Strawberries and Cream Tart

White and Dark Chocolate Raspberry Tart

For a pretty garnish, make white chocolate curls (see Chocolate Curls, page 611).

PREP 1 hr **TOTAL** 4 hr 50 min • 10 servings

One-Crust Pastry (page 586) or Press-in-the-Pan Tart Pastry (page 589)
2 tablespoons orange juice
1 teaspoon unflavored gelatin
1½ cups whipping cream
1 package (6 oz) white chocolate baking bars, chopped
1 bag (12 oz) frozen raspberries, thawed, drained and juice reserved
1 tablespoon cornstarch
1 tablespoon sugar
1 cup fresh raspberries, if desired
2 oz semisweet baking chocolate, cut into pieces
2 tablespoons butter

1 Heat oven to 450°F. Place pastry in 10-inch tart pan with removable bottom or 10-inch springform pan, pressing 1 inch up side of pan. Bake as directed for Baked One-Crust Pie (page 587). Cool completely.

2 Pour orange juice into 2-quart saucepan. Sprinkle gelatin over juice; let stand 5 minutes to soften. Stir in ¾ cup of the whipping cream; heat over low heat, stirring frequently, until gelatin is dissolved. Stir in white chocolate until melted and smooth. Transfer to medium bowl; refrigerate about 30 minutes, stirring occasionally, until cool but not set.

3 In blender or food processor, place thawed raspberries and reserved juice. Cover and blend until pureed. Set strainer over 2-cup measuring cup. Press puree with back of spoon through strainer to remove seeds. If necessary, add water to raspberry puree to measure ½ cup. In 1-quart saucepan, mix cornstarch and sugar. Gradually add raspberry puree. Cook and stir over low heat until thickened. Fold in fresh raspberries. Spread into cooled baked crust. Refrigerate 15 minutes.

4 Meanwhile, in chilled small, deep bowl, beat remaining ¾ cup whipping cream with electric mixer on high speed until stiff peaks form. Fold whipped cream into white chocolate mixture. Spoon and spread over raspberry layer. Refrigerate 1 hour or until filling is set.

5 In 1-quart saucepan, melt semisweet chocolate and butter over low heat, stirring frequently; carefully pour and spread over white chocolate layer. Refrigerate at least 2 hours or until set. Remove from refrigerator 30 minutes before serving to soften chocolate layers. Remove tart from side of pan (if using springform pan, remove side of pan). Cover and refrigerate any remaining tart.

1 Serving: Calories 390; Total Fat 27g (Saturated Fat 16g, Trans Fat 0g); Cholesterol 50mg; Sodium 135mg; Total Carbohydrate 33g (Dietary Fiber 2g, Sugars 19g); Protein 3g **Exchanges:** 1 Starch, 1 Other Carbohydrate, 5½ Fat **Carbohydrate Choices:** 2

Tiny Caramel Tarts

These rich and creamy caramel custard bite-size tarts are a perfect choice for a crowd.

PREP 25 min **TOTAL** 4 hr 25 min • 75 tarts

- 2 cups sugar
- ½ cup cold butter, cut into pieces
- 6 tablespoons all-purpose flour
- 4 egg yolks
- 2 cups milk
- 5 boxes (1.9 oz each) frozen mini phyllo (filo) shells (75 shells)
- 4 cups Sweetened Whipped Cream (page 622) Grated chocolate, if desired

1 In 10-inch heavy skillet, heat 1 cup of the sugar over medium heat 6 to 8 minutes, stirring constantly, until sugar is melted and golden brown. Stir in butter until melted. Remove from heat.

2 In 3-quart heavy saucepan, stir together flour, egg yolks, milk and remaining 1 cup sugar with wire whisk. Heat to simmering over low heat, stirring constantly. Add melted sugar mixture; cook 1 to 2 minutes, stirring constantly, until thickened. Spoon mixture into large bowl. Cover; refrigerate 4 hours.

3 To serve, spoon caramel mixture into phyllo shells; top with each with about 2 rounded teaspoons whipped cream and a sprinkle of grated chocolate.

1 Tart: Calories 270; Total Fat 17g (Saturated Fat 3.5g, Trans Fat 0 g); Sodium 115mg; Total Carbohydrate 25g (Dietary Fiber 0g, Sugars 0g); Protein 3g **Exchanges:** 1 Starch, ½ **Other Carbohydrate:** 3½ Fat Carbohydrate Choices: 1 ½

Salted Cashew–Bittersweet Chocolate Tart

Salted Cashew–Bittersweet Chocolate Tart

PREP 25 min **TOTAL** 2 hr 40 min • 16 servings

  One-Crust Pastry (page 586) or Press-in-the-Pan Tart Pastry (page 589)
- 1¼ cups whipping cream
- 12 oz bittersweet baking chocolate, chopped*
- ½ cup cashew halves and pieces, coarsely chopped
- 1 can (13.4 oz) dulce de leche (caramelized sweetened condensed milk)
- 2 tablespoons cashew halves and pieces
- ¼ teaspoon coarse (kosher or sea) salt

1 Heat oven to 450°F. Place pastry in 9-inch tart pan with removable bottom. Bake as directed for Baked One-Crust Pie (page 587), except do not prick crust. Cool completely.

2 Meanwhile, in 2-quart saucepan, heat whipping cream over medium-high heat just to boiling. Remove from heat; stir in chocolate with whisk until smooth. Stir in ½ cup chopped cashews. Pour into cooled baked crust. Refrigerate 2 hours or until firm.

3 Spread dulce de leche over chocolate layer. Sprinkle 2 tablespoons cashews and the salt evenly over top. Remove tart from side of pan. For easier cutting, use a thin, sharp knife, wiping it clean with paper towels and running it under hot water between cutting each slice.

*Semisweet baking chocolate can be substituted for the bittersweet chocolate.

1 Serving: Calories 370; Total Fat 26g (Saturated Fat 14g, Trans Fat 0g); Cholesterol 30mg; Sodium 150mg; Total Carbohydrate 28g (Dietary Fiber 4g, Sugars 13g); Protein 6g **Exchanges:** 1 Starch, 1 Other Carbohydrate, ½ Medium-Fat Meat, 4½ Fat **Carbohydrate Choices:** 2

Ginger–Lemon Curd Petite Pies

Lemon Meringue Pie

Ginger–Lemon Curd Petite Pies CALORIE SMART

PREP 40 min **TOTAL** 1 hr 10 min • 16 pies

LEMON CURD

- ½ cup granulated sugar
- 1 tablespoon cornstarch
- 2 teaspoons grated lemon peel
- ½ cup fresh lemon juice
- 2 eggs, slightly beaten
- 1 tablespoon finely chopped Crystallized Ginger (page 447) or crystallized ginger from 2-oz jar

CRUST

Two-Crust Pastry (page 586) or Easy Buttermilk Pastry (page 588)

GARNISH

Powdered sugar

1 In 1-quart saucepan, mix granulated sugar and cornstarch. Stir in lemon peel, lemon juice, eggs and ginger with whisk until blended. Cook over medium heat about 2 minutes, stirring constantly, until mixture thickens and boils. Remove from heat; transfer to bowl. Cover with plastic wrap and refrigerate 30 minutes or until completely cool.

2 Meanwhile, heat oven to 375°F. Line 2 cookie sheets with cooking parchment paper. On lightly floured surface, roll 1 pastry round to ⅛-inch thickness. With 3-inch round cookie cutter, cut out 16 rounds (you may need to reroll scraps to get 16 rounds). Place on cookie sheet. With fork, poke holes all over rounds. Repeat with second pastry—except don't poke with fork. With 1½-inch cookie cutter, cut out design

from center of second batch of rounds. Place on cookie sheet.

3 Bake 8 to 10 minutes or until golden brown. Remove from cookie sheets to cooling racks; cool completely.

4 To serve, place plain pastry rounds in jumbo paper baking cups or on individual dessert plates. Top each with about 1 tablespoon lemon curd. Sprinkle powdered sugar over rounds with cutouts; place over lemon curd.

1 Pie: Calories 180; Total Fat 9g (Saturated Fat 2.5g, Trans Fat 0g); Cholesterol 25mg; Sodium 160mg; Total Carbohydrate 21g (Dietary Fiber 0g, Sugars 7g); Protein 2g **Exchanges:** 1 Starch, ½ Other Carbohydrate, 1½ Fat **Carbohydrate Choices:** 1½

Lemon Meringue Pie

When you separate the eggs, be sure to save the egg whites to make the meringue. To speed up the beating, let the egg whites warm up to room temperature (about 30 minutes).

PREP 50 min **TOTAL** 3 hr 5 min • 8 servings

One-Crust Pastry (page 586), Easy Buttermilk Pastry (page 588) or Press-in-the-Pan Oil Pastry (page 588)

Meringue for 9-Inch Pie (below)

- 3 egg yolks (reserve whites for meringue)
- 1½ cups sugar
- ⅓ cup plus 1 tablespoon cornstarch
- 1½ cups water
- 3 tablespoons butter
- 2 teaspoons grated lemon peel
- ½ cup fresh lemon juice
- 2 drops yellow food color, if desired

1 Heat oven to 450°F. Place pastry in 9-inch glass pie plate. Bake as directed for Baked One-Crust Pie (page 587). Cool completely.

2 Make sugar mixture for meringue (recipe below). While sugar mixture is cooling, in small bowl, beat egg yolks with fork; set aside. In 2-quart saucepan, mix sugar and cornstarch. Gradually stir in water. Cook and stir over medium heat until mixture thickens and boils. Boil and stir 1 minute.

3 Immediately stir at least half of the hot mixture gradually into egg yolks, then stir back into hot mixture in saucepan. Boil and stir 2 minutes or until very thick. (Do not boil less than 2 minutes or filling may stay too soft or become runny.) Remove from heat. Stir in butter, lemon peel, lemon juice and food color. Press plastic wrap on filling to prevent tough layer from forming on top.

4 Heat oven to 350°F. Continue making meringue. Pour hot lemon filling into cooled baked crust. Spoon meringue onto hot lemon filling. Spread over filling, carefully sealing meringue to edge of crust to prevent shrinking or weeping.

5 Bake 12 to 15 minutes or until meringue is light brown. Cool away from drafts 2 hours. Store covered in refrigerator.

1 Serving: Calories 450; Total Fat 17g (Saturated Fat 6g, Trans Fat 1.5g); Cholesterol 95mg; Sodium 250mg; Total Carbohydrate 70g (Dietary Fiber 0g, Sugars 51g); Protein 5g **Exchanges:** 2 Starch, 2½ Other Carbohydrate, 3 Fat **Carbohydrate Choices:** 4½

Meringue for 9-Inch Pie In 1-quart saucepan, mix ½ cup sugar and 4 teaspoons cornstarch. Stir in ½ cup cold water. Cook and stir over medium heat until mixture thickens and boils. Boil and stir 1 minute; remove from heat. Cool completely while making filling for pie recipe. (To cool more quickly, place in freezer about 10 minutes.) In large bowl, beat 4 egg whites and ⅛ teaspoon salt with electric mixer on high speed just until soft peaks begin to form. Very gradually, beat in sugar mixture until stiff peaks form.

Spreading Meringue over Pie

Spread meringue evenly over hot filling, sealing to edge of crust to help keep meringue from shrinking.

Lemon Mascarpone Tart

PREP 30 min **TOTAL** 3 hr 35 min • 12 servings

    Easy Nut Crust (page 589)
¾ cup mascarpone cheese (from 8-oz container)
1 cup sugar
2 tablespoons grated lemon peel
⅓ cup fresh lemon juice
2 tablespoons whipping cream
1 teaspoon vanilla
2 whole eggs
1 egg yolk
1 cup whipping cream
3 tablespoons mascarpone cheese (from 8-oz container)
2 tablespoons honey
½ teaspoon vanilla
    Grated lemon peel or lemon peel twists

1 Make crust as directed, using pistachio nuts. Press crust evenly in bottom and up side of 10-inch tart pan with removable bottom. Refrigerate 30 minutes.

2 Heat oven to 350°F. In medium bowl, beat ¾ cup mascarpone cheese, the sugar and 2 tablespoons lemon peel with electric mixer on low speed until blended. Add lemon juice, 2 tablespoons whipping cream and 1 teaspoon vanilla; beat until well blended. Add eggs and egg yolk, beating on low speed just until combined. Spread filling evenly in chilled crust. Place cookie sheet on rack below tart in case of spillover.

3 Bake about 35 minutes or until filling is set but center still jiggles slightly when moved. Cool on cooling rack 1 hour. Refrigerate at least 1 hour.

4 In chilled large, deep bowl, beat 1 cup whipping cream and 3 tablespoons mascarpone cheese with electric mixer on high speed until soft peaks form. Stir in honey and ½ teaspoon vanilla. Spread over top of tart. Garnish with lemon peel. Remove tart from side of pan.

1 Serving: Calories 340; Total Fat 23g (Saturated Fat 13g, Trans Fat 0.5g); Cholesterol 110mg; Sodium 90mg; Total Carbohydrate 29g (Dietary Fiber 0g, Sugars 21g); Protein 3g **Exchanges:** 1 Starch, 1 Other Carbohydrate, 4½ Fat **Carbohydrate Choices:** 2

Pumpkin Pie

Be sure to use canned pumpkin puree, not pumpkin pie mix, in this recipe. The mix has sugar and spices already in it, so if you have purchased the pumpkin pie mix, follow the directions on that label. Or, if you like, use 1½ cups cooked, mashed fresh pumpkin.

PREP 30 min **TOTAL** 3 hr 45 min • 8 servings

> One-Crust Pastry (page 586) or Press-in-the-Pan Oil Pastry (page 588)
> 2 eggs
> ½ cup sugar
> 1 teaspoon ground cinnamon
> ½ teaspoon salt
> ½ teaspoon ground ginger
> ⅛ teaspoon ground cloves
> 1 can (15 oz) pureed pumpkin (not pumpkin pie mix)
> 1 can (12 oz) evaporated milk
> Sweetened Whipped Cream (page 622), if desired

1 Heat oven to 425°F. Place pastry in 9-inch glass pie plate. After fluting edge, carefully line pastry with double thickness of foil, gently pressing foil to bottom and side of pastry. Let foil extend over edge to prevent excessive browning. Bake 10 minutes; carefully remove foil. Bake 2 to 4 minutes longer or until pastry just begins to brown and has become set. If crust bubbles, gently push bubbles down with back of spoon.

2 In medium bowl, beat eggs slightly with whisk. Beat in remaining ingredients except whipped cream.

3 Pour filling into hot crust. (To prevent spilling, place pie plate on oven rack before adding filling.) Cover edge with pie crust shield ring or 2- to 3-inch-wide strip of foil to prevent excessive browning; remove shield or foil during last 15 minutes of baking.

4 Bake 15 minutes. Reduce oven temperature to 350°F. Bake about 45 minutes longer or until knife inserted in center comes out clean. Cool on cooling rack 1 hour; refrigerate uncovered until completely chilled. Store loosely covered in refrigerator. Serve with whipped cream.

1 Serving: Calories 300; Total Fat 15g (Saturated Fat 5g, Trans Fat 2g); Cholesterol 65mg; Sodium 360mg; Total Carbohydrate 33g (Dietary Fiber 2g, Sugars 19g); Protein 7g **Exchanges:** 1 Starch, 1 Fruit, 3 Fat **Carbohydrate Choices:** 2

Praline Pumpkin Pie Make pie as directed, except decrease second bake time to 35 minutes. Mix ⅓ cup packed brown sugar, ⅓ cup chopped pecans and 1 tablespoon softened butter. Sprinkle over pie. Bake about 10 minutes longer or until knife inserted in center comes out clean.

Testing Pumpkin Pie for Doneness

Bake until knife inserted in center comes out clean.

Pumpkin Pie

Banana Cream Pie

PREP 30 min **TOTAL** 2 hr 30 min • 8 servings

> One-Crust Pastry (page 586), Easy Buttermilk
> Pastry (page 588) or Press-in-the-Pan Oil
> Pastry (page 588)
> 4   egg yolks
> ⅔   cup sugar
> ¼   cup cornstarch
> ½   teaspoon salt
> 3   cups milk
> 2   tablespoons butter, softened
> 2   teaspoons vanilla
> 2   large ripe but firm bananas
> 1   cup Sweetened Whipped Cream (page 622)

1 Heat oven to 450°F. Place pastry in 9-inch
glass pie plate. Bake as directed for Baked
One-Crust Pie (page 587). Cool completely.

2 Meanwhile, in medium bowl, beat egg
yolks with fork; set aside. In 2-quart saucepan,
mix sugar, cornstarch and salt. Gradually
stir in milk. Cook over medium heat, stirring
constantly, until mixture thickens and boils.
Boil and stir 1 minute. Immediately stir at least
half of the hot mixture gradually into egg yolks,
then stir back into hot mixture in saucepan.
Boil and stir 1 minute; remove from heat. Stir in
butter and vanilla; cool filling slightly.

3 Slice bananas evenly into cooled baked crust;
pour warm filling over bananas. Press plastic
wrap on filling to prevent a tough layer from
forming on top. Refrigerate at least 2 hours or
until set. Remove plastic wrap. Top pie with
whipped cream. Store covered in refrigerator.

1 Serving: Calories 410; Total Fat 22g (Saturated Fat 8g, Trans Fat 2g);
Cholesterol 135mg; Sodium 370mg; Total Carbohydrate 46g (Dietary
Fiber 1g, Sugars 27g); Protein 7g **Exchanges:** 1 Starch, 1 Fruit, ½ Other
Carbohydrate, ½ Low-Fat Milk, 4½ Fat **Carbohydrate Choices:** 3

Butterscotch Cream Pie Substitute packed
brown sugar for the granulated sugar.
Omit bananas.

Chocolate-Banana Cream Pie Make
Chocolate Cream Pie filling (below). Cool
slightly. Slice 2 large ripe but firm bananas
evenly into cooled baked crust; pour warm
filling over bananas. Continue as directed.

Chocolate Cream Pie Increase sugar to
1½ cups and cornstarch to ⅓ cup; omit
butter and bananas. Stir in 2 ounces chopped

unsweetened baking chocolate after stirring
in milk.

Coconut Cream Pie Increase cornstarch to
⅓ cup. Substitute 1 can (14 ounces) coconut
milk (not cream of coconut) and milk to equal
3 cups for the milk. Stir in ¾ cup toasted coconut with the butter. Omit bananas. Refrigerate
pie 3 hours or until set. Top with whipped
cream; sprinkle with ¼ cup toasted coconut.

Pecan Pie

PREP 20 min **TOTAL** 1 hr 10 min • 8 servings

> One-Crust Pastry (page 586), Easy Buttermilk
> Pastry (page 588) or Press-in-the-Pan Oil
> Pastry (page 588)
> ⅔   cup sugar*
> ⅓   cup butter, melted
> 1   cup light or dark corn syrup
> 3   eggs
> 1   cup pecan halves or broken pecans

1 Heat oven to 375°F. Place pastry in 9-inch
glass pie plate.

2 In medium bowl, beat sugar, butter, corn
syrup and eggs with whisk until well blended.
Stir in pecans. Pour into pastry-lined pie plate.

3 Bake 40 to 50 minutes or until center is set.
Serve warm or chilled.

*Or use ⅓ cup packed brown sugar for half of the sugar.

1 Serving: Calories 530; Total Fat 29g (Saturated Fat 8g, Trans Fat 2g);
Cholesterol 100mg; Sodium 420mg; Total Carbohydrate 62g (Dietary
Fiber 2g, Sugars 33g); Protein 5g **Exchanges:** 2 Starch, 2 Other
Carbohydrate, 6 Fat **Carbohydrate Choices:** 4

Kentucky Pecan Pie Add 2 tablespoons
bourbon or 1 teaspoon brandy extract or vanilla
with the corn syrup. Stir in 1 cup semisweet
chocolate chips with the pecans.

Pecan Pie

Roasted Sweet Potato Pie

PREP 30 min **TOTAL** 6 hr 20 min • 8 servings

- 1½ lb dark-orange sweet potatoes (about 2 medium-large)
- One-Crust Pastry (page 586)
- ½ cup butter, softened
- ½ cup packed brown sugar
- ½ cup granulated sugar
- ½ cup whipping cream
- 2 tablespoons bourbon or 1 teaspoon bourbon extract, brandy extract or vanilla
- ½ teaspoon ground cinnamon
- ½ teaspoon ground nutmeg
- ¼ teaspoon salt
- 2 eggs

1 Heat oven to 400°F. Line cookie sheet with foil. Pierce sweet potatoes with fork; place on cookie sheet. Roast 1 hour or until tender. Cut potatoes in half. Scoop out pulp into medium bowl; discard skins. Reduce oven temperature to 350°F.

2 Place pastry in 9½-inch glass deep-dish pie plate. Beat sweet potato pulp with electric mixer on medium speed until creamy. Add remaining ingredients; beat 1 minute or until well blended. Pour filling into pastry-lined pie plate.

3 Bake 45 to 50 minutes or until knife inserted near center comes out clean. Cover edge with pie crust shield ring or 2- to 3-inch-wide strip of foil during last 15 minutes of baking if necessary to prevent excessive browning. Cool completely on cooling rack, about 4 hours. Store in refrigerator.

1 Serving: Calories 440; Total Fat 24g (Saturated Fat 14g, Trans Fat 0.5g); Cholesterol 100mg; Sodium 360mg; Total Carbohydrate 51g (Dietary Fiber 2g, Sugars 29g); Protein 3g **Exchanges:** 3 Other Carbohydrate, 1 Vegetable, 5 Fat **Carbohydrate Choices:** 3½

Roasted Sweet Potato Meringue Pie While pie is baking, make Meringue for 9-Inch Pie (page 603). Remove from oven; spread meringue over hot filling, carefully sealing meringue to edge of crust to prevent shrinking or weeping. Bake 12 to 15 minutes or until meringue is light brown. Cool as directed.

Roasted Sweet Potato Pie

Key Lime Pie

PREP 15 min **TOTAL** 2 hr 50 min • 8 servings

- Graham Cracker Crust (page 589)
- 4 egg yolks
- 2 cans (14 oz each) sweetened condensed milk (not evaporated)
- ¾ cup bottled or fresh Key lime juice or regular lime juice
- 1 or 2 drops green food color, if desired
- 1½ cups Sweetened Whipped Cream (page 622)

1 Heat oven to 375°F. Make crust as directed but do not bake.

2 In medium bowl, beat egg yolks, condensed milk, lime juice and food color with electric mixer on medium speed about 1 minute or until well blended. Pour into unbaked crust.

3 Bake 14 to 16 minutes or until center is set. Cool on cooling rack 15 minutes. Cover and refrigerate until chilled, at least 2 hours. Spread with whipped cream. Store covered in refrigerator up to 3 days.

1 Serving: Calories 430; Total Fat 23g (Saturated Fat 13g, Trans Fat 1g); Cholesterol 165mg; Sodium 230mg; Total Carbohydrate 48g (Dietary Fiber 0g, Sugars 38g); Protein 7g **Exchanges:** ½ Starch, 2½ Other Carbohydrate, 1 High-Fat Meat, 3 Fat **Carbohydrate Choices:** 3

Elegant Pear Custard Pie

PREP 1 hr **TOTAL** 6 hr 10 min • 12 servings

POACHED PEARS

- 1 cup sugar
- 1 cup water
- 1 cup pear vodka*
- ½ cup elderflower liqueur*
- 1 vanilla bean
- 3 lb Bosc or Bartlett pears, peeled, cut in half

CRUST

One-Crust Pastry (page 586)

CUSTARD

- ½ cup whipping cream
- ¼ cup reserved poaching liquid
- ¼ cup sugar
- Dash salt
- 4½ teaspoons cornstarch
- 1 whole egg
- 1 egg yolk
- ½ teaspoon vanilla

GLAZE

- 1 tablespoon reserved poaching liquid

1 In 4-quart saucepan, stir together 1 cup sugar, the water, vodka and liqueur. Cut slit down center of vanilla bean; scrape out seeds. Discard bean; add seeds to mixture in saucepan. Heat to boiling over medium-high heat; add pears. Reduce heat to low. Cover loosely and simmer 25 to 45 minutes or until pears are tender. (Poaching time will vary depending on ripeness of pears.) Remove from heat. Let pears cool in liquid 1 hour.

2 Meanwhile, heat oven to 425°F. Place pastry in 9-inch glass pie plate. Bake as directed for Partially Baked One-Crust Pie (page 587). Cool crust 10 minutes. Reduce oven temperature to 350°F.

3 Remove pears from liquid to cutting board. Strain poaching liquid through fine-mesh strainer; set liquid aside. Thinly slice pears; arrange in layers in decorative pattern in partially baked crust.

4 In large bowl, beat all custard ingredients with whisk just until combined. Slowly pour over pears. Carefully place pie in oven (pie plate will be full). Place cookie sheet on rack below pie in case of spillover. Cover crust edge with pie crust shield ring or 2- to 3-inch-wide strip of foil to prevent excessive browning; remove shield or foil during last 15 minutes of baking.

5 Bake 1 hour 10 minutes or until knife inserted in center comes out clean. Brush top of pie with 1 tablespoon reserved poaching liquid. Cool on cooling rack 1 hour. Refrigerate 2 hours or until completely cool.

*Pear nectar can be substituted for both the vodka and liqueur.

1 Serving: Calories 310; Total Fat 10g (Saturated Fat 4g, Trans Fat 0g); Cholesterol 45mg; Sodium 125mg; Total Carbohydrate 48g (Dietary Fiber 3g, Sugars 32g); Protein 2g **Exchanges:** 1 Starch, ½ Fruit, 1½ Other Carbohydrate, 2 Fat **Carbohydrate Choices:** 3

Elegant Pear Custard Pie

CALORIE SMART = See Helpful Nutrition and Cooking Information, page 643   FAST = Ready in 30 minutes or less
EASY = Prep in 10 minutes or less **plus** five ingredients or less   LIGHTER = 25% fewer calories or grams of fat
MAKE AHEAD = Make-ahead directions   SLOW COOKER = Slow cooker directions

DESSERT AND FRUIT BASICS

Fruit can be the dessert or can be showcased in delicious dessert recipes—either way, it's a perfect choice when you're looking for a lighter ending to your meal. Look here for how to buy and store fresh fruit so it will be at the peak of ripeness when you are ready to enjoy or use it in dessert recipes. Want to make your desserts just a bit more polished? Try one of our easy chocolate decorations.

BUYING AND STORING FRESH FRUIT

Purchase fruit that is bright in color, heavy for its size (indicating juiciness) and firm to the touch for the variety. Fresh fruit should not show any sign of decay or have soft spots. For berries, check for mold, which can occur in closed containers.

Fruits such as berries, pineapples, watermelon, cherries and apples will not ripen after purchase, so look for ripe fruit.

Fruit such as bananas, pears, peaches, cantaloupe and kiwifruit will ripen after purchase.

To ripen fruits after purchase, place them in a paper bag at room temperature 1 to 2 days. Don't use a plastic bag, as mold can form.

EASY CHOCOLATE DESSERT GARNISHES

Next time you want your dessert to look extra special, try one of these garnishes:

Chocolate-Covered Confections: Melt chocolate (right). Dip dried apricots, fresh strawberries, cherries with stems, pretzels, marshmallows or whole nuts three-fourths of the way into chocolate; shake or gently wipe off excess. If desired, sprinkle or roll confections in candy sprinkles, finely chopped nuts or shredded coconut. Place on cookie sheet lined with waxed paper. Refrigerate 10 minutes to set; chill until serving.

Chocolate Curls: Let milk chocolate bar stand at room temperature about 15 minutes. (Semisweet chocolate can also be used, but curls will be smaller.) Pull swivel vegetable peeler or thin sharp knife across block, using long, thin strokes. (Make chocolate shavings by using shorter strokes.) Use a toothpick to lift curls to prevent breakage.

Chocolate Swirls and Filigree: Melt chocolate (below). Place chocolate in resealable plastic food-storage bag. Cut off tiny corner of bag. Squeeze bag to pipe swirls inside stemware to use for shakes or ice cream drinks or as a clever way to serve mousse or pudding. Refrigerate 10 minutes to set; chill until serving. For filigree, pipe designs (such as stars, trees, letters, numbers or random patterns) onto cookie sheet lined with waxed paper. (Print out or draw designs on paper and place underneath waxed paper to trace with the chocolate.) Refrigerate until chocolate is set. Gently remove designs from paper; chill. Garnish desserts with filigree just before serving.

> ### Melting Chocolate
> In 1-quart saucepan, heat 1 cup semisweet or dark chocolate chips with 1 teaspoon shortening over low heat, stirring constantly until melted; remove from heat.

Raspberries

Golden Raspberries

Blackberries

Cranberries

Red Currants

Blueberries

Strawberries

Cape Gooseberries

BERRIES

Choose firm, plump berries; avoid moldy, mushy or soft spots. Remove any moldy or damaged berries before refrigerating unwashed. Very perishable; use within a few days. Available year-round but best when in season locally for superior flavor.

Blackberries: Largest wild berry. Best used immediately but can be refrigerated up to 2 days.

Blueberries: Juicy and sweet; range from tiny wild blueberries to large cultivated ones.

Cranberries: Available fresh September to December (avoid discolored, shriveled ones); also frozen, dried. Fresh berries are very tart. Dried are sweetened; use like raisins.

Gooseberries: Varieties include green, white, yellow or red with smooth or fuzzy skins. Limited season (March to June) depending on region; also canned. Great in jams, jellies, desserts.

Raspberries (Red, Golden, Black): Most intensely flavored berry. Red are available year-round; yellow from June to September; black from mid-June to mid-August.

Red Currants: Related to gooseberries. Available June to August in red, black, white. Black typically used for preserves, syrups, liqueurs. Use red or white as snacks or for preserves.

Strawberries: Choose berries that are all red, brightly colored, with bright green tops. Great in salads, desserts, snacks.

Colorado Peaches

Peaches

Pluots

Black Plums

Nectarines

Prune Plums

Red Plums

Sweet Cherries

STONE FRUITS

Choose plump stone fruits; free of bruises, soft or shriveled spots; not excessively hard. Avoid any greening (in lighter-colored fruit). Refrigerate 3 to 5 days.

Cherries: Sweet cherries are available fresh (choose firm—not hard—cherries), dried, frozen. Stemmed cherries last longer. Eat out of hand or cooked. **Sour cherries**, also known as *tart cherries*, are smaller and typically too tart to eat fresh. They are, however, delicious in main dishes, jams, jellies and pies, such Cherry Pie, page 596, the recipe featured on the cover of this book. Fresh sour cherries have a very short harvesting season and are typically found only at farmer's markets and roadside stands. Dried, frozen and canned tart cherries are available year around.

Nectarines: Sweeter, richer, firmer flesh than peaches. Available mid-spring to late September; peak season is July to August. Choose fragrant fruit that gives to gentle pressure.

Peaches: Fuzzy-skinned varieties range from lightly shaded pink/creamy white to red-shaded yellow. Flesh ranges from pink-tinged white to yellow-gold. U.S. varieties available May to October in most regions (or imports available during off-season). Choose intensely aromatic fruit that gives to gentle pressure.

Plums: Japanese varieties: larger, rounder; juicy; soft flesh; good for eating. European varieties (including prune plums or sugar plums): smaller; less juicy; firmer flesh; good for baking and drying. **Plumcots** and **Pluots** are varieties of plums crossed with apricots.

Mango

Red Plantain

Plantain

Dates

Coconut

Quince

Mangosteen

Kiwano
(Horned Melon)

Papaya

Pomegranate

Lychee

Carambola
(Star Fruit)

Figs

Guayaba

Kiwifruit

Longan

Pineapple

Dragon Fruit

Cherimoya

Rambutan

Grapefruit

Lime

Valencia Orange

Clementine
Orange

Navel Oranges

Minneola Tangelos

Meyer Lemon

Lemon

Key Limes

TROPICAL FRUITS

Exotic tropical fruits are available at different times of year. Look for new and interesting varieties that are firm, with great color and a fresh aroma.

Cherimoya: Creamy white flesh; sweet custard taste (discard large black seeds). Ripen unwashed at room temperature until fruit yields to gentle pressure. For more intense flavor, chill before serving.

Dragon Fruit: Pink skin (white or red flesh) or yellow skin (white flesh). Kiwi-pineapple flavor; edible seeds. Choose evenly colored skin with few blotches; avoid very dry, brown stem or brown-tipped "leaves." Fruit should yield to gentle pressure. Eat plain, in salads or smoothies.

Kiwano (Horned Melon): Bright, lime-green pulp; banana-cucumber taste; jellylike texture; edible seeds. Golden-orange at peak ripeness. Store at room temperature up to 2 weeks.

Mango: Golden-orange flesh with large center seed; very sweet flavor. Chill before serving.

Pineapple: Firm yellow flesh; very fragrant with sweet/tart flavor. Choose firm fruit with a crisp green top and no sign of decay.

Plantain: "Cooking banana." Less sweet; more firm than bananas. Popular in Latin American and some Asian and African cuisines. Avoid those with bruises. Green: mild, squash-like flavor. Ripened: soft, spongy texture. Use both types in side dishes. Store at room temperature.

CITRUS

Choose fruit heavy for size, with smooth-textured skin. Store unwashed at room temperature or refrigerate up to 2 weeks.

Blood Orange (Moro Orange): Deep red; sweet, juicy flesh. Peel is smooth or pitted with red blush. Peak season: December to May. Refrigerate up to 2 weeks.

Kumquat: Entirely edible; skin is sweet, pulp is tart. Peak season: December to May. Store unwashed at room temperature up to 2 days or refrigerate up to 2 weeks.

Meyer Lemon: Mild, juicy. Sweeter than common lemons; rind isn't bitter. Peak season: November to May. Refrigerate in plastic bag up to 2 weeks.

Tangelo: Cross between grapefruit and tangerine. Range of sizes. Yellow-orange to deep orange; smooth skin. Sweet-tart; juicy; few seeds. Minneola is most common variety. Peak season: November to March. Refrigerate up to 2 weeks.

Golden Delicious Apple

Red Delicious Apples

Red Bartlett Pears

Cortland Apples

Ginger Gold Apples

Pink Lady Apple

Jonathan Apple

Bosc Pears

Granny Smith Apple

Bartlett Pear

Honeycrisp Apple

Apple Pears

Braeburn Apple

Seckel Pears

Gala Apple

Comice Pear

French Butter Pears

McIntosh Apples

APPLES

Choose firm, smooth-skinned apples without bruises, blemishes or musty smell. Choose apples based on purpose—eating, baking or cooking. Store refrigerated in plastic bag up to 1 month.

Sweet: Crispin/Mutsu (crisp), Fuji (crisp), Gala (crisp), Ginger Gold (crisp), Golden Delicious (crisp), Honeycrisp (crisp), Honey Gold (slightly crisp), Red Delicious (slightly crisp), Regent (crisp)

Slightly Sweet: Fireside (slightly crisp), Prairie Spy (crisp)

Sweet-Tart: Braeburn (crisp), Jonagold (crisp), Jonamac (tender), McIntosh (tender)

Slightly Tart: Cortland (slightly crisp), Ginger Gold (crisp), Ida Red (slightly crisp), Jonathan (crisp), Newtown Pippin (crisp), Northern Spy (crisp), Paula Red (slightly crisp), Rome (crisp), Winesap (crisp)

Tart: Granny Smith (crisp), Haralson (crisp)

PEARS

Choose blemish-free pears. Ripen at room temperature; store in refrigerator 1 month.

Cooking/Baking Pears: Anjou (green, red when slightly ripe), Bosc, French Butter, Seckel

Eating/Salad Pears: Anjou (green, red when ripe), Asian, Bartlett, Cornice, French Butter

Caramel-Maple Pears

Baked Apples CALORIE SMART • EASY

Often overlooked, baked apples make a perfect last-minute dessert. Use the larger amount of brown sugar for very tart apples.

PREP 10 min **TOTAL** 50 min • 4 servings

- 4 large unpeeled tart cooking apples (Granny Smith or Rome)
- 2 to 4 tablespoons packed brown sugar
- 4 teaspoons butter
- ½ teaspoon ground cinnamon

1 Heat oven to 375°F. Core apples to within ½ inch of bottom. Remove 1-inch strip of peel from around middle of each apple, or peel upper half of each apple to prevent splitting. Place apples in ungreased 8-inch square (2-quart) glass baking dish.

2 In center of each apple, place 1½ teaspoons to 1 tablespoon sugar, 1 teaspoon butter and ⅛ teaspoon cinnamon. Sprinkle with additional cinnamon if desired. Pour water into baking dish until ¼ inch deep.

3 Bake 30 to 40 minutes or until apples are tender when pierced with fork. (Time will vary depending on size and variety of apple.) Spoon syrup in dish over apples several times during baking if desired.

1 **Serving:** Calories 200; Total Fat 4.5g (Saturated Fat 2g, Trans Fat 0g), Cholesterol 10mg; Sodium 25mg; Total Carbohydrate 39g (Dietary Fiber 5g, Sugars 28g); Protein 0g **Exchanges:** 2 Fruit, ½ Other Carbohydrate, ½ Fat **Carbohydrate Choices:** 2½

MICROWAVE Directions Prepare apples as directed. Place each apple in 10-ounce custard cup or individual microwavable casserole or bowl. Do not add water. Microwave uncovered on High 5 to 10 minutes, rotating cups half turn after 3 minutes, until apples are tender when pierced with fork.

Applesauce CALORIE SMART • FAST • EASY

PREP 20 min **TOTAL** 20 min • 3 cups

- 4 medium apples (1½ lb), peeled, quartered
- ½ cup water
- ¼ cup packed brown sugar or 3 to 4 tablespoons granulated sugar
- ¼ teaspoon ground cinnamon
- ⅛ teaspoon ground nutmeg

1 In 2-quart saucepan, heat apples and water to boiling over medium heat, stirring occasionally; reduce heat. Simmer uncovered 5 to 10 minutes, stirring occasionally to break up apples, until tender.

2 Stir in remaining ingredients. Heat to boiling; boil and stir 1 minute. Serve warm or chilled. Store covered in refrigerator.

½ **Cup:** Calories 90; Total Fat 0g (Saturated Fat 0g, Trans Fat 0g); Cholesterol 0mg; Sodium 0mg; Total Carbohydrate 22g (Dietary Fiber 2g, Sugars 18g); Protein 0g **Exchanges:** 1 Fruit, ½ Other Carbohydrate **Carbohydrate Choices:** 1½

Caramel-Maple Pears

SLOW COOKER • EASY

PREP 15 min **TOTAL** 2 hr 15 min • 6 servings

- 6 yellow- or red-skinned pears, cored from bottom leaving stems attached
- 1 cup caramel ice cream topping
- ⅓ cup real maple syrup
  Grated lemon peel

1 Spray 5- to 6-quart slow cooker with cooking spray. Place pears upright in cooker. (If all pears do not fit in bottom of cooker, place remaining pears suspended between 2 others in cooker.)

2 In small bowl, mix brown ice cream topping and syrup; pour over pears.

3 Cover; cook on High heat setting 2 hours to 2 hours 30 minutes to 3 hours 30 minutes.

4 Remove pears from slow cooker; place upright in individual dessert dishes. Spoon about ¼ cup topping mixture over each pear; sprinkle with lemon peel.

1 **Serving:** Calories 310; Total Fat 0g (Saturated Fat 0g, Trans Fat 0g); Cholesterol 0mg; Sodium 190mg; Total Carbohydrate 76g (Dietary Fiber 6g, Sugars 55g); Protein 1g **Exchanges:** 1 Starch, ½ Fruit, 3½ Other Carbohydrate **Carbohydrate Choices:** 5

Apple Dumplings

The recipe for apple dumplings was available free in Gold Medal™ flour bags, as noted in a 1938 advertisement, and has also been included in many of the company's cookbooks over the years, beginning with the 1904 Christmas edition of Gold Medal Flour Cook Book.

PREP 55 min **TOTAL** 1 hr 35 min • 6 servings

> Two-Crust Pastry (page 586)
>
> 6 small cooking apples (Golden Delicious, Braeburn or Rome), about 3 inches in diameter*
>
> 3 tablespoons raisins, dried cranberries or dried cherries, if desired
>
> 3 tablespoons chopped nuts, if desired
>
> 2½ cups packed brown sugar
>
> 1⅓ cups water
>
> 2 tablespoons butter, softened
>
> ¼ teaspoon ground cinnamon
>
> Cream or Sweetened Whipped Cream (page 622), if desired

1 Heat oven to 425°F. Make pastry as directed, except roll two-thirds of the pastry into 14-inch square; cut into 4 (7-inch) squares. Roll remaining pastry into 14x7-inch rectangle; cut into 2 (7-inch) squares.

2 Peel and core apples; place 1 apple on each pastry square. Mix raisins and nuts; fill apples with mixture. Moisten corners of pastry squares. Bring 2 opposite corners up over apple and

pinch together. Repeat with remaining corners, and pinch edges of pastry to seal.

3 Place dumplings in ungreased 13x9-inch (3-quart) glass baking dish. In 2-quart saucepan, heat brown sugar, water, butter and cinnamon to boiling over high heat, stirring frequently. Carefully pour syrup around dumplings.

4 Bake about 40 minutes, spooning syrup over dumplings two or three times, until crust is golden and apples are tender when pierced with small knife or toothpick. Serve warm or cool with cream.

*Dough squares will not be large enough to seal larger apples.

1 Serving: Calories 680; Total Fat 32g (Saturated Fat 9g, Trans Fat 5g); Cholesterol 10mg; Sodium 450mg; Total Carbohydrate 94g (Dietary Fiber 4g, Sugars 45g); Protein 5g **Exchanges:** 2 Starch, 4 Other Carbohydrate, 6 Fat **Carbohydrate Choices:** 6

Making Apple Dumplings

Moisten corners of pastry squares. Bring 2 opposite corners up over apple and pinch together.

Repeat with remaining corners; pinch edges of pastry to seal.

Apple Dumplings

Apple Crisp

Fresh Berry Crisp

Apple Crisp

PREP 20 min **TOTAL** 1 hr • 6 servings

- 6 medium tart cooking apples (Granny Smith or Rome), peeled, sliced (about 6 cups)
- ¾ cup packed brown sugar
- ½ cup all-purpose flour
- ½ cup quick-cooking or old-fashioned oats
- 1 teaspoon ground cinnamon
- ½ teaspoon ground nutmeg
- ⅓ cup cold butter
   Cream or ice cream, if desired

1 Heat oven to 375°F. Spray bottom and sides of 8-inch square (2-quart) glass baking dish with cooking spray.

2 Spread apples in baking dish. In medium bowl, mix brown sugar, flour, oats, cinnamon and nutmeg. Cut in butter, using pastry blender or fork, until mixture is crumbly. Sprinkle evenly over apples.

3 Bake 35 to 40 minutes or until topping is golden brown and apples are tender when pierced with fork. Serve warm with cream.

1 Serving: Calories 330; Total Fat 11g (Saturated Fat 7g, Trans Fat 0g); Cholesterol 25mg; Sodium 85mg; Total Carbohydrate 55g (Dietary Fiber 4g, Sugars 38g); Protein 3g **Exchanges:** 1 Starch, 1 Fruit, 1½ Other Carbohydrate, 2 Fat **Carbohydrate Choices:** 3½

Blueberry Crisp Substitute 6 cups fresh or frozen (thawed and drained) blueberries for the apples.

Caramel Apple Crisp Toss apples with ½ cup butterscotch caramel topping before spreading in pan.

Rhubarb Crisp Substitute 6 cups chopped fresh or frozen (thawed and drained) rhubarb for the apples. Sprinkle ½ cup granulated sugar over rhubarb; stir to combine. Continue as directed in Step 2.

Fresh Berry Crisp

PREP 15 min **TOTAL** 45 min • 6 servings

- 3 cups fresh strawberries, sliced
- 3 tablespoons cornstarch
- 2 tablespoons granulated sugar
- 1 pint (2 cups) fresh blueberries
- 1 pint (2 cups) fresh raspberries
- ⅔ cup packed brown sugar
- ½ cup whole wheat flour
- ½ cup old-fashioned or quick-cooking oats
- ½ teaspoon ground cinnamon
- ¼ teaspoon salt
- ⅓ cup butter, softened
   Ice cream or Sweetened Whipped Cream (page 622), if desired

1 Heat oven to 350°F. In 2-quart saucepan, mash 2 cups of the strawberries. Stir in cornstarch and granulated sugar. Cook over medium heat, stirring constantly, until mixture boils. Boil and stir 1 minute.

2 Carefully stir in blueberries, raspberries and remaining 1 cup strawberries. Pour mixture into ungreased 8-inch square (2-quart) glass baking dish or 9-inch glass pie plate.

3 In small bowl, mix brown sugar, flour, oats, cinnamon, salt and butter with pastry blender or fork until crumbly; sprinkle over berry mixture.

4 Bake about 30 minutes or until topping is golden brown and filling is bubbly. Serve warm with ice cream.

1 Serving: Calories 370; Total Fat 12g (Saturated Fat 7g, Trans Fat 0g); Cholesterol 25mg; Sodium 180mg; Total Carbohydrate 62g (Dietary Fiber 7g, Sugars 39g); Protein 5g **Exchanges:** 1 Starch, 1 Fruit, 2 Other Carbohydrate, 2½ Fat **Carbohydrate Choices:** 4

Fresh Berries

1. Raspberry Sangria Pops: In medium bowl, whisk together 1 cup raspberry sherbet, 1 single-serve container raspberry yogurt, and ½ cup each fresh raspberries and sangria. Divide between 4 (5-ounce) paper cups. Cover cups with foil; insert flat craft sticks with rounded ends through foil into center of pops. Freeze 4 to 6 hours or until firm. Remove cups to serve.

2. Creamy Strawberry-Poppy Dressing: For 4 servings, in small bowl, whisk together ⅓ cup canola oil, 2 tablespoons raspberry vinegar, 3 tablespoons sugar, 1 tablespoon sour cream, 1½ teaspoons Dijon mustard and ¼ teaspoon poppy seed. Fold in ⅓ cup finely chopped fresh strawberries. To serve, drizzle over salad greens and sprinkle with chopped walnuts and sliced strawberries.

3. Blueberry-Ginger Scones: Make Scones (page 490) as directed, except—increase whipping cream to ½ cup. Stir in ¾ cup fresh blueberries with egg. Omit kneading step. Sprinkle 8-inch round with 1 tablespoon coarse sugar mixed with 2 teaspoons finely chopped crystallized ginger; press lightly into dough.

4. Blackberry-Thyme Cocktail: For 3 cocktails, place thyme leaves from 1 fresh stem in food processor. Add ½ cup fresh blackberries. Process until almost smooth; place in pitcher; stir in 3 shots blackberry vodka, 1 tablespoon fresh lemon juice and 2 cups tonic water. Refrigerate at least 2 hours to blend flavors. Pour into sugar-rimmed glasses; garnish with additional fresh blackberries and thyme stem if desired.

5. Fresh Berries and Greens Smoothie: For 2 smoothies, place ½ cup orange juice in blender. Add 1 cup kale or spinach leaves, 1 tablespoon flaxseed, 1 small banana, 1 cup fresh berries and ½ teaspoon coconut oil. Add 1 to 2 cups water; blend until smooth.

6. Cucumber-Avocado-Berry Salad: For 4 to 6 servings, in medium bowl, mix ¼ cup olive oil, 4 teaspoons red wine vinegar, ¼ teaspoon salt and ⅛ teaspoon pepper; toss with 1 chopped avocado. Add 1 sliced English cucumber, 2 cups bite-size pieces fresh berries and ½ cup crumbled queso fresco or feta cheese; toss. Serve immediately.

7. Berry-Chia Breakfast Pudding: For 2 servings, mix 1 cup almond milk, ¼ cup chia seeds and 2 tablespoons honey. Cover and refrigerate overnight to soften seeds. To serve, spoon into bowls; top each with ½ cup fresh berries and ½ teaspoon grated lime peel.

Blueberry-Ginger Scones

Peach Cobbler

PREP 25 min **TOTAL** 55 min • 6 servings

- ½   cup sugar
- 1   tablespoon cornstarch
- ¼   teaspoon ground cinnamon
- 4   cups sliced peeled fresh peaches (6 medium)*
- 1   teaspoon lemon juice
- 1   cup all-purpose flour
- 1   tablespoon sugar
- 1½   teaspoons baking powder
- ½   teaspoon salt
- 3   tablespoons cold butter
- ½   cup milk
- 2   tablespoons sugar, if desired
-    Cream, if desired

1 Heat oven to 400°F. In 2-quart saucepan, mix ½ cup sugar, the cornstarch and cinnamon. Stir in peaches and lemon juice. Cook over medium-high heat 4 to 5 minutes, stirring constantly, until mixture thickens and boils. Boil and stir 1 minute. Pour into ungreased 2-quart casserole; keep peach mixture hot in oven.

2 In medium bowl, mix flour, 1 tablespoon sugar, the baking powder and salt. Cut in butter, using pastry blender or fork, until mixture looks like fine crumbs. Stir in milk. Drop dough by 6 spoonfuls onto hot peach mixture. Sprinkle 2 tablespoons sugar over dough.

3 Bake 25 to 30 minutes or until topping is golden brown. Serve warm with cream.

*Or substitute 4 cups frozen sliced peaches (from two 1-pound bags), thawed and drained, for the fresh peaches.

1 Serving: Calories 300; Total Fat 13g (Saturated Fat 7g, Trans Fat 0.5g); Cholesterol 40mg; Sodium 240mg; Total Carbohydrate 44g (Dietary Fiber 4g, Sugars 31g); Protein 3g **Exchanges:** 1½ Starch, 1½ Fruit, 1 Fat **Carbohydrate Choices:** 3

Apple Cobbler Substitute 4 cups sliced peeled tart cooking apples (Granny Smith or Rome) for the peaches.

Fresh Blueberry Cobbler Substitute 4 cups fresh blueberries for the peaches. Omit cinnamon.

Fresh Cherry Cobbler Substitute 4 cups pitted tart red or sweet fresh cherries for the peaches. Increase sugar in cherry mixture to 1¼ cups for tart cherries and 1 cup for sweet cherries, and cornstarch to 3 tablespoons. Substitute ¼ teaspoon almond extract for the lemon juice.

Raspberry-Peach Cobbler Substitute 2 cups fresh raspberries for 1 cup of the peaches.

Peach Cobbler

Strawberry Shortcakes

PREP 15 min **TOTAL** 2 hr • 6 servings

    1 quart (4 cups) fresh strawberries, sliced
    1 cup sugar
    2 cups all-purpose flour
    1 tablespoon baking powder
    ½ teaspoon salt
    ½ cup cold butter
    ⅔ cup milk
    1 egg, slightly beaten
       Sweetened Whipped Cream (right), if desired

1 In large bowl, stir strawberries and ½ cup of the sugar until well mixed. Let stand about 1 hour so juice forms.

2 Heat oven to 375°F. Grease bottom and side of 8- or 9-inch round cake pan with shortening; lightly flour.

3 In medium bowl, mix flour, remaining ½ cup sugar, the baking powder and salt. Cut in butter, using pastry blender or fork, until mixture looks like coarse crumbs. Stir in milk and egg just until blended. Spoon and spread batter in pan.

4 Bake 30 to 35 minutes or until toothpick inserted in center comes out clean. Cool 10 minutes.

5 Place cooling rack upside down over pan; turn rack and pan over and remove pan. Carefully invert shortcake onto serving plate. Cut shortcake into 6 wedges. If desired, split each wedge horizontally in half. Fill and top with strawberries and whipped cream.

1 Serving: Calories 490; Total Fat 18g (Saturated Fat 8g, Trans Fat 1g); Cholesterol 80mg; Sodium 570mg; Total Carbohydrate 75g (Dietary Fiber 4g, Sugars 41g); Protein 7g **Exchanges:** 2 Starch, 1 Fruit, 2 Other Carbohydrate, 3½ Fat **Carbohydrate Choices:** 5

Cutting Shortcake

Cut shortcake into 6 wedges.

If desired, split each wedge horizontally in half.

Drop Shortcakes Heat oven to 425°F. Make dough as directed. Onto ungreased cookie sheet, drop dough in 6 mounds about 2 inches apart. Bake 12 to 14 minutes or until golden brown.

Sweetened Whipped Cream Chill bowl and beaters in freezer or refrigerator 10 to 20 minutes. In chilled medium, deep bowl, beat ½ cup whipping cream, 1 tablespoon powdered or granulated sugar and ½ teaspoon vanilla with electric mixer on low speed until mixture begins to thicken. Gradually increase speed to high and beat just until soft peaks form. Do not overbeat or mixture will curdle. Makes 1 cup. Double ingredients to make 2 cups.

Broiled Pineapple CALORIE SMART • FAST

PREP 15 min **TOTAL** 15 min • 4 servings

    1 can (20 oz) sliced pineapple in juice, drained, or 12 slices (½ inch thick) fresh pineapple
    1 tablespoon packed brown sugar
    2 tablespoons lime juice
    2 tablespoons honey
    ½ cup vanilla fat-free yogurt
    1 teaspoon honey
    ½ teaspoon grated lime peel

1 Set oven control to broil. Place pineapple slices on ungreased broiler pan. In small bowl, mix brown sugar, lime juice and 2 tablespoons honey; drizzle over pineapple. Broil with tops of pineapple 4 inches from heat 6 to 8 minutes, turning once, until light brown.

2 In another small bowl, mix yogurt, 1 teaspoon honey and the lime peel.

3 For each serving, top 3 pineapple slices with 2 tablespoons yogurt mixture.

1 Serving: Calories 150; Total Fat 0g (Saturated Fat 0g, Trans Fat 0g); Cholesterol 0mg; Sodium 20mg; Total Carbohydrate 35g (Dietary Fiber 1g, Sugars 34g); Protein 2g **Exchanges:** 1 Fruit, 1½ Other Carbohydrate **Carbohydrate Choices:** 2

Broiled Grapefruit Omit lime. Cut 2 medium grapefruits in half. Place halves, cut sides up, on broiler pan. Top each grapefruit half with brown sugar mixture. Serve with yogurt mixture.

Strawberry Shortcake

Gingerbread

PREP 10 min **TOTAL** 1 hr 5 min • 9 servings

2⅓ cups all-purpose flour
 1 teaspoon baking soda
 1 teaspoon ground ginger
 1 teaspoon ground cinnamon
 ½ teaspoon salt
 ½ cup butter, softened, or shortening
 ⅓ cup sugar
 1 cup molasses*
 ¾ cup hot water
 1 egg
   Lemon Sauce (page 641), if desired
   Sweetened Whipped Cream (page 622),
   if desired

1 Heat oven to 325°F. Grease bottom and sides of 9-inch square pan with shortening; lightly flour.

2 In large bowl, beat all ingredients except lemon sauce and whipped cream with electric mixer on low speed 30 seconds, scraping bowl constantly. Beat on medium speed 3 minutes, scraping bowl occasionally. Pour batter into pan.

3 Bake 50 to 55 minutes or until toothpick inserted in center comes out clean. Serve warm with lemon sauce and whipped cream.

*Full-flavored (dark) molasses will result in a bold and robust flavor. For milder flavor, use mild-flavored (light) molasses. For extra-mild molasses flavor, use ½ cup light molasses and ½ cup real maple syrup.

1 Serving: Calories 370; Total Fat 12g (Saturated Fat 3g, Trans Fat 2g); Cholesterol 25mg; Sodium 360mg; Total Carbohydrate 60g (Dietary Fiber 1g, Sugars 28g); Protein 4g **Exchanges:** 1 Starch, 3 Other Carbohydrate, 2 Fat **Carbohydrate Choices:** 4

Pumpkin Pudding Cake

PREP 15 min **TOTAL** 1 hr 15 min • 9 servings

1½ cups all-purpose flour
 ¾ cup granulated sugar
 1 teaspoon baking powder
 ½ teaspoon baking soda
 ½ teaspoon salt
1½ teaspoons ground cinnamon
 ½ cup buttermilk
 ½ cup canned pureed pumpkin (not pumpkin
   pie mix)
 ¼ cup butter, melted
 ⅓ cup chopped pecans
1½ cups water
 ¾ cup packed brown sugar

1 Heat oven to 350°F. In large bowl, mix flour, granulated sugar, baking powder, baking soda, salt and cinnamon. Add buttermilk, pumpkin and butter; mix well with spoon. Spread in ungreased 8- or 9-inch square pan. Sprinkle with pecans, pressing into top.

2 In small saucepan, mix water and brown sugar. Heat over medium heat until simmering, stirring until sugar is dissolved. Carefully pour over batter. (Nuts may float, but will settle as cake bakes.)

3 Bake 35 to 45 minutes or until toothpick inserted in center comes out clean. Cool 15 minutes. Serve warm, spooning sauce from bottom of pan over cake.

1 Serving: Calories 300; Total Fat 9g (Saturated Fat 3.5g, Trans Fat 0g); Cholesterol 15mg; Sodium 320mg; Total Carbohydrate 53g (Dietary Fiber 1g, Sugars 36g); Protein 3g **Exchanges:** 1 Starch, 2½ Other Carbohydrate, 1½ Fat **Carbohydrate Choices:** 3½

Gingerbread

Pumpkin Pudding Cake

English Trifle

PREP 30 min **TOTAL** 3 hr 30 min • 10 servings

- ½ cup sugar
- 3 tablespoons cornstarch
- ¼ teaspoon salt
- 3 cups milk
- ½ cup dry sherry or other dry white wine or white grape juice
- 3 egg yolks, beaten
- 3 tablespoons butter, softened
- 1 tablespoon vanilla
- 2 packages (3 oz each) ladyfingers (24 ladyfingers)*
- ½ cup strawberry preserves
- 2 cups fresh strawberries, sliced, or 1 box (10 oz) frozen sliced strawberries, thawed, drained
- 1 cup whipping cream
- 2 tablespoons sugar
- 2 tablespoons slivered almonds, toasted (page 23)

1 In 3-quart saucepan, mix ½ cup sugar, the cornstarch and salt. Gradually stir in milk and sherry. Heat to boiling over medium heat, stirring constantly. Boil and stir 1 minute.

2 Gradually stir at least half of the hot mixture into egg yolks, then stir back into hot mixture in saucepan. Boil and stir 1 minute; remove from heat. Stir in butter and vanilla. Press plastic wrap on surface of pudding to prevent tough layer from forming on top. Refrigerate about 3 hours or until chilled.

3 Split ladyfingers horizontally in half. Spread cut sides with preserves. In 2-quart trifle bowl or glass serving bowl, layer one-fourth of the ladyfingers, cut sides up, half of the strawberries and half of the pudding; repeat layers. Arrange remaining ladyfingers around edge of bowl in upright position with cut sides toward center. (It may be necessary to gently ease ladyfingers down into pudding about 1 inch so they remain upright.) Cover and refrigerate until serving time.

4 In chilled large, deep bowl, beat whipping cream and 2 tablespoons sugar with electric mixer on low speed until mixture begins to thicken. Gradually increase speed to high and beat until stiff peaks form. Spread over trifle. Sprinkle with almonds. Cover and refrigerate any remaining trifle.

*Or substitute 2 packages (10.75 ounces each) frozen (thawed) pound cake for the ladyfingers. Place each pound cake on its side; carefully cut each cake lengthwise into 3 slices. Lay slices cut-side down; cut each slice crosswise into 4 slices (to total 24 slices). Spread one side of each slice with preserves and layer as directed.

1 Serving: Calories 360; Total Fat 16g (Saturated Fat 8g, Trans Fat 1g); Cholesterol 110mg; Sodium 180mg; Total Carbohydrate 46g (Dietary Fiber 1g, Sugars 35g); Protein 6g **Exchanges:** 2 Starch, 1 Other Carbohydrate, 3 Fat **Carbohydrate Choices:** 3

Individual English Trifles Prepare as directed through step 2. Do not split ladyfingers; omit preserves. Cut ladyfingers in half crosswise; layer 3 halves in the bottom of 8 (10 oz) glasses. Divide 1 cup of the strawberries among glasses; top each with about 3 tablespoons of the pudding. Repeat layers, except reserve 8 ladyfinger halves for garnish, if desired (using only 2 ladyfinger halves for second layer). Divide whipped cream and almonds among glasses. Garnish each glass with a sliced strawberry and reserved ladyfinger half.

New York Cheesecake

Cheesecake seems so special to your guests, they'll think you went all out. But don't say a word. We've worked hard to find the secrets to a perfectly baked crust and a creamy, rich filling— now you will know them, too.

PREP 45 min **TOTAL** 15 hr 45 min • 16 servings

CRUST

1 cup all-purpose flour
½ cup butter, softened
¼ cup sugar
1 egg yolk

CHEESECAKE

5 packages (8 oz each) cream cheese, softened
1¾ cups sugar
3 tablespoons all-purpose flour
1 tablespoon grated orange peel, if desired
1 tablespoon grated lemon peel, if desired
¼ teaspoon salt
¼ cup whipping cream
5 whole eggs
2 egg yolks
¾ cup whipping cream
⅓ cup slivered almonds, toasted (page 23), or fresh fruit, if desired

1 Heat oven to 400°F. Spray bottom and side of 9-inch springform pan with cooking spray; remove bottom. In medium bowl, mix crust ingredients, using pastry blender or fork, until dough forms; gather into a ball. Press one-third of the dough on bottom of pan. Place on cookie sheet. Bake 8 to 10 minutes or until light golden brown; cool 10 minutes.

2 Assemble bottom and side of pan; secure side. Press remaining dough 2 inches up side of pan. Wrap outside bottom and side of pan with heavy-duty foil to prevent leaking.

3 Increase oven temperature to 450°F. In large bowl, beat cream cheese, 1¾ cups sugar, 3 tablespoons flour, the orange peel, lemon peel and salt with electric mixer on medium speed about 1 minute or until smooth. On low speed, beat in ¼ cup whipping cream, the eggs and egg yolks just until blended. Pour into crust.

4 Bake 15 minutes. Reduce oven temperature to 200°F. Bake 1 hour 25 minutes to 1 hour 40 minutes longer or until cheesecake is set at

least 2 inches from edge of pan but center of cheesecake still jiggles slightly when moved and surface is golden brown. (Cheesecake will become firm during refrigeration.) Do not insert knife into cheesecake because the hole may cause cheesecake to crack. Turn off oven; leave cheesecake in oven 30 minutes longer. Remove from oven and cool in pan on cooling rack away from drafts 30 minutes.

5 Without releasing side of pan, run knife around side of pan carefully to loosen cheesecake. Refrigerate uncovered about 3 hours or until chilled; cover and continue refrigerating at least 9 hours or overnight before serving.

6 Run knife around side of pan to loosen cheesecake again; remove side of pan. Leave cheesecake on pan bottom to serve. In chilled medium, deep bowl, beat ¾ cup whipping cream with electric mixer on low speed until mixture begins to thicken. Gradually increase speed to high and beat until stiff peaks form. Spread whipped cream over top of cheesecake. Sprinkle with almonds. Store covered in refrigerator. To cut cheesecake, use long, thin-bladed, non-serrated knife. Dip knife into hot water after each cut, cleaning it off with paper towel.

1 Serving: Calories 520; Total Fat 38g (Saturated Fat 22g, Trans Fat 1g); Cholesterol 215mg; Sodium 310mg; Total Carbohydrate 35g (Dietary Fiber 0g, Sugars 27g); Protein 9g **Exchanges:** 2½ Other Carbohydrate, 1 High-Fat Meat, 6 Fat **Carbohydrate Choices:** 2

LIGHTER Directions For 19 grams of fat and 330 calories per serving, omit crust. Move oven rack to lowest position. Heat oven to 425°F. Lightly grease side only of 9-inch springform pan with shortening. Mix ¾ cup graham cracker crumbs, 2 tablespoons melted butter and 2 tablespoons sugar; press evenly in bottom of pan. Use reduced-fat cream cheese (Neufchâtel); increase flour to ¼ cup. Omit ¼ cup whipping cream. Substitute 1¼ cups fat-free egg product for the 5 eggs. Continue as directed in Step 3. Omit ¾ cup whipping cream and the almonds. Serve with fruit if desired.

Chocolate Chip New York Cheesecake Fold 1 cup miniature semisweet chocolate chips into cream cheese mixture before pouring into crust.

Making Cheesecake

Press one-third of the dough evenly on bottom of springform pan. Place on cookie sheet. Bake 8 to 10 minutes.

Assemble bottom and side of pan; secure side. Press remaining dough 2 inches up side of pan.

Wrap outside and bottom of pan with foil to prevent leaking during baking.

Without releasing side of pan, run knife around side of pan to loosen baked cheesecake.

Spread whipped cream over top of cheesecake. Sprinkle with almonds.

Cut with long, thin-bladed, non-serrated knife. After each cut, dip knife into hot water and clean it off with towel.

New York Cheesecake

Caramel-Cappuccino Cheesecake

PREP 30 min **TOTAL** 8 hr 50 min • 16 servings

CRUST

1¼ cups chocolate cookie crumbs (from 15-oz box)

¼ cup butter, melted

FILLING

2 tablespoons instant espresso coffee powder or granules

2 teaspoons vanilla

4 packages (8 oz each) cream cheese, softened

1½ cups granulated sugar

4 eggs

1 teaspoon ground cinnamon

¼ cup caramel topping

TOPPING

1 cup whipping cream

2 tablespoons powdered sugar or granulated sugar

¼ cup caramel topping

1 Heat oven to 300°F. Wrap outside of 10-inch springform pan with foil. To minimize cracking, place shallow pan half full of hot water on bottom oven rack.

2 In small bowl, mix cookie crumbs and butter with fork. Press mixture evenly over bottom of pan. Refrigerate crust while preparing filling. In another small bowl, stir espresso powder and vanilla until dissolved; set aside.

3 In large bowl, beat cream cheese and granulated sugar with electric mixer on medium speed until light and fluffy. Beat in eggs, one at a time, just until blended. Add espresso mixture, cinnamon and ¼ cup caramel topping; beat about 30 seconds or until mixture is well blended. Pour over crust.

4 Bake 1 hour 10 minutes to 1 hour 20 minutes or until cheesecake is set at least 2 inches from edge of pan but center of cheesecake still jiggles slightly when moved. Turn oven off; open oven door at least 4 inches. Let cheesecake remain in oven 30 minutes. Run small metal spatula around edge of pan to loosen cheesecake. Cool in pan on cooling rack 30 minutes. Refrigerate at least 6 hours or overnight.

5 Just before serving, run small metal spatula around edge of pan; carefully remove side of pan. In chilled medium, deep bowl, beat 1 cup whipping cream and powdered sugar with electric mixer on high speed until soft peaks form. Spread whipped cream over top of cheesecake; drizzle with ¼ cup caramel topping. Cover and refrigerate any remaining cheesecake.

1 Serving: Calories 440; Total Fat 30g (Saturated Fat 18g, Trans Fat 1g); Cholesterol 140mg; Sodium 300mg; Total Carbohydrate 35g (Dietary Fiber 0g, Sugars 29g); Protein 7g **Exchanges:** ½ Starch, 2 Other Carbohydrate, 1 High-Fat Meat, 4 Fat **Carbohydrate Choices:** 2

Cream Puffs

PREP 30 min **TOTAL** 2 hr 40 min • 12 cream puffs

PUFFS

½ cup butter, cut into pieces

1 cup water

1 cup all-purpose flour

4 whole eggs

FILLING

⅓ cup granulated sugar

2 tablespoons cornstarch

2 cups milk

2 egg yolks, slightly beaten

2 tablespoons butter, softened

2 teaspoons vanilla

Powdered sugar, if desired

1 Heat oven to 400°F. In 2-quart saucepan, heat ½ cup butter and the water over high heat, stirring occasionally, until boiling rapidly. Stir in flour; reduce heat to low. With wooden spoon, beat vigorously over low heat about 1 minute or until mixture forms a ball; remove from heat.

2 Add eggs, one at a time, beating vigorously with spoon after each addition until mixture is smooth and glossy.* Onto ungreased cookie sheet, drop dough by slightly less than ¼ cupfuls in mounds about 3 inches apart.

3 Bake 35 to 40 minutes or until puffed and golden. Remove from cookie sheet to cooling rack; prick side of each puff with tip of sharp knife to release steam. Cool away from drafts 30 minutes.

4 Meanwhile, in 2-quart saucepan, stir granulated sugar and cornstarch with whisk;

gradually stir in milk. Cook and stir over medium heat until mixture thickens and boils. Boil and stir 1 minute. Gradually stir at least half of the hot mixture into egg yolks, then stir back into hot mixture in saucepan. Boil and stir 1 minute; remove from heat. Stir in 2 tablespoons butter and the vanilla. Press plastic wrap on surface of filling to prevent tough layer from forming on top. Refrigerate at least 1 hour or until cool.

5 Using sharp knife, cut off top third of each puff; reserve tops. Pull out any strands of soft dough from puffs. Just before serving, fill bottom of each puff with about 2 rounded tablespoons filling; replace tops. Sprinkle with powdered sugar. Store cream puffs covered in refrigerator.

* Or beat in eggs with electric mixer on medium speed. Beat 1 minute after adding each egg.

1 Cream Puff: Calories 210; Total Fat 13g (Saturated Fat 7g, Trans Fat 0g); Cholesterol 135mg; Sodium 140mg; Total Carbohydrate 17g (Dietary Fiber 0g, Sugars 8g); Protein 6g **Exchanges:** 1 Starch, ½ Medium-Fat Meat, 2 Fat **Carbohydrate Choices:** 1

Éclairs After dropping dough onto cookie sheet, shape each mound into finger shape, 4½x1½ inch, with metal spatula. Bake and cool as directed. Fill éclairs with filling. Drizzle with Vanilla Glaze (page 581).

Ice Cream Puffs Omit filling. Fill cream puffs with your favorite flavor of ice cream (page 638). Cover and freeze until serving. Serve with Chocolate Sauce (page 642), Hot Fudge Sauce (page 642) or Caramel Sauce (page 642).

Profiterole and Cream Puff

Profiteroles Fill cream puffs with filling or ice cream (page 638). Drizzle with Chocolate Sauce (page 642).

Whipped Cream Puffs Omit filling. Make Sweetened Whipped Cream (page 622), using 2 cups whipping cream and ¼ cup granulated or powdered sugar and a large, deep bowl. Fill puffs with cream.

Double-Chocolate Puffs Prepare Cream Puffs as directed, except reduce flour to ¾ cup plus 2 tablespoons. Mix flour with 2 tablespoons unsweetened baking cocoa and 1 tablespoon sugar. Continue as directed, baking puffs 35 to 40 minutes or until puffed and darker brown on top. Substitute about 2¼ cups Chocolate Mousse (page 632) for the filling.

Eggnog Puffs Prepare Cream Puffs as directed, except reduce vanilla to 1 teaspoon. Add 1 teaspoon rum extract, ½ teaspoon ground nutmeg and ⅛ teaspoon ground ginger with the vanilla.

Making Cream Puffs and Eclairs

Beat vigorously with wooden spoon after adding the flour until mixture forms a ball.

To shape cream puffs, drop dough by slightly less than ¼ cupfuls in mounds about 3 inches apart.

To shape éclairs, shape each mound into finger shape, 4½x1½ inch, with metal spatula.

Cut off top third of each cooked puff; pull out any strands of soft dough.

Tiramisu

Mascarpone is a rich double- or triple-cream cheese that originated in the Lombardy region of Italy. It has a delicate, buttery flavor with just a hint of sweetness. Look for it in the cheese case in large supermarkets, specialty cheese shops or gourmet food stores.

PREP 35 min **TOTAL** 5 hr 35 min • 8 servings

- 6 **egg yolks**
- ¾ **cup sugar**
- ⅔ **cup milk**
- 2 **containers (8 oz each) mascarpone cheese or 2 packages (8 oz each) cream cheese, softened**
- 1¼ **cups whipping cream**
- ½ **teaspoon vanilla**
- ¼ **cup cold brewed espresso or very strong coffee**
- 2 **tablespoons rum***
- 2 **packages (3 oz each) ladyfingers (24 ladyfingers)****
- 1½ **teaspoons unsweetened baking cocoa**

1 In 2-quart saucepan, beat egg yolks and sugar with whisk until well mixed. Beat in milk. Heat to boiling over medium heat, stirring constantly; reduce heat to low. Boil and stir 1 minute; remove from heat. Pour into medium bowl; press plastic wrap on surface of custard mixture. Refrigerate about 1 hour or until chilled.

2 Add cheese to custard mixture. Beat with electric mixer on medium speed until smooth; set aside. Wash and dry beaters. In chilled large, deep bowl, beat whipping cream and vanilla with electric mixer on low speed until mixture begins to thicken. Gradually increase speed to high and beat until stiff peaks form; set aside.

3 In small bowl, mix espresso and rum. Split ladyfingers horizontally in half.

4 In ungreased 11x7-inch (2-quart) glass baking dish, arrange half of the ladyfingers in single layer. Brush with espresso mixture (do not soak). Spread half of the cheese mixture over ladyfingers; spread with half of the whipped cream. Repeat layers with remaining ladyfingers, espresso mixture, cheese mixture and whipped cream. Sprinkle with cocoa. Cover and refrigerate at least 4 hours to develop flavors but no longer than 24 hours. Store covered in refrigerator.

* Or substitute ⅛ teaspoon rum extract mixed with 2 tablespoons water for the rum.

** Or substitute 2 packages (10.75 ounces each) frozen (thawed) pound cake for the ladyfingers. Place each pound cake on its side; carefully cut each cake lengthwise into 3 slices. Lay slices cut-side down; cut each slice crosswise into 4 slices (to total 24 slices). Brush each slice with espresso mixture. Arrange 3 slices crosswise in baking dish. Spread half of the cheese mixture over cake; spread with half of the whipped cream. Repeat layers with remaining pound cake, espresso mixture, cheese mixture and whipped cream.

1 Serving: Calories 540; Total Fat 38g (Saturated Fat 22g, Trans Fat 1.5g); Cholesterol 270mg; Sodium 260mg; Total Carbohydrate 39g (Dietary Fiber 0g, Sugars 32g); Protein 9g **Exchanges:** 2 Starch, ½ Other Carbohydrate, 7½ Fat **Carbohydrate Choices:** 2½

Making Tiramisu

Separate ladyfingers horizontally; brush with espresso mixture.

Spread half of cheese mixture over ladyfingers; spread with half of whipped cream.

Tiramisu

Butterscotch, Chocolate and Vanilla Pudding

Vanilla Pudding

PREP 10 min **TOTAL** 1 hr 10 min ● 4 servings

⅓ cup sugar

2 tablespoons cornstarch

⅛ teaspoon salt

2 cups milk

2 egg yolks, slightly beaten

2 tablespoons butter, softened

2 teaspoons vanilla

1 In 2-quart saucepan, mix sugar, cornstarch and salt. Gradually stir in milk. Cook over medium heat, stirring constantly, until mixture thickens and boils. Boil and stir 1 minute.

2 Gradually stir at least half of the hot mixture into egg yolks, then stir back into hot mixture in saucepan. Boil and stir 1 minute; remove from heat. Stir in butter and vanilla.

3 Pour pudding into dessert dishes. Cover and refrigerate about 1 hour or until chilled. Store covered in refrigerator.

1 Serving: Calories 220; Total Fat 11g (Saturated Fat 5g, Trans Fat 0g); Cholesterol 130mg; Sodium 170mg; Total Carbohydrate 26g (Dietary Fiber 0g, Sugars 23g); Protein 5g **Exchanges:** 1½ Other Carbohydrate, 1 Low-Fat Milk, 2 Fat **Carbohydrate Choices:** 2

Butterscotch Pudding Substitute ⅔ cup packed dark or light brown sugar for the granulated sugar; reduce vanilla to 1 teaspoon.

Chocolate Pudding Increase sugar to ½ cup; stir ⅓ cup unsweetened baking cocoa into sugar mixture. Omit butter.

Panna Cotta EASY

PREP 10 min **TOTAL** 4 hr 20 min ● 4 servings

2 cups cold half-and-half

1½ teaspoons unflavored gelatin

¼ cup sugar

1 teaspoon vanilla

Dash salt

Raspberry Sauce (page 641), if desired

1 Pour half-and-half into 1½-quart saucepan. Sprinkle gelatin evenly over half-and-half. Let stand 10 minutes.

2 Heat mixture over medium-high heat 5 to 7 minutes, stirring constantly, until gelatin is dissolved and mixture is just beginning to simmer (do not boil). Remove from heat. Stir in sugar, vanilla and salt until sugar is dissolved.

3 Pour mixture into 4 (6-oz) ramekins or custard cups.* Cover tightly with plastic wrap; refrigerate about 4 hours or until set.

4 When ready to serve, run thin knife around edge of each panna cotta. Dip bottom of each ramekin into bowl of very hot water for 5 seconds. Immediately place serving plate upside down over each ramekin; turn plate and ramekin over and remove ramekin. Serve with raspberry sauce.

* Or, instead of using ramekins and having to unmold them, pour the custard into 4 parfait glasses, making sure to leave room at the top for the raspberry sauce.

1 Serving: Calories 210; Total Fat 14g (Saturated Fat 9g, Trans Fat 0g); Cholesterol 45mg; Sodium 125mg; Total Carbohydrate 18g (Dietary Fiber 0g, Sugars 18g); Protein 4g **Exchanges:** 1 Other Carbohydrate, ½ High-Fat Meat, 2 Fat **Carbohydrate Choices:** 1

Panna Cotta

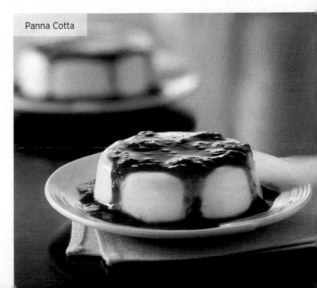

Chocolate Mousse

Chocolate Mousse

PREP 20 min **TOTAL** 2 hr 20 min • 8 servings

- 4 egg yolks
- ¼ cup sugar
- 2½ cups whipping cream
- 8 oz semisweet or dark baking chocolate, chopped

1 In small bowl, beat egg yolks with electric mixer on high speed 3 minutes or until thick and lemon colored. Slowly beat in sugar.

2 In 2-quart saucepan, heat 1 cup of the whipping cream over medium heat just until hot. Gradually stir at least half of the hot cream into egg yolk mixture, then stir back into hot cream in saucepan. Cook over low heat about 5 minutes, stirring constantly, until mixture thickens (do not boil).

3 Stir in chocolate until melted. Cover and refrigerate about 2 hours, stirring occasionally, just until chilled.

4 In chilled large, deep bowl, beat remaining 1½ cups whipping cream with electric mixer on low speed until mixture begins to thicken. Gradually increase speed to high and beat until stiff peaks form. Fold chocolate mixture into whipped cream.

5 Pipe or spoon mixture into 8 dessert dishes or stemmed glasses. Refrigerate until serving. Store covered in refrigerator.

1 Serving: Calories 460; Total Fat 41g (Saturated Fat 24g, Trans Fat 0.5g); Cholesterol 190mg; Sodium 35mg; Total Carbohydrate 17g (Dietary Fiber 4g, Sugars 9g); Protein 6g **Exchanges:** ½ Starch, ½ Other Carbohydrate, ½ Medium-Fat Meat, 7½ Fat **Carbohydrate Choices:** 1

LIGHTER Directions For 14 grams of fat and 255 calories per serving, substitute 2 whole eggs for the 4 egg yolks, and half-and-half for the 1 cup whipping cream in Step 2. Substitute 3 cups frozen (thawed) fat-free whipped topping for the 1½ cups whipping cream.

Rice Pudding CALORIE SMART

Leftover cooked rice can be used in this recipe. Use 1½ cups cooked rice and increase the bake time by about 5 minutes because the rice will be cold.

PREP 15 min **TOTAL** 1 hr 30 min • 8 servings

- ½ cup uncooked regular long-grain white rice
- 1 cup water
- 2 whole eggs or 4 egg yolks
- ½ cup sugar
- ½ cup raisins or chopped dried apricots
- 2½ cups milk
- 1 teaspoon vanilla
- ¼ teaspoon salt
  Ground cinnamon or nutmeg
  Raspberry Sauce (page 641), if desired
  Sweetened Whipped Cream (page 622), if desired

1 In 1½-quart saucepan, heat rice and water to boiling, stirring once or twice; reduce heat to low. Cover and simmer 14 minutes (do not lift cover or stir). All water should be absorbed; if not, drain excess water.

2 Heat oven to 325°F. In ungreased 1½-quart casserole, beat eggs with whisk or fork. Stir in sugar, raisins, milk, vanilla, salt and hot rice. Sprinkle with cinnamon.

3 Bake uncovered 45 minutes, stirring every 15 minutes. Top of pudding will be very wet and not set (overbaking may cause pudding to curdle).

4 Stir well; let stand 15 minutes. Enough liquid will be absorbed while standing to make pudding creamy. Serve warm, or cover and refrigerate about 3 hours or until chilled. Serve with raspberry sauce and whipped cream. Store covered in refrigerator.

1 Serving: Calories 180; Total Fat 3g (Saturated Fat 1g, Trans Fat 0g); Cholesterol 60mg; Sodium 125mg; Total Carbohydrate 33g (Dietary Fiber 0g, Sugars 22g); Protein 5g **Exchanges:** 2 Starch, ½ Fat **Carbohydrate Choices:** 2

Almond-Cherry Rice Pudding Substitute dried cherries for the raisins and ½ teaspoon almond extract for the 1 teaspoon vanilla. Omit raspberry sauce.

Baked Custard CALORIE SMART • EASY

PREP 10 min **TOTAL** 1 hr 25 min • 6 servings

    3 eggs, slightly beaten
    ⅓ cup sugar
    1 teaspoon vanilla
       Dash salt
    2½ cups very warm milk or half-and-half
       (120°F to 130°F)
       Ground nutmeg

1 Heat oven to 350°F. In medium bowl, beat eggs, sugar, vanilla and salt with whisk or fork. Gradually stir in milk.

2 Pour mixture into 6 (6-oz) ramekins or custard cups. Sprinkle with nutmeg. Place ramekins in 13x9-inch pan; place pan in oven. Carefully pour very hot water into pan to within ½ inch of tops of ramekins.

3 Bake about 45 minutes or until knife inserted halfway between center and edge comes out clean. Carefully remove ramekins from water using tongs or grasping tops of ramekins with pot holder. Cool about 30 minutes. Serve warm or cool. If desired, unmold custard onto individual plates. Store covered in refrigerator.

1 Serving: Calories 130; Total Fat 5g (Saturated Fat 2g, Trans Fat 0g); Cholesterol 115mg; Sodium 120mg; Total Carbohydrate 16g (Dietary Fiber 0g, Sugars 17g); Protein 7g **Exchanges:** 1 Low-Fat Milk, 1 Fat **Carbohydrate Choices:** 1

Caramel Custard (Crème Caramel)

Caramel Custard (Crème Caramel) Before making custard, in heavy 1-quart saucepan, heat ½ cup sugar over low heat 10 to 15 minutes, stirring constantly with wooden spoon, until sugar is melted and golden brown (sugar becomes very hot and could melt a plastic spoon). Immediately divide syrup among 6 (6-oz) custard cups before it hardens in saucepan; carefully tilt cups to coat bottoms (syrup will be extremely hot). Let syrup harden in cups about 10 minutes. Make custard as directed in Step 1; pour over syrup in cups. Bake as directed in Steps 2 and 3. Cool completely. Cover and refrigerate until serving or up to 48 hours.

To unmold, carefully loosen side of custard with knife or small spatula. Place dessert dish on top of cup and, holding tightly, turn dish and cup upside down. Shake cup gently to loosen custard. Caramel syrup will drizzle over custard, forming a sauce.

Unmolding Custard

Run thin knife around edge of each baked custard; dip bottom of each ramekin into hot water for about 5 seconds.

Immediately place serving plate upside down onto each ramekin; hold both ramekin and plate firmly. Turn ramekin upside down onto plate; remove ramekin.

Learn to Make
CRÈME BRÛLÉE

This elegant dessert, loved for its contrast in textures—the creaminess of the custard with the brittle caramelized sugar topping—is a popular star on restaurant menus. It's a great dessert to make ahead and dazzle your guests with because it's actually easy to make when you know the secrets to success.

Tips for Making Crème Brûlée

- Use whipping cream (not half-and-half or milk) to correctly set the custard and achieve the velvety smooth texture and creamy richness crème brûlée is known for.

- Use ceramic ramekins, not glass custard cups or glass pie plates, which may not be able to withstand the heat from the kitchen torch or broiler and break.

- Slightly beat the eggs with a whisk to break them up before adding to the cream mixture. Whisk eggs with cream mixture until well blended so the custard will be smooth when baked.

- Add enough boiling water to the pan until it comes up to two-thirds of the height of the ramekins in order to protect the custard from the direct heat of the oven during baking.

- Don't allow any boiling water to splash into the ramekins, which could affect the custard texture.

- Blot any condensation from the tops of the chilled custards before sprinkling with sugar.

- Use a kitchen torch (see right for directions) or broiler to caramelize sugar. **To broil topping**, sprinkle 2 teaspoons brown sugar over each chilled custard. (Brown sugar melts much more evenly under the broiler.) Place ramekins in 15x10x1-inch pan or on cookie sheet with sides. Broil with tops 4 to 6 inches from heat 5 to 6 minutes.

- Caramelize the sugar on top of the custard until sugar is melted and light golden brown, watching carefully so the sugar doesn't burn and forms a glaze.

Crème Brûlée

PREP 20 min **TOTAL** 7 hr • 4 servings

    2 cups whipping cream
    ⅓ cup sugar
    1 teaspoon vanilla
    6 egg yolks, slightly beaten
       Boiling water
    8 teaspoons sugar

1 Heat oven to 350°F. In large bowl, stir whipping cream, ⅓ cup sugar and the vanilla until well mixed. Add egg yolks; beat with whisk until evenly colored and well blended.

2 In 13x9-inch pan, place 4 (6-oz) ceramic ramekins. Pour cream mixture evenly into ramekins. Carefully place pan in oven. Carefully pour boiling water into pan to within ½ inch of tops of ramekins.

3 Bake 30 to 40 minutes or until tops are light golden brown and sides are set (centers will be jiggly). Carefully transfer ramekins to cooling rack, using tongs or grasping tops of ramekins with pot holder. Cool 2 hours or until room temperature. Cover tightly with plastic wrap; refrigerate until chilled, at least 4 hours but no longer than 2 days.

4 Uncover ramekins; gently blot any condensation on custards with paper towel. Sprinkle 2 teaspoons sugar over each custard. Holding kitchen torch 3 to 4 inches from custard, caramelize sugar by heating with torch about 2 minutes, moving flame continuously over sugar in circular motion, until sugar is melted and light golden brown. (Or caramelize under broiler; see left.) Serve immediately, or refrigerate up to 8 hours before serving. If served immediately, custard will be softer.

1 Serving: Calories 540; Total Fat 45g (Saturated Fat 25g, Trans Fat 1g); Cholesterol 450mg; Sodium 50mg; Total Carbohydrate 29g (Dietary Fiber 0g, Sugars 29g); Protein 7g **Exchanges:** 2 Other Carbohydrate, 1 High-Fat Meat, 7½ Fat **Carbohydrate Choices:** 2

Lemon Crème Brûlée Reduce sugar in custard to ⅓ cup. Add 1 tablespoon grated lemon peel with the vanilla. After caramelizing sugar, top each ramekin with 1 tablespoon fresh raspberries, if desired.

Apple-Fig Bread Pudding Cupcakes with Maple Sauce

heat, stirring occasionally. Remove from heat; stir in maple flavor.

5 Remove warm cupcakes from pan to individual serving plates. Spoon warm sauce over cupcakes. Garnish with maple candies.

1 Serving: Calories 660; Total Fat 26g (Saturated Fat 16g, Trans Fat 1g); Cholesterol 140mg; Sodium 450mg; Total Carbohydrate 98g (Dietary Fiber 3g, Sugars 74g); Protein 9g **Exchanges:** 2½ Starch, ½ Fruit, 3½ Other Carbohydrate, 5 Fat **Carbohydrate Choices:** 6½

Apple-Fig Bread Pudding Cupcakes with Maple Sauce

PREP 30 min **TOTAL** 1 hr 5 min • 6 servings

CUPCAKES

- 7 cups cubes (1 inch) day-old French or Italian bread (from 1-lb loaf)
- 1 large tart cooking apple (Braeburn, Cortland or Granny Smith), peeled, chopped (1½ cups)
- ½ cup chopped dried figs
- 1 cup packed brown sugar
- 1 cup milk
- ¼ cup butter, cut into pieces
- 1 teaspoon ground cinnamon
- ½ teaspoon vanilla
- 2 eggs, beaten

SAUCE

- ⅓ cup granulated sugar
- ⅓ cup packed brown sugar
- ⅓ cup whipping cream
- ⅓ cup butter, cut into pieces
- ½ teaspoon maple flavor
   Maple candies, if desired

1 Heat oven to 350°F. Grease 6 jumbo muffin cups with shortening.

2 In large bowl, mix bread cubes, apple and figs. In small saucepan, cook 1 cup brown sugar, the milk and ¼ cup butter over medium heat until butter is melted. Remove from heat; stir in cinnamon and vanilla. Pour over bread mixture in bowl. Add eggs; toss to coat. Spoon mixture evenly into muffin cups, filling to tops of cups.

3 Bake 30 to 34 minutes or until center is set and apples are tender. Cool while making sauce.

4 In 1-quart saucepan, stir granulated sugar, ⅓ cup brown sugar, the whipping cream and ⅓ cup butter. Heat to boiling over medium

Bread Pudding with Whiskey Sauce

PREP 25 min **TOTAL** 2 hr 20 min • 12 servings

BREAD PUDDING

- 4 whole eggs
- 1 egg yolk
- ¾ cup sugar
- 2½ cups milk
- 2½ cups whipping cream
- 1 tablespoon vanilla
- 1½ teaspoons ground cinnamon
- 12 oz French or other firm bread, cut into ½-inch slices, then cut into 1½-inch pieces (10 cups)
- ½ cup raisins, if desired
- 2 tablespoons sugar
- 2 tablespoons butter, melted

WHISKEY SAUCE

- ½ cup butter, cut into pieces
- 2 tablespoons water
- 1 whole egg
- 1 cup sugar
- 2 tablespoons whiskey or bourbon or 1 teaspoon brandy extract or vanilla

1 Heat oven to 325°F. Grease bottom and sides of 13x9-inch (3-quart) glass baking dish with shortening or cooking spray.

2 In large bowl, beat 4 eggs, 1 egg yolk and ¾ cup sugar with whisk until well blended. Beat in milk, whipping cream, vanilla and 1 teaspoon of the cinnamon until well blended. Stir in 7 cups of the bread pieces and the raisins. Let stand 20 minutes. Pour into baking dish. Lightly press remaining 3 cups bread pieces on top of mixture.

3 In small bowl, mix 2 tablespoons sugar and remaining ½ teaspoon cinnamon. Brush top of bread mixture with melted butter; sprinkle with cinnamon-sugar. Bake uncovered 55 to

Bread Pudding with Whiskey Sauce

Chocolate–Sour Cream Fondue

65 minutes or until top is puffed and light golden brown (center will jiggle slightly). Cool 30 minutes.

4 Meanwhile, in 1-quart saucepan, melt ½ cup butter over low heat (do not allow to simmer). Remove from heat; cool 10 minutes. In small bowl, mix water and 1 egg; stir into butter until blended. Stir in 1 cup sugar. Cook and stir over medium-low heat until sugar is dissolved and mixture begins to boil; remove from heat. Stir in whiskey. Cool at least 10 minutes before serving.

5 Serve sauce over warm bread pudding. Store bread pudding and sauce covered in refrigerator.

1 Serving: Calories 500; Total Fat 30g (Saturated Fat 16g, Trans Fat 1.5g); Cholesterol 190mg; Sodium 300mg; Total Carbohydrate 50g (Dietary Fiber 0g, Sugars 36g); Protein 8g **Exchanges:** 2 Starch, 1½ Other Carbohydrate, 5½ Fat **Carbohydrate Choices:** 3

LIGHTER Directions For 7 grams of fat and 300 calories per serving, substitute 2 eggs and ½ cup fat-free egg product for the 4 eggs and 1 egg yolk. Substitute 4 cups fat-free (skim) milk and 1 cup half-and-half for the milk and whipping cream. Instead of whiskey sauce, stir 1 tablespoon bourbon or 1 teaspoon brandy extract into 1 cup fat-free caramel topping; heat if desired.

Bread Pudding with Lemon Curd Make bread pudding as directed, except—omit whiskey sauce. Serve Lemon Curd (page 602) or purchased lemon curd over warm bread pudding.

Chocolate–Sour Cream Fondue FAST

PREP 15 min **TOTAL** 15 min • 12 servings

- 4 cups milk chocolate or semisweet chocolate chips (about 24 oz) or 6 packages (4 oz each) sweet baking chocolate, chopped
- 1 cup sour cream
- ½ cup half-and-half
- 1 tablespoon instant coffee powder or granules or ½ teaspoon ground cinnamon
- 4 cups cut-up fresh fruit
- 4 cups cubed angel food cake (to make your own, see page 572) or pound cake (to make your own, see page 564)

1 In 2-quart saucepan, heat chocolate, sour cream, half-and-half and coffee powder over low heat, stirring constantly, until chocolate is melted and mixture is smooth; remove from heat.

2 Pour chocolate mixture into fondue or chafing dish to keep warm. Spear fruit and cake with fondue forks; dip and swirl in fondue with stirring motion. If mixture becomes too thick, stir in small amount of half-and-half.

1 Serving: Calories 410; Total Fat 22g (Saturated Fat 13g, Trans Fat 0g); Cholesterol 25mg; Sodium 180mg; Total Carbohydrate 48g (Dietary Fiber 3g, Sugars 42g); Protein 6g **Exchanges:** 1 Starch, 2 Other Carbohydrate, 4½ Fat **Carbohydrate Choices:** 3

Funtastic Dippers

Here are some other fun foods to dunk in chocolate fondue:

- Mini cupcakes (page 574)
- Doughnuts (page 492)
- Marshmallows (page 550)
- Cooked bacon slices
- Pretzels
- Mini chocolate chip cookies
- Mini cereal-marshmallow bars

Individual Meringues filled with Lemon Curd (page 602)

Meringue Shell EASY

A meringue shell bakes up crisp yet melts in your mouth when you bite into it. Just before serving, fill with fresh fruit, ice cream, Chocolate Mousse (page 632), Lemon Curd (page 602) or Vanilla Pudding (page 631).

PREP 10 min **TOTAL** 4 hr 40 min • 8 servings

> 3 egg whites
> ¼ teaspoon cream of tartar
> ¾ cup sugar

1 Heat oven to 275°F. Line cookie sheet with cooking parchment paper.

2 In medium bowl, beat egg whites and cream of tartar with electric mixer on high speed until foamy. Beat in sugar, 1 tablespoon at a time; continue beating until stiff peaks form and mixture is glossy. Do not underbeat. On cookie sheet, shape meringue into 9-inch round with back of spoon, building up side.

3 Bake 1 hour 30 minutes. Turn off oven; leave meringue in oven with door closed 1 hour. Finish cooling at room temperature, about 2 hours.

1 Serving: Calories 80; Total Fat 0g (Saturated Fat 0g, Trans Fat 0g); Cholesterol 0mg; Sodium 20mg; Total Carbohydrate 19g (Dietary Fiber 0g, Sugars 19g); Protein 1g **Exchanges:** 1 Starch **Carbohydrate Choices:** 1

Individual Meringues Drop meringue by ⅓ cupfuls onto cookie sheet. Shape into rounds, building up sides. Bake 1 hour. Turn off oven; leave meringues

Shaping Individual Meringue Shells

Shape each meringue with back of spoon into desired shape, building up side.

in oven with door closed 1 hour. Finish cooling at room temperature, about 2 hours. Makes 8 to 10 meringues.

Chocolate Meringue Shell After beating egg white mixture, sprinkle 2 tablespoons unsweetened baking cocoa through strainer over top; fold cocoa into mixture. Bake as directed.

Vanilla Ice Cream EASY

PREP 10 min **TOTAL** 2 hr 40 min • 1 quart

> 3 egg yolks, slightly beaten
> ½ cup sugar
> 1 cup milk
> ¼ teaspoon salt
> 2 cups whipping cream
> 1 tablespoon vanilla

1 In 2-quart saucepan, stir egg yolks, sugar, milk and salt until well mixed. Heat just to boiling over medium heat, stirring constantly (do not allow mixture to continue to boil or it will curdle). Immediately remove from heat.

2 Pour milk mixture into chilled bowl. Refrigerate uncovered 2 to 3 hours, stirring occasionally, until room temperature. At this point, mixture can be refrigerated up to 24 hours before completing recipe if desired.

3 Stir whipping cream and vanilla into milk mixture. Pour into 1-quart ice cream freezer and freeze according to manufacturer's directions.

½ Cup: Calories 270; Total Fat 21g (Saturated Fat 12g, Trans Fat 0.5g); Cholesterol 150mg; Sodium 110mg; Total Carbohydrate 16g (Dietary Fiber 0g, Sugars 16g); Protein 3g **Exchanges:** 1 Starch, 4 Fat **Carbohydrate Choices:** 1

Chocolate Ice Cream Increase sugar to 1 cup. Beat 2 ounces unsweetened baking chocolate, melted and cooled, into milk mixture before cooking. Reduce vanilla to 1 teaspoon.

Eggnog Ice Cream Add ¼ teaspoon ground nutmeg with the sugar. Add 1 teaspoon rum extract with the vanilla.

Fresh Blueberry Ice Cream Reduce vanilla to 1 teaspoon. Mash 2 cups fresh blueberries and an additional ⅓ cup sugar with potato masher or process in food processor until slightly chunky (not pureed); stir into milk mixture after adding vanilla.

Fresh Peach Ice Cream Reduce vanilla to 1 teaspoon. Mash 4 or 5 peeled fresh peaches with potato masher or process in food processor until slightly chunky (not pureed) to make 2 cups; stir into milk mixture after adding vanilla.

Fresh Raspberry Ice Cream Substitute ½ teaspoon almond extract for the vanilla. Mash 2 cups fresh raspberries with potato masher or process in food processor until slightly chunky (not pureed); stir into milk mixture after adding almond extract.

Fresh Strawberry Ice Cream Reduce vanilla to 1 teaspoon. Mash 2 cups fresh strawberries and an additional ½ cup sugar with potato masher or process in food processor until slightly chunky (not pureed); stir into milk mixture after adding vanilla. Stir in a few drops red food color if desired.

Caramel Ice Cream

PREP 15 min **TOTAL** 2 hr 45 min • 1 quart

- ½ cup sugar
- 2 cups whipping cream
- 1 cup milk
- 3 egg yolks, slightly beaten
- ¼ teaspoon salt
- 2 teaspoons vanilla

1 In 2-quart saucepan, heat sugar over medium heat until sugar begins to melt. Stir until sugar is completely dissolved and becomes deep golden brown to amber in color. Remove from

Caramel Ice Cream

heat; carefully and gradually stir in 1 cup of the whipping cream (mixture will boil and splatter at first). Heat over low heat, stirring frequently, until any hardened sugar bits dissolve; remove from heat.

2 With whisk, stir in remaining 1 cup whipping cream, the milk, egg yolks, salt and vanilla until well mixed. Heat just to boiling over medium heat, stirring constantly (do not allow mixture to continue to boil or it will curdle). Immediately remove from heat.

3 Pour milk mixture into chilled bowl. Refrigerate uncovered 2 to 3 hours, stirring occasionally, until room temperature. At this point, mixture can be refrigerated up to 24 hours before completing recipe if desired.

4 Pour mixture into 1-quart ice cream freezer and freeze according to manufacturer's directions.

½ **Cup:** Calories 300; Total Fat 25g (Saturated Fat 15g, Trans Fat 1g); Cholesterol 160mg; Sodium 110mg; Total Carbohydrate 16g (Dietary Fiber 0g, Sugars 16g); Protein 3g **Exchanges:** 1 Other Carbohydrate, ½ Medium-Fat Meat, 4½ Fat **Carbohydrate Choices:** 1

Caramelizing Sugar for Caramel Ice Cream

Heat sugar in saucepan over medium heat until sugar begins to melt.

Stir until sugar is completely dissolved and is deep golden-brown to amber colored.

Gradually stir in whipping cream.

Heat over low heat, stirring frequently, until hardened sugar bits dissolve.

Watermelon Granita

Very Berry Frozen Yogurt

CALORIE SMART • EASY

PREP 5 min **TOTAL** 40 min • 12 servings

- 2 cups fresh strawberries or raspberries
- ⅓ cup sugar
- 4 cups vanilla low-fat yogurt

1 In large bowl, mash berries with sugar. Stir in yogurt.

2 Pour mixture into 2-quart ice cream freezer. Freeze according to manufacturer's directions. Scoop into serving dishes or ice cream cones.

1 Serving: Calories 100; Total Fat 1g (Saturated Fat 0.5g, Trans Fat 0g); Cholesterol 0mg; Sodium 55mg; Total Carbohydrate 19g (Dietary Fiber 0g, Sugars 18g); Protein 4g **Exchanges:** ½ Fruit , ½ Other Carbohydrate, ½ Low-Fat Milk **Carbohydrate Choices:** 1

Watermelon Granita   CALORIE SMART

Granita is the Italian term for an "ice" or frozen dessert made with fruit or fruit juice. The texture will be grainier than a sorbet—very similar to a slush.

PREP 20 min **TOTAL** 4 hr 25 min • 10 servings

- 3 tablespoons lime juice (2 to 3 limes)
- 1 cup water
- ½ cup sugar
- 6 cups 1-inch cubes seeded watermelon

1 In 1-quart saucepan, mix lime juice, water and sugar. Cook over low heat about 5 minutes, stirring occasionally, until sugar is dissolved. Cool slightly, about 5 minutes.

2 In blender or food processor, place watermelon. Cover and blend on high speed about 2 minutes or until smooth. Add lime juice mixture. Cover and blend until well mixed. Pour into 13x9-inch (3-quart) glass baking dish. Cover and freeze 1 hour.

3 Scrape with fork to distribute ice crystals evenly. Freeze at least 3 hours longer, repeating scraping procedure every 30 minutes, until mixture is consistency of fine ice crystals. To serve, scoop into chilled dessert cups.

1 Serving: Calories 70; Total Fat 0g (Saturated Fat 0g, Trans Fat 0g); Cholesterol 0mg; Sodium 0mg; Total Carbohydrate 17g (Dietary Fiber 0g, Sugars 16g); Protein 0g **Exchanges:** ½ Fruit, ½ Other Carbohydrate **Carbohydrate Choices:** 1

Lemonade Sorbet   CALORIE SMART • EASY

PREP 5 min **TOTAL** 4 hr 5 min • 4 servings

- 1½ cups cold water
- 1 cup lemonade concentrate (to make your own, see page 72, or thawed from 12-oz can)
- 3 tablespoons honey
  Lemon slices, if desired
  Fresh blueberries, if desired

1 In blender or food processor, place water, lemonade concentrate and honey. Cover and blend on low speed about 30 seconds or until smooth. Pour into 8-inch square (2-quart) glass baking dish.

2 Cover and freeze about 4 hours or until firm, stirring several times to keep mixture smooth. Garnish with lemon slices and blueberries.

1 Serving: Calories 190; Total Fat 0g (Saturated Fat 0g, Trans Fat 0g); Cholesterol 0mg; Sodium 0mg; Total Carbohydrate 47g (Dietary Fiber 0g, Sugars 43g); Protein 0g **Exchanges:** 1 Fruit, 2 Other Carbohydrate **Carbohydrate Choices:** 3

Cranberry-Raspberry Sorbet Substitute cranberry-raspberry concentrate for the lemonade concentrate.

Limeade Sorbet Substitute limeade concentrate for the lemonade concentrate.

Orange Sorbet Substitute orange juice concentrate for the lemonade concentrate.

Lemonade Sorbet

Pineapple Sorbet Substitute pineapple juice concentrate for the lemonade concentrate.

Raspberry Sauce

Lemon Sauce CALORIE SMART • FAST • EASY

PREP 10 min **TOTAL** 10 min • 1¼ cups

- ½ cup sugar
- 2 tablespoons cornstarch
- ¾ cup water
- 1 tablespoon grated lemon peel
- ¼ cup fresh lemon juice
- 2 tablespoons butter, softened

1 In 1-quart saucepan, mix sugar and cornstarch. Gradually stir in water. Cook over medium heat, stirring constantly, until mixture thickens and boils. Boil and stir 1 minute; remove from heat.

2 Stir in remaining ingredients. Serve warm or cool. Store covered in refrigerator up to 10 days.

1 Tablespoon: Calories 35; Total Fat 1g (Saturated Fat 0.5g, Trans Fat 0g); Cholesterol 0mg; Sodium 10mg; Total Carbohydrate 6g (Dietary Fiber 0g, Sugars 5g); Protein 0g **Exchanges:** ½ Fruit **Carbohydrate Choices:** ½

Raspberry Sauce

CALORIE SMART • FAST • EASY

PREP 10 min **TOTAL** 10 min • 1 cup

- 3 tablespoons sugar
- 2 teaspoons cornstarch
- ⅓ cup water
- 1 box (10 oz) frozen raspberries in syrup, thawed, undrained

1 In 1-quart saucepan, mix sugar and cornstarch. Stir in water and raspberries with syrup. Cook over medium heat, stirring constantly, until mixture thickens and boils (mixture will become translucent during cooking). Boil and stir 1 minute.

2 Strain sauce through fine-mesh strainer into bowl to remove seeds if desired. Serve sauce warm or cool. Store covered in refrigerator up to 10 days.

1 Tablespoon: Calories 30; Total Fat 0g (Saturated Fat 0g, Trans Fat 0g); Cholesterol 0mg; Sodium 0mg; Total Carbohydrate 7g (Dietary Fiber 0g, Sugars 6g); Protein 0g **Exchanges:** ½ Fruit **Carbohydrate Choices:** ½

Strawberry Sauce Substitute frozen strawberries in syrup for the raspberries.

Cranberry Sauce CALORIE SMART • EASY

The natural pectin in the cranberries thickens this easy homemade sauce. Be sure to cook the cranberries until they pop so the pectin is released and the sauce gels as it cools.

PREP 15 min **TOTAL** 3 hr 15 min • 4 cups

- 4 cups fresh or frozen cranberries
- 2 cups sugar
- 2 cups water
- 1 tablespoon grated orange peel, if desired

1 Wash cranberries; remove any stems and discard any blemished berries.

2 In 3-quart saucepan, heat sugar and water to boiling over medium heat, stirring occasionally. Boil 5 minutes.

3 Stir in cranberries. Heat to boiling; boil about 5 minutes or until cranberries pop. Stir in orange peel. Cover and refrigerate about 3 hours or until chilled. Store covered in refrigerator up to 1 week.

¼ Cup: Calories 110; Total Fat 0g (Saturated Fat 0g, Trans Fat 0g); Cholesterol 0mg; Sodium 0mg; Total Carbohydrate 28g (Dietary Fiber 1g, Sugars 26g); Protein 0g **Exchanges:** 2 Fruit **Carbohydrate Choices:** 2

Making Raspberry Sauce

Stir water and raspberries into sugar and cornstarch.

Cook, stirring constantly, until mixture thickens and boils and becomes translucent.

Rhubarb Sauce   CALORIE SMART • FAST

Rhubarb varies in sweetness, so add sugar to taste. Serve it for dessert, either by itself or over pound cake or ice cream. Or serve as a sweet-tart accompaniment to pork or chicken.

PREP 20 min **TOTAL** 20 min • 3 cups

- ½ to ¾ cup sugar
- ½ cup water
- 1 lb fresh or frozen rhubarb, cut into 1-inch pieces (3 cups)
  Ground cinnamon, if desired

1 In 2-quart saucepan, heat ½ cup sugar and the water to boiling over medium heat, stirring occasionally. Stir in rhubarb; reduce heat to low. Simmer uncovered about 10 minutes, stirring occasionally, until rhubarb is tender and slightly transparent, adding up to ¼ cup more sugar, if desired.

2 Stir in cinnamon. Serve sauce warm or chilled. Store covered in refrigerator up to 1 week.

½ **Cup:** Calories 80; Total Fat 0g (Saturated Fat 0g, Trans Fat 0g); Cholesterol 0mg; Sodium 0mg; Total Carbohydrate 20g (Dietary Fiber 1g, Sugars 17g); Protein 0g **Exchanges:** 1 ½ Other Carbohydrate **Carbohydrate Choices:** 1

Strawberry-Rhubarb Sauce Substitute 1 cup fresh strawberries, cut in half, for 1 cup of the rhubarb. After simmering rhubarb, stir in strawberries; heat just to boiling.

Hot Fudge Sauce   CALORIE SMART • EASY

PREP 10 min **TOTAL** 40 min • 3 cups

- 1 can (12 oz) evaporated milk
- 2 cups semisweet or dark chocolate chips (about 12 oz)
- ½ cup sugar
- 1 tablespoon butter, softened
- 1 teaspoon vanilla

1 In 2-quart saucepan, heat milk, chocolate chips and sugar to boiling over medium heat, stirring constantly; remove from heat. Stir in butter and vanilla until mixture is smooth and creamy.

2 Cool about 30 minutes or until sauce begins to thicken. Serve warm. Store sauce covered in refrigerator up to 4 weeks. Sauce becomes firm when refrigerated; heat slightly before serving (sauce will become thin if overheated).

1 **Tablespoon:** Calories 60; Total Fat 2.5g (Saturated Fat 1.5g, Trans Fat 0g); Cholesterol 0mg; Sodium 10mg; Total Carbohydrate 7g (Dietary Fiber 0g, Sugars 7g); Protein 0g **Exchanges:** ½ Starch, ½ Fat **Carbohydrate Choices:** ½

Chocolate Sauce

CALORIE SMART • FAST • EASY

PREP 10 min **TOTAL** 10 min • 1½ cups

- 1½ cups light corn syrup
- 3 oz unsweetened baking chocolate, chopped
- 1 tablespoon butter, softened
- ¾ teaspoon vanilla

1 In 1-quart saucepan, heat corn syrup and chocolate over low heat, stirring frequently, until chocolate is melted; remove from heat. Stir in butter and vanilla.

2 Serve warm or cool. Store covered in refrigerator up to 10 days. Reheat slightly before serving if desired.

1 **Tablespoon:** Calories 90; Total Fat 2.5g (Saturated Fat 1.5g, Trans Fat 0g); Cholesterol 0mg; Sodium 30mg; Total Carbohydrate 17g (Dietary Fiber 0g, Sugars 8g); Protein 0g **Exchanges:** 1 Other Carbohydrate, ½ Fat **Carbohydrate Choices:** 1

Caramel Sauce   CALORIE SMART • EASY

What else besides ice cream is caramel sauce great on? Drizzle it over cheesecake or sliced bananas and sprinkle with chopped pecans. Or you can use it as a dip for apple slices or cubes of pound cake.

PREP 10 min **TOTAL** 40 min • 2½ cups

- 1 cup light corn syrup
- 1¼ cups packed brown sugar
- ¼ cup butter, cut into pieces
- 1 cup whipping cream

1 In 2-quart saucepan, heat corn syrup, brown sugar and butter to boiling over low heat, stirring constantly. Boil 5 minutes, stirring occasionally.

2 Stir in whipping cream; heat to boiling, stirring constantly. Cool about 30 minutes. Serve warm. Store covered in refrigerator up to 10 days. Reheat slightly before serving if desired.

1 **Tablespoon:** Calories 80; Total Fat 3g (Saturated Fat 1.5g, Trans Fat 0g); Cholesterol 10mg; Sodium 20mg; Total Carbohydrate 13g (Dietary Fiber 0g, Sugars 10g); Protein 0g **Exchanges:** 1 Other Carbohydrate, ½ Fat **Carbohydrate Choices:** 1

HELPFUL NUTRITION AND COOKING INFORMATION

We provide nutrition information for each recipe that includes calories, fat, cholesterol, sodium, carbohydrate, fiber and protein. Individual food choices can be based on this information.

Criteria Used for Calculating Nutrition Information

- The first ingredient was used wherever a choice is given (such as ⅓ cup sour cream or plain yogurt).

- The first ingredient amount was used wherever a range is given (such as 3- to 3½-pound cut-up whole chicken).

- The first serving number was used wherever a range is given (such as 4 to 6 servings).

- "If desired" ingredients and recipe variations were not included (such as sprinkle with brown sugar, if desired).

- Only the amount of a marinade or frying oil that is estimated to be absorbed by the food during preparation or cooking was calculated.

Criteria Used for Calculating Lower-Calorie Recipes

Recipes designated as Lower Calorie were determined using the following guidelines:

- Main dishes: 350 calories or less

- Chilies, stews, plain meats: 250 calories or less

- Soups, breads, side dishes, appetizers: 175 calories or less

- Desserts: 200 calories or less

- Condiments, beverages, dips, sauces, dressings: 80 calories or less

Ingredients Used in Recipe Testing and Nutrition Calculations

- Ingredients used for testing represent those that the majority of consumers use in their homes: large eggs, 2% milk, 80%-lean ground beef and canned ready-to-use chicken broth.

- Fat-free, low-fat or low-sodium products were not used, unless otherwise indicated.

- Solid vegetable shortening was used to grease pans, unless otherwise indicated.

Equipment Used in Recipe Testing

We use equipment for testing that the majority of consumers use in their homes. If a specific piece of equipment (such as a wire whisk) is necessary for recipe success, it is listed in the recipe.

- Cookware and bakeware without nonstick coatings were used, unless otherwise indicated.

- No dark-colored, black or insulated bakeware was used.

- When a pan is specified in a recipe, a metal pan was used; a baking dish or pie plate means ovenproof glass was used.

- An electric hand mixer was used for mixing only when mixer speeds are specified in the recipe directions. If a stand mixer is necessary, the recipe will call for that appliance. When a mixer speed is not given, a spoon or fork was used.

INDEX

Note: Page numbers in *italics* indicate photographs.